A Handbook for Teaching and Learning
in Higher Education

A Handbook for Teaching and Learning in Higher Education is sensitive to the competing demands of teaching, research and scholarship, and academic management. Against these contexts, the book focuses on developing professional academic skills for teaching. Dealing with the rapid expansion of the use of technology in higher education and widening student diversity, this fully updated and expanded edition includes new material on, for example, e-learning, lecturing to large groups, formative and summative assessment, and supervising research students.

Part 1 examines teaching and supervising in higher education, focusing on a range of approaches and contexts.

Part 2 examines teaching in discipline-specific areas and includes new chapters on engineering, economics, law, and the creative and performing arts.

Part 3 considers approaches to demonstrating and enhancing practice.

Written to support the excellence in teaching required to bring about learning of the highest quality, this will be essential reading for all new lecturers, particularly anyone taking an accredited course in teaching and learning in higher education, as well as all those experienced lecturers who wish to improve their teaching. Those working in adult learning and education development will also find it a particularly useful resource.

Heather Fry is the founding Head of the Centre for Educational Development at Imperial College London.

Steve Ketteridge is Director of Educational and Staff Development at Queen Mary, University of London.

Stephanie Marshall is Director of Programmes at the Leadership Foundation for Higher Education and is currently Visiting Professor at Queen Mary, University of London.

A Handbook for Teaching and Learning in Higher Education

Enhancing Academic Practice

Third edition

Edited by
Heather Fry
Steve Ketteridge
Stephanie Marshall

Routledge
Taylor & Francis Group

NEW YORK AND LONDON

First edition published 1999
Second edition published 2003
by Routledge
This edition published 2009
by Routledge
270 Madison Ave, New York, NY 10016

Simultaneously published in the UK
by Routledge
2 Park Square, Milton Park, Abingdon, Oxon OX14 4RN

Routledge is an imprint of the Taylor and Francis Group, an informa business

Typeset in Palatino by
Keystroke, 28 High Street, Tettenhall, Wolverhampton
Printed and bound by
MPG Books Ltd, Bodmin

Library of Congress Cataloging in Publication Data
A handbook for teaching and learning in higher education : enhancing academic
practice / [edited by] Heather Fry, Steve Ketteridge, Stephanie Marshall.–3rd ed.
p. cm.
Includes bibliographical references and index.
1. College teaching–Handbooks, manuals, etc. 2. College teachers. 3. Lecture method
in teaching. I. Fry, Heather. II. Ketteridge, Steve. III. Marshall, Stephanie. IV. Title:
Teaching and learning in higher education.
LB2331.H3145 2008
378,1′25–dc22
2008009873

ISBN 10: 0–415–43463–7 (hbk)
ISBN 10: 0–415–43464–5 (pbk)
ISBN 10: 0–203–89141–4 (ebk)

ISBN 13: 978–0–415–43463–8 (hbk)
ISBN 13: 978–0–415–43464–5 (pbk)
ISBN 13: 978–0–203–89141–4 (ebk)

Contents

Illustrations

FIGURES

TABLES

Contributors

THE EDITORS

Heather Fry is the founding Head of the Centre for Educational Development at Imperial College London. After teaching and lecturing in Nigeria she worked at the Institute of Education, London, and the Barts and Royal London School of Medicine and Dentistry at Queen Mary, University of London. She teaches, researches and publishes on academic practice in higher education. Her particular passions are how teaching, curriculum organisation and manipulation of 'context' can support and expand learning, especially in medical and surgical education. She has also been involved in the development of several innovative programmes including a Master's in Surgical Education and another in University Learning and Teaching.

Steve Ketteridge is the first Director of Educational and Staff Development at Queen Mary, University of London. His academic career began with a university lectureship in microbiology. Subsequently he established the Postgraduate Certificate in Academic Practice at Queen Mary and has developed strategy in areas such as learning and teaching, skills and employability. He is a key reference point on supervision of doctoral students in science and engineering, and advises universities and research institutes across the UK. Recently he has been involved in international work on the development of performance indicators for university teaching.

Stephanie Marshall is Director of Programmes at the Leadership Foundation for Higher Education, where she has worked since 2003, and is currently Visiting Professor at Queen Mary, University of London. Prior to this, she worked at the University of York, where she taught and researched in the Department of Educational Studies, moving on to set up the university's first Staff Development Office. Subsequently she became the Provost of Goodricke College, and worked in the Centre for Leadership and Management. She has published widely.

THE AUTHORS

Sylvia Alexander is Director of Access and Distributed Learning at the University of Ulster. She has a wide knowledge of current practice in teaching, learning and assessment resulting from previous involvement in a variety of national initiatives including the Higher Education Academy.

Carol Arlett is the Manager for the Engineering Subject Centre and oversees the Centre's range of activities that aim to provide subject-specific support for engineering academics. She has a particular interest in employer engagement and skills development.

Liz Barnett is Director of the London School of Economics (LSE) Teaching and Learning Centre. At the LSE she has collaborated with colleagues both in supporting graduate teaching assistants and encouraging innovatory teaching approaches. She previously worked at the University of Southampton and has lectured on international health.

Denis Berthiaume is Director of the Centre for Learning and Teaching at the University of Lausanne, Switzerland. His research interests include discipline-specific teaching in higher education, reflective practice in teaching, and the assessment of learning in higher education.

Sam Brenton is Head of E-Learning at Queen Mary, University of London. He is particularly interested in the social uses and effects of new media and virtual worlds. He has been an author, broadcaster, critic, journalist, poet and educational developer.

John Dickens is Director of the Engineering Subject Centre. He is also Professor of Engineering Education, Associate Dean (Teaching) for the Faculty of Engineering, and Director of the Engineering Centre for Excellence in Teaching and Learning (CETL) at Loughborough University. He has 25 years of teaching experience in civil and structural engineering design and received a National Teaching Fellowship in 2006.

Linda Drew is the Dean of Academic Development at the University of the Arts London, UK. Linda is founding editor of the journal *Art, Design and Communication in Higher Education*. She is also a Fellow and Vice-chair of the Design Research Society and Vice-chair of the Group for Learning in Art and Design.

Adam Feather is a Consultant Geriatrician at Newham University Hospital Trust and a Senior Lecturer in Medical Education at Barts and The London, Queen Mary's School of Medicine and Dentistry. He is married to the most understanding woman in the world and has a Weapon of Mass Destruction, aged 4.

Della Freeth is Professor of Professional and Interprofessional Education within City Community and Health Sciences, contributing to the CETL on Clinical and Communication Skills developed jointly by City University and Queen Mary, University of London.

David Gosling has written widely on topics relating to learning and teaching in higher education and in applied philosophy. Formerly Head of Educational Development at the University of East London, he is now Visiting Research Fellow at the University of Plymouth. He works as an independent consultant with many universities in the UK and internationally.

Carol Gray is Senior Lecturer in Modern Languages in Education, University of Birmingham. She is involved in the development of initial and in-service training for modern languages and publishes on a range of related topics.

Sandra Griffiths was formerly a Senior Lecturer in Education at the University of Ulster. She has wide experience of supporting and researching learning and teaching and of developing, teaching, reviewing and consulting globally on postgraduate certificates for university teachers. She is President of the All-Ireland Society for Higher Education and a member of the International Council for Educational Development. In 2005 she was awarded a National Teaching Fellowship.

Sherria L. Hoskins is a Principal Lecturer at the University of Portsmouth where she is Course Leader for the B.Sc. Psychology and an operational member of the ExPERT (Excellence in Professional Development through Education, Research and Technology) CETL. In 2004 she was awarded a University Learning and Teaching Fellowship. She is an active researcher, focusing on social cognitive aspects of learning success, from school to university and beyond.

Dai Hounsell is Professor of Higher Education at the University of Edinburgh and previously Director of the Centre of Teaching, Learning and Assessment at that university. He publishes and advises widely on teaching and learning matters.

Ian Hughes is a National Teaching Fellow, Professor of Pharmacology Education, University of Leeds, and has directed the Higher Education Academy Centre for Bioscience, as well as other EU and UK projects, for example developing educational software.

Peter Kahn is Educational Developer in the Centre for Lifelong Learning at the University of Liverpool. He publishes widely on teaching and learning in higher education, and is co-editor (with Joe Kyle) of *Effective Learning and Teaching in Mathematics and its Applications*, also published by Routledge.

John Klapper is a Professor and Director of the Centre for Modern Languages, University of Birmingham, where he also teaches in German Studies. He is a National Teaching Fellow and publishes widely on various aspects of foreign language pedagogy and teacher development.

Pauline Kneale is Professor of Applied Hydrology with Learning and Teaching in Geography at the University of Leeds. She became a National Teaching Fellow in 2002 and is well known in the UK for her work on curriculum development and student employability.

Joe Kyle was formerly Senior Lecturer and Director of Learning and Teaching in the School of Mathematics and Statistics at Birmingham University. Mathematics coordinator for the Higher Education Academy Mathematics, Statistics and Operational Research Network, he is an editor of *Teaching Mathematics and its Applications*.

Ursula Lucas is Professor of Accounting Education at Bristol Business School, University of the West of England. Her research interests are in the development of a reflective capacity within higher education and workplace learning. In 2001 she was awarded a National Teaching Fellowship.

Gerry McAllister holds a B.Sc. and M.Sc. in Electronic Engineering and Ph.D. in Computer Science. He is currently Director of the Subject Centre for Information and Computer Sciences at the University of Ulster, where he is Professor of Computer Science and Head of the School of Computing and Mathematics.

Judy McKimm works at the Centre for Medical and Health Sciences Education, University of Auckland, New Zealand. She was formerly a Visiting Professor at the University of Bedfordshire. She has a long-standing interest and involvement in quality enhancement.

Philip W. Martin is Pro Vice-chancellor of De Montfort University. He has responsibility for Academic Quality and for all Learning and Teaching across the university. His remit also includes the student experience. He is a Professor of English and was formerly Director of the English Subject Centre (for the teaching of English in universities) at Royal Holloway, University of London.

Peter Milford is Interim Associate Director of Education for the South West Strategic Health Authority. Before rejoining the NHS in 2002, he was a Principal Lecturer in Accounting and Finance at Bristol Business School, University of the West of England.

Ann Morton is Head of Staff Development at Aston University. She was previously Programme Director for the Postgraduate Certificate in Learning and Teaching at the University of Birmingham and continues to teach on the similar programme for new lecturers at Aston.

Stephen E. Newstead is Professor of Psychology at the University of Plymouth, though recently he has ventured into management territory as Dean, Deputy Vice-Chancellor and even Vice-Chancellor. Back in the days when he had time to do research, his interests focused on cognitive psychology and the psychology of higher education, especially student assessment.

Lin Norton is a National Teaching Fellow (2007), Professor of Pedagogical Research and Dean of Learning and Teaching at Liverpool Hope University. Her research interests include student assessment which she pursues through her role as Research Director of the Write Now CETL.

Tina Overton is Professor of Chemistry Education at the University of Hull and Director of the Higher Education Academy Physical Sciences Centre. She has published on critical thinking, context-based learning and problem solving.

Pam Parker spent many years in the School of Nursing and Midwifery, City University, focusing on learning, teaching, assessing and curriculum development. She is now co-director of CEAP (Centre for Education and Academic Practice) at City University.

Gus Pennington now works as a consultant in the areas of change management and quality enhancement. He is Visiting Professor at Queen Mary, University of London, and a former chief executive of a national agency for promoting professional development throughout the UK higher education sector.

Morag Shiach is Vice-principal (Teaching and Learning) at Queen Mary, University of London. She has extensive experience of supervising research students and of examining doctoral dissertations in English and cultural history. She has published widely on cultural history, particularly in the modernist period.

Alison Shreeve is Director of the Creative Learning in Practice CETL at the University of the Arts London, UK. She is currently engaged in doctoral research investigating the experience of the practitioner tutor in art and design.

Lorraine Stefani is Director of the Centre for Academic Development at the University of Auckland, New Zealand. Her particular interests are curriculum design and development for a twenty-first-century university education; innovative strategies for assessment of student learning, and institutional strategies to promote student engagement.

Tracey Varnava is Associate Director of the UK Centre for Legal Education, the Higher Education Academy Subject Centre for Law based at the University of Warwick. Before moving to Warwick, she was a Lecturer in Law at the University of Leicester.

Shân Wareing is Dean of Learning and Teaching Development at the University of the Arts London, UK, where she leads the Centre for Learning and Teaching in Art and Design. She is also a Fellow and Co-Chair of the Staff and Educational Development Association.

Julian Webb is Director of the UK Centre for Legal Education and Professor of Legal Education at the University of Warwick, where he also leads the UK's only Master's degree in Legal Education.

Case study authors

Chapter authors who have written case studies have not been re-listed. National attribution has been assigned if outside the UK. Academic titles and departments can be found within the case studies.

Julie Attenborough, City University
Juan Baeza, now King's College London
Simon Bates, University of Edinburgh
Mick Beeby, University of the West of England
Simon Belt, University of Plymouth
Paul Blackmore, now King's College London
Chris Bolsmann, Aston University
Melanie Bowles, University of the Arts London
Jim Boyle, University of Strathclyde
Margaret Bray, London School of Economics and Political Science
David Bristow, Peninsula Medical School
Peter Bullen, University of Hertfordshire
Liz Burd, University of Durham
Christopher Butcher, University of Leeds
Rachael Carkett, now at University of Teesside
Hugh Cartwright, Oxford University
Marion E. Cass, Carleton College, USA
Tudor Chinnah, Peninsula Medical School
Elizabeth Davenport, Queen Mary, University of London
Matt Davies, Aston University
Russell Davies, Peninsula Medical School
Val Dimmock, City University
Roberto Di Napoli, Imperial College London
Caroline Elliott, University of Lancaster
John Fothergill, University of Leicester
Ann Gilroy, University of Auckland, NZ
Christopher Goldsmith, De Montfort University
Anne Goodman, South West and Wales Hub (Cardiff University)
Nuala Gregory, University of Auckland, NZ
Louise Grisoni, University of the West of England
Mick Healey, University of Gloucestershire
Iain Henderson, Napier University
Sarah Henderson, University of Auckland, NZ
Siobhán Holland, Royal Holloway, University of London
Desmond Hunter, University of Ulster
Andrew Ireland, Bournemouth University
Tony Jenkins, University of Leeds
Mike Joy, University of Warwick
Sally Kift, University of Queensland, Australia

Chris Lawn, Queen Mary, University of London
Jonathan Leape, London School of Economics and Political Science
David Lefevre, Imperial College London
David Lewis, University of Leeds
Ian Light, City University
Gary Lock, University of Bath
Lynne MacAlpine, McGill University, Canada, and University of Oxford
George MacDonald Ross, University of Leeds
Peter McCrorie, St George's Medical School, University of London
Neil McLean, London School of Economics and Political Science
Karen Mattick, Peninsula Medical School
Caroline Mills, University of Gloucestershire
Ebrahim Mohamed, Imperial College London
Clare Morris, University of Bedfordshire
Office of the Independent Adjudicator for Higher Education
Fiona Oldham, Napier University
James Oldham, Peninsula Medical School
Alan Patten, Princeton University, USA
Ben Pontin, University of the West of England
Steve Probert, Business, Management, Accounting and Finance Subject Centre (Oxford Brookes University)
Sarah Quinton, Oxford Brookes University
Lisa Reynolds, City University
Sarah Richardson, Warwick University
Andrew Rothwell, Coventry University
Mark Russell, University of Hertfordshire
Henry S. Rzepa, Imperial College London
Andrew Scott, London School of Economics and Political Science
Stephen Shute, University of Birmingham
Alan Simpson, City University
Teresa Smallbone, Oxford Brookes University
Adrian Smith, Southampton University
Simon Steiner, formerly University of Birmingham
Stan Taylor, University of Durham
Tanya Tierney, Imperial College London
Guglielmo Volpe, London Metropolitan University
Digby Warren, London Metropolitan University
Charlotte K. Williams, Imperial College London
Matthew Williamson, Queen Mary, University of London

Acknowledgements

The editors wish to acknowledge all those who have assisted in the production of the third edition of this handbook. We are especially grateful, as always, to our team of expert contributing authors and those who have supplied the case studies that enrich the text.

A special word of thanks is due to Mrs Nicole Nathan without whose organisational skills and help this book would have been much longer in coming to fruition.

We particularly wish to acknowledge the role of Professor Gus Pennington in supporting and encouraging the editors at all stages in the creation of the handbook and most recently in the production of this third edition.

Heather Fry
Steve Ketteridge
Stephanie Marshall

Foreword

It is a pleasure to write this foreword to the third edition of the highly successful *Handbook for Teaching and Learning in Higher Education*. While its contributors are mainly British and there are places where it necessarily addresses a specifically British context, this is a collection which has genuine international appeal and relevance. For, across much of the globe, the world of teaching and learning in higher education is being shaped by similar phenomena: a larger, more demanding and more diverse student body, a pervasive language of quality and accountability, rapidly changing technological possibilities yet uneven levels of student familiarity with them, more demanding arrangements with governments, and expectations by students and employers that graduates will be equipped for rapidly changing and globalising workplaces.

This is a handbook which offers higher education professionals both sage advice on the essentials of effective teaching and research-based reflection on emerging trends. It is a precious collection of core chapters on lecturing to large groups, teaching and learning in small groups, teaching and learning for employability, assessment, and supervision of research theses. At the same time, there are chapters on e-learning, effective student support, and ways of providing evidence for accredited teaching certificates and promotion, including the expanding use of teaching portfolios. Specialists from the creative and performing arts and humanities through business and law to the physical and health sciences will benefit from discipline-specific reflections on challenges in teaching, learning and assessing. Specific case studies, actual examples of successful practice, and links to helpful websites add to the *Handbook*'s usefulness.

This is thus a volume to which young academics will turn for lucid, practical advice on the essentials of effective classroom practice, while their experienced colleagues will find it a rich compendium of challenges to refresh their knowledge and rethink their assumptions. Teachers and students all over the world will have cause to be grateful to the co-editors Heather Fry, Steve Ketteridge and Stephanie Marshall, and to the score of contributors they have expertly assembled. Never before has there been such a need for sound but stimulating advice and reflection on teaching in higher education, and this is a splendid contribution to meeting that need.

Professor Peter McPhee,
Provost,
University of Melbourne,
Australia

Part 1
Teaching, supervising and learning in higher education

1

A user's guide

Heather Fry, Steve Ketteridge
and Stephanie Marshall

SETTING THE CONTEXT OF ACADEMIC PRACTICE

This book starts from the premise that the roles of those who teach in higher education are complex and multifaceted. Teaching is recognised as being only one of the roles that readers of this book will be undertaking. It recognises and acknowledges that academics have contractual obligations to pursue excellence in several directions, most notably in teaching, research and scholarship, supervision, academic administration and management and, for many, maintenance of standing and provision of service in a profession (such as teaching or nursing). Academic practice is a term that encompasses all these facets.

The focus of this book is on teaching and the supervision of students. The purpose of both of these activities, and all that is associated with them (for example, curriculum organisation and assessment), is to facilitate learning, but as our focus is on what the teacher/supervisor does to contribute to this, we have stressed the role of the teacher in both the title and the text of this handbook. However, effective teaching (and supervision, assessment, planning and so on) has to be predicated on an understanding of how students learn; the objective of the activities is to bring about learning, and there has to be insight and knowledge about learners' needs for teaching to be successful.

The authors recognise the fast pace of change in higher education. The past decade has seen continuing increase in student numbers, further internationalisation of the student population, and wider diversity in the prior educational experience of students. All these factors have placed yet more pressure on resources, requirements for income generation, improved flexibility in modes of study and delivery (particularly in distance and e-learning) and continuing scrutiny in relation to quality and standards. Commonly, academics will now work with students who are not only based on campus but also at a distance. A further challenge facing the higher education sector is the expectation to prepare students more carefully for the world of work. For many students the need to take on paid employment during term time is a financial reality. Other themes within teaching include the pressure to respond to local and national student opinion surveys of teaching and the total learning experience, compliance with the **Bologna** Declaration and extending the work and impact of universities out into the local community.

PURPOSE OF THIS BOOK

This book is intended primarily for relatively inexperienced teachers in higher education. Established lecturers interested in exploring recent developments in teaching, learning and assessment will also find it valuable. It will be of interest to a range of staff working in higher education, including those working with communications and information technology, library and technical staff, graduate teaching assistants and various types of researchers. It has much to offer those working outside higher education (for example, clinicians) who have roles in teaching and learning. Those joining universities after having worked in a different university tradition/context (perhaps in a different country), or from business, industry or the professions, will find this volume a useful introduction to current practice in teaching and learning in universities in a wide range of countries. Many of the authors work, or have worked, in the UK (and in other countries), and the UK experience is foregrounded in the text, but there are many ideas that are transferable, albeit perhaps with a slightly different emphasis.

The book is informed by best practice from many countries and types of institutions about teaching, learning, assessment and course design, and is underpinned by appropriate reference to research findings. The focus is primarily (but not exclusively) on teaching at undergraduate level. A particular strength of this book is that it reviews generic issues in teaching and learning that will be common to most practitioners, and also explores, separately, practices in a range of major disciplines. Importantly these two themes are linked in a dedicated chapter (15).

It is likely that those in higher education taking university teaching programmes or certificates or diplomas in academic practice will find the book useful and thought provoking. It supports those in the UK whose university teaching programme is linked to gaining national professional recognition through obtaining a fellowship or associate fellowship of the **Higher Education Academy (HEA)**.

The third edition of the book has been revised and updated. It now better reflects the changing world of higher education in the UK and beyond. It also includes new research and publications, incorporates case studies based on contemporary practice and considers teaching and learning across a broader range of disciplines. The authors have carefully integrated links and information from the UK HEA **Subject Centres**.

The book draws together the accumulated knowledge and wisdom of many experienced and influential practitioners and researchers. Authors come from a range of disciplinary backgrounds and from a range of higher educational institutions. They have taken care in writing to avoid overuse of jargon, but to introduce key terminology, and to make the text readily accessible to staff from all disciplines. The book aims to take a scholarly and rigorous approach, while maintaining a user-friendly format.

The book has been written on the premise that readers strive to extend and enhance their practice. It endeavours to offer a starting point for considering teaching, provoking thought, giving rationales and examples, encouraging reflective practice, and prompting considered actions to enhance one's teaching.

For the purposes of this book the terms 'academic', 'lecturer', 'teacher' and 'tutor' are used interchangeably and should be taken to include anyone engaged in the support of student learning in higher education.

NAVIGATING THE HANDBOOK

Each chapter is written so that it can be read independently of the others, and in any order. Readers can easily select and prioritise, according to interest, although Chapter 2 should be early essential reading. The book has three major parts and a glossary.

Part 1: Teaching, supervising and learning in higher education

This, the introductory chapter, describes the features of the book and how to use it. Chapter 2 lays essential foundations by putting an understanding of how students learn at the heart of teaching. Part 1 has 12 further chapters, each of which explores a major facet of teaching and/or learning. Each is considered from a broad perspective rather than adopting the view or emphasis of a particular discipline. These chapters address most of the repertoire essential to teaching, supervising, curriculum development, assessment and understanding of the student experience of higher education.

Part 2: Teaching in the disciplines

This section opens with a chapter that considers and explores how teaching in higher education draws on knowledge of three areas, namely knowledge about one's discipline, generic principles and ideas about teaching and learning (Part 1) and specific paradigms and objectives particular to teaching and learning in one's own disciplinary area (Part 2). It suggests that as experience and knowledge of teaching grows, so are teachers more inclined/able to link these areas together. Subsequent chapters draw out, for several major disciplinary groupings, the characteristic features of teaching, learning and assessment. These chapters are most useful when read in conjunction with the chapters in Part 1. They also provide the opportunity for an individual working in a particular discipline to explore successful practices associated with other disciplines that might be adapted to their own use.

Part 3: Enhancing personal practice

This section is concerned with how teachers can learn, explore, develop, enhance and demonstrate their teaching expertise. It describes frameworks and tools for professional development and demonstrating experience in teaching, be it as part of a programme to enhance individual practice or about sustaining career development.

Glossary

The final section is a glossary of educational acronyms and technical terms. This may be used in conjunction with reading the chapters or (as many of our previous readers have found) separately. In the chapters the meaning of words or terms in bold may be looked up in the glossary.

DISTINCTIVE FEATURES

Interrogating practice

Chapters feature one or more instances where readers are invited to consider aspects of their own institution, department, course, students or practice. This is done by posing questions to the reader under the heading 'Interrogating practice'. This feature has several purposes. First, to encourage readers to audit their practice with a view to enhancement. Second, to challenge readers to examine critically their conceptions of teaching and workplace practice. Third, to ensure that readers are familiar with their institutional and departmental policies and practices. Fourth, to give teachers the opportunity to develop the habit of reflecting on practice. Readers are free to choose how, or if, they engage with these interrogations.

Case studies

A strength of the book is that each chapter contains case studies. These exemplify issues, practices and research findings mentioned in the body of the chapters. The examples are drawn from a wealth of institutions, involving everyday practice of authors and their colleagues, to demonstrate how particular approaches are used effectively.

FURTHER READING

Each chapter has its own reference section and suggested further reading, including current web-based resources.

IN CONCLUSION

This third edition of the handbook builds upon and updates the previous editions, while retaining the features which have contributed to the success and wide usage of the book. There are new chapters which introduce further expert authors and provide a greater wealth of case study material. The editors are confident that this approach, combined with a reflection of the changing world of higher education (especially in the UK), offers a worthwhile handbook for teaching as part of academic practice.

2 Understanding student learning

Heather Fry, Steve Ketteridge
and Stephanie Marshall

INTRODUCTION

It is unfortunate, but true, that some academics teach students without having much formal knowledge of how students learn. Many lecturers know how they learnt/learn best, but do not necessarily consider how *their* students learn and if the way they teach is predicated on enabling learning to happen. Nor do they necessarily have the concepts to understand, explain and articulate the process they sense is happening in their students.

Learning is about how we perceive and understand the world, about making meaning (Marton and Booth, 1997). But 'learning' is not a single thing; it may involve mastering abstract principles, understanding proofs, remembering factual information, acquiring methods, techniques and approaches, recognition, reasoning, debating ideas, or developing behaviour appropriate to specific situations; it is about change.

Despite many years of research into learning, it is not easy to translate this knowledge into practical implications for teaching. There are no simple answers to the questions 'how do we learn?' and 'how as teachers can we bring about learning?' This is partly because education deals with specific purposes and contexts that differ from each other and with students as people, who are diverse in all respects, and ever changing. Not everyone learns in the same way, or equally readily about all types of material. The discipline and level of material to be learnt have an influence. Students bring different backgrounds and expectations to learning. Our knowledge about the relationship between teaching and learning is incomplete and the attitudes and actions of both parties affect the outcome, but we do know enough to make some firm statements about types of action that will usually be helpful in enabling learning to happen. In this chapter some of the major learning theories that are relevant to higher education are introduced. In the discipline of education a theory is something built from research evidence, which *may* have explanatory power; much educational research is not about proving or disproving theories, but about creating them from research data.

Increasingly teaching takes place at a distance or electronically rather than face-to-face, but the theories and ideas outlined in this chapter still need to be considered.

Motivation and assessment both play a large part in student learning in higher education and these topics are considered in more detail in Chapters 3 and 10.

This chapter is intended to give only a general overview of some key ideas about student learning. It describes some of the common learning models and theories relevant to higher education, presents case studies in which lecturers relate their teaching to some of these ideas, and indicates broad implications of these ideas for teaching and assessing. We hope readers will consider the ideas, and use those that are helpful in organising, understanding and enhancing their teaching in their discipline and context.

Interrogating practice

As you read this chapter, note down, from what it says about learning, the implications for teaching in your discipline. When you reach the last section of the chapter, compare your list with the general suggestions you will find there.

MAJOR VIEWS OF LEARNING

In psychology there are several schools of thought about how learning takes place, and various categorisations of these. Rationalism (or idealism) is one such school, or pole, of learning theory still with some vogue. It is based on the idea of a biological plan being in existence that unfolds in very determined directions. Chomsky was a foremost member of this pole. Associationism, a second pole, centres on the idea of forming associations between stimuli and responses. Pavlov and Skinner belong to this pole. Further details may be found in Richardson (1985). In the twenty-first century cognitive and social theories are those used most widely, with **constructivism** being the best known.

Many ideas about learning in the early twentieth century tended to consider the development of the individual in isolation, but by the 1920s and 1930s ideas looking at the influence of the wider context in which learning occurs and at emotional and social influences and affects became more common. These ideas continue to gain ground and some are mentioned later in this chapter.

Constructivism

Most contemporary psychologists use constructivist theories of varying types to explain how human beings learn. The idea rests on the notion of continuous building and amending of structures in the mind that 'hold' knowledge. These structures are known as schemata. As new understandings, experiences, actions and information are assimilated and accommodated the schemata change. Unless schemata are changed, learning will not occur. Learning (whether in **cognitive, affective, interpersonal** or **psychomotor domains**) is said to involve a process of individual transformation. Thus people actively construct their knowledge (Biggs and Moore, 1993).

Piaget (1950) and Bruner (1960, 1966) are two of the twentieth century's most eminent educationalists, with views that are largely congruent with constructivism. For example, Bruner's ideas relating to inducting students into the modes of thinking in individual disciplines and his notion of revisiting knowledge at ever higher levels of understanding, leading to the idea of a spiral curriculum, have been very influential. In the discipline of history, for instance, Bruner is often cited as the inspiration for changing the focus of history teaching in schools in England. This shifted the balance from regurgitation of factual information to understanding. Some of the ways in which this was done were to encourage learners to understand how the past is reconstructed and understood, for example by learning how to empathise and to work from primary sources.

Constructivism tells us that we learn by fitting new understanding and knowledge into and with, extending and supplanting, old understanding and knowledge. As teachers, we need to be aware that we are rarely if ever 'writing on a blank slate', even if prior understanding is rudimentary, or wrong. Without changes or additions to pre-existing knowledge and understanding, little learning will occur.

Very frequently learning is thought of in terms only of adding more knowledge, whereas teachers should be considering also how to bring about change or transformation to the pre-existing knowledge of their learners (Mezirow, 1991). Additions to knowledge, in the sense of accumulated 'facts', may sometimes be possible without substantial transformation, but any learning of a higher order, involving understanding or creativity, for example, can usually only happen when the underlying schemata are themselves changed to incorporate new, more refined understanding and linkages. Such change will itself be likely to facilitate retention of facts for the longer term (see Approaches to study, below).

APPROACHES TO STUDY

In the 1970s, Marton (1975) conducted empirical work that has subsequently gained much credibility and currency in higher education. Considerable further work has taken place, including in and across a range of disciplinary contexts (e.g. Lizzio *et al.*, 2002). Marton's research, investigating the interaction between a student and a set learning task, led to the conclusion that students' approaches to the task (their intention) determined the extent to which they engaged with their subject and this affected the quality of outcomes. These were classified as deep and surface **approaches to learning**.

The **deep approach** to learning is typified by an intention to understand and seek meaning, leading students to attempt to relate concepts to existing understanding and to each other, to distinguish between new ideas and existing knowledge, and to critically evaluate and determine key themes and concepts. In short, such an approach results from the students' intention to gain maximum meaning from their studying, which they achieve through high levels of cognitive processing throughout learning. Facts are learnt in the context of meaning. There is some evidence that lecturers who take a **student-focused approach** to teaching and learning will encourage students towards a deep approach to study (Prosser and Trigwell, 1999).

The **surface approach** to learning is typified by an intention to complete the task, memorise information, make no distinction between new ideas and existing knowledge; and to treat the task as externally imposed. Rote learning is the typical surface approach. Such an approach results from students' intention to offer the impression that maximum learning has taken place, which they achieve through superficial levels of cognitive processing. 'Facts' are learnt without a meaningful framework.

The following illustrates these concepts. The learning outcomes for, say, social science students, who adopt a deep approach to the task of reading a set text, would include full engagement with the central theme of the text and an understanding of contributing arguments. In contrast, those who adopt a surface approach would fail to identify the central themes – primarily because they would be engrossed in progressing through the text sequentially, attempting to remember the flat landscape of facts.

The conceptions of deep and surface approaches to learning have increased in sophistication with further research, most notably the work of Biggs (1987) and Ramsden (1988). Ramsden (2003: 47–48) provides helpful, illustrative examples of statements from students in different disciplines exhibiting deep and surface approaches.

Biggs and Ramsden turned learning theory on its head in that rather than drawing on the work of philosophers or cognitive psychologists, they looked to students themselves for a distinctive perspective. Ramsden (1988) suggested that approach to learning was not implicit in the make-up of the student, but something between the student and the task and thus was *both* personal and situational. An approach to learning should, therefore, be seen not as a pure individual characteristic but rather as a response to the teaching environment in which the student is expected to learn. Biggs (1987) identified a third approach to study – the **strategic** or **achieving approach**, associated with assessment. Here the emphasis is on organising learning specifically to obtain a high examination grade. With this intention, a learner who often uses a deep approach may adopt some of the techniques of a surface approach to meet the requirements of a specific activity such as a test. A learner with a repertoire of approaches can select – or be guided towards – which one to use. Approaches need not be fixed and unchanging characteristics of the way a person learns.

A misconception on the part of many students entering higher education is their belief that a subject consists only of large amounts of factual knowledge or a mastery of steps or rules, and, to become the expert, all one need do is add knowledge to one's existing store. It is the responsibility of the lecturer to challenge and change such limited conceptions and to ensure that their teaching, curricula they design, and assessments they set, take students into more stretching areas such as critical thinking, creativity, synthesis and so on. Biggs (1999) is one of the foremost proponents of the view that approaches to learning can be modified by the teaching and learning context, and are themselves learnt. He has also popularised the term **constructive alignment** to describe congruence between what the teacher intends learners to be able to do, know or understand, how they teach, and what and how they assess.

> ## Case study 1: Encouraging Master's level students to take a deep approach to learning through a combination of teaching and learning methods

There are 150 students on my MSc Management course. These students come from different countries, academic backgrounds, cultures, and teaching and learning traditions. It is a challenge to ensure sufficient exposure and learning for the diverse group; along with 'information', they need a deeper understanding of the concepts involved. However, because the entrance criteria for this course are high I can be confident that the students are 'quick' learners. I therefore include a lot of information in the formal lecture part of the two-hour sessions. I start from first principles, making few assumptions of prior knowledge, but go through the material quite quickly, which, coupled with comprehensive lecture notes, enables the whole group to be at a similar level in terms of the information they need. I then make the second half of the session as flexible and informal as possible so that students can work at different speeds and modes depending on their background. I encourage group work to harness the heterogeneity of the group and for students to learn from each other.

I am conscious that the lectures develop a surface approach to learning, which can be contrasted with the interactive sessions that promote a deeper approach to learning. All the students seem comfortable with the lecture part of the sessions while many of them struggle with the more interactive sessions; however, the group style of these sessions seems to ease this process. I find it worthwhile to remind myself that developing a deeper approach to learning can be a gradual and sometimes unsuccessful process.

(Dr Juan Baeza, Tanaka Business School, Imperial College London)

Interrogating practice

Consider occasions when you have wanted your students to really think about something or take it on board in a fundamental way, but they have taken a surface approach. Why do you think this was?

The SOLO taxonomy of levels of understanding

SOLO stands for Structure of the Observed Learning Outcomes. The taxonomy is based on the study of a variety of academic content areas and the principle that, as students learn, the outcomes of their learning pass through stages of increasing complexity (Biggs and Collis, 1982; Biggs, 1999). The changes are in the amount of detail and the quality of learning. Quantitative changes occur first, and then the learning changes qualitatively. It may be used as a framework for classifying learning and achievement especially in the cognitive domain; **learning outcomes** may be mapped on to it. It may also be mapped against other learning taxonomies (for example, Bloom's taxonomy, given in more detail in Chapter 4).

The SOLO taxonomy is a hierarchical classification in which each level is the foundation for the next:

- *Prestructural*: understanding at the individual word level. Students at this level may miss the point or use tautology to cover lack of understanding. Here, students show little evidence of relevant learning. Such understanding should be rare in the context of higher education.
- *Unistructural*: responses deal with terminology. They meet only part of the task and miss out important attributes.
- *Multistructural*: many facts are present, but they are not structured and do not address the key issue/s.
- *Relational*: consists of more than a list of details, addresses the point and makes sense in relation to the topic as a whole. This is the first level at which understanding is displayed in an academically relevant sense. It involves conceptual restructuring of components.
- *Extended abstract*: a coherent whole is conceptualised at a high level of abstraction and is applied to new and broader contexts; a breakthrough has been made, which changes the way of thinking about issues, and represents a high level of under-standing.

The SOLO taxonomy may be used to inform curriculum development and the articulation of learning outcomes and assessment criteria. (It is important not to confuse Biggs' 'levels' with other classifications, such as the **levels** of the Framework of Higher Education Qualifications – see Chapter 13.) One implication of Biggs' work is that higher levels of the SOLO taxonomy are unlikely to be achieved by those adopting a surface approach to learning.

THRESHOLD CONCEPTS

Meyer and Land (2006) have developed the idea of **threshold concepts** which has been taken up by many teachers in different disciplines. (Chapter 24, for example, briefly considers threshold concepts in business studies and accountancy.) Threshold concepts are those key ideas, concepts or processes in a discipline that need to be understood by students before they can understand other parts of the subject that follow from them. (Approaches to learning *might* be such a threshold concept in learning and teaching in higher education.) Not every key concept in a discipline is a threshold concept. The language Meyer and Land have developed thus talks of 'troublesome knowledge' that represents a 'portal' or 'gateway', which once the learner has passed through it will illuminate and underpin much subsequent understanding. Students can get 'stuck' in a state of 'liminality', not being able to get through the portal. The idea of threshold concepts is useful, as it helps teachers to identify very important areas that it is vital to help students understand; it can also help to identify past misunderstandings that may prevent the learner from making current progress. For example, diagnostic tests may commonly be given to students entering higher education to ascertain if there are areas they need to improve before embarking on degree work. These might focus on selected threshold concepts.

ADULT LEARNING THEORY

It is questionable how far there really are *theories* of adult learning and whether adult learning differs in character from that of children. Despite these doubts there are propositions concerning the learning of adults which have had much influence on higher education, if only to cause teachers in this sector to re-examine their premises and adjust some of their views. Adult learning theories are thought by some to be particularly relevant to an ever more diverse student body (whether considered by age, mode of study, or ethnic, economic or educational background) and to postgraduate work.

Malcolm Knowles is associated with using the term **andragogy** (despite its much earlier aetiology) to refer to adult learning and defining it as the 'art and science of helping adults learn' (Knowles and Associates, 1984). A complication is that he has changed his definition over decades of work. Andragogy is considered to have five principles:

- As a person matures he or she becomes more self-directed.
- Adults have accumulated experiences that can be a rich resource for learning.
- Adults become ready to learn when they experience a need to know something.
- Adults tend to be less subject-centred than children; they are increasingly problem-centred.
- For adults the most potent motivators are internal.

There is a lack of empirical evidence to support this differentiation from childhood learning. Despite many critiques of andragogy (e.g. see Davenport, 1993) it has had considerable influence because many university lecturers recognise characteristics they have seen their learners exhibiting. Many 'types' of learning that are often used and discussed in higher education, including **experiential learning**, student **autonomy** and **self-directed learning**, belong in or derive from the tradition of adult education.

Furthermore, considerable areas of work in higher education around the student experience, supporting students and widening participation are closely linked to work and ideas in adult education (e.g. barriers to entry, progression and empowerment).

EXPERIENTIAL LEARNING AND REFLECTION

It is self-evident that experience gained through life, education and work should play a central role in learning; this, constructivist, perspective on learning is called experiential learning. The most widespread theory of learning from experience is associated with David Kolb (1984), who developed ideas from earlier models of experiential learning; the Kolb model appears most frequently in the literature.

An appreciation of experiential learning is a necessary underpinning to many of the different types of teaching and learning activity discussed elsewhere in this book, including **work-based** (or **placement**) **learning, action learning,** teaching **laboratory work** and **reflective practice**. The provision of vicarious experience, such as by using case studies or **role play**, and many types of **small group** use experiential learning as an underlying rationale.

Experiential learning is based on the notion that understanding is not a fixed or unchangeable element of thought and that experiences can contribute to its forming and re-forming. Experiential learning is a continuous process and implies that we all bring to learning situations our own knowledge, ideas, beliefs and practices at different levels of elaboration that should in turn be amended or shaped by the experience – if we learn from it.

The continuously cycling model of learning that has become known as the 'Kolb Learning Cycle' requires four kinds of abilities/undertaking if learning is to be successful (see Figure 2.1).

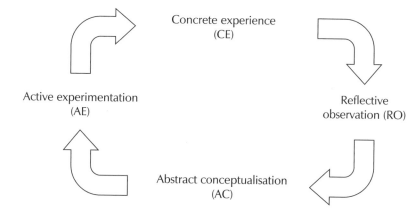

Figure 2.1 The Kolb Learning Cycle

First, learners are involved fully and freely in new experiences (CE). Second, they must make/have the time and space to be able to reflect on their experience from different perspectives (RO). Third, learners must be able to form, re-form and process their ideas, take ownership of them and integrate their new ideas and understanding into sound, logical theories (AC). It is these middle two elements in the cycle that can be strongly influenced by **feedback** from others. This moves towards the fourth point (AE), using the enhanced understanding to make decisions and problem-solve, and test implications and usage in new situations. The experiential cycle does not simply involve having an experience, or 'doing', but also reflecting, processing, thinking and furthering understanding, and usually 'improvement' the next time something is encountered or done.

By extension, this cyclical process has a part to play in even the most abstract and theoretical disciplines where the academic is concerned to help the learner acquire the 'tools of the trade' or the modes of thinking central to the discipline, such as in philosophy or literary criticism.

The teacher needs to be aware that in practice learners do not cycle smoothly through the model, but may get stuck, fail to progress or 'jump about'. The way in which the learner resolves these tensions will have an effect on the learning outcome and the development of different types of strength in the learner and, as will be seen, may pertain to personality traits and/or disciplinary differences.

Reflection is a key part of experiential learning as it 'turns experience into learning' (Boud *et al.*, 1985). Because of misunderstanding, overuse and its passive and negative connotations, reflection has had a worse press than it deserves, but it is also true that the research evidence about how it works is lacking. To learn from experience we need to examine and analyse the experience; this is what reflection means in this context. It may be a similar action to the one that we may consciously or subconsciously use when taking a deep approach to learning.

Reflection and reflective practice are not easy concepts. With regard to higher education they may be applied to the learning of students, and equally to the professional development of the lecturer (see Part 3). Schön (1987), in examining the relationship between professional knowledge and professional **competence**, suggests that rather than looking to another body of research knowledge, practitioners should become more adept at observing and learning through reflection on the artistry of their own particular profession. 'Reflection on practice' (on experience) is central to learning and development of knowledge in the professions. Recognised 'experts' in the field exhibit distinct artistry. This artistry cannot be learned solely through conventional teaching methods – it requires role models, observation of competent practitioners, self-practice, mentors, experience in carrying out all the tasks of one's job and reflection upon that practice. Support in developing reflection is often necessary, for example by using prompts and feedback. Such reflective practice is a key aspect of **lifelong learning**.

Interrogating practice

Call to mind some occasions when conscious reflection on something has enhanced your understanding or ability to carry out a particular task.

Case study 2: Using experiential learning and reflection with first year medical students learning communication skills

Teaching of patient-centred communication skills at Imperial is supported by repeated opportunities for students to practise, using role play. Role play provides a safe environment for students without risk of harm to a real patient. The effectiveness of role play is maximised by taking time for briefing (to put the role play in context and identify students' individual needs) and debriefing (to provide opportunity for reflections and feedback) (Nestel and Tierney, 2007).

Towards the end of Year 1, we provide three occasions for role play, using these 'concrete experiences' to encourage experiential learning. Students role play with each other, perform three five-minute interviews with volunteers and interview a professional 'simulated patient' (SP).

After each role play, students are encouraged to reflect. For the role plays with each other and volunteers, they complete 'boxes' in their notes in response to the following questions:

- What communication skills did you use effectively?
- What communication skills did you use less effectively?
- How will you maintain your strengths?
- How will you develop your weaknesses?

Reflection is supported by feedback. Students are given guidance on giving and receiving feedback so that they can provide effective feedback to each other; the volunteers give feedback on a short rating form.

However, the richest opportunity for students to receive feedback (and thus be guided in their reflections) is after their interview with a professional SP. Each student has 20 minutes with an SP and an experienced facilitator. After interviewing the SP, the student is encouraged to reflect on his or her own performance before receiving feedback from the SP. SPs and facilitators are trained to give feedback that is high challenge/high support to maximise benefit. The facilitator then summarises the students' reflections and the SP's feedback and encourages the students to consider how they will maintain and develop their skills and apply them in future interviews with patients (Kolb's abstract conceptualisation, active experimentation). To encourage active experimentation, students may be offered the chance to repeat sections of the role play to see if a different approach would have been more effective.

By encouraging reflection after role plays we aim to develop students' attitudes to reflective practice so that they will continue to use it in encounters with real patients, not only while they are studying, but throughout their professional lives.

(Dr Tanya Tierney, Faculty of Medicine, Imperial College London)

LEARNING STYLES AND RELATED IDEAS

Learning styles is one of the most widely used terms in relation to student learning. However, the notion of learning styles is problematic. There are several categorisations of 'styles'; research-based evidence of their existence is sparse (Coffield *et al.*, 2004); the term is sometimes misused to mean approaches to learning, or the two are conflated. However, even though learners may have preferences it may be that they should be encouraged to use a range of learning styles, in which case those responsible for organising learning should create opportunities for learning that are sensitive to different styles, and do not simply reflect how they or their students *like* to learn.

Three categorisations of learning style are mentioned below. Pask (1976) identified serialist and holist learning styles. A serialist is said to prefer a step-by-step approach and a narrow focus while holists prefer to obtain the 'big picture' and to work with illustrations and analogies.

Perhaps the best-known categorisation of learning style is that of Honey and Mumford (1982). They offer a fourfold classification of activist, pragmatist, reflector and theorist:

- *Activists* respond most positively to learning situations offering challenge, to include new experiences and problems, excitement and freedom in their learning.
- *Reflectors* respond most positively to structured learning activities where they are provided with time to observe, reflect and think, and allowed to work in a detailed manner.
- *Theorists* respond well to logical, rational structure and clear aims, where they are given time for methodical exploration and opportunities to question and stretch their intellect.
- *Pragmatists* respond most positively to practically based, immediately relevant learning activities, which allow scope for practice and using theory.

They suggest that the preferred learning style of any individual will include elements from two or more of these categories.

Wolf and Kolb (1984) suggested that learners develop different learning styles that emphasise preference for some modes of learning over others, leading to particular characteristics (see Table 2.1).

Table 2.1 Learning styles

Learning style	Strengths	Dominant learning ability
Convergent	Practical application of ideas	AC and AE
Divergent	Imaginative ability and generation of ideas	CE and RO
Assimilation	Creating theoretical models and making sense of disparate observations	AC and RO
Accommodative	Carrying out plans and tasks that involve new experiences	CE and AE

Source: Based on Wolf and Kolb (1984)

Learning and teaching in the disciplines

There are teaching norms that attach to disciplines (see e.g. Neumann 2001). Earlier sections have mentioned disciplinary-specific research around a number of learning theories. How far students are aware of, drawn to, or shaped by disciplinary norms and how far their perception is shared by academics is unclear (see e.g. Breen *et al.*, 2000; Neumann *et al.*, 2002). The idea that the preferred learning style of an individual may have a relationship to the particular disciplinary framework in which the learning is taking place is one that still warrants further research.

Becher and Trowler (2001) consider the clustering and characteristics of disciplinary knowledge, drawing on the 'Kolb-Biglan Classification of Academic Knowledge', and on earlier work by Becher. The classification suggests that the preferred learning style might be attributable to a relationship with a particular disciplinary framework. This may need to be taken into account when planning learning opportunities in different disciplines.

The distribution in the four quadrants shown in Table 2.2 is interesting, in that those studying the disciplines in quadrants 1 and 2 are described as showing some preference for reflective practice. However, we must ask ourselves, noting that some of the disciplines mentioned in quadrants 3 and 4 are now strongly associated with reflective practice, just how useful this classification is. Perhaps the lesson to learn is that there are likely to be disciplinary differences in these characteristics that may be difficult to classify. How far students acquire, are attracted to, or bring with them to a subject any of the associated ways of thinking, or 'frames of mind', is a difficult matter (see Gardner's classic work, (1985)), but not unimportant from a teaching perspective.

These views might lead to the supposition that students in particular disciplines may have considerable difficulty in developing, for example, employability skills that relate

Table 2.2 Classification of academic knowledge

1. **Abstract reflective**	2. **Concrete reflective**
AC-RO	CE-RO
Hard pure	Soft pure
Natural sciences	Humanities
Mathematics	Social sciences
3. **Abstract active**	4. **Concrete active**
AC-AE	CE-AE
Hard applied	Soft applied
Science-based professions, engineering	Social professions
Medicine and other healthcare	Education, social work
professions	Law

Source: Based on the Kolb-Biglan Model and subsequent work by Becher and Trowler (2001)

to a different quadrant (e.g. numeracy by humanities students or team working by mathematicians) (academics may also feel disconnection if asked to incorporate 'alien perspectives' into their teaching). However, we know of no robust research evidence to support or refute this hypothesis.

Approaches and styles

When encountering the term 'learning style', it is important to be clear about exactly which categorisation, if any, is being referred to, and whether or not learning style is being confused with approaches to study (for which the research evidence is more robust). It is also important to remember that a major contrast between styles and approaches, at least in the view of their main proponents, is the degree of immutability of these qualities. The contrast is between approaches to study (which are modifiable) and learning styles (which are usually held to be part of personality characteristics and traits and therefore more fixed). The current state of play dictates that neither approaches nor styles should be regarded as fixed, i.e. both may be modifiable, but that both may be habituated and hard to change. Teachers may wish to encourage their students to employ a range of strategies on different occasions.

Many of those who have worked with learning styles and approaches to learning have developed questionnaire-type taxonomies, or inventories, for identifying the approach (e.g. Marton *et al.*, 1997, originally 1984) or style being used by the learner. These should be used appropriately and interpreted with caution if one regards the underlying concepts or characteristics as in a state of flux. This has not prevented lecturers from using them to 'diagnose' student learning. Their use does have the advantage of helping students to think about how they best learn and whether they would benefit from trying to modify their behaviour; and for the teacher to consider if changing the curriculum design, especially the assessment, would change student behaviour.

A consideration of learning preferences is important for the lecturer planning a course module, as a variety of strategies to promote learning should be considered. Teachers also need to be aware that changing firmly established patterns of behaviour and views of the world can prove destabilising for the learner who is then engaged in something rather more than cognitive restructuring (Perry, 1979).

VYGOTSKY AND ASSOCIATED IDEAS

The ideas of the psychologist Lev Vygotsky (e.g. 1978) were little known outside the Soviet Union during his lifetime, and for decades remained largely buried in the mists of Stalin's Russia. They have subsequently become very influential.

Vygotsky is associated with emphasising the role of social and cultural context and process in development and learning, as opposed to a more exclusive focus within the individual. His ideas about the 'zone of proximal development' (ZPD) in children, the gap between what individuals can understand by themselves and what can be understood with help, emphasise that a learner can be taken more quickly up a learning curve, and their ZPD continuously advanced, with appropriate help. This notion is central to concepts such as 'scaffolding' learning, i.e. providing help and support. This idea has of course always underpinned, if not consciously, much teaching, including that in universities. In higher education there are often balanced judgements needed about tapering support so as to avoid spoon feeding and to promote the ability to think independently. Other ideas derived at least in part from Vygotsky's work include those associated with Engeström (2001), including **activity theory** and **expansive learning**.

Lave and Wenger (e.g. 1991) are associated with a social theory of learning called **situated learning**. Situated learning focuses on understanding knowledge and learning in context, and emphasises that the learner (or worker) engages with others to develop/create collective understanding as part of a **community of practice**. Their view of learning is thus relational, and downplays the importance of the continuous reformation and transformation of the schemata by single effort alone or within individuals, or of learning certain types of things through books or out of context. Situated learning views learning as a social practice and considers that new knowledge can be generated from practice. The idea of a community of practice is widely used in the development of professional knowledge and practice (e.g. in nursing and engineering). The concept also applies to research groups in science and engineering, even though many members may be unfamiliar with the term.

TEACHING FOR LEARNING

'It is important to remember that what the student does is actually more important in determining what is learned than what the teacher does' (Sheull, cited in Biggs, 1993). This statement is congruent with a constructivist view and also reminds us that students in higher education must engage with and take considerable responsibility for their learning. It is important that learners structure information and are able to use it (Biggs, 1999). The teacher cannot do all the work if learning is to be the outcome; congruently, the teacher must ensure that course design, selection of teaching and learning opportunities and assessment help the learner to learn. As designers of courses and as teachers, we want to 'produce' graduates of higher education capable of critical thought, able to be creative and innovate at a relatively high level. Learning requires opportunities for practice and exploration, space for thinking or reflecting 'in your head' and for interaction with others, and learning from and with peers and experts. These imperatives, coupled with those of our discipline, should affect our view of how we teach (and design courses) in our particular higher education context (see also Chapter 15). Case study 3 (opposite) shows three teachers creatively exploiting technology to assist learners to grasp the symmetry of molecules.

Turning theory into practice

Selection of teaching, learning and assessment methods should be grounded in and considered alongside an understanding of theories about learning. Notable among the precepts that emerge from what we understand about how students learn are the following:

- Learners experience the same teaching in different ways.
- Learners will approach learning in a variety of ways and the ways we teach may modify their approaches.
- Prior knowledge needs to be activated.
- Learners have to be brought to 'engage' with what they are learning so that transformation and internalisation may occur.
- Learners bring valuable experience to learning.
- Learners may be more motivated when offered an element of choice.
- Learners need to be able to explain their answers, and answer and ask 'why?' questions.
- Learners taking a discipline that is new to them may struggle to think in the appropriate manner (an important point in modular programmes).
- Teachers need to understand where learners are starting from so that they can get the correct level and seek to correct underlying misconceptions or gaps.
- Teachers and learners are both responsible for learning happening.
- Teachers need to be aware of the impact of cultural background and beliefs on learner behaviour, interpretation and understanding.
- Feedback and discussion are important in enabling the teacher and learner to check that accommodations of new understanding are 'correct'.
- Formal and informal discussion of what is being learnt in a peer (small) group can be a powerful learning tool.

Case study 3: Using technology to aid complex learning

Three colleagues teamed up to create interactive, dynamic visualisations as a supplement to lectures to help chemistry undergraduates learn about the symmetry of molecules. Understanding molecular symmetry requires that students develop good three-dimensional visualisation skills; most do not find this easy. Physical models aid learning, but have some limitations. Students can move a model, but can accidentally or deliberately break bonds (which changes the structure and therefore the symmetry) and there is no way to control what orientation is seen. In addition, the number of model kits available is limited, as are secure locations for storage and off-hour access for students. Creating 3D web images of molecules, using opensource software, gave several learning advantages. First, students can access them at any time for as long as they want, and all can access them simultaneously. Students can manipulate the molecules in 3D space to view the molecules from different orientations, and use 'buttons' to force the molecule to reorient – in such a fashion as to illustrate our point. By manipulating the molecules to align them in different orientations students can test for properties of symmetry. Fourth, if we then add a computational laboratory component, students can estimate the (often relative) energies of the molecules and get a feel for stability. Students using our interactive tools, we have observed, pick up symmetry concepts more quickly and get to the essence of the subject with less angst.

After our first animations, colleagues asked for visualisations and animations of dynamic molecular processes. This launched a second project in which our animations aided our teaching as well as our research. Our animations have been published in chemical education and research journals (for an online teaching example see Cass *et al.*, 2005).

(Professor Marion E. Cass, Carleton College, Northfield, MN,
on leave at Imperial when she became involved in this work, Professor Henry
S. Rzepa and Dr Charlotte K. Williams, Imperial College London)

- Learning best takes place in or related to a relevant context (to facilitate the 'making of meaning').
- When planning, specifying outcomes, teaching or assessing, lecturers need to consider all appropriate domains and be aware of the level of operations being asked for.
- The learning climate/environment in which learners learn (e.g. motivation, interaction, support) affects the outcomes.

- Teachers should consider reducing the amount of didactic teaching.
- Teachers should avoid content overload; too much material will encourage a surface approach.
- Think about possible threshold concepts in your discipline and how these can be taught for optimal learning, including how they can be relearnt when earlier understanding is inadequate.
- Basic principles and concepts provide the basis for further learning.
- Assessment has a powerful impact on student behaviour.

OVERVIEW

What is important about teaching is what it helps the learner to do, know or understand. There are different models of learning that it is useful for the university lecturer to be aware of. What we do as teachers must take into account what we understand about how students learn, generally and in our own context. The rationale for the choice of teaching and assessment methods needs to consider how students learn, and the make-up of our student intake, rather than infrastructure or resource constraints, or inflexible 'requirements'.

REFERENCES

Becher, T and Trowler, P (2001) *Academic Tribes and Territories*, Buckingham: Society for Research in Higher Education/Open University Press.

Biggs, J (1987) *Student Approaches to Learning and Studying*, Hawthorn, Victoria: Australian Council for Educational Research.

Biggs, J (1993) 'From theory to practice: a cognitive systems approach', *Higher Education Research and Development*, 12(1): 73–85.

Biggs, J (1999) *Teaching for Quality Learning at University*, Buckingham: Society for Research in Higher Education/Open University Press.

Biggs, J and Collis, K F (1982) *Evaluating the Quality of Learning: The SOLO Taxonomy*, London: Academic Press.

Biggs, J and Moore, P (1993) *The Process of Learning*, New York: Prentice-Hall.

Boud, D, Keogh, R, Walker, D (eds) (1985) *Reflection: Turning Experience into Learning*, London: Kogan Page.

Breen, R, Lindsay, R, Jenkins, A (2000) 'Phenomenography and the disciplinary basis of motivation to learn', in C Rust (ed.) *Improving Student Learning Through the Disciplines*, Oxford: Oxford Centre for Staff and Learning Development.

Bruner, J S (1960) *The Process of Education*, Cambridge, MA: Harvard University Press.

Bruner, J S (1966) *Towards a Theory of Instruction*, Cambridge, MA: Harvard University Press.

Cass, M E, Rzepa, H S, Rzepa, D R, Williams, C K (2005) 'An animated/interactive overview of molecular symmetry', *Journal of Chemical Education, Online*, 82(11): 1742–1743. Link:

http://jchemed.chem.wisc.edu/JCEDLib/WebWare/collection/reviewed/JCE2005p1742 WW/jcesubscriber/symmetry/index.htm (last accessed November 2007).

Coffield, F, Moseley, D, Hall, E, Ecclestone, K (2004) *Learning Styles for Post 16 Learners. What Do We Know? A Report to the Learning and Skills Research Centre*, Newcastle: University of Newcastle, School of Education.

Davenport, J (1993) 'Is there any way out of the andragony morass?', in M Thorpe, R Edwards and E Hanson (eds) *Culture and Process of Adult Learning*, London: RoutledgeFalmer.

Engeström, Y (2001) 'Expansive learning at work: toward an activity theoretical consideration', *Journal of Education and Work*, 14(1): 133–156.

Entwistle, N and Ramsden, P (1983) *Understanding Student Learning*, London: Croom Helm.

Gardner, H (1985) *Frames of Mind*, London: Paladin.

Honey, P and Mumford, A (1982) *The Manual of Learning Styles*, Maidenhead: Peter Honey.

Knowles, M and Associates (1984) *Andragogy in Action*, Houston, TX: Gulf Publishing.

Kolb, D A (1984) *Experiential Learning*, Englewood Cliffs, NJ: Prentice-Hall.

Lave, J and Wenger, E (1991) *Situated Learning: Legitimate Peripheral Participation*, Cambridge: Cambridge University Press.

Lizzio, A, Wilson, K, Simons, R (2002) 'University students' perceptions of the learning environment and academic outcomes: implications for theory and practice', *Studies in Higher Education*, 27(1): 27–52.

Marton, F (1975) 'On non-verbatim learning – 1: Level of processing and level of outcome', *Scandinavian Journal of Psychology*, 16: 273–279.

Marton, F and Booth, S (1997) *Learning and Awareness*, Mahwah, NJ: Lawrence Erlbaum Associates.

Marton, F, Hounsell, D, Entwistle, N (1997, 2nd edn) *The Experience of Learning*, Edinburgh: Scottish Academic Press.

Meyer, Jan H F and Land, R (eds) (2006) *Overcoming Barriers to Student Understanding*, London: Routledge.

Mezirow, J (1991) *Transformative Dimensions of Adult Learning*, San Francisco, CA: Jossey-Bass.

Nestel, D and Tierney, T (2007) 'Role-play for medical students learning about communication: guidelines for maximising benefits', *BMC Medical Education*, 7:3. Available online at http://www.biomedcentral.com/1472–6920/7/3.

Neumann, R (2001) 'Disciplinary differences and university teaching', *Studies in Higher Education*, 26(2): 135–146.

Neumann, R, Parry, S, Becher, T (2002) 'Teaching and learning in their disciplinary contexts: a conceptual analysis', *Studies in Higher Education*, 26(2): 406–417.

Pask, G (1976) 'Learning styles and strategies', *British Journal of Educational Psychology*, 46: 4–11.

Perry, W (1979) *Forms of Intellectual and Ethical Development in the College Years*, New York: Holt, Rinehart and Winston.

Piaget, J (1950) *The Psychology of Intelligence*, London: Routledge and Kegan Paul.

Prosser, M and Trigwell, K (1999) *Understanding Learning and Teaching. The Experience in Higher Education*, Buckingham: The Society for Research into Higher Education and Open University Press.

Ramsden, P (1988) *Improving Learning: New Perspectives*, London: Kogan Page.

Ramsden, P (2003, 2nd edn) *Learning to Teach in Higher Education*, London: RoutledgeFalmer.

Richardson, K (1985) *Personality, Development and Learning: Unit 8/9 Learning Theories*, Milton Keynes: Open University Press.

Schön, D (1987) *Educating the Reflective Practitioner: Toward a New Design for Teaching and Learning in the Professions*, San Francisco, CA: Jossey-Bass.

Vygotsky, L (1978) *Mind in Society: The Development of Higher Psychological Processes*, Cambridge, MA: Harvard University Press.

Wolf, D M and Kolb, D A (1984) 'Career development, personal growth and experiential learning', in D Kolb, I Rubin and J McIntyre (eds) *Organisational Psychology: Readings on Human Behaviour*, 4th edn, Englewood Cliffs, NJ: Prentice-Hall.

FURTHER READING

Biggs, J and Tang, C (1999) *Teaching for Quality Learning at University* (3rd edn), Buckingham: SRHE/Open University Press. A readable exploration of student learning and how to constructively align this with teaching.

Merriam, S, Caffarella, R, Baumgartner, L (2006) *Learning in Adulthood*, San Francisco, CA: Jossey-Bass. This ranges widely and provides an excellent synopsis of much that we know about adult learning.

Perkins, D (2006) 'Constructivism and troublesome knowledge', in Meyer and Land (2006) as above, pp. 33–47. A very lucid exposition of some key ideas in learning theory.

Ramsden, P (2003) As above. Much valuable discussion of student learning.

Rust, C (ed.) (2003) *Improving Student Learning Theory and Practice – 10 Years on*, Oxford: Oxford Centre for Staff and Learning Development. Good mix of recent research and practice.

Encouraging student motivation

Sherria L. Hoskins and Stephen E. Newstead

INTRODUCTION

A few years ago, a research team with whom one of us was working had a strong suspicion that incidents of student cheating were related to their motivation for attending university. The research team wanted to test this hypothesis but were faced with the problem of how to measure student motivation. We were struck by how little research had been done in this area, by how few measures of student motivation there were, and in particular by how difficult it was to obtain a quick and readily usable indication of what students' motives were for studying at university. This led us to consider how we could identify, first, what motivates students, and, second, differences between types of motivation.

To this end, we devised a very quick and simple measure: we asked students to indicate their single main reason for studying at university. The responses were, of course, many and varied, but we were able to categorise the great majority of them into three main categories, which we called 'stopgap', 'means to an end' and 'personal development' (Newstead *et al.*, 1996). These categories are summarised in Table 3.1. The percentage figures give the proportion of students who were placed into each category out of a university sample of 844 students.

Those classed as means-to-an-end students wanted to achieve something through their degree, whether this was a better-paid or more interesting job or simply qualifications to put after their names. This was by far the most common category and may be explained by the fact that an undergraduate degree is required for entry into many jobs that might previously have been accessible without one, a phenomenon described by Professor Wolf as the 'tyranny of numbers' (Bekhradnia, 2006). Personal development students (nearly a quarter of our sample) were those who were interested in the academic subject itself or who wanted to use their degree to realise their own potential. The smallest proportion, those classified as stopgap students, were studying because they could think of nothing else to do, wanted to defer taking a decision, or simply wanted to enjoy themselves for three years.

Table 3.1 Reasons for studying

Percentage of students	
Means to an end (66%)	Improving standard of living. Improving chance of getting a job. Developing career. Getting a good qualification. Getting a worthwhile job.
Personal development (24%)	Improving life skills. Reaching personal potential. Gaining knowledge for its own sake. Furthering academic interest. Gaining control of own life. Being classified in this way.
Stopgap (10%)	Avoiding work. Laziness. Allowing time out to decide on career. Social life. Fun and enjoyment.

While the classification was largely post hoc, and was carried out with incomplete knowledge of existing educational theories of motivation, it is striking how similar our classification is to those arrived at by other researchers. For example, a key distinction is often made between intrinsic and extrinsic motivation. Intrinsically motivated students enjoy a challenge, want to master the subject, are curious and want to learn; while extrinsically motivated students are concerned with the grades they achieve, external rewards and whether they will gain approval from others (Harter, 1981). While the fit is not perfect, the parallels with our own classification system are clear, with intrinsic motivation corresponding closely to personal development and extrinsic motivation corresponding to means to an end.

Other major distinctions that have been made in the literature also map closely on to our categorisation. Dweck and Elliott (1983) have drawn the highly influential distinction between performance goals and learning goals. Performance goals are linked with means to an end (and extrinsic motivation), while learning goals are linked with personal development (and intrinsic motivation). Other distinctions in the literature related to Dweck's are those between ability and mastery goals (Nicholls, 1984). There are, of course, important differences in emphasis in all these approaches (see Pintrich (2003) for an overview) but there is enough similarity between them, and enough overlap with the distinctions made in our own characterisation, to conclude that the concepts underlying them are reasonably consistent and widespread.

AMOTIVATION AND ACHIEVEMENT MOTIVATION

Stopgap motivation was not especially common in our student sample, but it did occur. A related concept, **amotivation,** has received some attention in the literature. Ryan and Deci (2000) describe amotivated students as those who do not really know why they are at university, think themselves incompetent and feel that they have little control over what happens to them. In a real sense, then, these students show an absence of motivation.

This highlights that motivation has strength as well as direction. Thus far we have looked at motivational goals; in other words, what students' aims are, but even students with identical goals may have very differing strengths of that motivation.

Many educational writers discuss **achievement motivation** as a measure of the strength of motivation, rather than of its direction (see Entwistle and Ramsden, 1983). A student who is high in achievement motivation is seen as lying at the opposite end of the scale from an amotivated student. This cuts across many of the dimensions discussed earlier, in that both extrinsically and intrinsically motivated students can be high or low in achievement motivation.

It is a gross over-simplification, but nevertheless it seems reasonable to suggest that our own research and the existing literature have identified three main types of motivation: intrinsic, extrinsic and achievement motivation (with amotivation simply being the opposite end of the continuum to achievement motivation).

MOTIVES AND BEHAVIOUR

There is surprisingly little evidence as to the behaviour associated with different motives. Some fairly simplistic predictions can be made. For example, one might expect that students high in achievement motivation will actually achieve higher grades. Furthermore, one might expect that students with intrinsic motivation will perform better academically than those with extrinsic motivation. One might also predict that the study strategies would be different in different groups of students. For example, intrinsically motivated students might be expected to develop a deeper understanding of the material than extrinsically motivated students, and perhaps also to be more resistant to discouragement in the light of a poor mark. There is, surprisingly, little clear-cut evidence on any of these predictions.

One line of evidence concerning the relationship between motives and behaviour derives from the work on students' approaches to studying. Research using the **approaches to studying inventory** (Entwistle and Ramsden, 1983) is arguably the most extensively researched area in higher education in recent years. The main focus of this research has been on the distinction between **deep** and **surface** approaches to studying. A deep approach is concerned with conceptual understanding of the material, and incorporating this into one's existing knowledge; whereas a surface approach is characterised by rote learning of material, with the intention of reproducing this in another context (e.g. an examination). Each of these approaches is linked to a certain type of motivation, with deep approaches being associated with intrinsic motivation and surface approaches with extrinsic motivation.

Crucially, these associations were derived empirically, through the use of factor analysis. What this means is that specific types of motivation and specific approaches to studying tended to be associated with each other in the responses given by students to questionnaire items. Subsequent research has shown the main factors to be remarkably robust. However, the link between motives and strategies may not be as neat as it seems at first sight. Pintrich and Garcia (1991) found that intrinsically motivated students did indeed use strategies designed to develop a conceptual understanding of material, but that extrinsically motivated students did not, as would have been predicted, use more rehearsal strategies.

In addition to deep and surface approaches, another approach consistently emerges in the analysis of responses to the approaches to studying inventory. This is usually termed the **strategic approach,** and it is closely related to achievement motivation. Strategic students vary their approach depending on the circumstances; if they judge that a surface approach is necessary in one situation they will use it, but in others they may use a deep approach. Their main aim is to secure high marks and they will adapt their strategy in whatever way they see fit to try to achieve this aim. Certainly while deep and surface approaches have been inconsistently associated with academic achievement, a strategic approach is often associated with higher grades (e.g. Cassidy and Eachus, 2000). Interestingly Cassidy and Eachus (2000) also identified that students' self-perceptions play a role in the motivation–learning strategy–achievement relationship. They found that perceived proficiency was positively correlated with strategic learning and academic performance. Pintrich and Schunk (2002) go some way towards explaining this relationship. They found that more confident students are more likely to try harder (amount of effort and persistence) and thus perform better. However, while Duff (2003) too found that high scores on the strategic approach predicted performance in course work and project work it was less reliable in predicting closed-book examinations and oral presentations.

MEASURING STUDENT MOTIVATION

In addition to the original approaches to studying inventory developed by Entwistle and Ramsden (1983) there are now several revisions of this tool, including the revised approaches to studying inventory (RASI) that includes a further three dimensions thought to influence motivation: lack of direction, academic self-confidence and meta-cognitive awareness of studying (Entwistle and Tait, 1995). In a recent evaluation of this tool it was considered entirely appropriate for use by educational and research purposes alike (Duff, 2000). A small number of other motivation measures have been developed specifically for use with students in higher education. The three most important of these are explored below.

- The *academic motivation scale* developed by Vallerand *et al.* (1992) consists of 28 items which are designed to assess three types of intrinsic motivation, three types of extrinsic motivation, and amotivation. It would appear to have reasonable reliability and validity (Vallerand *et al.*, 1992), and its short length means that it can realistically be used in educational research.
- The *motivated strategies for learning* questionnaire developed by Pintrich *et al.* (1993) is a much longer scale containing 81 items (perhaps rather too long to be

ofgreat use in educational research). Although the scale has good reliability and validity it is US-oriented and thus far seems to have not been used in this country.

- The *study process questionnaire* originally developed by Biggs (1999) contained three factors (surface, deep and achieving, with achieving being similar to the strategic approach described by Entwistle and Ramsden). It contains 42 items but has recently been redeveloped (the revised two-factor study process questionnaire (R-SPQ-2F)) by Biggs *et al.* (2001) with acceptable levels of reliability. This version explores deep and surface processes with only 20 items, and so is extremely practical for use in learning and teaching contexts.

THE DEVELOPMENT OF MOTIVATION

We have seen the kinds of things that motivate students. Exploring the development of their motivation through the years of a degree course may shed light on whether or not we effectively promote and support desirable levels and direction of motivation in higher education.

Yet another adaptation of the original approaches to studying inventory is the approaches to study skills inventory for students (ASSIST) developed by Entwistle (1998). This tool has the advantage of including questions about students' reasons for entering higher education. In a study carried out at the University of Plymouth, this inventory was administered to some 600 first-year students on entry to university, with the results as given in Table 3.2.

These results are broadly consistent with the findings obtained using a very different method (and on students already in higher education) by Newstead *et al.* (1996). The main reasons for entering higher education were to get a good job and to develop useful skills (i.e. means to an end), followed by reasons relating to personal development and rather less frequently cited stopgap reasons. The only slight mismatch is in the high ranking given in the Magee study (Magee *et al.*, 1998) to an active social and sporting life. This is probably because this reason is seldom the single most important reason (the Newstead study asked simply for the single main reason for studying).

The similarity of the findings in these two studies might suggest that students' motives do not change a great deal over the course of their degrees. There is direct support for this contention in the research of Fazey and Fazey (1998). They used Vallerand's academic motivation scale to carry out a longitudinal investigation of students' motivation over the first two years of their degree courses at the University of Bangor. Their results indicated that students were high on both intrinsic and extrinsic motivation on entry to university but much lower on amotivation. From the current perspective, the interesting finding was that the levels of these three types of motivation showed virtually no change over the first two years at university. In a sense this is a disappointing finding since one might have hoped that higher education would have led to students becoming more intrinsically motivated by their subject. It is of course possible that this does happen to some students

Table 3.2 Percentage of students agreeing with questions on the ASSIST scale

Reason for entering higher education	
The qualification at the end of this course would enable me to get a good job when I finish	92%
The course will help me develop knowledge and skills which will be useful later on	89%
I wanted a chance to develop as a person, broaden my horizons and face new challenges	63%
The opportunities for an active social life and/or sport attracted me	63%
I would be able to study subjects in depth, and take interesting and stimulating courses	61%
I basically wanted to try and prove to myself that I could really do it	46%
Having done well at school, it seemed to be the natural thing to go on to higher education	39%
It would give me another three or four years to decide what I really wanted to do later on	37%
I suppose it was a mixture of other people's expectations and no obvious alternative	9%
I rather drifted into higher education without deciding it was what I really wanted to do	7%

Source: Based on Magee *et al.*, 1998

but they are offset by an equal number who become less intrinsically motivated. A similar finding emerged in a study by Jacobs and Newstead (2000), who found that students' interest in their discipline seemed, if anything, to decline over the course of their studies. A three-year longitudinal study of 200 undergraduates, ideally suited to detecting more complex change patterns in approaches to studying over the course of a degree, found that students' achieving approach gradually declines over the year of their degree, but that surface and deep approaches were changeable over the period of their degree (Zeegers, 2001). The Biggs study process questionnaire was completed early in the students' first year, then again at 4-, 8-, 16- and 30-month intervals. While there was no significant difference in deep approaches at the beginning of the students' period of study to the 30-month point, there was an early dip in scores at the 4-month point (continuing through to the 16-month point). This dip coincides with a rise in surface approaches, but with the final surface approaches proving lower than at the beginning of the degree.

The development of student motivation over the course of their degree is not simple and not always what we might expect, or hope for. It certainly indicates that there is a great deal of room for improvement, perhaps improvement that we can support.

ENCOURAGING STUDENT MOTIVATION

Lecturers frequently bemoan the lack of student motivation and ask what they can do to improve it. Most lecturers would agree that a complete lack of motivation of any kind – amotivation – is highly undesirable. Further, most lecturers would claim that intrinsic motivation is more desirable than extrinsic motivation. Hence these are the two principal questions that will be addressed in this section.

First, then, how can we avoid students becoming amotivated? For some students this will be next to impossible, since they may have entered higher education with the sole aim of enjoying the social life. But there is also evidence that what we do to students at university can lead to their becoming amotivated. In one of our research programmes investigating students' approaches to essay writing we discovered, through a combination of focus groups and questionnaires, that certain factors lead students to lose their motivation (Hoskins, 1999). Of particular importance is the feedback given, both in terms of the mark awarded and the written feedback provided.

One group of students approached essay writing with an understanding motivation (very similar to deep approaches to studying), in that they enjoyed writing, had an intrinsic interest in the essay, and read extensively in order to develop their own conclusions in response to the essay title. Because of the amount of reading they did, and their relative inexperience as writers, they often had problems focusing their essay, developing arguments that adhered to academic conventions including writing within the word limit. As a result they received poor marks but had difficulty in understanding where they had gone wrong. They felt that feedback was inconsistent, unclear and contained insufficient detail to be helpful. As a consequence, they avoided this understanding strategy on the grounds that it was unlikely to lead to a high mark. Furthermore, they tended to disengage with feedback, ignoring it altogether.

In addition, students were highly critical of what they regarded as a 'glass ceiling' – an unwritten rule which seemed to prevent them from achieving marks higher than a low upper second. Those who did try perceived effort (in essence, achievement motivation) to be the way to achieve this, but were disappointed with only small mark increases not worthy of the substantial increase in work. This simply reinforces the idea that poor feedback and support may promote mediocrity, even in those initially striving for more.

It is only part of the answer to this problem, but it would appear that one way of avoiding amotivation is to make sure that students are given full and appropriate feedback. When terms such as 'developing an argument' are used, there needs to be some explanation of what this means. One way of achieving this might be by setting up a database of examples, which could act as an essay feedback bank that staff could draw on. This would enable markers to demonstrate what aspects of an essay are likely to attract good marks in a personally meaningful way that could be used in future assessments.

The second issue is that of how to encourage intrinsic rather than extrinsic motivation. There is much evidence to suggest that the majority of students tend to adopt surface approaches (of which extrinsic motivation is a part) at university (Ramsden, 2004). There is some evidence to suggest that changes at a course level may be effective. Ramsden's course experience questionnaire (Ramsden, 1991) measures five subscales: good teaching (providing useful and timely feedback, clear explanations, making the course interesting and understanding students); clear goals and standards (clear aims, objectives and expectations regarding standard of work); appropriate assessment (extent to which assessment measures thinking and understanding rather than factual recall); appropriate workload (the extent to which workloads interfere with student learning); and generic skills (extent to which studies have supported the development of generic skills). Kreber (2003) found a positive correlation between generic skills and independence with deep approaches, and a negative correlation with heavy workload and deep approaches. Lizzio *et al.* (2002) found that students' perceptions of their learning environment were a stronger predictor of learning outcomes at university than prior achievement at school.

Again there is no easy or guaranteed solution to this, and some authors are rather pessimistic as to what can be achieved by individual lecturers or even groups of lecturers contributing to course perceptions. Biggs (1993) points out that university education is part of a system, and that most systems are resistant to change, instead tending to return to the state of balance that has developed within them. What this means is that students' approaches to study and their motives are determined by a number of aspects of the higher education system, including their perception of the department and university they are in, and even of the university system in general (Duff, 2004). Trying to change students' motives by changing the way one module or group of modules is taught is unlikely to be effective, since all the other aspects will be working against this change. Similar, rather disappointing conclusions come from attempts to train students to approach their studies in different ways. Norton and Crowley (1995) found that the training programme they devised had little effect on how students studied. Purdie and Hattie (1995) found that their training programme led to a temporary improvement in approaches to studying but that these rapidly reverted to their initial levels after the training came to an end. On a more positive note Cassidy and Eachus (2000) redefined a research methods module at the University of Salford. The redefined module used more seminars (and therefore, fewer mass lectures), was assessed by assignment work only, encouraged more feedback from tutors, more contact with tutors, and favoured independent learning. Self-reports of the students' research methods proficiency and their module grades were recorded. Findings illustrated that the students reported a higher level of proficiency after completion of the research methods module, indicating that the redefined module heightened the students' beliefs regarding their own capabilities. In addition, there was a positive correlation between students' perceived proficiency and marks on this programme. Whether or not this change was maintained for any length of time was not determined, but since students' post-module perceived proficiency increased, this type of programme may influence student motivation by improving their academic confidence (Bandura, 1997).

There is one other aspect of higher education which does seem to be crucially important in students' motivation, and that is the assessment system. Entwistle and Entwistle (1991) describe how final-year students start out with good intentions, are intrinsically motivated and attempt to adopt deep approaches to their studies. However, as examination time approaches they become increasingly extrinsically motivated and adopt surface, rote-learning approaches. Similar findings have emerged in research by Newstead and Findlay (1997), and a deep, strategic approach to studying appears to be associated with high levels of academic achievement only when the assessment focuses on and rewards personal understanding; in instances where this is not the case surface approaches will likely be more effective (Entwistle, 2000). The assessment system should be one that encourages conceptual understanding as opposed to rote learning. This might be achieved through the increased use of problem solving, case studies and the like, where knowledge has to be used rather than just learnt. What is more, such assessments could take place under formal examination conditions, thus avoiding some of the problems associated with continuous assessment (such as student cheating, which is where this chapter began).

In a review of research into motivation in learning and teaching contexts, Pintrich (2003) sums up concisely some of the actions we as teachers might take to support our students that have been explored and hinted at above (see Table 3.3). Each of the motivational generalisations cited in Table 3.3 should be considered in relation to both the academic task (e.g. writing an essay) and topic/academic content of the task (e.g. theories of moral development). It should be borne in mind that a student may be intrinsically interested in theories of moral development but lack confidence in essay writing as well as

Table 3.3 Motivational generalisations and design principles

Motivational generalisation	Design principle
Adaptive self-efficacy and competence beliefs motivate students.	• Provide clear and accurate feedback regarding competence and self-efficacy, focusing on the development of competence, expertise and skill. • Design tasks that offer opportunities to be successful but also challenge students.
Adaptive attributions and control beliefs motivate students.	• Provide feedback that stresses process nature of learning, including importance of effort, strategies and potential self-control of learning. • Provide opportunities to exercise some choice and control. • Build supportive and caring personal relationships in the community of learners.
Higher levels of interest and intrinsic motivation motivate students.	• Provide stimulating and interesting tasks, activities, and materials, including some novelty and variety in tasks and activities. • Provide content material and tasks that are personally meaningful and interesting to students. • Display and model interest and involvement in the content and activities.

(Continued)

Table 3.3 Motivational generalisations and design principles (*continued*)

Motivational generalisation	Design principle
Higher levels of value motivate students.	• Provide tasks, materials, and activities that are relevant and useful to students, allowing for some personal identification with learning. • Classroom discourse should focus on importance and utility of content and activities.
Goals motivate and direct students.	• Use organisational and management structures that encourage personal and social responsibility and provide safe, comfortable and predictable environment. • Use cooperative and collaborative groups to allow for opportunities to attain both social and academic goals. • Classroom discourse should focus on mastery, learning, and understanding course and lecture content. • Use task, reward and evaluation structures that promote mastery, learning, effort, progress and self-improvement standards and less reliance on social comparison or norm-referenced standards.

Source: Based on Pintrich (2003, p 672)

perceiving this task to be vocationally irrelevant. Hence providing an engaging assessment topic may not be enough to support and encourage the use of intrinsic motivation and high levels of achieving orientation if students have not been sufficiently supported in their development of essay-writing skills and thus writing confidence.

OVERVIEW

The question of how to explore and support the development of our students' motivation is far from simple. This research field can be a daunting one to navigate, with related research using disparate approaches and terminologies (Murphy and Alexander, 2000; Pintrich, 2003). This chapter has provided a brief insight into some of the research findings regarding student motivation.

Essentially, students can be motivated or amotivated, reflecting the extent to which they want to succeed. In addition, they can be intrinsically motivated and/or extrinsically motivated. Intrinsically motivated students want to learn for learning's sake, while extrinsically motivated students study for external rewards.

One might expect that motivation would correlate with both student behaviour and with academic achievement but research has produced inconsistent results. In addition, one might expect students to become more highly motivated and more intrinsically motivated during their time in higher education; once again, however, results are inconclusive.

In this chapter we hope to have highlighted the importance of ascertaining how motivated students are by the specific tasks set, and also of determining the kind of motivation these tasks elicit. We have no ready panacea for solving the problems of student motivation, but it seems reasonable to suggest that the learning context and specifically the provision of high-quality feedback and the adoption of appropriate assessment systems are at least part of the answer.

REFERENCES

Bandura, A (1997) *Self-efficacy: The Exercise of Control*, New York: Freeman.

Bekhradnia, B (2006) 'Review of the future sustainability of the HE sector', House of Commons Select Committee on Education and Skills.

Biggs, J (1993) 'What do inventories of students' learning processes really measure? A theoretical review and clarification', *British Journal of Educational Psychology*, 63, pp 3–19.

Biggs, J (1999) *Student Approaches to Learning and Studying*, Victoria: Australian Council for Educational Research.

Biggs, J, Kember, D and Leung, D Y P (2001) 'The revised two-factor study process questionnaire; R-SPQ-2F', *British Journal of Educational Psychology*, 71, pp 133–149.

Cassidy, S and Eachus, P (2000) 'Learning style, academic belief systems, self-report student proficiency and academic achievement in higher education', *Educational Psychology*, 20, pp 307–322.

Duff, A (2000) 'Learning styles measurement – the revised approaches to studying inventory (RASI)', *Bristol Business School Teaching and Research Review*, 3.

Duff, A (2003) 'Quality of learning on an MBA programme: the impact of approaches to learning on academic performance', *Educational Psychology*, 23, pp 123–139.

Duff, A (2004) 'The revised approaches to studying inventory (RASI) and its use in management education', *Active Learning in Higher Education*, 5, pp 56–72.

Dweck, C S and Elliott, E S (1983) 'Achievement motivation', in E. M. Hetherington (ed.) *Handbook of Child Psychology: Socialization, Personality and Social Development*, 4, pp 643–691, New York: Wiley.

Entwistle, N J (1998) 'Motivation and approaches to learning: motivating and conceptions of teaching', in S Brown, S Armstrong and G Thompson (eds) *Motivating Students*, pp 15–23, London: Kogan Page.

Entwistle, N J (2000) 'Promoting deep learning through teaching and assessment: conceptual frameworks and educational contexts'. Paper presented at TLRP Conference, Leicester, November.

Entwistle, N J and Entwistle, A (1991) 'Contrasting forms of understanding for degree examination: the student experience and its implications', *Higher Education*, 22, pp 205–227.

Entwistle, N J and Ramsden, P (1983) *Understanding Student Learning*, London: Croom Helm.

Entwistle, N J and Tait, H (1995) *The Revised Approaches to Studying Inventory*, Centre for Research on Learning and Instruction, Edinburgh: University of Edinburgh.

Fazey, D and Fazey, J (1998) 'Perspectives on motivation: the implications for effective learning in higher education', in S Brown, S Armstrong and G Thompson (eds) *Motivating Students*, pp 59–72, London: Kogan Page.

Harter, S (1981) 'A new self-report scale of intrinsic versus extrinsic motivation in the classroom: motivational and informational components', *Developmental Psychology*, 17, pp 302–312.

Hoskins, S (1999) 'The development of undergraduates' approaches to studying and essay writing in higher education', Ph.D. thesis, University of Plymouth.

Jacobs, P and Newstead, S E (2000) 'The nature and development of student motivation', *British Journal of Education Psychology*, 70, pp 243–254.

Kreber, C (2003) 'The relationship between students' course perceptions and their approaches to studying in undergraduate sciences: a Canadian experience', *Higher Education Research and Development*, 22, 1, pp 57–75.

Lizzio, A, Wilson, K and Simons, R (2002) 'University students' perceptions of the learning environment and academic outcomes: implications for theory and practice', *Studies in Higher Education*, 27, 1, pp 27–52.

Magee, R, Baldwin, A, Newstead, S and Fullerton, H (1998) 'Age, gender and course differences in approaches to studying in first year undergraduate students', in S Brown, S Armstrong and G Thompson (eds) *Motivating Students*, London: Kogan Page.

Murphy, P K and Alexander, P (2000) 'A motivated exploration of motivation terminology', *Contemporary Educational Psychology*, 25, pp 3–53.

Newstead, S E and Findlay, K (1997) 'Some problems in using examination performance as a measure of student ability', *Psychology Teaching Review*, 6, pp 14–21.

Newstead, S E, Franklyn-Stokes, A and Armstead, P (1996) 'Individual differences in student cheating', *Journal of Educational Psychology*, 88, pp 229–241.

Nicholls, J G (1984) 'Achievement motivation: conceptions of ability, experience, task choice and performance', *Psychological Review*, 91, pp 328–346.

Norton, L S and Crowley, C M (1995) 'Can students be helped to learn how to learn? An evaluation of an approaches to learning programme for first year degree students', *Higher Education*, 29, pp 307–328.

Pintrich, P R (2003) 'A motivational science perspective on the role of student motivation in learning and teaching contexts', *Journal of Educational Psychology*, 95, pp 667–686.

Pintrich, P R and Garcia, T (1991) 'Student goal orientation and self-regulation in the classroom', in M Maehr and P R Pintrich (eds) *Advances in Motivation and Achievement*, 7, pp 371–402, Greenwich, CT: JAI Press.

Pintrich, P R and Schunk, D H (2002) *Motivation in Education: Theory, Research, and Applications* (2nd edn), Upper Saddle River, NJ: Prentice Hall.

Pintrich, P R *et al.* (1993) 'Reliability and predictive validity of the motivated strategies for learning questionnaire (MSLQ)', *Educational and Psychological Measurement*, 53, pp 801–813.

Purdie, N M and Hattie, J A (1995) 'The effect of motivation training on approaches to learning and self concept', *British Journal of Educational Psychology*, 65, pp 227–235.

Ramsden, P (1991) 'A performance indicator of teaching quality in higher education: the course experience questionnaire', *Studies in Higher Education*, 16, 129–149.

Ramsden, P (2004) *Learning to Teach in Higher Education*, London: Routledge.

Ryan, R M and Deci, E L (2000) 'Self-determination theory and the facilitation of intrinsic motivation, social development, and well-being', *American Psychologist*, 55, pp 68–78.

Vallerand, R J *et al.* (1992) 'The academic motivation scale: a measure of intrinsic, extrinsic and amotivation in education', *Educational and Psychological Measurement*, 52, pp 1003–1017.

Zeegers, P (2001), 'Approaches to learning in science: a longitudinal study', *British Journal of Educational Psychology*, 71, pp 115–132.

FURTHER READING

Brown, S, Armstrong, S and Thompson, G (eds) (1998) *Motivating Students*, Kogan Page, London. This is an edited book stemming from a Staff and Educational Development Association (SEDA) conference on Encouraging Student Motivation, offering some interesting and useful contributions.

Dweck, B (2006) *Mindset: The New Psychology of Success*, London: Random House. Carole Dweck's research has focused largely on children in education – why they sometimes function well and, at other times, behave in ways that are self-defeating or destructive. In this evidence-based but more accessible book she looks more broadly at understanding other people's motivations and their reactions to challenges. Not only a must read for any lecturer, but a gripping read.

Hartley, J (ed.) (1998) *Learning and Studying: A Research Perspective*, London: Routledge. A well-written book covering a range of wider issues relevant to student motivation. It draws on up-to-date research, providing useful examples. It also provides good insight into how psychologists investigate learning to include their findings.

Race, P (2006) *The Lecturer's Toolkit* (3rd rev. edn), London: Routledge. An easy-to-digest and practical book giving advice on learning styles, assessment, lecturing, and large and small group teaching to name just a few.

USEFUL WEBSITES

Challenging Perspectives in Assessment is an online conference managed by the Open University where you can watch or read a series of thought-provoking presentations related to feedback and assessment. The speakers include Professor Sally Brown, Pro-Vice-Chancellor at Leeds Metropolitan University, and Professor Liz McDowell of Northumbria University, Newcastle. Available at http://stadium.open.ac.uk/perspectives/assessment/.

There are two Centres for Excellence in Teaching and Learning that have some excellent resources:

- Centres for Excellence in Assessment for Learning (Lead institution: University of Northumbria at Newcastle) has an excellent website that may be found at http://northumbria.ac.uk/cetl_afl/.
- Assessment Standards Knowledge Exchange *(ASKe)* Centre for Excellence in Teaching and Learning available at http://stadium.open.ac.uk/perspectives/assessment/.

4 Planning teaching and learning

Curriculum design and development

Lorraine Stefani

INTRODUCTION

Planning teaching and learning is a fundamental aspect of the role of academic staff. The activities involved are not carried out in a vacuum, but rather in accordance with the nature of the institution. Academic staff might reasonably be expected to have an understanding of the culture of the institution in which they operate: the mission and vision of the organisation; the aspirations, the ethos and values. The culture and the ethos of the institution inevitably influence the curriculum.

How we conceptualise the curriculum and curriculum design is important because of the impact of these conceptions on the way we consider, think and talk about teaching and learning. This in turn influences how we plan the learning experiences we make available to our students.

Our knowledge and understanding of student learning gleaned from the research literature indicates that the attention given to curriculum design and development, the planning of learning experiences and assessment of student learning all have a significant impact on students' approaches to learning. This is not surprising given that academics' conceptions of 'the curriculum' range from a focus on content or subject matter through to more sophisticated interpretations which encompass learning, teaching and assessment processes. When we interpret 'the curriculum' in a manner that includes the processes by which we facilitate student learning, not only are we taking a more scholarly approach to planning teaching and learning; we are also making more explicit to ourselves and to our students our respective roles and responsibilities in the teaching and **learning contract**.

The more attention we pay to curriculum design and development, the more likely it is we can provide transparency for our students regarding the intended **learning outcomes** for any course or programme, and the more clear we can be in aligning our assessment strategies and processes with the intended learning outcomes.

Interrogating practice

What is your conception of 'the curriculum'? What models or frameworks do you use when designing and developing courses or programmes for which you have responsibility?

A LEARNING OUTCOMES APPROACH TO CURRICULUM DESIGN

Most higher education institutions will within their mission statements give a sense of institutional objectives and **graduate attributes**. In essence this is stating in generic terms the intended learning outcomes for students pursuing courses and programmes at that college or university.

These institutional claims should of course be reflected in and tracked through the stated learning outcomes for specific disciplinary and interdisciplinary-based curricula.

The University of Auckland, for example, has a well-documented Graduate Profile. It states that:

> A student who has completed an undergraduate degree at the University of Auckland will have acquired an education at an advanced level, including both specialist knowledge and general intellectual and life skills that equip them for employment and citizenship and lay the foundations for a lifetime of continuous learning and personal development.

This statement is followed by the attributes it expects its graduates to have, categorised under three headings (Table 4.1).

The Graduate Profile lays out explicitly the shared expectations for student learning at both the institutional and the programme levels. The Profile is therefore a guiding document for more specific disciplinary-based learning outcome statements and curriculum design. The role of academics within faculties, schools and departments is to design the curriculum, the teaching methods and strategies, the pedagogy and the educational opportunities that intentionally promote these shared expectations (Maki, 2004). Most universities have or are developing a Graduate Profile or statements of Graduate Attributes.

A learning outcomes approach to curriculum development is still relatively new and many academics initially find it difficult to express learning outcomes in a manner that is meaningful to both staff and students. The next section of this chapter will address this issue.

Table 4.1 The University of Auckland: graduate profile

I Specialist knowledge

1 A mastery of a body of knowledge, including an understanding of broad conceptual and theoretical elements, in the major fields of study.
2 An understanding and appreciation of current issues and debates in the major fields of knowledge studied.
3 An understanding and appreciation of the philosophical bases, methodologies and characteristics of scholarship, research and creative work.

II General intellectual skills and capacities

1 A capacity for critical, conceptual and reflective thinking.
2 An intellectual openness and curiosity.
3 A capacity for creativity and originality.
4 Intellectual integrity, respect for truth and for the ethics of research and scholarly activity.
5 An ability to undertake numerical calculations and understand quantitative information.
6 An ability to make appropriate use of advanced information and communication technologies.

III Personal qualities

1 A love and enjoyment of ideas, discovery and learning.
2 An ability to work independently and in collaboration with others.
3 Self-discipline and an ability to plan and achieve personal and professional goals.
4 An ability to be leaders in their communities, and a willingness to engage in constructive public discourse and to accept social and civic responsibilities.
5 Respect for the values of other individuals and groups, and an appreciation of human and cultural diversity.

What do meaningful learning outcomes look like?

From the previous section it should be clear that student learning outcomes encompass a wide range of student attributes and abilities both **cognitive** and **affective**, which are a measure of how their learning experiences have supported students' development as individuals.

Cognitive outcomes include demonstrable acquisition of specific knowledge and skills gained through the programme of study. We might pose the questions: What do students know that they did not know before and what can students do that they could not do before? Affective outcomes are also important in eliciting questions such as: How has their learning experience impacted on students' values, goals, attitudes, self-concepts, worldviews and behaviours? How has it developed their potential? How has it enhanced their value to themselves, their friends, family and their communities? (Frye, 1999).

To have students achieve high-quality learning outcomes is one of the aims of most university teachers. Ideally we want our students to engage in **deep** (as opposed to **surface**) **learning** (Chapter 2). As Prosser and Trigwell (1999) state: 'deep learning is the type of learning that is sought because it is the learning that remains after lesser quality outcomes have been forgotten. This is the learning that can be drawn upon in other and new contexts.'

An (intended) learning outcome is an objective of the **module** or **programme** being studied. An objective is a succinct statement of intent. It signifies either a desired outcome to be achieved and/or a process that should be undertaken or experienced. Objectives can thus focus on outcomes/processes or a blend of each. An outcome usually comprises a verb and a context. An example of a subset of learning outcomes in a first-year theology module at the University of Auckland is shown below.

Upon completion of this module students should be able to:

- demonstrate their knowledge of a process of practising theology contextually;
- identify numerous sources, including the Treaty of Waitangi, for the practice of theology;
- evaluate differences in types of sources and starting points in theology and how they are used in theologising or theological reflection;
- undertake a simple theological process around a chosen topic.

In a second-year Bachelor of Fine Arts module, the following learning outcomes are presented to students.

At the end of this module students are expected to be able to:

- demonstrate an awareness of the broad historical, theoretical and contextual dimensions of the discipline(s) studies, including an awareness of current critical debates in their discipline(s);
- demonstrate an ability to critically analyse and evaluate art and/or design work;
- formulate independent judgements;
- articulate reasoned arguments through review, reflection and evaluation;
- demonstrate an awareness of issues that arise from the artist's or designer's relationship with audiences, clients, markets, users, consumers and/or participants.

Interrogating practice

Consider your general aim/s for a module you are teaching. Write specific learning outcomes for this course: what do you want students to learn?

Learning outcomes should be pitched at the right level so as to specify the complexity and/or significance of the situation in which the learner is expected to demonstrate the behaviour. An issue many academics struggle with is pitching the learning outcomes in accordance with levels of ability. The writing of learning outcomes should reflect the students' increasing competence (Bingham, 1999). Bloom's *Taxonomy of Educational Objectives* (1979) may be helpful in articulating levels of expected academic performance when writing learning outcomes.

Bloom's Taxonomy (1979) covers six levels of cognitive ability increasing from knowledge, comprehension, application, analysis and synthesis through to evaluation.

McLean and Looker (2006) at the Learning and Teaching Unit at the University of New South Wales in Australia have presented a list of verbs to enable academic staff to construct learning outcomes which align with Bloom's Taxonomy shown above. Some of the verbs they present are shown below, linked to the six levels of cognitive abilities. An interesting exercise may be to examine these verbs and consider how they could align with levels of learning.

1   Knowledge

What do we expect learners to know? The verbs indicated may, for example, be used in the stem of assignment questions:

record	examine	reproduce	arrange
define	outline	state	present
describe	identify	show	quote

2   Comprehension

This covers learners' ability to convey what they understand. Can learners interpret what they know? Can they extrapolate from what they know? Consider the use of the following verbs in work to be done by learners:

discuss	clarify	classify	explain
translate	extend	interpret	review
select	summarise	contrast	estimate

3   Application

This covers a learner's ability to use a theory or information in a new situation. Can learners see the relevance of this idea to that situation? Verbs to use may include:

solve	examine	modify	apply
use	practise	illustrate	choose
relate	calculate	classify	demonstrate

4 Analysis

This covers a learner's ability to break down material or ideas into constituent parts, showing how they relate to each other and how they are organised. Can learners analyse elements of the subject field? Can they analyse relationships in the field? Can they analyse organisational principles?

The following verbs may help you construct learning outcomes in response to these questions:

differentiate	investigate	categorise	appraise
criticise	debate	compare	contrast
distinguish	solve	analyse	calculate

5 Synthesis

This covers the learner's ability to work with elements and combine them in a way that constitutes a pattern or structure that was not there before. Can learners produce a unique communication in this field? Can they develop a plan or a proposed set of operations? Can they derive a set of abstract relationships?

The verbs shown below may help you construct learning outcomes in response to these questions:

assemble	organise	compose	propose
construct	design	create	formulate
integrate	modify	derive	develop

6 *Evaluation*

This covers the learner's ability to construct an argument, compare opposing arguments, make judgements and so on. Can learners make judgements based on internal evidence? Can they make judgements based on external evidence?

The following verbs may be useful in constructing learning outcomes in response to these questions:

judge	select	evaluate	choose
assess	compare	estimate	rate
measure	argue	defend	summarise

In using these verbs to form your learning outcomes it is useful to bear in mind that you may need to check that your students actually understand the meaning of the verbs. Do your students understand, for example, the difference between 'compare' and 'contrast'? Do they understand what it means to 'construct an argument'?

In writing learning outcomes, there are other factors relating to 'the curriculum' as students experience it that need to be taken into consideration. For example, learning outcomes should include a description of the kinds of performances by which achievement will be judged, either within the outcome or in an associated set of assessment criteria (Toohey, 1999).

CREDIT LEVEL DESCRIPTORS

One of the issues many staff find problematic is that of credit levels and level descriptors. There is a strong push within the UK higher education sector towards credit frameworks. For example, the Southern England Consortium for Credit Accumulation and Transfer (SEEC, 2001) has presented a set of guidelines on *Credit Level Descriptors*. These descriptors are grouped under four headings:

- Development of knowledge and understanding (subject specific)
- Cognitive/intellectual skills (generic)
- Key transferable skills (generic)
- Practical skills (subject specific).

Credit level descriptors may be used as the means by which each subject area can check the level of demand, complexity, depth of study and degree of learner autonomy expected at each level of an individual programme of study. While credit level descriptors are 'generic' as presented in available guidelines, the idea is that they will be translated according to discipline and context. It would be unusual to expect individual staff members to 'translate' generic credit level descriptors. It is more likely that this exercise would be carried out by a course team. The exercise involves mapping existing learning outcomes against the credit level descriptors.

Credit level descriptors would generally apply to modules within programmes of study and would be used in the context of curriculum design and development. The UK Quality Assurance Agency for Higher Education (QAA, 2001) has presented a framework for higher education qualifications in England, Wales and Northern Ireland. There are five levels of qualification within this framework from Certificate level through to Doctoral level qualifications. This framework is designed to ensure a consistent use of qualification titles. Key points relating to this framework are that: it is intended, first, to assist learners to identify potential progression routes, particularly in the context of lifelong learning, and second, to assist higher education institutions, their external examiners and the QAA's reviewers by providing important points of reference for setting and assessing standards.

Credit level descriptors and qualifications frameworks are inevitably linked to the development of learning outcomes, and academic staff should be aware of these frameworks within which higher education operates. Similarly, in the UK, academics need to be aware of the *Subject Benchmark Statements* (QAA, 2008) which set out the general academic characteristics and standards of degrees in a range of different subjects. These should be used as an external reference point when designing and developing programmes of study and provide general guidance for articulating the learning outcomes associated with the programme. Learning outcomes for any course or programme do not exist in isolation. They must be linked or aligned with the assessment processes, the learning tasks, the teaching strategies and the external drivers on quality.

In the following section we explore the issue of curriculum alignment and examine some models of curriculum development.

Interrogating practice

When you are raising student awareness of learning outcomes for your course or programme, how do you ensure students understand these outcomes in the way you intend them to be understood?

CURRICULUM DESIGN AND DEVELOPMENT

The principle of 'constructive alignment' is central to curriculum design and development. Biggs (1999) describes teaching as a balanced system in which all components support each other. Biggs outlines the critical components of teaching as follows:

- the curriculum we teach;
- the teaching methods and strategies we use to facilitate student learning;
- the assessment processes we use and the methods of reporting results;
- the climate we create in our interactions with students;
- the institutional climate, the rules and procedures we are required to follow.

It must be taken as a given that whatever institution we are working in, we should understand the mission and the regulations. These are factors not within our control. We do of course have control over the classroom climate we create. Are we accessible to our students, appropriately supportive, approachable? These issues matter, and do have a bearing on how students respond and engage with learning.

The teaching, learning and assessment strategies are issues with which we need to engage in a scholarly manner. It is our role to ensure that the learning outcomes we agree upon are achievable, that we are clear about the levels or standards expected at different stages and that the learning tasks and the assessment of learning are in alignment. If we do not pay due attention to these issues, we may actually encourage surface learning.

Case study 1: Aligning teaching, learning and assessment with learning outcomes in the creative arts

The National Institute of Creative Arts and Industries is a Faculty of the University of Auckland. A key aim of the Faculty is to build a culture of interdisciplinarity and collaboration at both institutional level (between the five areas of architecture, art, dance, music and planning) and at the educational level (among the programmes taught to students). In 2007, the Faculty launched an initiative to promote the importance of drawing skills within the curriculum of all disciplines, at undergraduate level. A series of staff workshops was held to determine how best to do this, involving staff and students from different disciplines.

The first task of the staff workshop was to determine a set of achievable learning outcomes that would support a common curriculum in drawing, and could also be 'exported' to cognate disciplines outside the Faculty. The aim was to include outcomes and processes with clear cognitive, practical and affective dimensions that could be delivered within relatively few teaching hours.

Learning outcomes

The staff team devised a two-hour intensive teaching project on completion of which students would be able to:

- demonstrate a professional standard of drawing skills in a number of set tasks;
- understand and apply key drawing principles and methods;
- communicate confidence in their ability to be creative through the medium of drawing;
- show understanding of drawing not only as a creative art but also as a technical skill, a tool for experimentation and research, and a tool for presentation and communication of ideas;
- evaluate the quality of drawings used as informational tools within their own discipline;
- show understanding of drawing as a method for initiating, recording and developing ideas around which to build and manage a studio practice.

Alignment of teaching with learning outcomes

The ideas for the intensive teaching unit were tested in workshops with students from a range of disciplines, including engineering and business. Students were asked to bring along two drawings of a tree, one freehand and one digital, which were pinned on to the wall. They were then asked to execute a series of 'small steps' in drawing which illustrated simple but key principles of drawing practice; at each stage outcomes were discussed, analysed and reflected upon by students. Within two hours, by following the principles, each of the students was able to produce drawings of a professional – indeed, exhibition – standard. By comparing their final workshop drawings with their pre-workshop efforts, they were able to identify and evaluate key points of development. And, importantly, for the non-art students, they felt sufficiently competent to explore visual languages and creativity.

Interaction with students and formative assessment

In observing the student workshops, teaching staff were able to reflect upon the process of formative assessment within the studio environment, based on the interactions that took place between students and the workshop leader. Other points of importance were the use of the 'small steps' method; critical diagnosis of drawings; and a group dynamics of high energy, motivation and enjoyment – contributing to a level of concentrated work that produced excellent results. Summative assessment was not a goal of the workshops, but could be incorporated within a fully developed drawing programme that concluded with exhibitions of works.

(Nuala Gregory, Creative Arts and Industry, University of Auckland)

There are a number of key steps to effective course and curriculum design. One model is as follows:

- Consider your general aims for the course/programme.
- Write specific learning outcomes (objectives): what do you want the students to learn?
- Plan the assessment framework to match your objectives.
- Plan the content, i.e. sequence of topics/readings.
- Plan the teaching/learning design – what kinds of activities will you and your students engage in together?
- Compile a list of resources.
- Write the course outline including readings.
- Consider evaluation of the course (formative and summative) and how best evaluation can be carried out.

It is important to bear in mind that the use of technology in teaching and learning is increasing all the time (Chapter 7). There is still some resistance to embedding the use of technology into the curriculum, with some academic staff believing it is more complex to design e-learning courses and programmes, or worse still believing that using technology is a simple matter of transferring one's course notes or PowerPoint presentations 'on to the web'.

Whatever the context of learning (be it traditional classroom-based or distance learning, e-learning or blended learning) the purpose of the course or programme, the design, development and mode of delivery and associated assessment strategies must be carefully considered (Stefani, 2006), as in Case study 2.

The models of curriculum design described above indicate that assessment strategies should be considered once the intended learning outcomes have been agreed upon and articulated. Designing the curriculum in this manner may be considered to be a 'logical' model of curriculum development as opposed to a chronological model. In the 'chronological' approach, assessment may be seen as being something bolted on at the end of 'content delivery' as opposed to being an integral aspect of student learning.

A logical model of curriculum development

To support staff in visualising 'the curriculum', a model first presented by Cowan and Harding (1986) is generally very helpful. Figure 4.1 on p. 52 shows their original logical model of curriculum development, which is deserving of detailed explanation.

First, the grey area around the development activity diagram is not an accident. It has significance in that it represents the constraints within which any development operates, which can and should have a powerful impact on what is and what is not possible within the institutional and learning community context. Within this grey area, the arrows pointing inward indicate inputs from peers and other stakeholders such as employers or representatives of professional bodies who have a vested interest in the curriculum being provided.

Case study 2: Course design and development

The University of Auckland has for a number of years offered a postgraduate certificate programme relating to learning and teaching. Completion of the Certificate in University Learning and Teaching (CULT) required presentation of a portfolio of evidence of reflection and scholarship on a range of topics. Course design and development was one of these topics and on the basis of my practice within my discipline I presented the following model of the Course Design Process.

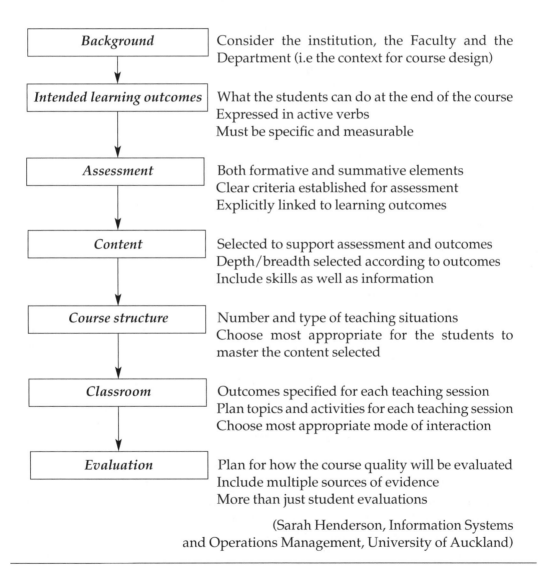

Background Consider the institution, the Faculty and the Department (i.e the context for course design)

Intended learning outcomes What the students can do at the end of the course
Expressed in active verbs
Must be specific and measurable

Assessment Both formative and summative elements
Clear criteria established for assessment
Explicitly linked to learning outcomes

Content Selected to support assessment and outcomes
Depth/breadth selected according to outcomes
Include skills as well as information

Course structure Number and type of teaching situations
Choose most appropriate for the students to master the content selected

Classroom Outcomes specified for each teaching session
Plan topics and activities for each teaching session
Choose most appropriate mode of interaction

Evaluation Plan for how the course quality will be evaluated
Include multiple sources of evidence
More than just student evaluations

(Sarah Henderson, Information Systems
and Operations Management, University of Auckland)

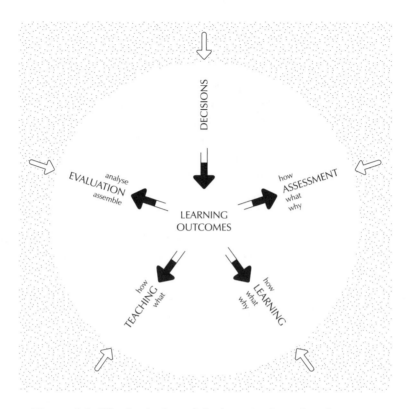

Figure 4.1 The logical model of curriculum development

The 'how?' and the 'what?' at each step in the development cycle also have significance. These are intended to encourage us to think through the point that the form of the programme or module should depend more on the type of content and expectation and learning outcomes than the actual nature of it.

For example, if our intention is to facilitate learning in such a way that students' abilities to analyse data, the method and approach taken, will have much in common with someone else who has a similar aim but within a different discipline, then 'how' is much more central to the design of the curriculum than 'what', which is particular to a discipline (Cowan, 2006, personal communication).

The model allows for and encourages an interrogation of 'how' to assess and 'what' to assess, how to facilitate learning and what sort of learning to encourage, and so on around the cycle.

A recent modification to this model is shown in Figure 4.2. This modified model puts learning outcomes at the centre of the development process, representing a minor change in the language reflecting aims and objectives for courses and programmes. The addition of the question 'why?' at each stage of the developmental process is intended to encourage staff to interrogate their classroom practice and to engage in reflection on curriculum development.

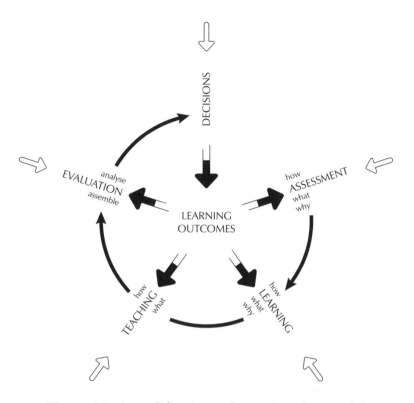

Figure 4.2 A modification to Cowan's earlier model

Using such a model is intended to enable staff to define learning outcomes clearly and in accessible language that supports students in thinking through their own learning strategies. It is also intended to encourage academic staff to consider how they will facilitate student learning to achieve the intended learning outcomes.

This logical model of curriculum development sits well with Biggs' model of alignment of teaching, learning and assessment (1999). There is much research to show that students tend to think about assessment first, rather than as their lecturers or tutors often do, as the last piece of course or curriculum development that needs to be considered. Biggs' model outlining the differences in students' versus staff perspectives on the curriculum is shown in Figure 4.3 on page 54.

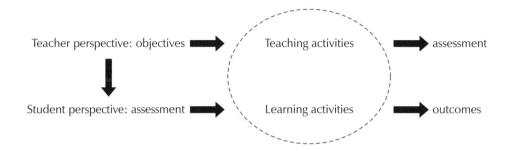

Figure 4.3 Views of the curriculum
Source: Biggs (1999: 142). Reproduced with permission from
the Open University Press Publishing Company.

Interrogating practice

Using any of the curriculum development models shown above, work through any module or programme for which you have some responsibility and consider whether or not you have an appropriate alignment between the intended learning outcomes and the assessment strategies you currently adopt or intend to adopt.

Curriculum design in an e-learning environment

In today's climate of embedding e-learning into the student learning experience, no chapter on curriculum design and planning would be complete without mention of learning activity design, or instructional design as it is often termed (see also Chapter 7).

Instructional design is defined as: the systematic development of instructional specifications using learning and instructional theory to ensure the quality of instruction. In essence the pedagogical principles of teaching and supporting student learning must be applied to the design and development of online or web-based modules, courses and programmes of study. Design is a useful term because it encompasses the entire process of analysis of learning needs and goals, and the development of a delivery system to meet those needs. It includes the development of learning materials, activities, practice elements (often using technology) and evaluation of all teaching and learning activities (Clark and Mayer, 2002).

Case study 3: Module design for an e-learning environment in theology

We used a team approach, of academic staff supported by the University's Centre for Academic Development (CAD), in the design and development of a curriculum for a Graduate Diploma of Theology qualification offered in an e-learning environment. Our potential students were university graduates who came new to the study of theology and e-learning but had previous learning and skills at advanced levels. Our main constraint was that the curriculum for the Graduate Diploma had to be drawn from the existing curriculum of the Bachelor of Theology programme which was delivered in a classroom environment. Our challenge was to design a curriculum that could work with flexibility in e-learning situations where the courses did not rely on the cumulative effects of sequential learning but could offer an integrative experience of theology. The courses were developed on the university e-learning platform which interfaced with the library catalogue and databases, the Student Learning Centre and other resources.

Learning outcomes, assessment and criteria

After identifying a selection of courses in the three subject areas of theology and planning an e-mode development timetable, we began designing courses by articulating the learning outcomes of each course and then relating the outcomes to appropriate assessment activities around which we eventually constructed criteria that directed students to the quality of their assessment activities in terms of deep learning, as well as to the literacy information skills needed to complete the assignment.

Content design and learning facilitation

We outlined the content topics that related to the learning outcomes and assessment activities of each course. Design decisions centred mainly on how best to transform topics into student e-learning experiences. As the academic team generated ideas for learning, the CAD team transformed them into audio and visual media components and the librarian searched out the electronic resources and created the course library pages.

The range of learning tasks and activities included in topics varied according to the level of the course. For example, in a level 1 course we built in teacher facilitation as a scaffold to learning by engaging students step by step in a theological process. At each step students participated in learning activities individually and in groups, such as guided reading, reflection and response to media, online group discussion and a weekly journal. Initially students received formative feedback on their journal entries, but in the latter weeks of the course the entries were given assessed feedback.

In contrast, courses at levels 2 and 3 focused more on student-directed learning around a topic, case study, and so on. This required students individually and in groups to research, reflect, share resources, engage in critical discussion and integrative activities online in order to be able to complete their assessment activities.

E-learning student–teacher communication

Introduction to teacher videos, course instructional materials, email and telephone contact information, announcement boards and quick feedback evaluations were designed to replicate the accessibility of 'face-to-face' communication in the e-environment.

(Dr Ann Gilroy, School of Theology, University of Auckland)

EVALUATION

Evaluation of student learning and the efficacy of the teaching processes is an integral aspect of curriculum design and it also serves as a quality assurance measure.

Different methods of evaluation are discussed in detail in Chapter 14. It is important to note here that an evaluation process is built into any curriculum development strategy. Evaluation carried out regularly and appropriately can give us feedback on student attainment (summative evaluation), student approaches to and understanding of the learning context and valuable data on which to make future decisions (formative evaluation), and supports the iterative process of curriculum design, development and delivery.

OVERVIEW

This chapter provides basic information for academic staff from all disciplines with responsibilities for planning learning and teaching activities and developing curricula. The link to UK frameworks on the academic infrastructure has also been made so that the reader is aware of the context in which higher education operates. The importance of the concept of alignment of learning, teaching and assessment has been identified as crucial for all staff involved in all types of curriculum design and development.

REFERENCES

Biggs, J (1999) *Teaching for Quality Learning at University*, Buckingham: SRHE/Open University Press.

Bingham, J (1999) *Guide to Developing Learning Outcomes*, The Learning and Teaching Institute, Sheffield: Sheffield Hallam University.

Bloom, B S (1979) *Taxonomy of Educational Objectives*, Handbook 1: *The Cognitive Domain*. New York: David McKay.

Clark, R C and Mayer, R E (2002) *E-learning and the Science of Instruction*. San Francisco, CA: Jossey-Bass/Pfeiffer.

Cowan, J and Harding, A (1986) 'A logical model of curriculum development', *British Journal of Educational Technology*, 17 (2), pp 103–109.

Frye, R (1999) *Assessment, Accountability, and Student Learning Outcomes*. Dialogue Issue 2. Available at <http://www.ac.wwu.edu/-dialogue/issue2.html> (accessed 10 May 2007).

McLean, J and Looker, P (2006) *Developing Learning Outcomes*, Learning and Teaching Unit, UNSW. Available at <http://www.ltu.unsw.edu.au/content/course_prog_support/outcomes.cfm?ss=0> (accessed 21 January 2008).

Maki, P (2004) *Assessing for Learning: Building a Sustainable Commitment Across the Institution*, Sterling, VA: Stylus Publishing, pp 10–11.

Prosser, M and Trigwell, K (1999) *Understanding Learning and Teaching*, Buckingham: SRHE/Open University Press.

QAA (2001) *The Framework for Higher Education Qualifications in England, Wales and Northern Ireland*. Available at http://www.qaa.ac.uk/academicinfrastructure/FHEQ/EWNI/default.asp (accessed 8 January 2008). For the Scottish Credit and Qualification Framework go to: <http://www.scqf.org.uk/the_framework.asp> (accessed 21 January 2008).

QAA (2008) *Subject Benchmark Statements*. Available at <http://www.qaa.ac.uk/academicinfrastructure/benchmark/default.asp> (accessed 7 January 2008).

SEEC (2001) *SEEC Credit Level Descriptors*. Available at <http://www.seec-office.org.uk/creditleveldescriptors2001.pdf> (accessed 21 December 2007).

Stefani, L A J (2006) *Effective Use of I.T. Guidance or Practice in the Biosciences*, Teaching Bioscience: Enhancing Learning Series, ed. Stephen Maw and Jackie Wilson, Higher Education Authority, pp 7–8.

Toohey, S (1999) *Designing Courses for Higher Education*, Buckingham: SRHE/Open University Press.

FURTHER READING

Biggs, J and Tang, C (2007) *Teaching for Quality Learning at University* (3rd edn), Buckingham: SRHE/Open University Press. This book is essential reading for a full analysis of the concept of constructive alignment of learning, teaching and assessment.

Cowan, J (2006) *On Becoming an Innovative University Teacher: Reflection in Action for all University Teachers* (2nd edn), Buckingham: SRHE/Open University Press. Key reading for all university teachers, particularly early career academics.

Stefani, L A J (2005) 'The scholarship of teaching and learning in higher education', in P. Ashwin (ed.) *An Outline of Changing Higher Education: The Development of Learning and Teaching*, London: RoutledgeFalmer pp 113–126. This chapter provides an overview of developing a scholarly approach to learning, teaching and curriculum design.

5 | Lecturing to large groups

Ann Morton

INTRODUCTION

Much of the writing in the late 1980s indicated that sitting in lectures was not always a particularly effective way for students to learn and predicted that the next few years would see the demise of the lecture. But lectures remain a significant part of the student learning experience, to the extent that even distance-learning students are often able to access recorded lectures over the web, or to receive the lecture in real time through video conferencing technology. There are those who would argue that the only reason the lecture has remained is because of significant growth in student numbers seen in the UK over the past decade. It is, after all, an efficient means of delivery. However, this view does a disservice to all those teaching staff who receive excellent feedback on their lectures from students.

This chapter will explore what makes an outstanding lecture that is able to promote student learning. In particular, three aspects – generating and maintaining interest, student engagement, and the importance of a good structure – will be considered in some detail. The case studies are used to illustrate how some teachers in different disciplines organise their teaching through lectures and achieve **active learning**.

As class sizes increase, two particular issues may arise that can be particularly difficult for the teaching team to manage. First, in modular systems the lecture may be attended by students from varied disciplines, often with very different skills and knowledge bases. This can provide significant challenges for the lecturer in knowing where to pitch the lecture and how to keep all students interested. Second, the lecturer may be faced with having to manage disruptive student behaviour in the class, which is now reported across disciplines in different universities.

The final section of this chapter will look at PowerPoint as a commonly used piece of presentation software, which now seems to be a ubiquitous part of the delivery of many lectures.

THE OUTSTANDING LECTURE

An outstanding lecture should have the following attributes:

- It is delivered in a way that is informative, interesting and engaging.
- The content is well organised and easy to follow. Students can understand the development of the argument, or the logic in the ordering of the information or ideas.
- Students feel involved. This may be through some type of active participation, use of relevant examples to which they can relate and by being made to think about what is being said. The ability to engage students through questioning, no matter what the class size, is an important way of getting students involved.
- Students leave wondering where the time has gone.
- Students leave knowing that they have learned something(s), and are often inspired to go off and find out more.

> ### Interrogating practice
>
> Do you believe that your lectures have these attributes? If you asked your students, what would they say?

Two studies involving history students (Evans, 2007) and engineering students (Davies *et al.*, 2006) are helpful in addressing the attributes for outstanding lectures in specific disciplines, such as the generating and maintaining of interest, student engagement, and structuring and organising lectures. These reinforce a number of published studies, such as those of Ramsden (1994).

There is significant literature, spread over many years, which discusses ways of making lectures more effective (e.g. Brown, 1987; Edwards *et al.*, 2001; Brown and Race, 2002; Race, 2007). A perusal of the Higher Education Academy's website also provides links to subject-specific resources. Many of the suggestions that follow are not new, and the list offered is not exhaustive. The ideas are selected for being practicable in lecturing to large groups, and for being able to promote much more learning than that simply associated with the transmission of information. Not all ideas will be relevant to every lecture, or to every discipline, but a selection of methods is likely to lead to a richer learning experience for the student. The case studies also give examples of how a variety of approaches can be effective.

Generating and maintaining interest

Gaining and maintaining students' interest in the lecture is likely to increase their motivation to learn (see Chapter 3). The start of the lecture is crucial and needs to interest students sufficiently to convince them that it is worth staying, or staying attentive, for the next hour.

At the very beginning you should:

- appear enthusiastic and interested yourself;
- be organised, and take control of the lecture room on your arrival;
- know how to use the presentation equipment.

During the first few minutes the lecturer could:

- go through the **learning outcomes** for the session, telling them what they should have learned by the end. This can be a little dry;
- describe a problem or scenario that is of relevance to the topic, and then go on to outline how the lecture will consider this;
- share their passion and enthusiasm for the subject by telling students why they are personally interested in this topic. Where possible, this could be a link to their personal research;
- link the lecture to some current news or activity. The lecturer could take this one step further by asking students to bring examples with them to the lecture, and inviting them to contribute.

To keep students interested during the remainder the lecturer could:

- use relevant and current examples to illustrate the point;
- where possible draw on the students' experiences;
- use rhetorical questions to encourage students to keep on track;
- change the demands on the student as the lecture progresses. Vary between note taking, listening, and active participation (considered later);
- use visual materials or artefacts that are relevant to the topic of the lecture;
- use live links to the web to demonstrate currency of the material being presented.

The lecturer's enthusiasm and interest is important at both the start and during the lecture, and this factor should not be underestimated in relation to the effectiveness of the lecture overall. It should also be remembered that there is a performance aspect to the craft of lecturing. A study by Hodgson (1984) highlighted the 'vicarious experience of relevance' whereby student interest in a topic is enhanced both by the lecturer's enthusiasm and through the use of examples which relate to the student's real-world experience. In a study by Brown (1987), students gave high ratings of interest to lecturers who adopted a narrative mode of delivery where informal language was used, and problems and findings were described as if telling a story. In addition, high interest ratings were given where examples related to both the topic and to the students. These studies are not new, but are still very relevant today. The study by Evans (2007), involving history students from four universities, concluded that students rated the enthusiasm of the lecturer very highly, and indicated they felt that it was a prerequisite for their involvement. Similarly, the smaller study with engineering students (Davies *et al.*, 2006) concluded that enthusiasm was one of the key features of a good lecturer. The evidence seems to confirm that a lecturer who is able to transmit their enthusiasm and interest through the lecture is providing a powerful stimulus for student learning. These types of study show that an effective lecturer can deliver far more than the transmission of information and ideas, and there is often a need to explain this to students. In particular, it may be important to explain to students why simply having a copy of the PowerPoint presentation is no substitute for lecture attendance.

Interrogating practice

- What approaches have you used to generate and maintain interest in your lectures?
- What links do you make between the particular topics in your lectures and the students' existing experiences and knowledge?
- Do you think that your students appreciate the benefit of attending lectures? If not, how might you make this clearer?

Organisation and structure

A lecture needs to be well organised in order for a student to make sense of it. Most texts on lecturing, or on giving presentations, talk about paying attention to the beginning, middle and end (i.e. the overall anatomy of the lecture), and these are aspects most lecturers are comfortable with. The case studies illustrate some strategies for structuring used by experienced academics in their lectures. However, difficulty can arise when the lecturer perceives the structure to be perfectly clear, but the students do not. This can happen because the lecturer, who knows the subject matter very well, fails to provide the signals and clues that guide the student through the lecture. Thus, despite the overall structure, the student gets lost or misses the key points. Brown (1987) has suggested a number of simple ways to give students the sorts of clues and signals they need (Table 5.1).

Interrogating practice

- How well structured are your lectures?
- Are the sections clearly organised and well linked?
- Will students know the key points to take away?

Table 5.1 Emphasising the structure of lectures using signals and clues

Signposts

These indicate the structure and direction of the lecture:

- *Last week we covered . . . and this week I will be developing those ideas further.*
- *Today I want to consider . . .*
- *First, we are going to look at . . .*
- *Second, I'll spend some time considering . . .*

There are also statements which indicate ends of the topics within the lecture:

- *So, that summarises the key features of . . .*

Links

These are phrases or statements that link part of a lecture together, and they often involve the use of rhetorical questions. Having just come to the end of a topic, you could say, for example:

So what does that mean in practice? Well, let's go on to have a look at . . .

So we can conclude then that . . . But what does that really tell us about . . . ? Well, if we go back to the first item we considered today . . .

So, you can see that this is the final step in the process. So what now? If we know that this happens in this way, what are the long term consequences? Well, we'll now go on to consider those.

Foci

These are statements that give emphasis and which highlight key points.

This is the most crucial step of the process,

There are three absolutely essential points that need to be made.

Adapted from Brown (1987)

Case study 1: Lecturing accounting to large groups of non-specialist students

I co-deliver an accounting module for M.Sc. programmes, which runs for two groups of 100-plus students, studying business-related but not specialist accounting. The module is taught through a series of nine weekly lecture sessions of three hours' duration. I have a simple philosophy: my aim is that the lecture session will be enjoyable for all involved – for the students and also for me. My experience is that more energy and force of personality is required for the sessions to be effective.

My priority is to engage the students immediately at the start of the lecture and then maintain their engagement throughout the session. I find the first few minutes of each session are vitally important to arouse interest and create the right atmosphere. The 'INTRO' mnemonic is particularly helpful to introduce the session:

Interest: I try to arouse some curiosity in the session by referring to a topical issue from the world of business that is relevant to the day's lecture material, or by posing a question that the lecture will ultimately resolve.

Need: I find it is particularly important to demonstrate why and how the day's lecture is important to the students. This includes making reference to the relevance of the material to the examination, but also, and of course more importantly, the real-world practical application of the ideas and concepts to be covered.

Timing: I try to make it clear how the three hours will be organised between the various elements of the session: lecture, activities, review of the previous week's exercises, and so on.

Range: The agenda for the session is explained to make clear what will be covered and indeed what will not be covered.

Outcomes: Of course, it is also important that students are aware of the learning outcomes they are expected to achieve as a result of the session.

I will often start the 'lecture' with some form of short activity for students to work on and discuss in pairs: in doing this students realise they have permission to interact with the subject, with me and with themselves. I then continue to use activities, questions and quizzes to maintain student engagement throughout the session.

To counteract the possibilities of non-engagement or of some students finishing the task before others, I use a number of techniques. (1) I tend to set some form of follow-up activity for those who finish the initial task early. (2) I move around the group to help ensure students are properly engaged in the desired activity. (3) I ensure the activities are relatively short, with clear time limits and reminders of the deadline. (4) I limit the amount of time spent for students to give responses, managing this process efficiently and in a manner that maintains everyone's interest. For example, I may split the audience into three parts and seek a response from each part. I will also repeat responses or questions from students to make sure everyone in the room has heard and understands what has been said.

(Matt Davies, Aston University)

Student engagement

There can be nothing more demotivating for students than sitting in a lecture where the lecturer is monotone, the PowerPoint presentation is a predictable list of bullet points and at no point do they feel part of the lecture. Student engagement allows them to feel involved. Lecturers should, through the techniques they employ, acknowledge that the lecture is for the students and that they are there to help them to learn.

There are different types and levels of student engagement. First, there is the simple acknowledgement of the students themselves. Build a rapport with the student group by communicating directly with some of the students. For example, chat to students as you are waiting to get started. Make sure students know how to contact you after the lecture if there are things they do not understand. Be approachable and friendly.

Second, some of the techniques mentioned thus far in this chapter will elicit student engagement by the very fact that the lecture is interesting, enthusiastically delivered and well organised. Attention span can be a particular problem in the lecture, particularly with a **didactic** delivery style. It is often suggested that students can only concentrate for about 20 minutes as passive learners in a lecture (Stuart and Rutherford, 1978) and that breaking the flow or changing actvity will help them overcome this problem.

The third and probably the most important aspect of student engagement is their active participation in the lecture. The following suggestions are examples of the ways in which this can be achieved in large lecture classes, as illustrated in the case studies.

- Pose questions for students to discuss in small groups, then take feedback from a few groups to hear what they think.
- Get the students to tackle problems individually, and then compare their answers with one or two others sitting next to them. You do not always need to elicit feedback.
- Ask the students to vote on a multiple choice question (MCQ) (see Chapter 26 for an example). Use a show of hands to check the responses, or use an electronic voting system. Wherever possible, the incorrect answers you offer should be derived from common mistakes that students make, and if they are chosen you can use the opportunity to talk the mistakes through with them.
- Show a DVD clip, but do ask the students to look for something specific that you can ask them about afterwards.
- Use demonstrations that can involve the students directly.
- Ask the students to do a mini-test, for example, to check student progress. This will need to be marked and could be based on an MCQ format.

Case study 2: Improving student learning in sociology lectures

This case study explores a technique used on an introductory sociology module to improve student learning. This first-year module of 40 students titled 'Global Society' explores introductory debates on globalisation. The underlying pedagogical approach is of a community of learning in which students are encouraged to participate and contribute to the learning experience. The lecturer uses a 2m by 1.5m laminated world map that is placed on the front wall or whiteboard in the lecture theatre.

In the first lecture 'Post-it' notes are distributed to all students. They are asked to remove their trainers/sneakers and see where they have been made. If students are uncomfortable about doing this or are not wearing such items, mobile phones or MP 3 players work perfectly well. Students write down the country where the product has been manufactured and come to the front of the venue and place the 'Post-it' on the map. Invariably the 'Post-its' cluster around countries in the Far East. This strategy works well to break the ice, especially if the lecturer wears trainers/sneakers and is prepared to remove them and place a 'Post-it' on the map. Whiteboard markers work well on laminated surfaces and the map may be used as a substitute for the whiteboard to make linkages to where products are made and where students purchased them. This exercise links students and their possessions to broader issues of globalisation.

A different strategy of engaging students is to ask them to bring a can of Coca-Cola to the lecture. Even if students refuse to bring a can for political reasons, this is an interesting point of discussion in itself. The lecturer asks students to compare different cans. One may find the product has been produced in a wide range of countries. Students can interrogate this and use the 'Post-its' on the map again. The lecturer can also ask where the can was purchased. From this we begin to look at issues of consumption, culture and globalisation.

Through these two examples, the students are placed at the centre of the learning experience. Rather than the lecturer telling the students where the trainers/ sneaker or cans of 'Coke' are manufactured, the student discovers this and makes linkages across the various processes. There is an element of risk in these two examples, as the lecturer may not always be in control of the situation. This is to be encouraged, since it allows for spontaneity and creativity to be generated. Students engage and the lecturer responds to their inputs.

(Dr Chris Bolsmann, Aston University)

LECTURING TO A VARIED STUDENT GROUP

It is not uncommon for individual modules to be offered on more than one degree programme, and this can lead to a student group that has a very varied background knowledge base. Despite these differences, the learning outcomes for the module will be the same and there is some skill in managing the diverse student group to the same end-point. Another possibility is that there may be students studying together in the same lecture group with slightly different learning outcomes. Use of other teaching methods alongside the lecture, such as small group work, projects, seminars and differing assessment strategies, can justify teaching the student group together.

To make the lecture a good learning experience for all students, the following suggestions may help:

- Find out as much as possible about the student cohorts who will be attending the lecture, in particular what they may already know about the subject so as to profile the range of knowledge and subject disciplines of the students.
- Acknowledge to the students at the start that you know they are a varied group and that the content, organisation and supporting materials for the lecture will reflect this.
- Use examples, or case studies, that are varied and reflect the subject disciplines of the group.
- When undertaking class tasks, suggest to the students that they work in their closest disciplinary cohorts.
- When appropriate, ask the students to work on different problems or consider different questions that are relevant to their knowledge base or subject discipline.
- Make explicit reference to specific additional resources each cohort can access for support after the lecture.

Case study 3: Bringing relevance to the lecturing of robotics

In teaching robotics to engineers, it is vital that the theory is learnt in context and that there is an understanding of its application. I therefore chose an approach whereby the students were encouraged into increasing levels of enquiry and enthusiasm through the consideration of possible solutions to actual robotics scenarios, linking this to the theory in the principles of robotics as the weeks progressed.

All lecture slots lasted for two hours. In the first lecture, the students were introduced to the topic of robotics through written case examples and relevant video material, showing illustrative applications that ranged from conventional (welding, paint spray, load/unload of processes, parts transfer) to newer (food and drink, medical, biomedical, roving/exploratory) applications. In doing this, students were made aware from the outset of the possibilities to use robotics in varied industrial contexts.

For future weeks, the students were organised into groups of five to eight. Each group was given a different scenario, with a company profile and a problem that the company sought to address by using robotics (e.g. skilled labour shortage, load handling issues, materials wastage rates). The format of the remaining lectures followed a similar pattern; I presented lecture material in the first hour to cover some theoretical aspects of robotics, and in the second hour the students (in their groups) worked on the application of the theory I had just presented to the scenario on which they were working. In some weeks, the students used their 'slot' to present their developing ideas to the rest of the class. This was particularly useful in helping me to identify and expand upon important learning points for the whole class as I explored the strengths and weaknesses of their ideas. The students readily appreciated the opportunity for 'free-thinking' on a potential robotics applications problem, addressing any necessary assumptions. This approach was far more effective than simply lecturing to the students, as I was able to interweave the robotics theory with the information that different groups had explored in their investigations.

This mix of input from me and activity by the students was well received, student feedback was extremely positive, and the quality of their assessed work showed that they had achieved the overall aim of understanding robotics theory when put into context.

(Dr Simon Steiner, Engineering Subject Centre, formerly Senior Lecturer, University of Birmingham)

MANAGING DISRUPTIVE BEHAVIOUR

The commonest causes of disruption by students in lectures seem to be upheaval caused by late arrivals, students talking to each other, or use of mobile phones (even though there will be a departmental policy on this). It is not usual for any of these behaviours to be extreme, but it can be annoying for those students who are trying to listen and learn. Sometimes student peer pressure will intervene to bring a halt to the disruption, but if this does not work then the lecturer will need to manage the situation. There are significant numbers of books on the causes and management of poor behaviour in schools and further education colleges, but much of the material is not relevant to higher education because we do not see the extremes of behaviour prevalent in other areas of education. The starting point for dealing with disruptive behaviour is to set out expectations or ground rules in the first lecture. These should be based on departmental rules or established custom and practice.

Late arrivals

Unless there is very good cause, the expectation must be that students arrive on time, as the lecture will start promptly. Although not generally acceptable, you may set a deadline that they may enter the lecture up to ten minutes late, but should come in quietly. You may wish to state that students should not come into the lecture theatre more than ten minutes after the start.

The key is then to enforce these rules from the outset. If students arrive late and are still chatting on entering the room, a hard stare may quieten them, or if this fails a pause will make the point that you are waiting for quiet before continuing. Use of humour to comment on late arrivals can be effective – it makes the point that it is not acceptable while not escalating the disruption. If there are significant numbers of late arrivals, it is worth checking why they are late. If there is no acceptable reason for their late arrival, remind them of the ground rules.

Students chatting

Students know that they are not meant to be chatting in the lecture so it is not necessary to make this a ground rule. Similar methods to those mentioned above – a hard stare, or a short pause, may be enough to stop it. If it continues, ask the students directly if they have any questions about what is being covered. In extreme cases, it might be necessary to ask troublesome students to leave the class.

Use of mobile phones

The lecturer can ask students at the start of every lecture to switch off their mobile phones – it could even be the first slide in your PowerPoint presentation. If a mobile phone does go off, pause, looking in the direction of the noise. Again, humour might help here, but use the occasion to remind students that they are breaking the ground rules and disrupting others.

It is important for the lecturer to remain calm and measured in the face of disruption. As already mentioned, humour can go a long way to prevent a problem from escalating. The lecturer should have a quiet word after the lecture with any individuals causing disruption. Dealing with disruptive behaviour can be stressful, and new lecturers may want to discuss the problems they are having with a more experienced member of staff, who can often give them advice and support.

If the disruption is so significant that the lecturer is unable to bring a lecture to order, the only recourse may be to leave, but this should really be a last resort and rarely used. Persistent and excessive disruption will have to be dealt with through more formal channels. All universities have regulations that govern the discipline of students, and for a very small minority of students this may be the only way to manage their behaviour.

EFFECTIVE USE OF POWERPOINT

PowerPoint in lecture presentations

PowerPoint can be a very effective tool for enlivening the lecture. It is easy to import graphics, photographs, charts, graphs, audio and video clips, and to insert live web links. Used well, it can generate interest and provide rich and varied information.

Unfortunately, PowerPoint presentations frequently exclude these features, and simply end up as long sequences of slides, each containing lists of bullet points through which the lecturer works in pedestrian fashion. A list of bullet points per se need not be a problem; a bullet point can be a useful starting point, providing a basis for elaboration and illustration with examples. Slides with bullet points, interspersed with other types of material, can work exceptionally well. However, lectures that use only slides with bullet point lists, often with more slides than is reasonable in the time available, do little to hold student interest. This can be exacerbated when the lecturer does little more than read out the bullet points. What is the lecturer contributing to learning that the students would not get from reading it for themselves? Furthermore, Sweller (2007) concluded from his research on cognitive loading that speaking the same words that are written decreases the ability to understand what is being presented. Because of this, he has been quoted (*The Times*, 18 April 2007) as saying that PowerPoint is a disaster and should be ditched. But the criticism would only be valid if the text on the slides is simply read out, which is rare.

To use PowerPoint effectively in lectures:

- Keep the number of slides to a minimum. Use slides to enhance and illustrate the presentation: if a slide does not really add anything, do not include it.
- Avoid using complex background images which detract attention. Ensure a good colour contrast between text and background.
- Do not use over-complex graphs.
- Use a sans serif font such as Arial or Verdana.
- Try to avoid lectures which use only slides with bullet points.
- Consider use of animations within PowerPoint to build graphic explanations of complex ideas if they enhance understanding.
- Import and use digitised images, sound or video material within the presentation, as appropriate and compliant with copyright.
- Use the active buttons feature or use the hyperlink function to allow non-linear progression through the material. This is particularly effective for question-and-answer slides, where clicking on the different answers to a posed question will take you to different slides, and then return you to the questions slide.

PowerPoint and handouts

Students now expect all lecturers to provide copies of the PowerPoint presentations from their lectures, often via a departmental website or **VLE** (virtual learning environment). The concern often expressed by lecturers is that students may see handouts, whether provided in hard copy or electronically, as a replacement for attending the lectures. The reality is that students may indeed think this, if attending the lecture gives them no added value over and above the PowerPoint presentation. Aspects such as generating and maintaining interest and student engagement give added value to the lecture. It is worth the lecturer making it clear to students from the outset that simply taking the handouts is not going to give them the best learning experience, and then letting their lecturing style speak for itself.

OVERVIEW

Lecturing to large groups of students is a challenging experience for the new lecturer. It is not sufficient to simply know the material. The lecturer needs to make the lecture interesting and engaging, well organised and structured, with clear guidance through the material, using relevant and topical examples and case studies. Getting the lecture right is a skill and can take time. The use of feedback from students and colleagues can be a starting point for **reflection** on your lecturing style, and you may wish to enhance your practice.

REFERENCES

Brown, G (1987) Lores and laws of lecturing. *Physics Bulletin,* 38: 305–307.

Brown, S and Race, P (2002) *Lecturing: A Practical Guide.* London: Kogan Page.

Davies, J W, Arlett, C, Carpenet, S, Lamb, F and Donaghy, L (2006) What makes a good engineering lecture? Students put their thoughts in writing. *European Journal of Engineering Education,* 31(5): 543–553.

Edwards, H, Smith, B and Webb, G (2001) *Lecturing, Case Studies, Experience and Practice.* London: Kogan Page.

Evans, E (2007) *Rethinking and Improving Lecturing in History.* Research Project 2001–07, Final Report. Available online at <http://www.hca.heacademy.ac.uk/resources/reports/eric_evans-Rethinking_and_Improving_Lecturing_in_History.pdf> (accessed 28 April 2007).

Hodgson, V (1984) Learning from lectures. In F Marston, D Hounsell and N Entwistle (eds) *The Experience of Learning:* 90–103. Edinburgh: Scottish Academic Press.

Race, P (2007) *The Lecturer's Toolkit* (3rd edn). London: Routledge.

Ramsden, P (1994) Current challenges to quality in higher education. *Innovative Higher Education,* 18(3): 177–187.

Stuart, J and Rutherford, R (1978) Medical student concentration during lectures. *The Lancet*, 2: 514–516.

Sweller, J (2007) Visualisation and instructional design. Available online at <http://lwm-kmrc.de/workshops/visualisation/sweller.pdf> (accessed 28 April 2007).

FURTHER READING

Evans, E (2007) See above. This is a compelling report of research undertaken over a period of time in four universities, which highlights how students value the lecture.

Race, P (2007) See above. A comprehensive hints and tips collection for effective lecturing.

Teaching and learning in small groups

Sandra Griffiths

BACKGROUND AND DEFINITION

In the UK there have been numerous attempts to define precisely what is meant by **small group teaching** in higher education (Abercrombie, 1970; Bligh, 1986). From a historical perspective, some of these attempts were linked to the fact that small group teaching often took place in association with the lecture method. Many of the aims and practices of small group teaching reflected this link. This led to the view that this approach existed only insofar as it supported the proper business of teaching: the formal lecture (see Chapter 5). Today 'small groups' are often larger than they were.

Attempts to define the concept using the words **'seminar'** and **'tutorial'** are problematic. These names are used both with different meanings and interchangeably. Some writers abandon their use in favour of the term 'group discussion'. The use of group discussion is congruent with a major objective of the activity, that is to teach students to think and to engage with their own and others' learning through the articulation of views and understanding (Stenhouse, 1972; Bligh, 1986).

In this chapter, consideration is given to the enormous and unique potential of the small group to promote learning. It is viewed as an exciting, challenging and dynamic method open to use in a variety of forms and to serve a range of purposes appropriate to different disciplines. Therefore terms will be explored in their most diverse and flexible forms. The process is identified not as a didactic one but rather as a participative experience, in which students are encouraged to take responsibility, along with tutors, for their own learning. Small group teaching and learning with similar aims can also take place online (see Chapter 7).

This chapter does not aim to embrace the topic of the assessment of student learning which emerges from small groups. This is considered further in Chapter 10, including in a case study. There are a number of useful peer assessment studies and case studies on the Higher Education Academy website (HEA, 2007). The report of a project on **peer tutoring** and **peer assessment** at the University of Ulster is also useful (Griffiths *et al.*, 1996), as is Boud *et al.*, (2001).

A HIGHLY SKILLED ACTIVITY

Many writers (Bligh, 1986; Griffiths and Partington, 1992) argue that small group teaching is among the most difficult and highly skilled of teaching techniques. In addition to the primary objective of teaching students to think, the tutor must have a number of subsidiary objectives if the small group is to function. Writers generally agree that the method requires a wide knowledge of subject matter and ability to attend to detail while keeping an eye on the overall picture. Appreciation of how groups function, openness of spirit, accommodation of different views, receptivity to new ideas and maturity to manage a group of students without dominating them are all necessary for effective small group teaching. These attributes are best thought of as skills to be developed over a period of time.

Not only do tutors have to learn how to teach using small group methods but students also have to learn how to work in small groups. Here, it is assumed that it is the tutor's job to assist students to learn, to equip them with self-confidence and facilitate group cohesion. Therefore, a tutor using these methods is much more than a subject matter expert.

In recognising that small group teaching is a difficult and highly skilled teaching technique, it is important to know that it is also one of the most potentially rewarding teaching and learning methods for tutors and students alike.

GROUP SIZE

Small group teaching, broadly speaking, is any teaching and learning occasion which brings together between two and 20 participants. The participants may be students and their tutors, or students working on their own. Because of the relatively small numbers of students involved, the financial cost of the method can be high.

CONTEXT

In recent years the experience of small group teaching and learning has come under threat. With the expansion of student numbers in higher education, class sizes have increased dramatically; tutored small group teaching is expensive when compared with the lecture. A resulting re-examination has had a profound impact on small group teaching and learning. It has led many tutors to re-evaluate critically the nature of the method and to maximise its potential to the full with some quite interesting and innovative results. Peer tutoring, peer assessment, peer learning and peer support have become more common (see e.g. Griffiths *et al.*, 1996). In defence of the method, it has been necessary for assurances to be made that time devoted to teaching in this format is well organised and well spent.

It is not only that there are more students participating in higher education than before; it is also the case that students are coming from more diverse backgrounds. Inclusion and internationalisation are matters to concern ourselves with, and, for example, there is a considerable culture shift towards providing a more diversified curriculum than used to be the case. Part of this shift involves a growing recognition by lecturers that they are responsible not only for what is taught but also, in part, for how students learn. All of these changes mean that the small group is now seen as a means of fostering student engagement, cooperative learning and collaborative learning.

LEARNING IN SMALL GROUPS

The interpersonal and interactive nature of small groups makes them a challenging and appropriate vehicle for engaging students in their own learning. Students are engaged in small groups, both as learners and as collaborators in their own intellectual, personal and professional development. Furthermore, there is strong evidence from students themselves that they benefit from, and enjoy, the experience in a range of different ways (Rudduck, 1978; Luker, 1989). These might best be summed up as both cognitive and affective in nature. Alongside understanding and knowledge benefits, students suggest that participation, belonging and being involved are important dimensions of the experience. The implications of these findings are that the process of building and managing groups, and assisting with the development of relationships, is of paramount importance.

The small group is viewed as a critical mechanism for exploring the development of a range of **key skills** (see Chapter 8). This revitalised interest in key skills has succeeded in according group work a new status.

It is within the small group that self-confidence can be improved, and teamwork and interpersonal communication developed. The development of group work and other skills is reported by students to foster conditions whereby they can observe their own **learning styles,** change these styles to suit different tasks and engage more deeply with the content of their subject (Griffiths *et al.*, 1996). These latter attributes are often cited as prerequisites for a **deep approach to learning.**

Interrogating practice

- How could you assist learners to organise small group sessions where you are not present?
- If you do this already, how could you improve on your practice?

Despite moves towards mass participation and larger classes in higher education, the quality of the learning experience, the need to deliver key skills and the potential for innovation have contributed to the retention and enhancement of the small group method. Small groups are used extensively, and in many different ways, for example in **problem-based learning (PBL)** approaches (see Chapter 26).

With the rapid growth in e-learning and blended learning approaches questions about facilitating groups in this relatively new environment have become very pressing (see Chapter 7). Jaques and Salmon (2006) offer excellent advice.

Interrogating practice

What particular problems do you think the e-learning environment poses for facilitating groups? In what ways do/might you monitor student interaction in electronic environments?

PLANNING

Successful small group teaching and learning does not happen by chance. Planning for effective small group teaching is as important as planning any other teaching activity. This point sometimes goes unrecognised because learning in small groups can at first glance appear unstructured. Some lecturers are put off by the seemingly informal, loose or open-ended nature of small group learning. Others fear this informality will be a recipe for chaos or that the group will develop into a therapy session. All types of teaching must be planned as part of a coherent package, with appropriate use of different methods within each component.

This appearance of informality is deceptive. Behind the facade of the informal group lies a backdrop in which all the learners are playing within a known set of rules which are spoken or unspoken. In other words, the creative flow of ideas is possible precisely because the lecturer or leader has a clear framework, deliberately planned to meet the **objectives** of the session. Within this framework, students feel sufficiently safe to develop their ideas. Equally important, staff feel safe to try out and practise the skills of small group teaching.

Planning for small group teaching may take many forms. It will have much in common with features of planning for any learning occasion. Typically the teacher might consider the intended **learning outcomes,** selection of a suitable type of small group teaching method and learner activity.

Beyond these general features the session plan will be dependent upon the requirements of specific disciplines, the culture of the institution, the overall context of the programme or module and the particular learning needs and prior knowledge of the students.

Whatever form the plan takes, it is critical that precise intentions for small group work are outlined. It is salutary to ask often whether what is being aimed at, and undertaken in small groups, is qualitatively different from that in other delivery modes. The gains for the students should justify the extra costs incurred. In short, the aims and content of the teaching session should dictate and justify the means.

Interrogating practice

Using your own experience as a learner in small groups, identify strengths and weaknesses of different approaches in your discipline.

PREPARING LEARNERS

In a study into peer tutoring in higher education (Griffiths *et al.*, 1996) staff indicated they had recognised the need for student preparation on the 'knowledge of subject' side but had not previously recognised the extent to which students would need training, and ongoing facilitation, to work in the new ways in groups. This finding concurs with other evidence (Griffiths and Partington, 1992), where students offering advice say that lecturers too often assume that they, the students, know how to work in groups. It is just as important for teaching staff to prepare students to work in groups as it is to prepare themselves.

Preparing students to work in small groups can mean providing specific training on how groups work. Such training will develop an understanding that all groups go through a number of stages. Hence, when conflict arises in the group, for example, it can be understood and dealt with as a natural feature to be resolved, rather than perceived as a descent into chaos. Preparation can also mean affording structured opportunities at strategic points within the teaching programme to examine how the group is functioning, what problems exist and how resolution can be achieved. Some lecturers achieve this by providing guidelines (ground rules) at the beginning of a small group session or at the beginning of a series of seminars or workshops. Some lecturers go further, believing that students (either individually or as a group) can themselves effectively be involved in establishing and negotiating ground rules and intended outcomes. Such activities may constitute a **learning contract** or agreement.

Such a learning contract is an important way of effecting a safe and supportive learning environment. Establishing the contract may involve tutors and students in jointly:

- setting, agreeing and understanding objectives;
- agreeing assessment procedures and criteria (if appropriate);
- allocating tasks to all participants, tutors and students;
- developing ground rules for behaviour within the group.

The staff/student contract provides a mechanism for continuing review. It is recommended that time be set aside every third or fourth meeting to evaluate the progress and process of the group's working against the original contract.

PHASES OF GROUP DEVELOPMENT

Social group theorists describe the initial phases in the life of a group using a variety of terms such as inclusion, forming and approach–avoid ambivalence (see e.g. Tuckmann, 1965; Adair, 1996). These works discuss the behaviour of individuals working in groups. What is also recognised is the conflicting tendency to avoid the situation of joining groups because of the demands, the frustration and even the pain it may bring about. This 'moving towards, pulling away' behaviour can easily create tension in the early stages of a group if it is not handled sensitively. Certain behaviours may be a natural part of the initial joining stages rather than a conscious act of defiance or withdrawal by a student. Understanding how students are likely to behave can assist the tutor to provide a framework that fosters confidence and allows trust to develop.

The ending of the group often brings to the surface many issues to do with termination. How intervention is handled at this stage will have a bearing on helping members move on. The tutor needs to be aware of appropriate ways of ending different types of group activity. For discussion and guidance on managing behaviour in groups see Jaques and Salmon (2006).

Interrogating practice

Consider small group teaching sessions you have facilitated. Think about the different types of individual and group behaviour you have witnessed. What were the possible causes?

SIGNIFICANCE OF THE SETTING

Our buildings should reflect our beliefs about learning and teaching and mirror our concerns about inclusion, participation and community. If we do not design our buildings to play to the wide variety of difference in our learners then we are continuing the practice of exclusive higher education.

(Watson, 2007)

This advice, given by one of those involved in designing the innovative Saltmire Centre at Glasgow Caledonian University, draws attention to the setting of group teaching. Few tutors in higher education work in an ideal setting with tailor-designed group workrooms. A great deal can be done, however, in setting up the room to encourage participation and interaction. The research into the influence of environmental factors on interaction has been fairly extensive and shows that physical arrangements have a powerful effect. For example, Korda (1976) documents the effect on encounters when one person is seated and the other is not.

It is well known that communication increases if the differences in social level or status are small. Therefore, part of the tutor's task is to play down the differences in roles and, in particular, play down his or her own authority. This will facilitate the free flow of discussion. It is not a straightforward matter, since the tutor must relinquish authority while all the time remaining in control. This knowledge about the need to minimise social status differences has an impact on where the tutor actually sits within the group.

In fact, it is possible to arrange a room so that certain desired effects are achieved. Three situations (Griffiths and Partington, 1992) serve as examples of this point:

- Nervous students can be encouraged to participate more readily if their place in the group is opposite (i.e. in direct eye contact) to either a sympathetic tutor or an encouraging, more voluble student peer.
- A dominating, vociferous student can be quietened by being seated immediately next to the tutor.
- The level of student participation and of student–student interaction can be affected by the choice of room itself. Is the tutor's own room with all his or her paraphernalia of authority likely to be more or less conducive to student participation? What is an unadorned, stark seminar room with a rectangular table and a special high-backed lecturer's chair at one end likely to dictate for the processes of the group?

Interrogating practice

Visualise yourself in a room where you teach small groups. Where should you sit to maximise your interaction with the group? Where might a student sit to avoid interaction with the tutor or other students? Where might a student sit if he or she wishes to persuade others of a point of view?

TYPES OF SMALL GROUP TEACHING

The specific method selected for small group teaching will derive from the objectives set. There are many different methods of small group teaching; some methods are more suited to certain disciplines than others. However, few methods are peculiar to one subject alone. A large number of methods can be adapted for use in any subject. It is important to remain flexible and open to try out a variety of methods drawn from a wide repertoire. It may be necessary to overcome a tendency to find one method that works well and to use this method frequently. The effect on learners of over-exposure to one method of teaching is worth considering.

Below is a brief description of various ways of working with small groups. It is not intended to be comprehensive, nor are all types mutually exclusive. Some methods are described in terms of a special setting that encourages the application of principles or techniques; for example, brainstorming takes place in a structured setting to encourage lateral thinking and creativity. Other methods are described in terms of their size or purpose.

Interrogating practice

Study the list, noting which methods you have used. Select one or two methods that you are less familiar with and decide how you could use them in the near future.

Examples of working with small groups

- *Brainstorm session* – generation of ideas from the group to foster lateral thinking; there is no criticism of ideas until they are logged.
- *Buzz group* – two or three people are asked to discuss an issue for a few minutes; comments are usually then shared with a larger group.
- *Cross-over groups* – used for brief discussions, then transfers between groups.
- *Fishbowl* – small groups are formed within a large observation group, followed by discussion and reversal.
- *Free discussion* – topic and direction come from the group; the tutor or leader observes.
- *Open-ended enquiries* – students determine the structure as well as reporting back on outcomes.
- *Peer tutoring* – students learn from one another and teach one another.
- *Problem-based tutorial group* – involves small groups using problem-based learning.
- *Role-play* – use of allocated or self-created roles. It is important to facilitate students to enter and come out of role.
- *Self-help group* – run by and for students; the tutor may be a resource.
- *Seminar* – group discussion of a paper presented by a student (note that this term is often used in different ways).
- *Simulation/game* – structured experience in real/imaginary roles. Guidelines on the process are important and feedback is critical.
- *Snowballing* – pairs become small groups and then become large groups.
- *Step-by-step discussion* – a planned sequence of issues/questions led by the students or tutor.
- *Structured enquiries* – the tutor provides lightly structured experiments and guidance.
- *Syndicate* – involving mini-project work, followed by reporting to the full class.
- *Tutorial* – a meeting with a very small group, often based on feedback to an essay or assignment (note that this term is often used in different ways).
- *Tutorless group* – the group appoints a leader and may report back; it may focus on discussion or completion of some other type of set task.

This list has been adapted from several sources, but owes much to Habeshaw *et al.* (1988), who also provide a more detailed description of particular methods.

There are several approaches not mentioned above that may be used in small or large groups. Case studies, **problem classes** and demonstrations fall into this category. The main determining factor is the amount of interaction that is desirable. Apart from this it is necessary to ensure that in a larger group all members can see, hear, and so on. Resource issues have forced some 'small groups' to become larger than is viable, thus risking a loss of much of the benefit.

Case study 1: The use of small groups on an undergraduate music degree at the University of Ulster

---

Course: B.Mus. (Hons)

Year of Study: 2

Module: Renaissance Studies

Delivery: lectures/classes, seminars and workshops

Class size: 20–25 students

Seminar programme

For this part of the **module** the class is divided into five groups. The tutor, ensuring a mix of personalities, determines the formation of the groups. Each group delivers two presentations to the whole class. The higher of the two marks awarded contributes towards the module assessment. The assessment criteria are negotiated with the class. Each group is asked to maintain a diary, recording meetings and discussions and their management of particular tasks.

Structure of each one-hour seminar

Group presentation (15–20 minutes). Listening groups consider presentation and agree questions (10 minutes). Questions and discussion (15 minutes). Reports completed (10 minutes).

As the presentation is a group endeavour, groups are encouraged to involve each member, not only in the presentation and delivery but also in the response to questions during the seminar. Students are reminded to think of interesting ways in which the presentation might be delivered to engage the attention of their audience. The 'presentation' might take the form of a panel discussion or a debate, or it might be modelled on a game show programme. Each presenting group is required to submit a one-page summary one week prior to the seminar. This is copied to the other groups to familiarise them with the treatment of the topic.

At the end of the seminar each of the listening groups completes a report which invites comments on the effectiveness of the presenting group's management of the situation and their knowledge of the topic, including their response to questions. The tutor monitors the proceedings and completes a separate report. The marks awarded by the students and the tutor are weighted equally in the final assessment.

(Dr Desmond Hunter, Module Tutor, University of Ulster)

SKILLS FOR EFFECTIVE SMALL GROUP TEACHING

Among important skills for teachers, those of listening, asking and answering questions and responding are paramount in small group settings.

Questioning

The skills of asking and answering questions are not as simple as they might appear. Many general teaching and social skills communication texts deal with the skill of questioning (see e.g. Brown and Atkins, 1988). Good questioning techniques require continuing preparation, practice and reflection by students and teachers alike. Preparation of a repertoire of questions in advance will allow the teacher to work effectively and flexibly in the small group. Similarly, student-to-student interactions in groups is enhanced if students prepare questions at the outset or end of a class. The confidence of students is often boosted through preparation of content in the form of key and incisive questions on a topic.

The type of question asked is also linked to promoting or inhibiting learning. Questions may be categorised in different ways, such as:

Open		Closed	
Broad	Reflective	Narrow	Recall
Clear	Probing	Confused	Superficial
Simple	Divergent	Complex	Convergent

Interrogating practice

How do you usually ask questions? Look at the list and see which categories your questions usually fit into.

Make a list of probing questions relevant to an important concept in your subject.

How you ask questions is important in fostering student responses. Body language displaying an indifferent, aggressive, closed or anxious manner will be less effective. An open, warm, challenging or sensitive manner may gain more responses of a thoughtful nature.

Interrogating practice

When you are asked a question by a student, what are some of the things you can do other than directly answering the question?

The above activity concentrates on your reactions to student questions. Some of these reactions may result in students being able to answer their own questions. However, there will be times when you will directly answer the question. Directly answering questions during a group meeting takes less time than attempting to encourage the student or group to come up with the answers. If you choose to answer directly, make your answer brief and to the point. After responding, you may wish to check that you have really answered the question by saying something like: 'Does that answer your question?'

The timing of asking questions and the use of pause and silence are also important in developing the skills of answering and asking questions. Taking these matters into consideration may in part address the common problem teachers in higher education report – that students do not contribute during small group sessions.

Listening

The mental process of listening is an active one that calls into play a number of thinking functions including analysis, comprehension, synthesis and evaluation. Genuine listening also has an emotional dimension since it requires an ability to share, and quite possibly understand, another person's feelings, and to understand his or her situation.

Intellectual and emotional meanings are communicated by the listener and speaker in both verbal and non-verbal forms. Thus how you listen will be observable through gestures and body language. Your listening skills may be developed by thinking about all the levels of a student's comment in this way:

- what is said: the content;
- how it is said: tone and feelings;
- when it is said: time and priority;
- where it is said: place and environment.

Listening attentively to individual students in the group and to the group's mood will heighten your ability to respond. This may demand that you practise silence; if you persevere you will find this an attainable skill through which remarkable insights can be gained.

Interrogating practice

Consider how much time you spend listening to students and encouraging students to listen to one another.

Responding

Listening in silence by paying undivided attention to the speaker is an active process, engaging and heightening awareness and observation. The other aspect of positive listening is of course to intervene in a variety of ways for a variety of purposes. The more intense our listening is, the more likely it is that we will know how to respond, when to respond and in what ways.

There are many ways of responding and many reasons for responding in a certain way. Appropriate responses are usually made when the tutor has considered not only the cognitive aims of the session but also the interpersonal needs of the group and the individual learner's level of confidence and knowledge. Different responses will have different consequences for the individual student and for the behaviour of the group as a whole. Therefore, an appropriate response can only be deemed appropriate in the context of the particular small group teaching session.

Interrogating practice

Along with a small group of colleagues, determine what skills you might usefully develop to increase effectiveness as a facilitator of groups.

OVERVIEW

This chapter has considered a selection of appropriate group methods; mentioned a range of group formats; referred to individual and group behaviour; and offered an opportunity for teachers and learning support staff to consider how they might develop and enhance their practice, including by offering suggestions for further reading.

REFERENCES

Abercrombie, M (1970) *Aims and Techniques of Group Teaching*, SRHE, London.

Adair, J (1996) *Effective Motivation*, Pan, London.

Bligh, D (ed.) (1986) *Teaching Thinking by Discussion*, SRHE and NFER Nelson, Guildford.

Boud, D, Cohen, R and Sampson, J (2001) *Peer Learning in Higher Education, Learning From and With Each Other*, Kogan Page, London.

Brown, G and Atkins, M (1988) *Effective Teaching in Higher Education*, Routledge, London.

Griffiths, S and Partington, P (1992) *Enabling Active Learning in Small Groups: Module 5 in Effective Learning and Teaching in Higher Education*, UCoSDA/CVCP, Sheffield.

Griffiths, S, Houston, K and Lazenbatt, A (1996) *Enhancing Student Learning through Peer Tutoring in Higher Education*, University of Ulster, Coleraine.

Habeshaw, S, Habeshaw, T and Gibbs, G (1988) *53 Interesting Things to Do in your Seminars and Tutorials* (3rd edn) Technical and Educational Services Ltd, Bristol.

Higher Education Academy (2007) website <www.heacademy.ac.uk>; access the case studies by going to the website and tapping on Resources (last accessed August 2007).

Jaques, D and Salmon, G (2006) *Learning in Groups: A Handbook for Face-to-face and Online Environments*, Taylor & Francis, London.

Korda, M (1976) *Power in the Office*, Weidenfeld & Nicolson, London.

Luker, P (1989) Academic staff development in universities with special reference to small group teaching (unpublished Ph.D. thesis), University of Nottingham.

Rudduck, J (1978) *Learning Through Small Group Discussion*, SRHE, University of Surrey.

Stenhouse, L (1972) Teaching through small group discussion: formality, rules and authority, *Cambridge Journal of Education*, 2 (1): 18–24.

Tuckmann, B (1965) Developmental sequences in small groups, *Psychological Bulletin*, 63 (6): 384–399.

Watson, L (2007) Personal communication, June.

FURTHER READING

Griffiths, S and Partington, P (1992) See above. An in-depth look at the topic. Useful interactive exercises and video to highlight skills.

Habeshaw, S, Habeshaw, T and Gibbs, G (1988) See above. Very useful for practical advice and activities.

Jaques, D and Salmon, G (2006) See above. Wide ranging, authoritative and up to date.

Race, P and Brown, S (2002) *The ILTA Guide, Inspiring Learning about Teaching and Assessment*, ILT in association with *Education Guardian*, York. Contains a lively and practical section on small group learning and teaching.

7 E-learning – an introduction

Sam Brenton

INTRODUCTION

The aims of this chapter are: to consider what we mean by e-learning; to give practical advice about approaches to e-learning; to introduce practitioners to key tools and technologies for use in effective e-learning; and to provide an overview of current issues in e-learning and direct the reader to further sources of information.

CONTEXT

Like the printing press, like mechanical flight, gunpowder, the telegraph, the telephone, the microchip, radio and television, the **internet** is a transformative technology. Across the planet, the **World Wide Web** is changing the way we do things, and allowing us to do things we could not do before. It is transforming the way we access information, enabling networks of interest and **communities of practice** to flourish across physical distance with an immediacy and breadth that were impossible less than a generation ago. There is informed speculation that it is changing the way in which today's younger generation learn and communicate, and the way they construct, not just their social networks, but their identities as social beings (e.g. Turkle, 1995).

The Web presents a challenge for formal education. In an age where there is ubiquitous access to high-quality content (once you know where to find it, how to spot it, or how to make it yourself), and where people can seek out and communicate with experts, practitioners and learners in any discipline, what becomes of our role as teachers, what are our libraries for, and what remains special about the physically situated learning communities of academe? Independent, non-formal education between people using the Web is occurring on an unprecedented scale across the globe. So the question we ask now is no longer 'does e-learning work?', but rather: how can we, in the formal, guided process of higher education, use the power and potential of recent electronic media to enable our students to learn better, from us, from each other and independently?

DEFINITIONS

The current trend is to define e-learning rather loosely. The 'e' prefix is unhelpful in that it implies (falsely) that the learning in 'e-learning' is of a special variety, distinct from 'normal learning'. And yet it allows useful semantic wriggle room, so that we don't encumber ourselves with restrictive definitions, which, in an era of rapidly developing technology and practice, might needlessly exclude useful tools or strategies. The Higher Education Funding Council for England (HEFCE), in its 2005 *Strategy for E-Learning*, addresses this question thus:

> We have debated whether we need to adopt a specific definition of e-learning at all, since it might curb exploration and restrict diversity. However, we believe we should limit the scope of our strategy, to be sufficiently focused, to the use of technologies in *learning* opportunities.
>
> (HEFCE, 2005)

It is likely that your institution will have its own e-learning strategy or policy. It may reflect this broad approach, or it may choose to interpret the 'e' in e-learning as pertaining purely to networked technologies, rather than including any and all computer-aided learning (**CAL**). In any case, the key implications of the HEFCE definition, and of many institutional e-learning strategies, are that:

- Rather than a series of systems and tools, e-learning is something that *happens* when students learn with information and communications technology (ICT).
- It may happen in distance learning courses or in campus-based courses (this latter is sometimes called '**blended**' or 'mixed-mode' learning).
- It will usually be defined sufficiently broadly to allow you as a practitioner in your discipline and a teacher of your students to employ a variety of approaches in the way you use it; there is no one way to 'do' e-learning.
- It is not something you 'deliver'. Rather, it is something you enable your students to do.

Acknowledging the breadth of useful definitions of e-learning, the remainder of this chapter presents some web-based technologies and pedagogical approaches which may be of practical use in teaching.

E-LEARNING PLATFORMS

The great majority of institutions have a virtual learning environment (**VLE**) of some kind. This may also be known as a learning management system or a course management system, or be part of a broader integration of web services and information systems usually known as a managed learning environment.

A VLE is a piece of web-based software that allows the running of all or part of a course or module online. It gives a menu-based or point-and-click interface for constructing an online course area without the need for specialist web development skills. These typically include: a chat room; a discussion board; a calendar; an announcements feature; a tool for building online assessments; a function for setting work, for the students to submit it and for you to grade it; a way to upload, order, index and time-release learning materials; a glossary; a tool for providing web links; a way to track your students' activity in the VLE; and a facility for displaying syllabus information. You can also make simple web pages in a VLE through a basic word processor-like interface (a WYSIWIG: 'What you see is what you get'). Note that a series of sophisticated, linked web pages, or any use of online video and other multimedia are created not within the VLE, but outside it and then uploaded; while VLEs make it easier to run a web-based course, these elements of web production remain a specialist, though learnable, skill. Your institution's VLE may also include a **blog**-like reflective journal, tools for you and your students to record, upload and download voice files, a messaging tool, perhaps an e-**portfolio** tool for your students to store and reflect on materials and information about their progress, and a 'Who's Online' tool. You log on to a VLE via a web address from any internet-enabled computer, and access to your course area/s is usually, though not exclusively, restricted to those students who are on your course.

You are under no obligation to use all of these tools and will be able to 'turn off' or hide features you are not using. You are likely also to have some control over basic design elements, and over the navigational structure of your course area/s. Over the past decade these tools have provided the staple functionality for running an online distance learning course or online elements within a blended learning course. VLEs do not usually provide 'out of the box' the more recent functionality associated with **'Web 2.0'** or **'social software'** (see below), but do give efficient access to a series of integrated tools which allow you to teach and guide your students' learning in ways you decide are appropriate.

The VLE may be accessed directly or through a student portal. It may be branded by your institution and integrated with other e-learning software (e.g. dedicated assessment software, messaging systems, plagiarism detection software such as **TurnItIn**). It may be that your department uses its own system or that your institution supports one central system. There are still some home-built systems within departments. In the UK, at the time of writing, the market leader in commercial VLEs is *Blackboard*, which acquired the other main commercial VLE company *WebCT*; the products are available in various flavours. **Open source** (free and freely modifiable) VLEs are becoming increasingly popular in UK HE, with growing interest in the *Moodle* platform, and other open source VLE products such as *Sakai* and *DrupalEd*. Whatever the case, it is almost certain there is an e-learning platform available in your place of work to use in your teaching. If you choose to explore e-learning as a field in itself, you are likely to encounter fervent debate about the merits of and educational philosophies behind the major platforms, but, broadly, though their design may foreground particular approaches, they allow you to do similar things.

Any VLE can be used well or poorly, for didactic teaching or for collaborative learning, for synchronous (live) or asynchronous (over time) activities, for arts or sciences, for assessment, reflection, blended or distance learning, course administration, individual and group work, for discussion or for provision of web-based materials, whether these are documents, web pages, interactive simulations, or use video or sound. Your challenge as a teacher is to examine closely your course, its learning outcomes, your students, the assessment structures and your own pedagogical ethos, and then to choose how to use these tools in a way that is going to be effective and will make best use of your time and skills. Once you start to do this, you may find yourself asking some fundamental questions about the ways in which your students learn, and about your role as a teacher.

Interrogating practice

First steps: a question of support

If you are new to your institution you may wish to find out the following:

- Is there any e-learning support in your department (as distinct from general IT support)?
- Is there an e-learning unit or team in your institution that can offer pedagogical and practical advice about getting started?
- Does your department and/or institution have an e-learning strategy?
- What software is available for use (e.g. a VLE, an e-assessment system, or blogging)?
- What facilities are available for your students to use as e-learners, and do the IT infrastructure and IT-enabled learning spaces encourage or hinder different types of study (e.g. computer-aided group study, multimedia playback)?
- If you are going to be involved in a course which already uses e-learning, how is it used and what will your role be?

E-LEARNING IN PRACTICE

Table 7.1 offers some possible e-learning activities which might usefully be integrated into a course. These combine things you could do within a VLE and tasks which might involve other tools. They are mapped to hypothetical educational challenges of a kind which a lecturer may encounter.

The activities suggested in Table 7.1 vary in scope and scale, and some require more technical skills than others. You may, if you are a new lecturer or a teaching assistant, not be able to re-engineer aspects of the course's teaching or assessment structure. However, with the assistance of experienced peers, or of any dedicated learning or educational

Table 7.1 Hypothetical teaching situations and possible e-learning responses

	Issue	E-learning activity
1	There is time pressure on lectures, where students sometimes arrive without sufficient background knowledge; more ground needs to be covered than time allows.	The lecturer records themselves speaking each week, for 20 minutes, on his or her mobile, covering background points. These are then uploaded as 'course podcasts' into either the VLE or podcast-enabling software. The students are invited to submit questions they have about the podcast content via the VLE discussion board, and the lecturer will address the most pertinent of these before the live lecture commences.
2	Students are taking incomplete notes, and are relying on the PowerPoint handouts (posted on the VLE) as their main record of the lectures.	The lecturer stops distributing the PowerPoint slides, and instead asks the students to take thorough notes and post these within the VLE discussion board for their peers to see, and to comment on inaccuracies. If the lecturer has control over the assessment structure, a small part of the assessment may be given to this posting and critiquing activity.
3	Student numbers are so high that the traditional format of seminars is strained to breaking point.	The lecturer asks students to post observations and comments in the VLE's discussion forum after the lecture, and to respond to each other's posts (the lecturer may kick-start this by introducing threads with particular questions or topics). The live seminar is used to conclude these discussions and to answer any outstanding questions that have arisen from them.
4	On a language course, students are not getting enough scheduled time to practise conversation, and are at different levels of comfort.	The lecturer posts a sound file of themselves, starting a debate or conversation about a relevant topic. Students are then required to reply, first to the lecturer and then to each other, and to post these files in either a discussion board or in a 'voice board' using either free recording software and microphones or with voice-recording software now found in many universities such as WIMBA Voice Tools (a sort of online language lab).
5	During a year abroad/on placements/in industry, it is clear that some students drift away from their peers and the university; data suggest that the drop-out rate climbs during this time.	The course teams sets up a discussion board within the VLE, or mailing list, or a social network, in order to encourage a continuing sense of cohesion among the cohort. This may end up being student-led and largely social, but with departmental news made available and any questions answered by staff.
6	In a first-year history course it becomes clear that there are two major problems: some students lack a basic knowledge of the period, and some students use sources indiscriminately and without reference.	The lecturer sets a task where students in small groups research a particular area of historical background, using the online library search tools to locate relevant electronic sources. The group then presents this as a written narrative on a **wiki** or within a VLE, and clearly references the sources. Other students are asked to comment and to critique the strength of these sources, and to suggest others where appropriate. This is assessed.

(Continued)

Table 7.1 Hypothetical teaching situations and possible e-learning responses (*continued*)

	Issue	E-learning activity
7	On a course that is assessed at the end of the semester by examination, it becomes clear only at the end that a percentage of students have not engaged with the reading or understood the topics.	Set required reading within the VLE and track which students are not accessing the material. Set short online tests at key intervals to see which students may be falling behind, and to make it difficult for them not to keep up with the reading.
8	On an engineering course, it is clear at the assessment stage that some students are having difficulty with sustained writing; writing is not focused on during the regular curriculum.	Devise problem-based learning scenarios. Students must present their solutions and reasoning in written form on their course blogs. Other students then give feedback to the author, explaining how passages might be made clearer (this process of writing and rewriting in public collaboration can be very effective online).
9	Lectures have become impractical with numbers of over 300.	The lecturer uses a tablet PC, a microphone and some **screen recording software** to pre-record the lecture. This is posted as video online, and the lecture slot is used for questions and answers. If the video is posted in the VLE, the lecturer can tell which students have and have not viewed it; thus it can become an attendance requirement, just as attending the live session may be.
10	On a distance-learning course, the students tend to contribute well, but miss the sense of collegiality and presence that a campus location would give them.	The lecturer decides to hold some tutorials, and even social networking events, within an online **3D virtual world**, such as *Second Life*, *There* or *Active Worlds*.
11	It becomes clear that some students are finding it difficult to organise their own learning, and are not confident that their progress has a structure to it. They find it difficult to express what they have learned so far, and how it relates to what they are assessed on.	The department decides that each student will have a reflective journal (or e-portfolio) where they are given the learning outcomes and updated information about their progress, and where they are required to reflect on their progress.
12	In assessed group projects, students are producing much good work, which may be useful to their current and future peers, but which languishes in a filing cabinet.	Require that the group work is published online, as a website, wiki or multimedia presentation (ensuring that any production skills involved are relevant and built into the course's stated transferable skills and learning outcomes).

technologists whose support you may be able to access, all of them should be possible. They are purely illustrative of the kinds of activities that academic staff may find successful, and are not, of themselves, recommended. The key thing to ask before embarking on any sort of e-solution is 'What is the purpose of this?' Higher education e-learning platforms and websites are littered with empty wikis, deserted discussion fora, rarely visited online course areas. This is usually due to three factors, of which the first is the most important:

1   There is insufficient purpose to the e-intervention; it is solving a problem that does not exist.
2   It is not built into the regular face-to-face teaching of the course or its assessment structures.
3   Insufficient time is available to set up and then diligently maintain the activities.

E-learning rarely works where it is regarded as simply a value-added extension of the main part of the course. It is also unlikely to flourish where there is little support or incentive available, or recognition that it is time-consuming (remember that e-learning is not automated learning; it requires the teacher's presence as much as other types of teaching). Lastly, as assessment drives student learning and is 'the most powerful lever teachers have to influence the way students respond to courses and behave as learners' (Gibbs, 1999, p. 41), so it follows that e-learning elements and activities will need to be integrated into the way the course is assessed (see Chapter 10 on assessment).

Once you start to approach the subject from the basis of your and your course's educational aims, you will inevitably find yourself thinking about learning design (see also Chapter 4). As you move from the basic provision of course management information and lecture materials made available via a VLE towards the knottier but more productive challenges of thinking what e-learning you want your students to actually do, you will need to consider how to design learning activities for your students, which have clear purpose and are integrated into the design of the course. The examples given in Table 7.1 are illustrative only; you will have your own challenges to surmount and your own answers and ideas.

There is much theory about design for e-learning, although one can also say that 'there are no models of e-learning *per se*, only e-enhancements of models of learning' (Mayes and de Freitas, 2004). In practice, we rarely start consciously from theoretical models of learning, but they are useful as you ask yourself some of the questions they try to answer or expand upon, and you may find that some have utility as you move from abstract consideration towards a practical solution. How we design for our students' e-learning, and what philosophical traditions we are acting within when we do so, is a fascinating and complex question but one which cannot be given further consideration in this chapter. The interested reader can find many excellent books which include overviews of learning models as applied to e-learning and useful checklists for the practitioner (e.g. Beetham and Sharpe, 2007) and online studies about mapping theory to practice in e-learning design (e.g. Fowler and Mayes, 2004).

Interrogating practice

Questions for e-learning design

- What are the learning outcomes of the course?
- What are your aims for the students? What do you want them to learn 'around the edges' of the formal outcomes? What skills and understanding do you want them to develop?
- Are there any particular learning activities you can think of to encourage the above? Can these be built into the design of the course?
- Do you and the students have access to any technologies or tools that might be used to craft and deliver these activities?
- Does the way the course is assessed encourage the students to meet the outcomes, and can you use any technologies discussed in this chapter to (1) make the assessment drive the students' learning, and (2) ensure timely **feedback** to assessment which can help the students develop as the course progresses?

Case study 1: Using VLE tools to promote feedback-driven learning experiences

At the Tanaka Business School, Imperial College London, all courses we teach are accompanied by a corresponding course area in the School's VLE. Learning technologists train us to use the various tools and assist in building or sourcing course content. I worked closely with our learning technologist, David Lefevre, to develop an online course area in our VLE for a postgraduate course in accounting management analysis.

In designing the area we were keen to avoid a technology-driven approach; we wanted to promote interactive and feedback-driven learning experiences. To this end our focus was on interactive content and assessment.

Our first step was to convert the traditional paper-based course booklet into a series of interactive multimedia activities. The introduction of new concepts (for example, the presentation of a financial statement) is followed by interactive activities in which students are given the opportunity to test and apply these concepts in a series of real-world tasks. I believe this ability to interact and play with the material leads to a deeper and more meaningful grasp of the content introduced on the course. While studying the materials students are able to contact either me or a teaching assistant through the VLE discussion boards. Students receive further feedback on their progress through a series of online formative tests which review and recycle the material.

For **summative assessment**, we retained a paper-based examination but took advantage of the VLE discussion boards when designing the coursework component. Prior to adopting the VLE, students were divided into groups and asked to produce an investment analysis. In the VLE-based coursework, students are given the same task but are asked to post their contributions on to a group discussion board. I am now able to assess not just the final product but also the process students have been through to get there.

The discussion boards created a transparency to the student learning process. It was very satisfying to know how much work the students put into their learning. Unsurprisingly the most active online students achieved the highest mark in the final closed book examination. However, whether this correlation indicates a causal relationship is a matter for further research.

Students who were not very vocal in class contributions now had an alternative forum in which to articulate their knowledge and learning. I received many comments on how much they had learned from each other during the discussions and how this had made the learning process far more engaging and effective.

(Ebrahim Mohamed, Director, Imperial Executive MBA Programme, with
David Lefevre, Senior Learning Technologist,
Tanaka Business School, Imperial College London)

THE ROLE OF THE TEACHER IN E-LEARNING

A course that makes extensive use of e-learning may break down the traditional academic role into several functions, which may be carried out by more than one person. One might, for example, have an online course in which there are:

- the 'lecturer', who works with a learning technology professional to produce suitable online content, be it text based or a lecture **podcast**;
- the 'e-moderator', who may be a teaching assistant with responsibility for the daily upkeep of the course's discussion forum, to stimulate discussion, and run learning activities based on the lecture material and reading (Salmon, 2000, 2002);
- group facilitators, who work with small groups of students on set collaborative activities, and may be students on the course themselves, or perhaps Ph.D. students in the department;
- a technical and/or administrative role responsible for answering practical student queries about the technology or course;
- the assessors, who may be brought in from outside the course to mark student work;

- one or more 'academic guests', supplying further specialist information, perhaps hosting a web conference or chat room discussion about a topic in which they have expertise (these can freshen up a course and give the student the feeling of being part of a larger faculty).

Many e-learning courses will features none or only some of these roles, but they give an idea of the roles that may need to be taken on/learnt by the teaching function in a typical distance learning or e-learning intensive course. We can see that it is vital to acknowledge (1) the multiplicity of roles the academic function must adopt in a successful e-learning course, and (2) the new skills that even the most experienced teachers may need to learn to fulfil these functions. It is also crucial that everyone is aware of the boundaries and obligations of their roles within such an arrangement.

BEYOND VLES

Web 2.0 and social software

One of the biggest developments in the use of the Web-at-large has been the emergence and widespread use of so-called 'Web 2.0' tools, or 'social software'. Unlike the traditional website where designers publish their pre-made content (or lecturers post their lecture notes), social software provides web users with tools that are more or less content-free, but which can be used collaboratively to generate, present and share user-made content. Popular examples of this sort of software include sites and services such as: *Flickr* (for sharing photographs); *Facebook, Bebo* and *MySpace* (for social networking); *YouTube* (for posting home-made movies and other clips). Tools such as blogs and wikis are also now a popular way to engage in a networked discourse over time. A further layer to this social activity is the persistence and growth of different kinds of grouping, networking and discussion tools (from the pre-Web internet e-mail groups to live messaging tools by MSN, *Yahoo*, *AIM* and many others, with peer-to-peer file-sharing applications). If we consider that interfaces which harvest information and present all these disparate services in an integrated manner are increasingly important to users (from a personalised *Google* home page, to a home-made web page which culls various **RSS** (really simple syndication) feeds from blogs and news sites, to a university's student portal pulling in various electronic services in a personalisable way (which some call a **'PLE'**)), we can see that the Web as it might have been perceived in HE a few years ago, of information-led websites, mail groups and monolithic e-learning platforms, is now a great deal more diverse and complex, and is humming with people, many of them undoubtedly our students, networking, talking, and creating and sharing resources.

It is possible to claim that effective learning is inherently a social activity, that we learn best from a social and experiential construction of knowledge (e.g. Vygotsky, 1978). If we adhere to that, then we may suggest that any effective e-learning will use software in a social manner, so chat room tutorials from the end of the last century are in a sense a precursor to this newer, social, user-led Web. It is certainly true that most of today's undergraduates are 'doing e-learning' in unofficial ways right beneath our noses. They chat on **MSN Messenger** in bedrooms, labs and libraries, share views and information on *Facebook*, search out journal articles and secondary sources through a popular search engine rather than through their institutions' e-journal subscriptions, and share comments, tips and even their work on mobile devices in the palms of their hands. This culture of collaboration, this ceaselessly social construction of shared knowledge across a multitude of platforms, presents a challenge and a huge opportunity. It is a challenge because it can stray very close to a culture of plagiarism, and because the wealth of readily available information may lead to a form of snow blindness, where the academic qualities of criticality, focused discourse, explicit recognition of sources become submerged in noise. But it is an opportunity because it allows us not always just to shun these sorts of interaction, but to harness their power, that our students may work together and by themselves in these familiar ways, but under taught guidance, to help them arrive at the requisite understanding of their subject and develop academic techniques.

Reusable learning objects (RLOs), free resources, open courseware

There are various schemes to enable e-learning content creators to share their creations across institutions. The shared resources are often called reusable learning objects (**RLOs**). These may be as atomised as a *Flash* animation of a bird's wing in flight, a traditional set of critical questions about Sir Gawain and the Green Knight, or a problem-based learning scenario with accompanying resources. The idea is that each may be taken and used by a teacher in the design and delivery of a course. A good example in medical education is *IVIMEDS*, the International Virtual Medical School (www.ivimeds.org/). It is also worth browsing the website for the Centre for Excellence in Teaching and Learning (CETL) in RLOs (http://www.rlo-cetl.ac.uk/), and exploring **Jorum**, established by the UK's **JISC** (a free online repository service for teaching and support staff in the UK). Two large-scale illustrative examples of this growing trend are:

1   the Open University's *OpenLearn* platform/website which allows anyone to register for free online courses, including access to materials and the ability to communicate with other learners (in LearningSpace), and also allows teachers to reuse and collaborate on educational resources (in LapSpace) (see http://www.open.ac.uk/openlearn);
2   *iTunesU*, a service run by Apple which enables educational institutions (only in the USA at the time of writing) to make educational content available through its iTunes software.

There has been a large growth in the amount of freely available, high-quality, online materials aimed at higher education across the globe. The Massachusetts Institute of

Technology, through its Open Courseware initiative, has materials from over 1,700 courses freely available under a **Creative Commons Licence** (http://ocw.mit.edu/OcwWeb/web/home/home/). The Open Courseware Consortium has participating member institutions across the globe (http://www.ocwconsortium.org/).

With the growth of **broadband** in some areas of the world, we see too a rise in the amount of audio and video content that is freely available to teachers and learners. Podcasts are proving a popular way to disseminate educational content (e.g. Warburton, 2007), so that students (and interested lay listeners) can subscribe and be notified of new releases via a blog, or by an RSS reader (such as may be found on **iGoogle** home pages), or via software such as **iTunes.**

Many colleagues are wary about using resources produced within other institutions, about the prospect of generic web-harvested content being treated as a ready-made solution, and about sharing their own resources with competing institutions. Legal, technical and social barriers remain. However, it is clear that there is a trend towards the availability and sharing of high-quality educational materials, and that if you make canny use of these resources at the course design stage you may be able to enrich your teaching and your students' learning. It is also apparent that with an increasing amount of material available this way, universities and their academics must offer an e-learning experience based on more than simply providing their (often fee-paying) students with access to excellent home-grown materials.

Interrogating practice

Selecting tools for e-learning

Once you have decided on the purpose and nature of your e-learning activities, and how you would like your students to engage with any e-content in the course, you might consider:

- What tools are supported and available in your institution (e.g. within the main VLE, or on departmental web space).
- Whether any of your activities require the use of other tools. Can you use freely available Web 2.0 or social software tools? Are there any copyright ownership implications or local policies about using external tools?
- Are there any technical or cultural barriers to overcome, and do you have support in your institution to help you with these (e.g. an e-learning team in your department or institution)?
- Will your students be absolutely clear about the purpose of the learning activities you are asking them to participate in through the use of these tools?

OVERVIEW

This chapter has looked at how changes in technology outside formal education open up new challenges and opportunities for us in our roles in higher education. Consideration has been given to various tools and technologies. Barriers to successful e-learning and some examples of possible e-learning activities have been presented, with the caveat that the key to making sure that e-learning will occur successfully is to consider the educational purpose first and the technology second.

E-learning tools and fashions date quickly. Back at around the turn of the century, large projects were in progress to revolutionise education through electronic media. Grand claims were made, and much money spent, for example on the UK e-University project. There was also something of a gold rush to repurpose learning materials and launch large-scale, content-led, broadly self-study distance-learning programmes. Today, the focus is returning to what makes good teaching, and thus encourages successful learning, whatever media are being used. In an era of widespread, free access to high-quality materials, a successful course – distance or blended – has to be about much more than high-quality electronic content. Rather, it will be distinguished by the quality and success of the interactions within it: how students work alone and with each other to make pertinent, visible contributions and progress; how the teacher moderates conversations, chooses appropriate uses of technology for key activities; how e-assessment elements keep the students learning and engaged in discourse; and how well the subject expert/s, be they lecturers, teaching assistants or professors, use the media and tools available to instruct, guide, interest and inspire their students.

Thus these tools, used appropriately, give one the opportunity for:

- synchronous and asynchronous interaction and communication (student–student and student–teacher);
- the sharing and generation of tutor-made and student-made materials;
- a richness of media involving sound, image, 3D simulation, video, flat text and graphical representations;
- a flexible way to embed formative and summative assessments into a course;
- a set of tools and techniques for teaching students on campus or anywhere where there is an internet connection.

Far from being automated learning or purely self-directed learning, it is clear that where effective e-learning takes place, it does so with the guidance and presence of a successful and thoughtful practitioner. That is, the role of the teacher in e-learning is just as important to student learning as it is in the seminar room or lecture hall.

REFERENCES

Beetham, H and Sharpe, R (eds) (2007) *Rethinking Pedagogy for a Digital Age: Designing and Delivering E-learning*. Oxford: Routledge.

Fowler, C and Mayes, T (2004) *Mapping Theory to Practice and Practice to Tool Functionality Based on the Practitioners' Perspective*. Available online at <http://www.jisc.ac.uk/uploaded_documents/Stage%202%20Mapping%20(Version%201).pdf> (last accessed 30 September 2007).

Gibbs, G (1999), 'Using assessment strategically to change the way students learn', in S Brown and A Glasner (eds) *Assessment Matters in Higher Education*. Buckingham: Society for Research into Higher Education and Open University Press.

HEFCE (2005) *HEFCE Strategy for E-Learning 2005/12*. Bristol: Higher Education Funding Council for England (HEFCE). Available online at <http://www.hefce.ac.uk/pubs/hefce/2005/05_12/> (last accessed 30 September 2007).

Mayes, T and de Freitas, S (2004) *Review of E-learning Theories, Frameworks and Models*. Available at <http://www.elearning.ac.uk/resources/modelsdeskreview/view> (last accessed 30 September 2007).

Salmon, G (2000) *E-moderating: The Key to Teaching and Learning Online*. London: Kogan Page.

Salmon, G (2002) *E-tivities: The Key to Active Online Learning*. London: Kogan Page.

Turkle, C (1995) *Life on the Screen: Identity in the Age of the Internet*. New York: Simon & Schuster.

Vygotsky, L (1978) *Mind in Society*. London: Harvard University Press.

Warburton, N (2007) *Philosophy: The Classics: An Introduction to Some of The Great Philosophy Books Read by the Author Nigel Warburton*. Available online at <http://www.philclassics.libsyn.com/> (last accessed 30 September 2007).

SUGGESTIONS FOR FURTHER READING

Beetham, H and Sharpe, R (eds) (2007) See above.

HEFCE (2004) *Effective Practice with E-Learning – A Good Practice Guide in Designing for Learning*. Available online at <http://www.jisc.ac.uk/media/documents/publications/effective practiceelearning.pdf> (last accessed 30th September 2007).

JISC (2003–2007) E-Pedagogy Programme (website with various publications). Available online at <http://www.jisc.ac.uk/elearning_pedagogy.html> (last accessed 30 September 2007).

Salmon, G (2002) See above.

8 Teaching and learning for employability

Knowledge is not the only outcome

Pauline Kneale

INTRODUCTION

Self-confident students who think about the processes they have gone through in higher education, as well as the knowledge they have gained, should be more effective students and researchers. From an entirely selfish point of view, happy, self-confident, employable students are good for university business in the short and long term. Students who enter the graduate job market and repay student loans at speed are more likely to look back and think fondly of the academic elements of their university experience.

Graduate employment ought to be a powerful motivator of students seeking to reduce debts by entering the graduate job market as speedily as possible. However, student motivation to to university careers services for support, physically or online, will be low unless they are aware of the opportunities. Many students find term-time and vacation jobs without too much effort, so obtaining employment after university is not perceived as a hurdle. Urgency is generally low. 'I will worry about a job when I've got a 2.1.' Academic tutors and careers staff are not always seen as necessarily the right people to give advice as 'they don't have graduate jobs'.

It is worth remembering that many students are motivated more by assessments than by an intrinsic love of learning and spend time in the library because the curriculum is cleverly designed to involve reading. Similarly, students are unlikely to engage with teaching that focuses on their future employability in a **deep learning** manner without there being a tangible and reasonably immediate benefit. Neither can they be expected to divert to campus careers offices without significant carrots or sticks, especially if that service is in an out-of-the-way location and lacking a coffee bar and comfortable chairs.

Without academic intervention and support, student awareness of employability and careers services facilities is unlikely to increase. External pressures on academic staff to raise awareness include league tables where employability is an indicator. Placing students effectively in the graduate workforce can be as important an outcome for an institution as the number of upper-second-class and first-class degrees.

The main emphasis of this chapter is on ways in which all staff can contribute in all modules to raise the profile of employability skills and attributes that will be inclusive of all students. It comments on issues regarding where this learning occurs, including that in specialist 'careers' modules. The case study material is all provided by the author.

Interrogating practice

Understanding what prompts student engagement with employability

- What motivated you and your colleagues to use a careers service as a student? What does the campus careers service offer to staff and students?
- What motivates students to go to careers service events?
- What is available on the careers website? How is it linked to departmental websites?

THE CONCEPT OF EMPLOYABILITY

Employability is a term that has multiple definitions. For some people employability is about skills, for others it is an activity which prepares individuals for long-term employment. The two roles were brought together in the definition of employability, adopted by ESECT, the Enhancing Student Employability Coordination Team, as 'A set of achievements – skills, understandings and personal attributes that make graduates more likely to gain employment and be successful in their chosen occupations' (Knight and Yorke, 2003: 5).

Knight and Yorke (2004: 25) identify seven employability definitions with numbers 5 to 7 having the 'greatest appeal to us':

1 Getting a (graduate) job.
2 Possession of a vocational degree.
3 Possession of 'key skills' or suchlike.
4 Formal work experience.
5 Good use of non-formal work experience and/or voluntary work.
6 Skilful current career planning and interview technique.
7 A mix of cognitive and non-cognitive achievements and representations.

Stephenson (1998: 10) links employability to capability. In his words, 'Capable people have confidence in their ability to':

1   take effective and appropriate action;
2   explain what they are seeking to achieve;
3   live and work effectively with others, and
4   continue to learn from their experiences both as individuals and in association with others in a diverse and changing society.

Stephenson recognises that individuals have their own specialist knowledge derived from their degree and other experiences, but more importantly they know how to apply that knowledge, and to acquire new knowledge. They have the aptitude to continue to learn and to develop their skills and knowledge so as to become continuously employable.

The Australian approach in defining 'graduate qualities' is tailored in many university strategies. For example, a University of South Australia graduate:

- can operate effectively with and upon a body of knowledge of sufficient depth to begin professional practice;
- is prepared for lifelong learning in pursuit of personal development and excellence in professional practice;
- is an effective problem-solver, capable of applying logical, critical and creative thinking to a range of problems;
- can work both autonomously and collaboratively as a professional;
- is committed to ethical action and social responsibility as a professional and citizen;
- communicates effectively in professional practice and as a member of the community;
- demonstrates international perspectives as a professional and as a citizen.

(Curtis and McKenzie, 2001)

For further insights into the range of definitions, descriptions of practice, employability case studies and institutional employability strategies, see Rooney *et al.* (2006); Association of Graduate Careers Advisory Services – AGCAS (2006, 2007); Higher Education Academy (2007); Harris Committee (2000), and Maguire (2005).

Interrogating practice

- What are the skills and employability ambitions of your university learning and teaching strategy and employability strategy?
- How are these institutional strategies linked to departmental practices?

OWNERSHIP OF EMPLOYABILITY

Ideally, employability is delivered by a partnership of academic staff and 'careers' staff who are usually located outside departments. The status of careers staff within departments varies within and between universities but they are likely to be invisible to students unless their role is promoted by departments and valued by tutors. Ideally, careers colleagues have a place on faculty and department teaching committees to enable seamless communication and raise everyone's awareness of emerging employability agendas and opportunities. Knight and Yorke (2004: 20–21) tabulate in detail the concerns which surround the notion that employability is a challenge to academic values and their text explores a variety of answers to this challenge.

Employability, like any other academic process, needs to persuade people to act through evidence. What, for example, is the proportion of graduates each year that moves to graduate jobs or postgraduate education? University league tables of graduate destinations and retention numbers motivate some of the stakeholders. Knowing who has these data is helpful, and posting it in student handbooks may be useful in promoting the department and discipline.

Maximising discipline relevance is powerful. Some academics promote connections to students between their discipline and its application in the 'real world', through a genuine interest in students' plans postgraduation and involving students in applied research activities. Graduates provide excellent role models in the classroom, explaining where their degree activities are relevant at work. There are also opportunities to include research-led module assignments for assessment. Examples to enhance disciplinary understanding could include researching the employment market for the discipline, entrepreneurship among recent graduates, and the range of national and international work-placement opportunities.

EMPLOYABILITY AND YOUR DISCIPLINE

Where employability is critical is in recruitment and retention. Raising awareness of the employability aspects of a particular discipline should be advantageous. The Student Employability Profiles (Higher Education Academy, 2006; Forbes and Kubler, 2006) give detailed information on the employability attributes and abilities for graduates of every discipline. Using this information at all stages, from recruitment to final-year careers advisory tutorials, gives students the information and appropriate language for describing the skills and attributes they have acquired through the degree, but perhaps this is not recognisable as making them employable.

For example, with linguistics students unsure of their position, ask them to discuss the following points selected at random from their profile.

Students with linguistics degrees can:

- assess contrasting theories and explanations, including those of other disciplines, think hard about difficult issues, and be confident in trying to understand new systems;
- critically judge and evaluate evidence, especially in relation to the use of language in social, professional and other occupational contexts, translation and interpretation;

- acquire complex information from a variety of sources and think creatively about and build complex systems.

(Higher Education Academy, 2006: 102)

Asking students to evidence concepts from their experience will help to build confidence in their abilities.

The Employability Profiles are equally relevant for students on vocational degrees. Dentistry has 12 bullet points but only one is directly related to clinical practice. All the others are competencies which can be expected of any graduate, for example:

- exercise initiative and personal responsibility;
- use IT for communication, data collection and analysis and for self-directed learning;
- analyse and resolve problems and deal with uncertainty;
- manage time, set priorities and work to prescribed time limits.

(Higher Education Academy 2006: 68)

Case study 1: Developing awareness

Here is a tutorial activity. To focus attention, ask students to explain, in a curriculum vitae or interview, the qualities, skills and experiences they have to offer to employers as a graduate of their own discipline.

Interrogating practice

How does the Employability Profile for your discipline appear in your undergraduate student handbook, on departmental websites, and in pre-university promotional materials?

DEVELOPING CONSCIOUS AWARENESS OF SKILLS AND ATTRIBUTES

An unaware student might explain that the absence of presentations from their curriculum vitae (CV), despite having given upward of 25 presentations to groups of five to 60 people, is because 'they don't count, they are just university presentations'. Experience shows that unless they are prompted (Case study 1), students concentrate on recounting their knowledge at the expense of appreciating that they have also acquired skills in data interpretation, project management, development of structured documents, and independent and critical thinking.

Case study 2: Exploring student misconceptions

- 'I can't apply to . . . because they want critical thinking and commercial awareness. In my course we don't do that. It's all research and projects.'
- 'No one tells you about what businesses want before you apply to uni. My degree just doesn't have any use, unless you want to do research and that needs a 2.1 or first. And research is all my tutor can talk about.'

Making the link between personal reflection and workplace application is easier for students who encounter **personal development planning** (PDP) in their vacation or term-time employment. Where students struggle to see the relevance of reflection, tutorial activities that begin with interviews with people who use personal development planning at work may be helpful (Kneale, 2007), as would asking students to read and reflect on Cooper and Stevens (2006).

Giving students the opportunity to practise making personal evaluative statements, before encountering them at work, is an employability skill in its own right. The lack of confidence of both students and academics with personal development processes exists partly because they are asked to articulate in an unfamiliar language information about which they feel self-conscious (Case study 2). Introducing students from **level** 1 onward to the discipline Employability Profiles and the Skills and Attributes Maps (Higher Education Academy, 2006) has the potential to develop the confidence of both students and staff in openly discussing these matters.

Finding the language

To make employability links clear to students, and to expand their employability vocabulary, it is suggested that the skills and competency terms and synonyms employers use should also be used in **module** descriptors and outcomes. If this seems to be pandering to the employment agenda, it is worth remembering that these terms are commonly used in research and academic job advertisements.

Critical thinking

Data analysis to find patterns and trends and draw conclusions is one aspect of critical thinking. This involves taking complex information, breaking it down into subunits, performing statistical and other data analyses, and then reflecting on the results. The keywords to describe these processes might include reasoning, logical thinking, integrating, developing insights, and finding relationships, all of which could replace the ubiquitous 'research skills' in a module or session descriptor.

Creativity

Employers seeking evidence of creativity might expect to find words like innovation, invention, originality, novelty, brainstorming, making connections, generating new concepts. A student of art and design should find creativity easy to articulate, but science students are equally involved in discovery activities, seeking to create new ways of looking at data and information. Brainstorming ideas in groups and teams is a familiar technique for scientists, but if creativity is never mentioned in the learning outcomes of a degree or module, a student is unlikely to describe his or her work as creative.

Problem-solving

In some students' minds being asked to articulate their problem-solving skills requires them to think of a problem which they have defined and solved themselves. An employer is looking at this in a much broader sense, in which the problem is any issue or activity that has been worked on. The processes involved might include seeing an issue from a variety of viewpoints, researching evidence to support or refute a particular position, and considering whether there are more deep-seated issues. Keywords here might include identifying issues, analysing, evaluating, thinking, generating ideas, brainstorming, group discussion.

Decision-making

Decision-making is a ubiquitous activity. An employer is seeking evidence that an employee will look into a position (research), think about it (evaluation), decide if the relevant facts are available, and propose and implement a reasoned course of action. The decision-maker needs to explain and defend his or her choices by describing a process that is evidence-led and transparent. The keywords might include consider, select, reason, reflect, evaluate, timescales considered. A tutor can help to articulate the process by asking for the reasoning behind a particular approach in delivering an assignment, and teasing out the decisions made consciously and unconsciously.

Personal effectiveness

Planning, time management and organisation are related skills that most employers like to see evidenced. Keywords include coordination, prioritisation, scheduling, efficiency, effectiveness, competence, capability, on time, on target. Essentially, planning and organisation require a person to create a process which enables a task to be completed on time to the best possible standard. This is vital in dissertation or project planning, so these keywords are potential learning outcomes of dissertation and project modules. At level 1 the same processes are required to deliver essay, poster or web page assessments on time. The employability bonus here is to discuss and reflect on the planning processes students use in assessment production, and to make the link to planning research and extended writing, and to CV or interview discussions.

Commercial awareness

Commercial awareness essentially revolves around being aware of the ways in which organisations operate and people interact with them. A commercially aware person can reflect on the possibilities and issues of business situations from a variety of perspectives. Themes include business planning, customer relationships, cash flow processes, strategic decision-making, SWOT (strengths, weaknesses, opportunities and threat) analysis, advertising and marketing, target setting, and understanding the mission and aims of an organisation. Employers are interested in reflection and understanding of the processes and approaches operating in businesses where applicants have worked or been **volunteering.** Experience of many of these themes is acquired as a normal part of life, through school, student societies, clubs and so on, as in Case study 3.

Case study 3: Exploring student misconceptions

Student: I'm a physics student; we do nothing on commercial awareness.

Academic: But your CV says you are a bar manager. You cash up after shifts, you collate the brewery orders. You organised club nights, recruiting staff, doing the promotions and the finances. These are all evidence of commercial experience and awareness.

Personal competencies

Under personal competencies, a person can talk about their motivation, energy to promote and start new initiatives, perseverance with difficult tasks, and ensuring tasks are completed on schedule. Keywords might include self-awareness, initiative, innovation, decision-making, flexibility, patience, care, rigour, meticulous. When prompted, most students realise that they have often used these skills and demonstrated these attitudes but have so far not articulated the experience and realised their value.

Interrogating practice

- Where do the discipline Employability Skills and Attributes Maps link with your teaching?
- How are students made aware of the skills and attributes they gain in the modules you teach?
- Do students comment on the skills and attributes listed in the module outcomes in their personal development planning, reflection and evaluation of your module?

TEACHING AND LEARNING OPPORTUNITIES

In a 2007 Universities UK publication on employability, recommendation 16 states: 'If students are to take employability in the curriculum seriously, institutions should consider including it in the assessment and grading process.' However, making space in the curriculum for accredited employability learning can conflict with perceived disciplinary needs.

In some departments employability issues are addressed through careers sessions within skills modules, careers sessions within discipline-specific modules (e.g. Tang and Gan, 2005; Heard and Hole, 2006), in modules addressing preparation for work placements (Bovea and Gallardo, 2006; Freestone and Thompson 2006), and in stand-alone modules (Maguire and Guyer, 2004). Recent examples of innovative approaches and activities may be found in Knight and Yorke (2004), Cockburn and Dunphy (2006), and Macfarlane-Dick and Roy (2006). Careers education in higher education is generally based broadly around a skills and competencies agenda, and sometimes theorised through the DOTS model – Decision learning, Opportunity awareness, Transition learning and Self-awareness (Watts, 1977; McCash, 2006).

There is real debate about the most appropriate place for such teaching and whether it should be optional or compulsory. The regular drip, drip approach argues for small bites in each level of study, regularly reminding students about career opportunities and providing space for reflection on their current experiences and the skills involved. In year-by-year engagements the focus can move from raising awareness of internships and the local job market at level 1, preparation for work placements at level 2, to refining techniques for graduate **assessment centres** and interviews at level 3. Timing is crucial, as targeting first-year students with information about graduate employment three or four years down the line falls on stony ground. Graduation is too far ahead for researching graduate jobs to be meaningful.

A specialist module approach presupposes space for two to five credits of assessment in each of three years. Where space is available for a single, 10- or 20-credit module there are good arguments for its placement at level 2. At this stage, applying for summer internships is a possibility, organisations which have application deadline dates in the September before students graduate can be highlighted, and there is time for students to undertake individual or group research projects in particular occupational sectors. For those students who have no idea about what do next, level 2 is a good time to start research.

Where 'careers modules' do exist, should they be compulsory? Short engagements in each year taken by everyone give a consistent and benchmarked provision to every student. The individual module is more problematic. Experience suggests that where such modules are compulsory there is disengagement from students. 'I know I want to be a teacher/estate agent/accountant so I don't need to do this module', 'I am not interested in this now, I will explore the career after I have finished my degree and taken a gap year', and 'I am a mature student, I have been employed for the past ten years, my

CV is fine, I hire people, I don't want to waste time on this'. Academics and careers service staff will appreciate that such comments are potentially short-sighted, but if the module is compulsory these students may be disruptive. Where the module is an elective or option some students who really need career support potentially miss out.

It may be helpful to consider what is unlikely to work with students. One-off events can be great fun and get good feedback on the day, but they fade quickly in people's memories, as will anything where students are not required to follow up with a piece of personal research, reflection and writing. Placing information about employment in the curriculum in the final year can be unhelpful, as by this stage it is too late to find a placement or internship, many application deadlines have passed, and examinations and assessments are distracting.

Assessment for modules or units with a career and employability focus must be at least as demanding and comparable with parallel discipline assessments. Creating a curriculum vitae and letter of application in response to a specific advertisement is a standard assessment, but a relatively mechanical activity, with support and advice available at universities and online. Arguably, it deserves a relatively small proportion of summative marks.

Employability assessments should give participants opportunities to practise the skills recognised as having employability dimensions. Group work, researching using the web and written sources, developing interview and assessment templates, researching career areas in general and particular organisations in detail to compare and contrast workplace cultures and processes are all appropriate. The style of assessment can develop posters, web pages, scenario development or research reports, ideally produced in groups. There is merit in mirroring assessment centre activities where there is pressure to produce group solutions quickly with instant poster and PowerPoint presentations. These activities prepare students for assessment centres and show them that they can work quickly to meet deadlines.

WORK PLACEMENTS

Work placements and experience appear in many university strategies with different emphases reflecting the nature of the institution. The relevance of work placements in non-vocational degrees is always a source of debate (Nixon *et al.*, 2006). Pressure to include such experiences comes in part from government initiatives. Universities UK (2007) recommendation 17 is 'Work experience, either as part of a programme of study, or as an external extracurricular activity, should be recognised in some way and formally accredited where possible'. The National Council for Work Experience is a major source of expertise in this area. This enlarges on the useful point that most students have paid employment in term-time and vacations; many have undertaken voluntary work at home and increasingly abroad during gap experiences. There is plenty of material for these students to reflect upon and trawl for examples of employability skills and attributes.

Interrogating practice

- What is the role of work placements and international placements in your department and university?
- Where do work placements fit in the university and department Learning and Teaching Strategies?
- How can these strategies be linked to your teaching?

Case study 4: Exploring student misconceptions

The visibly upset student, seriously worried that she had nothing to offer on her CV, turned out after discussion of her extracurricular activities to have led an Operation Raleigh group, done two stints on tall ships as an able-bodied helper to disabled crew members and spent three months doing voluntary work in a hospice. She had a significant list of employability skills and practice but had failed to make the connections, or count these activities as developing placement skills.

Work placements may be specialist modules, but they have a broader role, and in this case can encompass the year abroad or year in industry, the short-term placement such as a vacation internship or Shell Step (2007) project. They may be part of the recognised curriculum or they may be extracurricular. In practice, it is important that students know what they are doing, why they are doing it and have the tools to reflect on the practice the experience is giving them. Language departments where students take a year abroad often lead good practice, with reflective logging as part of the assessment. Similar practice is well established in education, psychology and healthcare departments where placements are normal curriculum elements.

LINKING EMPLOYABILITY TO YOUR TEACHING

The depth of engagement with employability taken by a member of staff will vary depending on the nature and level of a module, and the activities that students undertake in other modules. What follows are possibilities to prompt further engagement.

- The skills and attributes taught or practised in the module are clearly stated in the module outcomes in language that maps on to Employability Profiles (Higher Education Academy, 2006) and Subject Benchmark Statements (QAA, 2007). Students are required to reflect on module skills and attributes, possibly through personal development plans.

- Students are made aware of exactly how the skills and attributes practised in a module are relevant in dissertation or project research, and work placements.
- The value placed on the acquisition of skills and processes as well as knowledge is recognised through the assessment of the majority of skills.
- Every level 1 undergraduate can articulate the skills gained in each module in their curriculum vitae and letter of application for a vacation or term-time job.
- Every level 2 and 3 undergraduate is aware of and knows how to use the skills and attributes from a module as evidenced in a curriculum vitae and letter of application, and has had an opportunity to articulate these skills as practise for an interview.
- Taught and research postgraduate students can articulate the skills gained in their curriculum vitae and letters of application for a graduate, vacation or term-time job.
- Research postgraduate students understand that being able to articulate the skills gained through their research training and research experience, in their curriculum vitae and letters of application, will help to secure graduate employment in university and non-university sectors.

OVERVIEW AND CONCLUSION

This chapter has emphasised the benefits to students of being consciously aware of how they approach tasks as well as the knowledge that they gain from them. It argues that the ability to reflect on how you operate will both benefit current degree performance and build lifelong learning skills.

It suggests that tuning the curriculum (Knight and Yorke, 2004: 179) through many small-scale, awareness-raising activities and employability-aware reflection can be very powerful. In addition, specialist modules may be offered. While this is an important and valuable approach it runs the risk of being a packaged unit, with students missing the broader relevance of all modules to their employment and lifelong learning. As curricula evolve, whole modules are more vulnerable as staff move to other projects, whereas embedded discussion and reflection on module-learning processes and skills are likely to survive for the long term.

Generally it is thought that graduates will be more effective in the workplace and make a greater impact in their careers if lifelong learning skills and deep learning are part of their practice. Many degrees prompt the development of these approaches, students have some autonomy and responsibility for their own learning (Boud, 1988), and there is shift towards the tutor as adviser and facilitator (Stanier, 1997). University learning may be moving in ways that help employability, but do students realise that there is a change, and do they appreciate the value of reflecting on how they learn as well as what is learned?

Methods for integrating engagement must be backed up by positive support from the teaching community. Researching a career opportunity is as effective a way of practising research skills as any other student research activity, and can be assessed on the same basis. This agenda gives students the opportunity to meet appropriate experts, alumni, careers staff and those in discipline-related organisations for teaching and for work experience, helping to bridge the gap between university and work.

REFERENCES

AGCAS (2006) Careers Education Benchmark Statement, AGCAS, Sheffield. Available online at <http://www.agcas.org.uk/quality/careers_education_bs.htm> (accessed 22 April 2007).

AGCAS (2007) Institutional Approaches – Employability Case Studies, AGCAS, Sheffield. Available online at <http://www.agcas.org.uk/employability/strategic_approaches/index.htm@se> (accessed 22 April 2007).

Boud, D (ed.) (1988) *Developing a Student Autonomy in Learning* (2nd edn), London: Kogan Page.

Bovea, M D and Gallardo, A (2006) Work placements and the final year project: a joint experience in the industrial engineering degree, *International Journal of Engineering Education*, 22(6): 1319–1324.

Cockburn, D and Dunphy, J (2006) Working together: enhancing students' employability, Quality Assurance Agency, Gloucester. Available online at <http://www.enhancementthemes.ac.uk/documents/employability/Employability_Overview_QAA113.pdf> (accessed 22 April 2007).

Cooper, J and Stevens, D (2006) Journal keeping and academic work: four cases of higher education professionals, *Reflective Practice*, 7(3): 349–366.

Curtis, D and McKenzie, P (2001) Employability Skills for Australian Industry: Literature Review and Framework Development. Available online at <http://www.dest.gov.au/archive/ty/publications/employability_skills/literature_research.pdf>.

Forbes, P and Kubler, B (2006) *Degrees of Skill, Student Employability Profiles*, A Guide for Employers, The Council for Industry and Higher Education, London. Available online at <http://www.cihe-uk.com/publications.php>.

Freestone, R and Thompson, S (2006) Student experiences of work-based learning in planning education, *Journal of Planning Education and Research*, 26(2): 237–249.

Harris Committee (2000) *Developing Modern Higher Education Careers Services*, Report of the Review, Manchester University, Department for Education and Skills. Available online at <http://www.dfes.gov.uk/hecareersservicereview/report.shtml> (accessed 22 April 2007).

Heard, S and Hole, M (2006) Designing effective learning opportunities and promoting employment skills through a range of continuous assessments, *Planet*, 17: 40–41. Available online at <http://www.gees.ac.uk/planet/#P17> (accessed 22 April 2007).

Higher Education Academy (2006) *Student Employability Profiles: A Guide for Higher Education Practitioners*, The Higher Education Academy, York. Available online at <http://www.heacademy.ac.uk/profiles.htm> (accessed 22 April 2007).

Higher Education Academy (2007) *Employability and Enterprise*. Available online at <http://www.heacademy.ac.uk/Employability.htm> (accessed 22 April 2007).

Kneale, P E (2007) Introducing workplace PDPs, *PDP-UK Newsletter*, 10: 3–5. Available online at <http://www.recordingachievement.org/pdpuk/default.asp> (accessed 22 April 2007).

Knight, P T and Yorke, M (2003) *Assessment, Learning and Employability*, Maidenhead: Society for Research into Higher Education and Open University Press.

Knight, P T and Yorke, M (2004) *Learning, Curriculum and Employability in Higher Education*, London: Routledge Falmer.

McCash, P (2006) We're all career researchers now: breaking open career education and DOTS, *British Journal of Guidance and Counselling*, 34(4): 429–449.

Macfarlane-Dick, D and Roy, A (2006) *Enhancing Student Employability: Innovative Projects from Across the Curriculum*, Gloucester: Quality Assurance Agency for Higher Education. Available online at <http://www.enhancementthemes.ac.uk/documents/employability/Employability_Innovative_Projects_Across_Curriculum.pdf> (accessed 22 April 2007).

Maguire, M (2005). *Delivering Quality: Quality Assurance and Delivery of Careers Education, Information and Guidance for Learning and Work Within Higher Education*, London: Department for Education and Skills. Available online at <http://www.agcas.org.uk/quality/docs/delivering-quality-executive-summary.pdf.

Maguire, S and Guyer, C (2004) Preparing geography, earth and environmental science (GEES) students for employment in the enterprise culture, *Journal of Geography in Higher Education*, 28(3): 369–379.

Nixon, I, Smith, K, Stafford, R and Camm, S (2006) Work-based learning: illuminating the higher education landscape, York: The Higher Education Academy. Available online at <http://www.heacademy.ac.uk/research/WBL.pdf> (accessed 22 April 2007).

QAA (2007) Subject Benchmark Statements. Available online at <http://www.qaa.ac.uk/academicinfrastructure/benchmark/default.asp> (accessed 22 April 2007).

Rooney, P, Kneale, P, Gambini, B, Keiffer, A, Vandrasek, B and Gedye, S (2006) Variations in international understandings of employability for geography, *Journal of Geography in Higher Education*, 30(1): 133–145.

Shell Step (2007) Shell Step – students and businesses in step. Available online at <http://www.step.org.uk/> (accessed 22 April 2007).

Stanier, L (1997) Peer assessment and group work as vehicles for student empowerment: a module evaluation, *Journal of Geography in Higher Education*, 21(1): 95–98.

Stephenson, J (1998) The concept of capability and its importance in Higher Education. In J Stephenson and M Yorke (eds) *Capability and Quality in Higher Education*, London: Kogan Page.

Tang, B L and Gan, Y H (2005) Preparing the senior or graduating student for graduate research, *Biochemistry and Molecular Biology Education*, 33(4): 277–280.

Universities UK (2007) Enhancing employability, recognising diversity: making links between higher education and the world of work. Available online at http://www.universitiesuk.ac.uk/employability/> (accessed 22 April 2007).

Watts, A G (1977) Careers education in higher education: principles and practice, *British Journal of Guidance and Counselling*, 5(2): 167–184.

9 Supporting student learning

David Gosling

INTRODUCTION: LEARNING WITHIN A DIVERSE SECTOR

Not only are there more students in UK higher education than ever before, they are also more diverse than at any time in the past. Students vary enormously in their financial status, social class, family circumstances and age; their previous educational experience, reasons for attending higher education, and aspirations and ambition; their religion, ethnicity and nationality; their abilities and disabilities and special needs.

Closely connected to these trends towards greater diversity and 'widening participation' is a recognition that the system is recruiting more students who need significant help if they are to succeed in their studies. Students are increasingly heterogeneous and have multiple identities which in turn create a multiplicity of learning needs. We can no longer assume that there is a common understanding by students of the purposes of higher education or of the nature of studying at higher levels. Many students come from backgrounds without the cultural capital that would enable them to have an understanding of the key demands being made on them by their teachers at the point of entry. This has led to increasing concern about retention rates of students recruited.

Because students now pay fees (in England at any rate) and take on substantial loans for the duration of study, they and their families have to make greater financial sacrifices for higher education. More students are also working, sometimes for many hours per week, while also pursuing full-time studies. Students are therefore being regarded, and regard themselves, as consumers of higher education who are entitled to expect good standards of teaching and support for their studies. Their opinions as consumers are being collected through the **National Student Survey**, which is without doubt influencing the provision of support services in many institutions.

This chapter looks at how universities and colleges can effectively tackle ways of supporting the learning of students to meet the expectations of students themselves and improve their chance to stay on and succeed in their chosen studies. It will consider the role not only of academic staff but of all staff across institutions who support student learning. It will consider the notion of *learning development* and how this can be promoted for all students using both face-to-face and virtual learning and how learning support can be targeted at those students who are judged to be most at risk. Targeted learning support is also essential for students with disabilities and special needs. Legislation (Special Educational Needs and Disability Act 2001) requires universities to provide genuinely equal opportunities for students whether or not they have a disability. It is argued that greater cultural and ethnic diversit, among home and international students also requires strategies for supporting learning within a multicultural environment.

LEARNING NEEDS

In the changing context of higher education the need for a more systematic approach to supporting student learning becomes ever more important. A simple transmission model of teaching is even less adequate to meet the needs of students than it was in the past. In recent times, the sector has witnessed a significant change in emphasis from understanding teaching as a process in which academic staff simply lecture, to seeing it as one in which students are supported in their learning. Higher education no longer operates entirely on a teacher-centred model of teaching and is shifting, albeit slowly and hesitantly, towards a more student-centred model (see Chapter 1).

Part of being 'student centred' is recognising that although there is a subject content which all students must learn in order to pass, each student approaches the subject from their own perspective, their own unique past experience and their own understanding of themselves and their aspirations. A useful concept here is the idea of 'learning needs'. All students must undertake a personal journey from their level of knowledge and skills at the point of entry to the level required to succeed in their chosen courses. All students have their own learning needs that must be met if they are to complete this journey successfully.

Learning development is the process of meeting these needs. Structured learning support is designed to provide assistance to help students' learning development. For some this means developing their IT skills, for others their language skills, for others their employability skills and so on (Cottrell, 2001). The object is for each student to build on and develop his or her existing abilities, capacities and skills in a way that is personal and relevant to their own studies and aspirations.

The LearnHigher Centre for Excellence is a partnership of 16 institutions committed to improving student learning through practice-led enquiry, and building a research base to inform the effective use of learning development resources. 'Learning development' is defined by LearnHigher (2008) as:

> the process by which learners develop their abilities to think for themselves, develop their knowledge, understanding and self awareness, and become critical thinkers able to make the most of formal and informal educational opportunities that they

encounter. By extension 'learning development' also refers to the processes (including curriculum design, teaching strategies, support services and other resources) that are designed to help them do so.

Students need help to recognise their own learning needs and to find strategies to meet them. The university or college also has a responsibility for recognising these needs and making provision to meet them. Traditionally this has happened through the interaction between teaching staff and students in lectures, seminars, the studio, laboratory, field trips and so on, and through feedback provided to students informally or as part of the assessment process. But support through these types of staff–student contact is no longer enough. Student numbers have increased and staff student ratios have declined. There is increasing use of e-learning and modular schemes which can create a more fragmented and isolated student experience. Furthermore, students are both working and studying off-campus for longer hours.

Clearly other forms of learning support are needed, provided through online resources, forms of peer support and by central or faculty/campus-based service departments. Higher education institutions today provide a wide range of services designed to supplement the role of academic tutors. These include centres for academic writing and maths support, library and information services, disability support units, international student centres, and special projects to support the development of employability skills, writing skills and internationalising the curriculum.

A distinction may be made between services that support students as people and those that support students' learning development and learning resources (Simpson, 1996). The student services are designed to meet day-to-day needs for food, accommodation, medical advice and support including mental health, childcare, counselling, financial support and advice, recreational and sporting facilities, careers advice, chaplaincy and world faith advisers, and so on.

Learning development services are about helping students to be more successful in their programme of study. The goal of institution or campus/faculty-wide learning development services is to enhance students' learning and develop their skills through a variety of strategies – including confidential advice and counselling, drop-in centres, tailored courses, individual and group referrals, integrated provision with academic courses – designed to create an approach that should ideally integrate the role of teaching and support staff.

Learning resources are those facilities and materials which students make use of in their learning – books, learning packages, audio-visual materials (CDs and DVDs), artefacts and interactive online materials often made available through the university's **VLE** (see chapter 7), as well as **podcasts**, MP 3 and texting services – and the infrastructure which makes these available – libraries, laboratories, studios and IT networks. Many institutions have invested in attractive flexible learning spaces, where group work and social learning can occur and which have wi-fi networks, video-conferencing facilities, interactive whiteboards, and a variety of interactive resources.

But student services, learning development and learning resources are not independent of each other. There are is a long list of problems – stress, anxiety, eating disorders, drug use, difficulties with accommodation and finances, bereavement and other family issues – which clearly impact on students' study as well as their more general well-being. For this reason academic advice and guidance is sometimes provided alongside other services in what are often called 'one-stop shops' based within faculties or on each campus. The key to success is confidential and impartial advice followed by appropriate referral to those with specific expertise.

Supporting student learning is not simply the sum of the services and learning opportunities provided. It is also essentially about an ethos, which recognises that:

- Students are individuals, each with their own learning needs.
- Support is available to all through a variety of face-to-face and virtual means.
- Learning development is not stigmatised as 'remedial'.
- All tutors have a responsibility to provide support.
- Learning development specialists have an important role.
- Students need to be inspired and motivated.
- Successful support systems involve many departments and will require good communication between different parts of the institution.

Now let us look at various aspects of supporting student learning within teaching departments and higher education faculties or schools.

LEARNING DEVELOPMENT WITHIN ACADEMIC PROGRAMMES

Pre-entry guidance and support

- The process of supporting student learning begins as soon as students are recruited. Before students even arrive at the university they can be helped to understand the aims and structure of the course they have been accepted on to through some initial reading, and/or activity which they can undertake, using communication via e-mail or texts.
- Pre-entry guidance should also give students the opportunity to check that their choice of course, or chosen modules, are consistent with their career plans.
- If entering students are known to have special needs they should be referred to the disability service for their needs to be assessed as early as possible in order that support can be put in place – involving, for example, scribes, signers or a buddy to help with personal requirements.
- For some mature students, or those entering courses at levels 2 or 3, it is also necessary to agree the basis for any **AP(E)L** claim or credits being transferred, any course requirements that will need additional assessment, and those which have already been met.

- Where there are identified language needs (e.g. with students recruited from overseas), additional English classes can be agreed as part of the programme of study (see below for further details).

Student induction

Student induction is normally thought of as being the first week of the academic year, but some induction processes need to extend for the whole of the first term or semester, or the first level of study. New students transferring into levels 2 and 3 and into postgraduate programmes also need tailored induction programmes.

Induction, as illustrated in Case study 1, serves four main purposes:

1 *Social*: to provide a welcoming environment which facilitates students' social interaction between themselves and with the staff teaching on the programme of study upon which they are embarking.
2 *Orientation to the university*: to provide students with necessary information, advice and guidance about the university, its facilities, services and regulations.
3 *Registration and enrolment*: to carry out the necessary administrative procedures to ensure all students are correctly enrolled on their course of study.
4 *Supporting learning*: to provide an introduction to a programme of study at the university and to lay the foundations for successful learning in higher education.

Case study 1: Induction programmes

Drawing upon the literature survey, 15 characteristics of an ideal induction programme are identified which institutions could use for benchmarking, reflection, debate and development. It is suggested that an ideal induction programme would:

- be strategically located and managed
- address academic, social and cultural adjustments that students may face
- provide time-relevant targeted information
- be inclusive of all student groups
- address special needs of particular groups
- make academic expectations explicit
- include teaching staff at a personal level
- develop required computing and e-learning skills
- recognise existing skills and experience
- recognise different entry points and routes into higher education
- be inclusive of students' families
- be student centred rather than organisation centred

- be an integrated whole
- be part of an ongoing extended programme
- be evaluated with outcomes and actions communicated to relevant stakeholders.

(QAA Enhancement Themes: Responding to Student Needs
(http://www.enhancementthemes.ac.uk/documents/studentneeds/student_
needs_A5_booklet.pdf) (accessed 28 January 2008))

As has been argued above, it can no longer be assumed that students have a full understanding of the nature of higher education, the demands tutors expect to make on them, and the requirements of the subject they are studying. It is therefore necessary to be explicit about all these matters and take nothing for granted. Early tasks should induct students into processes of enquiry, searching for information, working in groups and using the **VLE**. Subject-specific projects should be set early to engage students and establish high expectations of them.

Furthermore, the importance of the emotional state that many students are in when they enter higher education needs to be recognised. Typically they are anxious, they lack confidence in their own ability to cope, they are full of uncertainty about what will be expected of them, and nervous about their relationships with other students as well as with staff. One survey reported that 58 per cent of students claimed that 'since being a student I feel under a lot more stress than before' (MORI, 2005).

Students typically ask themselves many questions when they enter higher education – as illustrated in Table 9.1. Rather than ignore students' self-doubt and uncertainty, it is better to address these legitimate questions in induction and throughout the first year.

Table 9.1 Questions students ask themselves

Questions	Learning support
How do I know . . .	*Response*
What to do?	Information to allow students to plan
	Clarification of expectations
	Skills development
If I'm doing it right?	Feedback on work in progress
How well I'm doing?	Feedback on assessed work
If I'm studying the right modules/courses?	Academic advice
What I've learnt?	Records of achievement
Where I'm going?	Career information and personal development planning (PDP)

Students' confidence can be enhanced by clearly valuing their prior experience and knowledge in discussion and writing assignments.

Study skills and academic integrity

The skills and capabilities required of students in higher education are complex and vary to some extent between different subjects. Many of these skills are acquired over the whole period of study and cannot be learnt as separate and identifiable skills at the beginning of a course. However, it can be valuable to introduce some fundamental study skills, particularly when students are unfamiliar with the demands of studying at higher education level. It is important that the skills are perceived by students to be timely, useful, appropriate and relevant.

Study skills that are specific to higher education include conventions of academic writing, styles for references and bibliographies, searching for and selecting information in libraries and using the internet, note taking from lectures, making presentations, and revision and exam techniques. In order to reduce the incidence of plagiarism, increasing importance is being attached to introducing students to the notion of 'academic integrity' and helping them to appreciate that using material from sources other than their own work requires appropriate referencing.

Research has also shown that it benefits students to pay attention to their meta-cognitive development and belief in their own self-efficacy (Knight and Yorke, 2003). This means providing opportunities for students to reflect on what they know, how they are learning and how they can make a difference to their success through, for example, learning journals, discussion and reflective writing.

Online course handbook

A component of responding to students' anxieties about the course they are embarking upon is having all the information they need on the university's intranet or within a virtual learning environment. This is an online student handbook that can be regularly updated. It should be an important point of reference for students, containing all the essential information they need to pursue their studies. This will include course structure, options and information on credit accumulation, descriptions of modules, their content and assessment methods – typically with learning outcomes and assessment criteria specified. It will also contain information about teaching staff, their availability and how to contact them; libraries and ICT facilities, location and opening times; bibliographic and referencing conventions; calendar for the year with significant dates and timetable for assessments; any special regulations relating to laboratories, studies, field trips; and support services which are available.

The VLE is also a portal to the internet and to the library, with access to journals and other materials, including course-specific learning materials, a noticeboard and discussion forums. Used carefully and in close association with the course, the VLE can be an important place for interactive learning and debate. It can, however, be badly used if it is simply a dumping ground for handouts and presentations.

Diagnostic screening

Early in the first term, students should be set a piece of work that will act as a diagnostic tool to enable tutors to identify students with weaknesses that might justify referral to a service department. Such diagnostic tests can reveal students who may be suspected to have specific learning difficulties (e.g. dyslexia), significant weaknesses in their use of English, problems with numeracy or early warning signs about their ability to meet deadlines and organise their work. However, diagnostic tests are only valuable if the opportunity is taken either to refer students to central services or to provide additional support within the programme of study.

Personal development planning (PDP)

PDP is defined as 'a structured process undertaken by individuals to reflect on their own learning, performance and/or achievement and to plan for their personal, educational and career development' (HEA, 2006). PDP goes under a variety of names (Gosling, 2002), but normally students are encouraged (or required, if it is a mandatory scheme) to keep a record of their learning achieved, both on the course and through their personal experience of work, voluntary activities, or other life experiences. They are also encouraged to reflect on how their learning matches the demands that will be made on them in the future by employers. Higgins (2002) suggests that personal development planning benefits students in that it:

- integrates personal and academic development, including work experience or other activities outside the curriculum, improving capacity to plan own learning;
- promotes reflective practice, effective monitoring and recording achievement;
- encourages learning from experience, including mistakes;
- promotes deeper learning by increasing awareness of what students are learning, how and to what level;
- requires explicit recognition of strengths and required improvements;
- provides a mechanism for monitoring career-related capabilities to prepare for seeking professional practice, building confidence;
- establishes lifelong learning habits, encompassing continuing professional development.

PDP provides a vehicle for a more synoptic overview of what is being learnt and an opportunity to plan ahead to construct a programme of study that suits each student. It can also provide feedback to students on their progress and create a record of transferable and employability skills acquired (but not formally assessed) which can aid career planning and CV writing. Such schemes can operate in dedicated professional learning modules or by regular meetings with a personal tutor or academic guidance tutor – say, once a term or semester.

In order to create greater flexibility, online portfolios are now being used as a vehicle for PDP. These can encourage students to create 'personal learning spaces' within the VLE in which they can both record and reflect on their learning.

Providing formative feedback to students

One of the most important aspects of supporting student learning is the feedback that students receive on their work. A not uncommon fault, particularly within a semester system, is that students only find out how well, or how badly, they have done when their assessed work is returned with a mark and comment at the end of the semester. By that time it is too late to take any remedial action. From the tutor's point of view it is difficult to give formative feedback to large classes in the short time available within a semester.

There is no easy answer to this problem, but some suggested solutions may include the following. Students submit a part of the final assessed work midway through the term, or they submit their planning work. Alternatively a short piece of assessed work can be set for early on in the semester with a return date before the final assessed work is completed. In some subjects online assessments can be used which can be marked electronically to provide rapid feedback to students on their progress. Such assessments may be done in the students' own time and feedback is provided automatically. Peer and self-assessment can also be useful for providing feedback on learning if these are well structured and the assessment criteria are well understood – for example, by discussing these with students.

Peer support

Supporting student learning is not only the province of tutors. Students can contribute through a variety of peer support mechanisms. Supplemental instruction (SI) is one such mechanism (Wallace, 1999) and Peer Assisted Learning (PAL) is another (Fleming and Capstick, 2003). Another is the use of online discussion groups provided within VLEs which have the advantage that tutors can monitor what is being discussed. Peer mentoring schemes can operate well if students are motivated to support other students and there is a structure within which they can work. It helps if the student mentors receive some credit or recognition for their efforts.

The role of teachers and the curriculum

There are many opportunities for supporting students in their learning through teachers recognising and monitoring the approaches to study being taken. This is as much to do with creating an ethos between tutor and student as it is about using specific methods. Students should feel that they can admit to needing support without risking the tutor's disapproval, although this does not mean that it is appropriate for tutors to be available for their students all the time. Set aside specific times when you can be available and advertise these to the students. Support may also be given via e-mail or through discussion groups on the VLE.

The design of the curriculum is an essential aspect of supporting student learning. The following are some of the key principles of course design that supports student learning:

- Begin where the students are: match course content to the knowledge and skills of the intake. Course content is sometimes regarded as sacrosanct but it is pointless teaching content that students are not ready to receive. Students must be challenged and stretched, but the starting point needs to reflect their current level of understanding.
- Make skill development integral to the curriculum. Do not assume that skills already exist. Make space for skills to be acquired in a risk-free environment.
- Pay attention to learning processes and not simply to the content or products. Design in the steps that students need to be taken through to get them to the desired learning outcome.
- Demonstrate the valuing of different cultures by building on students' own experience wherever possible. Knowledge and values cannot be taken for granted as higher education becomes more internationalised. Be on the lookout for cultural assumptions reflected in the curriculum and allow for alternative 'voices' to be heard.
- Avoid content and assessment overload which is liable to produce a surface approach to learning (see Chapter 2).

Useful texts that elaborate on these ideas are Biggs (2003) and Ramsden (2003).

Subject-specific skills

Each subject has its own set of specialist skills and processes that students need to be able to use. These need to be identified and students given the opportunity to develop and practise them. Examples of subject-specific skills include laboratory techniques, use of statistical methods, interpretation of texts, performance and making skills in the arts, investigative skills/methods of enquiry, field investigations, data and information processing/IT, and professional skills (SEEC, 2002).

It is important to recognise that academic writing is also a subject-specific skill. The types of writing demanded by academics reflect a variety of specialist genres. For example, essays required by each discipline have developed as part of the 'community of practice' (Wenger, 1998) of each subject and reflect subtle differences in the ways in which arguments should be presented and authorities referenced, the extent to which personal opinion is acceptable or quotations are expected, the use of specialist terminology (or jargon?), and many other subtleties that are rarely made explicit to students. Other forms of English, such as the laboratory report, legal writing and research reports, are all context-specific forms of social practice.

Higher-level cognitive and analytical skills

Higher education is distinguished by the demands it makes on students to operate at higher levels of thinking, creativity, problem-solving, autonomy and responsibility.

The QAA Qualification Descriptors state that 'typically, successful students at honours level will be able to critically evaluate arguments, assumptions, abstract concepts and data (that may be incomplete), to make judgements, and to frame appropriate questions to achieve a solution – or identify a range of solutions – to a problem' (QAA, 2001).

It is sometimes only too easy to take for granted that students know what is meant by terms such as analysis, critical understanding, interpretation, evaluation, 'argument'. The meanings of these terms are quite subject specific and tutors within the same discipline can have different expectations about what students need to do to demonstrate them in their work. Greater transparency may be achieved by using learning outcomes and assessment criteria, but it is essential that tutors take the time to discuss with students the meanings of the words used and give feedback using the same vocabulary.

Case study 2: History Department, Warwick University

The basic principle is to integrate skills into core modules – to have a spine running through the course so that all the students have the opportunity to acquire the skills they need.

We do not assume that students have got those skills or can acquire them without any direction. Certainly part of the reason we went down this route in the first place is that we found in the second year that some students still did not know where periodicals were, or tools such as referencing, critical analysis, or putting together bibliographies and using numerical techniques. Students tend to think that as historians they do not do numbers.

We were not checking that they were clear about these essential elements and we found that they did not just pick it up from comments on essays like 'You should have looked at a journal' and 'You can't reference properly'.

The skills-rich essays are very focused on historical sources compared with standard essays which may be more to do with historical problems or interpretations. This is a more source-orientated exercise and is very much focused on questions of analysis and criticism. There are also database-orientated projects looking more at quantification skills.

Some of the skills teaching is totally online, so the students work through an online package, but still supported by tutors. For example, one package is on essay writing and reflection, so the students do this online while they write their first essay. They will receive feedback from tutors, they will receive feedback on their essay and also benefit from their experience of acquiring the skills package as well.

The student reaction has been quite positive. Students feel they come with a lot of skills when they arrive, but they can also recognise the difference between how they have been taught at school, and what they need here. So while they thought they were very IT literate, for example, they had not been exposed to some of the sorts of information resources they get when they are at university. They also get rewarded because it feeds into assessment, so isn't an extra thing they have to do. Thus they can see the benefits.

(Dr Sarah Richardson, Associate Professor of History, Warwick University)

It is also important for students to be given the opportunity to learn and demonstrate key, generic and employability skills (see Case study 2).

LEARNING DEVELOPMENT: CROSS-INSTITUTIONAL, FACULTY- OR CAMPUS-BASED SERVICES

Library/resource centres

The role of library staff in supporting student learning is sometimes as important as the role of tutors themselves. This is because they are often more available at the time when students feel most in need of support and also because libraries are now far more than repositories of texts. While it remains the case that paper-based texts (books and journals) are the most important sources of information and knowledge, in this digital age libraries are also places where students can access electronic databases and multimedia packages. Resource centres also provide services for students including materials for presentations, guides to the use of information technology (IT), study skills materials, learning aids for the disabled, and IT facilities.

Libraries are daunting places for many (perhaps all) students. Library staff have a special role in supporting students to help them understand not only the regulations about loans, fines and opening times, but more importantly about how to access information effectively, how to make judgements about the relevance, currency and authority of the texts they access, and how to select what they need from the vast array of resources available on any topic. All students will need support in acquiring these skills in 'information literacy', not only at the introductory level but also as they progress to more sophisticated literature searches for dissertations and theses.

Information technology

While a greater numbers of students now arrive in higher education with excellent IT skills which can sometimes outstrip those of their tutors, a substantial number (particularly mature students) do not have these skills or the level of confidence in using IT that their course demands. All courses need to provide introductions to the use of basic word processing, spreadsheets, databases, presentation software, and using e-mail and the internet. Not all students will need introduction to all these elements. A diagnostic test may be used to determine which students need to develop their IT skills further to match the needs of the course. IT staff play an important role in supporting students throughout their studies, since the demands on students' IT skills typically rise as they progress to using more sophisticated subject-specific software.

Increasingly important are VLEs. These provide a vehicle for online learning by enabling tutors to make learning materials, online journals and assessments available via the Web (internet) or an internal network (intranet). VLEs are also means by which students can communicate with each other and with their tutors. Tutors can trace students' use of the VLE, while students have the advantage that they can access the course from any computer at any time. IT staff have a role in providing training, and supporting the use of VLEs for both staff and students (see Chapter 7).

Interrogating practice

Consider how you could build into your course learning development in IT and library skills. For example:

- using students' self-assessment of relevant IT skills – with follow-up courses for those who need them;
- requiring students to communicate using the VLE;
- searching literature that tests information skills;
- incorporating websites in your course handbook;
- including discussion of library use within seminars.

Academic literacy, English language and study skills support

Different subjects make different levels of demands on students' written and oral skills, but all programmes should make demands which require all students to develop their communication skills, both in writing and speaking. When students have difficulties meeting this demand, it can be for a variety of reasons. A common reason is the obvious one that English is not the students' first or home language. Second, there are students whose first or home language is English, but whose skills in the use of English do not match those required by their course. This is not just a matter of students whose spelling or grammar is idiosyncratic, since, as we noted above, writing is a subject-specific skill. Typically, when students exhibit poor writing skills this reflects a more general weakness in their approach to study. For this reason English language support is most effective when it is part of a holistic approach to developing students' academic literacy and study skills.

There is an important exception to this general rule, however, namely those students who have specific learning difficulties (e.g. **dyslexia**). Students with dyslexia have problems with writing which are the result of a disability rather than any reflection on their ability or grasp of the subject. Any student believed to be dyslexic needs to be professionally diagnosed and assessed, as we shall discuss in the next section.

The role of a central academic literacy service is to provide support which goes beyond anything that subject specialists can provide. Teaching English for these special purposes is a skilled matter which is best tackled outside the normal classroom. Some materials may be made available online or through multimedia language packages, but face-to-face classes are also needed. However, this specialist support needs to be provided in close collaboration with subject departments to ensure that the subject-specific requirements are adequately met.

Supporting students with disabilities

Disability may be regarded as a medical condition or a consequence of barriers created by the society we live in. Many people have some disabilities, although they may be such that they rarely prevent them doing what they want to do, or it is relatively easy to compensate for the disability (e.g. by wearing spectacles). But others have disabilities which are more significant because of the way so-called 'normal' life is organised; for example, steps and staircases constitute a barrier to those with mobility problems, whereas if there is a ramp or a lift the same person will no longer be disabled from getting where he or she wants to go.

The definition of a disability in UK legislation is: 'A physical or mental impairment which has a substantial and long-term adverse effect on (his/her) ability to carry out normal day-to-day activities' (DDA, 1995).

This includes:

- Learning difficulty
- Deaf/partial hearing
- Need personal care support
- Mental health difficulties

- Blind/partial sight
- Wheelchair/mobility
- Autistic disorder
- Unseen (e.g. diabetes, epilepsy, asthma)

Universities are now required to make provisions to remove the barriers which prevent students with disabilities from having an equal opportunity to succeed on their courses. The Special Educational Needs and Disability Act 2001 places duties on the bodies responsible for providing post-16 education and related services. These duties are:

- not to treat disabled people and students less favourably, without justification, than students without a disability;
- to take reasonable steps to enable disabled people and students to have full access to further and higher education.

In addition, the legislative duty (Disability Discrimination Act 2005) requires educational providers to be proactive in not discriminating against disabled people, which means we cannot wait until a disabled person applies to do a course, or tries to use a service, before thinking about what reasonable adjustments can be made.

Students with disabilities are under-represented in higher education. The reasons for this may be to do with underachievement and low aspiration as children at school, but may have as much to do with their social class, or their ethnicity or a combination of these factors. But we cannot rule out the possibility that prejudice against disabled students and ignorance about what they are capable of, with appropriate support, has also contributed to their under-representation.

Embedding disability provision is largely a matter of establishing a culture which values equality and diversity and integrates thinking about disabilities into standard procedures and thinking by all staff. Variation in support available to students persists and there continues to be a lack of awareness by staff of the special needs of certain students. There is still a stigma attached to some illnesses and disabilities – to forms of mental illness, HIV and even to dyslexia. The result is that students are sometimes reluctant to reveal their disability or have anxieties about who knows about it. However, in recent years the number of learners not disclosing any information about disability to their institution has decreased significantly. Colleges and universities have also improved methods for gathering data and nowadays provide several opportunities to disclose information (Action on Access, 2007).

Taking a proactive approach to disability support means continually anticipating the requirements of disabled people or students and the adjustments that could be made for them. Regular staff development and reviews of practice are an important aspect of this (DfES, 2002). All publicity and information about courses must be made available in alternative formats, provision must be made to ensure accessibility to university facilities if at all possible and adaptations, such as hearing loops, be provided in teaching rooms. The Disabled Students Allowance is available in the UK to pay for study support – for example, equipment, tutorial support, personal helpers, scribes or whatever is determined to be necessary through the process of 'assessment of needs' and the subsequent personal learning plan.

Advice and guidance for disabled students will normally be provided through a university service which would normally offer the following:

- coordination of the support available to students with disabilities, monitoring institutional policy and compliance with legal requirements;
- administration of needs assessments (or making provision for assessment of needs at a regional access centre) and administrative support for students claiming the Disabled Students Allowance;
- a team of specialist tutors available to provide tutorial support – particularly for students with specific learning difficulties (e.g. dyslexia);
- clearly understood and well-publicised referral by subject tutors;
- a systematic procedure for identifying students with disabilities at enrolment and early diagnostic tests to identify unrecognised problems – particularly dyslexia;
- regular audit of accessibility to buildings, and safety procedures;
- provision of physical aids and facilities for students with disabilities, for example in libraries.

Dyslexia typically accounts for between one-third and a half of all students reporting a disability. For this reason alone it needs particular attention. Screening for students needs to be available for both students who think they may be dyslexic and those referred by their tutor. When screening suggests that a student may be dyslexic, an assessment should be conducted by a psychologist or appropriately trained person. If dyslexia is confirmed, an assessment of the student's study needs must be administered, so that an appropriate level of tutorial support and specialist equipment or software can be provided. Adjustments to the student's assessment regime may also be necessary. This will need to be negotiated with the student's subject tutors. Raising tutors' awareness of the needs of dyslexic students is an important role for the central service.

There is a growing awareness of the impact of mental health difficulties such as depression, **Asperger's Syndrome** and eating disorders. The aim here must be to be supportive without necessarily labelling an individual. While some students will talk about their disability, others may be less willing, or may not perceive themselves as having a disability. Sensitivity to the individual's feelings is essential, as it is possible to cause stress by offering assistance which is viewed as unnecessary or intrusive (Martin, 2006).

Further advice on improving provision for disabled students is available through The Disability Equality Partnership (Action on Access, the Equality Challenge Unit and the Higher Education Academy).

THE MULTICULTURAL UNIVERSITY

Universities in the UK are becoming more multicultural for two main reasons. First, the composition of the student body reflects the racial and ethnic diversity of multicultural Britain (although the distribution of students from so-called ethnic minority groups tends to be clustered in particular institutions). Second, higher education has become a global market and the UK attracts many international students from virtually every country in the world. The Race Relations (Amendment) Act (2000) requires institutions to have an active policy to promote good race relations and ensure that no student is disadvantaged or suffers harassment or discrimination because of his or her race or ethnicity.

Responding to cultural and ethnic diversity requires a whole institution response which should:

- recognise cultural diversity in the curriculum;
- ensure that bibliographies reflect a range of perspectives;
- use teaching methods which encourage students from all cultures to participate;
- monitor assessment and results to check that fairness to all groups is demonstrated;
- consider the university calendar to ensure that major cultural and religious holidays are recognised;
- ensure that university publications do not contain assumptions about the ethnicity of the readers;
- develop proactive policies against discrimination and harassment;
- provide specialist counselling, advice and support services;
- provide places for all faiths to carry out acts of worship.

In these ways promoting equality of opportunity and good relations between multicultural groups contributes towards achieving a more supportive and enriched learning environment for all students.

Recent events have created headlines about Islamic groups within universities as a potential 'recruiting ground for terrorists'. Universities need to be vigilant about student societies and also about potential conflicts among ethnic groups. Clear principles need to be publicised and enforced about the values of free speech and tolerance. The institutional anti-harassment policy should clearly ban religious and racial hatred as well as gender harassment. But universities also need to educate its staff about 'cultural literacy'. As a contribution to this goal, the Higher Education Academy Subject Centre for Philosophical and Religious Studies has produced a series of Faith Guides which aim to assist in addressing 'issues relating to teaching people of faith in a higher education environment'.

International students

There are over 300,000 international students in UK higher education of whom about one-third are from the EU (Vickers and Bekhradnia, 2007). Institutions are part of an international market attempting to attract students from around the globe. The quality of support they receive is therefore important, not only for the benefit of the individual students but for the institution. International offices offer advice on immigration procedures, accommodation, family support, finance and scholarships, and security, and general counselling about living in the UK. They often welcome students and provide a specialist induction programme, and they can also offer learning support, particularly English language courses, sometimes before registration on a programme of study and sometimes in parallel with it. There are also issues relating to the curriculum, teaching methods and assessment which need to be considered from the perspective of international students. Staff development opportunities need to be provided to help teaching staff understand the difficulties faced by students, from China for example, who come from very different learning cultures from those found in the UK. 'Internationalising' the curriculum requires systematic review of the current syllabus to consider whether it is UK- or eurocentric.

WIDENING PARTICIPATION AND ACCESS

Some higher education institutions and all further education institutions have had long experience of providing support for so-called 'non-traditional' students. For others it may be a new experience to have mature students, part-time students, or students from ethnic minority groups or from the lower income groups. Many institutions have a widening participation office responsible for access courses, arranging the accreditation of prior learning, partnerships with local colleges, and 'Aim Higher' programmes. Such offices often have a predominantly outward focus liaising with local further education providers, but they can also play an important part in running bridging or summer courses, in supporting students with the transition to higher education and in advising academic departments on ways in which teaching or the curriculum may need to be modified to take account of students with non-traditional educational experiences.

CONCLUSION

Supporting student learning requires a multifaceted approach involving all parts of the university. Good liaison needs to exist to ensure that there are ways of referring students for additional help, whether this be, for example, due to a disability, a need for study skills or English language support or to use the IT and library facilities. But supporting learning is primarily about having an ethos in all learning and teaching interactions which recognises that all students have learning needs and that all students are undergoing learning development in relation to the skills that their courses demand of them.

REFERENCES

AoA (2007) *Disability: A Rough Guide, Action on Access*. Available online at http://www. actiononaccess.org/index.php?p=2_5.

Biggs, J (2003) *Teaching for Quality Learning at University: What the Student Does* (2nd edn), Buckingham: SRHE and Open University Press.

Cottrell, S (2001) *Teaching Study Skills and Supporting Learning*, Basingstoke: Palgrave Study Guides.

DDA (1995) *Higher Education Funding and Delivery to 2003–04*, DDA.

Disability Discrimination Act (2005) Available online at <http://www.opsi.gov.uk/ACTS/acts2005/20050013.htm> (accessed 7 August 2007).

DfES (2002) *Finding Out about People's Disabilities, A Good Practice Guide for Further and Higher Education Institutions*. Available online at <http://www.lifelonglearning.co.uk/findingout/> (accessed 7 August 2007).

Fleming, H and Capstick, S (2003) 'Peer assisted learning in an undergraduate hospitality course', *Journal of Hospitality, Leisure, Sport and Tourism Education*, 1 (1), 69–75.

Gosling, D (2002) *Personal Development Planning*, SEDA Paper 115, Birmingham: Staff and Educational Development Association.

HEA (2006) *Personal Development Planning*, York: Higher Education Academy. Available online at <http://www.heacademy.ac.uk/resources/detail/resources/publications/web0276_pdp_leaflet> (accessed 7 August 2007).

Higgins, M (2002) *Personal Development Planning: A Tool for Reflective Learning*. Available online at <http://www.heacademy.ac.uk/resources/detail/resources/casestudies/cs_080> (accessed 11 October 2007).

Knight, P and Yorke, M (2003) *Assessment, Learning and Employability*, Buckingham: SRHE/Open University Press.

LearnHigher (2008) Available online at <http://www.learnhigher.ac.uk/LearningDevelopment/index.html> (accessed 28 January 2008).

Martin, N (2006) Empowering students with Asperger's Syndrome, *Resources Directory*. Available online at <http://www.actiononaccess.org/index.php?p=1_3_3> (accessed 11 October 2007).

MORI (2005) *Student Experience Report* (5th edn), UNITE in association with HEPI.

QAA (2001) *The Higher Education Qualification Framework*, Quality Assurance Agency for Higher Education, Gloucester: QAA.

Ramsden, P (2003) *Learning to Teach in Higher Education* (2nd edn), London: RoutledgeFalmer.

SEEC (2002) *Credit Level Descriptors 2001, Southern England Consortium for Credit Accumulation and Transfer*, London: SEEC.

Simpson, R (1996) 'Learning development: deficit or difference?', in J Corbett and S Wolfendale (eds) *Opening Doors: Learning Support in Higher Education*, London: Cassell.

Vickers, P and Bekhradnia, B (2007) 'The economic costs and benefits of international students', Higher Educational Policy Unit. Available online at www.hepi.ac.uk.

Wallace, J (1999) 'Supporting and guiding students', in H Fry, S Ketteridge, and S Marshall, (eds) *A Handbook for Teaching and Learning in Higher Education* (1st edn), London: Kogan Page.

Wenger, E (1998) *Communities of Practice, Learning, Meaning and Identity*, Cambridge: Cambridge University Press.

10 Assessing student learning

Lin Norton

INTRODUCTION

Assessment is one of the most controversial issues in higher education today. Guidelines and principles abound. The UK Professional Standards Framework for teaching and supporting learning in higher education (2006) has 'assessment and giving feedback to learners' as one of six areas of activity, and the UK **Quality Assurance Agency** (QAA, 2006a) has recently revised its section on assessing students in its **code of practice**. Few topics create such divided opinions and raise such passions as assessment and yet, in higher education, we still seem relatively bad at it. The National Student Survey (2006 and 2007) indicated that assessment and feedback were areas that students were least satisfied with. In the recently published outcomes of their audit of 123 institutions, QAA commented: 'For a substantial number of institutions, further work in the development of assessment arrangements was judged either advisable or desirable' (QAA, 2006b: 13).

This is a serious indictment of a fundamental aspect of our professional work. This chapter explores some of the reasons behind this current state of affairs by considering some of the constraints that operate within universities and across the sector. Within this wider framework, some principles and methods will be explored by considering the two essential elements of assessing student learning: assessment design and **feedback**. Assessment design is concerned with pedagogical philosophy, disciplinarity, models of assessment and what we know about ways students learn. In other words, it is assessment to influence learning. Assessment as feedback is focused more on practices to improve student learning. A third major area in assessment is marking, which will be mentioned relatively briefly, because the focus of the chapter will be on assessment *for* learning in both undergraduate and taught Masters programmes rather than on assessment *of* learning (Birenbaum *et al.*, 2005).

Throughout the chapter, reference will be made to the relevant empirical and theoretical literature on assessment using the perspective of the **reflective practitioner** (Campbell and Norton, 2007). This involves examining our own beliefs about assessment and how they fit with the mores of our discipline, and the culture of the university in which we work.

BELIEFS ABOUT ASSESSMENT

Interrogating practice

What, in your view, is the purpose of assessment? Does this belief come from how you were taught and assessed yourself, or from your subject discipline practices, or from what you have read in the assessment literature? Looking at these three sources, do you think they constrain you in different ways, making it difficult to change your assessment practice if you wanted to?

Relatively little research appears to have been carried out to find out academics' beliefs about assessment and yet this is fundamental if we are serious about making changes in our practice and persuading colleagues to do the same. A notable exception has been the work of Samuelowicz and Bain (2002) who interviewed 20 academics from seven different disciplines in an Australian university about their assessment practice. Of the 20 interviewees, only eight appeared to have an orientation to assessment that was about transformation of knowledge rather than reproduction of knowledge. This is a disturbing finding, since it means that for these academics at least, there was a powerful conservatism operating in thinking about learning in terms of passive and incremental rather than active and transformational conceptions of learning (Saljo, 1979; Marton *et al.*, 1993).

Maclellan (2001) conducted a questionnaire study with 80 lecturers and 130 third-year undergraduates in an education faculty to establish their views about the purpose of assessment. The most frequently endorsed purpose, perceived by both staff and students, was to grade or rank student achievement. Interestingly, whereas staff thought assessment to be a motivator of learning, students did not agree, with 25 per cent actually stating it was never motivating. Lecturers believed assessment should be developmental and that feedback had a valuable role to play, whereas students thought it was more about grading and had very little to do with improving their own learning. Maclellan also found that although staff believed in the importance of assessment to promote learning, their feedback practices were not consistent with such a view. Assessment was not carried out at the start of a module, students were not allowed to be assessed when they felt ready to be assessed, nor were peer and self-assessments often practised. Similarly, staff believed they were assessing a full range of learning but in practice there was a heavy emphasis on the essay and short answer assignment. Clearly, there are mismatches occurring not only between staff and students but also between what staff believed and what they actually did.

PURPOSES OF ASSESSMENT

The QAA revised code of practice for the assessment of students determines four main purposes (classifications and additional comments by the author are indicated in italics):

1   Pedagogy: promoting student learning by providing the student with feedback, normally to help improve his or her performance (*but also to determine what and how students learn*).
2   Measurement: evaluating student knowledge, understanding, abilities or skills.
3   Standardisation: providing a mark or grade that enables a student's performance to be established. The mark or grade may also be used to make progress decisions.
4   Certification: enabling the public (including employers) and higher education providers to know that an individual has attained an appropriate level of achievement that reflects the academic standards set by the awarding institution and agreed UK norms, including the **Framework for Higher Education Qualifications**. This may include demonstrating fitness to practise or meeting other professional requirements.

(QAA, 2006a: 4)

Inevitably, there is some overlap between these four purposes but there is also potential for conflict, particularly when the need for certification, standardisation and measurement makes flexibility and changing assessment practice for pedagogical reasons slow and difficult.

PRINCIPLES OF ASSESSMENT DESIGN

It is now widely accepted that assessment tends to shape much of the learning that students do (Brown *et al.*, 1997), so if we want to change the way our students learn and the content of what they learn, the most effective way is to change the way we assess them. Birenbaum *et al.* (2005) argue persuasively for a paradigm shift in assessment practices. Although their paper is concerned with assessment in schools, their arguments apply equally to the university context for undergraduates and taught postgraduates. One of the powerful points they make is that in spite of the advent of technology, most education systems are still relying on an out-of-date information transmission model, which means that the assessments do not address the needs of learners in our modern complex and globalised societies. Authentic assessment which focuses on the development of real-world skills, active construction of creative responses, and the integration of a variety of skills into a holistic project has an additional benefit of designing out opportunities for **plagiarism**.

Many current assessment systems do not allow learners to improve their own learning because the assessments are 'considered to be an endpoint instead of a beginning or a step forward' (Birenbaum *et al.*, 2005: 3). This means that the assessment is summative (testing what has been learned) and therefore tends to drive the teaching (teaching for the test).

Assessment *for* learning places more emphasis on the formative, is integrated into the curriculum and is context embedded and flexible.

In practical terms this means assessment design which focuses on **learning outcomes** (see Chapter 4). Prosser and Trigwell (1999) use the term 'high-quality learning outcomes', which they define as involving 'an understanding that can be drawn upon in other and new contexts' (p.108). This is what is commonly recognised as a **deep approach to learning**, where the intention is to understand through an active constructivist engagement with knowledge, as opposed to a **surface approach to learning**, where the intention is to reproduce through a passive incremental view of knowledge (see also Chapter 2). It is important to note the keyword 'intention' here for, after the original and much-cited work of Marton and Saljo (1976), the higher education sector grasped the metaphor of deep and surface, and ironically began to characterise students as deep or surface. Nothing could be further from the truth and there is an oft-quoted example in Ramsden (1992), which clearly shows that students can readily adopt a surface or a deep approach depending on how they perceive the learning context, and most crucially how they perceive the assessment task.

Embedding assessment in curriculum design

Typically, when lecturers are given the opportunity to develop a module or course they tend to start with the content. The teaching metaphor tends to revolve around 'covering' the subject area rather than facilitating students' learning. Such a seemingly simple difference hides a fundamental distinction between approaches to teaching being either, in Prosser and Trigwell's (1999) terminology, 'conceptual change/**student focused**' or 'information-transmission/teacher-focused approach'. There is a growing body of research which shows that students tend to adopt a deep approach to learning while their lecturers adopt a more student-focused approach. In other words, when designing a module we need to think about what we want the students to learn, rather than what we teach. Taking this perspective is one of the main drives behind the current insistence in the sector on determining learning outcomes, as they have the potential to foster a preferred learning experience (such as higher-order cognitive skills and abilities as well as a conceptual understanding of the subject matter) by shifting the focus from what we teach to what our students learn. Learning outcomes, however, are contentious in that they appear to lend a precision and a measurable specificity to the learning process that cannot exist (Hussey and Smith, 2002). The unfortunate consequence is that learning outcomes and **constructive alignment**, as put forward by Biggs (1996, 2003), have been enthusiastically taken up by higher education management and by QAA. This has resulted in the current trend to slavishly match assessment tasks with learning outcomes in a formulaic way which tends to be operationalised in 'rules' from institutional quality assurance offices. This is unfortunate because learning outcomes have become hidebound by quality assurance practices, which do nothing to help the lecturer construct a meaningful learning experience for her or his students, not at all what Biggs intended.

The key principle is to design assessment *before* designing the content of the module as part of an integrated assessment system which serves the purposes of both assessing for learning and the assessing of learning. The main aim of such a system is to ensure that both students and lecturers are informed about how they (the students) are progressing, which in turn enables more flexible and planned teaching (Ramsden, 2003; Birenbaum *et al.*, 2005).

Constructive alignment

Biggs (1996) argues that any learning takes place in a system in which if you change one element of the system all the others must necessarily change in order to effect the desired learning. In poorly integrated systems, it tends to be only the most able students who are able to engage in learning at a deep level. In well-integrated systems, all students are enabled to achieve the desired learning outcomes, although this is not to say that all students will achieve them, as there is much individual variation. Constructive alignment is an example of an integrated system, in which the constructive aspect refers to the students constructing meaning through their learning activities and alignment refers to the activities that the teacher does in order to support the desired learning outcomes. Put very simply, the main principle is that there is a *consistency* between the three related components of curriculum design:

1   what you want your students to learn (i.e. what learning outcomes will they achieve?);
2   what teaching methods you will use to enable them to achieve these learning outcomes;
3   what assessment tasks and criteria you will use to show that students have achieved the learning outcomes you intended (and how you will arrive at an overall grade/mark).

Assessment methods

Helping students to achieve learning outcomes means setting assessment tasks that support learning. Choosing an appropriate task is not easy, which is why the most commonly used assessment tasks still tend to be the essay and/or the traditional timed unseen examination, whatever its format, such as **MCQs**, short answers or mathematical problems. The best advice is to make sure that the method chosen is relevant to the learning outcome it is supposed to test. For example, if we want to test students' ability to construct a coherent and reasoned argument, then the essay would be appropriate, but if we were more concerned with science students' laboratory skills, an observed performance assessment scheme might be more appropriate. Computer-based assessment is increasingly being used to motivate students to learn, enable them to practise disciplinary skills and abilities, broaden the range of knowledge assessed and increase opportunities for feedback, but like all methods of assessment it has disadvantages as well as advantages (Bull and McKenna, 2004).

Interrogating practice

What are the most frequently used assessment methods in your department? Do they reflect a conceptual-change student-focused or information-transmission teacher-focused approach?

Feedback to support learning

Another important element of assessment design is incorporating feedback. This is a complex matter, involving the distinction between **formative** and **summative** assessment. Summative assessment is defined as that which contributes to a grade and overall calculation of the degree classification, whereas formative assessment is defined as that which enables students to see how well they are progressing and gives them feedback. It is perfectly possible for summative assessment to have a formative component; indeed, that might be more desirable than much common assessment practice, when the assessment (either coursework or exam) comes at the end of the course. This means students are sometimes not concerned to pick up their marked work, as it has little relevance to them to either improve their learning or to improve their grades for the next assessment (often of a different course or module). The problem with students not taking any notice of feedback can be pretty exasperating for lecturers but this is not always the case. Higgins *et al*. (2002) found that students were 'conscientious consumers' of feedback, so one of the problems may well reside in the timing of both assessment and feedback (see Maclellan, 2001).

Yorke (2003) argues that although there is a wide acceptance of the importance of formative feedback, it is not generally well understood and we need to be far more aware of its theoretical underpinning. In so doing we should take into account disciplinary epistemology, theories of intellectual and moral development, stages of intellectual development and the psychology of giving and receiving feedback. Thinking through the implications of Yorke's comments, the author has taken the widely cited 'seven principles of good feedback' put forward by Nicol and Macfarlane-Dick (2006), and added her own interpretations. In so doing she has focused on coursework, but readers are encouraged to think through how such principles might be applied to examinations or tests in their own discipline.

1 Facilitates the development of self-assessment (*reflection*) in learning

This might be more appropriate at later stages in a student's degree than perhaps at the start of their programme as they progress through stages of intellectual development

(Perry, 1970; King and Kitchener, 1994). When students start degree work their aim is not to challenge the boundaries of knowledge but to understand the discipline, join the culture and become a fledgling historian, chemist or sociologist, much in the same way that students following vocational courses are encouraged to begin thinking and behaving like dentists, musicians or doctors. This may be one of the reasons why encouraging students to reflect on their learning, particularly when they are new to degree study, has proved difficult. There is much good advice about helping students to do this (Brockbank and McGill, 1998; Moon, 1999), some of it involving fellow students to react to and promote self-reflection.

2 Promotes peer and tutor dialogue around learning

The concept of dialogue between students first of all means collaborative work so that they can share understandings of what is required. Group work is sometimes readily embraced by students and sometimes, it has to be said, absolutely detested, but this is usually when summative assessment is involved. To help overcome this, the first requirement must be to ensure that the criteria by which the group is being assessed are known by students and assessors alike. Going even further, it is desirable that the levels of attainment leading to particular grades are also publicised. At the very least, this gives the assessors a proper basis for discussion in the event of disagreements.

> ### Case study 1: Development of 'grade-related assessment criteria' for group projects in a Masters of Engineering programme

Group projects occupy half of the fourth and final year of the Masters of Engineering course at Queen Mary, University of London, and so are a significant part of the students' assessment. The criteria for these group projects are broader than those of the individual projects that all engineering students undertake, usually in their third year. They are driven to a large extent by the requirements of the Institution of Mechanical Engineers for the accreditation of courses in accordance with the UK Standard for Professional Engineering Competence for Chartered Engineers. These requirements are aligned with the QAA Benchmark Statement for Engineering. They not only place great emphasis on the graduates having a 'wide knowledge and comprehensive understanding of design processes and methodologies and the ability to apply and adapt them in unfamiliar situations', but also on their having good transferable skills, such as communication and teamworking.

A difficulty in formulating the criteria to meet these requirements lies in the diverse nature of the projects being undertaken, ranging from 'Development of new arthroscopic meniscal repair system', to 'Energy and exergy balances in green, renewable systems', to 'Design of a solar-powered racing car'. Moreover, the activity of the individual students within the groups ranges from literature search, to computation, theory or experiment, although ideally it is a blend of all these. The criteria that were ultimately developed for the assessments were under the headings:

- Technical
- Personal/practical/organisational/initiative
- Teamworking and management
- Presentational

Under each heading about six characteristics were identified and the performance at grades A, B and C with respect to these characteristics was described. In demarcating the grades, it was borne in mind that all students on this programme had been assessed as being capable of an upper-second-class degree (average of Bs) or better. For all the technical criteria, the challenge therefore is to identify real flair, and to distinguish this from competent hard work (see Table 10.1).

It is emphasised that it is not expected that students will meet every criterion in each grade to be awarded it overall, and indeed in practice a blend of two, or even three, grades may be found. Judgement must be exercised in weighting them. To distinguish relative performance within the grades, marks are assigned on the usual scale (e.g. Grade B spans the scale from 60 per cent to 69 per cent).

The description of the transferable skills, which all students have at some level, is perhaps more difficult, but the approach here is to identify all the ways in which a contribution is likely to be made and to be more punitive when some elements are lacking. So for 'Teamworking and management', Grade A performance is said to be:

1 Works to an agreed plan.
2 Communicates clearly in tutorial sessions.
3 Is persuasive, but receptive, in arguing his or her point of view.
4 Contributes an appropriate share or more of the team effort.
5 Coordinates fellow team members, either formally as the leader, or informally in relation to his or her designated activities.
6 Is supportive of other team members.
7 Interfaces effectively with the outside world.

A Grade C performer would probably not contribute under items 5 or 6, but would have most of the other attributes to a lesser degree.

These criteria were developed some years after the M.Eng. project programme had been established, but they are now advertised in the project handbook. To some extent, they can be criticised for being a 'post-hoc rationalisation' of what the assessors had been doing instinctively. However, they are clearly useful in

Table 10.1 Characteristics of grades A, B and C

	Grade A > 70 %	Grade B > 60 %	Grade C > 50 %
Technical criteria	1 Uses taught courses as a starting point for development of advanced comprehension of complex issues and shows originality in either approach or analysis.	1 Uses material covered in taught courses to develop comprehension of the issues involved in the project and applies this material to the problem.	1 Uses material covered in taught courses to develop comprehension of the issues involved in the project, but has some difficulties in applying it.
	2 Moves beyond a comprehensive literature review to draw novel conclusions or to present comparative data in an innovative way.	2 Presents a comprehensive literature review.	2 Includes a literature review which covers the suggested sources.
	3 Selects and applies appropriate mathematical methods for modelling and analysing novel situations.	3 Applies mathematical models appropriately to project situations.	3 Attempts to apply mathematical models for the project.
	4 Successfully deploys a suitable computer program and shows critical insight into the way in which the program works.	4 Successfully deploys a suitable computer program.	4 Is partially successful in deploying a computer program.
	5 Displays analytical insight in the presentation of experimental data.	5 Conducts accurate analysis of experimental data.	5 Analyses experimental data, but with some misconceptions.
	6 Adapts test and measurement techniques for unfamiliar situations.	6 Uses appropriate tests and measurement techniques.	6 Uses suggested tests and measurement techniques.
	7 Draws conclusions that are relevant, valid, appropriate and critically evaluated.	7 Draws relevant, valid and appropriate conclusions.	7 Draws some relevant and valid conclusions.

inducting new staff into the assessment procedure and in getting experienced ones to reflect on just why they rate particular work as they do. Moreover, the weighting of performance to reach an overall grade for a student's contribution to a report, for example, still leaves considerable room for (unrationalised) judgement. Whether even this degree of prescription could be applied to assessment in arts and humanities subjects is an interesting question for debate.

(Professor Chris Lawn, Queen Mary, University of London, based on work by
Dr Matthew Williamson, Educational and Staff Development)

The publishing of criteria should also be helpful if **peer assessment** is part of the overall process. Peer assessment is often seen as unfair because students do not trust each other's judgements, worry about favouritism and friendship influencing marks, feel it is the responsibility of the lecturer and so on. There are, however, many solutions to ensuring that a group mark is fair to all, such as moderation by the lecturer, or estimation of each individual's contribution to the task where lower or higher than average contribution alters the group mark for that particular student, by a pre-agreed number of marks. Other psychometric solutions include having sufficient scores contributing to the overall mark to reduce the effect of each mark, or using a system that discounts the one or two highest and lowest scores. Whichever system you use, it is important to communicate to students an awareness of their concerns about unfairness, and the steps that have been taken to address them. Perhaps, though, the most effective way of using peer assessment is to use it formatively so that students can be relieved of anxieties about the marks counting and concentrate instead on the learning opportunities this process affords them (see also Case study 1 in Chapter 22).

Peer and tutor dialogue would seem at first glance to be costly in terms of tutor time, especially if this were to be carried out with each individual student, but Ramsden (2003) is unequivocal that it is an essential professional responsibility. Many tutors are happy to write feedback on assignments and then go through these on a one-to-one basis if students make an appointment to see them. The advances in technology are also enabling swifter, individualised feedback such as tablet PCs where tutors can write on electronically submitted assignments, and audio blogs where the tutor records her feedback and posts it on a **Virtual Learning Environment (VLE),** so that students can download and listen in their own time and convenience. The methods that suit will, as Yorke intimates, be largely a question of disciplinary epistemology. In performance-based subjects, for example, it is usual for the teacher to give feedback in class almost continuously, and students are required to self-critique/assess as well as critique each other's work. In many science-based, medical and health-related subjects where skills and competencies are routinely practised and assessed, feedback can also be given in this manner.

3 Helps clarify what good performance is (goals, criteria, expected standards)

Underlying this seemingly straightforward principle is a substantial literature around assessment criteria which highlights the paradox between making the goal of the task clear but at the same time making the *performance* of the task outweigh any actual learning that takes place (Norton, 2004). This is particularly the case for strategic students who are achievement orientated and will do whatever is required to achieve the best possible marks (Entwistle, 1998). Making assessment criteria explicit does not, of itself, enable students to produce better work (O'Donovan *et al.*, 2001) because unless they engage actively in some way with the criteria, they are unlikely to benefit. This is a further argument for encouraging students to self-assess; to have some part to play in devising assessment criteria and indeed in the assessment tasks themselves. Providing workshops on core assessment criteria can be helpful but, if voluntary, these are attended by relatively few students (Norton *et al.*, 2005).

4 Provides opportunities to close the gap between current and desired performance

This can be done mainly through staged assessment and/or formative assessment, since feedback which is given at the end of the course is likely to have little effect on students' learning – a problem that is exacerbated with provision of a higher education experience in modules, where the learning is fragmentary and the opportunities for slow learning as advocated by Yorke (2003) may be non-existent. Prowse *et al.* (2007) developed a feedback process carried out in four stages: (1) first submission of written work, (2) written feedback, (3) viva on student understanding of the feedback, (4) final submission of written work. Grade points increased as did student satisfaction but the authors were faced with resistance from the school quality committee. Research such as this shows that it can sometimes be very difficult to bring about change even when it demonstrably enhances student learning.

5 Delivers high-quality information to students about their learning

Feedback that is written can lead to all kinds of misinterpretation but there are many other ways of informing students about their progress such as the **personal response system**, sometimes known as 'clickers'. Students are given electronic handheld devices and choose answers out of a given array, results are displayed instantly and electronically and feedback given as to the right answer as well as, if necessary, an explanation. This not only enables lecturers to correct misunderstandings but also gives them a good idea of how students are learning.

6 Encourages positive motivational beliefs and self-esteem

This can, in practice, be very difficult to do when students tend to be more influenced by the grade they receive than the feedback comments (Hounsell *et al.*, 2005). This leaves us with a dilemma, as we cannot give high grades to boost self-esteem, but we can be very careful indeed with our written remarks and if, at all possible, support with verbal feedback, which is much easier to moderate, if a student appears discomfited, puzzled or demoralised.

7 Provides information to teachers that may be used to help shape the teaching

In thinking about effective feedback to give to students there is a double pay-off in that it enables us to realise very directly how and what our students are learning. A useful way of gauging how students are learning that may be used in class is Angelo and Cross' (1993) one-minute paper, in which students are requested to write answers to two questions at the end of a lecture: 'What is the single most important thing you have learned in this session?' and 'What is the single most important thing you feel you still have to learn?' The answers are handed in when the students leave and the tutor is then enabled to correct any misapprehensions at the beginning of the next lecture, giving very direct and immediate feedback to students.

Interrogating practice

What can you do to improve your feedback using the seven principles articulated above? How can you monitor/evaluate whether there has been any improvement?

Assessment as marking

There are six basic principles of marking and grading.

1   Consistency according to QAA (2006a) means ensuring that marking and grading across all departments and faculties is appropriate and comparable by institutional guidance on:

- grades or numerical marks;
- defining and treating borderline grades or marks;
- appropriateness of anonymous marking;
- when and what system of double or second marking should be used.

(QAA, 2006a:16–18)

2   **Reliability** means that any two markers would assign the same grade or numerical mark to the same piece of work. It is usually ensured by using assessment criteria and/or a marking scheme. In some disciplines where there is more objective testing, such as MCQs, this will be easier to accomplish than in others where there is more subjective judgement, such as music performance. Even in areas which are recognised as being very difficult to mark objectively, such as laboratory work and fieldwork, considerable efforts have been made to produce marking schemes which are reliable (Ellington and Earl, 1997).

3   **Validity** essentially means establishing that the marking measures what it is supposed to measure. This is a difficult principle, especially when assessing higher order skills such as critical thinking, formulating, modelling and solving problems in written work, which is why markers sometimes focus on lower order skills such as referencing, grammar and spelling. In science and practitioner disciplines where competencies are essential, validity may be established through competency models but there are also competencies which are hard to quantify (Knight, 2007).

4   Levelness means assessing learning outcomes that are appropriate for each **level** of study, as described in the QAA (2001) academic framework:

- Certificate
- Intermediate
- Honours
- Masters
- Doctoral

The framework gives generic qualification descriptors for each level based on learning outcomes, with further subject-specific information in the QAA **subject benchmark statements**.

5   Transparency is perhaps the principle that is most closely aligned with students' perceptions of the fairness of the assessment system, and is also the principle that is the easiest to ensure in practice. It includes:

- making sure that the assessment criteria and marking schemes for each assessment task are published and open to all;
- ensuring that assessment tasks are published in good time;
- having a fair and equitable appeals and complaints process that is accessible to all.

6   Inclusivity means making reasonable adjustments in assessing students who have disabilities. The Special Educational Needs and Disability Act (SENDA, 2001) states that disabled students are not to be substantially disadvantaged in comparison with students who are not disabled. In terms of assessment this means making reasonable adjustments; for example, students with:

- dyslexia should not be penalised for grammar and spelling in marking;
- a hearing disability should not be unfairly penalised in oral assessments for communication skills;
- a visual impairment may have to be assessed orally.

Fundamental to these principles is the concept of objectivity which assumes that marking is a science. This may be true in some disciplines but is hard to defend in others; nevertheless, it is important to be as rigorous as possible in this most important facet of being a university teacher. Unfortunately, little account is taken of the vast body of research on assessment and on students' experience of it (Rust, 2002, 2007). We know, for example, that students are well aware of the inconsistencies between individual markers and that their view is well founded. Small wonder that they rapidly become cynical and that the rate of plagiarism and cheating is so high (Franklyn-Stokes and Newstead, 1995).

Rust (2007) claims that much current practice in marking is unfair, statistically invalid and intellectually indefensible in spite of quality assurance procedures. He challenges the view held by some academics in humanities and social sciences that it is possible to make judgements about the quality of work to the precision of a percentage point, even were lecturers to use the whole of a 100-point scale, which is relatively rare. He also casts doubt on the effectiveness of double marking, a point supported by research, such as that by Cannings *et al.* (2005) in a medical context, and Gary *et al.* (2005) in politics. Markers give different marks for different reasons and when coming together to agree a mark, one may yield to the other in terms of experience or seniority or, equally unfairly, they may agree on a mid-point between their two marks, which then represents neither of the two markers' views.

Other examples of bad practice cited by Rust (2007) include the meaninglessness of marks unless they are stated in terms of norms or the objectives mastered; combining scores which hide the different learning outcomes being judged and/or which are using different scales (like trying to combine apples and pears) and distorting marks in combinations of subjects or by types of assessments, which can have an effect on the actual degree classification. Ecclestone (2001) suggests that this depressing state of affairs may be a consequence of current higher education being a mix of various/newer modes of study (e.g. distance learning). However, the same situation still exists in traditional non-modularised assessment, so fragmenting assessment communities, which means that increasing reliance on quality assurance procedures, assessment guidelines and assessment criteria cannot be the whole answer. Ecclestone's conclusions are pertinent to both modularised and non-modularised systems when she suggests that there are problems in communicating objective standards even when specified in precise detail, and there is a need for face-to-face discussion between colleagues to arrive at shared understandings. Assessors need assistance, and training in assessment and criteria can be very helpful in this process. Being inexperienced in marking can feel somewhat threatening for new lecturers, but a good understanding of the assessment literature on marking and an experienced mentor can do much to help develop this most important part of professional practice.

Interrogating practice

To what extent do colleagues in your department share an assessment community of practice? If they do not, you may want to consider establishing one, particularly since you have a valid reason for wanting to benefit from their shared expertise in marking practice.

OVERVIEW

In this chapter most of the emphasis has been on assessment design for learning because this is an area in which the individual can have some influence. Throughout, a reflective practitioner approach has been taken to encourage in the reader some active thinking to turn research findings into actions that will impact on the quality of his or her students' learning experience. In so doing, the intention of the author has been to encourage a healthy scepticism in some of the 'holy cows' that sometimes go unchallenged. Much of the research evidence in this chapter has come from the author's own subject discipline of psychology, but readers are encouraged to check the applicability of these findings by consulting pedagogical research in their own disciplines and contexts. Many of the HEA subject centre networks publish their own journals which would be a good starting point, as are many of the chapters in Part 2 of this book. In this chapter, the reader has also been encouraged to look at their own beliefs about assessment. In considering assessment design, the place of learning outcomes, assessment methods and constructive alignment has been examined as a way of thinking strategically about what and how we want our students to learn (conceptual change, student focused, or information transmission, teacher focused?). Feedback, in particular, has been given close attention, since this is key to helping students learn, yet so often we do not do it as well as we might. In terms of pedagogical impact, this is quite possibly the area where individual lecturers can have the greatest effect.

REFERENCES

Angelo, T A and Cross, K P (1993) *Classroom Assessment Techniques*, San Franciso, CA: Jossey-Bass.

Biggs, J (1996) Enhancing teaching through constructive alignment, *Higher Education*, 32: 1–18.

Biggs, J B (2003) *Teaching for Quality Learning at University* (2nd edn), Buckingham: Society for Research into Higher Education and the Open University Press.

Birenbaum, M, Breuer, K, Cascallar, E, Dochy, F, Ridgway, J, Dori, J and Wiesemes, R (2005) 'A learning integrated assessment system', in R. Wiesemes and G Nickmans (eds) EARLI (European Association for Research on Learning and Instruction) series of position papers.

Brockbank, A and McGill, I (1998) *Facilitating Reflective Learning in Higher Education*, Buckingham: Society for Research into Higher Education and the Open University Press.

Brown, G, Bull, J and Pendlebury, M (1997) *Assessing Student Learning in Higher Education*, London: Routledge.

Bull, J and McKenna, C (2004) *Blueprint for Computer-assisted Assessment*, London: RoutledgeFalmer.

Campbell, A and Norton, L (eds) (2007) *Learning, Teaching and Assessing in Higher Education: Developing Reflective Practice*, Exeter: Learningmatters.

Cannings, R, Hawthorne, K, Hood, K and Houston, H (2005) Putting double marking to the test: a framework to assess if it is worth the trouble, *Medical Education*, 39(3): 299–308.

Ecclestone, K (2001) I know a 2:1 when I see it: understanding criteria for degree classifications in franchised university programmes, *Journal of Further and Higher Education*, 25(3): 301–313.

Ellington, H and Earl, S (1997) Assessing laboratory, studio, project and field work. A guide prepared for and hosted on the GCU intranet by Glasgow Caledonian University with the permission of The Robert Gordon University. Available online at <http://apu.gcal.ac.uk/ciced/Ch27.html> (accessed 25 August 2007).

Entwistle, N (1998) 'Approaches to learning and forms of understanding', in B B Dart and

G M Boulton-Lewis (eds) *Teaching and Learning in Higher Education*, Melbourne: Australian Council for Educational Research.

Franklyn-Stokes, A and Newstead, S E (1995) Undergraduate cheating; who does what and why?, *Studies in Higher Education*, 20(2): 39–52.

Gary, J, McCool Jr, M A and O'Neill, J (2005) Are moderators moderate?: Testing the 'anchoring and adjustment' hypothesis in the context of marking politics exams, *Politics*, 25(3): 191–200.

Higgins, R, Hartley, P and Skelton, A (2002) The conscientious consumer: reconsidering the role of assessment feedback in student learning, *Studies in Higher Education*, 27(1): 53–64.

Hounsell, D, Hounsell, J, Litjens, J and McCune, V (2005) Enhancing guidance and feedback to students: findings on the impact of evidence-informed initiatives. Available online at <http://www.tla.ed.ac.uk/etl/docs/earliHHLM.pdf> (accessed 25 August 2007).

Hussey, T and Smith, P (2002) The trouble with learning outcomes, *Active Learning in Higher Education*, 3(2): 220–233.

King, P M and Kitchener, K S (1994) *Developing Reflective Judgment: Understanding and Promoting Intellectual Growth and Critical Thinking in Adolescents and Adults*, San Francisco, CA: Jossey-Bass.

Knight, P (2007) Fostering and assessing 'wicked' competences. Available online at <http://www.open.ac.uk/cetl-workspace/cetlcontent/documents/460d1d1481d0f.pdf> (accessed 25 August 2007).

Maclellan, E (2001) Assessment for learning: the differing perceptions of tutors and students, *Assessment and Evaluation in Higher Education*, 26(4): 307–318.

Marton, F and Saljo, R (1976) On qualitative differences in learning. I – Outcome and process, *British Journal of Educational Psychology*, 46: 4–11.

Marton, F, Dall'Alba, G and Beaty, E (1993) Conceptions of learning, *International Journal of Educational Research*, 19: 277–300.

Moon, J A (1999) *Reflection in Learning and Professional Development*, Abingdon: RoutledgeFalmer.

National Student Survey (2006) <http://www2.tqi.ac.uk/sites/tqi/home/index.cfm> (accessed 25 August 2007) http://www.unistats.com/?userimagepref (2007 and onwards) (last accessed 1 November 2007).

Nicole, D J and Macfarlane-Dick, D (2006) Formative assessment and self-regulated learning: a model and seven principles of good feedback practice, *Studies in Higher Education*, 31(2): 199–218.

Norton, L S (2004) Using assessment criteria as learning criteria. A case study using Psychology Applied Learning Scenarios (PALS), *Assessment and Evaluation in Higher Education*, 29(6): 687–702.

Norton, L, Harrington, K, Elander, J, Sinfield, S, Lusher, J, Reddy, P, Aiyegbayo, O and Pitt, E (2005) 'Supporting students to improve their essay writing through assessment criteria focused workshops', in C Rust (ed.) *Improving Student Learning 12*, Oxford: Oxford Centre for Staff and Learning Development.

O'Donovan, B, Price, M and Rust, C (2001) 'Strategies to develop students' understanding of assessment criteria and processes', in C Rust (ed.) *Improving Student Learning 8: Improving Student Learning Strategically*, Oxford: Oxford Centre for Staff and Learning Development.

Perry, W G (1970) *Forms of Intellectual and Ethical Development in the College Years*, New York: Holt, Rinehart & Winston.

Prosser, M and Trigwell, K (1999) *Understanding Learning and Teaching. The Experience in Higher Education*, Buckingham: Society for Research into Higher Education and the Open University Press.

Prowse, S, Duncan, N, Hughes, J and Burke, D (2007) '. . . do that and I'll raise your grade'. Innovative module design and recursive feedback, *Teaching in Higher Education*, 12(4): 437–445.

QAA Subject benchmark statements <http://www.qaa.ac.uk/academicinfrastructure/benchmark/default.asp> (accessed 25 August 2007).

QAA (2001) The framework for higher education qualifications in England, Wales and Northern Ireland – January 2001. Available online at <http://www.qaa.ac.uk/academicinfrastructure/FHEQ/EWNI/default.asp> (accessed 25 August 2007).

QAA (2006a) *Code of Practice for the Assurance of Academic Quality and Standards in Higher Education* (2nd edn), Section 6 Assessment of students. Available online at <http://www.qaa.ac.uk/academicinfrastructure/codeOfPractice/section6/COP_AOS.pdf> (accessed 17 July 2007).

QAA (2006b) Outcomes from institutional audit. Assessment of students. Available online at <http://www.qaa.ac.uk/reviews/institutionalAudit/outcomes/Assessmentofstudents.pdf> (accessed 25 August 2007).

Ramsden, P (1992) *Learning to Teach in Higher Education*, London: Routledge.

Ramsden, P (2003) *Learning to Teach in Higher Education* (2nd edn), London: RoutledgeFalmer.

Rust, C (2002) The impact of assessment on student learning: how can the research literature practically help to inform the development of departmental assessment strategies and learner-centred assessment practices?, *Active Learning in Higher Education*, 3(2): 145–158.

Rust, C (2007) Towards a scholarship of assessment, *Assessment and Evaluation in Higher Education*, 32(2): 229–237.

Saljo, R (1979) Learning about learning, *Higher Education*, 8: 443–451.

Samuelowicz, K and Bain, J (2002) Identifying academics' orientations to assessment practice, *Higher Education*, 43: 173–201.

Special Educational Needs and Disability Act SENDA (2001) <http://www.opsi.gov.uk/acts/acts2001/20010010.htm> (accessed 25 August 2007).

The UK Professional Standards Framework for teaching and supporting learning in higher education (2006) <http://www.heacademy.ac.uk/assets/York/documents/ourwork/professional/Professional_Standards_Framework.pdf> (accessed 17 July 2007).

Yorke, M (2003) Formative assessment in higher education: moves towards theory and the enhancement of pedagogic practice, *Higher Education*, 45: 477–501.

FURTHER READING

Boud, D and Falchikov, N (2007) *Rethinking Assessment in Higher Education: Learning for the Longer Term*, London: Routledge. Directs attention to what is important in assessment.

Bryan, C and Clegg, K (eds) (2006) *Innovative Assessment in Higher Education*, London: Routledge. Contributions from practitioners showing how assessment can be changed.

Elton, L and Johnston, B (2002) Assessment in universities: a critical review of the research. Available online at http://ltsnpsy.york.ac.uk/docs/pdf/p20030617_elton_johnston-assessment_in_universities_a_critical_view_o.pdf (accessed 25 August 2007). Highly recommended as a comprehensive and challenging view of assessment in higher education.

Gibbs, G and Simpson, C (2002) Does your assessment support your students' learning? Available online at <http://www.brookes.ac.uk/services/ocsd/1_ocsld/lunchtime_gibbs_3.doc> (accessed 17 July 2007). Widely cited source of guidance describing 11 principles of good practice.

Heywood, J (2000) *Assessment in Higher Education. Student Learning, Teaching, Programmes and Institutions.* Higher Education Policy Series 56, London: Jessica Kingsley. A thorough text which gives useful background on the history and philosophy of assessment.

Pickford, R and Brown, S (2006) *Assessing Skills and Practice* (Key Guides for Effective Teaching in Higher Education), London: Routledge. Ideal for any lecturer new to this form of assessment.

Race, P, Brown, S and Smith, B (2004) *500 Tips on Assessment* (2nd edn), London: RoutledgeFalmer. Useful for 'dipping in'.

WEBSITES

CETLs

Assessment for Learning Enhancement (http://northumbria.ac.uk/cetl_afl/).
Assessment and Learning in Practice Settings (ALPS) (http://www.alps-cetl.ac.uk/).
Assessment Standards Knowledge Exchange (ASKE) (http://www.business.heacademy.ac.uk/projects/cetls/cetl_aske.html).
Write Now (http://www.writenow.ac.uk/index.html).

Plagiarism

The JISC plagiarism advisory service. Provides generic advice including assessments which design out plagiarism (http://www.jiscpas.ac.uk/index.php).

Generic resources

The HEA website also allows access to subject centre links related to assessment (http://www.heacademy.ac.uk/ourwork/learning/assessment).

11 Supervising projects and dissertations

Stephanie Marshall

When considering what constitutes good project and dissertation supervision the waiter analogy is useful: a good waiter in a good restaurant is around enough to help you when you need things but leaves you alone enough to enjoy yourself (Murray, 1998). Readers will undoubtedly agree with the sentiments expressed above, as would students reflecting on their desired role for their supervisors in the supervision of projects and dissertations as an integral part of taught programmes (for research student supervision, see Chapter 12). But how is such a fine balance achieved, and is it really possible for a supervisor to attain the ideal of knowing when to be 'hands-on' and when to be 'hands-off'? This chapter seeks to explore this question, first by providing a background to the use of projects and dissertations in teaching, moving on to consider a working definition; and second, by mapping out the terrain – that is, the key issues supervisors need to think through and be clear about prior to introducing such a strategy for promoting learning. Finally the chapter will summarise the key management and interpersonal skills required of the supervisor in order to promote efficient and effective supervision of projects and dissertations.

WHY PROJECTS AND DISSERTATIONS?

Over the past decade, the use of projects and dissertations in university curricula, both undergraduate and taught postgraduate, has been seen as increasingly important. First, projects and dissertations have been seen as a means of encouraging more students to think about 'staying on' as research students and thus contributing to the research productivity of departments and schools. Second, projects and dissertations are deemed to be an important means of bringing about an effective research culture to underpin all undergraduate and postgraduate curricula. Third, projects and dissertations have come to be seen as an important component of degree programmes across the disciplines, because of the clear emphasis they place on the learners taking responsibility for their own learning, and engaging with the production of knowledge. The importance of students being able to understand and, to some extent, plan and undertake research and knowledge generation is of greater importance than a few decades ago, as Barnett (2000) might argue, due to the 'supercomplexity' of society. Increasingly, the introduction of projects and dissertations is seen as a way of promoting the teaching–research nexus, at the same time as assisting in the attainment of increasing targets for postgraduate research students.

In summary, the so-called 'knowledge economy' requires students to graduate capable of engaging with and analysing research, which thus requires careful thought when planning and designing appropriate curricula.

Projects and dissertations have always been viewed as an effective means of research training and of encouraging a discovery approach to learning, through the generation and analysis of primary data. Such an approach is aimed at the development of higher-level cognitive skills, such as analysis, synthesis and evaluation. Alongside this obvious rationale, projects and dissertations are also seen as an effective means of:

- diversifying assessment;
- addressing concern to promote skills and employability (see Chapter 8);
- empowering the learner;
- motivating students;
- promoting links between teaching and research;
- 'talent spotting', i.e. identifying potential research students/assistants.

DEFINITIONS

Projects and dissertations have often been discussed as one in the educational development literature (Day *et al.*, 1998; Wilkins, 1995). It is worth considering both distinctions and similarities prior to offering a working definition.

A project, as distinct from a dissertation, is generally defined as aimed at generating primary data (Williams and Horobin, 1992). Dissertations, on the other hand, are categorised as generating secondary data, often in the form of a long essay, review or report (Parsons and Knight, 2005). Henry researched extensively the use of projects in teaching on behalf of the Open University. She offers a six-point definition of a 'project' which is not dissimilar to a dissertation, stating that:

> The student (usually) selects the project topic; locates his or her own source material; presents an end product (usually a report and often for assessment); conducts an independent piece of work (though there are also group projects). The project lasts over an extended period and the teacher assumes the role of adviser.
>
> (Henry, 1994: 12)

The similarities between projects and dissertations are obvious in that both require project management skills: scheduling, action planning, time management, monitoring, delivery of a product on time and evaluation. Over recent years the term 'dissertation' in the context of undergraduate work has come to be employed less, and the use of the term 'project', incorporating the notion of project management, employed more. Case study 1, drawing on the University of York 2007 prospectus, exemplifies this trend.

Case study 1: Definitions of project as offered in the University of York *Undergraduate Prospectus* 2007

Electronics

In their final year B.Eng. students carry out a personal project supervised by a member of staff. Each year a large number of possible projects are offered to students and there is also the opportunity for students to propose their own project. The final B.Eng. project contributes about one-fifth of the final degree marks.

History collaborative projects

All students on a module may work together to select and define more closely a project which will form a major part of the term's work. . . . When such a project is undertaken, the tutor will always be available for advice and assistance, but seminars, and the ultimate outcome of the term's work, the written project, will be shaped by the group of students taking the module. It is their responsibility to allocate the research, presentations and writing that will need to be done.

Music

Our ground-breaking project system permits you to select one course module in each term from a wide range of choices. . . . Choices vary from year to year, although some projects (such as composition, ensemble performance, music in the community) are run every year. . . .

Most projects are assessed by a submission at the end of the module. The nature of the submission is flexible, and may consist of an essay, seminar paper, composition, performance or analysis; often a combination of these will be required.

All three explanations of project work offered in Case study 1 emphasise project management skills on the part of the student. Such a definition suggests that both projects

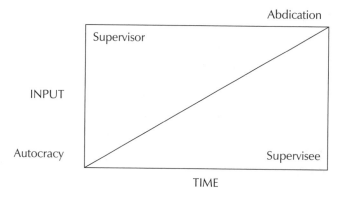

Figure 11.1 Supervisor–supervisee relationship in project supervision

and dissertations are a piece of project management with an emphasis on the students determining the parameters within which they will operate to deliver a time-bound, externally described output – a project or dissertation of a certain length and format. Within this specified time framework students are offered the potential to pursue their own interests within a given discipline area. The role of the **supervisor** thus moves away from that of teacher, providing the format within which students will be expected to perform, to that of **facilitator**, thus promoting a different sort of relationship with a subtly different skills set.

There is a distinction between the supervision of projects and dissertations and the routine supervision of students by teaching staff. The former requires a time-bound, managed activity that demands project management skills on the part of both supervisor and supervisee. The latter requires self-awareness (e.g. of one's personality style, gender, class and race), combined with an ability to engage in reflective practice and acute sensitivity to the needs of the student. It is this distinction that warrants further consideration.

Projects and dissertations clearly offer a teaching and learning strategy which passes the onus for learning on to the students, requiring supervisors to reposition themselves away from the role of teacher, moving vertically up the axis to that of facilitator, as illustrated in Figure 11.1. However, such a figure can offer too simplistic a picture, as effective supervisors would suggest that intense periods of time have to be deployed with supervisees, both at the commencement of the project and as the project is being pulled together at the end. Nevertheless, the implications of this shift in role offer the greatest potential for student learning, at the same time as offering the greatest potential for role conflict on the part of the supervisor. As Day *et al.* (1998: 51) suggest, 'avoiding the twin traps of over- or under-supervising is never easy'.

Establishing and agreeing the appropriate working relationship between supervisor and supervisees – a highly complex and underexplored area at the undergraduate level – offers the key to maximising the learning capacity of projects and dissertations. How to achieve such a working relationship is explored in detail in the next section.

MAPPING THE TERRAIN

Prior to embarking on the introduction of projects or dissertations, supervisors should review their own project management skills. There would appear to be four key questions that supervisors need to address:

1 their own motivation in choosing a project or dissertation as a learning strategy;
2 whether to opt for a structured or unstructured project or dissertation;
3 their role as supervisor;
4 ways of broadening support for supervisees.

THE AIMS AND OBJECTIVES OF THE LEARNING STRATEGY

In planning any project or dissertation, supervisors must be clear as to why they are choosing such a method of teaching and learning to promote the aims of the learning programme. The labour, intensity and potential for undue pressure on the supervisor further to pursuit of the project method have been discussed elsewhere (Henry, 1994). Cullen (2007) suggests that there is still debate about the role (and nature) of the dissertation within courses, with a particular focus on what form the learning should take, and how best the desired outcome can be achieved.

It is common to find that projects and dissertations form an important part of any departmental learning and teaching strategy. Furthermore, projects and dissertations do appear to feature as distinct evidence of a significant piece of student-centred learning in course programmes which might otherwise appear rather traditional. There is general agreement that projects and dissertations are best left until the latter part of the degree programme (Jaques, 1989; Thorley and Gregory, 1994; Hammick and Acker, 1998) and, indeed, for most students, the single most significant piece of work carried out is the final-year research project or dissertation. Not only can it assist with the integration of subject material, but it provides an introduction to research techniques and methods. Both Baxter Magolda (1999) and Blackmore and Cousin (2003) argue that students involved in research-based enquiries develop more sophisticated levels of intellectual development, with Healey (2005) suggesting that designing curricula which develop the teaching–research nexus requires a shift from teacher focused to students as participants in the research process. It is this unique feature of projects and dissertations (i.e. the shift in control from supervisor to supervisee) which can offer the greatest challenge to both student and supervisor. This shift is explored further in the next section.

Interrogating practice

Reflect on projects or dissertations you have supervised or, indeed, have recently completed. How was the learning strategy used to promote the aims of the curriculum?

STRUCTURED VERSUS UNSTRUCTURED

There has been much written in favour of both structured and unstructured projects and dissertations. At one end of the spectrum it is agreed that providing students with a structure reduces the risk of failure at the same time as making the supervisory role easier in the sense that the supervisor will be able to monitor student progress through clearly prescribed stages (Race and Brown, 1998). The main critique of such a method is that projects and dissertations can appear insufficiently open-ended, thus being too prescriptive, offering a rationalist approach to learning rather than a constructivist approach and presenting a number of students with little real challenge. However, provided the purpose of this approach is clear, significant value added can be gained.

At the other end of the spectrum, it is agreed that providing students with extended project and dissertation work allows them to collect a range of evidence, proceeding on to test a range of theories and explanations, to promote a deep approach to learning and allowing the potential for students to progress along a hierarchy of understanding, such as that offered by the SOLO taxonomy outlined in Chapter 2. The result should thus be a demonstration of familiarity with key theories (which at best will be conceptualised at a high level of abstraction), and an awareness of the importance of using sufficient evidence. However, the main criticism of adopting the unstructured approach is that students, in being given too much choice and scope, may flounder. Alongside student autonomy, academic staff will be forced to supervise too great a range of projects, thus testing the facilitatory supervision skills of some staff. Both of these factors may result in a compromise of quality.

Interrogating practice

Reflect on the parameters offered for projects within your department. Would you classify these as structured or unstructured? What are the strengths and weaknesses of the approach adopted by your department?

THE ROLE OF PROJECT AND DISSERTATION SUPERVISOR

Determining how to supervise projects and dissertations may offer a great challenge to the academic. As with any project, 'front loading' (putting most time and effort in at the beginning) at the planning stage – both initially on one's own and then with the supervisee(s) – is essential. Equally important, 'end loading' (putting much time in at the end) is often essential to ensure the written output accurately reflects the knowledge, understanding and new skills that have been acquired in the process of undertaking the project or dissertation.

Stone (1994) refers to the 'walk-through' approach as offering an essential planning tool. By this he means that the supervisor should mentally walk through every step of the project, considering such issues as phasing and likely time allocation. It would seem most appropriate to pursue this method to promote dialogue with supervisees, particularly as one of the regular complaints from supervisors with respect to unstructured projects and dissertations is that students choose overly ambitious topics, being wholly naive as to the breadth of the topic but also as regards phasing and costing out the different activities within a fixed time-scale (e.g. literature review, research, writing up).

There are four key features of the supervisory framework which will require planning for and sharing with the supervisee(s). First, determine and agree educational objectives; second, determine and agree specific objectives to include formative deadlines; third, agree set targets; and, finally, review and ensure understanding of the assessment criteria (see Case studies 3 and 4). Within this framework, time allocation for supervision needs to be made clear so as to avoid any possible future confusion and many departments encourage supervisors to do this through set office hours. Within these dedicated supervisory hours, the supervisor needs to consider equity of quality time for supervisees, and thus should spend some time going through a few simple calculations.

Interrogating practice

Reflect on how much time, including planning, delivery, supervision and review, you would normally spend on a taught course which equates in credit value to the project or dissertation you are or will be supervising. What does this mean in terms of the hours per week you should make available for project or dissertation supervision? What does this means in terms of time allocation for each of your supervisees?

Once a framework for supervision has been determined as above, legal (e.g. health and safety regulations, special educational needs and disability requirements), ethical (e.g. issues of confidentiality) and financial (e.g. restricted budgets for experimental science work) constraints should be addressed. Such issues will undoubtedly be addressedin departmental guidelines for project and dissertation completion, and can be reviewed elsewhere (Williams and Horobin, 1992). As more additional guidance data to informthe execution of projects and dissertations are gathered, it will save the supervisor much time in the long run by establishing and codifying his or her own clear guidelines and criteria, offering these to supervisees as either a handout or a web page, or both.

Supervising unstructured or semi-structured projects and dissertations implies assisting students in formulating research questions; second, choosing methods; and finally, scoping the means of data collection. As the end-product should be the supervisees' intellectual property, the supervisor must be sensitive to the supervisees' ability to determine these for themselves. There is a fine line between guiding and telling, and much will depend on the ability and vision of the student, combined with the sensitivity of the supervisor. A supervisor-led approach emphasises the transmission of research knowledge to the student, whereas supervisee-focused approaches emphasise the student constructing his or her own knowledge. In the case of the latter, able students may be encouraged to write up their reports or dissertations for publication, which requires a different sort of supervisory support.

Interrogating practice

Reflect on your role. At which stage(s) of the project or dissertation will you take on a 'teaching' role and at which stage(s) a facilitatory role? Consider the skills required at both ends of the spectrum.

Focusing on the facilitatory role should prompt a response which includes asking supervisees open-ended questions, reflecting questions back and encouraging supervisees to explore strategies to take their work forward. Facilitation skills have been written about extensively, as they do not necessarily require supervisors to demonstrate their own technical skills but rather demand interpersonal skills, which can prove far more difficult to learn (Williams and Horobin, 1992; Hammick and Acker, 1998). Furthermore, with increased student numbers, it is likely that supervisors will be required to supervise a group of students working outside what the supervisor might comfortably perceive to be his or her own area of research expertise.

Interrogating practice

Reflect on your own departmental practices. How do students choose their supervisor, or are students allocated to a supervisor? Will you be expected to supervise students outside your area of expertise?

Further to supervisory responsibility being determined, the supervisor and supervisee should establish an agreed, appropriate working relationship. At the first meeting, the supervisor and supervisee should discuss expectations in terms of apportioning responsibility. The most recognised formal approach to agreeing a working relationship is that of a **learning contract**, or what Williams and Horobin (1992: 43) refer to as creating a 'we culture'. Ryan (1994) offers a template for a supervisor checklist and student contract which itemises the range of responsibilities to which both parties agree (e.g. agreed times for meetings, writing up supervisory meeting notes, dealing with ethical issues, submission of progress reports for formative assessment and involvement in peer group support).

WAYS OF BROADENING SUPPORT

With the 'massification' of higher education, and the recognition of the value of teamwork, peer support has been increasingly viewed as a learning strategy that should be promoted within the curriculum for a range of reasons (Thorley and Gregory, 1994). Working in project teams provides moral support at the same time as promoting teamwork skills. Such an approach is becoming more widespread (e.g. in problem-based medical education) (see Chapter 26). Moore (2007) uses the term PBL, which he uses in relation to the teaching of electronics, to refer to '*project*-based learning', suggesting it not only improves students' knowledge, understanding and transferable skills, but additionally enhances their employability. A group of, say, five or six has a greater range of total experience and skills than any one individual. It is particularly beneficial to be able to draw on a range of students' skills such as an exceptionally IT literate student, a student capable of sophisticated statistical analysis, or a student capable of maintaining morale when the going gets tough. It could be a requirement of the department that peer support teams meet at prescribed times to provide feedback. Jaques (1989: 30) advocates this method, suggesting that:

> Many of the issues to do with the progress of a project can be just as well dealt with by students themselves, provided they have a reasonably clear structure to work with. In the case of individual projects, students can report and be quizzed in turn by the rest of a peer group at regular meetings on matters like: . . . What are you proposing to do? . . . How can you break that down into manageable steps? . . . What or who else could help you?

He advocates using a similar set of guidance questions towards the end of the project, moving on to suggest ways of engaging these peer groups in summative evaluation prior to formal submission of the project.

Chelford and Hopkins (2004) advocate the use of group projects in Built Environment curricula and explore how best to address assessment issues. A range of disciplines are now moving to group projects, and Case study 2 provides a useful illustration of managing the assessment of the range of learning outcomes such projects can promote.

Case study 2: Year Two group project for single Honours History students

Single Honours History students at the University of Southampton devote a quarter of their second year to the group project. Groups of eight choose a topic, the nature of which depends upon the interests of designated supervisors. Their capacity for collective and independent historical investigation is tested via differently weighted modes of assessment: project proposal; group log; group presentation; public outcome; group historical essay; and individual reflective essay (facilitating differentiation as all other elements provide a joint mark). Teamwork and individual research provide valuable employment/life skills as well as preparation for the final year dissertation. The group presentation taps sophisticated IT/media skills and encourages less extrovert students to talk about process and outcomes, while a diversity of public outcomes reflects a conscious engagement with 'public history'. The course has proved universally popular, and has demonstrated how effectively today's students can utilise new technology to gather, disseminate and analyse/interpret information.

(Dr Adrian Smith, Southampton University)

Ways of broadening student support include the use of a Virtual Learning Environment (**VLE**) and a website poster board giving guidance notes (e.g. on format, word length) and frequently asked questions (FAQs), and encouraging students to post up queries. However, the supervisor will need to monitor the poster board to make appropriate interventions, ensuring that accurate resolution of problems takes place. The Higher Education Academy Subject Centres for Sociology, Anthropology and Politics, and Social Work and Policy (http://www.socscidiss.bham.ac.uk/) provides an excellent web resource for undergraduate students in social sciences on all aspects of dissertations in social sciences. It addresses common questions, concerns and practical issues such as research design, ethics, access and writing skills. The resource also provides some useful information for academic staff supervising undergraduate dissertations. There are an increasing number of books on the market targeted at students undertaking projects (e.g. Bell, 2005; Parsons and Knight, 2005).

Finally, Clark (1992: 7), writing about the supervision of group work projects in the History Department at the University of York, advocates the supervisor being close on hand to offer interventions if requested by students, noting that when he dropped in on his first-ever project group to offer advice on writing up, he was told with much amusement, 'Go away, we don't need you.'

MANAGING SCHEDULING

The pressure of time will be felt by both supervisors and supervisees when working to deadlines. In order to keep projects and dissertations on track, a range of documentation may prove useful. The use of guideline criteria and learning contracts as initial documentation was referred to in the previous section. Schedules, action plans and checklists similarly are useful tools. Some useful examples are provided by Day *et al.* (1998), and a simplistic version of a checklist offering a 'walk-through' approach to supervision is illustrated in Case study 3. Checklists and documentation are most useful for the supervisor to avoid memory overload, providing a written record of meetings to include agreed action points. Such written records are invaluable in cases of student appeals.

Case study 3: Checklist for preparation for project and dissertation supervisory meetings

The checklist that follows results from brainstorming sessions with academics enrolled on a staff development workshop aimed at promoting professional supervision of dissertation and projects.

Planning for the supervision – how will you tackle the following?

- discussing current strengths and weaknesses;
- encouraging the student to plan for taking the work forward;
- setting short-term objectives (to include contingency planning) within an action plan;
- setting up a more detailed time and action framework.

What will your agenda be?

- agree action plan and/or review progress against action plan;
- give feedback on performance;
- troubleshoot, problem-solve;
- revisit assessment criteria;
- revisit and redefine action plan and time-scale.

What information do you need to refer to?

- supervisee's written progress reports;
- supervisee's draft material;
- departmental project regulations and assessment criteria.

Arrangements for the supervisory meeting:

- ensure 'quality time' free from interruption;
- ensure the venue is conducive to open discussion.

The supervision meeting must be structured and well organised:

- opening – use this to clarify the purpose and agree the agenda;
- middle – you should facilitate discussion of ideas, discuss specific issues;
- monitor progress, give constructive feedback, question effectively, set and agree objectives leading to the next supervision meeting;
- end – you should record an action plan, to include short-term objectives and end on a positive note.

(Professor Stephanie Marshall, University of York)

By adopting such methods as offered in Case study 3 and checklists presented elsewhere (Wilkins, 1995; Day *et al.*, 1998), both supervisor and supervisee will share a sense of purpose and progress. Another means of assisting rigour in approach is to ensure that there are open and transparent assessment criteria, which will aid the supervisor to assist the supervisee in ensuring that adequate attention is paid to the weighting of various components. An example of such rigour is offered in Case study 4, which offers a marker's assessment pro forma (see pages 162–163).

By supervisors adopting a rigorous approach to project and dissertation completion that entails, first, transparency in formative and summative assessment criteria, combined with, second, professional supervisory skills, supervision will be viewed as a constructive means of monitoring the milestones on the route to successful project and dissertation completion.

Case study 4: UCL Computer Science project assessment form

INSTRUCTIONS: Use the general comments box below to note the particular strengths and weaknesses of the project and any factors that are not covered by the rest of the form. Fill in a per cent mark for each of the 5 named areas below. *Underline key phrases* in the descriptions that apply to this project where appropriate (also overleaf). Average 5 marks to get a final per cent mark. All parts of the form are mandatory. See overleaf for more guidance.

Student Surname: . . . .

Student Forename: . . . .

Project Name: . . . .

Supervisor Name: . . . .

Marker Name: . . . .

General comments

Mark (%)

1 Background, aims and organisation

The student has not understood the aims of the project. The student has failed to place the work in the context of the surrounding literature. The student has failed to identify suitable subgoals.

vs.

The student has clearly understood and stated the aims of the project. There is a suitable literature review which relates to the task. The project is well organised with suitable subgoals.

2 Achievement

The student failed to achieve basic aims. Goals were not sufficiently ambitious to warrant a whole project. Quality of the work is insufficient. The student has not produced sufficient deliverables.

vs.

The student has achieved all of the stated aims. The project is complex and challenging. The student has produced a considerably body of deliverables in terms of both software and write-up.

vs.

vs.

3 *Clarity*

The report is unclear or written badly. The write-up is disorganised. Figures and figure legends are of insufficient quality. The presentation is poor. It is hard to understand the core ideas.	*vs.*	Report is carefully written. Clear structure with a flowing, logical argument. Figures and legends are helpful for understanding the project. It is easy to understand the core ideas.

4 *Analysis/testing*

For a *software-based* project there is insufficient testing. Documentation is poor. For a *research-based* project there is no critical analysis of the results. Weaknesses and improvements are not considered.	*vs.*	For *software-based* projects there is thorough testing. Analysis of strengths/weaknesses present. Detailed documentation. For *research-based* projects there is critical analysis of method and results. Weaknesses and possible extensions are discussed.

5 *Difficulty level and supervision*

The project was easy to understand and implement. The student required close supervision and did not work independently.	*vs.*	The project was conceptually and practically difficult. The student worked independently and did not overly rely on the supervisor.

Your mark (average of above):

Agreed mark:

(Taken from the Computer Science website at University College London. See the same site for details of the grade-related criteria used when allocating per cent marks to each of sections 1 to 5. http://www.cs.ucl.ac.uk/staff/ s.prince/IndivProject/UG2007/ProjectAssessment.pdf> (accessed 19 December 2007))

OVERVIEW

This chapter examined the greater use made of projects and dissertations across disciplines and endeavoured to provide a working definition. Projects and dissertations were described as offering a unique learning opportunity in that:

1   they are sufficiently time-bound to afford students the opportunity to demonstrate their project management skills;

2   they are clearly a student-centred learning experience which requires the supervisor to take on the role of facilitator;
3   they afford students the opportunity to make an original, intellectual or creative contribution to knowledge.

It was argued that for supervisors to offer effective and efficient supervision of projects and dissertations, they would have to examine and refine their own management and interpersonal skills. In the case of the former, a range of planning tools was offered. In the case of the latter, it was suggested that the supervisor should broaden support for the student so that the supervisor could take on the role of facilitator, prompting and encouraging the student to seek out his or her own solutions and strategies for moving forward and undertaking and making sense of their own research. It is this combination of unique features which makes projects and dissertations such a powerful learning tool.

REFERENCES

Barnett, R (2000) Supercomplexity and the curriculum, *Studies in Higher Education*, 25(3): 255–265.

Baxter Magolda, M B (1999) *Creating Context for Learning and Self-authorship*, Nashville, TN: Vanderbilt University Press.

Bell, J (2005) *Doing Your Research Project* (4th edn), Berkshire: Open University Press.

Blackmore, P and Cousin, G (2003) Linking teaching and learning and research through research-based learning, *Educational Developments*, 4(4): 24–27.

Chelford, T and Hopkins, A (2004) Sizing the Slice: Assessing Individual Performance in Group Projects, Higher Education Academy project. Available online at <http://www.he academy.ac.uk/resources/detail/resources/casestudies/cs_096> (accessed 30 December 2007).

Clark, C (1992) Group projects in the Department of History, *Staff Development and Training Newsletter*, Staff Development Office, University of York.

Cullen, S (2007) Dissertation Supervision: Enhancing the Experience of Tourism and Hospitality Students. Available online at <http://www.heacademy.ac.uk/hlst/projects/detail/ourwork/dissertation_supervision_enhancing_the_experience_of_tourism_and_hospitality_students> (accessed 19 December 2007).

Day, K, Grant, R and Hounsell, D (1998) *Reviewing Your Teaching*, University of Edinburgh: CTLA and UCoSDA.

Hammick, M and Acker, S (1998) Undergraduate research supervision: a gender analysis, *Studies in Higher Education*, 23(3): 335–347.

Healey, M (2005) 'Linking research and teaching: exploring disciplinary spaces and the role of inquiry-based learning', in R. Barnett (ed.) *Reshaping the University*, Berkshire: SRHE and the Open University Press.

Henry, J (1994) *Teaching Through Projects*, London: Kogan Page.

Jaques, D (1989) *Independent Learning and Project Work*, Oxford: Open Learning.

Moore, A (2007) PBLE: Project Based Learning in Engineering, Higher Education Academy Project 43/99. Available online at <http://www.heacademy.ac.uk/projects/detail/projectfinder/projects/pf1611> (accessed 30 December 2007).

Murray, R (1998) *Research Supervision*, Centre for Academic Practice, University of Strathclyde.
Parsons, T and Knight, P (2005) *How to Do Your Dissertation in Geography and Related Disciplines*, Abingdon, Oxon: Routledge.
Race, P and Brown, S (1998) *The Lecturer's Toolkit* (3rd edn), London: Routledge.
Ryan, Y (1994) 'Contracts and checklists: practical propositions for postgraduate supervision', in O Zuber-Skerritt and Y Ryan (eds), *Quality in Postgraduate Education*, London: Kogan Page.
Stone, B (1994) 'The academic management of group projects', in L Thorley and R Gregory (eds) *Using Group-based Learning in Higher Education*, London: Kogan Page.
Thorley, L and Gregory, R (1994) *Using Group-based Learning in Higher Education*, London: Kogan Page.
Wilkins, M (1995) *Learning to Teach in Higher Education*, Warwick: Coventry Printers.
Williams, M and Horobin, R (1992) *Active Learning in Fieldwork and Project Work*, Sheffield: CVCP USDTU.

FURTHER READING

Barnett, R (ed.) (2005) *Reshaping the University*, Berkshire: SRHE and the Open University Press. A range of useful Chapters, particularly Chapter 5 by Mick Healey (as above), which explores the bringing together of research and teaching (i.e. the teaching–research nexus), by engaging students as participants as opposed to as the audience.
Day, K, Grant, R and Hounsell, D (1998) See above. Chapter 7 deals specifically with supervising projects and dissertations, and includes some examples of useful pro forma.
Henry, J (1994) *Teaching Through Projects*, London: Kogan Page. A comprehensive and thorough examination of the use of project work to inform extension of this practice by the Open University.

WEBSITE

Companion for Undergraduate Dissertations Sociology, Anthropology, Politics, Social Policy, Social Work and Criminology – A Survival Guide for Coping with your Dissertation. Higher Education Academy Centre for Sociology, Anthropology and Politics, Centre for Social Policy and Social Work, and Sheffield Hallam University. Available online at <http://www.socscidiss.bham.ac.uk/> (accessed 19 December 2007). Much useful information for students and supervisors across a wide range of disciplines.

12 Supervising research students

Steve Ketteridge and Morag Shiach

INTRODUCTION

The growth in number of students in the UK higher education sector over recent years has included an increase in numbers of students enrolled for research degrees. For the majority of academics working in UK universities, supervision of research students is now an integral part of their academic practice; indeed for many it will be an explicit requirement of their role and clearly identified in the terms and conditions of employment or job description, using phrases such as 'to supervise research students through to completion'. This chapter provides an introduction to the supervision of research students reading for research degrees of different types, but with an emphasis on the Doctor of Philosophy (Ph.D.) and Master of Philosophy (M.Phil.). It will also have relevance to those supervising similar doctorates with thesis requirements, such as the Doctor of Medicine (MD or MD [Res]) and **professional doctorates** (e.g. Ed.D.).

This chapter is built on two premises. The first is that research supervision is a specialist form of teaching. For some disciplines this has always been thought to be the case, but for others, research has been considered very much as part of the research side of the business. James and Baldwin (2006: 3) at the University of Melbourne set out a number of principles of effective supervision which should inform effective practice, including:

> Supervision involves the fundamentals of good teaching, among them, concern for students, interest in their progress, and the provision of thoughtful and timely feedback. Good supervisors exemplify the characteristics of good teachers in any setting.

> Supervision is an intensive form of teaching, in a much broader sense than just information transfer. The sustained complexity involves much time and energy. Good supervisors are aware of this and of the professional commitment necessary to every student they agree to supervise.

The second premise on which this chapter builds is that a key factor to success in supervision is the development of the relationship between the student and the supervisor. Many experienced supervisors will know this intuitively. As Delamont *et al.* (1997: 14) comment:

> Having a reasonable experience with higher degree students is dependent on the relationship with you, and, if there are any other supervisor(s). You need to sort out a good working relationship with your supervisee. Relationships have to be worked at, and discussed, because most of the problems stem from a failure to set out the expectations both parties have for the relationship, agree them or agree to disagree.

This chapter will consider different stages in the supervision of research students, indicating some key points for consideration by supervisors. The scope of the chapter is limited and, for more details of other aspects of supervision, readers are referred to the excellent *Handbook* by Taylor and Beasley (2005).

CODES OF PRACTICE

One of the major changes to research degrees in the UK has been increased regulation. Up to the late 1990s, research students working in universities, colleges and research institutes were working in environments where their learning experience was determined primarily by university policies, custom and local practice. Some of the funding bodies (e.g. PPARC [now Science and Technologies Facilities Council], ESRC) published guidelines on good supervisory practice, as had other bodies (e.g. The Wellcome Trust, National Postgraduate Committee) and these set out basic expectations of the supervisory process for both supervisor and student. Even so, the quality of the student experience was variable.

In 1999 the Quality Assurance Agency published its Code of Practice on Research Programmes which was subsequently updated (QAA, 2004). The QAA Code contains 27 precepts covering all aspects of the research student experience and, from these, UK universities have derived their own Codes of Practice on research degrees. Institutional Codes for research students and their supervisors set out guidelines for the conduct of the supervisory relationship in the university context and are intended to ensure the quality of the research student experience. They also serve as a standard for external **Audit** and in research degree appeals. Codes of Practice differ between universities, and supervisors need to be sure that they have the Code for their own university.

Interrogating practice

Do you have a copy of your University Code of Practice on research degrees? As you read this chapter and go through the research student life cycle, check to see what requirements you have to meet to comply with your Code.

RESEARCH DEGREES IN THE UK

Most universities offer a range of research degrees. A research degree is distinguished from taught degrees in the following ways:

- there is a substantial dissertation or thesis;
- individual examiners are appointed for the student;
- the student is supervised by a 'supervisory team' rather than by a course director.

The typical periods of study required for research degrees are shown in Table 12.1. Research degrees may include some 'Masters by Research' (e.g. M.Sc.) as well as doctorates, but not usually the Master of Research (M.Res.) which has a large taught component.

At the University of East Anglia (UEA, 2007) the period of study is the time in which the research work is undertaken and in which it is desirable that the thesis is submitted. Research should be completed by the end of the period of study. For some degrees the university allows a 'registration-only' period (sometimes called a 'writing-up period') within which the student may complete and submit the work. However, the norm is that the degree should be completed within the period of study and this applies in all universities. The period of study for part-time Ph.D. and M.Phil. degrees is six years and four years respectively and for the Masters by research two years.

Supervisors need to be aware of what is required for the award of the research degrees that they supervise and should discuss these with the students at an early stage. All universities will have their own regulations which will include criteria, requirements for the thesis and **viva voce examination** ('the viva'), and these are broadly similar across the sector. For the London Ph.D., there are a number of requirements for the thesis (University

Table 12.1 University of East Anglia: full-time research degrees

	Period of study	Registration-only period	Total period of registration
Doctor of Philosophy	3 years	1 year	4 years
Doctor of Philosophy (integrated studies)	4 years	1 year	5 years
Doctor of Philosophy (with rotational year)	4 years	–	4 years
Doctor of Social Work	3 years	1 year	4 years
Doctor of Clinical Psychology	3 years	–	3 years
Master of Philosophy	2 years	1 year	3 years
Master degrees by research (MA, M.Sc., LLM, M.Mus.)	1 year	1 year	2 years

of London, 2007: 3) including the key requirement: 'the thesis shall form a distinct contribution to the knowledge of the subject and afford evidence of originality by the discovery of new facts and/or by the exercise of independent critical power'. The requirement for an 'original' contribution is common to most universities and the meaning of originality is something which supervisors will need to discuss with their students and put in a disciplinary context. Most universities set a word limit on thesis size – 100,000 words for the Ph.D., and for a professional doctorate (e.g. Ed.D.) a maximum of 60,000 words. Universities also make statements on the scope of the thesis and the University of East Anglia (2005: 501) states: 'Examiners shall take into account that the substance and significance of the thesis should be of a kind which might reasonably be expected of a capable and diligent student after three years of full-time (or equivalent) study.' This focuses on the fact that the Ph.D. represents a three-year project. However, supervisors need to be aware that this does not imply three years of full-time research, but three years to include writing up and integration of other essential skills training into the programme, as will be discussed later.

Growing numbers of doctoral students

There has been steady growth in the numbers of doctoral students in the UK and, over the five years to 2005, the numbers expecting to graduate increased by about 15 per cent. Earlier growth over the five-year period to 2003 was 31 per cent. Table 12.2 shows the numbers of doctoral qualifications obtained in the UK over the period to 2005, classified as full-time and part-time, and by UK domiciliary (UK), other European Union (EU ex UK) domiciliary and non-EU overseas domiciliary.

For those graduating in 2005, the gender balance between total numbers is about 43.3 per cent female and 56.7 per cent male. When considering numbers of full-time students separately there is little difference. With part-time students there is a slight shift in the balance to 44.6 per cent female graduates. Of the 2005 graduating cohort 40 per cent of students are from EU countries other than the UK and non-EU countries, indicating the diversity of doctoral students in the UK.

These figures show the continued growth of full-time and part-time students from outside the UK to be greater than those from the UK. Of these, the greater proportion comprises non-EU overseas students, and experienced supervisors are well aware of this change, especially as represented by Chinese students.

Graduate schools and the Researcher Development Programme

The changing world of doctoral supervision and the increasing number of students have led many universities to establish graduate schools. These are generally responsible for:

- managing resources for research students;
- assuring quality of the student learning experience;
- delivering elements of skills training which form part of the research degree.

Table 12.2 Doctoral qualifications obtained in the UK, 2001 to 2005

Registered in final year	Full-time			Part-time			Full- and part-time			Total
	UK	EU ex UK	Non-EU overseas	UK	EU ex UK	Non-EU overseas	UK	EU ex UK	Non-EU overseas	
2005	7215	1745	3990	2650	335	580	9865	2080	4570	16565
2004	6870	1700	3460	2700	365	610	9570	2065	4070	15705
2003	6670	1560	3110	2570	345	615	9240	1905	3725	14870
2002	6460	4200		2670	875		9130	5075		14205
2001	6400	4115		2740	865		9140	4980		14120
5-year growth	11.3%	28.2%		−3.4%	5%		7.3%	25%		14.5%

Source: Adapted from UK GRAD Programme and **HESA** View statistics online (see references).

Note: The split between EU and non-EU international doctoral students was not available before 2003. UK Grad comment that the figures also include 'dormant' researchers who are due to complete Ph.D.s but do not do so, and consequently overestimate the numbers of graduates. This may account for 15 to 20 per cent of the total.

Graduate schools differ widely across institutions, and the graduate schools at Imperial College London were winners of the Times Higher Award in 2006 for 'Outstanding Support for Early Career Researchers'. Some universities have a single graduate school which covers the whole institution, while others have separate schools looking after different groupings of disciplines. Graduate schools may provide an institutional focus in the form of a 'Graduate Centre' with PCs and learning spaces in which students can also network, enhance social cohesion and come to feel valued and a vital part of the university research community. On a practical level graduate schools may also be responsible for ensuring appropriate monitoring of student progress and completion, and the development of research degree programmes.

A useful support network for both supervisors and students has been the UK GRAD (see also Case study 2) which is funded by Research Councils UK (RCUK), organised around eight regional hubs.

The main emphasis for research students has been on the development of personal and professional skills and integration of these into research degree programmes, alongside the formal research studies. However, at the time of writing the UK GRAD Programme has come to the end of its five-year contract and a new replacement body will be responsible for supporting postgraduate researchers and for the personal, professional and career development of post-doctoral research staff. The new programme will be called the Researcher Development Programme and will be launched in September 2008.

POSTGRADUATE RESEARCH EXPERIENCE SURVEY

The Postgraduate Research Experience Survey (PRES) is an annual online survey designed to collect feedback from research students. PRES is a national survey supported by the **HEA,** and universities can choose whether or not to participate. Unlike the **National Student Survey** for undergraduates, the information published by PRES is not attributed to individual institutions. The public data are a snapshot of the collective experience of research students from the institutions that took part in PRES. For a given university, the PRES data are meant to provide an evidence base from which to enhance the quality of the student experience and it is becoming increasingly useful in benchmarking performance within the institution and against information from across the sector.

Looking at the overview results for 2007 (Park *et al.*, 2007), the headlines reveal that Ph.D. students consistently identify the level and quality of supervision they receive as the most important contributor to the successful completion of their Ph.D. Intellectual climate was also an important factor in overall satisfaction. Research students were also positive about their overall experience, with 81 per cent indicating that the programme as a whole met or exceeded their expectations. The authors' PRES findings are similar to those from the Australian Postgraduate Experience Questionnaire on which PRES is based.

FORMING THE STUDENT–SUPERVISOR RELATIONSHIP

This part of the chapter will review some of the early stages in the research student life cycle and will draw out some essential aspects which are important in starting to build an effective and professional relationship.

Entry requirements, selection and induction of students

Entry requirements

Entry requirements vary between disciplines and also to some extent between institutions. It is increasingly common to require students to complete a programme at Masters level before they embark on a research degree. This may be a programme such as an M.Eng. where the Masters-level work is integrated within an undergraduate programme, a free-standing Master's programme which provides broad disciplinary preparation for research or alternatively a more specialised research training programme, such as an MRes. Some students are still admitted to a research degree following successful completion of an Honours degree. There is no robust evidence to demonstrate that any of these routes is consistently associated with higher levels of completion. However, it is clear that institutions need to recognise the different forms of research preparation offered by these different routes and to develop a personalised approach to supporting and training students appropriately at the beginning of their research degree programmes.

Selection

Selection procedures for research students should be based on institutional recruitment and selection principles. Studentships should be advertised and interview processes should align to equal opportunities policies and procedures. It is the selection process that many new supervisors find particularly challenging, trying to counterbalance the academic qualifications, experience, research potential and motivations of the applicants. All Codes of Practice will require the selection process to include at least two members of academic staff experienced in making selection decisions, often with a requirement that they should be 'research-active'. This requirement applies to overseas applicants where it is now commonplace to interview using Voice over Internet Protocol (VoIP). In making decisions, it is usual to consider applicants' undergraduate work, such as final-year dissertations, and it is usually a requirement to use references to inform decisions.

Induction

Induction is increasingly seen as vital in establishing a relationship with the new student. Formal induction is meant to provide students with the information they need to enable them to begin their studies with an understanding of the academic and social environment in which they will be working (QAA, 2004). Induction events usually take place at institutional or graduate school level, at departmental and/or team level, and each has its different role to play. It is essential that supervisors take a supportive attitude to institutional induction and make clear its value. In many institutions this part is often followed by a social event and so begins the social cohesion and integration of the student. Supervisors will need to be sure that the induction needs of any international student who arrives late can be met if they miss scheduled induction activities. Institutional induction events vary greatly. In its Code of Practice, Aberystwyth University (2007) sets out information (in English or Welsh) about the registration and induction for research postgraduates which provides comprehensive information about the organisation and facilities of the university.

Supervision

> ### Interrogating practice
>
> Reflect on your own experience of being supervised for a research degree. How would you rate the experience? What aspects of that supervision would you wish to import into you own practice and what aspects would you reject?

Arrangements for supervision vary somewhat between institutions and details of supervisory arrangement are clearly set out in Codes of Practice. In the majority of cases, two designated supervisors are appointed, or a 'supervisory team' of two or more. Whatever the arrangements, there must be one designated supervisor who is clearly the first point of contact for the student. This principal, main or primary supervisor will normally be an experienced supervisor who has seen at least one student through to completion, has overall responsibility for the student and will be the line of communication with the university. The secondary supervisor or other main member of the supervisory team may not necessarily be fully experienced in supervision, will have a supporting role, may be required to stand in for the primary supervisor in his or her absence and/or provide support to the student in specific aspects of the research degree.

In all Codes there is a statement of responsibilities for the principal supervisor. This formally sets out the full range of responsibilities, such as:

- providing satisfactory advice and guidance on the conduct of the research and preparation of the thesis;
- being accountable to the relevant department, faculty or graduate school for monitoring the progress of the research;
- establishing and maintaining regular contact with the student and being accessible at appropriate times for consultation;

- having input into the student's development needs and ensuring the student has access to appropriate education and training opportunities;
- reading drafts produced by the student and providing timely, constructive and effective feedback on the student's work and overall progress within the programme;
- ensuring that the student is aware of the need to exercise probity and to conduct research according to ethical principles, and of the implications of research misconduct;
- helping the student to interact with others working in the field of research, for example by helping to identify funding;
- providing effective pastoral support and/or referring the student to other sources of support if relevant;
- maintaining necessary supervisory expertise, including the skills to perform the role satisfactorily, supported by relevant professional development activities;
- being sensitive to the diverse needs of students.

Apart from these formal requirements, there are some other practices which will help ensure that the student–supervisor relationship is built on firm foundations.

Agreeing supervisory guidelines

It is important to set out guidelines for the student–supervisor relationship, just as in other forms of teaching. This means that at the beginning, both parties should agree what the supervisor will do, what the student is responsible for, what both agree to do and what the supervisor will not do. These should be documented and signed by both sides. This sets out clarity over roles, responsibilities and expectations. Also at this time, there should be some discussion about supervisor accessibility and what the student should do if there is a problem that cannot be dealt with by the principal and/or secondary supervisor. When problems develop later in supervisory relationships, it is sometimes because these discussions have not taken place.

Frequency of supervisory meetings

At the outset, students and supervisors need to set out and agree the intervals at which they should meet for formal supervisions and dates should be recorded for the next few months at least. Many universities in their Codes specify the minimum frequency at which supervisions take place. Thus, for example, the University of York (2006: section 6d) specifies: 'Formal supervisory meetings at which substantial discussion of research progress normally takes place, should be held at least twice a term' and that: 'A meeting with the supervisor, if requested by a student, should take place within one week, if this is practicable'. The purpose of these formal meetings should be discussed with students and the difference between formal and informal meetings made clear. This type of clarity may help to prevent any confusion at a later stage.

Records of supervisory meetings

It is considered good practice for the student to write records of supervisory meetings in which topics discussed are logged, progress against milestones monitored and future objectives set. These should be dated and then e-mailed to the supervisors to sign off. This helps students to take an interest in managing their own work and seeing progress being made. It is important for the supervisor to keep such action plans as records of their own performance, should this be challenged. There is a positive correlation between establishing a routine of keeping effective records of supervision and successful outcomes of supervision.

Skills for supervision

Supervision is a professional relationship. How supervisors work with their students may vary according to custom and practice, from one discipline to another. In its key principles for research degree supervision, the University of East Anglia (UEA, 2007: 3) says of supervision that: 'It should be guided by the principles of intellectual and inter-personal integrity, fairness, respect, clarity about roles and responsibilities, student autonomy and working in the best interest of the student.' A discussion of ways of conceptualising the supervisor–student relationship is given by Taylor and Beasley (2005).

The approach to the supervision of research students is not dissimilar to that for supervision of undergraduate projects and dissertations (Chapter 11). Supervision is a front-loaded activity which requires significant input in the early stages to be effective. Towards completion there is another major commitment in supporting writing. Research supervision is about **facilitation**, nurturing and where appropriate challenging students to ensure development of their critical understanding and self-evaluation. In this way they can take responsibility for the development of their own research over the period of the degree. The process involves being able to let the students go and take chances as they move through the research.

Supervision requires high-level teaching skills that have developed from the same skill set as may be used in other settings, such as small group teaching (Chapter 6). In addition, it requires empathy. In supervision the skills set includes effective questioning, active listening and responding. Supervisors need to provide effective **feedback** on when things are going well and, importantly, if things are not going so well. The PRES data mentioned earlier indicate the importance research students attach to prompt and high-quality feedback. Owens (2008) outlines expectations of students starting their Ph.D. programmes for their own role and that of their supervisors, and how these may be used to start building the student–supervisor relationship.

Case study 1 shows an approach used by the University of Durham to acknowledge and set criteria for excellence in research degree supervision.

Case study 1: Vice-Chancellor's award for excellence in doctoral supervision

Context

Over the past two decades or so, virtually all UK universities have adopted awards for excellence in teaching and learning, but not for doctoral supervision. This is in marked contrast to universities in Australia and the USA, where such awards are common. In 2005, and with the strong encouragement and support of the then Vice-Chancellor Sir Kenneth Calman, Durham University instituted such awards. These have attracted a significant number of high-quality applications and have helped to raise the status of doctoral supervision.

The purpose of this award is to promote, recognise and reward excellence in doctoral supervision. The award will be made to members of the university's staff who can demonstrate excellence in the supervision of doctoral students, including those studying for the Ph.D., the DBA and the Ed.D.

Eligibility

Academic and research staff who have normally participated in the supervision of at least three doctoral students to successful completion and who have not previously won an award.

Nomination

Nominations are invited from heads of department, in consultation with directors of postgraduate research. Agreement should be obtained from prospective nominees to their names going forward for consideration for the award.

The university expects all of its supervisors to enable their students to:

- where appropriate, initiate and plan a research project;
- acquire the research skills to undertake it and gain adequate access to resources;
- complete it on time;
- produce a high-quality thesis;
- be successful in examination;
- disseminate the results;
- lay the basis for their future career.

It would expect that an excellent supervisor would also be able to demonstrate:

- a strong interest in, and enthusiasm for, supervising and supporting research students;

- the ability to recruit and select good candidates and establish effective working relationships with them and, where appropriate, with co-supervisors;
- the ability to offer appropriate support to students' research projects, including encouraging and supporting them to write up their work, giving useful and prompt feedback on submitted work, advising on keeping the project on track, and monitoring progress;
- a concern to support the personal, professional and career development of doctoral students;
- an ability to support students through the processes of completion of their thesis and final examination;
- an ability to critically evaluate their practice as supervisors and, where appropriate, disseminate it.

Awards

Three awards, each to the value of £1,000, will be available to successful staff to support their academic development in the field of doctoral supervision.

Procedure

For details go to: http://www.dur.ac.uk/academicstaffdevelopment/vcsawards/.

The statements of successful candidates will be published in the newsletter *Quality Enhancement in Durham*, and on the university's website as examples of good practice in doctoral supervision.

(Dr Stan Taylor, Academic Staff Development Officer, University of Durham)

SUSTAINING THE RELATIONSHIP

Integrating skills training into research degree programmes

There is now a requirement that doctoral students receive a coherent skills set as part of their training. The background to this is reviewed in Case study 2. All research students funded by the UK Research Councils (2001) and some other funding bodies must receive training which covers the research skills and techniques that are appropriate to their areas of research (A to C in the list below) and a wider set of employment-related skills or high-level **transferable skills** (D to G). This common skills set is known as the Joint Skills Statement (JSS) and is organised under the following headings:

[A] Research skills and techniques;
[B] Research environment;

[C]   Research management;
[D]   Personal effectiveness;
[E]   Communication skills;
[F]   Networking and team working;
[G]   Career management.

Under each heading is a short set of competencies that the student must be able to meet by the end of the training period. Although the JSS comes from RCUK and other funders, it is recognised that all students, both full-time and part-time, should receive this type of skills training.

> **Case study 2: The skills agenda: background information and support for supervisors**

Supervising your first postgraduate researcher can be a daunting prospect.

As well as grappling with all the internal policies and procedures, you are suddenly subject to a whole new range of external drivers, policies and jargon.

An area which may be new to you, and which you may not have experienced while doing your own Ph.D., is that of skills development for Ph.D. researchers. A slew of reports and recommendations around this issue were published in the early years of the new millennium.

Background information

In 2001 the UK Research Councils in collaboration with UK GRAD and the HE sector identified a set of competencies that postgraduate researchers should have or develop during the course of their Ph.D. degree programme (QAA, 2004). Known as the Joint Skills Statement, this is now the accepted framework for doctoral competencies.

Sir Gareth Roberts (2002) published a key report *SET for Success*. Briefly, the report recommended increasing Ph.D. stipends and the average length of a Ph.D. degree and introducing skills development, aimed at improving the attractiveness of research careers.

Crucially, this report was followed by government funding (commonly known as 'Roberts' Money'). The Research Councils issued included guidance on the allocation, use and monitoring of the additional funds for postgraduate and postdoctoral training – recommending two weeks' training in skills development.

Their joint policy was to seek to embed personal and professional skills development within doctoral degree programmes, rather than treat it as an adjunct.

In parallel to these initiatives, the QAA revised its Code of Practice for research degrees. It incorporated the principles of using training needs analyses (TNA) and personal development planning (PDP). The aim of the code was to achieve a consistently good experience for research students.

UK GRAD

One of the aims of the 'researcher development' programme is to support supervisors by providing access to information and resources, and to national and regional networks. The current UK GRAD website hosts an excellent Database of Practice where higher education institutions post examples of how they are dealing with different aspects of implementing the skills agenda.

The website is also a useful place to read about policy relating to researchers in the UK and in Europe. Downloadable resources for supervisors and postgraduate researchers are also available.

Other opportunities to share good practice are provided by the Regional Hub network. The hubs host a range of local events, and provide relevant information about national events, materials and courses.

Finally, there are a range of national events, bulletin board discussions and more which can help you keep in touch with others who are getting to grips with this issue.

(Anne Goodman, South West and Wales Hub, Cardiff University)

Student complaints

All universities have formal procedures for dealing with student complaints and these are described fully in Codes of Practice. If the complaint cannot be resolved using the institutional procedures the student may ask the Office of the Independent Adjudicator for Higher Education (OIA) to investigate the matter. Case study 3 is an illustration of a real complaint (anonymised) considered by the OIA. It illustrates the importance of proper monitoring procedures, adequate feedback mechanisms and the need for strict compliance with university Codes of Practice. In their report for 2006, it was noted that applications to the OIA rose by 11 per cent and that 39 per cent of them were from postgraduates.

Case study 3: Doctoral supervision – a complaint considered by the OIA

Student A was registered as a doctoral student for seven years. After two years he transferred from M.Phil. to Ph.D. status. After eight extensions to the deadline for his submission he withdrew voluntarily from the course and complained to the university about his supervision. He sought compensation of £250,000; the university identified defects in its procedures and offered £500. A complained to the OIA about his supervisor's failure to warn him that his work was not of the required standard; that he did not receive annual appraisals; and that he was not given appropriate support and communication by the university. The OIA found the complaint justified on the grounds that there should have been earlier warnings about the failure to progress and the failure to submit written work. Although A did not complain about his supervision during the seven years, nor did he complete a single chapter of his thesis, firmer control should have been exercised by his supervisor, who should not have repeatedly supported requests for extensions. The student also bore responsibility and should have taken steps to ensure that his difficulties were being addressed. The OIA recommended that the university offer £1,000 compensation, improve its appraisal and upgrade procedures, and show how it would monitor those procedures to ensure compliance in the future.

(Office of the Independent Adjudicator for Higher Education, UK, with permission)

Building a culture of completion

The importance of timely and successful completion of postgraduate research programmes is increasingly clear, both to students and to higher education institutions. Students recognise that their employment prospects are considerably enhanced if they have demonstrated their intellectual and professional abilities by gaining their postgraduate research qualification within the expected timeframe. They also recognise that funding opportunities to continue research beyond three years are scarce and insecure. In 2005, the **HEFCE** published for the first time comparative qualification rates for research degrees: these showed that 57 per cent of full-time students who started Ph.D. programmes in 1996–7 completed within five years, rising to 72 per cent after seven years and 76 per cent after ten years of beginning their research in English higher education institutions. In doing this, HEFCE referred explicitly to the need for all research degree programmes it supports to meet minimum standards as set out in the QAA Code of Practice for postgraduate research programmes. HEFCE did not identify minimum standards specifically in relation to qualification rates. Research Councils and other institutions funding postgraduate research students specify very clear minimum standards and they expect a four-year completion rate of at least 70 per cent. Completion rates below this level jeopardise chances of securing continuing funding from the Research Councils and other bodies. For further information on completion, see HEFCE (2007).

Supporting students to timely completion is key to the supervisory relationship. It involves ensuring that the detailed design of their research project is compatible with the time-scale specified within the degree programme; that all aspects of research and writing are planned in detail; and that all milestones towards completion are met. Research degrees take place over a number of years, and students are unlikely to have had prior experience of planning a project over this length of time. They may need some time to adjust to this and to realise the importance of using all the time they have intensely and productively. The experience of a supervisory team in identifying all aspects of the work that requires to be done in planning, acquiring relevant research and generic skills, undertaking research, developing relevant professional skills through presenting research nationally and internationally, publishing selected outputs, exploring potential for knowledge transfer or commercialisation of research, disciplinary networking or teaching, and then successfully writing a dissertation is fundamental to any student's success.

More nebulous than this, however, is the importance of creating within any given research environment a 'culture of completion'. This means creating an unambiguous expectation of timely completion, and giving all students the confidence that they will be supported by all those involved in their supervision to achieve this. A culture of completion requires explicit monitoring and reporting of the progress being made by all students; regular sharing of research outputs through informal or formal seminars; clear acknowledgement of all milestones met, and collective celebration of successful completions. It also means resisting the temptation to romanticise non-completion. Many supervisors themselves may have taken a long time to complete their dissertations and there can be a tendency retrospectively to associate this with the ambition, originality and importance of their research. Students can pick up an unspoken message that the more brilliant they are the less likely they are to complete on time. There is no evidence for such a belief, but if it is communicated to students it can substantially undermine their chances of success.

The culture of completion described above is much easier to achieve within a reasonably large student cohort, which allows for more effective sharing of research outputs and progress, more opportunities for informal support, and more opportunities for networking. Where postgraduate research is being undertaken within a small or very specialist unit, it is advisable for a supervisor to identify possible networking opportunities beyond the level of academic department, or even beyond the institution. It is also advisable for supervisors to share as much information as possible with students about research completion rates within the discipline in order to benchmark individual students' progress.

Monitoring

All universities have robust procedures for reviewing research student progress. The minimum requirements are for a major review at least once each year and this may be organised at departmental, faculty or graduate school level. The review process will require the student to prepare a written submission. Often it will involve disciplinary specialists outside the formal supervisory arrangements and the student may make a presentation or be given an oral examination. Where students register for the M.Phil. degree and wish to be transferred to the Ph.D., this will normally occur during the first 12 to 18 months of registration.

MOVING TOWARDS THE END OF THE RELATIONSHIP

Submission and preparation for the viva

Examination of a research degree involves scrutiny of the submitted dissertation by experts in the field who also conduct a viva voce examination of the candidate. The purpose of this is to confirm the authorship of the dissertation and also to provide an opportunity for examiners to explore issues that may not have been fully or satisfactorily discussed in the dissertation. This second aspect can be particularly stressful for students as it is very likely that they have not experienced such a prolonged and intense scrutiny of their ideas and arguments before. Supervisors have a key role to play in preparing students for this examination by providing opportunities for them to present and defend their ideas. Many institutions now appoint independent chairs for viva examinations to ensure that students are treated fairly and that all questions posed are relevant and appropriate. The University of Birmingham has been doing this for a number of years. They reassure students that: 'the chair is not an examiner. He or she ensures that the viva is run properly and fairly, taking notes and helping where necessary to clarify misunderstandings' (University of Birmingham, 2006). For further information on the examination of doctoral degrees, see Tinkler and Jackson (2004).

Career development

For many supervisors, a measure of success of the doctoral training will be that the student is capable of applying independently for grant funding. However, it has to be recognised that although the 'education sector' is the largest employer of Ph.D.s immediately after graduation, over 50 per cent of Ph.D. graduates take employment outside the HE sector (Metcalfe and Gray, 2005). Accordingly, Codes of Practice quite often say something about supervisors supporting students in finding a job. Interestingly, over ten years ago, PPARC (1996) in its good practice guide on supervision stated that supervisors should 'advise and help students secure a job at the end of it all, remembering that many will move away from academia'. Finally, the supervisory relationship frequently continues after the viva, shifting and becoming a professional relationship between peers.

OVERVIEW

This chapter has presented an overview of the changing world of supervision of research degrees. It has aimed to highlight points in the research student life cycle that require careful attention by the supervisor. It has viewed the student–supervisor relationship as key to success of the Ph.D. A particular feature of this chapter is the attention given to creating a culture of completion which has much relevance not just for new supervisors but for those staff responsible for managing research degrees at departmental or school level.

REFERENCES

Aberystwyth University (2007) Code of Practice for research degrees – registration and induction. Available online at <http://www.aber.ac.uk/postgrads/en/Code per cent20Research per cent20PG per cent20E.pdf> (accessed 5 February 2008).

Delamont, S, Atkinson, P and Parry, O (1997) *Supervising the PhD*, Buckingham: SRHE and the Open University Press.

HEFCE (2007) Research degree qualification rates. Available online at http://www. hefce.ac.uk/pubs/hefce/2007/07_29/ (accessed 5 February 2008).

HESA. View statistics online, Table 14 HE qualifications obtained in the UK. <http:// www.hesa.ac.uk/index.php/component/option.com_datatables/task,show_ file/defs,1/Itemid,121/catdex,3/disp,disab0506.htm/dld,disab0506.xls/yrStr,2005+to+2 006/dfile,studefs0506.htm/area,disab/mx,0/> (accessed 5 February 2008).

Imperial College London, Graduate Schools. <http://www3.imperial.ac.uk/graduate schools> (accessed 5 February 2008)

James, R and Baldwin, G (2006) *Eleven Practices of Effective Postgraduate Supervisors*, Centre for the Study of Higher Education and The School of Graduate Studies, Australia: The University of Melbourne. Available online at <http://www.sche.unimelb.edu.au/ pdfs/11practices.pdf> (accessed 5 February 2008).

Metcalfe, J and Gray, A (2005) *Employability and Doctoral Research Postgraduates*, Learning and Employability Series Two, York: The Higher Education Academy. Available online at <http://www.heacademy.ac.uk/assets/York/documents/ourwork/tla/employability/i d431_employability_and_doctoral_research_graduates_593.pdf> (accessed 5 February 2008).

Office of the Independent Adjudicator for Higher Education. <http://www.oihe.org.uk> (accessed 5 February 2008).

Owens, C (2008) New PhD students explore the student–supervisor relationship. Available online at <http://www.esd.qmul.ac.uk/acprac/research/Owens_Case_Study.pdf> (accessed 5 February 2008).

Park, C, Hanbury, A and Harvey, L (2007) *Postgraduate Research Experience Survey – Final Report*, York: The Higher Education Academy. Available online at <http://www.heacademy.ac.uk/assets/York/documents/ourwork/research/surveys/pres/PRES.pdf> (accessed 5 February 2008).

Particle Physics and Astronomy Research Council (1996) *An Approach to Good Supervisory Practice for Supervisors and Research Students*, Swindon: PPARC.

Quality Assurance Agency for Higher Education (2004) *Code of Practice for the Assurance of Academic Quality and Standards in Higher Education: Postgraduate Research Programmes*, Gloucester: QAA. Available online at <http://www.qaa.ac.uk/academicinfrastructure/codeOfPractice/section1/postgrad2004.pdf)> (accessed 5 February 2008).

Roberts, Sir Gareth (2002) *SET for Success*, HM Treasury. Available online at http://www.hm-treasury.gov.uk/documents/enterprise_and_productivity/research_and_enterprise/ent_res_roberts.cfm (accessed 5 February 2008).

Taylor, S and Beasley, N (2005) *A Handbook for Doctoral Supervisors*, Abingdon: Routledge.

Tinkler, P and Jackson, C (2004) *The Doctoral Examination Process*, Maidenhead: SRHE and the Open University Press.

UK GRAD programme. UK PhD degrees in context. Available online at <http://www.grad.ac.uk/cms/ShowPage/Home_page/Resources/What_Do_PhDs_Do__publications/What_Do_PhDs_Do_/UK_PhD_degrees_in_context/p!ecdXXji> (accessed 5 February 2008).

UK Research Councils (2001) *Joint Skills Statement of Training Requirements*. Available online at <http://www.grad.ac.uk/cms/ShowPage/Home_page/Policy/National_policy/Research_Councils_training_requirements/p!eaLXeFl#Joint per cent20Statement per cent20of per cent20Skills per cent20Training per cent20Requirements per cent20of per cent20Research per cent20Postgraduates per cent20(2001)> (accessed 5 February 2008).

University of Birmingham (2006) *School of Computer Science, Research Student Handbook*. Available online at <http://www.cs.bham.ac.uk/internal/research_students/submitting_a_thesis.php> (accessed 5 February 2008).

University of East Anglia (2005) *2005–2006 Calendar, Regulations PhD*, Norwich: UEA.

University of East Anglia (2007) *Research Degrees Code of Practice*, Norwich: UEA. Available online at <http://www1.uea.ac.uk/cm/home/services/units/acad/ltqo/pgresearch/copandregs> (accessed 5 February 2008).

University of London (2007) *Regulations for the Degrees of MPhil and PhD*, London: Senate House. Available online at <http://www.london.ac.uk/fileadmin/documents/students/-postgraduate/phd_regs_200708.pdf> (accessed 5 February 2008).

University of York (2006) *Code of Practice on Research Degree Programmes*. Available online at <http://www.york.ac.uk/admin/gso/exams/researchcode.htm#Supervision> (accessed 5 February 2008).

FURTHER READING

Finn, J (2005) *Getting a PhD: An Action Plan to Help Manage Your Research, Supervisor and Your Project*, Abingdon: Routledge. Useful to students and their supervisors, taking a project management approach.

James, R and Baldwin, G (2006) See above. A detailed practical guide on supervision from Melbourne.

Taylor, S and Beasley, N (2005) See above. A comprehensive and practical handbook outlining all aspects of supervision and well researched.

Teaching quality, standards and enhancement

Judy McKimm

INTRODUCTION

Managing and ensuring educational quality is one of the key responsibilities of educational institutions and of those who work in them. Demands from external agencies define part of what is considered to be good practice, and these demands combine with discipline-based practices and institutional culture and requirements to set the context for lecturers.

This chapter aims to offer an overview of current thinking about quality and standards from a UK perspective, and demystify some of the terminology. The intention is to provide a context within which lecturers can develop their understanding of quality issues in higher education, and consider their roles and obligations in relation to maintaining and enhancing quality and **standards**.

Interrogating practice

What is your role in maintaining and enhancing educational quality in your institution?

DEFINITIONS AND TERMINOLOGY

Definitions and usage of terminology about the concepts of academic 'standards' and 'quality' vary depending on the aims and purposes of the educational provision or country and historical context. These concepts underpin the thinking behind the design, delivery, evaluation and review of educational provision. In the UK, the term 'academic standards' has been described as 'the level of achievement that a student has to reach to gain an academic award' (QAA, 2007).

'Quality' is a broader term used with variable meanings, referring, for example, to individual student performance, the outputs of an educational programme, the student learning experience or the teaching provided. The **Quality Assurance Agency** (QAA), which has responsibility for assuring the quality of higher education in the UK, defines 'academic quality' as 'describing how well the learning opportunities available to students help them to achieve their award' (QAA, 2007). 'Learning opportunities' include the provision of teaching, study support, assessment and other aspects and activities that support the learning process.

The concept of quality can be subdivided into several categories or types, as Harvey *et al.* (1992) demonstrate, including:

- *Quality as excellence* is the traditional (often implicit) academic view which aims to demonstrate high academic standards.
- *Quality as 'zero errors'* is most relevant in mass industry where detailed product specifications can be established and standardised measurements of uniform products can show conformity to them. In HE this may apply to learning materials.
- *Quality as 'fitness for purpose'* focuses on 'customers' (or stakeholders') needs' (e.g. students, employers, the academic community, government as representative of society at large). The quality literature highlights that operational definitions of quality must be specific and relate to a specific purpose. There is no 'general quality'.
- *Quality as enhancement* emphasises continuous improvement, centres on the idea that achieving quality is essential to HE and stresses the responsibility of HE to make the best use of institutional autonomy and teachers' academic freedom. All Western European HE evaluation procedures focus more on quality as enhancement than as standards and may be seen as a sophisticated version of the 'fitness for purpose' concept.
- *Quality as transformation* applies to students' behaviour and goals being changed as a result of their studies or to socio-political transformation achieved through HE. The latter is more difficult to measure.
- *Quality as threshold* defines minimum standards, usually as broad definitions of desired knowledge, skills and attitudes of graduates (e.g. subject benchmarking; see below). HEIs are usually expected to surpass these minimum standards.

Quality assurance (QA) refers to the policies, processes and actions through which quality is maintained and developed. Accountability and enhancement are important motives for quality assurance. Accountability in this context refers to assuring students, society and government that quality is well managed, and is often the primary focus of external review. QA is not new in higher education; for example, the involvement of external examiners in assessment processes, and the peer review system for evaluating research publications, are well established QA processes. **Evaluation** is a key part of quality assurance; see Chapter 14. **Quality enhancement** refers to the improvement of quality (e.g. through dissemination of good practice or use of a continuous improvement cycle).

Accreditation grants recognition that provision meets certain standards, and may in some instances confer a licence to operate. The status may have consequences for the institution itself and/or its students (e.g. eligibility for grants) and/or its graduates (e.g. making them qualified for certain employment).

Performance indicators (PIs) are a numerical measure of outputs of a system or institution in terms of the organisation's goals (e.g. increasing employability of graduates, minimising drop-out) or educational processes (e.g. maximising student satisfaction, minimising cancelled lectures). In developing PIs, there needs to be a balance between measurability (reliability), which is often the prime consideration in developing indicators, and relevance (validity). Indicators are signals that highlight strengths, trends and weaknesses, not quality judgements in themselves.

BACKGROUND AND CONTEXT

Higher education in the UK has undergone rapid change over the past two decades. Globalisation, widening participation, the impact of new technology and the falling unit of resource have each contributed to concern about maintaining and enhancing educational quality. There is increased emphasis on accountability for public money, on demonstrating quality, and on increasing transparency through specification of outcomes.

The UK National Committee of Inquiry into Higher Education **(NCIHE)** published its findings and recommendations in the Dearing Report (1997). The wide-ranging recommendations established the framework for a 'quality agenda' focusing on enhancement; with amendments, this framework is still in use ten years later, including the QAA.

The QAA was formed in 1997 to provide an integrated quality assurance framework and service for UK higher education. It is an independent body funded through contracts with the main UK higher education funding bodies and by subscriptions from UK universities and colleges of higher education. The QAA has a responsibility to:

> safeguard the public interest in sound standards of higher education qualifications, and to encourage continuous improvement in the management of the quality of higher education . . . by reviewing standards and quality and providing reference points that help to define clear and explicit standards.
>
> (QAA, 2007)

The **Bologna** Declaration (1999) emphasised the importance of a common framework for European higher education qualifications. In the UK this has been addressed by a number of initiatives aiming to bring comparability between programmes in terms of standards, levels and credits. In the UK the focus is on the quality of the outcome rather than time spent.

The NCIHE foreshadowed the creation of the **Higher Education Academy** (HEA) that was formed in May 2004 by the merger of several previous organisations. The HEA supports HEIs in educational activities and in enhancing the student experience;

supporting and informing the professional development and recognition of staff in teaching and learning in higher education against **national professional standards**, funding educational research and development projects. The Academy also supports enhancement initiatives such as the National Teaching Fellowship Scheme (NTFS), the Scottish Quality Enhancement Framework and the CETLs (**Centres for Excellence in Teaching and Learning**).

THE CONTEMPORARY QUALITY AGENDA

The current quality agenda aims to reduce external scrutiny and bureaucracy and to increase institutional autonomy and self-regulation, seeking to emphasise enhancement rather than inspection. QA methods coordinated by the QAA have been streamlined based on lessons learned from earlier subject reviews and quality audit. The current quality assurance arrangements are locked into externally determined and audited standards and norms, but with a lighter 'inspectorial' touch. The quality agenda is like a 'jigsaw' comprising interdependent and interlocking processes that emphasise increasing transparency, accountability and specification.

The main elements of the external quality framework in England and Northern Ireland are a combination of institutional **audit** (at the level of the whole organisation) and investigation at discipline level. **External examiners** also provide impartial advice on performance in relation to specific programmes, offering a comparative analysis against similar programmes, evaluating standards and considering the soundness and fairness of assessment procedures and their execution.

The external quality framework for teaching and learning includes 'Major Review' of NHS-funded healthcare programmes, involving the QAA and relevant health professions' councils. Other programmes of study (such as law, engineering, medicine or accountancy) lead to professional or vocational qualifications and are subject to accreditation by the relevant professional or statutory body. Further education colleges offering higher education programmes also undergo review. In Scotland, Enhancement-Led Institutional Review (ELIR) is central to the enhancement-led approach to managing standards and quality which focuses on the student learning experience. In Wales, a process of institutional review is carried out across all institutions offering higher education provision and is part of a wider QA framework.

The Research Assessment Exercise (RAE) is a separate activity evaluating the quality of research in universities and colleges.

Internal quality processes

Higher education institutions are responsible for the standards and quality of their provision and each has its own internal procedures for assuring and enhancing the quality of its programmes. Internal procedures include assessment of students, processes for the design and approval of new programmes and regular monitoring and periodic review of continuing programmes. Regular monitoring considers how well programmes and students are achieving the stated aims and learning outcomes, taking into account external examiners' reports, student feedback, assessment results and feedback from employers. Periodic programme review (typically five-yearly) may involve external reviewers and consider the currency and validity of programmes or services as well as achievement against stated aims and outcomes.

Case study 1: Staff development through quality assurance at the University of Bedfordshire

One of the explicit aims of academic QA and enhancement at the university is to 'foster subject, pedagogical and staff development'. This happens in three key ways.

- Template documentation for programme validation and review aligns with external and internal QA mechanisms. Programme specification templates map against QAA subject benchmark statements, requiring clear identification of QAA defined skills. At module level, templates ensure mapping of the external programme specification to internal module specification and include a framework that aligns module outcomes with learning, teaching and assessment methods.
- By adopting a 'developmental' approach to programme development and validation, academic, administrative, learning resource and learning technology staff work together in developing programmes, supporting documentation and engaging in peer review. This fosters an interdisciplinary dialogue and exchange of ideas as well as a 'team approach' to design and delivery, aligned with the university's educational strategy.
- A 'staged' approach to programme accreditation and review includes 'Faculty-level validation' prior to university validation. This provides an opportunity to review the quality of documentation, identify resource issues and 'rehearse' the validation process with colleagues. This in turn enables staff to develop understanding and skills in QA processes, better preparing them to take part in external and institutional QA events.

(Clare Morris, Associate Dean (Curriculum), Bedfordshire and Hertfordshire Postgraduate Medical School, University of Bedfordshire)

Internal quality assurance procedures and development activities to enhance educational quality include the evaluation of individual staff members through systems such as student feedback questionnaires, peer review systems, mentoring for new staff or regular appraisals.

Institutional audit

QAA quality assurance processes include:

- submission of a self-evaluation document (SED) or reflective analysis (Scotland only) by the institution or programme which describes and analyses internal monitoring and review procedures;
- scrutiny of the information published by the institution about its provision;
- visit(s) to the institution, involving discussions with senior managers, staff and students;
- peer review involving external scrutiny by auditors and reviewers (academics, industry and professional body representatives);
- a published report on the review activities.

Up-to-date information on QAA arrangements, including guidance documents and review reports, may be found on the QAA website (see Further reading).

One institutional audit visit is usually carried out to each HEI by an external review team every six years. The audit is based around production of a SED followed by a briefing visit and a longer audit visit. Audits consider examples of internal QA processes at programme level and across the institution, selecting the particular focus of attention (which may be at subject level) depending on the findings and concerns of the audit team. The main aim of the audit is to verify that internal QA processes are robust enough to ensure and enhance educational quality across all the provision that the institution manages. Review by professional statutory bodies (PSBs) continues alongside institutional audit. Following the visit a public report is published summarising the main findings and recommendations, and stating the level of confidence the audit team has in the provision. If there are serious weaknesses, follow-up visits and scrutiny are arranged. For institutions that demonstrate sound QA and enhancement mechanisms, audit will have a 'lighter touch' in future.

Audit and review place considerable demands on lecturers and other staff. Audit teams require details of internal assurance processes, student evaluations, student satisfaction surveys, employers' evaluations and input to programmes, examiners' reports (internal and external), intake and graduate data and detailed information concerning programme content and assessment. Provision and take-up of staff development and training are considered (particularly around teaching and learning) including numbers attaining the **UK professional standards** for teaching or belonging to professional organisations.

Institutions are required to publish a **Learning and Teaching Strategy.** In addition to consideration of the student learning experience and internal monitoring and review procedures, the QAA review teams consider how institutions demonstrate adherence to the Learning and Teaching Strategy and effectively use any associated Teaching Quality Enhancement Funds (TQEF). Teams will also consider the development, use and publication of **programme specifications** and **progress files** and how well institutions and programme teams have used external reference points, including:

- the **Code of Practice** for the assurance of academic quality and standards in higher education;
- the **Frameworks for Higher Education Qualifications**;
- **subject benchmark** statements.

Teaching Quality Enhancement Funds (TQEF)

Since 2000, HEFCE has provided enhancement funds (TQEF) for learning and teaching strategies; supporting professional standards; student and staff volunteering; and new funding to support teaching informed by research. The main strategic purpose of this funding is to embed and sustain learning and teaching strategies and activities, and to encourage future institutional investment in continuous improvement. At national level, TQEF has supported the CETL and National Teaching Fellowship Scheme (NTFS) programmes.

Programme specifications

Programme specifications were introduced in 1999 to make the outcomes of learning more explicit and to relate programmes and awards to the qualifications frameworks.

Teaching teams are required to produce programme specifications for every programme that an HEI runs, often using a specified template. The specifications require the essential elements of a programme to be synthesised into a brief set of statements, however complex. The elements include the intended **learning outcomes** of a programme (specific, measurable intentions expressed as what learners will be able to do in terms of knowledge, understanding, skills and other attributes); teaching and learning methods; assessment; career opportunities and relationship of the programme to the qualifications framework. Programme specifications also provide a basis for the university (through quality assurance committees and boards), students, employers and external reviewers to assure quality at programme level.

Progress files

The student progress file helps students and employers understand the outcomes of learning in higher education. It comprises three interlinked elements:

1 transcript – a formal record of learning and achievement provided by the institution;
2 personal and development planning (PDP) – a process owned and produced by the student in liaison with staff;
3 individual students' personal records of achievements, progress reviews and plans.

Progress files help students to monitor, build and reflect on their development and to produce personal statements such as CVs. Institutions must provide the opportunity for students to undertake PDP, and staff need to ensure that adequate, appropriate and timely assessment information is provided for the transcript. The involvement and encouragement that teachers or other staff provide varies between institutions and disciplines. PDP may be used as a means of structuring tutorials or meetings with students, and different types of paper-based or electronic progress files may be developed, ranging from a reflective 'journal' to a more descriptive record of development and skill acquisition. Issues of confidentiality and responsibility need to be addressed.

Interrogating practice

How useful do students find progress files/PDP as a tool for developing a reflective approach to study and development? How do/might you as a teacher help students to use PDP for personal and professional development?

Code of Practice for the assurance of academic quality and standards in higher education

The Code of Practice sets out precepts or principles that institutions should satisfy relating to the management of academic standards and quality with guidance as to how they might meet the precepts. The Code covers ten areas of provision:

1 postgraduate research programmes
2 collaborative provision
3 students with disabilities
4 external examining
5 academic appeals and student complaints
6 assessment of students
7 programme approval, monitoring and review
8 career education, information and guidance
9 placement learning
10 student recruitment and admissions.

Frameworks for Higher Education Qualifications

There is a single qualifications framework for England, Wales and Northern Ireland and a separate one for Scotland. The frameworks aim to simplify the range of awards, informing employers, students and other stakeholders about the meaning and level of qualifications and the achievements and attributes that may be expected of holders of qualifications, and aim to provide assurance that qualifications from different institutions and for different subjects represent similar levels of achievement.

The higher education qualifications awarded by universities and colleges in England, Wales and Northern Ireland are at five levels: the Certificate, Intermediate, Honours, Masters and Doctoral levels. Generic 'descriptors' indicate the expected outcomes at each level and provide a reference point for course development and review, whatever the subject. Lecturers and institutions need to ensure that their programmes match the appropriate level (see also Chapter 4).

Subject benchmark statements

Produced by senior academics in consultation with the sector, subject benchmark statements are statements about the 'threshold quality' or 'minimum standards' of graduates' achievements, attributes and capabilities relating to the award of qualifications at a given level in each subject.

The statements are used alongside qualifications frameworks so that for any programme there is compatibility between the intended learning outcomes and the relevant programme specification. The benchmark statements are regularly reviewed to reflect developments in the subject and the experiences of institutions and others of working with them.

Lecturers need to be aware of the benchmark statements for their own subjects, particularly if they are involved in curriculum design or the production of programme specifications. Statements are one reference point for designing new programmes or when reviewing the content of existing curricula. The benchmark statements are also used by external bodies as reference points for audit and review.

Student satisfaction surveys

Higher education institutions are charged with providing timely, accurate and relevant public information but they must also demonstrate engagement with and consideration of the student, employer and other stakeholders' 'voice' (Cooke, 2002). The **National Student Survey**, which began in 2005, systematically gathers and reviews student feedback on programmes and institutions to improve the quality of the student learning experience (see also Chapters 9 and 10 for further consideration of the impact of the surveys).

Lecturers (and administrators) need to be aware of national, institutional and departmental requirements for the collection of data from students and employers, to respond to the comments received, and to ensure that information is made available for public consumption.

Interrogating practice

How are the processes of institutional audit and academic review impacting on your work?

ENHANCING AND MANAGING QUALITY: THE ROLE OF THE LECTURER

It is often hard for individual academics to make connections between their fundamental concern to do a good job for their own and their students' satisfaction, and the mechanisms and requirements associated with 'academic quality'. Educational quality is everyone's responsibility.

At institutional level, arrangements must be set in place for the formal management of quality and standards in accordance with the national agenda described above. External reviews by the QAA and PSBs (e.g. in medicine or engineering) can provide a framework for internal quality management and a focus and milestone towards which many institutions work.

All institutions have a formal committee structure, part of whose function it is to manage and monitor quality, including external examining. This is supported by an administrative function (often in Registry) to collect and collate data relating to academic quality (e.g. student feedback questionnaires, annual course reviews, external examiner reports, admissions or examination statistics). Structures and processes vary between institutions, but they should enable issues concerning educational quality to be identified and addressed in a timely and appropriate way. One of the senior management team(e.g. a pro-vice-chancellor) often has a remit for ensuring educational quality and maintaining academic standards. Clear mechanisms for the approval of new programmes, a regular system of programme reviews and a means of enabling feedback (from students, staff, employers and external reviewers) to be considered should be in place.

Additional formal mechanisms usually operate at faculty and departmental level in order to enable the consideration of more detailed issues and to quickly address concerns. Committees (such as teaching and learning committees) include representatives from programmes. They act to promulgate, interpret and implement organisational strategy, policies and procedures; to develop and implement procedures for managing the monitoring and review of faculty/departmental programmes and procedures; and to respond to demands from review, accreditation or inspection bodies. Staff–student liaison committees are another example of committees operating at programme level.

Interrogating practice

Do you know how the systems of feedback and quality management (including committee structures, course review, external examining and feedback loops) work in your department and institution?

It is at programme level that the individual teacher will be mainly involved in ensuring the quality of provision. All those who teach need to understand the purposes and context of the programmes on offer, and to be aware of the elements that comprise a 'quality' learning experience for students. They will also need to be familiar with and understand the use of programme specifications, levels, benchmarking and internal audit requirements. Teachers will be required to participate in formal monitoring and review of activities relating to learning and the learning environment. These include procedures such as ensuring that evaluation feedback and student assessment results are collected and analysed or that course materials are distributed in a timely fashion. Delivering a good 'student learning experience' requires a high level of competence in and understanding of teaching and learning in higher education and the development of reflective practice and peer review of teaching (see Part 3).

Interrogating practice

Has your view of your role in maintaining and enhancing educational quality changed after reading this chapter? How?

CONCLUSION AND OVERVIEW

Assuring and enhancing educational quality and academic standards can be seen as complex and multifaceted activities, geared towards ensuring that UK higher education and graduates compete successfully in a global market. But at the centre of these wide-ranging activities are the individual learner and lecturer and what happens in their classroom and programmes. It is often hard to maintain a balance between 'quality as inspection' and 'quality as enhancement' and between 'requirements' and what makes good sense in terms of effective teaching practices.

Higher education in the UK is largely funded by public money, and students as fee payers have a set of often ill-defined expectations relating to their programme of learning. The current national quality agendas firmly set out to define the outcomes of learning programmes and to make higher education more transparent and accountable.

Awareness of the concepts, terminology and expectations of national agencies concerned with quality, coupled with increasing competence and understanding of teaching and learning processes, can help the individual teacher and course team member to feel more engaged with and contribute more effectively towards the development and enhancement of a quality culture in higher education.

REFERENCES

Bologna Declaration (1999) and further information at: <ec.europa.eu/education/policies/educ/bologna/bologna_en.html> (accessed July 2007).

Cooke, R (2002) *Information on Quality and Standards in Higher Education* (The Cooke Report, 02/15), Northhaven: HEFCE.

Harvey, L, Burrows, A and Green, D (1992) *Criteria of Quality: Summary Report of the QHE Project*, Perry Barr, Birmingham: University of Central Birmingham.

National Committee of Inquiry into Higher Education (1997) (Dearing Report) *Higher Education in the Learning Society*, London: NCIHE, HMSO.

QAA (2007) <www.qaa.ac.uk/aboutus/qaaintro/intro.asp> (accessed 4 May 2007).

Quality Assurance Agency (QAA) *A Guide to Quality Assurance in UK Higher Education.* Available online at <www.qaa.ac.uk/aboutus/heGuide/guide.asp> (accessed 29 March 2007).

Quality Assurance Agency (QAA) *Policy on Programme Specification.* Available online at http://www.qaa.ac.uk/crntwork, <www.qaa.ac.uk/aboutus/qaaintro/intro.asp> (accessed 4 May 2007).

FURTHER READING

The Higher Education Funding Council for England's website contains publications relating to academic quality and standards: <www.hefce.ac.uk>.

The Scottish Funding Council's website includes details of review and quality assurance procedures: <www.sfc.ac.uk>.

The Higher Education Funding Council for Wales has responsibility for assuring the quality of provision in Welsh colleges and universities: <www.hefcw.ac.uk>.

In Northern Ireland, responsibilities for assuring educational quality are distributed between the Department for Employment and Learning in Northern Ireland at <www.delni.gov.uk/index/further-and-higher-education/higher-education.htm> and the Northern Ireland Higher Education Council at <www.delni.gov.uk/index/further-and-higher-education/higher-education/nihec.htm>.

The Quality Assurance Agency (QAA) <www.qaa.ac.uk>. Includes information on codes of practice; national qualifications frameworks; latest information on educational review and institutional audit (including handbooks); programme specifications; progress files and subject benchmark statements.

The Higher Education Academy also provides information about educational quality at <www.heacademy.ac.uk>.

<table>
<tr><td>14</td></tr>
</table>

14 Evaluating courses and teaching

Dai Hounsell

> Evaluation is a way of understanding the effects of our teaching on students' learning. It implies collecting information about our work, interpreting the information and making judgements about which actions we should take to improve practice. . . . Evaluation is an analytical process that is intrinsic to good teaching.
>
> (Ramsden, 1992: 209)

INTRODUCTION

It is almost 40 years since the publication of *The Assessment of University Teaching* (Falk and Dow, 1971), the first book of its kind to appear in Britain. Initially, the very idea that teaching in higher education might be evaluated proved highly controversial. Some academics considered it an affront to their academic autonomy, while others viewed it as needless kowtowing to student opinion. Nowadays, evaluation raises very few eyebrows. It is widely seen not only as a necessary step towards accountability, but also as an integral part of good professional practice and the systematic development of teaching expertise. From this contemporary standpoint, excellence in teaching and learning is not simply the product of experience. It depends on the regular monitoring of teaching performance to pinpoint achievements, build on strengths, and identify areas where there is scope for improvement.

Alongside acceptance of the indispensability of evaluation have come sharper differentiation of purposes and, accompanying that shift, greater methodological sophistication. For many years, approaches to evaluation were strongly influenced by practices in the USA, where standardised student ratings questionnaires had been developed chiefly for **summative** purposes: to compare the teaching performance of different individuals in making decisions about tenure and promotion (D'Andrea and Gosling, 2005). But in universities in the UK and Australasia, evaluation purposes have predominantly been **formative** and developmental (i.e. to enhance quality), and the focus is typically on courses and course teams as well as individual lecturers – on the script as well as the actors, to paraphrase Biggs (2001). What has therefore been called for are more broadly based approaches that could be tailored to differences in subject areas, course structures and teaching-learning and assessment methods, and these began to appear from the late 1980s onwards (e.g. Gibbs *et al.*, 1988; Hounsell *et al.*, 1997; Day *et al.*, 1998). It is these broader approaches to evaluation which are explored in this chapter.

Interrogating practice

What recommendations or guidelines do you have in your institution or department on collection and analysis of feedback from students?

MOTIVES AND CONTEXTS

There are many motives for evaluating the impact and effectiveness of courses and teaching. New lecturers are usually keen to find out whether they are 'doing OK', what their strengths and weaknesses are as novice teachers, and how their teaching compares with that of other colleagues. Module coordinators need to find out how smoothly their course units – whether new or well established – are running, or that, for instance, a fresh intake of students is settling in reasonably well. And those staff who oversee a degree programme or suite of programmes may want to check how well the various component units hang together, and whether there are sufficient opportunities for choice and progression. But the drivers of feedback are extrinsic as well as intrinsic. With the gradual professionalisation of university teaching have come expectations that new and experienced lecturers will formally document the quality of their teaching – the former as part of the assessment requirements of accredited learning and teaching programmes, the latter to support bids for promotion or awards for excellent teaching (Hounsell, 1996). At the same time, the advent of **quality assurance** has brought with it procedures within institutions for the regular monitoring and review of modules and programmes, and sector-wide guiding principles and precepts (see e.g. QAA, 2006a, 2006b). And following the recommendations of the Cooke Report (HEFCE, 2002), the inception of the National Student Survey (NSS) has made data freely and publicly available on graduates' satisfaction with their degree programmes, by subject area and by university (HEFCE, 2007; Richardson, 2007). As has reportedly occurred in Australia following a similar initiative, the nationally administered *Course Experience Questionnaire* (see e.g. Wilson *et al.*, 1997; McInnis *et al.*, 2001), we can expect British universities to respond in two ways: by ensuring that questions asked in the NSS questionnaire are echoed in in-house surveys; and by more strategic support to enhance teaching quality in departments or faculties where NSS ratings have been lower than expected.

FOCUS AND TIMING

The kinds of evaluative feedback which are sought will depend on both motives and focus. Thus feedback which is collected for extrinsic purposes usually has to fulfil a set of formal requirements, at least in part, whereas individuals or course teams collecting feedback for their own purposes usually have much greater scope over what kinds of feedback they collect and in what form. In either case careful consideration has to be given to what would be the most appropriate focus for feedback in any given instance. If, for example, the intention is to capture as full and rounded a picture as possible of teaching in its various guises, then the equivalent of a wide-angle lens will be needed. This can encompass questions of course design and structure, teaching-learning strategies, academic guidance and support, and approaches to assessment, together with interrelationships between these. But there may also be occasions when the overriding concern is with a specific aspect of teaching such as an e-learning activity or a new approach to giving students feedback on their assignments, and where only a close-up will capture the kind of fine-grained information being sought.

These considerations will be influential in determining not only how and from whom feedback is to be sought (as will be apparent below) but also *when* it is to be elicited – a dimension of evaluation that is often overlooked. There is the widespread but questionable practice, for example, of waiting until the end of a course before canvassing student opinion, usually on the grounds that the students need to have experienced the whole course before they can effectively comment on it. But one consequence is that students often find it difficult to recall with much precision a series of practical classes, say, or a coursework assignment that took place several months previously. A second consequence is that none of the issues or concerns that students raise will be addressed in time for them to derive any benefit – a situation which is not conducive to good teaching and likely to undermine students' interest in providing worthwhile feedback. No less seriously, especially in universities where exams continue to carry a substantial weighting in overall assessment, students' perceptions of exams frequently go unsurveyed because evaluation questionnaires are usually distributed and completed before examination diets get underway (Hounsell *et al.*, 2007).

Interrogating practice

At what points in your teaching do you gather feedback from students? Does this give you time to respond to issues they raise?

SOURCES OF FEEDBACK

In contemporary practice in higher education, there are three principal sources of feedback that are widely recognised. These are:

1   feedback from students (by far the commonest source of feedback);
2   feedback from teaching colleagues and professional peers (see Chapter 28);
3   self-generated feedback (which comprises reflections and observations by an individual or a group of colleagues on their teaching).

If it is to be considered appropriately systematic and robust, any feedback strategy is likely to make use of at least two – and preferably all three – of these sources, since each has its own distinctive advantages and limitations. Feedback from students, for instance, offers direct access to the 'learners' eye-view', and students are uniquely qualified to comment on matters such as clarity of presentation, pacing of material, access to online resources or library facilities, 'bunching' of assignment deadlines and helpfulness of tutors' feedback on written work. But there are some issues where departmental teaching colleagues may be better equipped to comment: for instance, on the appropriateness of course aims, content and structure; on the design of resource materials; or on alternatives in devising and marking assignments, tests and examinations. And third, there is self-generated feedback, which is grounded in the day-to-day teaching experiences, perceptions and reflections of the individuals concerned. The aim of self-generated feedback is not to enable university teachers to act as judge and jury in their own cause, but rather to promote self-scrutiny and cultivate reflection. It can open up valuable opportunities to 'capitalize on the good things' and to 'repair mistakes quickly before they get out of hand' (Ramsden and Dodds, 1989: 54).

Over and above these three main sources of feedback, there is a fourth which, though readily available, is often underexploited or goes unnoticed: the 'incidental feedback' which is to be found in the everyday routines of university teaching and course administration and therefore does not call for the use of specific survey techniques. It includes readily available information such as attendance levels; pass, fail, progression, transfer and drop-out rates; patterns of distribution of marks or grades; the nature of the choices that students make in choosing between assignment topics or test and examination questions; and the reports of external examiners or subject reviewers. It can also encompass the kinds of unobtrusive observations which can be made in a teaching-learning situation, such as a lecture: how alert and responsive the students are; whether many of them seem tired, distracted or uninvolved; to what extent they react to what is said by looking at the teacher or avoiding his or her gaze (Bligh, 1998).

Interrogating practice

How do you make use of incidental feedback? Does it form part of your own reflective practice?

METHODS OF FEEDBACK

The question of the source from which feedback is to be obtained is closely related to the question of how it is to be sought (see Figure 14.1). Indeed, any such overview of sources and methods in combination highlights the rich array of possibilities that are currently available to university teachers in seeking and making use of feedback.

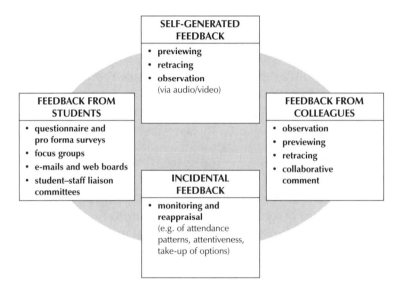

Figure 14.1 Sources and methods of feedback

As far as methods of obtaining feedback from students are concerned, questionnaires remain extremely popular – largely, we may suspect, on two grounds. First, there is the widespread availability of off-the-shelf questionnaires, which can be broad-brush or geared to particular areas or aspects of teaching (e.g. Day *et al.*, 1998), and which are regularly bartered and cannibalised by course teams and individuals alike. Second, there are the attractions of a method that offers every student the chance to respond while at the same time generating data which are quantifiable. However, in an age when mass higher education has led to much greater student diversity, it is important to ensure that questionnaires – particularly to first-year students – log some information about students' backgrounds and aspirations, so that course teams can verify whether the needs of different student constituencies are being equally well served (Hounsell and Hounsell, 2007). The *Monash Experience Questionnaire* (CHEQ, 2007) provides an excellent illustration of how this kind of background information can be readily collected in periodic university-wide student surveys. Similarly, Queensland University of Technology's First-year experience survey (Case study 1) offers a good example of a questionnaire that is both tailored to the expectations and experience of its target audience while also tapping into distinctive features of the mission of the university concerned – for example, QUT's commitment to 'real-world learning' and graduate employability.

Case study 1: Queensland University of Technology

First-year experience survey

The extract below is taken from Section C of the questionnaire, which focuses particularly on students' academic experiences. Other sections of the questionnaire relate to students' wider experiences of university life and their interactions with staff and with their fellow-students.

Survey page:

QUT **Queensland University of Technology**
Brisbane Australia

DEV Environment

a university for the **real** world*
QUT Virtual

Help

Close browser window

First Year Experience Survey (FYES)
Make a difference to the student experience at QUT.

This survey and your privacy

The survey includes a mixture of open-ended questions and scale-based questions.

To answer the open-ended questions, please enter your comments in the fields provided. Open-ended questions are optional.

To answer the scale-based questions, please select the option that most accurately reflects your response to each statement. You must answer every statement, but you have the option to select 'Not Applicable / No Comment' if you wish. Some scale-based questions also include a comments field to enable you to clarify your selected response (these comments are optional).

Section C - Course - This section asks you about your overall course experience as a first year student (eg teachers, curriculum, workload, assessment, etc).

	Strongly Disagree	Disagree	Neutral	Agree	Strongly Agree	Not Applicable / No Comment
	1	2	3	4	5	N/A
17 The staff make a real effort to understand difficulties I might be having with my work.	○	○	○	○	○	○
18 The course is developing my practical skills eg problem solving, critical thinking, team work, and communication.	○	○	○	○	○	○
19 I usually have a clear idea of where I am going and what is expected of me in this course.	○	○	○	○	○	○
20 I am finding my course engaging and stimulating.	○	○	○	○	○	○
21 I consider what I am learning from this course to be valuable for my future.	○	○	○	○	○	○
22 In my course, I feel part of a group of students and staff committed to learning.	○	○	○	○	○	○
23 I am confident that my course is helping me prepare for the workforce.	○	○	○	○	○	○
24 The workload for my course is appropriate.	○	○	○	○	○	○
25 The assessment for my course is appropriate.	○	○	○	○	○	○
26 The course materials and resources are relevant and up to date.	○	○	○	○	○	○
27 The teaching staff normally give me helpful feedback on how I am going.	○	○	○	○	○	○
28 My course makes appropriate use of technology in its online learning environments.	○	○	○	○	○	○
29 Overall I am satisfied with the quality of my course.	○	○	○	○	○	○
30 I am satisfied that I have chosen the right course for me.	○	○	○	○	○	○
31 I am thinking seriously about withdrawing from my course.	○	○	○	○	○	○

QUT

32	I am satisfied with the usage of group assessment within the course.	○	○	○	○	○	○	
33	I am thinking seriously about changing my course next year.	○	○	○	○	○	○	
34	What is your understanding of the term 'Real World Learning'?							
35	What are the best aspects of your course?							
36	What aspects of your course are most in need of improvement?							

PRIZE DRAW

Would you like to enter the draw to win a $200 Myer Gift Voucher or an iPod Shuffle? ○ Yes ○ No

[SUBMIT]

Close browser window

CRICOS Institution Code: 00213J   Help

Questionnaires can also have their downsides. Overenthusiastic canvassing of student opinion in some universities has led to 'questionnaire fatigue', while among staff there has been a growing awareness of the considerable time and expertise needed, not only to design questionnaires which are salient and to the point, but also to process and analyse the resulting data. Happily, there is a growing range of alternative approaches to gathering feedback (e.g. Harvey, 1998; Morss and Murray, 2005; Kahn and Walsh, 2006). These include:

- 'instant' questionnaires, 'one-minute' papers (Stead, 2005) and pro formas, many of which side-step questionnaire fatigue by combining brevity with opportunities for student comment;
- **focus groups**, student panels and structured group discussion, which can offer students more informal and relatively open-ended ways of pooling thoughts and reactions;
- web-based discussion boards on which students post their comments and queries for open display.

Methods of obtaining feedback from colleagues and peers are equally varied. Probably the best-known method is direct observation, where a colleague or 'buddy' is invited to sit in on a lecture, seminar or practical and subsequently offer comments as a knowledgeable third party (Chapter 28). But there are likely to be situations – especially in small classes and in one-to-one tutorials or supervisory meetings – where the presence of a colleague would be obtrusive and inhibiting. It is here that the techniques of previewing and retracing come to the fore (Day *et al.*, 1998: 8–9). Previewing involves looking ahead to a forthcoming class and trying to anticipate potential problem areas and explore how they might best be tackled. Retracing, on the other hand, is retrospective and is intended to review a specific teaching session, while it is still fresh in the mind, in order to pinpoint successes and areas of difficulty. Both techniques entail the use of a colleague as a 'critical friend', prompting reflection and the exploration of alternatives. Colleagues can adopt a similarly thought-provoking role in joint scrutiny of course materials or collaborative marking and commenting on students' written work.

In today's higher education, inevitably, the advice of busy colleagues and peers can only be sought periodically and judiciously, but many of the same techniques may also be adapted for use in compiling self-generated feedback. Video- and audio-recordings make it possible for us to observe or revisit our own teaching, while previewing and retracing are equally feasible options for an individual, especially if good use is made of an appropriate checklist or pro forma to provide a systematic focus for reflection and self-evaluation. Case study 2 gives an example of a pro forma which may be used in retracing a fieldwork exercise. Checklists can be helpful to underpin previewing, retracing, or direct or indirect observation.

Case study 2: A pro forma that may be used for retracing fieldwork

The University of Edinburgh

Fieldwork is a typical case where feedback from direct observation or teaching is not usually feasible. Here the most appropriate way to obtain feedback is by retracing. This method readily lends itself to other teaching situations; for example, pro formas can be adapted for one-to-one sessions in creative arts that may run for several hours in which a one-hour sample observation would not yield useful feedback.

A pro forma for retracing fieldwork

Record by ticking in the appropriate column the comments which come closest to your opinion.

How well did I . . . ?	Well	Satisfactory	Not very well
• make sure that students had the necessary materials, instructions, equipment, etc.			
• get the fieldwork under way promptly;			
• try to ensure that all the set tasks were completed in the time available;			
• keep track of progress across the whole class;			
• handle students' questions and queries;			
• provide help when students encountered difficulties;			
• respond to students as individuals;			
• help sustain students' interest;			
• bring things to a close and indicate follow-up tasks.			

ANALYSING AND INTERPRETING FEEDBACK

Any technique for obtaining feedback is going to yield data that need to be analysed and interpreted. Some techniques (e.g. structured group discussion) can generate feedback in a form which is already categorised and prioritised, while questionnaires can be designed in a format which allows the data to be captured by an **OMR (optical mark reader)** or, in some institutions, processed by a central support service. Increasingly, Web-based systems are being introduced which invite students to respond to multiple choice questions (MCQs) and enter comments in text boxes. From these, different types of report can be generated. Yet while possibilities such as these do save time and effort, there are few or no short-cuts to analysis and interpretation, since these are not processes that can be delegated to others. There is a body of thought, as Bligh has noted, which contends that the actions of a lecturer and the students' response to that lecturer (as represented in the feedback they provide) are not accessible to an outside observer or independent evaluator, but can only be properly understood 'in the light of their intentions, perceptions and the whole background of their knowledge and assumptions' (Bligh, 1998: 166). While this may risk overstating the case, it does make a telling point: the teacher of a course is in a unique position to make sense of feedback and to weigh its significance against a knowledge of the subject matter in question, the teaching aims and objectives, and the interests, aspirations and capabilities of the students who provided the feedback.

Equally crucially, it has to be acknowledged that analysing and interpreting feedback can benefit from the involvement of others – those without a direct stake in teaching or assessing on the course concerned. First, interpreting feedback from our students is an emotional business (Hendry *et al.*, 2005), and it is easy to fall into one of two traps:

dismissing unwelcome feedback too readily, or dwelling gloomily on less favourable comment to the neglect of those features of teaching which have attracted praise. In circumstances such as these, calling on the 'second opinion' of a seasoned teaching colleague can provide a much-needed counterweight. Second, specialist help may often be required in analysing and interpreting findings – and especially so when a standardised student questionnaire has been used and results for different individuals are being compared. Research at the London School of Economics (Husbands, 1996) draws attention to the complexity of the issues raised. Third, the interrelationship of information and action is far from unproblematic. Good feedback does not in itself result in better teaching, as US experience has suggested (McKeachie, 1987; Brinko, 1990). Improvements in teaching were found to be much more likely when university teachers not only received feedback but could draw on expert help in exploring how they might best capitalise upon strengths and address weaknesses.

Interrogating practice

In your department, what happens to feedback data from student questionnaires? Is it made public to the students involved? How do staff analyse, review and act upon the findings from this source? How are students informed about changes made in response to their views?

ACTING ON FEEDBACK

This last point is a crucial one, especially given that not all university teachers will have easy access to a teaching-learning centre or educational development unit offering specialist guidance and support. It is therefore important to acknowledge that acting on feedback constructively entails recognition of its practical limitations. Sometimes feedback produces unclear results which only further investigation might help to resolve, or it may be necessary to explore a variety of possible ways of both interpreting and responding to a given issue or difficulty.

Three examples may help to illustrate this. In the first of these, feedback on a series of lectures has indicated that many students experienced difficulties with audibility. But where exactly might the problem lie? Was it attributable to poor acoustics in the lecture theatre, or was it because many of the students were reluctant to sit in the front rows, or because the lecturer spoke too softly or too rapidly? And what would be the most appropriate response: installing a microphone and speakers, encouraging the students to sit nearer the front, better voice projection and clearer diction by the lecturer, or greater use of PowerPoint slides and handouts, so that students were less reliant on the spoken voice?

The second example is one in which pressures on resources have led to larger tutorial groups, and a module evaluation has revealed that students are dissatisfied with the limited opportunities they have to contribute actively to the discussion. One way forward might be to halve the size of tutorial groups by scheduling each student to attend tutorials at fortnightly rather than weekly intervals. Another might be to experiment with new strategies to maximise tutorial interaction and debate (e.g. through greater reliance on preparatory and follow-up exercises carried out by the students in their own time).

In the third example, a student questionnaire has pointed to shortcomings in the provision of feedback to students on their coursework assignments. But where exactly are the major trouble spots, given recent research evidence that students' concerns about feedback and guidance can take many different forms (Hounsell *et al.*, 2008), and since remedial action needs to match diagnosis if it to be effective?

As these three examples make clear, in many teaching-learning situations there is no one obvious or ideal response to feedback, but rather an array of options from which a choice has to be made as to what is appropriate and feasible. Some options may have resource implications that necessitate consulting with colleagues; some may necessitate further probing to pinpoint more precisely the nature of the concerns expressed; and some may best be resolved by giving the students concerned an opportunity to express their views on the various options under consideration.

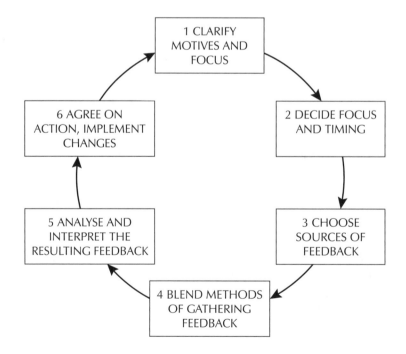

Figure 14.2 The evaluation cycle

OVERVIEW

This chapter has looked at the principal factors to be considered in evaluating teaching. The sequence followed was not fortuitous, as Figure 14.2 suggests. The processes involved, when viewed collectively, may be seen as a series of interlocking steps which together comprise an integrative cycle of evaluation. Overlooking any one of these steps is likely to be dysfunctional. Neglecting to clarify focus and purposes, for example, may result in feedback which is unhelpful or of marginal relevance. Similarly, failing to respond to issues which have arisen by not implementing agreed changes risks alienating those who have taken the trouble to provide feedback.

It would be misleading, none the less, to see this cycle of evaluation as a counsel of perfection. No university teacher can realistically subject every aspect of his or her day-to-day practice to constant review or modification. Nor can workable evaluation strategies be devised in isolation from careful consideration of the resources of time, effort and expertise which would be called for. Indeed, effective evaluation is not simply a matter of technique. It also calls for the exercise of personal and professional judgement.

REFERENCES

Biggs, J (2001) The reflective institution: assuring and enhancing the quality of teaching and learning. *Higher Education*, 41 (2): 221–238.

Bligh, D (1998) *What's the Use of Lectures?* (5th edn), Intellect, Exeter.

Brinko, K T (1990) Instructional consultation with feedback in higher education. *Journal of Higher Education*, 61 (1): 65–83.

Centre for Higher Education Quality (2007) *Monash Experience Questionnaire*, Monash University, Victoria. Available online at <http://www.adm.monash.edu.au/cheq/reports/> (accessed 14 January 2008).

D'Andrea, V and Gosling, D (2005) *Improving Teaching and Learning in Higher Education: A Whole Institution Approach*, Open University Press, Maidenhead.

Day, K, Grant, R and Hounsell, D (1998) *Reviewing Your Teaching*, TLA Centre, University of Edinburgh/UCoSDA, Sheffield. Available online at <http://www.tla.ed.ac.uk/resources/ryt/index.htm> (accessed 14 January 2008).

Falk, B and Dow, K L (1971) *The Assessment of University Teaching*, Society for Research into Higher Education, London.

Gibbs, G, Habershaw, S and Habershaw, T (1988) *53 Interesting Ways to Appraise Your Teaching*, Bristol: Technical and Educational Services.

Harvey, J (ed.) (1998) *Evaluation Cookbook*, Learning Technology Dissemination Initiative, Heriot-Watt University, Edinburgh. Available online at <http://www.icbl.hw.ac.uk/ltdi/cookbook/contents.html> (accessed 14 January 2008).

Hendry, G, Peseta, T and Barrie, S (2005). How do we react to student feedback? *Synergy*, 22. Available online at <http://www.itl.usyd.edu.au/synergy/article.cfm?print=1&articleID=262> (accessed 14 January 2008).

Higher Education Funding Council for England (HEFCE) (2002) *Information on Quality and Standards in Higher Education*. Final report of the Task Group chaired by Sir Ron Cooke (HEFCE Report 02/15).

Higher Education Funding Council for England (HEFCE) (2007) *National Student Survey*. Available online at http://www.hefce.ac.uk/learning/nss. See also: <http://www.unistats.co.uk/> (accessed 14 January 2008).

Hounsell, D (1996) Documenting and assessing teaching excellence, in *Evaluating Teacher Quality in Higher Education*, ed. R Aylett and K Gregory, Falmer, London, pp 72–76.

Hounsell, D and Hounsell, J (2007) Teaching-learning environments in contemporary mass higher education, in *Student Learning and University Teaching* (British Journal of Educational Psychology Monograph Series II, no. 4), ed. N J Entwistle *et al.*, British Psychological Society, Leicester, pp 91–111.

Hounsell, D, Tait, H and Day, K (1997) *Feedback on Courses and Programmes of Study*, TLA Centre, University of Edinburgh/UCoSDA, Sheffield/IHEDSA, Johannesburg.

Hounsell, D, Xu, R and Tai, C M (2007) *Monitoring Students' Experiences of Assessment* (Scottish Enhancement Themes: Guides to Integrative Assessment, no. 1), Quality Assurance Agency for Higher Education, Gloucester. Available online at <http://www.enhancementthemes.ac.uk/publications/> (accessed 14 January 2008).

Hounsell, D, McCune, V, Hounsell, J and Litjens, J (2008) The quality of guidance and feedback to students. *Higher Education Research and Development*, 27 (1): 55–67.

Husbands, C T (1996) Variations in students' evaluations of teachers' lecturing and small-group teaching: a study at the London School of Economics. *Studies in Higher Education*, 21 (2): 187–206.

Kahn, P and Walsh, L (2006) *Developing Your Teaching: Ideas, Insight and Action*, Routledge, London.

McInnis, C, Griffin, P, James, R and Coates, H (2001) *Development of the Course Experience Questionnaire (CEQ)*, Department of Education, Training and Youth Affairs, Canberra. Available online at http://www.dest.gov.au/sectors/higher_education/publications_resources/profiles/archives/development_of_the_course_experience.htm> (accessed 14 January 2008).

McKeachie, W J (1987) Instructional evaluation: current issues and possible improvements. *Journal of Higher Education*, 58 (3): 344–350.

Morss, K and Murray, R (2005) *Teaching at University. A Guide for Postgraduates and Researchers*, Sage, London.

Quality Assurance Agency for Higher Education (2006a) *Code of Practice for the Assurance of Academic Quality and Standards in Higher Education. Section 7: Programme design, approval, monitoring and review* (2nd edn), QAA, Gloucester.

Quality Assurance Agency for Higher Education (2006b) *Guidelines for Preparing Programme Specifications* QAA, Gloucester (see esp. p 5).

Queensland University of Technology (2007) *First Year Experience Survey*. Available online at <http://www.yourfeedback.qut.edu.au/qut_surveys/fyes/> (accessed 28 January 2008).

Ramsden, P (1992) *Learning to Teach in Higher Education* (2nd edn), Routledge, London.

Ramsden, P and Dodds, A (1989) *Improving Teaching and Courses: A Guide to Evaluation* (2nd edn), University of Melbourne, Melbourne.

Richardson, J (2007) The National Student Survey: development, findings and implications. *Studies in Higher Education*, 32 (5): 557–580.

Stead, D R (2005) A review of the one-minute paper. *Active Learning in Higher Education*, 6 (2): 118–131.

Wilson, K L, Lizzio, A and Ramsden, P (1997) The development, validation and application of the Course Experience Questionnaire. *Studies in Higher Education*, 22: 33–53.

FURTHER READING

The following are practical guides, each approaching evaluation in a distinctive and contrasting way.

Angelo, T A and Cross, K P (1993) *Classroom Assessment Techniques: A Handbook for College Teachers* (2nd edn), Jossey-Bass, San Francisco, CA.
Day, K, Grant, R and Hounsell, D (1998) See above.
Kahn, P and Walsh, L (2006) See above.

Part 2
Teaching in the disciplines

15 Teaching in the disciplines

Denis Berthiaume

INTRODUCTION

Teaching in higher education is a rather interesting profession. To enter it, people are trained for years in one area of their occupation (i.e. research) while most often not trained in another (i.e. teaching). Yet the latter area takes up much time in an academic's day-to-day activities. University teaching staff are often left to develop their understanding of teaching and learning on their own. But anyone teaching in higher education knows that it is not so easy to decide what works and what does not work when teaching in their discipline.

For some time now, educational researchers have investigated the idea that, in order to be effective, higher education teaching may have to be 'discipline-specific'. In other words, teaching in higher education has to take into account the specific characteristics of the discipline being taught. This means that developing an understanding of teaching and learning is not sufficient to become an effective teacher in higher education. Rather, one must also develop understanding of the teaching and learning requirements of one's own discipline. This has been termed 'discipline-specific pedagogical knowledge' (Berthiaume, 2007; Lenze, 1995). Otherwise, the pedagogical knowledge developed either through accredited academic practice programmes for new lecturers or through continuing professional development activities lies alongside one's disciplinary knowledge, but the two types of knowledge are not necessarily integrated with one another. In such a scenario, the university teacher remains a disciplinary specialist with some knowledge of teaching, but does not necessarily become a disciplinary specialist who knows how to teach and foster learning within his or her own discipline.

This chapter introduces you to the notion of discipline-specific pedagogical knowledge (DPK) in order to help you build bridges in your mind, and between the first two sections of the book. In Part 1, you were presented with various ideas and materials related to learning and teaching in general, thus helping you develop what is called 'generic pedagogical knowledge' or the knowledge of teaching and learning that is applicable to all academic disciplines. In Part 2, you are presented with ideas and materials related to learning and teaching in various different disciplines, thus helping you to develop DPK. In this chapter, a model for linking your generic knowledge of learning and teaching with the specific characteristics of your discipline is presented. This is done to provide you with tools to relate what you have learnt about learning and teaching in general with the requirements of learning and teaching in your discipline. In the end, this should help you grow as a disciplinary specialist who knows how to teach and facilitate learning in a specific disciplinary area.

A MODEL OF DISCIPLINE-SPECIFIC PEDAGOGICAL KNOWLEDGE (DPK)

In educational research, the notion of DPK has traditionally been examined within one of two distinct lines of research: research on the **knowledge base for teaching** (e.g. Hiebert *et al.*, 2002; Munby *et al.*, 2001; Shulman, 1986) or research on **disciplinary specificity** in university teaching (e.g. Becher and Trowler, 2001; Donald, 2002; Neumann, 2001). Within research on the knowledge base for teaching, three components have been found to play a particularly crucial role in guiding an academic's thinking about teaching. These components include the teacher's knowledge about teaching (the body of dynamic, relatively consensual, cognitive understandings that inform skilful teaching – many of which are considered in Part 1), his or her beliefs relating to teaching (personal and most often untested assumptions, premises or suppositions about instruction that guide one's teaching actions), and his or her goals relating to teaching (what a teacher is trying to accomplish, his or her expectations and intentions about instruction, be they short- or long-term).

Within research on disciplinary specificity, two types of characteristics have been found to affect what one can do when teaching a given discipline. These include the socio-cultural characteristics of the discipline (characteristics that are socially constructed through the establishment of norms, practices or rules within a group of individuals) and the epistemological structure of the discipline (characteristics that directly depend upon how the field is structured) – see below and other chapters in Part 2.

Yet each of these two lines of research is limited in its ability to represent the notion of DPK in its full complexity. Neither are they consistently brought together, either in professional development activities, in educational research or through the **reflection** of university teachers. However, using these two lines simultaneously enables us to examine the phenomenon of DPK more accurately, since linking elements of the knowledge base for teaching with elements of disciplinary specificity provides a way to consider internal and external factors contributing to the formation of DPK.

This is what the empirical model of DPK presented in this chapter does. But the model goes further by including elements from a third source, namely the teacher's **personal epistemology** – his or her beliefs about knowledge and its development (e.g. Baxter-Magolda, 2002; Hofer and Pintrich, 2002; Perry, 1998; Schommer-Aikins, 2002). This dimension is essential to articulating the link between the knowledge base for teaching and disciplinary specificity since, for instance, beliefs that are present about teaching may interact with the body of knowledge that is formed by an academic's discipline. As such, an academic's way of seeing knowledge and its development (their personal epistemology) may act as a mediator between his or her thought processes about teaching and the specific characteristics affecting teaching that he or she perceives in his or her discipline. For example, this could explain why chemists do not necessarily all think alike with regard to chemistry and therefore end up teaching similar topics differently.

Within research on personal epistemology, three aspects have been found to play a particularly important role, namely an individual's beliefs about knowledge and knowing (how one views what constitutes knowledge and the various actions associated with being able to know), his or her beliefs about knowledge construction (how one views the development or accumulation of knowledge), and his or her beliefs about the evaluation of knowledge (how one attributes more value to certain forms of knowledge than others).

The model of DPK presented in this chapter thus incorporates the three lines of research identified above and their various components. In this sense, the DPK a university teacher develops corresponds to a complex web of relationships between the various components coming from these three sources (see Figure 15.1 on p. 219). The model of DPK presented in this chapter was validated by interview research described in Case study 1.

Interrogating practice

Consider the sources of information and inspiration you draw from when teaching. In light of these, think of instances in which you seem to be making links between your knowledge base for teaching, the disciplinary characteristics of your field, and/or your personal epistemology.

Consider how much the institutional/departmental context in which you find yourself affects your thoughts and teaching actions.

Case study 1: The DPK research

The model of DPK outlined in Figure 15.1 was validated with the help of a multi-case study of four university professors from four disciplines. Their disciplines represented each of the four groupings of university disciplines identified in the Biglan (1973) and Becher (1989) taxonomy, namely Hard-Pure (Mathematics), Hard-Applied (Civil Engineering), Soft-Pure (Political Theory), and Soft-Applied (Social Work) (see Chapter 2 for further explanation of these groupings).

Interviews – some of which were part of another research project (McAlpine *et al.*, 1999) – were used and focused on different moments in teaching, namely at the beginning of a course, immediately before a class, immediately after a class, and at the end of a course. One additional interview did not specifically focus on any teaching moment but focused rather on the various aspects of DPK. All interviews addressed both thoughts and actions, thus ensuring that what came out of the interviews was representative of the four professors' actions, not just their intentions.

Through content analysis of the various interview transcripts, several dimensions emerged in relation to each component of the DPK model. A further examination of these dimensions led to the identification of relationships between components of the DPK model. This is why the discipline-specific pedagogical knowledge of an academic can be assimilated to a complex web of relationships between components associated with all three sources mentioned above.

The four participants in the study were all in the first ten years of their career as university teachers. They were all trained in the British-inspired Anglo-Saxon tradition. Two were men and two were women. They were also selected for the differences associated with the disciplines they teach. There is no reason to think the four are atypical. As such, even though the sample for validation was small, the fact that they were purposefully chosen for their difference increases the validity of the model of DPK that is derived from their experience.

(Dr Denis Berthiaume, University of Lausanne)

Interrogating practice

While reading Tables 15.1 to 15.3, reflect on the 'dimensions' and see if yours would be similar. By doing this consciously you are starting to construct your own DPK and may reach a much greater and quicker understanding about teaching your discipline than leaving development of your understanding to chance.

RECONCILING KNOWING HOW TO TEACH WITH KNOWING WHAT TO TEACH

The empirical DPK model (Figure 15.1) provides insights into how a university teacher may relate their generic understanding of learning and teaching to the specific characteristics or requirements of their discipline. Tables 15.1 to 15.3 describe the dimensions which emerged from the interviews that are described in Case study 1.

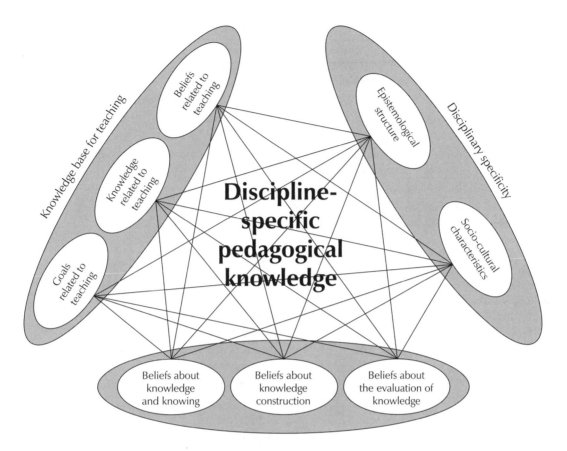

Figure 15.1 Model of discipline-specific pedagogical knowledge (DPK) for university teaching

Table 15.1 Dimensions associated with components of the knowledge base for teaching

In Tables 15.1–3 dimensions with an asterisk are likely to be 'core' dimensions, important for most university teachers, whatever their academic discipline.

Component	Emerging dimension and description
Goals related to teaching: What a teacher is trying to accomplish, his or her expectations and intentions about instruction, be they short or long term.	***Course-level goals:** What the teacher wants to achieve during the course. ***Class-level goals:** What the teacher wants to achieve during a given class. **Ordering of goals:** The precedence or importance of goals for a particular course, class or programme.

(Continued)

Table 15.1 Dimensions associated with components of the knowledge base for teaching (*cont'd*)

Component	Emerging dimension and description
	*Accomplishment of goals: The attainment of the teacher's goals, at the course or class level; the means by which the goals are accomplished.
	New/future goals: Goals related to future iterations of the course, arising after the course or class is over.
Knowledge related to teaching: The body of dynamic, relatively consensual, cognitive understandings that inform skilful teaching.	***Knowledge of the content:** Knowledge of the discipline, the dimensions of the subject matter taught and/or learned.
	*Pedagogical-content knowledge: Knowledge of teaching specific aspects of content in specific contexts or situations.
	Knowledge of self: Certain aspects of the teacher's persona that may impact on his or her teaching (specific feelings or states of mind), how he or she perceives him or herself.
	*Knowledge of teaching and teachers: Knowledge of principles and methods of teaching or dealing with university teachers.
	*Knowledge of learning and learners: Knowledge of learner characteristics and actions, or evidence of learning on their part.
	*Knowledge of assessment of learning: Knowledge of the principles and/or methods of assessment.
	*Knowledge of curricular issues: Knowledge of how a given topic or course fits within a larger educational programme, the relationship between one's specific course and the courses taught by colleagues.
	Knowledge of human behaviour: Knowledge of how human relations or reactions may affect teaching and/or learning (group dynamics, interpersonal relations, non-verbal communication).
	Knowledge of the physical environment: Knowledge of how the physical arrangements or location of the class may affect teaching and/or learning.
	Knowledge of logistical issues: Knowledge of how administrative dimensions may impact on teaching and/or learning.

Component	Emerging dimension and description
Beliefs related to teaching: Personal and most often untested assumptions, premises or suppositions about instruction that guide one's teaching actions.	**Beliefs about the purpose of instruction:** The teacher's views about the long-term finalities of higher education systems, his or her expectations directed at graduates. **Beliefs about the conditions for instruction:** The teacher's views about the basic requirements or conditions for effective university teaching and/or learning to take place. ***Beliefs about teaching and teachers:** The teacher's views about the role and responsibilities of the university teacher or what constitutes 'good' university teaching. ***Beliefs about learning and learners:** The teacher's views about the roles and responsibilities of a learner in the university context.

Table 15.2 Dimensions associated with components of disciplinary specificity

Component	Emerging dimension and description
Socio-cultural characteristics: Characteristics that are socially constructed through the establishment of norms, practices or rules within a group of individuals.	***Teaching in the discipline:** Norms, conventions, or rules about teaching that seem to prevail among colleagues teaching the same discipline and/or students learning that discipline. ***Learning in the discipline:** Norms, conventions, or rules about learning that seem to prevail among colleagues teaching the same discipline and/or students learning that discipline. ***Knowing in the discipline:** Norms, conventions, or rules about knowing that seem to prevail among colleagues teaching the same discipline and/or students learning that discipline. **Practising in the discipline:** Norms, conventions, or rules about practising that seem to prevail among colleagues teaching the same discipline and/or students learning that discipline.
Epistemological structure: Characteristics that directly depend on the epistemological structure of the field.	***Description of the discipline:** The nature of the teacher's discipline or what their discipline is about (the level of complexity or difficulty of the discipline). **Organisation of the discipline:** What the main branches and/or sub-branches of the teacher's discipline are, how these have evolved over time. **Relation to other disciplines:** How the teacher's discipline relates or compares to other disciplines (similarities and/or differences, changes in the relative status of the discipline in relation to others).

Table 15.3 Dimensions associated with components of the personal epistemology

Component	Emerging dimension and description
Beliefs about knowledge and knowing: How one views what constitutes knowledge and the various actions associated with being able to know.	**Beliefs about the nature of knowledge:** The teacher's views on what constitutes knowledge in general, not necessarily in his or her discipline. ***Beliefs about the act of knowing:** The teacher's views on what people do when they know or how people know in general (not about acquiring knowledge but rather the action of knowing).
Beliefs about knowledge construction: How one views the development or accumulation of knowledge.	***Beliefs about how people learn in general:** The teacher's views on issues of learning and knowledge construction that are applicable to all individuals, not just about them or specific to their discipline. ***Beliefs about how one learns specifically:** The teacher's views on issues of learning and knowledge construction that are specific to them only, how one believes people learn, not specific to their discipline.
Beliefs about knowledge evaluation: How one attributes more value to certain forms of knowledge over others.	***Beliefs about the relative value of knowledge:** The teacher's views on the ordering or relative importance of certain types or sources of knowledge. **Beliefs about how to evaluate knowledge:** The teacher's views on how one makes judgements on the relative importance of certain types or sources of knowledge, how the teacher him or herself evaluates knowledge.

Some dimensions were present in all four university teachers, despite the fact that these individuals came from different disciplines. Such dimensions may therefore be thought of as 'core' dimensions or ones that are likely to be important to develop for most university teachers, regardless of their academic discipline. In Tables 15.1 to 15.3 core dimensions are identified with an asterisk. Table 15.1 corresponds, broadly speaking, to elements presented in Part 1 of the book whereas Table 15.2 corresponds to elements presented in Part 2.

Case study 2 provides illustrations of the DPK of a particular university teacher who took part in the DPK study.

Case study 2: Developing pedagogical knowledge specific to political theory

Professor Alan Patten teaches political theory in the Department of Political Science at Princeton University, USA. Political theory is the subfield of political science that looks at political ideas. At the time of the interviews, Alan had been teaching at university level for seven years. His teaching experience has spanned two continents, as he had taught at the University of Exeter, UK, and then at McGill University, Canada. The particular undergraduate course that was the focus of the interviews is an introductory course to political theory which attracted between 200 and 300 students.

One aspect of Alan's DPK brings together components from his knowledge base for teaching and the disciplinary specificity of his field. For instance, when reflecting upon the assessment of his students' learning, Alan draws from his *knowledge related to teaching*, namely his *knowledge of assessment of learning*. As an illustration, he says that his approach is to examine 'how well students are achieving the goals of the course' as opposed to merely getting them to 'reproduce the material of the course'. Therefore, Alan has deep reservations about the use of multiple choice exams – particularly in political theory – as that would encourage the students simply 'to learn facts'. He prefers to use essays rather than 'poorly designed multiple choice exams'.

In a parallel fashion, Alan reflects on the learning to be achieved by his students and draws from the *socio-cultural characteristics* of his discipline in doing so. More specifically, he draws upon what he sees as requirements for *teaching in the discipline*. As an illustration, Alan says that three elements would constitute good teaching in general: imparting knowledge, giving students tools, and triggering motivation. He adds that different disciplines would put 'more or less weight on each of these'. But Alan feels that in political theory 'giving students tools and exciting them about the subject is more important than the knowledge'.

Alan's DPK thus comprises a relationship between his *knowledge of assessment of learning* and what he sees as requirements for *teaching in the discipline*. On the one hand, Alan chooses to assess learning that goes beyond the reproduction of facts. On the other hand, he says that *teaching in the discipline* of political theory requires focusing on something beyond imparting knowledge; that is, giving students tools and helping them become proficient in their use of such tools. These two ideas are closely related, thus linking his pedagogical and disciplinary knowledge.

(Alan Patten, Princeton University; Denis Berthiaume, University of Lausanne)

Case study 2 provides an illustration of the DPK model by showing how various components come together to form a university teacher's discipline-specific pedagogical knowledge, their DPK. The case study shows that the richness of a teacher's DPK is particularly dependent upon the quality of the relationships between its various components.

Interrogating practice

If you have completed the previous two IPs, you will have a good idea of which dimensions are present in each component of your DPK. Now consider the relationships that might exist between the various components of your DPK.

- Which relationships seem to be most important for you when thinking and/or making decisions about your teaching? Why are these relationships so important?
- How does your institutional or departmental context, or the level of course you might be considering, affect them?

OVERVIEW

This chapter has aimed to introduce the notion of 'discipline-specific pedagogical knowledge' (DPK) in order to help you build bridges between the first and second part of this book and your own, perhaps currently separated, fields of knowledge. In order to do so, a model for linking your generic knowledge of learning and teaching with the specific characteristics of your discipline was presented. This was done in order to provide you with tools to relate what you have learnt about learning and teaching in general with the requirements of your discipline with regard to learning and teaching. One way to ensure that you grow as a disciplinary specialist who knows how to teach and foster learning in your disciplinary area could be to set aside a certain amount of time, regularly, to reflect upon the various dimensions and relationships of your DPK; a point to bear in mind if you are wishing to demonstrate and develop your teaching expertise, as touched on in Part 3. The chapter in Part 2 of this book that most relates to your discipline should be helpful in assisting you with this process.

REFERENCES

Baxter-Magolda, M B (2002) 'Epistemological reflection: the evolution of epistemological assumptions from age 18 to 30', in B K Hofer and P R Pintrich (eds), *Personal Epistemology: The Psychology of Beliefs about Knowledge and Knowing* (pp. 89–102), Mahwah, NJ: Lawrence Erlbaum.

Becher, T (1989) *Academic Tribes and Territories*, Buckingham: Society for Research into Higher Education and Open University Press.

Becher, T and Trowler, P R (2001) *Academic Tribes and Territories: Intellectual Enquiry and the Cultures of Disciplines*, Buckingham: SRHE/Open University Press.

Berthiaume, D (2007) What is the nature of university professors' discipline-specific pedagogical knowledge? A descriptive multicase study (unpublished Ph.D. dissertation), Montreal: McGill University.

Biglan, A (1973) 'The characteristics of subject matter in different academic areas', *Journal of Applied Psychology*, 57(3): 195–203.

Donald, J G (2002) *Learning to Think: Disciplinary Perspectives*, San Francisco, CA: Jossey-Bass.

Hiebert, J, Gallimore, R and Stigler, J W (2002) 'A knowledge base for the teaching profession: what would it look like and how can we get one?', *Educational Researcher*, 31(5): 3–15.

Hofer, B K and Pintrich, P R (2002) *Personal Epistemology: The Psychology of Beliefs about Knowledge and Knowing*, Mahwah, NJ: Lawrence Erlbaum.

Lenze, L F (1995) 'Discipline-specific pedagogical knowledge in Linguistics and Spanish', in N Hativa and M Marincovich (eds), *Disciplinary Differences in Teaching and Learning: Implications for Practice* (pp. 65–70), San Francisco, CA: Jossey-Bass.

McAlpine, L, Weston, C, Beauchamp, J, Wiseman, C and Beauchamp, C (1999) 'Building a metacognitive model of reflection', *Higher Education*, 37: 105–131.

Munby, H, Russell, T and Martin, A K (2001) 'Teachers' knowledge and how it develops', in V. Richardson (ed.), *Handbook of Research on Teaching* (pp. 877–904), Washington, DC: American Educational Research Association.

Neumann, R (2001) 'Disciplinary differences and university teaching', *Studies in Higher Education*, 26(2): 135–146.

Perry, W G (1998) *Forms of Ethical and Intellectual Development in the College Years: A Scheme*, San Francisco, CA: Jossey-Bass (originally published in 1970, New York: Holt, Rinehart and Winston).

Schommer-Aikins, M (2002) 'An evolving theoretical framework for an epistemological belief system', in B K Hofer and P R Pintrich (eds), *Personal Epistemology: The Psychology of Beliefs about Knowledge and Knowing* (pp. 103–118), Mahwah, NJ: Lawrence Erlbaum.

Shulman, L (1986) 'Those who understand: knowledge growth in teaching', *Educational Researcher*, 15(2): 4–14.

FURTHER READING

Gess-Newsome, J and Lederman, N G (eds) (1999) *Examining Pedagogical Content Knowledge: The Construct and its Implications for Science Education*, Dordrecht: Kluwer. A thorough examination of the notion of pedagogical content knowledge, the primary/secondary school equivalent to DPK.

Hativa, N and Goodyear, P (eds) (2002) *Teacher Thinking, Beliefs, and Knowledge in Higher Education*, Dordrecht: Kluwer. The various chapters present the elements forming the knowledge base of university teachers.

Hativa, N and Marincovich, M (eds) (1995) *Disciplinary Differences in Teaching and Learning: Implications for Practice*, San Francisco, CA: Jossey-Bass. Comprehensive examination of the various aspects of disciplinary specificity at university level.

Minstrell, J (1999) 'Expertise in teaching', in R J Sternberg and J A Horvath (eds), *Tacit Knowledge in Professional Practice* (pp. 215–230), Mahwah, NJ: Lawrence Erlbaum. Thorough explanation of the link between expertise and teaching.

16

Key aspects of learning and teaching in experimental sciences

Ian Hughes and Tina Overton

This chapter draws attention to distinctive features of teaching and learning in experimental sciences, which primarily include the physical sciences and the broad spectrum of biological sciences, and it will review:

- issues surrounding the context in which teaching and learning are delivered;
- teaching and learning methods, particularly important in science;
- other current teaching and learning issues in these sciences.

CONTEXT

Teaching and learning in the experimental sciences in the UK have to take account of a number of critical issues. These are:

1   the extent of freedom for curriculum development and delivery;
2   employer involvement in course specification and delivery;
3   recruitment imperatives/numbers of students;
4   enhanced degrees (e.g. the M.Sci.);
5   increased participation, varied aspirations of students and differentiated learning.

Freedom for curriculum development and delivery

In common with engineering disciplines, within the experimental sciences the curricula, and even learning and teaching methods, may be partially determined by professional bodies and employers. With some professional bodies, recognition or accreditation of undergraduate programmes may simply indicate a focus on the scientific discipline involved without making any judgement about content or standards. Other professional bodies may provide indicative or core curricula as guidance with no requirement that such guidance is followed, though providers may find such guidance helpful in maintaining the content of their programmes against institutional pressures. However, professional bodies in the experimental sciences differ from engineering, where they are more definitive; their accreditation may be vital for future professional practice and may determine entry standards, detail curricula and assessment methods and minimum requirements for practical work.

There are also QAA Subject Benchmarking statements (Quality Assurance Agency, 2000–2002), and institutions are increasingly introducing module 'norms' for hours of lectures, laboratory classes and tutorials, and may also define the extent and type of assessments. Determination of the 'what and how' of teaching is no longer under the complete control of the individual teacher. Furthermore, discipline knowledge is expanding and undergraduate curriculum overload is a real issue in all the experimental sciences. Disciplines are becoming less well demarcated and significant knowledge of peripheral disciplines is now required if the integrated nature of science is to be understood.

Employer involvement in course specification and delivery

The increasing involvement of employers in the design and delivery of courses and the development of work-based learning illustrate how outside influences affect courses. In part, the impetus has been to improve student **employability** as many organisations look to Higher Education to produce graduates with the range of skills which will enable them to make an immediate impact at work (see also Chapter 8).

Interrogating practice

Do you work in a discipline in which curricula are influenced by the requirements of a professional body, learned society or employer?

- What is the attitude of that relevant professional body/learned society to the accreditation of undergraduate programmes?
- What are the specific requirements which must be in place for your programmes to be accredited?
- How does this affect your own teaching?

Recruitment imperatives

A major challenge for the experimental sciences in the UK is undergraduate recruitment, as the 18–21-year-old age group is set to fall 13 per cent from 2.06m in 2010 to 1.79m by

2020 (Higher Education Policy Institute, 2002). In addition, experimental science subjects are increasingly seen as 'difficult' and unfashionable alongside the plethora of new disciplines. Accordingly, the rise in student numbers during the past two decades has not been matched by a proportionate rise of numbers within experimental science disciplines (Institute of Physics, 2001) and the proportion of students studying science AS and A2 courses is decreasing. The need for universities to fill available places inevitably means that entry grades are falling and students are less well prepared. This has serious implications for curriculum design, for approaches to learning and teaching, and for systems for student support and retention. How the changing science A level curriculum and the move towards the baccalaureate examination will affect this issue remains to be seen.

Enhanced degrees

During the 1990s, science and engineering disciplines in the UK developed the 'enhanced' undergraduate degree, an 'undergraduate Masters' programme (e.g. M.Chem., M.Phys., M.Biol., M.Sci.). These grew from a need for more time at undergraduate level to produce scientists and engineers who can compete on the international stage. Many programmes remain similar to the B.Sc./B.Eng. with a substantial project and some professional skills development in the final year. Others use a '2-plus-2' approach, with a common first and second year for all students and distinctive routes for year 3 of the B.Sc. and years 3 and 4 at Masters level. In the latter case there are issues related to the distinctiveness ofthe Bachelors and Masters routes and the need to avoid portraying the B.Sc. as a second-rate degree. Harmonisation of European qualifications through the implementation ofthe **Bologna** agreement may influence these developments (*The Bologna Declaration*, 1999).

Widening participation, aspirations and differentiated learning

The percentage of the 18–24 age group participating in university education has grown from about 3 per cent (1962) to about 45 per cent (2004) and is set to increase to 50 per cent (2010). This increase has been accompanied by a diversification in student aspiration, motivation and ability. The increased focus on the development of generic (**transferable**) skills has increased the employability of students in areas outside science (as well as within science) and less than 50 per cent of graduates may now take employment in the area of their primary discipline.

The decline in the mathematical ability of young people is well researched and documented (e.g. *Making Mathematics Count*, 2004). The recruitment pressures mentioned above mean that departments accept students who have not achieved AS or A2 mathematics. Useful ideas and resources on mathematics support for students may be obtained from the UK Higher Education Academy Subject Centres and **Centres** for **Excellence in Teaching and Learning** (CETLs) such as the 'Mathcentre' (http://www.mathcentre.ac.uk). The ability to write clear and correct English has also diminished and students often do not know how to present a practical report or structure an essay.

The increasing diversity of ability at entry leads to problems at the edges of the range as illustrated by a quote from a student: 'You know there are three groups in the class – those who are bored, those who are OK and those who are lost.' Universities have moral and contractual obligations to their paying customers, as well as a need to retain students,and all should have in place multiple support mechanisms to help struggling students.

The very able students often receive no additional provision though they should have equal entitlement to be developed to their full potential. 'Differentiated learning' is, therefore, an emerging issue and may be taken as:

- the intention to differentiate learning opportunities and outcomes;
- differentiation by ability;
- focus on the most able.

This is a newly emerging issue in higher education and as yet there has been no full exploration of its implications or how it could be achieved.

LEARNING AND TEACHING

Some learning and teaching methods are particularly important for the experimental sciences which are often heavily content driven. For example:

1 the lecture;
2 small group teaching;
3 problem-based learning;
4 industrial work experience;
5 practical work.

The lecture

The lecture is still the most widely used way of delivering 'content' in experimental sciences, in which curricula are predominantly linear and progressive in nature with basic concepts that have to be mastered before further study can be considered. However, in recent years many lecturers have introduced more opportunities for student interaction and participation, and use lectures to generate enthusiasm, interest and involvement with the subject (see also Chapter 5).

Interrogating practice

- What are the aims and objectives of your next lecture?
- What do want your students to achieve?
- Design one short activity in which your students can participate during the lecture.

Case study 1: The use of electronic voting systems in large group lectures

The traditional lecture is essentially a one-way transmission of information to students, especially in large classes (over 100 students). The challenge is to make the lecture more akin to a two-way conversation. One solution is to promote interactive engagement through technology, via handheld, remote devices.

An early decision relates to the type of handsets; infrared handsets generally cost less than those using radio-frequency communications. In Edinburgh, the large class sizes determined that we bought the cheaper alternative: an IR-based system known as PRS (personal response system). All systems come with software to collate and display student votes, some (e.g. the PRS software) with a plug-in for Microsoft PowerPoint that enables questions to be embedded within a slideshow. It needs the entire display screen to project a response grid which enables the students to identify that their vote has been received. Display of the question on which the students are voting, which must be clearly visible during thinking time, necessitates the use of a second screen, overhead projector or board. The logistics of providing the students with handsets must be considered. We issue handsets at the beginning of the course and collect them at the end, which avoids time lost through frequent distribution and collection of handsets.

We have exclusively used multiple choice questions **(MCQs)** as interactive engagement exercises within our lectures. The electronic system has provided us with valuable insight into what makes a 'good question', i.e. one where a spread of answers might be expected or where it is known that common misconceptions lurk. A poor question, by contrast, might be a deliberate trick question, or one that is distracting from the material at hand.

We have employed these interactive question episodes throughout our first-year physics and biology courses in a variety of ways:

- To simply break up the lecture, to regain audience focus and attention and as a mild diversion timed around halfway through.

- To serve as a refresher or test of understanding of key points from material previously covered (e.g. a question at the beginning of a lecture, addressing material covered at the last lecture).
- As a vehicle for peer instruction, capitalising on the social context of discussion and peer interaction. The process for one of these episodes is that a question is posed and voted on individually. Following display of the class responses, students are invited to talk to neighbours and defend or promote their own viewpoint and why they think it is correct. The class is then re-polled and the revised response distribution is displayed.
- In 'contingent teaching' the interactive engagement episodes act as branch points in the lecture. Subsequent progression is contingent on the response from the students. A question which, for example, 80 per cent of the students get wrong would indicate either a fundamental misunderstanding associated with the material, or a lack of clarity in the exposition of it, or both. Some corrective action is clearly necessary and, in this respect, the lecture truly becomes a two-way experience.

It is important not to rush through these episodes, but to give adequate thinking time (usually about two minutes). A cycle of peer instruction can take 10 to 15 minutes, perhaps longer if preceded by an orientation to the topic.

One the most difficult things to evaluate after using this methodology is the effect it has on student learning. Our own investigations of the correlation between lecture attendance in a first-year physics class (more accurately 'participation', as evidenced by a recorded vote from a handset) with end-of-course examination performance has yielded a positive correlation, albeit rather weak ($R^2 = 0.18$). We have extensively evaluated the attitudinal aspects of the use of this methodology, from the perspectives of both students and staff. In a physics course the handsets and their use often rated as one of the best things about the course: 'The questions make you actually think about what the lecturer has just said, which helps 'cos sometimes it just goes in one ear and out the other', 'I find I am even having to think in lectures'.

(Dr Simon Bates, University of Edinburgh)

Small group teaching

The traditional small group tutorial (see also Chapter 6) is increasingly under pressure as group sizes grow. It may be a difficult form of teaching for new staff. **Small group teaching** can be particularly challenging in sciences where the discipline itself does not always present obvious points for discussion and students often think there is a single correct answer. If problem solving is an aspect of small group work, then it is worth designing open-ended or 'fuzzy' problems to which there may not be a single correct answer. This provides opportunities for students to discuss multiple responses rather than simply work out where they 'went wrong', but this is not always easy to accomplish (Garratt *et al.*, 1999).

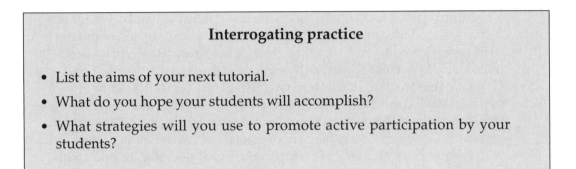

Interrogating practice

- List the aims of your next tutorial.
- What do you hope your students will accomplish?
- What strategies will you use to promote active participation by your students?

Problem-based learning

Problem-based learning (PBL) is well established in medical education (Chapter 26) and is now being adopted in other 'professional' disciplines (Raine and Symons, 2005). It is a style of learning in which the problems act as the driving force for student-directed learning (Boud and Feletti, 1998). All learning of new knowledge is done within the context of the problems. PBL differs from 'problem solving' in that in PBL the problems are encountered before all the relevant knowledge has been acquired and solving problems results in the acquisition of knowledge and problem-solving skills. In problem solving, the knowledge acquisition has usually already taken place.

It is claimed that a PBL approach:

- produces better-motivated students;
- develops a deeper understanding of the subject;
- encourages independent and collaborative learning;
- develops higher-order cognitive skills;
- develops a range of skills including problem solving, group working, critical analysis and communication.

In PBL the curriculum is organised around the problems which must be matched to the desired learning outcomes. Students work in groups to solve the problems. There are no lectures; instead, students engage in self-directed learning and the tutor acts as a facilitator, mentor or guide.

There are disadvantages in a wholly PBL approach. The content is reduced compared to the amount that can be covered in lecture-based courses. PBL takes more staff time because the group sizes have to be restricted and strategies have to be put in place to ensure inclusive group working. Many institutions may be short of the sort of learning spaces that helps PBL to work well – flat seminar rooms with movable furniture.

Problems that are used for PBL should address curriculum objectives, be real and engaging, be 'fuzzy' and place the group in a professional role, i.e. as physicists or chemists. It is not a trivial task to develop effective 'problems' for PBL, but many academics think the initial investment is worth the effort (Overton, 2001).

Industrial work experience

Industrial placements, varying from a few months to a full year, are increasingly a feature of experimental science programmes. Employers value work experience and students who return from industrial placements are generally highly motivated and have developed a range of transferable and personal skills and appropriate attitudes. Many academic departments have identified members of staff who are responsible for building partnerships with employers, placing students and supporting them during their work placement. The aims of the work experience have to be clear to all three parties. If the placement is credit bearing, there have to be outcomes that can be assessed (Murray and Wallace, 2000). Ensuring consistency among multiple assessors in multiple workplaces is difficult, as is ensuring that all students projects are of equal difficulty and that help is provided in the workplace on an equal basis.

There is a QAA Code of Practice for Placement Learning (QAA, 2007), and the Association for Sandwich Education and Training (Wilson, 2001) has also defined good practice and expected standards. Generically applicable formative audits of good practice in work-based learning and placement learning are also available from the HEA Centre for Bioscience (2007). Key stages in a successful work placement scheme include the following.

Finding the placement

Students may be required to find and apply for their own placement (a useful learning experience) or they may be fully supported through a departmental system which finds placements for them and thereby provides the best service to students.

The partnership: the company, the university, the student

A successful partnership will have defined statements of responsibilities, expected learning outcomes and behaviours. These should be set out in a handbook, sectionalised for students, visiting tutor and industrial supervisor.

Preparing the student

Students need to be informed (optimally by presentations from industrialists or students returning from placement) of the benefits of work placements, the time-scale and methods of application and the normal requirements of the workplace (such as dress code). Courses on writing CVs, application forms and interview techniques are important.

Maintaining contact with the student

Students should be encouraged to contact the university to discuss problems and successes, are best supported by a visit by academic staff and will benefit from electronic support, either between staff and students or between peer groups of students.

Assessment

Students need to be conscious of their development and should assess their own progress via a portfolio, personal development log or other form of **personal development planning**. Essays or project reports may also form a major part of the assessment process.

Practical work

Laboratory/practical classes and workshops play a major role in the education of experimental scientists (Boud, 1986; Exley, 1999). In this environment students learn to be scientists and develop professional skills and attitudes. Sciences are practical subjects and academics see this practical experience as vital and non-negotiable. Such learning experiences are very expensive in terms of staff time, support staff, consumable materials and equipment, and are vital for the development of practical, discipline-specific skills, as well as providing rich opportunities for the development of intellectual and transferable skills.

Although students are carrying out an investigation or producing a design, the learning objectives for practical sessions are usually much broader and might include the following:

- gain practical skills;
- gain experience of particular techniques or pieces of equipment;
- produce a design;
- plan an experiment;
- make links between theory and practice;
- gather, manipulate and interpret data;
- make observations;
- form and test hypotheses;
- use judgement;
- develop problem-solving skills;
- communicate data and concepts;
- develop personal skills;
- develop ICT skills;
- develop safe working practices;

- motivate and enthuse students;
- simulate professional practice.

Practical work may take very many forms. It may be very constrained, where students follow detailed instructions with little scope for independent thinking. These experiences have their place in developing basic practical skills and giving students confidence. Practical work may take a more open-ended approach, developing practical and technical skills, as well as design skills, problem solving and application of theory to practice. Assessment is an issue since it is often the ability to write up laboratory exercises (several dozen times!) that is assessed rather than acquisition of practical skills and appropriate attitudes.

Graduates have made it clear that they are generally ill-prepared for the practical issues they have to address in their early employment (Brown *et al.*, 2005), possibly because of reduced quantity and quality of practical work offered on courses. The final year project has also undergone a change. For example, literature reviews, computer-based modelling, desktop impact assessments and surveys of all sorts are now offered as alternatives to the laboratory-based project. Such alternative projects may better prepare students for the career to which they aspire.

Fieldwork has been a strong feature of courses in many disciplines but has come under pressure in some institutions as it is expensive and time consuming and may present health and safety challenges. Many graduates value their experience of fieldwork and any decision to reduce fieldwork availability or practical content should be taken carefully (Brown *et al.*, 2005).

The module teacher does not always plan a laboratory class from scratch. It is not uncommon for new academics to inherit activities and to be constrained in what they can do by available resources and equipment. When planning a practical session or final year project it is vital to obtain clarity of intended learning outcomes and to ensure the learning experience can deliver those outcomes and there is matched assessment.

Students should come to a laboratory, workshop or field trip already familiar with the activity they are about to perform and relevant background theory. Unless this requirement is made explicit, students will turn up not having read through their schedule or manual. The easiest way to ensure that students think about the practical before they arrive is to set a pre-practical exercise (Carnduff and Reid, 2003) which may be fairly short and consist of a few questions, based on the manual or handout they will use. The students should be required to complete the exercise before starting the session. Such 'pre-pracs' or 'pre-labs' may be paper based or automated, via the web or a **VLE**, or use a simulation.

Case study 2: Preparing for fieldwork in environmental sciences

---

Fieldwork plays a central role in most modern environmental science courses. It provides students with opportunities to develop their discipline-specific and transferable skills, including techniques/methods for sampling and data analysis, and invaluable training in problem-solving within 'real life' scenarios.

There remains, however, a challenge in fieldwork with undergraduate students in the early stages of their degree courses. The reasons for this are not simply limited to the subject material that needs to be covered, which often demands some subject interdisciplinarity. The *process* of fieldwork is unfamiliar to most students, and as a result, an appreciation of demands and expectations is often lacking.

In order to address this issue, a number of methods can be useful, including introductory lectures and supporting documentation. Unfortunately, student feedback suggests that such methods are often inadequate at delivering the most valuable 'message' and there can be a risk of information overload. As an alternative, web-based materials offer the possibility of combining various elements of preparative fieldwork in a flexible and interactive format.

The B.Sc. Environmental Science degree at the University of Plymouth includes weekly local fieldwork, together with an integrated, week-long study of the Teign catchment of South East Devon. This involves an assessment of the effect of land use (both ancient and modern) on water quality in the Teign district. To better prepare students we have developed an interactive website which is far from being a substitute for the hands-on nature of the fieldwork, but focuses more on the preparative components that are required in order for the fieldwork to be effective. Along with suitable graphics and links between the different site visits, each section has an interactive self-assessment section that enables students to evaluate their own level of understanding, become more aware of their own learning and develop independence. The website is accessible at all times, and a scheduled session, approximately one week before the fieldwork, replaces introductory lectures.

In terms of student feedback, in their responses to the question 'How effective was the introductory talk/session in preparing you for the field week?', the percentage of returns scoring 'Very high' has risen from 50 per cent (introductory lecture) to 90 per cent (website session).

(Professor Simon Belt, University of Plymouth)

Another issue vital to an effective practical session is the quality of support from postgraduate students or postdoctoral workers used as demonstrators. In order to be effective they have to be familiar with the activity, well briefed, have a good rapport with the students and be willing and able to deal with any problems. Most universities organise generically applicable training sessions for demonstrators, but lecturers involved in practical classes are well advised to hold a briefing session immediately before the activity to ensure demonstrators are familiar with the purpose of the class and with equipment and have sufficient background knowledge to deal with any queries. If demonstrators are involved in marking students' work, then detailed marking schemes should be available to ensure consistent standards.

Interrogating practice

Write down a list of the qualities of an ideal postgraduate demonstrator.

Ask the demonstrators assigned to your next practical session to do the same. How do the two lists compare?

If there are major differences, discuss these with your demonstrator.

Find out how your department/institution trains postgraduate demonstrators.

OTHER ISSUES

Other issues that are pertinent to the teaching of experimental science subjects include:

- skills and employability;
- teaching ethics;
- assessment;
- use of information technology.

Skills and employability

All *Subject Benchmark Statements* (Quality Assurance Agency, 2000–2002) include statements about transferable skills acquisition. The Dearing Report (NCIHE, 1997) argued that there are four skills key to the future success of graduates, whatever they intend to do in later life:

1 communication skills;
2 the use of information technology;

3   numeracy;
4   learning how to learn.

It is well documented that while employers highly value personal skills they commonly note inadequacies in one or more aspects of communication and presentation (Ketteridge and Fry, 1999). Most providers have now embedded explicit and progressive teaching, practice and assessment of such skills in their courses.

In recent years the 'skills' list has expanded to include enterprise and entrepreneurship and broadened to include such generic elements as ethics, sustainability, citizenship and the development of appropriate attitudes (professionalism). The advent of progress files and personal development planning may do much to encourage staff and students to pay attention to these areas and to make time for reflection on their development.

Case study 3: Enhancing employability aspects of a bioscience degree programme

One tool to help programme teams to enhance employability aspects of their course is the generically applicable employability audit, developed by the Centre for Bioscience. The audit is formative and consists of a number of headings:

1   Graduate employment;
2   Career path development ;
3   Relationship with employers;
4   Options for work experience;
5   Does your curriculum promote employability?
6   Are students helped in obtaining and developing careers?
7   Extra-curricular activities;
8   General.

Each heading covers a set of questions; for example, under 4 (Options for work experience) questions include:

- Work experience encouraged during vacations?
- Sandwich placements encouraged as part of the course?
- Can student carry out in-course project work in real settings with employers?
- Are work experience/placements available in areas *not* involving your specific discipline?

For each item the team then considers:

- What options could improve the provision?

- Do resource constraints make any of these unrealistic?
- Can these be made before the next intake of students?

Application of this audit identified 14 areas where improvements could be made. Some (e.g. circulation to staff and students of details of the employment taken by graduates over the last three years) were easy to correct. Others (e.g. provision of work experience placements in areas not involving the discipline) were more difficult and controversial. The audit was easy to carry out and staff felt the course was significantly improved by the process.

(Professor Ian Hughes, University of Leeds)

Interrogating practice

Find out the strategy for skills development in your institution and department.

List the transferable skills development opportunities available in the courses you teach.

- Are your students aware of these opportunities?
- Are the transferable skills developed reflected within the assessment?

Teaching ethics

The issue of ethics is increasingly prominent, as illustrated by some quotes:

- Supermarket chain annual report: 'Expect staff to take into account ethical and sustainability issues when making decisions and choices.'
- Engineering firm: 'Project management must take ethical and environmental issues into account.'
- Marketing training video: 'The PR cost of ethical irresponsibility can be huge and often unrecoverable'.

Professional organisations also require ethical behaviours in their codes of conduct, and within the experimental sciences the nature of the disciplines exposes a host of ethical issues. Graduates need to be able to recognise ethical issues, and be acquainted with the aspects of constructing an argument based on ethical principles (e.g. autonomy, beneficence, non-maleficence, fairness and greatest good to largest number).

Assistance on this topic may be available from several of the Centres for Excellence in Teaching and Learning (CETLs). For example, the IDEA CETL has available a structured set of tutorials providing support material for teacher and student to deliver a basic understanding of ethical principles and thinking. Generic case studies are available as well as some that are more focused on individual disciplines (http://www.idea.leeds.ac.uk/). See also Athanassoulis (2007).

Case study 4: Teaching the ethics of biomedical research

Students in the Faculty of Biological Sciences participate in laboratory exercises or final-year projects in which they or their colleagues act as subjects. However, they receive little or no training in the UK law governing the use of humans as subjects. To address this lack of knowledge and to increase student awareness of the ethical issues involved, students enrolled on the B.Sc. Human Physiology programme were required to attend a lecture and accompanying seminar on the use of human subjects in biomedical research. The lecture provided information on current UK legislation governing clinical trials, but focused primarily on the guidelines and quasi-legal regulations governing non-therapeutic biomedical research. In the following seminar, which was co-taught with a colleague from the Interdisciplinary Ethics Applied Centre of Excellence in Teaching and Learning (IDEA CETL), the students were divided into small groups to discuss and debate what they understood by 'informed consent', their deliberations being fed into a subsequent plenary session. They were also provided with case studies in which, within their small groups, they had to discuss whether the subjects had given their 'informed consent'.

The co-teaching of the seminar by a biological scientist and an ethicist enabled both the scientific and ethical issues surrounding the use of humans as subjects in research to be fully addressed. Feedback on the lecture and seminar was sought both from staff who were observing this new provision and from the students themselves, both groups finding them extremely educational and informative. As a result, in 2007 to 2008, other undergraduate and postgraduate degree programmes within the Faculty, in which students participate in practical work in which they or others act as subjects, will be provided with this training.

(Dr David Lewis, University of Leeds)

Assessment of student learning

Even with modules of equal credit rating there are huge variations (Hughes, 2006) in the amount of:

- staff time spent on assessing students;

- student time spent on being assessed;
- time spent on giving and receiving feedback.

While some universities are attempting to standardise assessment across modules, variations must be expected since the assessment should be linked to the learning objectives and to the teaching methods.

The main assessment tools encountered in experimental science disciplines are:

- unseen written examinations;
- written assignments or essays;
- multiple choice questions and other forms of objective testing;
- laboratory/practical/fieldtrip reports;
- project reports and software developed;
- portfolios and personal development plans;
- poster/oral presentations.

Unseen written examinations still remain the principal means of summative assessment within experimental sciences. For new academics, one of the most daunting tasks is to write their first examination questions, often before the course has been taught. Many academics consider unseen written examinations to be the only rigorous form of assessment, even though such assessments cannot measure the range of qualities and skills demanded of a professional scientist.

One distinctive feature of experimental sciences is the assessment of large numbers of written laboratory or practical reports. The value of repeatedly assessing such exercises, which may not measure practical skills at all, is not always questioned, and alternative possibilities are reviewed elsewhere (Gibbs *et al.*, 1997; Hughes, 2004).

Interrogating practice

List the objectives of your next laboratory/practical class or workshop.

How will you assess the knowledge and skills developed in this work?

Check that your assessment protocol is valid and that it measures what it is supposed to measure.

THE USE OF INFORMATION TECHNOLOGY

Apart from the generic use of C&IT in word-processing, spreadsheets and so on, increasing use is being made of electronic resources to support learning and teaching in experimental sciences (e.g. molecular modelling and computer animation). This includes the use of software packages, managed or virtual learning environments or web-based resources.

One of the common uses of software is for mathematics support where a software or web-based resource can be accessed as needed by the students (e.g. Mathcentre, http://www.mathscentre.ac.uk). There are many such mathematics support packages, and for details see any of the relevant Higher Education Academy Subject Centre websites.

Simulations of experiments are another area where the use of C&IT can be beneficial. Laboratory use of expensive equipment is not always available to all students and so a simulation can provide large numbers of students with some experience of a specialised technique, perhaps through distance learning. Simulations may enable students to generate a large number of results in a fraction of the time it would take to generate them in a laboratory and can allow students to use learn by discovery methods. Making mistakes in execution or design of experiments can be too costly or dangerous to be allowed in the laboratory but may be allowed on a simulation. Experimental design can also be taught using trial-and-error methods. The Higher Education Academy Subject Centres can provide details of simulations available in each discipline.

Case study 5: Developing an online experiment in chemistry

In an ideal world, the content of a university science practical course would be determined entirely by what is academically desirable. In reality, we are restricted by space limitations and to what is physically and financially achievable.

The practical course in physical chemistry at Oxford University exemplifies this. Chemistry has a large student intake – some 190 per year. The cost of providing multiple sets of experiments is significant, so, several years ago, when the equipment required replacement, we decided it would be most cost-effective if wide access to a single experimental rig could be offered. We decided to create an experiment which could be accessed and controlled through the internet, one instrument being used simultaneously by several groups of students.

A number of practical difficulties arise when real equipment is to be controlled through the web. There may be contention between different users who are trying to access equipment simultaneously; malicious or inexperienced users might cause damage to the equipment; if chemicals are required, overzealous online users might consume large quantities of chemicals. We have chosen, for the first experiment we have placed online, to work with equipment which has no moving parts and consumes no chemicals. Through a hidden queuing system we ensure that users' requests cannot clash. Since a web request automatically comes tagged with the user's IP address, it is straightforward to give high priority to users within defined institutions, while giving unrestricted access to other users at times of low demand.

Although the aim was initially to provide an updated experiment for our own course, there is much to be gained by the creation of a network of many different web-based experiments shared among institutions. Advantages of such an arrangement include reduced cost, broadening of the curriculum, access to real (as opposed to simulated) experiments for those who suffer from disabilities or who are pursuing a remote-learning course and access to expensive or unusual equipment.

The web was not designed as a medium for running experiments, so practical difficulties remain. However, the advantages of the creation of a pool of experiments, widely accessible through the internet, are very substantial.

(Dr Hugh Cartwright, Oxford University)

WHERE TO FIND MORE SUPPORT

Some of the most useful support can be obtained from colleagues in the same discipline and many professional bodies and learned societies have considerable teaching resources available from their websites.

The Higher Education Academy Subject Centres provide discipline-specific support for all teachers in higher education. Their services are free and many also provide services specifically for new academics.

- The Higher Education Academy, http://www.heacademy.ac.uk/
- Centre for Bioscience, http://www.bioscience.heacademy.ac.uk/
- Engineering Subject Centre, http://www.engsc.ac.uk/
- Geography, Environmental and Earth Science (GEES), http://www.gees.ac.uk/
- Maths, Stats and OR Network, http://www.mathstore.ac.uk/
- UK Centre for Materials Education, http://www.materials.ac.uk/
- Physical Sciences Centre, http://www.physsci.heacademy.ac.uk/

There are approximately 70 CETLs, many directly or indirectly engaged with experimental science education. A full listing of links to CETLs may be found at http://www.heacademy.ac.uk/3591.htm.

REFERENCES

Athanassoulis, N (2007) *An Introduction to Ethical Thinking*. Available online at <http://www.idea.leeds.ac.uk/EthicalThinking/ > (accessed 5 November 2007).

The Bologna Declaration (1999) <http://ec.europa.eu/education/index_en.html> (accessed 5 November 2007).

Boud, D (1986) *Teaching in Laboratories*, SRHE/Open University Press, Buckingham.

Boud, D and Feletti, G (1998) *The Challenge of Problem-based Learning*, Kogan Page, London.

Brown, A, Calvert J, Charman, P, Newton, C, Wiles, K and Hughes, I (2005) 'Skills and Knowledge Needs Among Recent Bioscience Graduates – How Do Our Courses Measure Up?', *Bioscience Education e-Journal*, vol. 6, no. 2.

Carnduff, J and Reid, N (2003) *Enhancing Undergraduate Chemistry Laboratories*, Royal Society of Chemistry, London.

Exley, K (1999) 'Key Aspects of Teaching and Learning in Science and Engineering', in *A Handbook for Teaching and Learning in Higher Education: Enhancing Academic Practice*, ed. H Fry, S Ketteridge and S Marshall, Kogan Page, London.

Garratt, J, Overton, T and Threlfall, T (1999) *A Question of Chemistry*, Longman, Harlow.

Gibbs, G, Gregory, R and Moore, I (1997) *Labs and Practicals with More Students and Fewer Resources*, Teaching More Students 7, Oxford Centre for Staff Development, Oxford.

Higher Education Academy Centre for Bioscience (2007) *Work Related Learning Audit*. Available online at <http://www.bioscience.heacademy.ac.uk/ftp/Resources/wrlaudit.pdf> (accessed 22 November 2007).

Higher Education Policy Institute (2002) *Demand for Higher Education to 2002*. Available online at <http://www.hepi.ac.uk/downloads/22DemandforHEto2020.pdf> (accessed 5 November 2007).

Hughes, I E (2004) 'Coping strategies for staff involved in assessment of laboratory write-ups', *Bioscience Education e-Journal*, vol. 3, 3–3. Available online at <http://bio.ltsn.ac.uk/journal/vol3/> (accessed 5 November 2007).

Hughes, I E (2006) 'Development of an assessment audit', *Bioscience Education e-Journal*, vol. 7, 7–1. Available online at <http://www.bioscience.heacademy.ac.uk/journal/vol7/> (accessed 5 November 2007).

Institute of Physics (2001) *Physics – Building a Flourishing Future – Report of the Inquiry into Undergraduate Physics*. Available online at <http://www.iop.org/activity/policy/Projects/Archive/file_6418.pdf> (accessed 5 November 2007).

Ketteridge, S and Fry, H (1999) *Skills Development in Science and Engineering*, Final Project Report to the Department for Education and Employment. Available online at <http://www.innovations.ac.uk/btg/projects/theme2/digests/project9.htm. (accessed 5 November 2007).

Making Mathematics Count, The Report of Professor Adrian Smith's Inquiry into Post-14 Mathematics Education (2004) HMSO, London. Available online at <http://www.mathsinquiry.org.uk/report/> (accessed 5 November 2007).

Murray, R and Wallace, R (2000) *Good Practice in Industrial Work Placement*, Higher Education Academy Physical Sciences, York.

NCIHE (1997) (The Dearing Report) *Higher Education in the Learning Society*, National Committee of Inquiry into Higher Education, HMSO, London.

Overton, T (2001) *Web Resources for Problem Based Learning*, Higher Education Academy Physical Sciences, York.

Quality Assurance Agency for Higher Education (2000, 2001, 2002) *Subject Benchmark Statements*. Available online at <http://www.qaa.ac.uk/academicinfrastructure/benchmark/default.asp> (accessed 5 November 2007).

Quality Assurance Agency for Higher Education (2007) *Code of Practice for the Assurance of Academic Quality and Standards in Higher Education, Section 9: Work-based and Placement Learning.* Available online at <http://www.qaa.ac.uk/academicinfrastructure/code OfPractice/default.asp> (accessed 5 November 2007).

Raine, D and Symons, S (2005) *PossiBiLities – Problem-based Learning in Physics and Astronomy,* Higher Education Academy Physical Sciences, York.

Wilson, J (2001). *A Code of Good Practice for the Operation of Placement Elements of Sandwich Courses in Higher Education,* Association for Sandwich Education and Training, York.

FURTHER READING

Moore, I and Exley, K (eds) (1999) *Innovations in Science Teaching,* SEDA Paper 107, Staff and Educational Development Association, Birmingham.

Planet Special Edition 2 (2001) *Case Studies in Problem-based Learning (PBL) from Geography, Earth and Environmental Sciences,* Higher Education Academy GEES, York.

Planet Special Edition 1 (2001) *Embedding Careers Education in the Curricula of Geography, Earth and Environmental Sciences,* Higher Education Academy GEES, York.

Race, P (2000) *Designing Assessment to Improve Physical Sciences Learning,* Higher Education Academy Physical Sciences, UK.

Reid, N and Mbajiorgu, N (2006), *Factors Influencing Curriculum Development in Chemistry,* Higher Education Academy Physical Sciences, York.

Savin-Baden, M (2000) *Problem-based Learning in Higher Education: Untold Stories,* SRHE/Open University Press, Milton Keynes.

Teaching Bioscience: Enhancing Learning Series, Higher Education Academy Centre for Bioscience, York.

<table>
<tr><td>

17

</td><td>

Key aspects of teaching and learning in mathematics and statistics

</td></tr>
</table>

Joe Kyle and Peter Kahn

INTRODUCTION

Recent years have seen a greater focus on learning and teaching in mathematics and its applications in higher education. Old assumptions are being re-examined and there are new political agendas to be addressed. What should the typical undergraduate programme contain and how should it be taught? How best do we serve the needs of those who require mathematics as part of their study of another discipline? There will, no doubt, be many valid answers to these questions and this chapter attempts to cover a good cross-section of the issues involved.

There are in the UK what might be referred to as 'official' answers for what a typical undergraduate programme should contain, as embodied in the Quality Assurance Agency for Higher Education (QAA) **subject benchmarking** statement which covers mathematics, statistics and operational research (QAA, 2002). A 'modal level' graduate should be able to:

- demonstrate a reasonable understanding of the main body of knowledge for the programme of study;
- demonstrate a good level of skill in calculation and manipulation of the material within this body of knowledge;
- apply a range of concepts and principles in loosely defined contexts, showing effective judgement in the selection and application of tools and techniques;
- develop and evaluate logical arguments;

- demonstrate skill in abstracting the essentials of problems, formulating them mathematically and obtaining solutions by appropriate methods;
- present arguments and conclusions effectively and accurately;
- demonstrate appropriate transferable skills and the ability to work with relatively little guidance or support.

The authors of this statement go to some lengths to qualify and set the context for this list. In particular it is stressed that 'students should meet this standard in an overall sense, not necessarily in respect of each and every one of the statements listed'. Clearly there has been no attempt to set a 'national curriculum'; rather we are presented with generic descriptions of the type of skills and qualities we should look to be fostering in our programmes.

We cannot, though, expect to find any 'official' answers to how we should teach or support student learning in mathematics and statistics. Mathematicians and statisticians, indeed, often find themselves challenging approaches to teaching that are advocated widely across higher education. Learning outcomes, personal development planning, reflective practice, key skills, and the 'value' of replacing blackboards with whiteboards, smartboards, overhead projectors, Powerpoint or whatever: we are well known for contesting such notions.

While we will address this debate in what follows, our underlying aim is to concentrate on discipline-specific issues facing those engaged in facilitating learning and teaching in mathematics and statistics at higher education level, drawing upon contributions that are firmly grounded in the discipline. The chapter considers these issues from the perspectives of pure mathematics, applied mathematics, statistics and the impact of technology. It is acknowledged that there has been major growth in service teaching for disciplines, but this is not dealt with in what follows. Nor do we provide a catalogue of immediately 'consumable' classroom resources. Up-to-date materials of this nature are available, in abundance, at the website of the Mathematics, Statistics and Operational Research (MSOR) Network that is part of the Higher Education Academy, located at www.mathstore.ac.uk.

Instead, this contribution to the book seeks to give examples of good practice from experienced facilitators in the field and to explain the challenges that are presented by mathematics and statistics education. However, we also offer avenues for exploration wherein readers may develop their own pedagogic principles. In this it is important to be aware of ways in which the nature of our discipline grounds approaches to teaching and learning, while also taking account of key challenges we face, such as the transition to university. It is to these issues that we thus first of all turn, before moving on to look at more specialist areas.

THE NATURE OF MATHEMATICS AND ITS APPLICATIONS

What we might term the standard approach to teaching mathematics and its applications is one that is relatively conservative. In the UK at least, 'most teaching comprises formal lectures', more innovative methods are used only 'occasionally' and most assessment strategies rely on formal examinations rather than a wider range of assessment methods (QAA, 2001). But there remains a significant basis for this standard approach in considering the nature of the discipline. If we view mathematics as a system of ideas that is underpinned by logic and applied to modelling the real world, then it makes sense to offer coherent explanations of this system to students. If, in addition, we include opportunities for students to work through a set of problems or examples so that they can themselves own this body of knowledge, then we have the natural defaults of lectures and tutorials based around the solution of problems. Mathematics is the science of strict logical deduction and reasoning, a severe taskmaster for both learner and teacher.

Challenges for the discipline

We also find that mathematics and statistics are often taught in schools as a collection of rules, procedures, theorems, definitions, formulae or applications that need to be unthinkingly memorised, and then used to solve problems. Of course, as the level of complexity increases such an approach becomes difficult to sustain; and universities find themselves coping with the legacy. If we simply present mathematics, though, as a logical system of thought, might we not fail to shift ingrained perceptions of mathematics as a collection of facts to be memorised?

What about the challenges we face in a system of mass higher education? The range and diversity of those engaged in learning the subject is considerable and is destined to become wider still in the near future. This will range from foundation-level material, preparing students for entry to other numerate disciplines, to advanced-level specialist mathematical study at or near the contemporary frontiers of the subject. And to what extent does the standard approach to teaching mathematics rely on the students themselves being able to pick up the essential strategies mathematicians employ in making sense of a proof or solving a problem? Will they even be motivated to tackle a problem for themselves?

We have the exploding breadth in the applicability of mathematics. Mathematics is fundamental not only to much of science and technology but also to almost all situations that require an analytical model-building approach, whatever the discipline. In recent decades there has been a huge growth of the use of mathematics in areas outside the traditional base of science, technology and engineering. How do we help to ensure that our students will be able to shape this new body of mathematically related knowledge, as well as be able to make sense of existing knowledge?

Whether it is changing policies affecting school mathematics, the need to recruit more students to our disciplines or the impact of rapidly developing technology, mathematicians and statisticians face many new challenges. There are clear signs that the wider world too is becoming aware of the issues that currently surround the discipline, many of them international; but we too need to respond as educators.

How much room for movement is there in our teaching?

In this response, we may well rely on the standard approach to teaching mathematics, recognising the robustness of mathematical knowledge in contrast to bodies of knowledge that are seemingly more relative. Put most starkly, young colleagues embarking upon a university career feel that they are obliged to embrace an ideology of learning that is completely foreign to the core values of the discipline. For example, faced with the assertion that *Hamlet* is a lousy play, it may be reasonable and effective to adopt a strategy which respects this as a valid personal view that should be respected and debated alongside other views – all deserving of equal respect. Consider, on the other hand, a new lecturer faced with the claim that the recurring decimal 0.99999 . . . is less than 1. One may sympathise with a student who might think this is true and adopt an understanding approach, but no one can, in all honesty, pretend that it has equal validity with the view that 0.99999 . . . is equal to 1.

Of course things need not be as extreme as may be implied here. All of us in the knowledge economy should treat students with sympathy and respect, whatever our subject. But at the same time, those charged with 'training' our new young colleagues must be aware that there is, within mathematics, restricted room for movement when attempting to allow students 'ownership' of the subject. Perhaps it is for reasons such as this that there has been the emergence of an interest in 'discipline-based' staff development, whether this is for new or experienced colleagues (see e.g. Durkin and Main, 2002).

But we will find that alternative approaches are still of value, and these may equally well be rooted in our understanding of mathematics and its applications. We can, for instance, also conceive of mathematics as a human activity, involving creativity and imagination, rather than simply seeing it as an abstracted system of thought. Teaching then takes its place as helping students to enter into this world of mathematical activity – rather than simply as an opportunity to present to students the finished products of our rigour. The challenge is to help students enter into the process of doing mathematics or applying it to the real world. Before looking at teaching and learning through specialist perspectives, it will thus help to give further consideration to the changing student body; and to the challenges students face in making the transition to higher education.

THE TRANSITION TO HIGHER EDUCATION

The transition from one educational stage to another can often be a fraught and uncertain process. In mathematics there has been ongoing publicity over many years about the issues around the transition to higher education. Notable among these are the Smith Report, *Making Mathematics Count* (Department for Education and Skills, 2004), and the earlier reports from the London Mathematical Society (1992) and the Engineering Council

(2000). Major factors include changes in school/pre-university curricula, widening access and participation, the wide range of degrees on offer in mathematical subjects, IT in schools, and sociological issues. The earlier establishment of the Advisory Committee on Mathematics Education (ACME) and current government initiatives indicate that there is still work to be done here. Various reports, including those listed above, point to the changes in schools as a key source of problems in the transition, and make recommendations as to how things could be put right there. Indeed, in response to wider concerns about literacy and numeracy, government initiatives have, perhaps, partially restored some of the skills that providers of numerate degrees need; over time these may feed into higher education. But it is doubtful that there will ever be a return to the situation where school qualifications are designed solely as a preparation for higher education.

However, if some of the difficulties in transition lie outside the control of those in higher education, others can be tackled, impacting as they do on the student experience. These include curriculum design and pastoral support, both of which may need attention if those who choose our courses are to have the best chance of success. We might also usefully consider what our students know about our courses when they choose them, and how they might prepare themselves a little before they come – in attitude as well as in knowledge. For example, Loughborough University sends new engineering students a pre-sessional revision booklet as part of its support for incoming students (Croft, 2001). Such approaches can be expected to influence student satisfaction with their course of study, an issue of increasing importance, given student fees. Since 50 per cent of providers were earlier criticised for poor progression rates in QAA Subject Reviews and as the government continues to prioritise widening participation *and* retention, there is much scope for other institutions adopting similar methods. A number of the reports and publications listed above offer more detailed suggestions, but common themes which emerge repeatedly include:

- use of 'pre-sessional' material before arrival;
- initial assessment (or 'diagnosis') of mathematical skills. This is a key recommendation of the report *Measuring the Mathematics Problem* (Engineering Council, 2000);
- ongoing attention to the design of early modules;
- strategic monitoring of early items of coursework;
- some overarching form of academic support: a recent report (Lawson *et al.*, 2001) shows that about 50 per cent of providers surveyed offer some form of 'mathematics support centre'.

Of course, the local circumstance of each institution will influence the nature of initial and continuing support. However, the following have been identified as effective and worthy of consideration.

Additional modules or courses

Some providers mount specific modules/courses designed to bridge the gap, ranging from single modules focusing on key areas of A level mathematics to one-year foundation courses designed to bring underqualified students up to a level where they can commence the first year proper. Specific modules devoted to consolidate and ease the transition to university should be integrated as far as possible with the rest of the programme so that lecturers on parallel modules are not assuming too much of some students. Foundation years should provide a measured treatment of key material; a full A level course is inappropriate in one year.

There are a number of computer-based learning and assessment packages that can help (e.g. *Mathwise*, *Transmath* and *Mathletics* are all described on the Maths, Stats and OR Network Website – www.mathstore.ac.uk). Again, these are best when integrated fully within the rest of the curriculum, linked strategically with the other forms of teaching and with the profiles and learning styles of the individual students. It is widely accepted that simply referring students with specific weaknesses to 'go and use' a computer-aided learning (**CAL**) package is rarely effective. On the other hand, many middle-ability students may be happy to work through routine material on the computer, thus freeing up teachers to concentrate on the more pressing difficulties.

Streaming

Streaming is another way in which the curriculum can be adapted to the needs of incoming students as a means of easing the transition. 'Fast' and 'slow' streams, practical versus more theoretical streams and so on are being used by a number of providers who claim that all students benefit (e.g. Savage, 2001).

Use of coursework

Regular **formative** coursework is often a strong feature of good support provision; it may help in this to find some way effectively to make this work a requirement of the course, as Gibbs (1999) suggests. Fast turnaround in marking and feedback is seen to be effective in promoting learning, with possibilities for students to mark each other's work through peer assessment (see Chapter 10). This area is of particular importance given that student satisfaction surveys regularly highlight feedback to students as an issue of concern. Another criticism in the earlier Subject Reviews was the similarity of coursework to examination questions. This and generous weightings for coursework may generate good pass rates, but often simply sweep the problem under the carpet. There is a nice judgement to make: avoid being too 'helpful' for a quick short-term fix, but encourage students to overcome their own weaknesses.

Support centres

Variously called learning centres, drop-in clinics, surgeries and so on, they all share the aim of acting as an extra-curricular means of supporting students in an individual and confidential way. Lawson *et al.* (2001) outline some excellent examples of good practice here, and the concept is commendable and usually a cost-effective use of resources. One can spread the cost by extending the facility to cover all students requiring mathematical help across the institution. An exciting recent development is the emergence of the UK Mathematics Learning Support Centre which will, through the agency of the Maths, Stats and OR Network, freely make available to all staff and students in higher education a large number of resources via a variety of media.

Interrogating practice

How does your department address the changing needs of students entering higher education? What else could you do to address 'gaps' in knowledge, skills and understanding?

Peer support

Mechanisms for students to support each other tend to be generic, but are included here, as mathematicians have been slow to adopt some of these simple and successful devices. There is a growing trend to the use of second- and third-year students in a mentoring role for new students, supporting, but not replacing, experienced staff. Such student mentors go under a number of names – peer tutors, 'aunties', 'gurus' – but the main idea is for them to pass on their experience and help others with their problems. In at least one institution such students receive credit towards their own qualifications in terms of the development of transferable skills that the work evidences. It is clear that both parties usually benefit – the mentors from the transferable skills they develop, and the mentored from the unstuffy help they receive. It is of course essential that the mentors are trained for their role, and that this provision is monitored carefully. Suggestions are enlarged and expanded upon in Appleby and Cox (2002).

ISSUES PARTICULAR TO PURE MATHEMATICS

What, then, are the special and particular problems that lie in the way of effective teaching and learning in pure mathematics? There are, of course, the issues of transition and mathematical preparedness touched upon above. Lack of technical fluency will be a barrier to further work in pure mathematics. However, there are deeper, more fundamental issues concerning reasoning skills and students' attitudes to proof. Certainly, within the context of higher education in the UK, there are a number of signals and signs that can be read. Among these are current issues in mathematical education, reported problems in contemporary literature (a good recent example is Brakes (2001)), and – to a lesser extent – the results of the QAA Subject Review reports.

So what can be done? There is little evidence that a dry course in logic and reasoning itself will solve the problem. Some success may be possible if the skills of correctly reading and writing mathematics together with the tools of correct reasoning can be encouraged through the study of an appropriate ancillary vehicle. The first (and some would still claim, the foremost) area was geometry. The parade of the standard Euclidean theorems was for many the *raison d'être* of logic and reasoning. However, this type of geometry is essentially absent from the school curriculum, geometry is generally in some state of crisis, and there is little to be gained from an attempt to turn the clock back. It is worth noting, however, that students' misuse of the <=> symbol and its relatives were less likely through exposure to the traditional proof in geometry – most commonly, lines were linked with 'therefore' or 'because' (with a resulting improvement in the underlying 'grammar' of the proof as well). Mathematicians may not want to bring back classical geometry, but should all regret the near passing of the proper use of 'therefore' and 'because' which were the standard features of geometrical proofs.

At one time, introductory mathematical analysis was thought to be the ideal vehicle for exposing students to careful and correct reasoning. Indeed, for many the only argument for the inclusion of rigorous analysis early in the curriculum was to provide a good grounding in proper reasoning. Few advance this case now. Indeed, some researchers in mathematics education have cast doubt on the need for proof itself in such introductions to mathematical analysis (see e.g. Tall, 1999). (We see here a case where research in mathematics education and actual practice are in step with each other. Concerns, though, have been expressed in recent years as to whether the gap between research and practice in mathematics education is widening. Perhaps if we all do our bit to 'mind the gap', we can improve the lot of those at the heart of our endeavours – our students.) Recently the focus has passed to algebra. Axiomatic group theory (and related algebraic topics) is thought by some to be less technical and more accessible for the modern student. Unfortunately, there is not the same scope for repeated use over large sets of the logical quantifiers ('for all' and 'there exists') and little need for contra-positive arguments. Number theory has also been tried with perhaps more success than some other topics.

Working within the comfort zone

However, most success seems to come when the mathematics under discussion is well inside a certain 'comfort zone' so that technical failings in newly presented mathematics do not become an obstacle to engagement with the debate on reasoning and proof. Examples might include simple problems involving whole numbers (as opposed to formal number theory), quadratic equations and inequalities and trigonometry. (At a simple level we can explore how we record the solutions of a straightforward quadratic equation.) We may see the two statements:

'$X=3$ or $X=4$ is a root of the equation $X^2-7X+12=0$'

'The roots of the equation $X^2-7X+12=0$ are $X=3$ and $X=4$'

as two correct uses of 'and' and 'or' in describing the same mathematical situation. But do the students see this with us? Is it pedantic to make the difference, or is there a danger of confusing the distinction between 'or' and 'and'? By the time the solution to the inequality:

$$(X-3)(X-4)>0$$

is recorded as the intersection of two intervals rather than the union, things have probably gone beyond redemption (see also Brakes, 2001).

Interrogating practice

What do you do to assist students to move beyond their 'comfort zone'? What do you do when it becomes apparent that students are floundering with newly presented mathematics? Are there any specific approaches you feel you would like to improve?

Workshop-style approaches

One possible way forward is to use a workshop-style approach at least in early sessions when exploring these issues. Good evidence exists now for the usefulness of such active approaches, as Prince (2004) argues. But a real danger for such workshops at the start of university life lies in choosing examples or counterexamples that are too elaborate or precious. Equally, it is very easy to puncture student confidence if some early progress is not made. Getting students to debate and justify proofs within a peer group can help here. One way of stimulating this is outlined in the workshop plan given in Kyle and Sangwin (2002).

Students can also be engaged by discussing and interpreting the phraseology of the world of the legal profession. Much legislation, especially in the realm of finance, goes to some lengths to express simple quantitative situations purely, if not simply, in words. Untangling into symbolic mathematics is a good lesson in structure and connection. Further, one can always stimulate an interesting debate by comparing and contrasting proof in mathematics with proof as it is understood in a court of law.

Teaching from the microcosm

If students are to see mathematics as a creative activity it will help to focus on the different strategies they themselves can employ to help make sense of mathematical ideas or problems. It may also help to focus on the process of learning mathematics more broadly. Specific teaching approaches, though, are required to realise this. Palmer (1998: 120), for instance, argues that every problem or issue can become an opportunity to illustrate the internal logic of a discipline. We can take a straightforward example of this. If you do not understand an initial concept, it will be virtually impossible to understand a more advanced concept that builds on the initial concept: to understand the formal definition of a group, for instance, you first need to understand the concept of a variable (as well as other concepts). But students cannot rely on the tutor always identifying these prior concepts for them. They themselves need to be able to take a look at an advanced concept and identify contributory concepts, so that they can then make sure they understand them. The same applies to other strategies, as Kahn (2001) further explores, whether generating one's own examples, visualising, connecting ideas or unpacking symbols. In terms of concrete teaching strategies, the tutor can model these strategies alongside a systematic presentation of some mathematics or require students to engage in such strategies as a part of the assessment process. We thus move away from an exclusive focus on the content, to more direct consideration of the process by which we might come to understand that content.

ISSUES PARTICULAR TO APPLIED MATHEMATICS

Given the more extensive experience of the authors in relation to pure mathematics, this section draws heavily on views expressed by others in writing and at conferences, particularly the work of Hibberd (2002). Mathematics graduates, whether they embark upon postgraduate study or enter a career outside academic life, are expected to possess a range of abilities and skills embracing subject-specific mathematical knowledge and the use of mathematical and computational techniques. They are also expected to have acquired other less subject-specific skills such as communication and teamworking skills. For most mathematics degree programmes within the UK, the acquisition of subject-specific knowledge, essential IT skills, the use of mathematical and statistical software and subject-specific problem-solving skills are well embedded in the curriculum (QAA, 2001). Typically these are delivered through formal lectures supported by a mixture of tutorials, seminars, problem classes and practical workshop sessions. As noted earlier, assessment is often traditional, making much use of examinations. Increasingly it is recognised that these approaches do not provide students with the non-mathematical skills that are much valued by employers. This has prompted a search for some variety of learning and teaching vehicles to help students develop both subject-specific and transferable skills. We introduce one such approach in Case study 1, which is based on experience at the University of Nottingham.

Case study 1: Mathematical modelling

A typical goal in implementing a modelling element is to stimulate student motivation in mathematical studies through 'applying mathematics' and to demonstrate the associated problem-solving capabilities. It also offers the chance to provide a synoptic element that brings together mathematical ideas and techniques from differing areas of undergraduate studies that students often meet only within individual modules. This in itself can lead students into a more active approach to learning mathematics and an appreciation and acquisition of associated key skills.

The underlying premise in this type of course can be accommodated through activities loosely grouped as 'mathematical modelling'. Associated assessments and feedback designed around project-based work, whether as more extensive coursework assignments or as substantial reports, can allow students to demonstrate their understanding and problem-solving abilities and enhance both mathematical and key skills. Often quoted attributes gained by graduates are the subject-specific, personal and transferable skills gained through a mathematics-rich degree.

Increasingly, students are selecting their choice of degree to meet the flexible demands of a changing workplace, and well-designed MSOR programmes have the potential to develop a profile of the knowledge, skills, abilities and personal attributes integrated alongside the more traditional subject-specific education.

A mathematical model is typically defined as a formulation of a real-world problem phrased in mathematical terms. Application is often embedded in a typical mathematics course through well-defined mathematical models that can enhance learning and understanding within individual theory-based modules through adding reality and interest. A common example is in analysing predator–prey scenarios as motivation for studying the complex nonlinear nature of solutions to coupled equations within a course on ordinary-differential equations; this may also extend to obtaining numerical solutions as the basis of coursework assignments. Such a model is useful in demonstrating and investigating the nature of real-world problems by giving quantitative insight, evaluation and predictive capabilities.

Other embedded applications of mathematical modelling, particularly within applied mathematics, are based around the formal development of continuum models such as those found, for instance, in fluid mechanics, electromagnetism, plasma dynamics or relativity. A marked success in MSOR within recent years has been the integration of mathematics into other less traditional discipline areas of application, particularly in research, and this has naturally led to an integration of such work into the modern mathematics curriculum through the development of mathematics models. Applied mathematics has always been a strong part of engineering and physical sciences but now extends to modelling processes in biology, medicine, economics, financial services and many more.

The difficulty often inherent in practical 'real-world' problems requires some preselection or guidance on initial problems to enable students to gain a threshold level of expertise. Once some expertise is gained, exposure to a wider range of difficulties provides students with a greater and more realistic challenge. In general, modelling is best viewed as an open-ended, iterative exercise. This can be guided by a framework for developing the skills and expertise required, together with the general principle 'solve the simple problems first', which requires some reflection on the student's own mathematical skills and competencies to identify a 'simple problem'.

As with most learning and teaching activities, the implementation of modelling can be at a variety of levels and ideally as an integrated activity through a degree programme. The learning outcomes that can be associated with an extensive modelling provision include:

- knowledge and understanding;
- analysis;
- problem-solving;
- creativity/originality;
- communication and presentation;
- evaluation;
- planning and organisation;
- interactive and group skills.

In practice most will only be achieved through a planned programme of activities.

(The Authors)

According to Hibberd (2002), mathematical modelling is the process of:

- translating a real-world problem into a mathematically formulated representation;
- solving this mathematical formulation; and then
- interpreting the mathematical solution in a real-world context.

The principal processes are about how to apply mathematics and how to communicate the findings. There are, however, many difficulties that can arise. For those with an interest in exploring the ideas offered in Case study 1, the article by Hibberd (2002) contains further case studies illustrating the application of these principles; while Townend *et al.* (1995) and Haines and Dunthorne (1996) offer further practical materials.

Interrogating practice

What different teaching and learning approaches are used to deliver your modules? Do these address, at various stages, the skills highlighted above? If not, consider how you might apply the use of modelling to your practice.

ISSUES PARTICULAR TO STATISTICS

Statistics is much younger than mathematics. Two strands can be identified in tracing its origins. First, discussions about the theory of gambling in the mid-seventeenth century led to the first attempts to found a theory of probability. Second, the gradual increase in the collection of what would nowadays be called official statistics throughout the nineteenth century led to new developments in the display, classification and interpretation of data. Many signal advances in public policy were made through the application of what might now be seen as very elementary techniques of descriptive statistics but which were at the time truly visionary. These included, famously, the identification of a single pump mainly responsible for a cholera outbreak in London, and the work of Florence Nightingale in establishing the antecedents of today's extensive medical statistics.

Given that society is being increasingly exposed to more and more data across a broad range of disciplines, it is vitally important that people involved in those disciplines achieve at least a basic understanding of what variability means. For many, an appreciation of how that variability within their subject area can be managed is vital for success. And yet statistics is often regarded as being difficult to understand, especially by non-specialist students of the subject. It is therefore important for teachers of statistics, whether specialist statisticians or other subject experts who teach it within their own curriculum area, to know how best to approach teaching the subject.

For this section we draw on many fruitful conversations with Professor N. Davies, Director of the Royal Statistical Society Centre for Statistical Education; as well as on a survey of teachers of statistics in the *Maths, Stats and OR Newsletter* (February 2000) and on the research literature.

How students learn statistics

In a wide-ranging paper, Garfield (1995) reports the results of a scientific study of how some students best learn statistics. Inter alia, she concluded that the following five scenarios needed to be part of the learning environment so that students could get the optimal learning gain for the subject:

1   activity and small group work;
2   testing and feedback on misconceptions;
3   comparing reality with predictions;
4   computer simulations;
5   software that allows interaction.

When the mathematical foundations of statistics are being studied, it is often necessary to go into the sometimes deep theoretical foundations of the subject. Students who have a strong mathematical background will be able to cope with this. However, many experienced teachers of statistics have come to the conclusion that these five points work best with a data-driven approach to the subject. Many would claim that this is the only method that is likely to work on a large scale with non-specialist students of the subject. Even so, some scholars advocate that, at the same time as teaching data handling, probability concepts must be taught as well, and as early as possible. See, for example, Lindley (2001), who argues convincingly that even at school level, probability concepts should be taught. Others maintain that probability is such a difficult and sophisticated topic to teach properly that its treatment should be left until students have reached a more mature appreciation of the subject (see e.g. Moore and McCabe, 1998). There appear to be little experimental data to support either claim at present.

Innovative use of real data

As well as a discipline in its own right, statistics is an essential science in many other subjects. Consequently, at some stage data will need to be collected for and on behalf of each of those disciplines. This could comprise primary and/or secondary data. When surveyed, the statistics community of teachers in higher education institutions expressed a need for exemplar data-based material for routine use both by themselves and by their students. They looked for realistic scenarios, useful to both the teacher for good practice teaching material and students for effective learning material. The Web-based random data selector, described in Davies (2002), provides a useful tool to create just such a rich learning and teaching material. The CensusAtSchool project is delivered from: http://censusatschool.ntu.ac.uk.

A Web facility permits the selection of a random sample of the raw data collected for CensusAtSchool. These data are for use in the classroom or in pupils' projects. Users may choose from databases consisting of responses from specific countries, including the UK, Queensland in Australia, South Africa, or a combined database of directly comparable responses. This may be a selection from all data of geographical regions of the chosen country. Selections may be restricted to responses from a particular age or gender. Sample sizes allowed are up to 200 per country and 500 from the combined database. A full range of graphical and spreadsheet accessories may be brought to bear upon the data.

THE ROLE OF TECHNOLOGY

There is an increasing focus on the use of technology in higher education and a lively debate on effective e-delivery and e-learning. Sadly we have to note that few of the generic developments in this area are well aligned with the needs of learners in mathematics and statistics. To a certain extent these problems also have an impact upon those studying engineering and the sciences. For example, most of the software for computer-based assessment is very restrictive when used in mathematics. Common problems are:

- inefficient or poor display of mathematical expressions;
- restricted choice of question types;
- failure to recognise mathematically equivalent solutions;
- difficulty in allowing students to input complex mathematical responses.

As a result, technological developments in the discipline have tended to follow a distinct but parallel path. The important extra ingredient which enhances the power and ease of access of computer technology usually involves some form of computer algebra system (**CAS**), by which is meant software systems that can perform symbolic as well as numerical manipulations and include graphical display capabilities. Examples include Maple, Mathematica, Macsyma and Derive. Some of these systems are available not only on personal computers but also on handheld 'super calculators' such as the TI-92 plus and the TI-89.

Much has been spoken and written about the use of a CAS in learning and teaching over the past few decades (see, e.g., the International Congress for Mathematics Education (ICME) Proceedings since 1984, and journals such as the *International Journal of Computer Algebra in Mathematics Education* (IJCAME)). Yet there still seems to be a range of views about the effectiveness of these systems in the learning and teaching of mathematics. Certainly, the strong emphasis on the use of calculator technology, especially in schools, has been blamed for 'the mathematics problem in society' and this 'bad press' has contributed to the debate on whether the use of technology such as a CAS may be linked to falling mathematical standards among graduates.

On the other hand, there have been several studies citing students gaining a better conceptual understanding of mathematics with no significant loss in computational skills. For example, Hurley *et al.* (1999) cite a National Science Foundation report which states:

> Approximately 50% of the institutions conducting studies on the impact of technology reported increases in conceptual understanding, greater facility with visualization and graphical understanding, and an ability to solve a wider variety of problems, without any loss of computational skills. Another 40% reported that students in classes with technology had done at least as well as those in traditional classes.

Further developments have occurred more recently in relation to assessment, where the power of computer algebra systems has been employed to ease issues of both question setting and marking. There are now a number of alternatives, including **AIM** (Alice Interactive Mathematics) and its related development STACK (System for Teaching and Assessment using a Computer Algebra Kernel), which we focus on in Case study 2. STACK offers advantages over AIM, which is no longer being developed, in that it employs the open-source computer algebra system Maxima instead of Maple.

Case study 2: Stack

STACK exploits the full power of a computer algebra system to offer significant flexibility in authoring tasks for students (see Sangwin and Grove, 2006). One may create random problems based on a given structure, provide worked solutions and assess student responses. Answers may involve arbitrary mathematical expressions couched in syntax employed for *Maxima*, allowing one to determine the mathematical properties of the answers that students provide. Feedback can also be linked to the student responses.

The software thus addresses many of the issues raised in the initial part of this section, and has been widely adopted in the USA, UK, Australia, Canada and Norway. STACK incorporates a range of features that are of particular relevance:

- free availability – STACK is owned by the academic community, there is no licence and the package can be freely downloaded (see http://stack.bham.ac.uk/);
- ease and flexibility of use – STACK can be easily customised to reflect the particular style of approach of the individual lecturer;
- ease of access for students – STACK allows for integration into the virtual learning environment Moodle.

(The Authors)

Sangwin (2002) considers the power of such software to help develop higher mathematical skills. This signals a major new role for technology in learning mathematics. In particular, it is now possible to challenge students to produce 'instances' (as Sangwin calls them), which is a task that has always probed more deeply into students' understanding, but has been seen to be very demanding on staff (for example, it is very instructive for a student to construct an example of a 4 by 4 singular matrix, with no two entries the same – but who wants to mark 200 when they can all be different and all still correct!). Other contributions to the role of technology (some with special reference to higher skills) in computer-aided assessment may be found at www.mathstore.ac.uk.

OVERVIEW

This chapter has concentrated on the discipline-specific issues facing those engaged in facilitating learning and teaching in mathematics and statistics in higher education, considering these issues from the perspectives of pure mathematics, applied mathematics, statistics and the impact of technology. In this we have taken particular care to consider the ways in which teaching and learning in mathematics and statistics may be grounded in the nature of these disciplines. While traditional methods enable us to present mathematics as a system of ideas that is underpinned by logic, and applied to modelling the real world, we have also seen that wider methods can help us to view mathematics as a creative activity; one that is carried out by students facing their own challenge in adjusting to study at higher education.

And now . . . Read the chapter again! Engage with it and reflect upon it. Consider how you might apply or adapt the ideas proposed to your own practice. There are plenty of other suggestions in the references. Disagree if you wish, but at least engage and know why you teach the way you do. If we have given you something to think about in your own approach, then we will be well on our way to improving the learning experiences of students as they study one of the most inspiring and challenging subjects in higher education.

REFERENCES

Appleby, J and Cox, W (2002) 'The transition to higher education', in P Kahn and J Kyle (eds), *Effective Learning and Teaching in Mathematics and its Applications*, pp 3–19, London: Kogan Page.

Brakes, W (2001) 'Logic, language and life', *Mathematical Gazette*, 85 (503), pp 255–266.

Croft, A (2001) *Algebra Refresher Booklet*, Loughborough: Loughborough University of Technology.

Davies, N (2002) 'Ideas for improving learning and teaching statistics', in P Kahn and J Kyle (eds), *Effective Learning and Teaching in Mathematics and its Applications*, pp 17–393, London: Kogan Page.

Department for Education and Skills (DfES) (2004) *Making Mathematics Count* (The Smith Report), London: DfES.

Durkin, K and Main, A (2002) 'Discipline-based skills support for first-year undergraduate students', *Active Learning in Higher Education*, 3 (1), pp 24–39.

Engineering Council (2000) *Measuring the Mathematics Problem*, London: The Engineering Council.

Garfield, J (1995) 'How students learn statistics', *International Statistics Review*, 63, pp 25–34.

Gibbs G (1999) 'Using assessment strategically to change the way students learn', in S Brown and A Glasner (eds), *Assessment Matters in Higher Education*, Maidenhead: Open University Press, pp 41–53.

Haines, C and Dunthorne, S (1996) *Mathematics Learning and Assessment: Sharing Innovative Practice*, London: Edward Arnold.

Hibberd, S (2002) 'Mathematical modelling skills', in P Kahn and J Kyle (eds), *Effective Learning and Teaching in Mathematics and its Applications*, pp 175–193, London: Kogan Page.

Hurley, J F, Koehn, U and Gantner, S L (1999) 'Effects of calculus reform: local and national', *American Mathematical Monthly*, 106 (9), pp 800–811.

Kahn, P E (2001) *Studying Mathematics and its Applications*, Basingstoke: Palgrave.

Kyle, J and Sangwin, C J (2002) 'AIM – a parable in dissemination', *Proceedings of the second International Conference on the Teaching of Mathematics*, New York: John Wiley and Sons.

Lawson, D, Croft, A and Halpin, M (2001) *Good Practice in the Provision of Mathematics Support Centres*, Birmingham: LTSN Maths Stats and OR Network.

Lindley, D V (2001) Letter to the editor, *Teaching Statistics*, 23 (3).

London Mathematical Society (1992) *The Future for Honours Degree Courses in Mathematics and Statistics*, London: The London Mathematical Society.

Moore, D and McCabe, G P (1998) *Introduction to the Practice of Statistics*, New York: W H Freeman.

Palmer, P (1998) *The Courage to Teach*, San Francisco, CA: Jossey-Bass.

Prince, M (2004) 'Does active learning work? A review of the research, *Journal of Engineering Education*, July, pp 223–231.

Quality Assurance Agency for Higher Education (QAA) (2001) *QAA Subject Overview Report for Mathematics, Statistics and Operational Research*, Bristol: QAA. Available online at www.qaa.ac.uk/revreps/subjrev/All/QO7_2000.pdf (accessed 5 May 2008).

QAA (2002) *Benchmarking Document for Mathematics, Statistics and Operational Research*, Bristol: QAA. Available online at www.qaa.ac.uk (accessed 29 September 2007).

Sangwin, C J (2002) 'New opportunities for encouraging higher level mathematical learning by creative use of emerging computer aided assessment', *International Journal of Mathematical Education in Science and Technology*, 34(6), pp 813–829.

Sangwin, C J and Grove, M J (2006) 'STACK: addressing the needs of the "neglected learners"', in *Proceedings of the First WebALT Conference and Exhibition*, 5–6 January, The Netherlands: Technical University of Eindhoven, pp 81–95.

Savage, M D (2001) 'Getting to grips with the maths problem', *A Maths Toolkit for Scientists*. Available online at http://dbweb.liv.ac.uk/ltsnpsc/workshop/reports/mathtoo2.htm (accessed 29 December 2007).

Tall, D O (1999) 'The cognitive development of proof: is mathematical proof for all or for some?', in Z Usiskin (ed.), *Developments in School Mathematics Education Around the World*, 4, pp 117–136, Virginia: National Council of Teachers of Mathematics.

Townend, M S *et al.* (1995) *Mathematical Modelling Handbook: A Tutor Guide*, Undergraduate Mathematics Teaching Conference Workshop Series, Sheffield: Sheffield Hallam University Press.

FURTHER READING

Baumslag, B (2000) *Fundamentals of Teaching Mathematics at University Level*, London: Imperial College Press. Based primarily on the UK higher education experience.

Kahn, P E and Kyle, J (2002) *Effective Learning and Teaching in Mathematics and its Applications*, London: Kogan Page. Based primarily on the UK higher education experience.

Krantz, S G (1999) *How to Teach Mathematics* (2nd edn), Providence, RI: American Mathematical Society. Offers a US perspective and is full of solid, down-to-earth, sensible advice.

18 Key aspects of teaching and learning in engineering

John Dickens and Carol Arlett

CONTEXT

Curricula in engineering have for many years been heavily influenced by the requirements of **accreditation** by the professional institutions. Historically, accreditation guidelines have prescribed minimum contents of subdisciplines, admissions standards and even contact hours. In recent years there has been a significant move away from prescription and admission standards to output standards. The **QAA Subject Benchmarking** statements for engineering, first published in 2000, defined a set of standards in terms of knowledge and understanding, intellectual abilities, practical skills and general transferable skills that an engineering graduate should have attained. Almost in parallel, the Engineering Professors' Council produced a set of output standards and in 2004 the Engineering Council published *UK-SPEC* (ECUK, 2004) which adopted output standards for professional accreditation for the first time. The existence of three sets of output standards, despite being broadly similar, caused concern that was resolved in 2006 when all three parties agreed to adopt *UK-SPEC* as the output standard and the QAA published a revised benchmark statement that formalised this (QAA, 2006). The move to output standards has led to degree programmes being defined in terms of a set of **learning outcomes** (see Chapter 4). This has had an impact on programme design and on **assessment** strategies that enable students to demonstrate the attainment of learning outcomes.

The majority of degree programmes are accredited as providing the educational base that allows a graduate to progress to Chartered or Incorporated Engineer status after a period of professional practice. Accreditation confirms that graduates from a degree programme meet the defined output standards. However, a programme does not have to be accredited for it to meet the standards specified in the QAA benchmark statement.

> ### Interrogating practice
>
> What are the specific requirements which must be in place for your programmes to be accredited by the relevant professional body? How does this affect your own teaching?

Degree programmes in the UK are generally a three-year Bachelor of Engineering (B.Eng.) or a four-year Master of Engineering (M.Eng.). The M.Eng. provides the full educational base for Chartered Engineer status, a B.Eng. provides the base for Incorporated Engineer or can be topped up with further learning to Master's level either through a one-year Master's degree (M.Sc.) or an alternative approved combination of training and learning. A number of universities offer the M.Eng. and B.Eng. with an optional one-year **placement** in industry usually after two years of study.

There are also two-year **Foundation degrees** in engineering, many of which are delivered through further education colleges; all must have an industrial element. Foundation degrees do not normally require high admissions grades and most offer the opportunity for able students to top up their degree to Bachelor level. The professional accreditation position of Foundation degrees had not been resolved at the time of writing.

Admission to engineering degrees (M.Eng., B.Eng., B.Sc.) generally requires students to have the equivalent of three GCE A levels, one of which must be mathematics; a number of disciplines also require physics. In the 1990s universities saw a decline in the number of applications for admission on to engineering programmes (Engineering Training Board, 2006) but this position has improved with increases, for example, in Civil, but more difficult recruitment patterns in Manufacturing engineering. There has been much public debate about the numbers of students taking maths and sciences in schools and about the mathematical ability of the students who offer a maths qualification for university entry (Engineering Council UK, 2000). This change in the skills base of students entering university has led to many universities providing additional support, particularly in mathematics, and modifying the curriculum (Sigma – Centre for Excellence in Mathematics and Statistics Support, 2007). Changes in 14–19 education are introducing vocational diplomas in England, with the highest level being intended for university entry. Consultation between the diploma development groups and universities has focused particularly on mathematical content (14–19 Engineering Diploma, 2007).

Engineering curricula are continually being refreshed to keep up with developments within engineering businesses (The Royal Academy of Engineering, 2007). This is to include recent advances in engineering knowledge and also to incorporate new and developing areas such as sustainable development and ethics. The needs of employers and the wider economy have produced increased emphasis on **employability** skills, entrepreneurship and the need for **internationalisation** to enable graduates to work in the global economy.

At the time of writing the European Union is moving towards the Europe-wide adoption of a common educational framework in 2010, generally referred to as the **Bologna Process**. The framework defines the first two degree stages as a first cycle Bachelor degree 180 **ECTS** (three years) and a second cycle Masters at 90–120 ECTS. The Bachelor degree in the UK meets the first cycle requirement and the UK one-year taught postgraduate Master's may meet the 90 ECTS requirement. At the time of writing there is still some uncertainty about the impact of the Bologna Process on the four-year M.Eng. degree which has 240 ECTS.

Engineering teaching in HE faces a number of challenges which include coping with a wider skills mix among the student cohort on entry, particularly in mathematics, the need to be able to articulate clearly the learning outcomes for modules and to devise assessments that enable students to demonstrate the attainment of these outcomes. The **National Student Survey** (Unistats, 2007) has shown that the greatest area of dissatisfaction is in assessment and **feedback,** so establishing good practice in this area in essential.

CURRICULUM DESIGN AND DELIVERY

The lecture

Traditionally, lectures have involved the one-way transmission of course content from academics to students often in large lecture groups. Many academics still see the lecture as an efficient way, in terms of time usage, to deliver large volumes of core knowledge. If it is done well then it can be effective but the quality of the student learning is heavily dependent on the quality of delivery; Chapter 5 elaborates on some of these themes in more detail. Students can become passive recipients of information, leading to failure to engage with the subject or gain much from the learning experience. In response to this, and to make use of new technologies, the lecture format in engineering has seen some changes in recent years as many lecturers have introduced more opportunities for student interaction, participation and activities. For example, skeletal notes may be used to improve attention by the students, which have key pieces of information missing, such as parts of an equation, diagram or graph. Tests and quizzes can be effective in making the lecture a more interactive process and provide feedback on the students' understanding. **Personal Response Systems** and facilities offered through **Virtual Learning Environments** (VLEs) can be used to give immediate feedback. Lectures should motivate and challenge students and relevant photographs and video clips may be useful, as demonstrated in Case study 1 from the University of Bath.

Case study 1: 21ST century engineering with a historical perspective

Fluid Mechanics with Historical Perspective is part of a series of modules covering the broader subject of thermodynamics at the University of Bath. At the start of each hour-long lecture the tutor gives a 15-minute input on an aspect of discoveries and developments related to flight. This historical background usually consists of a five-minute PowerPoint presentation, followed by a short video clip providing the context for the formulae and calculations that are to be explained in the lecture. For example, at the start of a lecture on compressible flow of gases, the presentation is on the story of the first supersonic flight. The tutor developed 24 'mini-history lectures' to accompany the lecture series which he hopes will make this largely theoretical-based subject more interesting for his students.

The lectures are supported by a set of notes given out at the beginning of each topic. The notes include visual images, as well as brief notes on the historical perspective shown and the theoretical concepts explored. The notes are not, however, complete and students are expected to bring them to the lecture each week to fill in the blanks.

A large collection of materials has been developed over a period of time, and the improved access to resources via the internet has helped to develop the library further. 'Remembering back to the lectures that I enjoyed at university, I wanted to add something interesting to these lectures.'

Students traditionally regard mathematically based subjects as difficult. The tutor aims to expose students to the colourful history of engineering through using videos and images in the lectures. It is hoped that seeing real applications will help students to understand the fundamentals of the science and mathematics being taught. Feedback from students indicates that the inclusion of historical examples made the course more interesting and they welcomed the 'real examples of theory in action', which made the theoretical elements easier to understand. They felt more motivated and were keen to learn because they had more interest in the subject. Students also commented on the lectures expanding 'beyond just engineering into social and political issues', with the tutor being happy to discuss the impact of engineering on society.

The students also appreciated the good-quality, up-to-date notes produced by the tutor and found that the gaps in the notes made them concentrate in the lectures. The reference sections in the notes helped if they wanted to learn more or go back over theory, and as the notes were illustrated with pictures and anecdotes, the students were more likely to read through them again.

(Gary Lock, Department of Mechanical Engineering, University of Bath)

Enquiry-based learning

Engineering is a practical subject and the engineering degree curriculum has for many years contained project work where students undertake substantive pieces of work either individually and/or in groups (see also Chapter 11). In recent years it has been recognised that students engage better with the student-centred learning which projects provide, and often develop a deeper **approach to learning**. It reflects an old adage that students learn by doing. Consequently there has been an increase in the proportion of the curriculum delivered through **enquiry-based learning**.

Approaches to enquiry-based learning include (CEEBL, 2007):

- project-based learning (research-based approach);
- **problem-based learning (PBL)** (exploration of scenario-driven learning experience);
- investigation-based learning (fieldwork or case study adapted to discipline context).

Project-based learning provides students with the opportunity to bring together knowledge-based skills from a number of subject areas and apply them to real-life problems. It also helps to reinforce existing knowledge and provides a context to the theory. Engineering is a subject which lends itself well to this type of learning where projects will typically address authentic, real-world problems (Crawford and Tennant, 2003; Project Squared, 2003).

Projects can operate within hugely diverse contexts and along a broad continuum of approaches. They may be used by a single lecturer or course team within a department that mainly uses more traditional methods of teaching, or they may be linked to a complete restructuring of the learning experience of all students. The choice of type of project work will depend on the intended learning outcomes, and on whether you are looking for depth or breadth of knowledge-based skills. Projects may be open or closed; individual or group; conducted over a day or a year; multidisciplinary; or industry based. Projects are often well suited to applied topics, where different solutions may have equal validity. Students will be required to discover new information for themselves, and to use that knowledge in finding solutions and answers, but students will need support to become **independent learners**.

Problem-based learning has been introduced in some engineering departments on the grounds that for an equivalent investment of staff time, the learning outcomes of students are improved, as students are better motivated and more independent in their learning and gain a deeper understanding of the subject (see Case study 4). It is a style of learning in which the problems act as the context and driving force for learning (Boud and Feletti, 1997). It differs from 'problem-solving' in that the problems are encountered before all the relevant knowledge has been acquired, and solving problems results in the acquisition of knowledge and problem-solving skills. (In problem-solving, the knowledge acquisition has usually already taken place and the problems serve as a means to explore or enhance that knowledge.)

The curriculum is organised around the problems. So problems have to be carefully matched to the desired learning outcomes. Where PBL has been fully taken on board there are no lectures; instead students, usually working in groups, engage in self-directed learning and the tutor acts as a facilitator, mentor or guide (see also Chapter 26).

There are some disadvantages to using a wholly PBL approach. The content covered in this way is reduced, compared to the amount that can be covered in lecture-based courses. In addition, many institutions may be short of the sort of space that helps PBL to work well (see Learning spaces, p. 272 below). It also requires considerable investment of staff time to manage the groups and to develop effective problems, but many academics think the initial investment is worth the effort.

The *CDIO Initiative* is an innovative educational framework for producing the next generation of engineers. In the education of student engineers it stresses engineering fundamentals set in the context of *C*onceiving – *D*esigning – *I*mplementing – *O*perating real-world systems and products. It was designed as a framework for curricular planning and outcome-based assessment that is universally adaptable for all engineering schools. The framework was initially developed in the USA and has been adopted by a number of universities around the world either as part of a complete redesign of the curriculum or as new elements in a modified curriculum (CDIO Initiative, 2007).

Practical work

Laboratory classes have always been an integral part of the curriculum, reflecting again that engineering is a practical subject. Lab sessions range through simple routine testing to give hands-on experience of how materials behave, to tests that prove the validity and limitations of theoretical concepts and culminate in research projects where students are devising their own laboratory testing programmes to determine new knowledge. Laboratory sessions are by their very nature student centred and deliver a wide range of learning outcomes that may include:

- gaining practical skills
- gaining experience of particular pieces of equipment/tools
- planning a testing programme
- making links between theory and practice
- gathering data
- analysis of data
- making observations
- forming and testing hypotheses
- using judgement
- developing problem-solving skills
- communicating data and concepts
- developing personal skills
- developing ICT skills

- conducting risk assessments
- developing health and safety working practices.

Laboratories are expensive to provide, maintain and equip. They also require high levels of staff contact time. It is therefore important that laboratory sessions are well planned and integrated into the curriculum if maximum benefit is to be gained from this expensive resource. Learning materials such as virtual labs are becoming available which have an important role in supplementing lab work but are unlikely to replicate the full benefits of the hands-on practical session in the foreseeable future.

e-learning

Engineers have long been at the forefront of change, exploiting advances in technology and related innovations, and now the computer is very much an integral part of life for the professional engineer. Hence many engineering academics have embraced the concept of e-learning which is about facilitating and supporting student learning through the use of information and communication technologies. Many different approaches to learning and teaching are being taken within engineering to keep pace with rapidly changing technical developments. It is important to consider and evaluate the pedagogical benefits to both students and staff. Examples of good e-practice within engineering may be found on the Engineering Subject Centre's website, such as: mobile and wireless technologies (use of PDAs, podcasts, mobile phones), online communication tools (e-mail, bulletin boards), flexible interactive computer-based learning (use of software, audio and video conferencing), and delivery through virtual learning environments (see also Chapter 7).

Case study 2: Implementations of optical fibre communications module in a virtual learning environment

The VLE, BlackBoard, is used as the sole means for delivering content and most of the assessments for a course taken by students studying a variety of degrees in Electrical and Electronic Engineering or Communication Engineering. The tutor wanted to find a flexible way of delivering his course without disadvantaging students. The bulk of the content delivery is now through 40 short lectures, which comprise an audio-video recording of the lecturer, slides, and a transcript of the lecture, supported by handouts. The recordings are accessible at any time, and can be paused, rewound, replayed and so on under the control of the student. The online resources also include other video clips and animations, video contributions from an external expert, 35 formative assessments (quizzes), online summative assignments, links to selected external resources, and a message board for queries.

The feedback from the students indicates that they are appreciative of the flexibility offered by the online course and of being able to work at a time and pace that suits them, with the majority finding that using the VLE increased their motivation to learn. The VLE enabled the use of different resource types and greater interaction with the tutor through the discussion board than was typical in a lecture.

For further information see http://www.engsc.ac.uk/downloads/optical.pdf.

(John Fothergill, Department of Engineering, University of Leicester)

Web-based laboratories

As described above, practical work is a key component of engineering degrees and laboratory sessions are one of the principal ways that engineers learn how to apply theory. However, with the increase in class sizes and the drain on resources to provide up-to-date equipment, universities and colleges are increasingly using web-based laboratories (also referred to as virtual or remote labs or e-practicals). Virtual labs can also help to develop laboratory skills in distance learning students and disabled students who may not be able to access traditional laboratories. The practical sessions can use a range of technologies including online movie clips, simulations and labs controlled over the internet. While virtual approaches cannot replace real-world experimentation in technology and engineering, if a sound pedagogic approach is adopted, they can be a valuable aid to understanding.

e-assessment or computer-aided assessment

There are plenty of examples of innovative and effective practice in e-assessment which can have advantages over traditional methods including greater speed of marking and immediate feedback, as well as increasing usability and accessibility for a diverse range of students. Case study 3 describes such an example.

> Case study 3: Improving student success and retention through greater participation and tackling student-unique tutorial sheets

In response to concerns about the poor examination pass rates and also about the students' understanding of the subject in a first-year Fluid Mechanics and Thermodynamics module, the tutors introduced student-unique, weekly-assessed tutorial sheets. Each week a new set of assessment sheets, made unique by embedding random factors into each student's tutorial sheet, are delivered to the students via the university's bespoke Learning Environment. The students have one week to submit their answers to a dedicated computer program, written specifically to support the requirements of this assessment. The process of marking and providing feedback is automated, using a Microsoft Excel spreadsheet.

The use of computer technologies made the regular and student-unique approach a viable proposition. The tutors found that short and regular assessments with prompt group and individual feedback can have a positive impact on student learning. This is evidenced by the increased levels of student engagement with the subject and also in their improved performance in the final examination. The students are positive about this uniqueness of the assessment which also indicates their willingness to help combat collusion and answer sharing.

More information available from http://www.engsc.ac.uk/resources/wats/downloads/wats_report.pdf.

(Mark Russell and Peter Bullen, School of Aerospace,
Automotive and Design Engineering, and
the Blended Learning Unit, University of Hertfordshire)

Learning spaces

The majority of university buildings were designed at a time when the delivery of the curriculum focused heavily on the lecture and so most have a stock of tiered lecture theatres with fixed seating. These will have been updated to provide better visual aids such as data projection and still allow appropriate space for the traditional lecture. However, as we have described above, delivery methods have moved towards more student-centred practices that require flat-floored, well-resourced flexible spaces, and often these may be in short supply. It follows that if students are set more project and PBL work, often in groups, they need space for informal working sessions. New lecturers should consider the learning space available and its effective use when planning their teaching.

There has been a move to redesign learning spaces in recent years, for example the interactive classroom at Strathclyde (see Case study 4). The Centres for Excellence in Teaching and Learning initiative in England included funding for the provision of new learning spaces, and for research and evaluation into their use. Some examples relevant to engineering may be found at the Engineering **CETL** at Loughborough University (http://engc4e.lboro.ac.uk/); InQbate at the University of Sussex (www.inqbate.co.uk); and the Reinvention Centre at the University of Warwick and Oxford Brookes (www.warwick.ac.uk/go/reinvention).

The Department of Mechanical Engineering in the University of Strathclyde has embarked upon a radical change in its teaching methods for first-year students. The aim was to introduce active and collaborative learning in the large lecture room through the use of peer instruction – a version of Socratic Dialogue ('teaching by questioning') as developed by Professor Eric Mazur at Harvard University. The standard lecture/tutorial/laboratory format of traditional instruction was replaced by a series of two-hour active learning sessions involving short mini-lectures, videos, demonstrations and problem-solving, all held together by classroom questioning and discussion. A custom-built lecture theatre – the InterActive ClassRoom – was constructed in 1998 to enable this style of teaching. The classroom – which holds 120 students – was designed for group seating, and, to assist peer instruction, included the first Classroom Feedback System in Europe, now replaced by the **Personal Response System** (PRS). Peer instruction was initially used in introductory mechanics and thermo-fluids classes, but was quickly extended to mathematics. This accounted for half the compulsory engineering elements of the first year.

The following year a version of PBL (mechanical dissection) was introduced into the design classes. Now students work in groups of four in the design classes, and also work together in the same groups in the InterActive ClassRoom. Finally in 2000 Strathclyde built the first of its new Teaching Clusters – a managed suite of teaching rooms that includes the first Teaching Studio in the UK. The Studio is based on a design developed by Rensselaer Polytechnic Institute in the USA. The first-year students now use the studio for engineering analysis classes and their learning experience is a mix of peer instruction, PBL and studio teaching.

Overall the change to active teaching styles, with collaborative learning, has been a huge success – in terms of both student performance and retention. An independent evaluation was carried out. Student reaction included the following:

> 'With 100 people in the class you normally just sit there without being involved . . . and add to your notes. In that class everybody's involved, you have to think about what's being said . . . you have to stay awake...but it's more fun, you get more from it . . . better than just sitting taking notes.'

> 'What fun it can be, it can be light-hearted, yet you still learn a lot.'

> 'How quickly a two-hour class passed compared to other one-hour lecture classes.'

'You can learn a lot easier from the people that are the same age as you . . . if they've just grasped it then they can explain it in sort of easier terms than the lecturer . . . you suddenly understand it when a minute before it was difficult.'

For more information see http://www.mecheng.strath.ac.uk/tandl.asp.

(Professor Jim Boyle, Department of Mechanical Engineering, University of Strathclyde)

Work-based learning

A work-based learning programme can be defined as a process for recognising, creating and applying knowledge through, for and at work which forms part (credits) or all of a higher education qualification (NEF, 2007).

Industrial placements

Work-based learning (WBL) is seen by the majority of university engineering departments as learning *for* work. Typically, this includes WBL undertaken by full-time undergraduate students as part of their degree course in the form of sandwich placements and work experience modules. There are challenges for university lecturers in structuring WBL into a taught degree programme, and in its assessment as part of the overall degree assessment. Ideally a **placement learning** contract is established against a competence assessment framework and in some cases the placement is credit bearing. The period of work experience can vary from a few months to a whole year. The QAA's Code on placement learning provides a set of precepts, with accompanying guidance, on arrangements for placement learning (QAA, 2001).

The vast majority of students will say that WBL activity has improved their generic and personal **transferable skills** (e.g. multi-tasking, working under pressure, communication, timekeeping, interpersonal and reflective skills). They also have the chance to use the theory and apply it to real-life projects. Lecturers report that WBL is important in improving student motivation, the generic skill set and specific engineering skills, and this is recognised by employers when it comes to graduation (Engineering Subject Centre, 2005; NEF, 2007).

Key stages in a successful work placement scheme include:

* Finding the placement. Building and maintaining links with industry so as to be able to offer students quality work experience takes a number of years, and many engineering departments have dedicated staff with responsibility for this and persuading employers about the potential business benefits of offering placements.
* Working in partnership – the company, the university, the student. A successful partnership will develop if there are clear statements of responsibilities, set out

in a handbook, sectionalised for student, visiting tutor and industrial supervisor. The university needs to provide channels of communications between all the partners.

- Health and safety. Universities need to consider the health and safety legislation very carefully. Risks to students are minimised by ensuring that the employer conforms to health and safety legislation. However, delegation of the procurement of placements to other agencies does not release universities from their legal responsibilities (CVCP, 1997).
- Preparing the student. Students need to be informed of the benefits of work placements, the time-scale and methods of application and the normal requirements of the workplace. Courses on writing CVs, application forms and interview techniques are important. Visiting lectures by industrialist recruitment specialists and presentations by careers staff and students returning from industry can all be useful.
- Maintaining contact with the student. Students should be encouraged to contact the university to discuss problems and successes. In the workplace, students are best supported by a visit from an academic member of staff. Students on placements might be further supported by electronic means, either between staff and students, or between peers.
- Assessment. Students gain most benefit from the placement if the formal assessment process is clear. However, the novel and innovative nature of WBL requires that non-traditional means are found for assessing it. Students need to be conscious of their development and to be encouraged to assess their own progress. This may be assessed via a **portfolio** or personal development diary. Students may be expected to support their placement work and prepare for return to university with some academic study. Many students in industry carry out project work and the project report may form a part of the assessment.

Workforce development

In order to realise the UK's higher skills agenda (Leitch, 2006), universities are considering how to respond to the possibility that a proportion of HE funding could be delivered through a demand-led mechanism, with employers having an influence on the content of courses. It is hence increasingly important that engineering departments continue to develop relationships with employers, possibly through Sector Skills Councils, and to develop flexible modes of delivery. Engineering departments are looking to enhance their capability and capacity to deliver innovative WBL solutions to support the skills agenda. If targets for numbers with higher-level qualifications are to be met, then many engineering lecturers may increasingly be delivering teaching within the workplace to non-traditional students.

SKILLS DEVELOPMENT

The requirements as set out by UK-SPEC and the QAA Benchmark Statement for Engineering cover specific learning outcomes in engineering that should be demonstrated by graduates (covered explicitly within the curriculum), as well as what engineers view as the 'softer (or transferable) skills', such as an awareness of ethical and environmental issues. Employers want graduates who demonstrate a wide range of attributes including analysis, reflection, critique and synthesis, but they also value the 'soft' personal skills, including communication and presentation skills (Harvey, 2003; Engineering Subject Centre, 2007a). This is a challenge for engineering academics as they seek innovative ways of integrating these into an already packed curriculum.

The most effective way of providing opportunities for students to develop these skills is by embedding them within a discipline context in a module. Not only does this help to overcome difficulties of fitting new material into an already full curriculum, but it also helps the students to learn within a context that is relevant.

- Communications skills occur within a context of giving a presentation about project work.
- Enterprise and entrepreneurship skills (risk assessment, risk-taking, creativity skills, business planning and overcoming fear of failure) may be included as part of a team project to design and develop an innovative product.
- Intellectual property awareness should be raised during the first year. Students can be encouraged to review IP of consumer items, technical assignment and patents and trademarks policy of their placement company (Engineering Subject Centre, 2007b).
- Ethical aspects of engineering are becoming an increasingly important theme. The curriculum map (Royal Academy of Engineering and the Engineering Professors' Council, 2005) provides a framework for ethics across each level of an undergraduate programme, defining the location within the curriculum, the learning outcomes, content and process. Case studies to support the teaching of ethics to engineering students have been developed by the Inter-disciplinary Ethics Applied CETL (IDEAS, 2007).
- Education for sustainable development should be a component of all courses to ensure students develop the skills and knowledge that will enable them to think and act critically and effectively about sustainability issues. This is often taught within design courses and a toolbox with teaching materials is available (Loughborough University, 2004).

Engineering departments would not usually expect their staff to have the expertise to cover all these areas, but delivery can be provided jointly with departments and services within the institution (business schools, enterprise units and careers services may be able to help with entrepreneurship; a law department will have experts on IP; a philosophy department may have ethicists to support teaching of ethics). External speakers from industry, professional bodies, government organisations and alumni can provide additional interest and expertise.

An audit of what you already do in the curriculum with respect to employability may help to highlight strengths and areas for improvement (Engineering Subject Centre,

2007c). Make sure that students are aware of the significance of aspects of learning and appreciate ways in which activities such as teamwork, projects and problem-solving offer opportunities for skills development. **Personal Development Planning,** progress files or e-portfolios can do much to encourage staff and students to pay attention to skills development and to make time for development and reflection within the curriculum (see also Chapter 8).

Interrogating practice

- How does the content and design of the modules/courses you teach address employability issues?
- What improvements could you make to integrate skills development within your teaching?

ASSESSMENT

Assessment and **feedback** to students are critical and significant parts of an academic's work (see also Chapter 10 on assessment, which includes a case study from engineering). The evidence that students meet the learning outcomes of their programme of study for internal **quality assurance** and external accreditation is found in students' work. It is therefore vital that the assignments set and the marking criteria used enable students to demonstrate this attainment. The National Student Survey (Unistats), sent to all final-year students in England, has consistently identified assessment and feedback as the area in which students are least satisfied.

The main assessment tools encountered in engineering disciplines are:

- unseen written examinations
- laboratory/practical/field trip reports
- analytical calculations
- multiple choice questions (especially at lower levels)
- project reports and software developed
- design project reports/outputs
- drawings (usually CAD)
- portfolios and personal development plans
- poster presentations
- oral presentations.

Unseen written examinations still comprise a substantial part of the assessment in engineering and are appropriate in many areas, particularly for assessing knowledge of underpinning engineering science in the early part of a traditionally structured degree programme. In areas where the learning outcomes are more focused on the application of knowledge and skills development, coursework assignments and project work are more appropriate. Care is needed when setting coursework assignments as the easy access to electronic information has led to an increase in **plagiarism**. All engineering will contain elements of group work, particularly in design projects, and it is important that the assessment can differentiate between the students within the group either by incorporating individual elements of work or by using peer assessment.

An underlying principle governing the selection of assignments is that the assessment should align with the teaching methods and learning outcomes for the module. This is known as **constructive alignment** (Biggs, 1999; Engineering Subject Centre, 2007d). Assignments should have clear marking criteria which should be communicated to students and they should enable students to show that they have achieved the outcomes for that element of learning (Moore and Williamson, 2005). It is also important that students receive feedback on submitted work that tells them where they could have improved the submission and why they have received the mark or grade awarded. While it is important that assignments align to the learning outcomes, it is also important that students are not over-assessed. The type and quantity of assessments needs careful planning at both module and programme level to ensure that they are sufficient but not excessive.

Interrogating practice

- Do the methods of assessment that you use align with the teaching methods for your module?
- Do your assessed assignments align with and deliver the learning outcomes for your module?
- Are you aware of how your module fits into the bigger picture of the overall programme assessment strategy?

WHERE TO FIND MORE SUPPORT

Many academics find that the most useful support comes from within their own discipline area. There are 24 subject centres within the subject network of the Higher Education Academy and the following are particularly relevant for engineers:

- Engineering Subject Centre, www.engsc.ac.uk
- UK Centre for Materials Education, www.materials.ac.uk
- Centre for Education in the Built Environment, www.cebe.heacademy.ac.uk

All subject centres provide subject-specific support and work closely with academics to enhance the student learning experience. Their websites are rich sources of information about relevant events, opportunities for funding, and learning and teaching resources. Programmes are run specifically for new lecturers, providing opportunities to draw on the expertise of colleagues within the same discipline area.

Many of the Centres for Excellence in Teaching and Learning (CETLs) have expertise on themes that are of interest to engineers, including ethics, assessment, creativity, blended learning and enquiry-based learning. The Engineering CETL (http://engc4e.lboro.ac.uk/) at Loughborough University supports industry-linked higher education across engineering, informed by research and evaluation.

The professional bodies provide some professional updating in teaching-related areas or organise conferences on teaching and learning. The Engineering Council (UK)'s website (www.engc.org.uk) has links to the 36 engineering institutions, as well as information about accreditation and getting registered.

The Engineering Professors' Council (www.epc.ac.uk) is a forum for senior academics responsible for engineering teaching and research in higher education, but its publications and activities will be of interest to all academics.

A wide variety of schemes and awards for undergraduates are run by the Royal Academy of Engineering (www.raeng.org.uk) to support engineering education.

OVERVIEW

This chapter provides a current view of the context for learning and teaching in engineering and outlines some approaches to curriculum design and delivery. The curricular requirements from professional bodies and skills required by employers are discussed. Case studies are used to give examples of practice in engineering from universities across the UK and references are provided to give the reader links to further information.

REFERENCES

14–19 Engineering Diploma (2007) <http://engineeringdiploma.com/ (accessed September 2007).

Biggs, J (1999) *Teaching for Quality Learning at University*, Buckingham: SRHE and the Open University Press.

Boud, D and Feletti, G (1997) *The Challenge of Problem-based Learning* (2nd edn), London: Kogan Page.

CDIO Initiative (2007) <http://www.cdio.org/index.html (accessed September 2007).

Centre for Excellence in Enquiry-Based Learning (CEEBL) (2007) The University of Manchester, <http://www.campus.manchester.ac.uk/ceebl/ebl/> (accessed May 2007).

Crawford, A and Tennant, J (2003) A *Guide to Learning Engineering through Projects*. Available online at <http://www.pble.ac.uk (accessed May 2007).

CVCP (1997) *Health and Safety Guidance for the Placement of HE Students*, London: CVCP.

Engineering Council UK (2000) *Measuring the Mathematics Problem*, London: ECUK.

Engineering Council UK (2004) *UK-SPEC Standard for Chartered Engineers and Incorporated Engineers*, London: ECUK.

Engineering Subject Centre (2005) *Guide to Industrial Placements*, Loughborough: Engineering Subject Centre.

Engineering Subject Centre (2007a) *Employability Briefing for Engineering Academics*. Available online at <http://www.engsc.ac.uk/er/employability/index.asp (accessed September 2007).

Engineering Subject Centre (2007b) *Intellectual Property in the Engineering Syllabus – a Model for Integrating Key but not Core Concepts across the Disciplines*. Available online at <http://www.engsc.ac.uk/resources/ipminiproj/index.asp (accessed September 2007).

Engineering Subject Centre (2007c) *Employability Audit*. Available online at <http://www.engsc.ac.uk/er/employability/audit.pdf (accessed September 2007).

Engineering Subject Centre (2007d) *How Can Learning and Teaching Theory Assist Engineering Academics?* Available online at <http://www.engsc.ac.uk/er/theory/index.asp (accessed September 2007).

Engineering Training Board (ETB) (2006) *Engineering UK 2006: A Statistical Guide to Labour Supply and Demand in Engineering and Technology*, London: ETB with ECUK.

Harvey, L (2003) *Transitions from Higher Education to Work*, York: ESECT/Higher Education Academy.

Inter-Disciplinary Ethics Applied: a Centre for Excellence in Teaching and Learning, University of Leeds (IDEAS) (2007) <http://www.idea.leeds.ac.uk/ (accessed September 2007).

Leitch Lord (2006) *Prosperity for All in the Global Economy – First Class Skills*, London: HM Treasury.

Loughborough University (2004) *Toolbox for Sustainable Design Education*. Available online at <http://www.lboro.ac.uk/research/susdesign/LTSN/Index.htm (accessed September 2007).

Moore, I and Williamson, S (2005) *Assessment of Learning Outcomes*, Loughborough: Engineering Subject Centre.

New Engineering Foundation (NEF) (2007) *The Path to Productivity: The Progress of Work-based Learning Strategies in Higher Education Engineering Programmes*, London: NEF.

Project Squared: A Guide to Project Work in Electrical and Electronic Engineering (2003) <http://www.eee.ntu.ac.uk/pp/ (accessed September 2007).

Quality Assurance Agency (2001) *Code of Practice for the Assurance of Academic Quality and Standards in Higher Education. Section 9: Placement Learning*, Gloucester: The Quality Assurance Agency for Higher Education.

Quality Assurance Agency (2006) *Subject Benchmark Statement Engineering*, Gloucester: The Quality Assurance Agency for Higher Education.

The Royal Academy of Engineering (2007) *Educating Engineers for the 21st Century*, London: The Royal Academy of Engineering.

The Royal Academy of Engineering and the Engineering Professors' Council (2005) *An Engineering Ethics Curriculum Map*, London: The Royal Academy of Engineering.

Sigma – Centre for Excellence in Mathematics and Statistics Support (2007) <http://www.sigma-cetl.ac.uk/ (accessed September 2007).

Unistats (2007) The college and university comparison site. Available online at <http://www.unistats.co.uk/ (accessed September 2007).

FURTHER READING

Baillie, C and Moore, I (eds) (2004) *Effective Learning and Teaching in Engineering*, Abingdon: Routledge.

Engineering Subject Centre (2005) *Guide to Lecturing*, Loughborough: Engineering Subject Centre.

Engineering Subject Centre (2007d) *How Can Learning and Teaching Theory Assist Engineering Academics?* See above.

19 Key aspects of teaching and learning in computing science

Gerry McAllister and Sylvia Alexander

THE COMPUTING PROFESSION

Information and computing skills are an essential component of all undergraduate programmes and the wider process of lifelong learning. In addressing the key issues of teaching and learning in computing science it is useful to have an insight into the short history of the subject in order to put it in context. Certainly no other subject community can claim that their industry or interest has had a greater impact on the everyday life of so many in the developed sector of our world. Likewise, no other subject discipline has been exposed to the rate of change that has occurred within computing science.

The computing industry itself has grown dramatically since the 1940s and was initially dominated by technology which provided large number-crunching and data-processing solutions within major commercial organisations or university research departments. The evolution of the technology progressed through a phase of lesser machines called mini-computers in the 1960s and 1970s, which both economically and physically facilitated functions such as industrial control and smaller commercial administrative operations, and were within the budgets of academic research projects. Thanks largely to the development of the single microprocessor chip, today we have desktop computers on practically every desk in every office and, through the merger of the computer and communications industries, a worldwide interconnection of computers.

Computing science is thus a discipline that has evolved at considerable pace, particularly throughout the second half of the past century. The impact of computers on everyday life may be commonly recognised in web browsing, electronic games and the everyday use of e-mail, spreadsheets and word processing. However, computing is now ubiquitous in every aspect of life, often invisible and thus unappreciated in the perception of the public. The mobile phone, iPod, MP 3 player, ATM machine, airline booking system, satellite navigation system and supermarket electronic scanning system are all perceived as being within and part of a greater company infrastructure, or technology developed as part of another industry (communications, music), rather than significant technological benefits to that infrastructure, or in fact a development of computer technology itself. Further confusion is caused by the role of ICT as used in everyday life and computing science as an academic discipline, two very different issues. These factors are believed to be considerable in the impressions which influence young people's decisions about entering the profession in the numbers industry currently seeks. Despite continued sector growth there has been a decline in applications to subject degree programmes over the past four years. This is not the reality of the computing industry where demand for graduates of the subject has continued to grow.

The software industry has had a significant impact on prosperity and growth in many Western economies (Sparrow, 2006). These economies have seen a shift in emphasis from industrialised manufacture of goods and selling services to one centred on the creation of wealth and jobs in a knowledge economy. This is driving many new opportunities. In the UK the benefits of software development are clear, with an estimated value of £13bn for own account software in 2006, an increase from £2.5bn in 2003. In total the UK software development industry employs one million people and produces an annual gross value added of £30bn.

Overall, computing science academics are tasked with considerable issues in maintaining a curriculum in the world's most rapidly changing industry, meeting the educational needs and expectations of 'digital native' students and adhering to numerous reports in skills issues such as greater employer engagement in the curricula (Leitch, 2006).

THE ACADEMIC ASPECT – COMPUTATIONAL THINKING

The 2007 revised QAA Subject Benchmark Statements for Computing (QAA) describes the subject as the understanding, design and exploitation of computation and computer technology and proposes it as one of the most significant advances of the twentieth century. It is a discipline that blends elegant theories with the solution of immediate practical problems. These theories are often derived from a range of other disciplines, such as mathematics, engineering, psychology and human behaviour, graphical design or experimental insight.

Computational thinking encompasses a significant number of somewhat unique cognitive tasks identified within the range of computing science, and seeks to address the fundamental question of what is computable. It has been suggested (Wing, 2006) that computational thinking should be added to every child's analytical ability to include thinking recursively, parallel processing, interpretation of data and code, type checking, analysing and numerous other analytical and cognitive skills associated with computer programming and large complex system design, until it becomes ingrained in everyone's lives.

Curriculum

Graduates of computing science require a blend of abilities encompassing not only technical but business acumen and interpersonal skills. Employers of graduates seek primarily good technical ability in all aspects of software development but also a mixture of other skills facilitating teamworking, communications and project management. Both the British Computer Society (BCS) and the Institution for Engineering and Technology (IET) are concerned that educational institutions maintain standards appropriate for those wishing to follow a career in computing. Both professional bodies offer systems of exemption and accreditation for appropriate courses, providing a route to membership. These schemes are valuable forms of recognition by professional bodies that courses offer appropriate curricula to meet the needs of industry and commerce. In considering courses for exemption or accreditation, evidence is required to show that course content aims to offer students sufficient breadth of coverage in appropriate computing topics to provide sound academic grounding in the discipline. The curricular guidelines produced by the validating bodies are not prescriptive with respect to core course content, thus enabling institutions to develop specialisms and provide a distinctive flavour to their course provision.

The scope of the field of computing is reflected in the varied titles and curricula that institutions have given to computing-related degree courses. The expanding inter-disciplinary and diverse nature of the subject causes overlap with areas of interest such as engineering, physics, mathematics, psychology, physiology, design and linguistics. Many institutions offer joint programmes of computing with these areas. However, with the rapid rate of development, study of different aspects of the subject is appropriate to a wide range of student interests and aspirations. Computer ethics, forensics, multimedia, games development and medical informatics are all emerging disciplines which present a spectrum of activity ranging from theory at one end to practice at the other. The QAA subject benchmarks define a body of knowledge indicative of the scope of the broad area of computing. However, despite the flexibility in programme design there are certain core elements which remain common, most notably the teaching of programming. Problems associated with the teaching (and more importantly the learning) of programming have generated considerable debate within the profession.

Teaching programming

Programming is a core skill in computing science. The teaching of programming is perceived to be problematic and programming modules are identified as having a detrimental effect on continuing enrolment rates within degree programmes. The cognitive difficulties in learning to program and the skills that make a good programmer are difficult to identify. Probably more time is invested in teaching programming than any other area of the discipline, yet students struggle as they try to master the skill. Many graduates of computing science will indeed seek employment where the need for the skill is minimal. Some institutions have developed programs where the curriculum is more focused on the application of software and software packages, with less focus on the design and development of software itself. Nevertheless, the demand for skilled programmers is increasing and academics must consider carefully how best to deal with the problems associated with programming in order to provide better student support.

Case study 1: Teaching programming

Teaching computer programming is indeed a problem. At the heart of the problem lies the very nature of the skill itself; programming is something that is best learnt over a long time and with a great deal of practice. This is not a learning model that fits happily in today's still prevailingly lecture-based and often semesterised higher education system.

There is a danger in any lecture setting that students can become little more than passive recipients of information conveyed by the lecturer. The old cliché has this information passing from the notes of the lecturer into the notes of the student, and passing through the minds of neither. This scenario might be acceptable, or even effective, in some disciplines, but it is absolutely fatal when programming is being taught or learnt.

The key to making lectures on programming more effective is for the 'lecturer' to make the students participate. The students should be active participants rather than passive recipients. There are many ways in which this can be done – the only limitation is the imagination of the lecturer. The following are some examples.

Parameter passing

There are usually two forms of parameter passing supported in a programming language, and the difference is subtle, especially for novices. The essential difference between parameters passed as values and those passed as references can be illustrated with a simple demonstration.

Armed with some sample functions, accepting a variety of parameters, the instructor can record the values of variables on the back of a collection of Frisbees. Different colours of Frisbee, or different sizes, can be used to indicate different variable types. The sample functions can be 'walked through', and a student (or group) is nominated to carry out this process; they are passed the appropriate parameters by the instructor. Where a value parameter is required, the instructor simply reads out the value. But if a reference parameter is used, the value (the Frisbee) must itself be passed to the students representing the function. If the function changes the value of the variable, the students must change the value recorded on the Frisbee, which is returned when they reach the end of the function call.

This simple strategy graphically illustrates the difference. An extension is to attach a piece of string to each passed Frisbee so that a swift tug can precipitate the return; this provides a further neat illustration of pointers!

Data structures

When they have mastered the basics of programming, students often move on to implementing simple data structures such as linked lists or stacks. A significant part of the battle in teaching these structures is to explain to the students what such a structure is and how pointers are usually used to implement and eventually traverse one. The students in a lecture room can be turned into a linked list. One student is nominated as the head of the list (effectively a pointer to the first item) and is equipped with a large ball of wool. The student throws this to another in the room, who forms the second element, and so on. When a suitable structure has been created, the instructor can show how to traverse the list to find certain values, and can show how it is vital not to lose the first element.

It is straightforward to extend this idea to explain more complex operations with these structures, such as the deletion of an element. This requires some temporary pointers (and scissors!) as the wool forming the list is cut and then tied back together.

A word of caution

The effectiveness of these techniques lies in their novelty. Lectures using ideas such as these will hopefully be memorable, and the subject of much discussion afterwards. That is important.

It is probably possible to devise demonstrations to illustrate most parts of an introductory programming course, but if they are overused they can lose their crucial novelty value.

(Dr Tony Jenkins, University of Leeds)

Teaching methods

Courses in computing provide a mix of both theory and practice, thus enabling transfer of knowledge and the development of skills. Case study 1 highlighted the need for active rather than passive learning. In order to involve students in active learning it is important that they are motivated, and this is best achieved in the learning environment by ensuring that they are stimulated and challenged. Problem-based learning often ensures that students acquire, in addition to problem-solving skills, additional wider knowledge outside the domain of the set problem. Individual institutions currently adopt a variety and diversity of curricular styles and a range of learning and teaching practices including lectures, tutorials, seminars and laboratory work, but with increasing emphasis being placed on the learning experiences gained through the examples noted, industrial placement (**work-based learning**), group work and individual projects. These new patterns of learning all facilitate the need to inculcate the **transferable skills** previously discussed, as well as develop subject specialist skills. However, this transfer requires the exploitation of new approaches to facilitate and manage the learning and support of students who spend a significant proportion of their time remote from the university and in isolation from their peers. There is therefore an increasing need to apply technologically based solutions.

While the conventional lecture theatre can serve to impart knowledge, many aspects of computing science demand laboratory provision and practical sessions are a key aspect of all courses. Scheduled laboratory classes are most often supervised by academic staff or graduate demonstrators, who encourage and support students in making independent progress without heavy supervision. In addition to supervised sessions, students also have opportunities to access equipment for personal study and independent learning outside formal class times.

Interrogating practice

Reflect on your current teaching methodologies. What is the rationale for their use? Does your current approach maximise learning opportunities for the student? What new methods might you try?

Information and computer sciences (ICS) is a major growth area within the national economic scene and the demand for skilled graduates continues to grow. Furthermore, the continuing change in technology and its consequence for the curriculum is having a considerable impact on the educational environment. The future demand for computing science education is therefore unlikely to be fully satisfied by conventional courses. Furthermore, qualified practitioners require access to short professional development courses in order to maintain currency, expand their skills base and keep abreast of new developments in the field. E-learning is viewed by many as an opportunity to support access to curricula and learning materials and providing short top-up courses covering areas of perceived need. Virtual Learning Environments (**VLE**s) are central to the delivery and management of e-learning programs, providing an exciting and intellectually challenging environment for teaching and learning, which stimulates students and encourages academics to vary their teaching style.

Interrogating practice

Consider how you might introduce a VLE to support a module which you teach. Would the communication/collaboration tools provide opportunities to extend and build upon the classroom-based teaching? Would this enhance the student experience?

Teaching large groups

Despite some decline in numbers entering the subject, computing remains a large discipline (in terms of staff and student numbers) and one of the largest within the STEM (science, technology, engineering and mathematics) disciplines. In contrast, conventional support for academic lecturers in computing has declined, due to decreasing per capita student funding resulting from, for example, the changing funding band introduced in the UK. Further difficulties ensue in attracting appropriate numbers of computing science research students, whose skills are generously rewarded in industry and commerce. The growth and diversification of the student population is producing an increasingly complex higher education structure (advancing in both size and scope), which challenges traditional delivery methods. At the same time technology is developing to a stage where it can provide sophisticated support for such complexity.

Interrogating practice

How does your department deal with the diverse range of experience of incoming students? Do you take into account their differing learning styles and requirements when planning your teaching and assessment? (See Chapters 10 and 11.)

Presenting lecture material to large numbers frequently results in a pedestrian, **didactic** style, the main purpose of which is to impart information. Tutorials and seminars have always been an important component of course delivery – they provide effective reinforcement to large group teaching and present opportunities for academic staff to emphasise the impact of research activity on curricular content. While the conventional classroom lecture can accommodate numbers limited only by physical space provision, in many cases small group tutorials have been abandoned, due largely to resource constraints. Academics must therefore identify other teaching methods that stretch students intellectually, challenging and stimulating them to consider facts and principles beyond the content delivered in the lecture theatre.

Group work

Today's employers have expressed a need for graduates to improve their group working and communication skills. Group working forms an integral part of computing programmes. With large student numbers, the ability to coordinate and manage group projects is a laborious task. The system is fraught with problems, including allocation of members to groups, delegation of tasks within the group, motivation of team members and attributing appropriate marks for individual effort. The problem is further exacerbated where a course is offered in mixed mode with part-time students/distance learners finding it difficult to engage in activities with their full-time counterparts. Furthermore, the pedagogic shift from the traditional teacher-centred to a student-centred approach requires a fundamental change in the role of the educator, from that of information provider to a facilitator of learning.

Team exercises and small group work enhance both the personal and professional skills of students and are often employed to inculcate transferable skills. Group projects are particularly useful for sharing ideas (and concerns), debating issues of mutual interest and learning to work to an agreed schedule. They can also help to promote confidence among quieter members of the team (see Chapter 12).

Collaboration is not easy but can provide added value in a number of areas, most notably the stimulation and motivation of students, who take responsibility for planning, and the generation of ideas. There are a number of examples of good practice in teamworking, especially where they have been used to develop both transferable and specialist skills. At Durham, second-year students undertake a group project in software engineering (see Case study 2). The organisation of this project is based on a tutor, supported by research students trained specifically for the purpose of acting as facilitators at group meetings. The students run the meetings and keep log-books and minutes, all of which are signed off weekly by the facilitator. This organisation is simple but effective. There are a number of examples of good practice in teamworking, especially where they have been used to develop both transferable and specialist skills.

Case study 2: Group working

Within computer science at Durham the organisation of the Software Engineering Group project is based on a customer who acts as the driver and academic overseer of the group. Since each group has different requirements there are substantial differences between the work of individual groups, and thus there are no issues of plagiarism. On the management side the students run the group work coordination meetings and keep log-books and minutes, all of which are reviewed by the academic facilitator. Thus a careful watch is taken of the contributions of members and the progress of the group as a whole. Unfortunately however, group work practices are not without their difficulties. Typical problems include the accurate assessment of group work products, the evaluation of individuals' contributions within the group which is usually not equal and thus should be reflected in the assessment marks, and finally controlling the project so that a good learning environment can be made available to all students. Solutions to three of the main issues that are adopted within the Durham system are now described.

Assessment

Assessment of group work projects is often made difficult by the freedom placed upon the group. In order to maximise the learning potential it is beneficial to minimise the control placed upon the group. The outcome of this is that frequently groups produce very varied products. Thus the assessment of such a varied field is difficult. Furthermore, since within Durham the assessment is conducted by the customer, who sets the requirements, there is also a need to ensure that the approaches and criteria for the marking process are consistently applied across each of the groups. Clearly what is required are detailed marking criteria that are relevant for all group work. This is aided in Durham by the setting of a basic specification upon which each customer sets each of the requirements. Since no individual supervisor has the power to modify the basic specification, a common set of marking criteria or tests may then be applied at some levels to all of the group's final systems.

Evaluating individual contributions

There are a number of strategies possible for arriving at an individual mark for the assessment of group work. Some institutions give all students within a group an equal grade for their group work activities. Within Durham individual contributions are assessed, which ultimately results in a specific mark being attributed to an individual student. The approach adopted involves a process of tutor, peer and self-assessment of the contribution that each member has made to specific phases of the group work project. Based on individuals' contribution, the group mark is modified for individual members but not changed. Thus for a group of three (students: A, B, C) with a group mark of 60 per cent, individuals within the group may receive marks based on their contributions of A=55, B=60 and C=65 per cent. From research conducted at Durham the best approach identified to establish such a mark is to ask the students and staff to rank students' contributions where the ranking position is significantly greater than the number of a group. Thus if a potential ranking set of 15 slots (slot_1 showing the highest potential contribution, slot_15 the lowest) is available, in the above example the slots may be used: A=slot_12, B=slot_7, C=slot_3. In this way the relative positioning of the students is demonstrated, along with the potential to show the significance of the differences between students.

Controlling the project

Experience at Durham has shown the importance of having someone to drive and control the process. Problems do occur with group work practices and are often associated with personality clashes between group members. It is important to deal with these problems quickly before they begin to affect the academic work of the group members. To date it has always been possible to provide resolutions to problems within groups without the necessity to modify the group structure. In most instances this is solved by greater involvement of the group's tutor within the decision-making processes.

The other significant issue that experience has shown is often attributed to group work projects within computing is that of the overenthusiasm of the students involved. While in most instances student enthusiasm is considered desirable, when taken to the extreme it may mean that students start to forsake their other modules. Within Durham, experience has shown that this issue is mainly concerned within the implementation phase when the students actually implement their ideas. Steps have been put into place to ensure that students work in a controlled manner via the issuing of tokens. When planning their implementation, students identify a phased implementation approach. This phased approach is then applied during the implementation phase, and in order to be able to move on to the next phase students must apply for a token. The basis of receipt of the token rests on the students' ability to show that the next proposed implementation phase has been adequately planned for.

A final word of encouragement

Many of the problems associated with group work may lead the reader to wonder if setting up group work activities is worth the bother. However, experience in Durham is that the skills and enjoyment that the students gain from this work far exceed additional considerations that such an approach requires. Furthermore, from responses from past students it seems that for computing at least, the skills they acquire are those that they perceive are most frequently used within industry.

(Dr Liz Burd, University of Durham)

Interrogating practice

What are the specific learning outcomes of your group work exercises? Do you assess transferable skills and what assessment criteria do you use? How will you know if the learning outcomes have been achieved? How do you resource and manage group work? What training did those providing the management/facilitation role receive?

Assessment

Students of computing science need to experience a range of assessment techniques throughout their learning experience. All major activities on an Honours degree programme in computing should be assessed, with progress or award the appropriate outcome. The assessment technique needs to correlate with the nature of the learning, and assessment is required to cover all learning outcomes of the programme. Formal examination, coursework submitted on time, and project work assessed partly by oral examination expose students to a variety of methods. Other challenges exist with equality and comparability when assessing aspects such as work-based learning. This of necessity must involve the student, visiting academic mentor and industrial supervisor. Students must be made aware of the individual elements of work-based learning and the contribution of each to the final mark.

The use of VLEs or other automatic methods for computer-assisted assessment (CAA) has a significant and increasing role, particularly in the earlier years of programmes where basic knowledge and understanding of factual information is being assessed. This has the role of providing rapid feedback to the student on performance but needs careful design to ensure appropriate formative feedback, a necessity if students are to get added value from the assessment and thus improve on their performance. CAA is particularly popular for assessment of large groups.

A compilation of student achievement in the form of **portfolios** is becoming another method of assessment. The portfolio can include evidence from sources such as tutor feedback on work and sections of completed project work. This is a suitable environment to allow students to reflect on and analyse past experience. The actual assessment criteria for a portfolio mainly evaluates organisational skills and evidence of critical and reflective analysis.

Self- and peer assessment has increased in higher education in recent years. These are particularly useful as formative assessment methods rather than **summative**. This is identified as students assessing the work of others at a similar level. While of limited use as a method of acquiring a formal mark it has the value of making estimates of others work and providing **feedback**.

Plagiarism is an increasing problem particularly in coursework and its detection presents considerable difficulty in assessment. The vast array of materials readily available via the internet makes it difficult to detect the work of others, submitted by students and passed off as their own. Computing science academics have long been concerned with issues relating to plagiarism detection and most departments have drawn up proactive anti-plagiarism policies. Clearly students are tempted to plagiarise in order to gain some advantage in their overall grading. The Joint Information Systems committee (JISC) has established a national plagiarism detection advisory service to aid detection (see www.jiscpas.ac.uk). In dealing with plagiarism institutions need a clear policy which both acts as a deterrent to the practice and also offers support and guidance to students.

Interrogating practice

What assessment methods do you use? Which are used for formative and which for summative purposes?

The problems of assessing group work projects have already been alluded to. Similarly, the increase in student numbers has resulted in large numbers of individual final-year and M.Sc. projects which need to be supervised and examined. The increase in staff numbers has not grown proportionately, resulting in academics being burdened with increased loads at already busy times (examination periods). As final-year projects are a universal requirement, some innovative approaches to the management and assessment of student projects, including the use of formative peer assessment and poster-based presentations, have already been adopted. Computing science programmes are challenged by resource constraints. As such, there is great demand for demonstration of exemplar practices that can be tailored to local needs.

Assessing practical work with large groups

Many departments operate informal mechanisms for offering extra assistance to students, thus placing responsibility on students to assess their own progress and judge when to seek assistance. Staff–student communication can be enhanced by employing technology-based solutions which facilitate efficient collection of some forms of coursework. Such systems have the potential to greatly assist learning and provide early warning of potential problems.

As mentioned above, programming is a core component of all computing programmes. Assessing the practical skills associated with programming is a time-consuming activity which is exacerbated by the need for regular submission and quick turn-around time. A further problem is the prevalence of plagiarism which can often go undetected due to the large numbers involved.

Interrogating practice

Are you familiar with your institutional policy on plagiarism? Do your students realise the implications of plagiarising work? How do you deal with issues relating to plagiarism within your particular course/module?

Systems to assist in the administration of courses, assignment marking and resource management all have a part to play in increasing the leverage of the human resource investment. At Warwick, a system has been developed facilitating online assessment methods to address the pressing problems associated with the management and assessment of large student numbers. The BOSS system, explored in Case study 3, provides students with 'instant' detailed feedback on their submitted coursework while enabling staff to monitor the students, automate assessment of their work, and generate reports about plagiarism possibilities. Using BOSS, students are able to complete more coursework with more efficient feedback.

Case study 3: Managing the assessment of large groups

Automated tools for the submission and assessment of programming assignments have been developed in the Department of Computer Science at the University of Warwick since 1994. The original motivation was the need to streamline the process of marking assignments, ensure accuracy and facilitate timely feedback.

Known as BOSS (The BOSS Online Submission System), the package began as a UNIX text-based utility, targeted specifically at two large Pascal programming modules. Since then, it has developed into a large platform-independent networked tool, and is used in over a dozen modules delivered by the Department of Computer Science and other academic departments. Modules include introductory programming (Pascal, Java, SML, C++, UNIX Shell) and advanced software modules (Software Engineering, Concurrent Programming), with class sizes up to 300.

BOSS allows any piece of work stored on a computer to be submitted online. A student's identity is verified against data held on the university's student database, and an electronic receipt for the assignment is returned to the student as an e-mail. Security measures are employed, such as the inclusion in each receipt of a hash code (which can be thought of as a digital signature) for each file submitted, in order to ensure the integrity of submitted work should a student later claim the system had corrupted his or her files.

If an assignment is a computer program, or is suitable for running automatic checks (for example, a style analyser in the case of an essay), then BOSS will run automatic tests in a secure environment, to prevent overenthusiastic students from accidentally or deliberately corrupting system data. Tests can be made available to students prior to submission in order for them to check that their assignment meets the criteria set. One or more markers are given access to an intuitive interface to allocate marks to various marking categories (including, but not restricted to, the automatic tests) set by the module leader, who subsequently moderates prior to feedback being e-mailed to the students. The use of slider bars, buttons and other graphical devices in the user interfaces speeds up the process as much as possible. Finally, BOSS contains a tool called 'Sherlock' which assists the module leader in detecting assignment submissions that have degrees of similarity, and are possible instances of plagiarism.

The response, both of staff and students, has been generally very favourable. The overall time taken to manage an assessment has been substantially reduced, and the consistency of marking is invariably high. The number of successful appeals against errors in marking has been reduced to almost zero. Regular use of a plagiarism detection tool has reduced the identifiable number of disciplinary offences to very small numbers. In situations where no tests are to be performed, and where BOSS is simply a device to facilitate assignment submission, it has proved to be a highly effective administrative tool.

The successful use of such a tool should not be a surprise to a computer scientist. What is of particular interest is the process of developing the tool, and the issues, both technical and pedagogic, encountered during its development and deployment.

BOSS was developed 'in-house' since no comparable tool was available to purchase (and even now there is none that would satisfy our current needs), and general issues about developing large-scale software are therefore relevant. For example, initial coding, maintenance and development of the software require suitably skilled programmers who are seldom willing to work for the remuneration which UK universities are able to afford. The software is 'mission-critical', and staff and students must have full confidence in it. Security is paramount (and must be demonstrably so), and thorough testing is crucial.

Automatic tests on computer programs are notoriously difficult to write, and even small programs yield unexpected surprises. Early versions of BOSS allowed such tests to be specified so that text output of programs was compared to the expected output. Variations in punctuation, white space, number presentation, and even spelling, could cause tests unexpectedly to fail for individual students. Tight specification of a program's behaviour gives rise to student criticism that the software is too 'picky', whereas the alternative reduces the effectiveness of the testing harness. The specification of tests in the context of graphical output or input is difficult (although the use of Java objects can be helpful).

If an assignment carries a significant proportion of a module's marks, it is undesirable for all of the marks to be awarded for automatic tests. Furthermore, there must be a manual check of any automatically awarded marks to ensure that no unforeseen system problem has accidentally penalised any students (and this is now a requirement of the university).

Perhaps the major lesson we have learnt is that computer systems are invariably much less reliable than we would desire. When 200 students are attempting to use a network application at the same time, and five minutes before a deadline, then the possibilities for system failure are immense. Computer crashes and network failures are common, and the scalability of the software is tested to the limit. Departmental processes, such as deadline enforcement, must be flexible to accommodate this, and it is prudent to have competent staff available at crucial times to deal with the unexpected. The software has been made open source, and documentation and software downloads are available at sourceforge.net/projects/cobalt/.

(Dr Mike Joy, University of Warwick)

Student support

ICS programmes attract entrants from a wide variety of traditional and vocational educational backgrounds, resulting in a diverse student population. Furthermore, as in many disciplines, an increasing percentage of the student population is international and in many cases English may not be their first language. Support mechanisms need to be in place to ensure that all students reach the recognised and accepted standards of attainment. How institutions support the student learning experience is a key issue in ensuring continuing enrolment of students on computing science programmes.

Student motivation is crucial to this and how students are motivated to learn can depend on the individual. Some are quite content with traditional learning of theoretical principles at lectures, others prefer practical activity; yet others respond to greater challenges and problems, to application-oriented or research activity. It is important that they encounter a diversity of activity in the learning environment. Active learning is recognised in computing science as a strong motivating force, and provides the challenges to stimulate learning. It is important that all assessment is structured to enhance learning through timely and constructive feedback in order to generate self-confidence.

The computing discipline demands high standards in a number of skills including report writing, software development, analytical thinking, teamworking and presentations. Students need to know what will be expected of them throughout their programme and student induction has a key role to play in conveying this to the student population. Student induction should take place at entry to higher education. This often has the necessary role of introducing them to the institution in general but students also need to be informed of what is expected of them in the discipline and this needs to be reinforced throughout their course. For example, as students progress they need to take greater responsibility for their own learning. Again, constructive feedback on completed work can continually convey the message over of how progression can be ensured and excellence achieved.

Technology within the domain of the student must be recognised as a tool to support student learning. Most students have mobile phones and many engage in social networking. The accessibility of information driven by modern technology has influenced student behaviour and their approach to learning. The expectation of students is that the tools available to them, whether mobile phone, laptop, iPod or MP 3 player, can deliver information anywhere any time. This has created an expectation of 'mobile learning' or m-learning (Vassell *et al.*, 2006). For example, audio podcasts and SMS messaging all provide methods of supporting students who often of necessity (e.g. part-time students or full-time students who cannot attend all lectures) need alternative means of accessing material. These mechanisms and their use as educational support tools are at an early stage and have currently been adopted in a piecemeal manner but provide the opportunity to further support student learning.

Widening participation

Widening participation takes two main forms: a general trend towards relaxing entry requirements and an increasing number of access course arrangements with further education colleges and foreign institutions, thereby facilitating transfer and progression from one course to another. The problems associated with widening participation are most acute in the further education sector. Higher education provision in further education is already an area of substantial growth within the computing discipline, further amplified by the introduction of **foundation degree** programmes. The associated problems of work-based learning and transfer routes into higher education are a cause for growing concern. Providers in further education find difficulty in maintaining currency due to their heavy teaching loads.

Despite differences in institutional structure and curriculum development, most departments are aware of the need to widen student access and are committed to increasing flexibility of both curriculum delivery and student choice within their courses. Most departments have already adopted flexible modular programmes which support credit accumulation and transfer schemes and enable students to transfer between different modes of study. Increased flexibility can lead to complex teaching programmes and students embarking on the course may lack the ability and prior experience required to achieve the objectives set by the programme of study. Academic staff must be careful to monitor individual progress and ensure that students are able to make the necessary links between discrete units or modules.

While the demands faced by computing science departments are daunting, technology-supported learning provides both possible solutions and new opportunities. Many departments are currently developing an e-learning strategy (see Chapter 7) which will incorporate advanced pedagogical tools into a technological framework, thus enabling departments to:

- continually improve the quality of course/programme provision;
- attract and retain students;
- widen participation by expanding campus boundaries;
- improve graduate employability.

However, it is widely acknowledged that in supporting a diverse range of students and student ability academic staff need to learn new skills to move from traditional to e-tutoring mode. In order to take full advantage of these emerging technologies, computing science academics must keep abreast of current good practice which will inform local developments and ensure effective exploitation of existing resources.

Learning environments and resources

Computing science education promotes independent learning as an important feature. However, it is no longer funded as a laboratory subject, although classroom and laboratory teaching are both important and integral parts of the educational provision.

As part of the overall learning environment, lectures, assessments, case studies, library material (conventional and digital), websites, videos, software, standards and laboratory provision have all contributed to students of computing science. The computing science curriculum further requires specialised material to support the teaching of the subject in the form of software libraries, programming language development tools, graphics packages, network analysers, multimedia development tools and project management tools. Even the basic resource material is comprehensive and expensive for departments to maintain and keep current. New versions of software frequently appear within the time-span of one programme. There is thus heavy reliance on equipment and software, which is expensive to purchase and subject to continual and rapid development. Developing the practical skills associated with programming can be particularly time and resource intensive: it is therefore important that there is access to adequate and appropriate resources for this purpose.

OVERVIEW

Future learning is most likely to embrace more electronic resources, online material and electronic communication. Students of computing science will be adept at recognising the computer as a tool to aid learning, in addition to their study of computing as an academic subject. Academic institutions are increasingly using VLEs to meet the diversity of student learning needs and particularly of students off-campus. Virtual worlds (e.g. Second life <http://secondlife.com>) are seen as a comprehensive multimedia and interactive environment, modelling the real world to the extent that a virtual classroom can be created.

Information and communication technologies, services and networks are rapidly transforming the way people live, work and learn. Preparing individuals with the knowledge and skills they need for the emerging 'Information Society' and for continued lifelong learning is becoming a priority task for educators at all levels. Competence in ICT is rapidly becoming a 'life skill' that ranks alongside basic literacy and numeracy. Computing science graduates clearly have the necessary IT skills. However, it is the 'communication' dimension which is assuming increasing importance in the sense of equipping young people to transfer their thoughts and ideas. Computing science educators need to develop awareness of how online teaching technologies and environments can become an integral part of the process and management of all teaching and learning; to enhance and enrich education; to provide access to electronic information sources and interactive learning resources; and to encourage flexible and effective patterns of learning.

REFERENCES

JISCIPAS Internet Plagiarism Services <http://www.jiscpas.ac.uk> (last accessed 1 February 2008).

Leitch, S (2006) 'Skills in the UK: the long term challenge'. Available online at <http://www.hm-treasury.gov.uk/independent_reviews/leitch_review/review_leitch_index.cfm> (accessed 1 February 2008).

Prensky, M (2001) 'Digital natives digital immigrants'. Available online at <http://www.marcprensky.com/writing/Prensky%20>%20Digital%20Natives,%20Digital%20Immigrants%20-%20Part1.pdf (accessed 1 February 2008).

QAA Subject Benchmark for Computing <http://qaa.ac.uk/academicinfrastructure/benchmark/honours/default.asp> (accessed 1 February 2008).

Second Life – an online 3D virtual world created entirely by its residents available at <www.secondlife.com> (last accessed 1 February 2008).

Sparrow, E (2006) *Developing the Future. A Report on the Challenges and Opportunities Facing the UK Software Development Industry*, Microsoft Corporation.

Vassell, C et al. (2006) 'Mobile learning: using SMS to enhance education provision'. Paper presented to the 7th Annual Conference of the Subject Centre for Information and Computer Sciences, 29–31 August, Trinity College Dublin, pp 43–48.

Wing, J M (2006) 'Computational thinking', *Communications of the ACM*, March 49(3).

FURTHER READING

See <http://www.ics.heacademy.ac.uk/> for a comprehensive overview of the work of the Higher Education Academy Subject Centre for Information and Computer Sciences to include links to other relevant sites.

<table>
<tr><td>20</td><td></td></tr>
</table>

Key aspects of teaching and learning in arts, humanities and social sciences

Philip W. Martin

INTRODUCTION

The purpose of this chapter is not to provide a catalogue of classroom techniques, but to ask a series of questions about what it is that we do in the classroom, and why we do it. Two axioms provide the basis for this chapter. First, at the centre is placed the student as active subject. That is to say that there is no presumption here, at any point, that passive learning, or the consumption of knowledge, is at all possible within the arts and humanities. No colleague teaching in these areas would demur from the legitimacy of this axiom, yet, at the same time, some would also see it as an ideal proposition. Second, arts, humanities and social sciences are disciplinary fields which are heavily value-laden. That all education may be value-laden is doubtless a contention to be taken seriously (see Rowland, 2000: 112–14) but the point to be stressed is that the academic subject areas addressed in this chapter are cored through and through with ethical issues, social concerns, judgement, and the recognition of human agency, in a way that hotel and catering management, for example, cannot be, and in a way that physics, for example, may not be. So discussion of teaching and learning in these subject areas consistently acknowledges the high degree of volatility that derives from a rich constitutional chemistry: in these classrooms the validity of personal opinion, subjectivity, individual experience and creative scepticism mix with judgements about right and wrong, truth and untruth, order and chaos. Our task as teachers is to ensure that such judgements as emerge are best provided for by being well informed, and that this threshold of information is also served by a schooling in argument, the careful presentation and interpretation of evidence, and the identification of the valuable questions that need to be asked.

CONCEPTS

Broadly, the arts and humanities have this in common: they understand themselves to be an education not primarily structured around the imparting of skills and competences, but one primarily structured around a series of engagements with a body of knowledge or (in the case of the practical arts) a body of practice. Although these 'bodies' are very difficult to define or delimit in precise terms, and are continuously disputed by academics and practitioners, this wide definition holds true.

Of course, a distinction such as this is to an extent artificial. Engaging with knowledge, or practice, requires the acquisition of methods of understanding, and those in turn require technical comprehension (in the analysis of language or data, for instance, or in the understanding of the processes whereby artefacts are made). A student cannot 'naturally' engage. He or she must learn the disciplines that govern, or make sense of, the ways in which we can approach and negotiate knowledge, and this learning could indeed be legitimately described as accomplishment in 'skills'. But it is not the imparting of this accomplishment, primarily, which governs the concept of the educational experience.

Here we discover a major paradox. For just as we cannot fix the centre of the education in skills, or the range of abilities needed to acquire and negotiate knowledge, neither – surprisingly – can it be fixed in the other quantity of my definition, the body of knowledge or practice. This is awkward, frustrating even, but it is essential to understand this if we are then to comprehend the key aspects of teaching and learning in the arts, humanities and social sciences. For across the whole spectrum, these subjects are concerned with acts of continuous reinterpretation and revision. Hence the use of the word 'engagement'. These subjects break up the bifurcation, or the conventional grammar, of knowledge and understanding, just as they break up the equivalent relations between teaching and learning. Let us explore this for a moment, beginning with the latter pairing.

It was not so long ago that our understanding of classroom practice in higher education was dominated by notions of teaching. Then the term 'teaching and learning' came into being as a means of acknowledging the student experience both within and beyond the classroom, and this, commonly, is now inverted (with a somewhat overbearing political correctness) to become 'learning and teaching', in order to give emphasis to the most powerful armature of the educational experience. Yet whichever way around this phrase is put, it is an awkward instrument, implying a division between the two elements that is uncomfortable. At its crudest, this division implies (for instance) an active projection (teaching) and a passive consumption (learning); or, less crude, synthesis and assimilation (learning) related to, or deriving from, an activity directed at, or to, or between, the two primary subjects (teaching the student, teaching the subject). It is clear that these linguistic structures, or even simply the vocabularies, are forcing awkward divisions. The term 'teaching and learning' can of course refer to an undivided practice involving both tutor and student: in such cases the force of the conjunction ('and') has to be read very strongly as a unifying force, rather than a yoking together of discrete elements. But even when this is the intention, the terms are still sufficiently powerful to imply their separate functions.

Similarly, understanding and knowledge operate within a charged semantic field. 'Knowledge', we could say, is out there to be 'understood'. It exists as a primary subject to be understood by a secondary practice. But of course we would dispute this: understanding, we would argue (since knowledge is not raw data), constructs knowledge; it does not simply operate in a purely interpretative function. Knowledge, or more precisely the division of knowledge, is a historical construct.

Interrogating practice

Is it possible to divide work in your discipline into categories of knowledge and categories of skills of analysis and understanding? Are such skills modes of knowing in themselves, and therefore a form of knowledge? In planning your classes what do you want students to know, and what do you want them to be able to do?

So 'teaching and learning' and 'knowledge and understanding' are awkward terms for the arts and humanities, which is not to say that we cannot use them, but that they will be used in a qualified way. For an arts and humanities education is understood primarily not as the imparting of knowledge, nor as the imparting of skills. Rather, student and tutor alike are involved in the revision and making of knowledge. As part of this process, 'skills' are to be seen also as constructs, as powerful determining agents in the making and unmaking of knowledge. In short, teachers in these areas do not tell their students what to think or how to think it; they try to encourage their students to think for themselves, and to understand this process as something operating within a broad academic rationale. In this way, tutor and student alike are engaged with the construction and revision of bodies of knowledge, and in the arts, in a strongly parallel way, bodies of practice. To those involved in these subjects this may seem like stating the obvious: if opinions and ideas did not change, for instance, we would still be teaching history through Macaulay; if literary interests were always to remain the same, then English departments up and down the country would not be teaching half the writers now featuring on curricula.

Unlike the sciences, wherein change in the subject is driven most strongly by discoveries altering underlying paradigms; or the technological subjects, in which such change derives from technological advances; or some vocational subjects wherein change derives from changes in professional practice in response to commercial or legislative shifts, the arts and humanities change continuously by virtue of their being elements of a culture always in a condition of transition. Thus they transform through internal dispute, contestation, revision of tastes and methods, discovery or recuperative research, politics and philosophies. These subjects are continuously in debate and discussion: as new writers or artists emerge (or are discovered) to challenge existing norms, a field of discursive activity is stimulated; as new historical theories, evidence or discoveries are made, different and challenging historical narratives follow which will then be tested in debate. All these subjects operate in these ways for student and tutor alike: they require active, participating students, since discussion and argument are fundamental to their practice but this, in itself, can present difficulties, as illustrated in Case study 1. In such dynamic fields, where new areas of work are continuously evolving, it is therefore vital to consider carefully how students are to be adequately supported.

Case study 1: Teaching contemporary literature

When students encounter contemporary fiction they often feel that they are being asked to let go of the handrails that have guided them through their programmes thus far. If they are preparing to comment on or write about Dickens' *Bleak House* or Jane Austen's *Pride and Prejudice* they can draw on their prior encounters with the author's work through novels, films and TV adaptations. Such classic texts and authors have, oddly, a kind of cultural currency which students can make use of in seminars and assignments. This familiarity often needs to be decentred by the tutor, as anyone who has tried to encourage readings of Jane Austen that reach beyond romance will know. Nevertheless, in many courses in English departments there is cultural capital to draw on and experiment with when the module begins.

Contemporary Irish prose is under-researched, compared with English fiction or even Irish poetry. While students generally enjoy reading it, studying it often produces a crisis of voice as students realise they will be required to comment on a text without the opportunity to weave their comments into a prior conversation about a novel conducted among critics, a conversation which is normally ratified as acceptable through its publication and presence in the library. Students often see their encounter with contemporary fiction as one which requires them to develop an unmediated response to the text in question. When the fiction also invites them to investigate a different culture this sense of vulnerability and the perceived risk of saying 'the wrong thing' can be acute.

There is a balance to be struck in these circumstances between giving students the sense of security they feel is lacking and encouraging the risk-taking that enables original work. I try to achieve this balance first by being clear about expectations. In a detailed handbook, I acknowledge anxiety and aim for clarity about what students are and are not expected to know. I then provide a glossary for dialect words and references to public figures or political acts that the text refers to, in addition to a bibliography, and students can propose additions to both as the course develops. I also provide brief seminar preparation exercises which give the students some guidelines about issues to look out for and possible reading strategies. Students have responded particularly well, for example, when they have been asked in advance to read Eavan Boland's passionate arguments about women in Irish writing 'against the grain', reflecting on rather than acquiescing to the poet's arguments in *Object Lessons* (London: Vintage, 2000). These exercises help students navigate their way through unfamiliar texts. They are in turn built into a course which is divided into three sections. The sections encourage the students to think of the course in terms of plateaux and progress so that they can develop a sense of achievement and development as the course proceeds.

In lectures and seminars, comparisons with texts students are already familiar with, through prior or synchronous modules, is helpful. If they are using Eve Kosofsky Sedgwick's ideas about sexuality elsewhere, they can be invited to summarise their understanding of their ideas for the benefit of other students. As in all seminars, students rely on the known to get to the unknown, but it is important for the tutor not to be the only guide in this process: the sole authority on interpretation when other direct sources of commentary on the texts in question are not available. Locating the students as fellow critics through the use of primary sources in the seminar can help you concentrate on developing students' independence. For instance, Bunreacht na hÉireann, the Irish Constitution, is available online and students can be asked to read it as a paratext for Colm Tóibín's *The Heather Blazing*, which focuses on a Supreme Court judge and his rulings on it. Short essays on Irish culture, like those to be found in the Attic Press series of 'LIP pamphlets', can form the basis for staged debates in the classroom, with groups of students adopting the position of one of the authors of the secondary texts. The advantage of this kind of approach is that it stages critical strategies for students and allows them to rehearse their critical voices before they have to prepare their readings of the fiction they have studied. Simple strategies, such as asking students to produce questions rather than answers in seminars, and asking them to answer each other's questions in small groups can help to raise students' awareness of the critical skills they already possess and those they need to develop.

I find it is crucial to stress that learning how to operate as an independent critic is as much the focus of a module as the fiction we are studying itself. This dual focus on the fiction and the student-critics is enabled in part by the theoretical issues with which my module of contemporary Irish fiction is concerned. The students are being asked to reflect on the different ways in which Irish authors draw on and move away from discourses associated with Irish nationalism. As students make their first attempt to respond to texts independently they are reflecting critically on how, and with what effects, the authors they are studying and they themselves are moving away from what John McGahern calls 'those small blessed ordinary handrails of speech' (1990: 52).

(Dr Siobhán Holland, English Subject Centre,
Royal Holloway University of London)

The description of active and engaged students involved in the contestation of knowledge may sound rather too much like a highly idealised notion of a community of learning without hierarchies or differentiations, in which a liberal or postmodern philosophy denies the validity of knowledge, because it can only ever be provisional, or relative. And perhaps in its most abstract sense, the concepts described amount to something of the kind. But we do not live in an abstract universe. We live in a material one, and the materialisation of these concepts, most obviously in the construction of a curriculum, in classroom practice, in the three or four years of a conventional undergraduate education, requires a good pragmatic response that is still capable of acknowledging the intellectual underpinning of our subjects. In this sense, perhaps, we can distinguish between the subject (as a concept) and the discipline (as a practice). Our first task, therefore, is to decide on strategies that are fit for purpose, and to consider curriculum design, and the context that such a design provides for the teaching which brings it to life.

CURRICULA AND CURRICULUM DESIGN

Designing curricula is in itself a predicate of change, since it offers the opportunity to reflect on past practice and assumptions, usually through the stimuli of student and staff feedback on the one hand, and research-generated change on the other. At the same time, because it is essential to conceive of the student as active participant, curricula need to be designed with the desiderata that the students following the curriculum should be stimulated by it. For some, or perhaps now only a benighted few, curriculum design is an odd, new concept. Believing that the values of the subject are sacrosanct and should therefore remain undisturbed, they might prefer, therefore, to teach the subject as a reified object (rather than a field of human activity), regardless of its context (an insistence, in other words, on teaching the subject rather than the students). Quite apart from this being an indefensible stance in the face of cultural and intellectual change, it is pedagogically irresponsible in its denial of the need to recognise the student and the contextualisation of student learning. Curricula in the arts, humanities and social sciences have a wide variation, for the scope of study is enormous. First, there are the conventional subdivisions within the conventional disciplines, which include cultural and period divisions, there are also subdisciplines (e.g. within language and linguistics), and in the practical arts, divisions of genre (e.g. drawing, performance, painting, printmaking, sculpture, ceramics). Second, there are interdisciplinary areas, some growing out of marriages between subjects (e.g. literature and history); others the result of relatively recent political, social or technological/cultural developments (gender studies on the one hand, media studies on the other); yet more that derive from theoretical challenges to conventionally conceived areas (there are, for example, many people working within the broad province of 'English' who will see themselves, primarily, as cultural historians, or cultural critics). Third, there are new, distinct areas growing out of more conventional regions of practice: thus visual culture is developing out of media and cultural studies on the one hand, and art history on the other; creative writing is developing out of English, and even as it does so, it is cross-fertilising with journalism, and script-writing from performance or film studies programmes. Although change is a constant condition of arts, humanities and social sciences, the pace of change is faster than ever before in this growing fluidity, this proliferation of cusps between subjects, as well as in the emergence of powerful new areas. Alternatively, the current context of change may be read less positively as a dissolution of the disciplines (Barnett, 1994: 126–39).

Interrogating practice

To what extent do you understand your subject as a practice whose borders are defined by particular disciplinary procedures? What do you think students expect of the subject, and how would you explain to them its coherence and/or its interdisciplinary connections?

The first question confronting us when we begin curriculum design is that of situating our programme within this intellectual ferment, and although the prospect of marking out such territory is exciting, it also has to be done with the utmost care, to ensure that our own enthusiasm for exploration does not result in chaos or confusion for the students. Potentially good programmes can be easily marred by the unconscious displacement of academics' intellectual enthusiasms, or crises, into the student experience.

So, marking out the territory is an essential first stage, but this must be done concurrently with an understanding of the student body, and a conceptualisation of what the whole programme may add up to. This, again, is challenging. There is a huge diversity in student intake nationally in these areas, and in some cases this diversity has almost as great a range in individual institutions. Academics now teach mixed-ability classes more than they ever used to, and all the signs are that this will continue and spread – even to institutions long accustomed to accepting only very highly qualified A level candidates. The implications for teaching and learning in general are considerable, but there are also very particular implications for curriculum design. Without a doubt, it is most usually the first level of a programme that deservedly receives the most attention in all curriculum design activities. Most academics have a clear idea about where they want their students to be upon completion of the degree, and their understanding of their discipline is such that they are confident about how a graduate in that discipline should be defined. Much less certainty now attends the understanding of how undergraduates should begin their degrees, and the reasons for this are manifold. First, the threshold of students' knowledge and abilities is no longer assumed to be stable or held in common (Haslem, 1998: 117–18). Second, every department will have its own understanding of the foundational experience required by the students. Third, institutional infrastructures and structures – and particularly those determined by modular schemes – would exert a strong logistical influence over what is possible. Each of these is addressed in turn below.

> ### Interrogating practice
>
> How can curricula be designed so as to serve the needs of students and tutors in monitoring progress in the early stages? What are the best practical means of providing feedback to students that will allow them to identify strengths and weaknesses?

Students' threshold knowledge and ability

The majority of students in these disciplines will be coming from a school or college experience with a highly structured learning environment, which apportions tasks and assessments in a phased programme of learning. Others will be coming from **access courses**, or the equivalent, which are traditionally more intimate learning environments in which peer and tutor support are key elements. In addition, most of them will be impelled to follow disciplines in the arts, humanities and social sciences not as a means to a specific end, but because they have elected for an education of personal development which marks them out as an individual, and not simply as a consumer of knowledge and skills. In this education, pleasure and satisfaction, those orphans of a utilitarian educational policy, are essential motivators, and they will have been developed in, and practised by, the students in many different curriculum contexts. Here, then, is a series of challenges for the curriculum designer: the students will find themselves in a learning environment that treats them as independent learners expected to construct, for the most part, their own particular interests and responses within the broad remit of their modules; they will find themselves less supported by peers or schooling; they will be seeking, amidst this, to sustain and develop further the pleasures and satisfaction that probably governed their choice of degree. All the time, during the first year, they will want to know how they are doing; their lecturers, in the meantime, will be concerned to know much the same thing, perhaps from another perspective. **Feedback**, therefore, is all-important, and is a vital agency to be used in the complex acculturation of the student in the early stages of higher education, where the new cultural forces at play are particularly volatile (see Barnett, 1990: 95–109).

Each department, ideally, will be agreed on how their students should develop in the first level of their study. Most will want to be assured that, whatever the students' prior experience, they will be well prepared for the second and third levels of their degrees, and able to choose an appropriate and coherent pattern of study where choice is an option. For most academics in these disciplines, the design of the early stages of the curriculum should be governed by the need to achieve an optimum balance between a grounding in knowledge and the establishment of the necessary tools of analysis, including the acquisition of a critical, theoretical or analytical vocabulary.

Grounding is important for the students' future location of their own work within the broad map; tools of analysis provide the essential means by which students can define themselves confidently as active learners, since the primary materials (texts, documents, data) are converted from an inert condition into the constituents of new meanings and ideas through the students' own work. Precisely how either area is designed will be determined by the particular programme's character and purpose, which may range from the highly theoretical through to the pragmatic. What is essential here is that this character, or philosophy, should be clearly visible to the student, and not something that he or she is left to work out through arbitrary encounters with tutors of different preferences.

Most universities and colleges now work under the pressure of a system in which space in their buildings and infrastructure is measured and accounted for in relation to student numbers and activities. In addition, a great many universities and colleges run modular schemes which offer student choice both within and across discipline areas. These common features have large and different effects on the teaching and learning of subject disciplines that should be acknowledged, and taken into account at the point of curriculum design: what it is that can be studied cannot be divorced from how it will be taught, and that, in turn, depends on the availability of resources and time. A curriculum designer may, for excellent reasons, require four-hour blocks of time only to discover that a modular timetable prohibits this; similarly, rooms where small groups of students can work in pairs or fours with adequate facilities may not be available. A further complication for the disciplines is that many degree structures now require or encourage students to explore a wide discipline base in their first year, thus minimising the time available for the foundational phase. Such structures have (probably unbeknown to themselves) produced a graphic template for curriculum design within the disciplines that is an inverted pyramid, with students' subject experience growing from a narrow base to a broad tip across the three years of their degree.

Foundational experience

Having explored these three critical elements impacting upon the start of students' studies, we can recombine them into a composite picture, and then develop this across the extent of the degree programme. Where students are studying a combination of subjects (and very large numbers of students are in these disciplines, particularly during the first year, or level), the inverted pyramid, or its near equivalent, is the key factor to be addressed, since it means that there is only a small proportion of the students' total study time available for the foundational phase in each subject. And in the arts, humanities and social sciences this foundational phase is commonly understood to be, of necessity, rich in content. Students studying English will usually be introduced to a range of genres, and some historical contexts, as well as methods of understanding; students of history will explore a range of periods and locations, or one rich period in depth, so as to maximise understanding of the different kinds of historical analysis, as well as comprehending the nature of sources, and historiography. Students of the practical arts will have an equivalent need to understand such breadth through their own practice (although the nature of such programmes usually means that their students have progressed somewhat further with this experience because of the benefit of the extra year provided by their foundation year, or its equivalent in access courses). Since this foundation is already compressed by the need to maximise feedback and concurrently build both knowledge and tools of analysis, curriculum designers are commonly forced into some hard, discretionary thinking that will focus on identifying essential components. In these subjects, such a phase is likely to have a broad and representative content rather than a narrow one, in order to allow the student sufficient introduction to the variety and kinds of materials to be discovered later in more depth. At the same time, a broad content will also provide sufficient range for the introduction of the different modes of analysis that will be refined as the students progress.

Interrogating practice

If the foundational phase of the programme is broad based, what are the implications for work at the subsequent levels in your discipline? Conversely, if it is narrow (part of the inverted pyramid), what are the implications?

For a great many departments, discretionary thinking comes down to difficult and practical choices. What can be achieved within the established resource? Can the resource (between the three levels of the student experience) be redistributed? Should first-year students receive more, intensive teaching, since so little time is available in which so much needs to be established?

These questions have an added urgency for those departments that are offering an undifferentiated second stage (that is to say where modules are not designated by progression at levels 2 and 3, but are offered to all students at both levels). Here, even more pressure is exerted on the first stage, since students will progress into classes in which the expectations attached to second-year full-time students will be the same as those in their third year. Where the curriculum designer is faced with a differentiated system at levels 2 and 3, however, there is an opportunity, and in the case of a steeply angled inverted pyramid structure, possibly an imperative, to push introductory work up into the second level.

Institutional infrastructure and levels

Levels are therefore useful devices for curriculum designers attempting to plot carefully student progression. Three levels will reduce the intense pressure of the first-level experience; they may also allow a steady gradient of assessment tasks to be plotted similarly, to allow, for instance, the nurturing of independent research skills, or the training required for oral assessments and presentations. Without levels, such diversity is not always possible, since there can be no acknowledgement of a stage in which some carefully accounted risk can be attached to the development of new techniques, which will then, in turn, be assessed when the student is properly prepared. Although there are doubtless imaginative ways around this, undifferentiated systems tend to be conservative in assessment styles, honing very high levels of abilities in specific areas, and founded upon a homogeneous student body, usually very highly qualified.

There is resistance to progressive-level structures in these disciplines in some quarters which stems from the essential nature of learning that they share, described at the beginning of this chapter. Since we are dealing here with content-laden bodies of knowledge, whose division into manageable portions is to a certain extent arbitrary, or conceptual, and not based on a linear knowledge pattern in which one stage necessarily predicates another, then levels are not, specifically, appropriate. Once a foundation has been established, there is no reason to suppose (for example) that the study of Picasso is intrinsically any more difficult than the study of Turner, or that the study of postcolonial ideologies is any more difficult than the study of medieval theology. While some credence would be attributed to the notion that some primary materials are more difficult, or less accessible, than some others, this does not immediately convert into the assumption that they might be, intrinsically, third-level subjects. Academics in these subjects therefore have strong intellectual grounds for their resistance to models of learning which derive from content rigidly ordered by standard prerequisites.

Interrogating practice

What is the rationale for progression in the programmes with which you are familiar? Is there, in your discipline, a convention or an understanding of the order of topics for study?

TEACHING AND LEARNING

Over the past decade or so, those teaching in the arts, humanities and social sciences have found their student numbers increasing at a high rate. Most of this increase occurred in the early 1990s, mirroring expansion within the sector as a whole. One effect of this was to stimulate reflection on student learning, as tutors discovered that the traditional techniques on which they had hitherto relied, predominantly the lecture, the seminar and the tutorial, were proving less effective. The prime reason for this, of course, was the group size: as tutors struggled to maintain high levels of participative discussion with their students, they discovered, unsurprisingly, that the seminar was not to be indefinitely distended, and that whole group discussion around a nominated theme or topic became more and more difficult. In subjects where the principle of learning itself relies so heavily on participation in discussion, and the exchange of ideas between peers, the advent of high student numbers, combining with the erosion of the unit of resource, produced something close to a crisis in the understanding of how students were to be best taught.

A whole stream of new techniques began to be adopted in the face of this difficulty, and these are perhaps best described as regenerative rather than revolutionary, since most were concerned not to alter radically the aim of the learning experience, but to sustain and continue to develop its best aspects. As a result, most subjects are now still operating within a framework of teaching delineated by the lecture, the seminar and the workshop (supplemented by tutorials in specific cases). These terms are capable between them of classifying most of the formal teaching contact, but, in reality, they cover a wide repertoire of teaching techniques. It is also the case that in themselves, lectures and seminars do not adequately describe the current learning environment, which, in practice, is made up of a much wider range of elements, many of which have developed as a response to harnessing technology to enhance the learning process. Disciplines such as history and archaeology were early advocates of the benefits to be accrued from the use of IT, and are discussed at length in the first edition of this *Handbook* (Cowman and Grace, 1999). Case study 2 looks at the harnessing of technology to support the teaching of philosophy.

Case study 2: Teaching the history of modern philosophy

I tell my students that philosophy is an activity that they can learn only by doing. This applies as much to its history as to any other aspect of the subject. Struggling through a difficult primary text is like climbing a mountain – and if I were teaching them mountaineering, they would feel cheated if all I did was to show them pictures of the view from the summit, and describe the wrong routes taken by other mountaineers. They need to get their boots on, and work up a sweat.

In teaching the history of philosophy, the easiest method (for teachers and students alike) is for teachers to give the students their own interpretation of the text. But then the students have no need or motive to read the text itself, and they are left feeling cheated. It isn't reasonable to expect them to plough through page after page of material which they don't have the background knowledge to understand. So how can they be helped? As with mountaineering, one can help by removing unnecessary obstacles, and by guiding them through the difficulties that remain.

One unnecessary obstacle for philosophy students (though not necessarily for students in other humanities disciplines) is linguistic. When I first gave a course comparing Descartes and Hobbes, students complained that they couldn't understand Hobbes' English. 'Why couldn't Hobbes write decent modern English like Descartes?' as one student put it. So I translated the Hobbes text into modern English, and ever since, most students report more satisfaction from reading Hobbes than Descartes.

As for guidance, students need to be led by the hand at the precise point where there are difficulties. It's not much use having a dense text on one part of the desk, and a running commentary beside it, if there is no easy way of relating the commentary to the text. The simplest solution is to provide all the material electronically, with a split screen. The text, broken up into short paragraphs, is presented in the upper frame, with a running commentary in the lower frame. Hyperlinks enable the student to summon up the relevant commentary from the text, or the relevant text from the commentary.

In order to make the students' learning experience more active, I encourage them to digest the material by creating a dossier of course notes. By splitting the screen vertically, they can have two portrait windows, one with text and commentary, and one with a word-processing package; and they can copy and paste from the former to the latter. They are guided in their note taking by a series of questions, which are also discussed in face-to-face seminars.

Needless to say, there are serious problems in getting students to participate actively in this approach to enhancing student learning. Too many students simply print out the documents (at considerable cost to themselves), and they lose the benefits of hyperlinking. The module is under continuous development, and my hope is that by adding more and more features that are available online only, future students will take full advantage of this mode of delivery.

(George MacDonald Ross, University of Leeds)

Virtual Learning Environments (VLEs) and other electronic resources for learning

In recent years, a great many universities in the UK and elsewhere have adopted the **VLE** as a primary tool in delivering learning materials to students across the institution. In the arts, humanities and social sciences the extent of such adoption by academics has been variable. Some tutors have embraced the VLE with great enthusiasm and innovation; some have been more sceptical, and some simply reluctant. Debates about the advantages and drawbacks of VLEs have been structured by old and new thinking: old thinking has expressed concern that the VLE (and other electronic resources) makes information too quickly attainable, thereby discouraging reflection, consideration and synthesis (at its most extreme this line of thought argues that information is replacing knowledge); new thinking expresses concerns that younger students are increasingly to be understood as 'digital natives' and that their tutors may be either 'digital immigrants' or even digital illiterates. Further concerns are expressed in both new and old thinking that the speed of developments in digital environments and the predominance and vigour of peer-to-peer interactions in the virtual spaces of the new social software are transforming the nature of literacy and understanding (see Brown and Duguid, 2002; Owen, 2004; Prensky, 2001).

Such debate easily leads to the generation of an overanxious pedagogy in subjects in the arts and humanities, primarily because these subjects have traditionally emphasised learning as individual labour, a model which has not predominated to quite the same extent in the social sciences, but which has had an enduring presence there also. In such a model learning is hard work, academic research is commonly imagined via the emblem of the lone scholar and the vast and intractable world of knowledge has to be mined or discovered by lengthy and time-consuming efforts, resulting in a highly personalised notion of intellectual property. In contrast, digital technologies render information in wonderfully tractable forms which promote almost instantaneous interactions, and the notion of individual intellectual property is rapidly weakening. Digital technologies can transform areas of learning and research, rendering previously impossible tasks – such as those now being undertaken in the field of corpus linguistics – entirely practical (Carter, 2006).

Doubtless, the new electronic technologies are transforming our understanding of the nature of learning, knowledge and the disciplines just as surely as did the previous dominant technology – print. The context in which we currently work therefore has to be understood as a time of practical adaptation, in which tutors will want to exploit the opportunities that new technologies offer. The VLE is one such opportunity. In itself, and as a form of organisation, it has no implicit pedagogic virtue. The VLE is a format (like any other form of structuring learning such as a seminar or a book) that can be adapted for pedagogic purposes. At the very least, it may be used as an effective and convenient organising tool through which materials and information can be made available to students at any time, but at its best, the VLE can exploit its capacity for flexibility and access to develop new learning opportunities and environments, but it is not just VLEs that can achieve this. Case study 3 exemplifies how an electronic tool such as the **wiki** can present new and flexible opportunities for students.

Case study 3: Teaching history and international relations with technology

I had always intended my final-year module on US Intervention and the Collective Memory of Vietnam to include a web-based group project as part of the assessment, but adopting a wiki to achieve this was the result of trial and error. During the second half of the module we examine US interventions overseas since the end of the Vietnam War, looking at the effects of the Vietnam Syndrome on both policy-makers and the public. The group project would allow students to study a specific intervention or administration in greater depth while developing student skills in basic web page creation.

Initially I asked the students to work in groups of four or five to produce a series of web pages investigating a particular case study. While some of the resulting student work was quite good, the process was not as creative as I had hoped. Feedback from the students also identified a number of problems. Many had found the technical process of creating pages in a basic web editor difficult and there were the perennial complaints about the difficulties of working with students who were not as academically strong or did not share the group's work ethic.

With this in mind I was open to the idea of adopting a wiki as an alternative. I hoped it would overcome the problems that students had identified the year before. Instead of small groups, the 35 students on the module would work together in the creation of a wiki on US foreign policy since 1975. They could choose to create pages about specific presidents, administrations or interventions. In addition, the wiki format would allow students to choose to work with others or work on their own sections individually. Both of these hopes were fulfilled: students found wiki style a flexible and simple format for creating pages and were quickly forming ad hoc working groups to work on topics that interested them.

However, there were other more subtle changes taking place that made the wiki a much more effective learning experience. It was a microcosm of the wider academic community, with students operating as authors, editors, reviewers and publishers of academic work. Students' responses to feedback on their work from their peers were much more passionate than when I commented on it. After some initial friction they became more effective at offering constructive criticism of each other's work and developed a method for collaborating on the development of specific pages. As a group they set their own standards for both content and presentation and policed content for plagiarism. By the end of the project they had not only built a very useful revision site, but they had a real sense of the issues that professional historians have to face up to in the process of publishing their work.

The wiki also threw up real challenges for me as a teacher. Judging the level of tutor intervention was difficult: initial progress was slow and I had to give an overall structure to the project. There were also real issues in terms of assessment. Should I reward outcomes or contributions to the process of making the wiki? How do you reward people who develop great skills in wiki style, but are weaker in terms of historical analysis? In the end I agreed a rubric for assessment after consultation with the student group, who felt that people who were active in the group processes should be rewarded. More practically it was a considerable task to work back through the myriad iterations of the wiki to evaluate who had contributed what to the final product.

This experience allowed students to participate in the process of making and remaking knowledge structures that lies at the heart of humanities education. For me, the lesson of the wiki was to remember that I am collaborating with fellow historians in the classroom rather than teaching students.

(Christopher Goldsmith, De Montfort University)

Lectures

Commonly denigrated by many educationalists as an inefficient technique for student learning, the lecture nevertheless continues to occupy an eminent position in many of these disciplines, but perhaps no longer as a theatrical experience, the dramatisation of the great mind at work. The arguments against lectures are powerful ones: they produce, potentially, an awkward relationship of an active teacher and a passive, consuming student; they make unreasonable demands upon the concentration span; they have the liability of being implicitly monological, and thereby construct alienating models of knowledge; they privilege a first-order discourse of speech, while initiating second-order recording devices through the writing of notes; they do not require, ostensibly, student participation. All of these objections have some validity, and moreover, they are underpinned by the certain knowledge that the bad lecture is surely, irrevocably, the very worst of all bad teaching experiences.

However, there are counter-arguments to be made on the lecture's behalf. None of them are strong enough to rescue the bad lecture, or to remove the risk of its occurrence, and none of them can be defended without being carefully related to the aims of such teaching. In this respect it is not possible to defend the lecture as an aggregated mode of teaching; it is only possible to defend the different kinds of lectures in relation to the purposes for which they might be fit. For this reason, more space is dedicated to a taxonomy of lecturing here than to any other teaching modes, since the different kinds of seminars, tutorials or workshops are probably familiar enough.

Lectures are adopted or retained partly because of the pressurised unit of resource which has encouraged departments to move towards large group sessions. At the simplest level, lectures offer an efficient mode of teaching large numbers of students all at once. Even so, the question must be asked: what is it that the lecture can offer? In turn, this can only be answered sensibly by stating first that there are many different kinds of lectures; the first principle here is to analyse what it is that we wish the lecture to achieve. The **exemplification lecture** is a lecture designed around a series of analytical examples. It will take, in the case of literature students for example, a literary text with which the student is familiar, and demonstrate different modes of interpretation. It will show the advantages and disadvantages of these modes, thereby calling on the students to be arbitrators of a kind, seeking simultaneously to explore the distinct intellectual or theoretical positions which underpin the different modes. The **thesis lecture** is, in contrast, a piece of argumentation, frequently contentious, possibly provocative, but always building a case. This mode of lecturing is designed to provoke a response, or to deliver a surprising perspective on a familiar subject. Closely related to this is the explicatory lecture, a lecture which seeks to mediate and make more comprehensible a difficult area, the value of which depends almost wholly on the opportunities therein for the lecturer to demonstrate how such concepts and ideas can be better understood, while simultaneously periodically checking on the students' progress.

Lectures can also be arranged around the provision or definition of context: the consolidation of relevant materials through which the object of study may be illuminated in different ways. The lecture may be a broad category, but it is constituted by several subgenres, each of which is characterised by specific aims and objectives. In each case, the lecture provides that which cannot be provided by other means: it offers the dramatisation of intellectual processes, by which I do not mean an extravagant performance, but the living exploration of questions, ideas, theories and counter-arguments.

Further, lectures not only come in a variety of forms deriving from their purpose; their styles or modes are various too. They can be informally interactive, inviting unscheduled interruptions and questions; formally interactive, with such slots built in – usually with predetermined lines of enquiry, and including discussion between the students as well; they can be 'dialogues' in which two lecturers present contrasting arguments; they can be one, or a series, of 'mini-lectures' where several lecturers may present for only five or ten minutes in a carefully coordinated series.

Seminars

In their purest form, seminars are, of course, very different. Deriving from the Latin term for seed-bed, ideally the seminar is precisely this, a place wherein students' ideas and intellectual development will be nurtured by way of discussion and reflection. Conceived in this way, the seminar should not be a place for tutor 'input' so much as a place for his or her guidance. In practice, seminars are not just this: the student group size frequently exceeds the sensible limit for discursive activity (around ten), and the term 'seminar' is used commonly to describe a one- to three-hour group event that may well include some formal input from the tutor, followed by general or structured discussion. 'Workshop' is an alternative name for such activity. Seminars and workshops, of course, may be further divided into subcategories.

The rationale for choice of teaching mode here is almost always guided by the principle of student engagement. Will students be best served by the structuring of group discussions within the seminar, by presentations from groups or individuals, or by a series of structuring questions set by the tutor? There is no single mode of teaching that is likely to prove intrinsically more effective than another: the essential question is whether it is fit for purpose.

A seminar itself (as the inert form) is just as likely to stifle discussion and exchange as promote it. Teaching forms are loose structures that need to be made taut around their purposes: if the aim of the seminar is to promote discussion between students on a given text or topic, then preparation for the seminar must be given proper priority, and the subsequent arrangement of the seminar requires careful planning to ensure proper interchange. Large groups, for example, need to be more orchestrated and structured than smaller groups.

If, on the other hand, the purpose of the seminar is to get students to explore a given topic, text or document together, then it is important to ensure that they will be in sufficiently small groups to ensure that their collective explorations are truly beneficial. There are no slick rules to be adopted here, but there are optima to bear in mind: a cryptic two-line poem by e e cummings, for example, may be underserved by discussion in pairs; an extended passage of literary theory, or a complex historical primary document, however, may be more effectively examined by just two people working together.

Today's higher education classrooms, with a wider range of mixed-ability students, many of whom are also from different educational backgrounds, require a far higher degree of organisation and preparation. Most tutors find that seminars are best served by a greater structuring of student time outside the classroom, and requirements for specific forms of preparation. Increasingly, tutors are discovering the advantages of supplementary forms, such as the **virtual seminar**, which provides the opportunity for students to reflect on points in the discussion, read, research and think, before replying. These synthetic processes, so important in these subjects, can be very well supported by the new technology. In addition, the virtual seminar can provide confidence-building for students uncertain of their oral abilities, reducing the performative anxiety that afflicts the large seminar group. In both respects, virtual seminars can bring benefits to live seminars, providing a structure for preparation, and an opportunity for shy students to discover the authenticity and acceptance of their own voices.

Interrogating practice

Bearing specific examples in mind, what might be the group size optima for particular seminar topics in your discipline, and how might these change in a typical programme from week to week? How can seminars be organised to provide sufficient flexibility?

ASSESSMENT

There is perhaps no more contentious area in teaching the arts, humanities and social sciences than the assessment of students, and no single area, perhaps, that has seen so much innovation of practice over the past decade (innovations that are being pulled back at the time of writing, in some universities, by an insistence on a proportion of assessment by examination, driven by fears of student plagiarism). Assessments now take a wide variety of forms, ranging from creative or practical work to illustrative and design work, discursive essays and theses, social science-style surveys and interpretation of data, performance and oral presentations conducted in groups or individually, online assessments and so on. Such forms of assessment also transform in their various modes, such as examinations, coursework, and formative or summative assessments. An interesting approach to assessment, and an interesting approach to consideration of gendered space, is illustrated in Case study 4.

No attempt will be made here to summarise this almost endless variety, since assessment catalogues in themselves are probably not particularly useful in these subjects. It is essential, nevertheless, for there to be a rationale for the assessment diet in any given programme, and for practitioners and tutors to reflect upon the purpose of the assessments set.

Case study 4: Teaching social geography

For most of my students, the level 2 module in social geography is their first taste of the subject. The aim of the module is to explore the significance of space to social life, and I select topics from current events debated in the media, or from areas of students' own experience, to engage their interest and to encourage them to feel that they have something valid to contribute. Mindful of the fact that they will need to start work on their dissertation at the end of the year, the module must develop research skills, including presenting and analysing social patterns via (carto)graphical and statistical techniques. Beyond this, I try to elicit an awareness of alternative ways of explaining such patterns, to question the 'taken-for-grantedness' of popular and other accounts of issues such as minority ethnic segregation, homelessness or crime.

This range of intended outcomes calls for a fairly imaginative mix of teaching modes. The usual format for my two-hour classes is a loose structure of lecture 'bites' interspersed with different activities. These activities might involve a practical exercise with maps or calculators. More frequently, I ask students to reflect on some material stimulus which I have brought to class – a video- or audio-tape, a newspaper article, or a set of questions. They jot down ideas, then share them in a plenary session which leads into a mini-lecture.

To give an example. Due to the limited opportunities to develop the topic in level 1, most students are barely aware that gender has any relevance to geography. So the session on gender and environment starts by asking students to work in small (mixed) groups to identify places where they feel 'out of place' because they are male or female, and (an idea I adapted from a recent student text) to think of the kinds of images typically used on birthday cards for 'Mum' and 'Dad'. By using their own diverse experiences to demonstrate how space might be gendered, students' own knowledge is both legitimised and gently challenged.

To explore how different theories are constructed, I present students with brief written accounts from semi-academic pieces. They must read these quickly, focusing not on the details of the argument, but on the language: 'underline those words or phrases which you find particularly striking'. For instance, one piece on urban gentrification might be couched in the language of 'urban pioneers' while another highlights flows of capital. I ask each student to call out one word or phrase which I write up on the board; later, this rather distinctive selection of words will be the vehicle for examining how knowledge is constructed in each written account. Similarly, in investigating how environment might contribute to crime, I focus on the case made in a influential book of the 1980s which has had a significant impact on public policy. After a brief introduction, students read (condensed versions of) a critical review of the book published in a geography journal, the rejoinder from the book's author, and the reviewer's response in return (each of these is written in a pretty vigorous style, which helps to spark their interest). Working in pairs, students identify two positive points and two negative points concerning the claims of the original book, and they write these on overhead transparencies; I collect these transparencies, cut them into strips, rearrange them and present them on the OHP. These then become my visual aid for a mini-lecture on the debate over how environmental design determines social behaviour. In a linked session, we debate the alternative strategies deployed to control street crime and urban incivilities in the context of their own experiences of the local nightlife, considering how these strategies reflect different underlying assumptions about the structure of social life (including prejudices about students), as well as different political agendas.

Students' learning is assessed in two ways. The seen examination is a conventional summative assessment of their capacity to engage with ideas. The other element of assessment is a project on the social geography of a selected social group in a particular locality, to be written up in the form of a journal article. Each student negotiates the choice of topic with me early in the module (at which stage I head off anything that sounds like a reworked A level project). Progress is checked in individual tutorials which direct them to sources of information they need to collect (statistics, field observations, interviews), and the books or articles to contextualise their primary research. Students' achievement on the project element is usually high, and they evaluate the task as challenging but fulfilling. I encourage them to think about expanding this topic for their dissertations, so that the summative assessment in this module becomes formative for the next level of study.

(Caroline Mills, University of Gloucestershire)

A key factor in Case study 4 is that of skills. This chapter has not emphasised the teaching of skills as something distinct from content, but in the area of assessment, due consideration must be given to student training in the mode of assessment. This is particularly so in these areas where an enthusiasm for diversification on the one hand, and the breaking down of discipline divisions on the other, can compound to produce potentially damaging effects on the students, and indeed, on standards.

Nowhere is this more obvious than in joint degrees or in modular schemes where students move across two or three subjects. Drama students, for example, may be highly competent in oral and presentational skills (having received practice and training) where other students may not be; design or media students may be particularly skilled in website exercises, where English students, for example, have had little prior support. Thus diversifying assessment in more traditional subject areas is a complex matter, requiring sensitivity: setting a website design task may be an exercise underpinned by a set of criteria that other subject areas may deem to be well short of an undergraduate standard. Similarly, tutors will need to satisfy themselves that they have adequate skills to advise and support the students in their assessment tasks, while simultaneously being sure that the new mode of assessment has the integrity to support the level of content required. Innovation is not intrinsically virtuous (Hannan and Silver, 2000: 1–13), and innovative or diversified assessment tasks should be achieved within a scale that pays due attention to training, support and the extent of the assessment tasks required of students, since too much variety will give insufficient practice and too little opportunity for students to refine their competences.

Essentially, my point here is an argument strongly in favour of a coherent assessment strategy focused around a broad agreement of the range of skills to be assessed (see Chapter 10). Once established, such a strategy provides a safe and well-mapped territory in which diversification may take place.

Interrogating practice

What are the advantages and disadvantages of the predominant modes of assessment in your discipline? If you were to design an assessment strategy for your department, what would be the chief factors to consider?

OVERVIEW AND OUTCOMES

This chapter has acknowledged the great diversity of practice and kinds of learning undertaken in these disciplinary fields, and attempted to stress the need to be sensitive to context while focusing on the prime aim of engaging the students as active participants. In these respects, it has argued for the importance of a rationale for all that we do, a rationale that is sufficiently broad and flexible to deal with – in most cases – the current student constitution of mixed ability.

It remains to make some cautionary remarks about rigidity in such a rationale or strategy. That teaching and learning should be carefully planned, and conceptualised within a framework that acknowledges pedagogical styles and preferences, and further, that it should be understood to be moving towards specific kinds of developments in understanding, is incontrovertible. At the same time, the disciplines covered in this chapter are not constructed as linear or accumulative patterns of knowledge, each stage predicated by a former stage, and it does not follow, therefore, that planning and structure map neatly on to the notion of specified 'outcomes' (Ecclestone, 1999). Indeed, a strong feature of these areas is that of unpredictability: there is a sense in which the very best teaching session is the one which usurps and transforms the tutor's anticipated outcome (Rowland, 2000: 1–2). In such instances the students, individually or otherwise, bring a form of analysis to bear on the object of study which radically transforms the knowledge produced; alternatively, they may recast it through modes of understanding shaped in another discipline, or indeed through forms of prior knowledge which have not been anticipated by the tutor. And even without these forms of intervention, anticipated outcomes can be subverted in other ways. The anticipated level of student understanding, for instance, may have been overestimated, or homogenised to an excessive extent. Such instances sometimes give rise to a series of fundamental questions at a basic level, which, even so, are of radical potential in terms of their ability to challenge received views (Seitz, 2002). The mixed-ability classroom is also a classroom in which casual assumptions about cultural knowledge, so prevalent in these disciplines, can no longer be made.

REFERENCES

Barnett, R (1990) *The Idea of Higher Education*, Buckingham: SRHE/Open University Press.

Barnett, R (1994) *The Limits of Competence: Knowledge, Higher Education and Society*, Buckingham: SRHE/Open University Press.

Brown, J S and Duguid, P (2002) *The Social Life of Information*, Boston, MA: Harvard Business School Press.

Carter, R (2006) 'Common speech, uncommon discourse: whose English is English', in P W Martin (ed.), *English: The Condition of the Subject*, Basingstoke: Palgrave.

Cowman, K and Grace, S (1999) 'Key aspects of teaching and learning in arts and humanities', in H Fry, S Ketteridge and S Marshall (eds), *A Handbook for Teaching and Learning in Higher Education* (1st edn), London: Kogan Page.

Ecclestone, K (1999) 'Empowering or ensnaring?: The implications of outcome-based assessment in higher education', *Higher Education Quarterly*, 53 (1), pp 29–48.

Hannan, A and Silver, H (2000) *Innovating in Higher Education*, Buckingham: SRHE/Open University Press.

Haslem, L S (1998) 'Is teaching the literature of Western culture inconsistent with diversity?', *Profession*, pp 117–30.

McGahern, J (1990) *The Pornographer*, London: Faber.

Owen, M (2004) 'The myth of the digital native'. Available online at <http://www.futurelab.org.uk/resources/publications_reports_articles/web_aricles> (accessed October 2007).

Prensky, M (2001) 'Digital natives, digital immigrants', *On the Horizon*, Vol 99, Issue 5, University of Nebraska: NCB University Press.

Rowland, S (2000) *The Enquiring University Teacher*, Buckingham: SRHE/Open University Press.

Seitz, D (2002) 'Hard lessons learned since the first generation of critical pedagogy', *College English*, 64 (4) March, pp 503–12.

FURTHER READING

Higher Education Academy (HEA) <http://www.heacademy.ac.uk/>. Click on 'Subject Centres' for all Subject Centre addresses, where subject-specific materials relating to the enhancement of teaching and learning will be found.

Brown, S and Knight, P (1994) *Assessing Learners in Higher Education*, London: Kogan Page.

Davies, S, Lubelska, C and Quinn, J (eds) (1994) *Changing the Subject: Women in Higher Education*, London: Taylor & Francis.

Downing, D B, Hurlbert, C M and Mathieu, P (eds) (2002) *Beyond English Inc.: Curricular Reform in a Global Economy*, Portsmouth, NH: Heinemann.

Gibbs, G, Habeshaw, S and Habeshaw, T (1988) *53 Interesting Things to do in your Seminars and Tutorials* (3rd edn), Bristol: Technical and Educational Services.

Martin, P W (ed.) (2006) *English: The Condition of the Subject*, Basingstoke: Palgrave.

Salmon, G (2004), *E-Moderating: The Key to Online Teaching and Learning*, London: Routledge.

21

Key aspects of teaching and learning in languages

Carol Gray and John Klapper

INTRODUCTION

The first sections of this chapter consider the following issues which are central to the effective learning and teaching of modern languages in higher education (HE):

- the changing face of language study in HE
- the implications for HE language learning of changes at secondary level
- insights from second language acquisition research
- communicative approaches to language teaching
- autonomous learning and learner differences
- communication and information technology (C&IT)
- translation.

A subsequent case study of a first-year post-A Level language course illustrates these issues in practice and provides a pointer to how they may be integrated into a coherent whole. The focus throughout is on language learning rather than the non-language elements of degree courses since the latter are covered elsewhere in this volume, in particular in Chapter 20.

LANGUAGES IN HIGHER EDUCATION

Developments in the teaching of foreign languages over the past 40 years have resulted partly from new methodological perceptions but also from the changing role of the higher education institution (HEI) as language provider. HE language courses were once characterised by a predominantly post-A Level intake, by translation into and out of the **target language**, academic essay writing, the study of phonetics, and 'conversation classes'. Nowadays languages are offered *ab initio* and there is considerably less emphasis on translation, especially in the early stages of the undergraduate degree. There have also been moves in several institutions towards increased use of the target language as the medium of instruction and towards broadening the range of activities employed to include oral presentations, group discussions, debates, précis, summaries, letters, reviews and reports.

'Non-language' components have also changed, with the downgrading of literature and the introduction of film and media studies, as well as socio-cultural, political and historical studies. Where literature is still taught, pre-twentieth-century writing features much less frequently and a wider range of authors is studied, including more women writers and writers from minority ethnic backgrounds. The extent to which the foreign language is used as the medium of tuition in such components is variable, in some cases because modularisation has mixed language and non-language students on Area Studies courses, in others because staff fear a 'watering down' of intellectual content.

There is increasing employment of part-time staff and postgraduate research students, and, in those institutions with sufficient funding to employ them, 'colloquial assistants' – now usually called foreign language assistants – are involved in the delivery of key course components. The likelihood that these categories of staff will receive training and support has increased in recent years but provision remains variable (Gray, 2001).

The number of students studying languages as the main part of their degree has fallen dramatically over the past ten years. **HESA** data for the UK suggest a 6 per cent decrease in language undergraduates from 2002/03 to 2005/06, following an even steeper decline over the previous five years; this at a time when total HE first-degree enrolments have increased substantially (CILT, 2006). Statistics for HE language study are notoriously difficult to pin down in view of the multiplicity of non-specialist study routes; however, an important DfES/AULC survey shows strong and increasing demand both for assessed study that accounts for less than 50 per cent of credits (38,194 students in 2005/06, up 37 per cent since 2003/04) and for extra-curricular language learning (30,402, up 20 per cent) (cited in Byrne and Abbott, 2006). This mushrooming of language courses for non-specialists on so-called **IWLPs** or **UWLPs** (Institution-/University-wide Language Programmes), often delivered by language centres, represents a major agent of change. Courses range from one-semester modules to full four-year degrees with a year abroad, and one of their key features, in contrast to much language teaching in academic departments, is the use of trained 'dedicated', full- or, more likely, part-time language teachers, often operating on non-academic contracts.

THE INCOMING STUDENT

One of the most widely accepted tenets of teaching is to start where the students are, with a view to using their strengths to build confidence, while simultaneously addressing their weaknesses. A clear understanding of the school context is important for all HE teachers. Over recent decades the secondary school system in England has experienced an unprecedented rate of change, for example:

- experimentation with a variety of school types, including privately owned and run academies and specialist colleges such as language colleges focusing on an international curriculum;
- new examinations to address a wider range of ability and purpose, including at 16 the GCSE vocational examinations such as the Certificate in Business Language Competence and Applied Language GCSEs, the AS and A2 to encourage study of a wider range of subjects at 16-plus, and the current piloting of new Diplomas to provide a vocational route for 40 per cent of 14- to 19-year-olds of all abilities;
- regulation of content and teaching style through National Curriculum orders and a range of national 'strategies' such as the Modern Foreign Languages (MFL) Framework (see below);
- swings in the status of MFL as a compulsory or optional subject from 14 to 16; the current National Languages Strategy aims for compulsory language learning from 7 to 14 from 2010;
- major investment throughout the compulsory education sector in the application of C&IT to teaching and learning, including a mass programme of teacher training and the introduction of C&IT Standards to be met by new trainee teachers; this has implications for student expectations in HE;
- a change in government emphasis from European languages for social cohesion to a focus on the economic needs of the country, for example by encouraging Japanese or Chinese.

These are both causes and symptoms of a drive to ensure that compulsory education meets the vocational and leisure needs of the country; the priority in compulsory education is to meet the needs of the majority rather than prepare a small élite for further academic study. This has consequences for HE colleagues who need to acknowledge the change in skills of incoming students and adapt their courses to address new needs.

A major factor in making language learning more relevant and more widely accessible was the introduction of a topic-based GCSE examination at 16. Although this has often been criticised for its uninspiring content and for shifting the balance too far from accuracy to fluency and improving neither, HE teachers should not underestimate its contribution to increased access; without it, numbers in HE might be lower still. Dissatisfaction throughout the system has led to changes which re-emphasise the development of grammatical knowledge and accuracy. Nevertheless, a topic-based syllabus, combined with minimal teaching time and high-stakes league tables, inevitably leads to a focus on 'topic coverage' rather than on language learning skills.

There have been attempts to lessen the washback effect of the GCSE examination by ensuring that firm foundations for language learning are set during Key Stage 3 (11–14).

Here, teaching style and content are determined by the National Curriculum (NC) and the various National Strategies. The NC for MFL broadly supports a **communicative approach,** stressing language as a means of communication rather than as an object of academic study. This is, however, balanced by recognition of the role of 'pre-communicative' work and the relationship between communication skills and more formal language-learning skills. The recent MFL Framework for Key Stage 3 accentuates this aspect still further and, in its specific objectives, places great emphasis on how language works, encourages the learning of high-frequency words and transferable phrases, and promotes mastery over broad topic coverage.

Beyond 16, a wide range of qualifications are offered by numerous approved bodies such as the Royal Society of Arts (RSA) and City and Guilds; the effects of the New 14 to 18 Diplomas will need to be monitored. The National Languages Strategy encourages a plurilingual approach to language learning, including the use of the Languages Ladder which measures accredited and informal achievement against the Common European Framework. This defines developmental stages of competence in language use, enabling the creation of a Languages Portfolio outlining skills attained in a range of languages. HEIs may find portfolios increasingly prevalent among their non-specialist candidates. Specialists are more likely to pursue the traditional A Level qualification route, though this also undergoes constant reform to ensure a smooth follow-on from earlier stages. There is an emphasis on **mixed skills teaching and testing**, on use of the target language as the main medium of communication and on encouraging the development of real-life language-learning skills through use of texts in examinations and individual control of tapes in listening components. In addition, the 'modular' nature of courses allows students to 'bank' modules over a limited period of time. AS qualifications reward a shorter period of study in a greater number of subjects which can stand alone or be developed into fully fledged A2 awards. In the private education sector the broader-based International Baccalaureate is gaining in popularity; despite strong interest in the state system, policy-makers have yet to be moved.

A recent comprehensive review of the national languages policy called for a 'powerful programme of action' and a 'renaissance in language learning' (Dearing and King, 2007), the cornerstone of which is compulsory language learning from 7 to 14. This has so far met with political approval (DfES, 2007) and language teachers throughout the sectors are holding their breath.

Interrogating practice

- To what extent does your department's current practice take account of the needs and skills of incoming learners?
- Think of three ways you might improve upon current practice.

INSIGHTS FROM WORK ON SECOND LANGUAGE ACQUISITION

Second language acquisition (**SLA**) has been the focus of considerable research in recent years (for an overview, see Mitchell and Myles, 2004). There is still no coherent agreed model, owing to the difficulties involved in separating out and evaluating the diverse elements which contribute to second or foreign language (**L2**) acquisition and disagreements over the role of a learner's mother tongue (**L1**) in this process.

Nevertheless, all language teachers need a basic understanding of the principal aspects of SLA. Towell and Hawkins (1994: 7–16) list these as:

- 'Transfer': learners' unconscious application of L1 grammatical features to their L2 grammar.
- 'Staged development': learners progress through a series of intermediate stages towards L2 acquisition.
- 'Systematicity': the broadly similar way L2 learners develop their ability in the target language; the majority of L2 learners go through the same developmental stages regardless of their L1 or the type of input they receive.
- 'Variability': during the developmental stages, learners' 'mental grammars of L2' allow alternative forms which may co-exist for a long period.
- 'Incompleteness': the failure of most L2 learners to attain a level of automatic grammatical knowledge of L2 comparable to that of native speakers.

One of the implications of these features of SLA is that error and inaccuracy are both inevitable and necessary. The traditional assumptions of language teaching that learners must master new forms in a conscious manner when they are first presented to them, that error should not be tolerated and indeed should be avoided at all costs, are misguided. SLA research reveals, on the contrary, that L2 competence both generally and in specific grammatical instances is *by its very nature* developmental, that it grows as a function of both conscious and unconscious learning and that error plays a major part at all stages of this process.

L1 acquisition depends on learners interacting with other L1 speakers and engaging with increasing amounts of new information which steadily builds on previous knowledge. It therefore seems reasonable to suggest that L2 acquisition will similarly be furthered by interaction with authentic language. While **immersion learning** (e.g. in Canada) and bilingual programmes in several countries have highlighted the dangers of 'fossilisation' if no formal learning takes place, they have also crucially demonstrated that learners need repeatedly to focus on meaning while being exposed for extended periods to L2. For this reason target language use in the classroom and the deployment of a wide range of authentic texts are now both recognised as crucial to the language-learning process at advanced levels. The real benefit of authentic texts is that they help shift the focus on interaction along the continuum of L1/L2 medium-oriented communication towards L2 message-oriented communication (see Dodson, 1985). That is to say, authentic texts and realistic tasks (e.g. preparing an address in a mock French election based on some aspect of a political party's programme) provide learners with an explicit, content-based learning purpose in which the focus is on the message and the achievement of the task. While not sufficient in themselves, such tasks do encourage *implicit* learning of syntactical, morphological and lexical features of the target language.

The above suggests that L2 acquisition resembles L1 acquisition in a number of important ways. However, most L2 learners clearly approach the target language with a degree of proficiency and literacy in their L1. This means that they can use reading and writing to help promote their L2 learning. Furthermore, they bring to the L2 learning process a capacity for exploring grammatical forms in a conscious and explicit manner, and are able to talk *about* language. These facts make L2 learning in a formal educational setting a much more deliberate and intentional process.

The difficulty is that knowing formal rules does not by itself guarantee the ability to formulate language which obeys these rules. This is a real problem for many learners, especially those combining languages with other disciplines in HE: in language learning, **inductive learning** processes are just as important as the more cognitive, **deductive approaches** typical of many other academic disciplines, in which it often *is* possible to learn things solely as a result of explicit rule teaching and error correction. Language learning, however, is not always a conscious activity dependent on the availability of explicit knowledge about the language and the way it functions; rather, it is the product of a complex process of both conscious learning and the gradual, unconscious development of an internal ability to use language naturally and spontaneously without reference to the conscious mind.

It is the challenge of the language classroom to develop learners' internalised linguistic competence; that is, their implicit knowledge of and capacity for appropriate language use, *in tandem and interactively with* explicit knowledge of grammatical and phonological rules. This requires the development of an expanding body of interlocking skills through imitation, repetition, drilling and frequent practice in extended contexts to the point where these skills become automatic and unconscious. Little and Ushioda's analogy with piano playing seems most apposite in this context:

> Just as the novice pianist must consciously learn finger placements and pedalling, so the language learner must consciously learn bits of language – words and phrases, pronunciation and patterns of intonation – that become embedded in memory and can be accessed spontaneously.
>
> (Little and Ushioda, 1998: 15)

Interrogating practice

- Does your current departmental practice take account of evidence from research into second language acquisition?
- How might the department address this issue in its language curriculum?

TOWARDS A COMMUNICATIVE APPROACH TO LANGUAGE LEARNING

These insights have contributed to the development of a communicative approach to the teaching of modern foreign languages which is nowadays to be found in various guises in all educational sectors. The past 40 years have seen a number of different approaches to modern language teaching. Grammar-based language teaching, such as **grammar-translation** and **audio-visual/audio-lingual methodology**, adopted a rigid, graded approach to structures. Textbooks written in these traditions (and there are still a lot of them about) present items in what is considered to be a logical sequence (e.g. present tense before past, nominative case before dative), intended to teach learners to acquire certain items before progressing to other, supposedly more complex ones. Such an approach fails to take account of the insights from SLA outlined above. It precludes, for example, the teaching of such central communicative expressions as *je voudrais* or *ich möchte* until learners have covered the conditional and the subjunctive respectively.

An approach to language based on communicative need starts instead from a consideration of what learners are likely to have to do in the foreign language and then builds in the vocabulary, expressions and grammar needed to perform these 'functions' (see Wilkins (1976) for an introduction to functional-notional syllabuses). As a result, the same grammar points are revisited frequently throughout a language course. This acknowledges that grammar is not acquired in a linear fashion or in discrete chunks digested one at a time, but rather in a developmental process which cannot be regimented or rushed. The difficulty of a functional-notional syllabus is, however, predicting precisely what learners' future needs in the language will be. In formal language-learning situations the teacher has often to work hard to contrive such needs, and it is vital that the learner also develops a generative system to cope with future unknown needs.

The principal aim of the communicative approach is to facilitate independent communication by the learner (Pachler and Field, 1997: 70). The communicative classroom is therefore characterised by the following:

- grammar as a facilitator of communication
- phased development from pre-communicative to free communicative exercises
- inductive learning of grammar
- maximum use of the target language
- a focus on meaning
- language used for a purpose
- the foregrounding of learners' needs
- personalisation of language
- the creative use of language
- learner interaction
- the use of authentic language and materials
- a mixed-skills approach to teaching and assessment.

In practice, therefore, instead of being built around a purely structural syllabus, a communication-based course sees form as a necessary tool for expressing and exchanging meaning. This does not preclude or diminish the role of grammar. On the contrary, advanced and skilful communication can only take place when learners have assimilated a range of complex structures together with understanding of their application and potential effects within a wide range of situations. Grammar and knowledge 'about' language are, however, no longer seen as ends in themselves.

Furthermore, grammar is not taught deductively by artificial isolation and presentation of a series of rules, but inductively by the identification of useful patterns within content-focused language. Attention is drawn to recurrent structures, with subsequent clarification and drilling exercises. The emphasis is, however, firmly on the context within which such structures occur and hence the meanings that they have the potential to convey. It is a question of identifying rules from examples rather than creating examples on the basis of a presented rule.

Interrogating practice

- Think of a point of grammar you have taught recently. Did students learn it successfully?
- Was it learnt deductively or inductively?
- In what contexts are the students most likely to meet this grammatical item, and what is its communicative function?
- Was this function explored fully during the learning process?
- Can you think of ways in which you might have presented and practised it more effectively to maximise learning?

One of the major tenets of a communicative approach is that of optimum use of the target language for instruction and interaction. If the language is not used whenever viable within the learning process, then not only is its status as a means of communication severely undermined, but learners are also denied their only genuine stimulus for developing coping strategies and learning to negotiate meaning. In addition, being surrounded by examples of the language in real situations exposes them to a far wider range of patterns and vocabulary than they would otherwise experience. Although target language use has caused much debate in the professional literature, discussion centres not on whether, rather on how much; the mother tongue is both a thinking tool and a vital reference point for language learners (see Klapper, 1998; Butzkamm, 2003) and should not be banned from the classroom. Its role, however, needs to be clearly defined, and delineated, and limited to what is necessary to support learning.

However, simple exposure to new language forms and vocabulary is not sufficient for learning to take place; learners need to notice and internalise the language patterns in use and put them to use for themselves, so form-focused instruction has also become accepted as an essential part of a communicative approach.

The focus of classroom interaction within a broad communicative approach must be the expression of meaning, for where nothing new or meaningful is being said, communication ceases. Consequently, whatever the learners' language level, the meanings which they themselves wish to express should form the core of the learning process. Content, materials and the sequence in which grammatical patterns are introduced therefore need to reflect students' interests, so that they can be encouraged to engage with them and to assimilate language through use. This necessarily also implies that, as far as possible, the language taught and learnt should be personalised so that it becomes the learner's own.

Essential to the development of a communicative course is the use of real or 'authentic' materials which reflect the social and cultural context of the language, although at early stages of the learning process texts may need to be adapted to make them accessible. A genuinely communicative classroom would encourage learners to find and bring to class materials which reflect their personal interests and to share and explore these with peers.

Finally, communicative language teaching involves the integration of the four language skills of listening, speaking, reading and writing. Real-life language incorporates a mixture of skills: we engage in conversations which require both listening and speaking; we respond to written stimuli by filling in forms, writing letters, making notes or discussing the content of our reading with others. Modern methods of teaching and assessment recognise this interdependence of skills and incorporate it into tasks for learners rather than creating artificial distinctions.

AUTONOMOUS LEARNING AND LEARNER DIFFERENCES

If the learner is to take increasing responsibility for progress and the teacher aims to facilitate, not control, the language-learning process, then autonomous learning becomes crucial. Autonomous learning does not mean self-instruction or learning without a teacher. Rather it is a way of complementing face-to-face tuition which makes learning more productive and develops independence. Educational research has long recognised that learning is less effective the more learners depend on the teacher and the less they take responsibility for their own learning. Therefore the emphasis currently being placed on the role of the learner in the pedagogical process is to be welcomed (see Chapter 2).

In a world which is changing so rapidly students need not so much to accumulate a set body of knowledge as to learn *how* to acquire knowledge both now and in the future. Language teaching thus implies the development of transferable language-learning skills based on an understanding of what makes an effective language learner. There are four essential elements here.

1 Understanding how languages are learnt

Providing students with an insight into the nature of language learning means explaining to them the reasons for engaging in particular classroom activities but also teaching them proven strategies for:

- *learning vocabulary:* for example, using word roots and affixes, guessing strategies, word cards, imagery or other mnemonics (Nation, 2001);
- *learning grammar*: colour-coding structures, using mnemonics for rules;
- *reading*: activating background knowledge, making use of titles or illustrations, skimming and scanning texts, spotting cohesive and coherence markers (Nuttall, 1996);
- *listening*: listening with a purpose, practising gist listening by using background knowledge, listening with and without a text (Broady, 2002);
- *writing*: producing drafts, checking written work, spotting errors (Sharpling, 2002);
- *speaking*: reading and repeating after a tape for pronunciation, learning phrases and techniques for seeking repetition/explanation, exploring ideas for increasing oral interaction outside the classroom (Tyler, 2003);
- *making the most of **CALL** and the internet*: working in pairs/individually, focusing on personal weaknesses, using FL spell-checkers, accessing online dictionaries and using the internet as a source of information and means of communication (Dudeney, 2000; Davies *et al.*, 2005).

Such strategies and techniques can usefully be listed in a course or module guide at the start of the year but should also be integrated into language-learning tasks themselves in order to demonstrate their relevance and applicability and to encourage their transfer to similar tasks beyond the classroom.

2 Identifying preferred learning style

Learning styles denote students' individual approaches to learning. They are largely determined by a person's psychological make-up but are also shaped, to a lesser extent, by upbringing and education. A distinction is normally made between **cognitive** styles (how we process information) and **learning styles** (how we acquire and retain information). Although research has found distinct strengths and learning preferences for such major cognitive styles as 'field independent/field dependent' and 'holistic/analytic', there appears to be no overall advantage in language learning for either style.

There have been various attempts to classify learning styles, including analytical, concrete, communicative and authority oriented or visual, auditory and haptic (for an overview and an established learning styles questionnaire, see Littlemore, 2002). We should remember, however, that any style identified in a particular student is only ever a 'preferred' style and that the most effective learners apply different styles strategically for different purposes, in different contexts. Furthermore, a learning approach can be strongly affected by such factors as assessment.

While style classifications can help explain elements of student behaviour that may otherwise remain perplexing, research suggests it is impossible to effect any significant change in students' learning styles. When confronted with a group of students who evince different learning styles, language tutors can therefore at best ensure that learning activities both in and out of the classroom are varied, so that all styles are accommodated for at least some of the time. (For a list of helpful ideas, see Littlemore, 2002: 13.3.4.)

3 Understanding the role of affective factors

Important though learning styles are, students' motivation is ultimately *the* major factor in successful language learning (Dörnyei and Csizer, 1998; Dörnyei, 2001; see also Chapter 3). Lambert and Gardner (1972) distinguish 'integrative' from 'instrumental' motivation; the former indicates a genuine interest in the foreign country and the speakers of L2, while the latter denotes greater concern for the practical benefits of learning the language, such as gaining a qualification or using it to further one's career. Integrative motivation and close identification with the target culture seem to be more successful in motivating learners to persist with the long, demanding process of L2 learning. The further students move towards the integrative end of this continuum, the more likely they are to succeed. However, the importance in HE of 'resultative' motivation should also not be forgotten: self-reinforcing successes and achievements are often a key motivator for advanced learners, suggesting that motivation often derives from successful language learning rather than being at the root of it and that the cause/effect model is thus often more blurred than many assume.

Unlike other disciplines, language learning requires students to forsake part of their own identity: their sense of self as defined by their relation to a particular language community. They also have to adopt once more the uncertain role of the imperfect speaker with its inevitable sense of insecurity and anxiety (see Oxford, 1999). Success will depend to a considerable extent on how they cope with these two factors.

Teachers need to be sensitive to all these motivational issues, both in the image they present of the foreign country and its people, and in the way they structure classroom activities to handle students' uncertainties.

4 Being involved in shaping the course

Involving students in the organisation of the course implies some or all of the following:

- seeking student preferences as to topics
- allowing students some say in the choice of materials
- engaging students in independent information-gathering

- involving them in individually chosen project work
- linking tuition to a range of activities in open learning facilities.

In summary, learners need to accept responsibility for their language learning, to develop the capacity to reflect on their individual learning style and to use that reflection to shape the content and process of subsequent learning.

Interrogating practice

In what ways are your students encouraged and provided with the tools to become independent learners with transferable language-learning skills?

USING TECHNOLOGY IN MODERN LANGUAGES

C&IT can also be a useful tool in the development of autonomous learning, and many HE colleagues are experimenting to harness the power of digital communication to enhance the learning experience of their students (see Chapter 7). Language teachers have often argued in the past that language means interpersonal communication and interaction, requiring face-to-face contact which allows language support mechanisms such as facial and body language to contribute to meaning. However, the growth of e-mail and texting as means of personal communication, the development of webcams and video phones, the expansion of the internet as an instant source of information and the increasing use of intranets and Virtual Learning Environments (**VLEs**) within institutions as means of dissemination, interaction and learning support (see Case study 1) cannot be ignored. The computer has valuable potential as one of a range of learning tools, and it is the teacher's duty to encourage learners to make full use of any appropriate tool.

The key question is: 'What is appropriate?' Any computer-based learning and teaching activity must be assessed according to its contribution to the learner's language skills and to how well it promotes the development of learner independence. Usage needs to be language rather than C&IT driven. One needs to be certain of the specific advantages brought by digital resources to ensure that valuable time is not wasted in the development and execution of activities which would be more effective in the traditional classroom environment or using paper and pen.

There are numerous ways in which appropriate software, both generic and language specific, can make a unique and valuable contribution to the learning process; for example:

- Features of the interactive whiteboard (IWB) may be used to demonstrate grammatical changes and patterning in a very clear and visual way.

- Voting systems may be used in conjunction with an IWB to engage students more actively in a lecture situation and provide instant feedback for the lecturer to allow misconceptions to be addressed (Beekes, 2006; Schmidt, 2006).
- The IWB may be used to project digital text or audio or video material for the class to work on, including performances produced by students.
- The IWB may be used to demonstrate and share the writing process, to present models of work in order to highlight good features and suggest improvements (this could be a particularly useful tool in the translation process suggested below).
- **Video-conferencing** may be used to link up with native speakers and bring reality to topic discussions.
- The creation of digital video vignettes and **podcasts** may be exploited to provide an end goal and a real audience for language use and production.
- Institutional intranets may be used as a means of communication and support for learners within a guided self-study scheme, for example by providing video and audio clips with related tasks; the use of remote drives linked to digital language laboratory software such as the popular Sanako system is a further extension of this.
- Concordancing may be used with more advanced learners to encourage heuristic learning approaches and develop sophisticated language skills.
- With appropriate guidance on where to look and how to evaluate the reliability and validity of information, the internet can be a useful source of authentic and interesting material for both lecturer and student, and in particular can help support research for projects.
- CD ROM collections may be used as a valuable source of research material for project work.
- Multimedia CD ROMs may be used to develop pronunciation and fluency.
- With tutorial guidance, students can make use of grammar-based programmes to diagnose learning needs and improve their accuracy through drilling and test exercises (see Case study 3).

This list is by no means exhaustive, and the speed of technological development means that none ever could be. A useful and regularly updated source of support is the ICT4LT website (Davies, 2005) which provides case studies and advice combined with a research-led rationale for various aspects of C&IT use. Further ideas may be found in Dudeney (2000), Gill (2000) and Coleman and Klapper (2005).

Case study 1: Languages online

Project background

Since 2002, the Department of Languages and Translation Studies has been delivering **FL** courses with an integrated online component. The aim in using a VLE (WebCT) was to extend and enhance the student learning experience by allowing greater reflection and autonomy. Thus, the system was designed to offer flexibility, independence and feedback. It was also intended to support a wide range of learning styles and encourage student interaction outside the classroom.

The project started with just a few courses and soon expanded to embrace other language programmes. It has focused on developing two areas within WebCT: language practice self-check exercises (*Hot Potatoes*) and interactive discussion tasks. Materials have been written by a team of tutors within the department, working collaboratively. The materials are peer reviewed during all stages of production, and specialist technical and pedagogical support is provided by the e-learning team. Tutors have received training in e-moderation and other specific issues, although virtual peer observation has also proved to be a highly effective training tool.

Courses

The multimedia exercises focus on grammar, vocabulary and receptive skills. Feedback is built into each exercise with back-up explanations and transcripts. The main courses are offered in 'blended' mode and tasks are assessed for participation and content; some are also offered as extra support but are not assessed. The integration of online work with face-to-face sessions has changed classroom work which is now largely devoted to oral skills and the presentation of new structures and vocabulary. Exercises and materials covered in class feed into the online interactive tasks, with students collaborating on their productive skills and using the target language creatively. These are communicative language tasks adapted to an asynchronous, written medium.

Feedback

Evaluation shows consistently that students rate online work positively due to its flexibility, ease of revision, collaborative learning dimension and enhanced tutor feedback. Negative aspects include the loss of face-to-face time and difficulties with group activities. Tutors have also observed a higher standard of linguistic output and greater participation on the part of quieter learners. Student interaction can be monitored more closely than in the classroom, making feedback more targeted, and there has been a shift towards greater learner independence, as students plan their learning, and reflect on and monitor their own language and that of their peers.

(Department of Languages and Translation Studies (LTS), University of Surrey)

TRANSLATION

In many universities, L1>L2 translation and L2>L1 translation (i.e. into and out of the foreign language) are still very common teaching and testing techniques. It is difficult to prove whether translation helps students to learn a language. Many now have doubts but still argue for the retention of L2 to L1 translation, at least for final-year students, as a **key skill**.

Reservations about the continued use of translation relate particularly to many departments' traditional approach: students write a translation in their own time and hand it in for marking by the lecturer, who then spends most of the class hour going over the piece, highlighting problems and possibly offering a 'fair' version (Klapper, 2006). Such an approach fails to make clear how students are to learn *about* translation (see Millan, 2002). Instead, it treats translation simply as a vague support to general language learning, and the process becomes in effect little more than repeated testing. An alternative approach, outlined in Case study 2, aims to encourage students to learn about translation.

Case study 2: Making translation a more effective learning process

Fourth-year German–English translation class for non-specialist learners

One of the basic principles of this course for students of law, politics or economics is that if they are to be able to approach the text in an effective manner, students must first be told the context of the extract being used (i.e. its significance within the whole work, the purpose for which it was written and its intended audience).

At the start of the module, students are shown that translation is not about simply transposing items from one language to another at the level of lexis and syntax, but that it is about conveying meaning. In order to take this first step in reconstructing meaning, short exercises are employed to encourage students to read the whole text thoroughly, actively and critically, addressing such questions as sentence length (can sentences be merged or split?), order of sentences/paragraphs, assumed cultural knowledge, and cultural/social/ political equivalence.

The novice translator needs to see himself or herself as a mediator between cultural worlds (i.e. as someone who helps those unfamiliar with a culture to understand and appreciate all the cultural nuances of the original text). Translation is therefore a communicative act: it is as much about en-coding as it is about de-coding.

Students are required to produce an occasional annotated translation, giving their reasons for the choices made. This forces them to focus consciously on the act of translation, thus helping to make them more reflective. Repeated translation without focus on the process provides no evidence of learning or progress.

In order to avoid literal and 'safe' translations, the course tutor repeatedly encourages students to focus on whole text and translation-task issues rather than just grammar and lexis. The following ideas are useful for this purpose:

- Students provide an L1 summary of an L2 text as a briefing to someone visiting the foreign country for a specific purpose; this focuses attention on relevance and appropriateness of material, the target audience's information needs and students' English versions.
- The tutor supplies a specific brief (e.g. to translate an article for inclusion in a particular British broadsheet) which requires clear explication of cultural references, foreign figures or events.
- Students translate a passage for inclusion in a specialist English language journal and adapt their translation to the particular 'house style'.
- Students correct an inaccurate translation which may include errors of fact, idiom, collocation or metaphor.

(Department of German Studies, University of Birmingham)

Translation *into L2* poses particular problems and can be both demotivating and a poor learning experience for many students. Often learners are asked to perform too many simultaneous tasks and there is insufficient focus on individual weaknesses. There are three alternatives. These are as follows.

1 Demonstration

A basic pedagogical principle is to demonstrate how to do something before asking learners to do it themselves. In translation this can be achieved by giving students a parallel L2 text which allows contrastive analysis of the two languages. This reveals how the translator has set about the task and highlights interesting discrepancies and even mistakes which are a source of fascination to learners. Students can then move beyond lexical and grammatical points to look for differences in tone, style and register. At the end of a class spent working on the parallel texts, the L2 text can be withdrawn and students required to translate the L1 version. Marking then involves a lot less correction and the process is less demotivating for everyone. Feedback using the original L2 text can focus on students' alternative renderings, thus emphasising that there is always more than one correct version and reinforcing the message that it is *meaning* that translators should be seeking to convey.

2 Comparison

Two L2 versions could be used and students asked to compare the two translations, focusing on, for example, lexis, grammar or even idiom. This is a demanding task but carries much potential for learning in the form of more sophisticated contrastive analysis. Setting up these tasks is not easy, but a bank of texts can be built up based on versions produced by two different language assistants or exchange students. It is also sometimes possible to find two L2 translations of English literary texts. (This exercise can, of course, work well the other way, comparing and contrasting two L1 versions of an L2 text.)

3 Collaboration

As an alternative to 'cold' translation, students may be asked to prepare a text in pairs by underlining any potentially problematic structures and circling any unknown vocabulary. Ideas are then pooled in fours, and groups subsequently brought together for plenary discussion. Vocabulary and structures can be shared on an overhead projector or IWB, all acceptable ways of translating a particular expression can be listed and dictionaries consulted collectively to further good reference skills. The text is then set for homework. The advantages of this approach are that the weaker benefit from collaboration with more able peers and marking time is reduced as less correction of common difficulties is required. The diagnosis of individual errors with ensuing provision of targeted advice thus becomes much easier.

These approaches to translation emphasise process, focus attention on *how* to translate and employ assessment and feedback for the purpose of learning. They thus avoid the tendency in some modern language programmes to use translation as a continual testing mechanism.

Many of the points discussed in this chapter are illustrated in the description of a language course aimed at bridging the gap between the skills of school leavers and the needs of university language studies (Case study 3).

> ## Case study 3: First-year language course for (specialist) post-A Level students of French

Background

A decade ago, the Department of French Studies of the University of Birmingham introduced a new first-year language course, which aimed to build on skills acquired at A Level by using 'real-life' situations, exposing students to authentic materials while encouraging accuracy and promoting autonomous learning.

Discovering where the students are

A diagnostic test was introduced so that tutors and students could obtain a snapshot of the latter's competence in key grammatical areas. It became clear that our cohorts were far from homogeneous and this, together with student feedback, has since led us to use the diagnostic test to stream students for their written language class. This was necessary, as the best students were complaining that they were not stretched enough, while the weaker ones felt intimidated by the better ones and did not engage fully in the classes. While streaming works well for the better students, it is not clear that it is entirely successful with the weaker students, as it sometimes creates a 'can't do' culture among students.

Grammar

Students are encouraged to work on the grammar topics of the diagnostic exercise by taking an assessed test in the second half of semester 1. We suggest that they make a revision plan, which they show to their language tutor. They work on these topics autonomously with the help of their grammar book (Hawkins and Towell, 2000) and its accompanying workbook (Hawkins *et al.*, 1997) as well as online exercises on WebCT. The latter may need to be reinforced to enable those who, despite their good A Level results, are now coming to university with very little knowledge of grammar and limited grammatical terminology.

In the first year we also have a weekly lecture on key grammatical topics. These lectures comprise a series of explanations given by the tutor which alternate with exercises that the students complete and that are corrected immediately. Students can ask questions, although some cohorts avail themselves of this opportunity more than others. The language of delivery of the lecture has gone full circle, from predominantly English to almost all French and back again, both as a result of student feedback and tutor experience. Reinforcement tasks are provided for students in their study pack to complete in their own time. Fair copies are available on WebCT.

Speaking and listening

Students also have one weekly *expression orale* class and one fortnightly language laboratory class, both taught by French foreign language assistants. Our old language course did not include any language laboratory component, but one oral and one written exercise linked to the lectures on Modern France which were given in French. When the language module was first revised, we introduced five laboratory sessions initially as part of the Modern France module. We subsequently felt that students needed more hours in the language laboratory and that these should form part of the language module – their number was increased up to their current frequency. These sessions take place in new digital laboratories (Sanako 300) and are used to foster both accurate pronunciation and good comprehension skills. In addition, through their study pack and WebCT, students are provided with exercises to complete autonomously (comprehension, pronunciation, vocabulary tasks). This year, for the first time, students were required to buy a vocabulary book (Lamy, 1998). At the end of each exercise it is suggested that students learn the vocabulary in the sections corresponding to the exercise.

VLE

WebCT is largely used to support guided autonomous work. However, we also use it as part of our assessed coursework. Students are required to complete a number of gap-filling exercises on verb forms in a variety of tenses and other key grammatical topics. We believe that such topics require regular practice and that WebCT is particularly appropriate for this type of practice. However, we also know that few students would do them regularly were it not for the fact that they contribute to the module mark.

Challenges faced

Several of the new challenges facing us seem to stem from the way assessments are undertaken in schools. Students now expect us more and more to coach them for their exams. Increasingly, they think classes should prepare them directly for particular assessments and they have a growing tendency to view as irrelevant exercises that do not seem to do this. Although they all say they want to become fluent in French, they would like us to provide them with a very clearly defined list of words to learn for each exam. In addition, students now think they should be allowed to retake particular assignments to improve on their grades, not realising that at university one can only retake (in the resit period) a module that has been failed overall, not individual components.

Another challenge is students' diminishing ability to read in French, which colleagues now notice in non-language modules, as growing numbers of students struggle to keep up with the reading they are given. There is undoubtedly a shift in culture as we move increasingly into an audiovisual world. However, reading remains a necessary skill, not only from a cultural or literary angle, but also because when students read more, they learn more vocabulary, become more aware of grammatical structures and avoid confusing basic words such as *assez/aussi* or *allé/allez/allait/aller*.

These developments and issues mean we need to review our course again, to incorporate reading comprehension exercises and better integrate vocabulary learning within the whole module, finding ways to foster more independent learning and make students realise that learning a language is about having a comprehensive approach, not one limited to passing a few tests.

(Department of French Studies, University of Birmingham)

Interrogating practice

Compare the approaches outlined in Case study 3 with your own department's first-year language programme. What differences are there?

- Does your department teach any aspects more effectively?
- Is there anything in the case study which your department could learn from?

OVERVIEW

HE language teachers need to respond both to recent changes in the understanding of how languages are learned and to developments in the secondary education system which provides their raw material. Perhaps the most significant change of focus in recent years has been towards content-based, meaning-driven language learning within which students are encouraged to explore topics relevant to their needs and interests via mixed-skill activities. This is in contrast to the traditional grammar-led approach focusing on the written language, which is now out of step with the prior learning experiences of many incoming students. The strengths and weaknesses of these students need to be addressed within a flexible learning package, which encourages language acquisition, develops transferable learning skills, promotes learner autonomy, and identifies and tackles individual formal weaknesses. As Case study 3 shows, C&IT can be a valuable tool in providing individual support for learners in this process, encouraging an independent approach to the all-important grammar drilling. Where translation remains part of the language curriculum, attention needs to be paid as much to the process as to the product.

REFERENCES

Beekes, W (2006) 'The "Millionaire" method for encouraging participation', *Active Learning in Higher Education*, 7(1): 25–36.

Broady, E (2002) 'Understanding and developing listening in a foreign language', DELPHI distance-learning module. Available online at <http://www.delphi.bham.ac.uk> (accessed 20 April 2007).

Butzkamm, W (2003) 'We only learn language once. The role of the mother tongue in FL classrooms: death of a dogma', *Language Learning Journal*, 28: 29–39.

Byrne, N and Abbott, J (2006) *Survey on University Students Choosing a Language Course as an Extra-Curricular Activity: Results from the First Year of a Planned Three-year Survey Conducted by AULC on Behalf of DfES*, London: Department for Education and Skills/Association of University Language Centres.

CILT (2006) 'Higher education statistics'. Available online at <http://www.cilt.org.uk/research/statistics/education/higher.htm> (accessed 20 April 2007).

Coleman, J and Klapper, J (eds) (2005) *Effective Learning and Teaching in Modern Languages*, London: Routledge.

Davies, G (ed.) (2005) *Information and Communications Technology for Language Teachers (ICT4LT)*, Slough: Thames Valley University. Available online at <http://www.ict4lt.org/en/en_mod1-4.htm> (accessed 26 April 2007).

Davies, G, Walker, R, Rendall, H and Hewer, S (2005) 'Introduction to computer assisted language learning (CALL)', Module 1.4, in G Davies (ed.), *Information and Communications Technology for Language Teachers (ICT4LT)*, Slough: Thames Valley University. Available online at <http://www.ict4lt.org/en/en_mod1-4.htm> (accessed 22 April 2007).

Dearing, R and King, L (2007) *Languages Review*, London: DfES. Available online at <http://www.teachernet.gov.uk/docbank/index.cfm?id=11124> (accessed 26 April 2007).

DfES (Department for Education and Skills) News Centre (2007) 'Johnson backs Dearing's blueprint for a Renaissance in language learning'. Available online at <http://www.dfes.gov.uk/pns/DisplayPN.cgi? pn_id=2007_0041> (accessed 12 March 2007).

Dodson, C J (1985) 'Second language acquisition and bilingual development: a theoretical framework', *Journal of Multilingual and Multicultural Development*, 6: 325–46.

Dörnyei, Z (2001) *Teaching and Researching Motivation*, London: Longman.

Dörnyei, Z and Csizer, K (1998) 'Ten commandments for motivating language learners: results of an empirical study', *Language Teaching Research*, 2: 203–29.

Dudeney, G (2000) *The Internet and the Language Classroom*, Cambridge: Cambridge University Press.

Gill, C (2000) *Improving MFL Learning through ICT*, Dunstable and Dublin: Folens.

Gray, C (2001) 'Training postgraduate and foreign language assistants: the DOPLA approach', in J Klapper (ed.), *Teaching Languages in Higher Education: Issues in Training and Continuing Professional Development*, London: CILT.

Hawkins, R and Towell, R (2000) *French Grammar and Usage* (2nd edn), London: Arnold.

Hawkins, R, Lamy, M-N and Towell, R (1997) *Practising French Grammar* (2nd edn), London: Arnold.

Klapper, J (1998) 'Language learning at school and university: the great grammar debate continues (II)', *Language Learning Journal*, 18: 22–8.

Klapper, J (2006) 'Translation as a learning experience', in J. Klapper (ed.), *Understanding and Developing Good Practice: Language Teaching in Higher Education*, London: CILT.

Lambert, W and Gardner, R (1972) *Attitudes and Motivation in Second Language Learning*, Rowley, MA: Newbury House.

Lamy, M-N (1998) *The Cambridge French–English Thesaurus*, Cambridge: Cambridge University Press.

Little, D and Ushioda, E (1998) *Institution-wide Language Programmes*, London/Dublin: CILT/Centre for Language and Communication Studies, Trinity College Dublin.

Littlemore, J (2002) 'Learner autonomy, language learning strategies and learning styles', DELPHI distance-learning module. Available online at <http://www.delphi.bham.ac.uk> (accessed 19 April 2007).

Millan, C (2002) 'Using translation in the language classroom', DELPHI distance-learning module. Available online at <http://www.delphi.bham.ac.uk> (accessed 21 April 2007).

Mitchell, R and Myles, F (2004) *Second Language Learning Theories* (2nd edn), London: Arnold.

Nation, I S P (2001) *Learning Vocabulary in Another Language*, Cambridge: Cambridge University Press.

Nuttall, C (1996) *Teaching Reading Skills in a Foreign Language* (2nd edn), London: Heinemann.

Oxford, R (1999) 'Anxiety and the language learner: new insights', in J Arnold (ed.), *Affect in Language Learning*, Cambridge: Cambridge University Press.

Pachler, N and Field, K (1997) *Learning to Teach Modern Foreign Languages in the Secondary School*, London: Routledge.

Schmidt, E C (2006) 'Investigating the use of interactive whiteboard technology in the English language classroom through the lens of a critical theory of technology', *Computer Assisted Language Learning*, 19(1): 47–62.

Sharpling, G (2002) 'Developing foreign language writing skills', DELPHI distance-learning module. Available online at <http://www.delphi.bham.ac.uk> (accessed 20 April 2007).

Towell, R and Hawkins, R (1994) *Approaches to Second Language Acquisition*, Clevedon/Philadelphia, PA: Multilingual Matters.

Tyler, E (2003) 'Promoting the development of speaking skills', DELPHI distance-learning module. Available online at <http://www.delphi.bham.ac.uk> (accessed 20 April 2007).

Wilkins, D A (1976) *Notional Syllabuses*, Oxford: Oxford University Press.

FURTHER READING

Coleman, J A (forthcoming) *Residence and Study Abroad: Research and Good Practice*, Clevedon: Multilingual Matters. An authoritative overview of this central element of the undergraduate degree.

Coleman, J and Klapper, J (2005) See above. Twenty-six concise chapters on key aspects of the discipline, combining insights from research with practical advice.

Davies (2005) See above. The result of a SOCRATES-funded project, this site provides a wealth of freely available training resources in C&IT for language teachers.

DELPHI Website of the DELPHI distance-learning project, <http://www.delphi.bham.ac.uk> (accessed 18 April 2007). Comprises 14 freely accessible modules designed specifically for HE language teachers with limited experience, along with supporting links and references.

Hervey, S and Higgins, I (2002) *Thinking Translation: A Course in Translation Method: French to English* (2nd edn), London: Routledge. Also available in Arabic (2002), German (2006), Italian (2000) and Spanish (1995).

Klapper, J (2006) See above. A substantial manual linking findings from pedagogical and applied linguistic research to the practicalities of the HE language classroom.

Lewis, T and Rouxeville, A (eds) (2000) *Technology and the Advanced Language Learner*, London: AFLS/CILT. A set of articles that look at innovative uses of technology such as video, CALL, e-mail tandem partnerships, bulletin boards and discussion lists.

Towell, R and Hawkins, R (1994) See above. One of the more readable surveys of the theoretical principles of SLA.

22

Key aspects of teaching and learning in the visual arts

Alison Shreeve, Shân Wareing and Linda Drew

INTRODUCTION

This chapter is concerned with issues relevant to teaching and learning in the visual arts. As with other subject areas, it is impossible to place clear and finite parameters around the discipline. Teachers of undergraduate and taught postgraduate art, media and design should find much they recognise; teachers of performing arts, publishing and communication will probably find some aspects of this chapter applicable and some less so. Teachers in other practice-based disciplines, such as medicine and engineering, may also find aspects of relevance.

The chapter begins by exploring the disciplinary context, dealing particularly with the tutor-practitioner, the student-practitioner, and equal opportunities. It proceeds to look at examples of learning activities which may be used as part of the curriculum, and considers theoretical approaches to understanding student learning within the discipline. Next, assessment is considered, and ideas to ensure the **crit** supports student learning effectively. This section includes a case study on peer assessment, illustrating the use of a computer programme to support the assessment process. The chapter deals next with skills development and the second case study is concerned with maximising students' opportunity to develop skills through an industry-based team project.

CONTEXT

While many of the educational traditions within visual arts higher education will be obvious, their implications for learning and teaching bear close analysis. For that reason, some of the main aspects are listed below. The list is numbered not to indicate priority but to make subsequent references back to the list easier.

1   Students are, from the outset of their higher education, practitioners in their subject of study.
2   Many courses are structured to include long periods of working on projects.
3   There is often a range of technical skills which students need to acquire.
4   Study time and contact hours frequently occur in studios and workshops, which provide opportunities for engaging in informal conversations about the work in progress among students and between tutors, technicians and students.
5   Assessment and feedback are often accomplished through the crit, or critique, a key component of most art and design education.
6   Opportunities to learn from peers and from the work of students in the years above are plentiful.
7   There is an emphasis on open-ended solutions and many possible ways of undertaking practice.
8   There is less emphasis than in many subjects on formal knowledge and more on procedures and ways of working which are more or less appropriate in specific situations. This knowledge is frequently held tacitly by practitioners (both teachers and students) and therefore may not be readily articulated.
9   The expectation that students will become independent, self-analytical, critical thinkers informs the entire period in higher education from the start of their course.
10 Students (and indeed staff) are often uncomfortable with the role of writing and theory within the subject; it is often seen as separate and unrelated.
11 The environment in which students learn is rich in opportunities to develop skills, usually referred to as personal and professional skills, **key skills** or skills for employability.

The implications of these features will be explored through the chapter.

The tutor-practitioner

Particular challenges for the visual arts educator often result from tutors combining teaching with active practice in their craft, art or industry (see point 8 in the list above); many are part-time or hourly paid staff with professional lives outside education. Combining two fulfilling professions which nourish each other, and flexibility in terms of hours and future career pathways, are undeniably positives, as are the sense of reward from bringing to the classroom relevant current knowledge, and a capacity to enthuse and mentor students. However, there is also a range of complicating factors which can be stressful for the tutor and have a negative effect on students' education unless well managed.

Part-time tutors can find it more difficult to obtain a thorough induction into institutional and departmental services and equipment to support teaching. Time to support students outside scheduled teaching time and to undertake core tasks other than teaching, such as attendance at examination boards, can be limited. It is easy to be left out of communication loops, and even accessing a university e-mail account or conventional mail may present practical difficulties. Part-time staff may also lack a sense of community and comradeship with colleagues, which many feel as a particular absence in their working environment.

Suggestions for managing this situation to minimise the difficulties include:

- Actively seek out an induction into institutional and departmental resources and support services, if you are not automatically given one.
- Even if the greater part of your inbox is spam and your mail is junk, take time to sort through it regularly for relevant communications, announcements and information.
- Find out about any interesting institutional staff development activities for which you are eligible: attending will help you get a sense of the wider institution and meet people from across the university or college.
- Ask if you can have a more experienced member of staff as a mentor, who can be a sounding board and a source of guidance.
- Visit ADEPTT, a website specifically developed as a resource for part-time teachers in art and design.

The student-practitioner

Students learn through engaging in activities which are either fully authentic examples or replicas of those undertaken by practitioners in the field and consequently may recognise themselves and be recognised by the visual arts community as junior but legitimate members of the community. Lave and Wenger's phrase to describe this is 'legitimate peripheral participation' in a **'Community of Practice'** (Lave and Wenger, 1991; Wenger, 1998). The tutor in this situation to some extent adopts the role of the more experienced 'old-timer', who explains and initiates the newer members into the ways of working and thinking in the community through enabling the practices to be mad⁻ ⁻sible and accessible to the student, which, as indicated in point 8 above, may be kn⁻   ⁻v but not explicitly.

Equal opportunities

The prevalence of tacit knowledge in art and design must be
extent mitigated because of its potential to undermine equal⁻
entering higher education will not all know and understand ⁻
practices, the words or concepts tutors use in the educat⁻
less well equipped initially than others to pick u⁻
educational experiences or countries of origin. Tak⁻

engagement is not necessarily a sign of lesser capability. In transition to a new situation everyone has to learn about new systems, practices and expectations. Students can be helped to make this transition by the provision of plentiful opportunities to become part of this community of practice, through formal processes such as written guidelines and induction briefings, and through informal processes such as teamwork, social networking and informal conversations.

LEARNING IN VISUAL ARTS

A range of the possible learning activities within visual arts education are listed below, to indicate the richness and variety which can be part of the student experience.

- *Live projects.* Projects set in conjunction with industry practitioners.
- *Event-based learning.* Learning off site, engaging in 'real-life' projects in the community, with schools, in galleries and industry.
- *Group learning.* Using role allocation in teams to replicate the conditions of practice (particularly essential in performing arts, media, and other team-based practices) to undertake projects, enter exhibitions or put on a show together.
- *Artists' talks.* Practitioner talks can offer opportunities for providing insights into the wider world of practice and give an insider view of the practice. Students should have opportunities to engage in conversations and activities based on these talks.
- *Consultancy.* Students can act as consultants to industry, working collaboratively with industry partners to solve issues they identify.
- *Simulating conditions of industry.* This offers equal access for all students to experience what it is like.
- *Peer learning.* Student-to-student mentoring.
- Learning in work. Through short-term activities or through longer-term accredited work placement opportunities.

Project work in art and design

Many of the activities described above are likely be experienced by students through project work, as indicated in point 2 above. Projects should be supported by a written brief, the function of which is to set the parameters for the work students will be engaged in. Briefs should be realistic, clearly set out the **learning outcomes**, what students are expected to learn as a result of the project, and how the project will be assessed (see Chapter 3 for more on learning outcomes). These should be an example of **constructive alignment** (Biggs, 1999); i.e. the project should enable the student to demonstrate the ___ing which is directly assessed. The brief can helpfully include information about ___sources, sources of inspiration or research, and the types of artefacts to be submitted in the portfolio or final presentation of the work. Dates, deadlines, tutorials, and information about any formative or progress crits should also be included.

Student approaches to learning

While the project is a most common form of engagement with learning for students in visual arts, students do not all approach project work identically. In a study of fashion textiles students it was found that Marton and Saljö's description of two approaches to learning, a **deep** or **surface approach** (1984) (see Chapter 2 for more on approaches to learning), needed modification in order to map on to student approaches to design-based project work (Drew *et al.*, 2002). The study identified four categories of variation in approach:

- a product-focused strategy with the intention of demonstrating technical competence, where the emphasis is a concern with remembering processes and techniques
- a product-focused strategy with the intention of developing the product through experimenting and practising to ensure competence
- a process-focused strategy with the intention of developing the design process through experimenting and engaging with others in order to explore the design process rather than just perfecting the product
- a concept-focused strategy with the intention of developing the student's own response and ideas in relation to the project, ultimately a search for intrinsic personal meaning.

Mapped on to Marton and Saljö's categories, these categories could be said to show a surface approach at one end of the scale and a deep approach at the other. However, there are also the categories of approach between the extremes, that seem to relate specifically to the kind of learning undertaken in practical and creative subjects, and that indicate a concern with learning being about practice and process. A similar structural approach to learning has been found in engineering students (Case and Marshall, 2004).

Approaches and concepts are not fixed traits of students and it is the role of tutors to try and expand students' awareness of ways to undertake their project work. Factors that can affect all students negatively include time pressures, not understanding assessment requirements, lacking confidence, and not understanding the reasons why they are failing. Any of these can damage a student's ability to take a deep approach to a project.

Practical changes to the curriculum to support students undertaking a deeper approach include opportunities for students to explore, visually and verbally, what it means to undertake research, what is important, how to do it and what 'good' research looks like. Making the brief as explicit as possible, including the marking criteria, setting interim deadlines, and following the guidelines suggested below for crits may all help.

> ### Interrogating practice
>
> Articulate what you understand by research in your discipline. Do you know whether your students understand research in the same way, and if not, how could you find out?
>
> What could you do to develop your students' understanding of research in the context of their project work?

ASSESSMENT

Assessment in the visual arts is usually accomplished through the presentation and examination of a collection of student work in a portfolio that contains evidence of the project process, research, drawings, artefacts, samples, sketches, thoughts, developmental ideas and finished products or recording of performances. It may be unclear to the student, and indeed to the new lecturer, what is actually being assessed. Assumptions vary and may include the product, the process, the person and the learning outcomes. This variation in belief can give rise to discrepancies in practice between tutors and difficulty on the part of students in understanding the nature and intention of assessment. This lack of clarity can inhibit student learning.

There have been criticisms of assessment in the visual arts as being subjective and lacking in rigour. Research has shown how tutors arrive at grades through discussion (Orr, 2006) in a process which is rigorous but socially negotiated and includes unwritten criteria. In order for students to understand the assessment process and develop the capacity for effective self-evaluation and development, opportunities must be provided for them to understand assessment practices through formal explication and through social learning, as happens for tutors (Drew and Shreeve, 2006). This can enable students to benefit and learn from assessment rather than seeing it as something that is 'done to them' (Shreeve *et al.*, 2004) (see also Chapter 10 for a discussion about the impact of assessment on learning).

The crit is a common assessment format encountered in the visual arts (point 5 above). It may be undertaken for both formative and **summative** assessment purposes and is an excellent opportunity for students to learn from other people's work. However, there can be some very real problems which reduce the effectiveness of the crit as an opportunity for students to learn. In critiques controlled by the tutor, research shows that students tend to learn less. Students report being nervous, anxious, even terrified, and unable to listen to comments made about others' work as they wait their turn to explain and defend their work. Afterwards they may be so relieved that they switch off from the rest of the session. The crit has been explored extensively through tutors' and students' perspectives by Blair (2006a, 2006b).

With some planning, the crit can become a useful opportunity for learning:

- *Prepare students.* Students should be provided with opportunities to practise speaking and presenting work in informal small group settings first.
- *Provide written prompts.* Students report finding worksheets with questions prompting the analysis of project work to be helpful in learning to assess their own and others' work.
- *Work in pairs or small teams.* Discussion and debate help to develop confidence in using critical vocabulary and in understanding what to look for and how to evaluate successful work.
- *Let the students do the talking.* Tutors should resist the temptation to take the role of expert and lead the discussion, and instead allow students to explore their responses first. Talking helps evaluation and engenders confidence and fluency in the discourse.
- *Take a back seat.* Tutors should avoid standing at the front in a commanding position; speaking from among the audience changes the power relations to a more collaborative position and contributes to students' confidence to talk.
- *Provide low-stakes opportunities for learning.* The crit should be used as an informal feedback opportunity as well as the end of project assessment.
- *Invite others to participate too.* The Fashion Studies course at the London College of Fashion, University of the Arts London, invited representatives from industry to come in and critique work in progress, thus providing contacts and comments from current practitioners in fashion design. Comments took the form of brief written notes or a discussion with individual students.
- *Keep everyone engaged.* Sessions should not be too long and students should be kept actively involved: they need a purpose to be there.

Case study 1: CASPAR, an online tool for self- and peer assessment

The Media School at Bournemouth University developed a computer-based solution for self- and peer assessment through a four-year **HEFCE**-funded project, GWAMP (Group Work and Assessment in Media Production).

The aims of CASPAR were:

- to support group work as a vocational key skill for employment;
- to recognise and implement peer assessment as a valid and valued method of assessment;
- to make easier the provision of formative assessment, recognising its importance to student learning;
- to reduce the impact of assessment on staff time, while maintaining the student learning experience.

CASPAR is a computer database, with a web front end. It can easily sort and manage data, providing students and tutors with immediate information. When CASPAR was designed, it was intended that it would become a 'one-stop shop' forthe organisation and assessment of group work, featuring the following functions:

- sort and manage students into groups;
- enable students to input marks and feedback comments on themselves and others;
- allow for multiple formative assessment points;
- enable students to view graphs depicting their development over the duration of the project;
- make peer feedback available to students (usually anonymously, at the tutor's discretion);
- provide an electronic group journal that helps student groups keep a record of their project as it develops;
- enable the tutor to view student feedback and mark it easily;
- incorporate a colour-coded system to point out potential marking discre-pancies to aid moderation;
- support the generation and retrieval of a large amount of feedback from every peer assessment undertaken.

CASPAR's pilot study was undertaken by first-year undergraduate television production students at Bournemouth University. The students collaborated in groups on a given brief. The pilot followed one seminar group (comprising two small production groups, each consisting of six students) through the completion of two pieces of work: a formative exercise in documentary skills and a summatively assessed short documentary. The groups were formed at the beginning of the academic year by alphabetical selection, and each group had previously worked together to produce four group projects. The size of each group is consistent with the number of key production roles, following an industry model: director, production manager, sound recorder, lighting, camera operator, editor. The students had not had any previous experience of peer assessment before undertaking the pilot.

Key findings included the following:

- The system needs to be sufficiently flexible to be moulded to how a tutor would like to operate a group project.
- CASPAR needs to have a system in place to help the tutor remind the students that a peer assessment deadline is approaching.
- Students in the pilot agreed unanimously that peer assessment should be anonymous.
- CASPAR was felt to instigate solving group issues, which should be followed up with a face-to-face discussion where possible. Where it is not possible,

CASPAR could provide a space where students could meet 'virtually' to resolve issues.

- CASPAR was felt by most students to be easy to access and use, and to have helped them learn about being a good group member.
- Students wrote fair and honest feedback about each other, usually attributing lower marks to themselves than to their peers.
- Although students could not agree on the weighting of peer assessment criteria, 'reliability to carry out allocated roles' was deemed the most important overall.
- Students really valued reading honest opinions about their performance from their peers, but were uncomfortable about writing it down.
- Students unanimously agreed that peer assessment should take place at multiple points over a project, and not just at the end, to allow them to reflect and change their practice.

The use of peer assessment throughout the project, rather than only at the end, was key to this study. The more feedback the student has, and the more often, the greater the opportunity to reflect, learn and evolve. Every student in the pilot expressed a preference for assessment throughout, not just at the end.

Marking and providing feedback is usually the work of a tutor, and ongoing assessment of this type would normally mean considerably more tutor work. CASPAR peer assessment involved little or no time from the tutor's perspective, and gave the students themselves some ownership in awarding marks and comments, and enabled learning through that process.

CASPAR has been further developed following the findings of the pilot and will soon be available for other institutions to use. Continuing investigations and piloting of the system in different scenarios will continue to improve it as we learn more about how students interact with it as a learning tool.

(Andrew Ireland, Subject Leader for Television Production, Bournemouth University, National Teaching Fellow 2004)

Interrogating practice

Think about the assessment processes you have experienced as a tutor and as a student. How involved were students in assessment?

What was the formative assessment which had most impact on you when you were a student?

SKILLS IN THE VISUAL ARTS

Technical skills

Technical skills for art and design are an important part of students' learning (point 3 above). Skills are required in order to engage in practice. Without technical skills, students are limited and frustrated in their attempts to express themselves. Furthermore, the health and safety aspects of working with equipment have to be addressed: organising demonstrations of technical equipment and alerting students to the associated health and safety issues are the tutor's responsibility, as is creating an ethos within a workshop of shared responsibility for everyone to work in an appropriate and safe way.

However, an emphasis on skills, as we have seen in the approaches to learning described earlier, is a limiting way to experience the learning environment. Too much time spent on perfecting skills can be frustrating for tutors and students. Moreover, skill is not the be-all and end-all of practice; not all employment opportunities depend on being able to do the skilled components of a practice. There are a number of ways in which skills acquisition can be eased:

- *Buddying.* In an open studio students can learn from more experienced students in a buddy system. Students can either be paired up with a buddy from a year above or groups can be created from all years of the course. The tutor has to initiate this but once social bonds are in place students can support each other to check on skills, or teach each other new skills such as computer programming.
- *Group working.* Having to achieve practical outcomes as a group can lead to more understanding of processes due to having to plan explicitly, articulate and agree the next steps forward. This is particularly important for art and design which traditionally emphasise individual work, unlike media practice which tends to be more team based.
- *Deconstruction of artefacts.* This can be undertaken either individually or as a group. As an illustration, unpicking a jacket and noting or describing the methods discovered in its construction can improve understanding of how its layers of linings, interlinings, padding and stitching were physically constructed to maintain its shape.
- *Using visual resources to explain processes.* Handouts have been used traditionally but step-by-step procedural diagrams can be replaced by digital photographs in interactive PowerPoint for technical skills. This can be accessed by students in the workshop and can be built up by the students themselves as they encounter technical problems that require inventive solutions.

Personal and professional skills

Project-based work provides excellent opportunities to learn personal and professional skills useful in a wide range of work opportunities beyond those of the physical practice of an artist or designer (point 11 above). There is an increasing focus now not only on skills for **employability**, but on entrepreneurial skills (see Chapter 8). In practice, there is no clear division between skills for employability and skills for entrepreneurship. Being an entrepreneur does not necessarily mean prioritising financial success over other goals and it is possible to be an ethical entrepreneur. The skills of entrepreneurship are as relevant to someone in employment as they are to someone who runs their own business. Students in creative arts subjects need to be enterprising to maximise their abilities and create opportunities for employment.

There is no definitive list of the skills which increase employability, or the ability to run a business, but skills which are frequently cited in this context include:

- adaptability;
- being proactive;
- communication skills;
- confidence;
- emotional intelligence;
- financial acumen;
- flexibility;
- networking;
- opportunism;
- problem-solving;
- project management;
- resourcefulness;
- self-efficacy;
- self-management;
- self-sufficiency;
- team working abilities;
- vision.

Although the practical and **experiential learning** (see Chapter 2) provided by a visual arts education offers plentiful opportunities for these skills to be developed, students will need to be reminded that they are acquiring them while they undertake other learning opportunities. Often these skills are tacitly acquired, and it is helpful to emphasise exactly what engagement in practice requires and what has been learned. Maximising the learning opportunities has to be engineered through curriculum planning. **Personal Development Planning (PDP)** is the sector-wide process for this. PDP is a structured and supported process through which individuals reflect upon their learning, experiences and performance and plan for the future. It is situated in social, personal, academic and work-related domains and encompasses the whole person, acknowledging the individuality of learners. It should be student owned and student led.

Case study 2: Developing students' personal and professional skills through active learning

Stage two students in the Textiles Department at Chelsea College of Art and Design, University of the Arts London, have the opportunity to show their work alongside professional companies at the high-profile annual international textile trade fair *Indigo* in Paris. This professional practice-based project gives students an insight into the commercial world of textiles within a global arena. The course values this experience for the students highly, but organising and preparing for it has in the past placed a huge strain on the departmental staff. The staff team considered ways that students could take on responsibility for some of the planning and organising of the project, giving them not only responsibility but also a real experience of organising the event, something that as professional designers they would have to do. The opportunity to encourage teamwork was also welcomed, as textile students often work in isolation.

The department initially looked at all aspects of the project from planning, preparation, organising and production and split this into seven tasks. From these, students were asked to assign themselves to work on one of the teams.

- *Fact-finding about Paris*
  To compile a Rough Guide to Paris with maps and essential information for all students.

- *Exhibition and site management*
  To take responsibility for portfolios, presentation and mounting the exhibition.

- *Sales and PR*
  To oversee the sales and public relations of the show.

- *Exhibition design*
  To design and produce a team brand/identity for stand, backdrop and graphics.

- *Documentation*
  To record and document the event prior to, during and after the event. To record student feedback and compile a newsletter, *Après Indigo*.

- *Database and archives*
  To build a database of existing and new clients and industry contacts.

- *Project*
  To write a design brief and present it to peers.

All these tasks had previously been done by the staff. Looking at all aspects of the project made the tutors aware of not only how complex the project is but also what a rich learning experience it offers. The team tasks were advertised as jobs with a list of skills required. Students were asked to sign up for a team, taking into careful consideration what skills they wished to develop. Each team had a tutor to support its role. Once the teams were briefed they were given an '*Indigo* Journal' to log all information such as meetings and time plans. This record provided a source to refer back to after the completion of the project when students are briefing the year below them to undertake the *Indigo* project again. Mentoring of the year below is a key way in which sustainability is built in: students become knowledgeable and in turn can support others. This adds to their own ongoing learning and reflection on the skills required to become professional designers.

The team tasks gave students the opportunity to extend, develop or even discover new skills that would otherwise go untapped. Student feedback was positive about teamwork and the experience of seeing themselves as textile designers within a professional arena:

- 'I realised my strengths lay in selling, not in design.'
- 'I was able to practise another language and improve my interpersonal skills and work with other students.'
- 'I don't normally tell people what to do, I worked with people I don't know very well.'
- 'Everyone played a part in the organisation of the event.'
- 'I enjoyed being part of a team and knowing I was helping towards the show.'
- 'Paris rocks!'

(Melanie Bowles, Senior Lecturer, Textiles,
Chelsea College of Art and Design, University of the Arts London)

Interrogating practice

How can you maximise the learning opportunities for personal and professional development in the curriculum? How can you encourage students to see how essential these skills are in relation to the practice?

Writing in the visual arts

As indicated above (point 10), writing in the visual arts can be difficult territory. This is partly because a relatively high proportion of students and tutors have specific learning difficulties (SpLD, commonly referred to as **dyslexia**), which can slow down reading and writing and make structuring written work more difficult. Even for staff and students unaffected by dyslexia, the written word can seem like a foreign language for people whose native preference is visual communication.

However, written communication skills are an essential transferable skill for life and employment, and core to aspects of visual arts disciplines and related areas (art history, cultural studies, media studies, journalism), and as such there has been considerable effort to find effective ways of supporting the development of literacy in the visual arts.

Key projects include the Writing PAD project (Writing Purposefully in Art and Design), based at Goldsmith's, University of London, and with 40 UK partner higher education institutions. The website includes examples of successful case studies, examples of students' work and discussion papers. Writing PAD is actively engaged in developing new models of academic writing which are more conducive to the visual arts.

ThinkingWriting is another project which supports academic writing across a range of disciplines with online resources. Based at Queen Mary, University of London, it has been very successful in improving student writing through structured writing tasks which allow the challenges of academic writing to be tackled one at a time. It is particularly strong on supporting reflective writing, which links into Personal Development Planning (PDP) discussed above, and to the use of sketchbooks in the visual arts.

Reflecting on learning

Reflection is increasingly recognised as essential to effective learning (see e.g. Moon, 2000). Learning journals are now common throughout higher education, although, as discussed above, because of discomfort with the medium of written communication, without well-planned support many reflective journals remain descriptive accounts of process. However, the sketchbook is a long-standing example of reflective learning in higher education, with its emphasis on enquiry, thinking and reflecting on product, process, audience and personal meaning. The form a sketchbook takes will be dependent on local expectations, but the purpose and function of a sketchbook is worth exploring with your students. It is not until it becomes a personal necessity and portable thinking tool that its purpose is really understood. Combining written and visual communication in a sketchbook may be one way to encourage students both to develop their writing skills and to deepen their learning through effective reflection.

Interrogating practice

How can you encourage your students to develop a personal ownership of their sketchbook and use it in productive ways? Apart from using a sketchbook, what other ways can students reflect on practice?

LOCATIONS FOR LEARNING

The studio

Most learning in the visual arts takes place in a studio, workshop or small communal space where the tutor traditionally interacts on a one-to-one basis with each student. This may be seen as the ideal learning environment where time is spent giving personal and relevant feedback to each student, but there is a danger of 'studio cruising', of tutors seen as experts dispensing pearls of wisdom as they pass through their domain. At best, the sensitive tutor will construct a lively and interactive situation in the studio where there are challenges set and conversations about learning taking place. Working on informal small group activities is just as important as the larger, more structured group project, which is now common in most courses. The studio can be an isolating space as well, with each person intent on his or her own work. New computer-based design practices also make conversations difficult and the tutor needs to structure exchanges, paired activities or small group tasks into teaching activities in order to maximise the opportunities for students to learn from each other.

Outside the institution

Not all learning has to take place in the studio or workshop environments provided by the university. There are many opportunities for students to engage in learning activities outside the university, in industry, the community or in practice.

The students themselves can arrange these off site, for example finding spaces to exhibit their work and organising and curating an exhibition as a group. Students benefit from the organisational experience this provides and although they need support and guidance, their entrepreneurial abilities are developed and their success can reinforce their self-efficacy, their belief in their own abilities to succeed. The tutor acts as a facilitator, setting up the situation so that students are enabled to take responsibility. This requires the tutor to prepare students: more experienced students, recent graduates or the tutor themselves should describe the processes and organisational skills or project management skills needed to succeed. These are also key components of the students' personal and professional development. Not only are the students developing their own practical work through the project, but they are also building on social, networking and organisational skills as they do this. They are learning what it means to be a practitioner in the world beyond the university, undertaking 'authentic activities' in context. The skills are supported by a social situation that provides relevance and helps to create meaning and understanding.

Work-based learning

In many courses work **placement**, or learning in work, will be an assessed part of the course. For **foundation degrees** this component is a fundamental part of student learning;

more information about these degrees is available from the Foundation Degree Forward website. There are important issues about student safety and the expectations of students and employers when arrangements are made to engage in learning on placement. There are national guidelines on placement learning (QAA, 2001), and the university or college will have its own regulations with which you should make yourself familiar. Students require support before and while they are undertaking learning in work. The Keynote Project is a good example and provides a series of support materials for students and tutors online.

Learning in museums and galleries

Museums and galleries are also traditional sites for student learning. They can provide sources of inspiration, ways to experience the latest developments in the practice, building on the traditions of craft subjects, and are also places in which to challenge preconceptions about visual arts practices. Tutors may need to help students derive maximum benefit from such visits, for example by exploring the reasons for visits to museums and galleries before asking students to spend a day drawing or visiting. Curator and artist talks in the gallery can provide a challenge to ways of perceiving artefacts.

Consultancy projects, schools and community links

Students can put their knowledge into practice through collaborative work with partners. These can be business, community or schools links, but the student takes on the role of practitioner with a client from the world beyond the university. These kinds of interactions enable students to feel that they are capable and are learning the additional social interaction skills that will be needed on graduation. Setting up such opportunities requires support from the tutor who can maximise the learning opportunities through preparing students with ideas about what to expect, through peer mentoring from students who have already experienced such projects and through constructing more permanent learning resources to explain processes, give examples and hear from employers, clients and the students themselves.

OVERVIEW

This chapter has considered the consequences of the discipline-specific aspects of the visual arts for learning and teaching. Some of these will be recognised as good practice across all disciplines (authentic learning activities, aligned curricula, practice-based work, team-based events, opportunities for skills development, the use of sketchbooks, and formative feedback inherent in the curriculum structure, for example). Other aspects need thoughtful responses to ensure effective student learning (for example, the prevalence of tacit knowledge which may exclude and inhibit some learners, the marginalisation of written communication, the consequences for some aspects of curriculum planning and delivery of the high proportion of part-time teachers). The challenge for the visual arts is to ameliorate the potential negative aspects of the discipline group while retaining and enhancing the inherent pedagogic strengths.

REFERENCES

ADEPTT <http://www.adeptt.ac.uk/> (accessed 14 August 2007).

Biggs, J (1999) 'Enhancing teaching through constructive alignment', *Higher Education*, 32, 347–364.

Blair, B (2006a) 'Does the studio crit still have a role to play in 21st-century design education and student learning?', in A Davies (ed.), *Proceedings of the 3rd International Centre for Learning and Teaching in Art and Design Conference*, London: CLTAD.

Blair, B (2006b) 'Perception, Interpretation, Impact: An Examination of the Learning Value of Formative Feedback to Students Through the Design Studio Critique', Ph.D. thesis, Institute of Education, University of London.

Case, D and Marshall, J (2004) 'Between deep and surface: procedural approaches to learning in engineering education contexts', *Studies in Higher Education*, 29(5): 605–614.

Drew, L and Shreeve, A (2006) 'Assessment as participation in practice', in C Rust (ed.), *Proceedings of the 12th Improving Student Learning Symposium*, Oxford: OCSLD.

Drew, L, Bailey, S and Shreeve, A (2002) 'Fashion variations: student approaches to learning in fashion design', in A. Davies (ed.), *Proceedings of the 1st International Centre for Learning and Teaching in Art and Design Conference*, London: CLTAD.

Foundation Degree Forward <http://www.fdf.ac.uk/> (accessed 14 August 2007).

Group Work and Assessment in Media Production (GWAMP) <http://www.cemp.ac.uk/resources/caspar> (accessed 4 September 2007).

Keynote Project <http://www.leeds.ac.uk/textiles/keynote/> (accessed 14 August 2007).

Lave, J and Wenger, E (1991) *Situated Learning: Legitimate Peripheral Participation*, Cambridge: Cambridge University Press.

Marton, F and Säljo, R (1984) 'Approaches to learning', in F Marton, D Hounsell and N Entwistle, *The Experiences of Learning*, Edinburgh: Scottish Academic Press.

Moon, J (2000) *Reflection in Learning and Professional Development: Theory and Practice*, London: RoutledgeFalmer.

Orr, S (2006) 'Studio based mark agreement practices: the said and the unsaid', in A Davies (ed.), *Proceedings of the 3rd International Centre for Learning and Teaching in Art and Design Conference*, London: CLTAD.

Quality Assurance Agency (QAA) (2001) Placement Learning, Section 9 of the Code of Practice for the assurance of academic quality and standards in higher education. Available online at <http://www.qaa.ac.uk/academicinfrastructure/codeOfPractice/section9/default.asp> (accessed 14 August 2007).

Shreeve, A, Bailey, S and Drew, L (2003) 'Students' approaches to the "research" component in the fashion design project: variation in students' experience of the research process', *Art, Design and Communication in Higher Education*, 2(3): 113–130.

Shreeve, A, Baldwin, J and Farraday, G (2004) 'Variation in student conceptions of assessment', in C Rust (ed.), *Proceedings of the 10th Improving Student Learning Symposium*, Oxford: OCSLD.

ThinkingWriting <http://www.thinkingwriting.qmul.ac.uk/> (accessed 14 August 2007).

Wenger, E. (1998) *Communities of Practice: Learning, Meaning and Identity*, Cambridge: Cambridge University Press.

Writing PAD <http://www.writing-pad.ac.uk/> (accessed 14 August 2007).

FURTHER READING

ADEPTT <http://www.adeptt.ac.uk/> (accessed 14 August 2007). The Art and Design-Enabling Part Time Tutors website is a mine of valuable information which includes advice on facilitation, working with students with disabilities, teaching large groups, health and safety, and much more.

23 Key aspects of teaching and learning

Enhancing learning in legal education

Tracey Varnava and Julian Webb

INTRODUCTION

This chapter is intended to encourage the use of pedagogical approaches that will underpin and develop student learning in law. The subject matter itself is a rich source of material and ideas, as an intrinsic and influential thread running through the fabric of everyday life. Law both shapes and reflects societal rules, norms and values. The boundaries of the discipline are, perhaps increasingly, indistinct, drawing, for example, on philosophy, politics, sociology and economics. This porosity affords plenty of scope to move beyond a narrow construction of the curriculum to a wider consideration of the place and status of law in society. One of the first challenges for the teacher is therefore to articulate through the syllabus a conception of law which takes students beyond their own assumptions about the parameters of the subject. A broader vision not only opens up new vistas for exploration but also offers exciting possibilities for enhancing learning. This chapter aims to outline some ideas and suggestions as to how this might be achieved.

The first section of the chapter gives a flavour of some of the issues that shape and define the study of law at university. These influences have the potential to both limit and liberate the way in which law is taught. In the next section, two innovative approaches to teaching law, namely problem-based learning and research-based learning, are described. These have been selected as examples that are particularly well suited to fostering the attributes that have been identified as characteristic of a law graduate (QAA, 2000). Approaches to assessment in law are also addressed. The chapter ends with an overview of the matters discussed and some suggestions for further reading.

CONTEXT AND BACKGROUND

There are a number of features of law as a discipline of study in higher education that have had a significant impact on the curriculum and the way in which it is taught. Many of these are shared with other discipline areas and include, for example: the impact of universities with different missions; the tension between teaching and research; and balancing knowledge and skills. However, in recent years perhaps the most influential factors as far as law is concerned have been the academic/vocational divide, the level of resource available to law schools, and the pressures, allied to attempts to counter the charge that law is 'elitist', of widening access.

The academic/vocational divide

Law as an academic discipline is a relative newcomer to the academy. Traditionally, study at university was always allied to training for the legal professions and it was not until the early to mid-twentieth century that it started to establish itself as an independent academic discipline (see Twining, 1994). Perhaps as a consequence of this, the discipline sometimes appears to be uncertain as to its status and focus, leading to ongoing debates and disagreements about the purpose of legal study at undergraduate level. Specifically, to what extent should the curriculum cater to the needs of the professional bodies? Many law academics feel strongly that it is not the place of the law school to prepare students for practice and that law is an academic subject in its own right which can be studied in isolation from any vocational concerns or influences. Others feel equally strongly that law cannot be properly understood without an appreciation of how it is applied and practised in the real world. Both arguments have their merits but are so vociferously stated and defended that they are each in danger of restricting the development of alternative positions which seek to draw on the strengths of both, combining academic rigour with an understanding of law in its practical context and recognising that to fully engage with law as a subject it has to be studied in all its forms, both theoretical and applied.

Professional bodies

Lying behind these debates about the purpose of legal education is the role of the Solicitors Regulation Authority and the Bar Standards Board in regulating the undergraduate law degree, which is currently represented primarily through the Joint Statement on Qualifying Law Degrees (Law Society/Bar Council, 2004). The main requirement of the Joint Statement is that the Foundation of Legal Knowledge subjects must be taught for a degree to have qualifying status. These subjects are:

1 Public law
2 Law of the European Union
3 Criminal law

4 Obligations
5 Property law
6 Equity and the Law of Trusts

Students are also expected to have received training in legal research.

Beyond specification of the subject areas that constitute a qualifying law degree, there are no requirements set with regard to the delivery or assessment of the degree course. However, despite what seems to be relatively light-touch regulation, there is a persistent concern among law schools about what the professional bodies might be inclined to do to strengthen their influence should they perceive that standards are slipping. There has been a tendency in the past for the professional bodies to focus on the academic stage when vocational providers and law firms make adverse comments about the qualities and abilities of law graduates. This concern about standards has inclined the professional bodies to advocate traditional pedagogic approaches, particularly in relation to assessment. This advocacy has been influential and perhaps chimes with the natural conservatism of the subject and those who teach it. Thus, at undergraduate level the lecture/tutorial format accompanied by closed-book examination remains the predominant approach. The challenge for those seeking to innovate has been to demonstrate that new approaches are no less rigorous and testing than more traditional approaches to teaching and assessment.

Law Subject Benchmark Statement

In the context of seeking to establish a distinct identity for the discipline, the **subject benchmarking** exercise which was undertaken in 2000 represented an opportunity for the academic community itself to articulate both the defining characteristics of the discipline and the academic qualities expected of a law graduate. However, the published statement does not delve into the fractious questions about the distinctiveness of the subject and focuses only on certain features of 'graduateness'. For the purposes of law these have been defined as: subject-specific knowledge; application and problem-solving; ability to use sources and research together with the ability to analyse and synthesise, exercise critical judgement and evaluation; demonstrate autonomy and the ability to learn. The Benchmark Statement was revised in 2006 with only minor amendments being made. In terms of the graduate characteristics identified, however, while they may seem relatively generic, it may be argued that law as a discipline is perhaps particularly suited to their development, providing fertile soil for a range of pedagogical approaches.

Both the Joint Statement and the Law Subject Benchmark Statement emphasise the acquisition of legal knowledge. However, an overcrowded curriculum is often cited as a deterrent to adding new topics or indeed to developing new forms of teaching and assessment. Given that in many areas of law the content changes rapidly, an approach which enables students to learn and update their own knowledge, while developing the skills and abilities identified in the Benchmark Statement, is more likely to result in an engaging and satisfying learning experience for all concerned.

> **Interrogating practice**
>
> How do you ensure that the knowledge and skills identified in the Benchmark Statement are developed and demonstrated?

Resourcing the law school

Law regularly attracts a high number of applications to university, including large numbers of overseas students, making it a profitable source of income for institutions. However, despite this, law schools do not find themselves well resourced. Vice-chancellors have had a tendency to view law as a 'cash cow', underwriting less popular and more resource-intensive discipline areas. Institutions persist in seeing law as primarily text based, with teaching delivered using the traditional lecture and tutorial/seminar format. Law schools have repeatedly argued that being regarded as a 'cheap' subject to resource has unfairly disadvantaged the creative development of law teaching (see e.g. Directions in Legal Education, 2004). But they have also been complicit in the perpetuation of the status quo by failing consistently to articulate an alternative vision. Nevertheless, at a discipline level, innovations do exist, with significant developments in e-learning and clinical legal education among the successes. Both of these, however, may need additional specialist skills or resources to establish effectively. The examples given below show how learning can be taken beyond the confines of the lecture and tutorial within a more conventional skills/resource envelope. This is not to doubt that law schools need to push for a higher unit of resource. To be successful, however, they need evidence that practices are changing and that there is a clear pedagogical case for more diverse learning environments.

Widening access

There are serious questions to be addressed by both law schools and vocational training providers about fair access to legal study. Linked to the government's drive to widen participation in higher education, the pressure on law schools as a whole to admit more students from more diverse backgrounds is intense, if differentially applied. There is no doubt that, overall, it is law schools in the post-92 institutions that have admitted higher student numbers in recent years. The pre-92 institutions that are able to select rather than recruit their students have had the scope to find other mechanisms for identifying those best suited to legal study. An example is the establishment of the Law National Admissions Test as a supplement to A Level results, which is now used as part of the admissions process by ten pre-92 university law schools. Even so, increasing student numbers and the need to adapt to the learning needs of a more diverse student body are necessarily having an impact on all law schools. Although resourcing issues, as discussed, are a significant (limiting) factor, this diversity can and should be seen as a useful spur for rethinking traditional approaches and seeking different ways of engaging students in the study of law.

Interrogating practice

What factors do you see as blocking change to learning, teaching and assessment practices? How can these 'blockers' be turned into opportunities to lever change?

In setting the context for this chapter a number of issues have been identified as having a potentially limiting effect on the development of the curriculum. Some of these are beyond the control of the individual lecturer to influence (for example, rising student numbers). However, the impact of these factors can be mediated and in some cases turned to positive advantage as traditional approaches perhaps prove too inflexible to deal with a wider range of student needs and demands. In the next section, two approaches to learning are described and examples of how they may be implemented are offered. Their respective advantages are highlighted, together with some particular challenges they may pose.

PROBLEM-BASED LEARNING

Defining problem-based learning

Although not unique, the focus on problem-solving activities is a strong and distinctive feature of legal education. **Problem-based learning (PBL)** encourages academics to place that aspect at the centre of the learning process.

PBL is where students are confronted with the materials and facts underlying a problem from which they have to work out both the nature of the problem and an appropriate solution, usually without (much) prior instruction in the necessary knowledge to solve it. The commonly acknowledged characteristics of problem-based learning are:

1 Stimulus materials are used to help students define and discuss an important problem, question or issue.
2 Problems are presented as a simulation of professional practice or a real-life situation.
3 Students are guided in critical thinking and provided with limited resources to help them learn from defining and attempting to resolve the given problem.
4 Students work cooperatively as a group, exploring information in and out of class with access to a tutor who knows the problem well.

5   Students are encouraged to identify their own learning needs and the appropriate use of available resources.
6   Students use the knowledge gained to solve the original problem *and* to define new learning issues for themselves.

(adapted from Boud and Feletti, 1997: 4)

In some disciplines, such as medicine and architecture, PBL has been adopted as a holistic approach to a complete programme. Elsewhere it often forms the basis for delivering a module or a substantial project.

It should be noted that there are a number of different approaches which may designate themselves as problem-based learning. Some commentators seek to identify an 'authentic' PBL approach which sticks closely to a set of principles and processes first systematised by medical educationalists at McMaster University, Canada. However, for the purposes of this chapter it is the intention rather than the model that is important: namely that problems, tasks and unexpected situations form the starting point for learning.

In 'traditional' curricula teachers tend to start by providing information and then expect students to use the information to solve problems. This is certainly a model that is prevalent in law where it is common for students to be set a problem in a seminar relating to law which has been previously covered in a lecture. The problem generally consists of an incident or set of incidents involving two or more characters. Based on the facts as presented, students are posed a number of questions about the law that applies and are generally asked to advise one or more of the characters involved accordingly.

In a problem-based approach to learning, the problem comes first. Students both define the problem and gather information to explore it. Working in self-directed groups, students thus take an active and systematic approach to defining and 'resolving' the problem. (They are not necessarily expected to reach the 'right' answer. There may not be a right answer.) The technique is characterised by team-based exploration and synthesis combined with individual research and analysis. An example of how this might be done in law is provided in Case study 1.

Case study 1: The estate agent's problem

Group A

Your office has recently been engaged by a Mr Alun Ash to advise on a dispute with the English Estate Agency Association. The EEAA is a private company that regulates the delivery of residential property services against a Code of Professional Practice.

An article concerning Mr Ash's experiences appeared in the regional newspaper last week. By this morning, in light of the publication of the newspaper article, the office had received a related enquiry from a Ms Catrin Cook. Both of these correspondents are keen to pursue an application for judicial review.

Group B

You have been engaged by the English Estate Agency Association (EEAA), with a view to defending it in case of any application for judicial review arising from the Ash/Cook grievances. You have had such material as is available to Group A made available to you.

In addition to the material gleaned from these prospective clients, your preliminary investigations have produced a number of seemingly relevant items:

- Membership of the EEAA is not legally necessary either for firms of estate agents or for individual practitioners working for them. However, the claim that such affiliation is widely recognised as a sign of integrity is largely true. Indeed, your investigations indicate that for those seeking to operate in the mainstream property market such accreditation approaches are imperative.
- Mr Ash has been a Fellow of the EEAA for five years.
- The Director General of Fair Trading (DGFT) was conferred with powers to regulate the estate agency sector in 1986. These powers appear, however, to be held in abeyance.
- The EEAA regulatory regime has received the government's explicit imprimatur on a number of occasions in recent times. Indeed, the Minister for Consumer Affairs stated recently that the EEAA had her 'full backing as a vital cog in the maintenance of good practice in the sector'.

Documentary evidence relating to facts mentioned in the brief is provided for reference. Each group (comprising seven to nine students) should work together to develop a substantiated legal argument concerning the disparate issues that arise, and reflecting the interests of the various clients. This solution is to be presented in a week three moot class in which each group should be prepared to discuss the main points in its solution for around 20 minutes. In advance of the moot class, each group is asked to submit a short skeleton argument on Blackboard (a **Virtual Learning Environment (VLE)**) in accordance with instructions to be provided. Full information on the tasks to be completed by the study groups and by each individual student is available on Blackboard.

(Example provided by Andrew Scott,
London School of Economics and Political Science)

Some advantages

As discussed above, law is very content-heavy and as traditionally taught can instil a surface approach to learning where there is insufficient time to reflect on, question and analyse what is being taught. A benefit of problem-based learning is that it can help students to cope with the extensive knowledge base of law but also enable them to apply it to the analysis of problems. In addition, the approach may be used to aid the development of problem-solving skills, self-directed learning skills and teamworking skills.

Problem-based learning is founded on a view of knowledge as something that learners construct for themselves. Educational research has shown that students learn more effectively when their prior learning is taken into consideration – students are not 'blank' slates, and encouraging them to use and apply knowledge already acquired helps to contextualise and embed new learning (see Ramsden, 2003).

A problem-based learning approach also enables students to be partners in the learning process rather than the recipients of it. The tutor plays a facilitative role, allowing students to explore a range of avenues rather than dictating their route.

The cognitive skills and abilities identified in the subject benchmark statement are also fostered by a problem-based learning approach and particularly the attributes of 'autonomy and the ability to learn' which have been described as 'emblematic' of graduateness in the Law Subject Benchmark Statement.

Finally, a problem-based learning approach helps students to appreciate that the law is messy and indeterminate, both a creator and a product of the social and economic conditions within which it is practised.

Some challenges

Ideally, any proposals to change learning, teaching and assessment practices will arise from regular review of the course or module concerned and will be widely discussed and debated. Changes should clearly support what the teaching team are trying to achieve in terms of student learning, and should be grounded in clear evidence and/or understanding of the educational research literature.

In working with colleagues it is important to seek agreement on the aims, objectives and desired outcomes of the module/course. Discussion about different assessment approaches should focus on choosing methods which are clearly designed to support and demonstrate learning. In relation to PBL, assessment should not only provide students with an opportunity to display their knowledge, understanding and application of the law, but also recognise the development of relevant skills and abilities, for example by rewarding effective teamworking.

The semi-structured nature of PBL makes different demands on tutor time and resources, and may well involve extensive preparation. The tutor will have to think about the different types of information resources the students might make use of, particularly given the increasing number of web-based resources. This may require the preparation of briefing notes for the students, a longer reading list, or advice on search strategies.

It is important to acknowledge that both staff and students involved in new learning approaches are likely to need to develop new skills and aptitudes. Staff used to a more didactic approach to teaching may find it difficult to step back and allow the students to follow their own route through the material. Students too may feel vulnerable and exposed in an environment where they are primarily responsible for their own learning. Therefore they need to be given the necessary tools and the confidence to work in ways that may not be familiar to them, for example as part of a team or as an independent researcher. The structure of the module or course may also need to be adjusted to allow a more flexible use of the time available.

RESEARCH-BASED LEARNING IN LAW

In the present university environment, academics are under pressure to deliver both quality research and quality teaching. The relationship between teaching and research is widely seen as important. For some, it is the proximity of teaching to the processes of knowledge creation that gives higher education its 'higher' quality. At the same time, discussions about the emergence of 'teaching-only' universities, and concerns that institutional Research Assessment Exercise strategies may actually distance research from undergraduate teaching in particular, reflect an alternative, but also common, view that teaching and research may be – and in practice often are – largely independent activities. Whatever else it may have achieved, this debate has helped to focus attention on what added value research can bring to the classroom.

Conventionally it has been assumed that, insofar as there is a connection between research and teaching, it lies in the subject expertise of staff. In other words, law teaching will be research-*led* where teaching and learning reflect and are directly based upon the specialist research interests of the staff delivering the curriculum. Such an approach can leave students in the position of spectators rather than participants. They can admire the scholarship from a distance, but not necessarily gain any deeper understanding of research itself as a process of learning. However, there are methods of enabling under-graduate students to participate in research through learning and teaching which are explicitly research-*tutored* or research-*based* (Jenkins et al., 2007: 29). The difference between these is that the former tends to focus on enabling students to engage critically and reflectively with research literature and data, whereas the latter actually enables students to do research and learn through the process of enquiry. Such methods, it is argued, add real value to undergraduate work for both learners and teachers. Learning becomes linked to the lecturer's research interests in ways that develop new and original research for the lecturer, while giving students direct experience of research, and increasing their motivation to learn.

A number of UK universities are developing institutional strategies to build the connection between research and undergraduate learning. Some of these are free-standing research initiatives, such as the Undergraduate Research Scholarship Scheme at Warwick University, which pays undergraduate students to work on research projects with faculty members. In 2006 to 2007, 57 such projects were funded, including two within the law school. Others may operate at the level of a department or course (see Jenkins et al., 2007). However, there are still relatively few discipline-specific examples in law, aside from the ubiquitous dissertation, of course. In the remainder of this section, through illustrations in Case studies 2 and 3, we focus on two recent UK examples of what can be done.

Case study 2: Using case studies and teamwork to develop research skills at the University of Birmingham

A pilot final-year module was launched using a multifaceted case study of a politically and/or legally contentious episode as a means of enabling students to design and evaluate research projects. Each student on the module was required individually to develop a project design, carry out their project and write an essay and reflective account of the process. Each student also received formative peer assessment of their project design during the module. At the end of the module, students came together in teams to devise a strategy for disseminating, to a non-academic audience, part or all of their research output. Each team then produced a strategy document together with any actual or proposed output, such as a press release, draft magazine or newspaper article, or plans for a website. Work on the formal development and introduction of the module is now continuing.

(Professor Stephen Shute, University of Birmingham)

Case study 3: Doing socio-legal history through environmental law at the University of the West of England

In 2006/2007 students taking a final-year module in environmental law undertook small group projects exploring the historical context of leading cases in the law of nuisance. The students were sent on field trips around England and Wales with the brief of discovering what inspired the claimants in these cases to bring their suit, including why attempts to settle may have failed, and what the practical outcome of these proceedings was for the communities in which they were situated. These mini-projects were made the subject of group presentations which constituted 30 per cent of the student's final mark: an essay of 20 per cent and exam of 50 per cent made up the remainder. Subsequently the five projects have all been written up and published, or submitted for publication (see e.g. Pontin *et al.*, 2007). This approach is being continued in 2007/2008 with a focus on legal issues of climate change.

(Dr Ben Pontin, University of the West of England)

Evaluation

Case studies 2 and 3, examples of research-based learning in law, are both recent innovations. Even so, they offer some relevant insights into what can be achieved, albeit on specialist options with relatively small student numbers. They show that it is possible to get students actively engaged with research in a way that gives them a different experience of learning about the living law. They show how assessment can be used to support the research-based character of the learning, while also enhancing the students' transferable skills (e.g. in the use of oral presentations, or writing in different formats and/or for different audiences than the norm). They also suggest a rather different dynamic and division of responsibilities between teacher and learner. As Ben Pontin has observed in correspondence with one of the present authors:

> Students are brilliant at gathering 'raw material' . . . detective work. However, where students needed input from an academic was in interpreting the significance of empirical findings. Great at treating law as a material object (a field or stately home protected against a polluting factory or sewage works), students struggled with law's ideas!

There are, of course, a range of practical matters to be considered:

- such courses may be relatively resource-intensive;
- there may be issues about ensuring the sustainability of the research element year on year;
- ethical issues need to be addressed as regards the form of research collaboration and the terms under which undergraduate students are engaged in research;
- research-based learning may create issues about managing student expectations in a relatively unfamiliar learning environment.

However, none of these are insurmountable problems.

Interrogating practice

Consider a module you are teaching or would like to teach:

- How might you make the learning more research-based?
- What will you do to address the practical design problems you might encounter?

EFFECTIVE AND INNOVATIVE ASSESSMENT

As discussions in Part 1 of this book have shown, assessment plays an enormously important role in shaping students' learning experiences. It can do much to shape motivation to learn and the capacity and opportunities for students to demonstrate **deep learning.** The downside of this, of course, is that ineffective or inappropriate assessment practices will equally influence the whole learning process for learner and teacher: for good or ill, the assessment tail tends to wag the learning dog.

If we look at the overall range of assessment mechanisms being used in UK law schools today, there is a wide variety. Aside from variations on the theme of the traditional examination and coursework essay, law schools are also using (for example):

- mooting tasks
- oral presentations (group or individual)
- client interview, negotiation or advocacy skills exercises
- reflective journals
- portfolios
- projects (mostly in written form, but some web-based or multimedia).

At the same time, however, it is also clear that, in overall terms, traditional modes of assessment still tend to dominate students' experience of learning at law school. Thus, a survey for UK Council on Legal Education on teaching, learning and assessment methods used in Scotland found essays (96 per cent) and examinations (94 per cent) were the commonest forms of assessment used by respondent lecturers, dissertations were the third most common (75 per cent) and oral presentations (58 per cent) next. Skills activities were used by 33 per cent and groupwork by 29 per cent of staff (see Maharg, 2007; Clegg, 2004: 27–28). Moreover, there is evidence that alternative modes of assessment are more likely to be used **formatively** than **summatively** (Clegg, 2004: 29) and, more anecdotally, a sense that, where used summatively, they are more likely to appear in optional subjects than in the legal foundations.

So why isn't there greater variation in assessment methods? The following four reasons are likely to be significant, though not necessarily exhaustive. None of them are entirely compelling.

First, there are genuine and widespread concerns about assessment **reliability** and **plagiarism**. Unseen examinations, in particular, are seen as least open to abuse. This in turn suggests there is quite a high degree of uncertainty among law lecturers about the ways in which alternative assessment processes can also be made to satisfy standards of authenticity. Second, there is a misapprehension that the professional bodies require certain modes or patterns of assessment in the foundation subjects. As we noted earlier, this is certainly not the case at present, though the Joint Academic Stage Board (JASB) has sought recently to extend its 'guidance' to law schools to formalise a traditional coursework/examination requirement for the foundations. This change is being resisted by the academic bodies consulted by the JASB. Third, there is still a belief that traditional examinations are more rigorous than other assessment mechanisms, despite the volume of educational literature which points to their shortcomings. Finally, there is also a tendency for higher education to replicate the experience of earlier generations, so that teachers tend, almost instinctively one suspects, to adopt the learning and assessment methods by which they learned.

This is not to suggest that well-designed examinations and coursework essays have no place in the system.

For example, as Bone (1999: 21) notes, examinations are:

- reasonably efficient
- reliable
- relatively plagiarism proof, and
- easy, in organisational terms, to moderate.

Like all methods, however, they have their shortcomings. Consider the following exercise as a way of identifying those limits, and, perhaps, beginning to think differently about assessment.

In Table 23.1 the column headings show a range of levels of performance (based on Anderson and Krathwohl, 2001) and a set of transferable/legal skills (based on the QAA Law Benchmark) that could be developed in the law degree. The levels indicate generically the different kinds of cognitive competence that students might be asked to demonstrate. These are not terms of art, they convey their ordinary everyday meaning. 'Remembering', it follows, is obviously the lowest level, representing the product of what amounts to memory testing, and 'creating' [new knowledge] is equally obviously the highest. This typology is also broadly reflected in the Benchmark's references to 'knowledge and understanding', 'application' and 'analysis, synthesis, critical judgement and evaluation'. (Note that Table 23.1 excludes the Benchmark's 'autonomy and ability to learn' as a separate category. It is, however, reflected in part in the emphasis on independent research under the heading 'Legal research'.)

The headings 'examination' and 'coursework' should be construed traditionally. That is, 'examination' should be understood to mean a summative unseen examination paper containing a mix of essay and problem questions, and 'coursework' means a free-standing essay or problem question to which the student produces a written answer outside any controlled environment, again assessed summatively.

You now have two tasks:

1 First place a tick in the relevant box, where you think a skill or cognitive level can be assessed (even in part) by that method; otherwise leave it blank.
2 Now focus on each cognitive level or skill and identify, by a different colour tick, which one(s) can be *particularly well assessed* by examination or coursework. Again, leave the others blank.

Table 23.1 Skills and cognitive levels assessed by law coursework and examinations

Cognitive levels

	Remembering	Understanding	Applying	Analysing	Evaluating	Creating
Coursework						
Examination						

Benchmark skills

	Legal research (including evidence of an ability to undertake independent legal research)	Written communication and literacy	Oral communication	Numeracy	IT skills	Teamwork
Coursework						
Examination						

When you have completed this exercise it is probable that the two sets of ticks will not be identical. It is also probable that you will have fewer ticks in the second set than the first, and that, in a few instances, your answer was prefaced by a 'well, it depends . . . '. What emerges from doing this exercise?

Some of the key issues that could have been considered are:

- Which kinds of assessments are going to be better at assessing the more complex or higher cognitive abilities?
- When assessing skills of evaluation, is it students' capacity to evaluate information against criteria they have come up with, or just their capacity to remember and apply someone else's criteria that is being assessed? The latter involves evidence of a different (and lesser) cognitive capacity.
- Are conventional assessments good at enabling students to create new knowledge? If not, is this just a matter of unsophisticated question design, a flaw in the mode of assessment, or a more fundamental problem in that the curriculum inadvertently discourages students from being creative and making connections across topic or subject boundaries?
- To what extent are legal research skills directly assessed rather than inferred from performance in traditional assessments?

Consequently it is suggested that there are two substantial challenges for law teachers: (1) to ensure that traditional assessments are well designed and used appropriately in the light of module and programme learning objectives (this is itself a complex issue – see e.g. Bone (1999: 17–20) for a brief introduction) and (2) to adopt a range of alternative assessments that are also appropriately aligned – again a complex issue – to their relevant learning objectives.

It is also not possible in an overview such as this to look exhaustively at the range of alternative assessment practices available. Therefore, the remainder of this section will offer some brief examples of assessment practices, with an example offered in Case study 4, that potentially add variety and breadth to the legal education experience, and could link with the innovative teaching approaches already discussed.

Case study 4: Assessing teamwork at the Queensland University of Technology (QUT)

The development of teamworking and group skills has increasingly been emphasised in UK legal education, first through the benchmarking process, and latterly, because such skills are highly valued by employers, as part of what is sometimes called the 'employability agenda' for higher education. Moreover, it is also argued that, independent of any such agenda, group learning has substantial intellectual benefits. Working together, students develop a deeper understanding of material by having to explain their knowledge for peers, and may be challenged on their understanding to an extent that may not happen in tutor-led or mediated interactions. The group may also provide an environment for more creative thinking, and for developing greater learner autonomy, self-confidence and motivation.

Building on curriculum development work begun in 2000, the Law Faculty at QUT has developed a sophisticated assessment framework to demonstrate achievement of what they describe as a set of 'graduate capabilities'. The framework focuses on embedding four areas of 'social, relational and cultural capability' across the curriculum, namely oral communication skills, teamwork, indigenous content and perspectives on law, and ethical knowledge and values. The approach to teamwork at QUT is integrated across a range of core modules, builds teamwork into classroom and independent learning activities and uses different group assessment tasks. For example, in *Corporate Law* (in Year 3), the major assessment task is a group assignment based on a teamwork portfolio which is completed by groups operating both face to face and in a virtual learning environment. Self- and peer evaluation of teamwork also forms part of the assessment for this module. The module *Law, Society and Justice* (Year 1) assesses teamwork via an oral group presentation. A formatively assessed Teamwork Reflection Sheet is also provided to support learning in this module. *Advanced Research and Legal Reasoning* (Year 4) requires students to work in groups to produce a range of written documents, such as memoranda of legal advice, client letters, and a client newsletter (Kift *et al.*, 2006).

(Submission for Carrick Award led by Professor Sally Kift)

Using reflective narratives as assessment tools

The value of developing students' capacity for reflection is widely acknowledged in higher education theory and practice, particularly as part of a strategy of making assessment more authentic. Assessment is authentic when the task has a degree of 'real-world' complexity, the learning it measures has value beyond the classroom and is (or becomes in the process) personally meaningful to the learner. Authenticity is more likely to be achieved where a variety of assessment mechanisms are deployed.

The use of reflective narrative in law has its origins in clinical legal education where it draws substantially on the literature of 'reflective practice' (see Maughan and Webb, 1996). In this context it is not surprising that reflective narratives are most often cited in the legal education as tools that are useful in the development of academic and practical skills, such as research, writing and legal literacy, presentation skills, group working (again), and so on. But its scope and value are broader than that. As Cowan (1999: 18) observes, reflection occurs whenever a student 'analyse[s] or evaluate[s] one or more personal experiences and attempt[s] to generalise from that thinking'. It thus constitutes a quite fundamental (self-)critical facility, which, it is argued, can be demonstrated by students 'surfacing' their reflection about any given learning experience. Looked at from this perspective, the scope for using reflective narratives is probably wider than we conventionally allow. Maughan and Webb (1996: 283), for example, have suggested that reflective narratives can be used to encourage students to record their reflection on:

- specific skills, attributes or behaviours demonstrated in a specific task;
- practical legal knowledge, focusing on the operation of substantive or procedural law 'in action';
- theories about the legal process.

Reflective narratives can take a variety of forms – short, independent summary sheets in which students record reflections on specific activities or tutorials; elements of a portfolio, or a fully fledged learning diary, in which students accumulate a rich articulation of their experience over an extended period of time (e.g. as part of a clinical or work placement). Narratives may also be private or relatively public documents. Information technology may be used to democratise reflective learning through e-portfolio tools and blogs, facilitating the creation and sharing of students' reflection with both peers and tutors. Given the sometimes quite personal nature of reflection, the decision to use such *fora* needs to be considered carefully, with the support of the students involved, though it may be that, with the growing popularity of social networking sites such as Bebo and Facebook, this is less of an issue than it once was.

Reflective narratives are valued for their ability to personalise learning and support development within what educationalists call the **affective domain** – the area of values, feelings, motivations – and this is largely how they add authenticity to assessment. Equally, some commentators acknowledge that, given the highly personalised nature of the learning involved, they generate problems of reliability that one does not encounter with more standardised assessment activities. Even some proponents of reflective narratives and journals question the appropriateness of assessing them summatively because this can distort the way they are used, i.e. students are conscious of the assessment context and may be more wary of reporting their full experience or accurate reflection if they feel such comments are inappropriate to or will not be valued in the formal assessment process.

Rethinking assessment

Assessment has tended to be the Cinderella topic when thinking about course design and development. New (and established) teachers wishing to innovate may find themselves confronted by a variety of challenges: resource or programme design constraints, sceptical colleagues, and sometimes sceptical students too. At the same time, there is growing recognition of the importance of variety in assessment practices, of ensuring that assessment is properly aligned with the range of learning objectives, and fit for purpose in a context where students have been skilled very differently by schools and colleges from preceding generations.

Interrogating practice

Look at the assessments in a module that you are delivering.

In the light of the above, what changes, if any, would you make to the assessment design and/or process?

OVERVIEW

The purpose of this chapter has been to review some of the challenges of taking law teaching seriously. It explores some of the practical constraints that exist, and acknowledges those that are largely self-imposed. It shows how both student and university expectations are changing, that effective legal academics are expected to be not only researchers and purveyors of legal scholarship, but also familiar with educational theory and practice, and willing to bring the same critical and reflective attitudes to their teaching as their research. It sets out to highlight, albeit briefly, some examples of good and innovative practice, and in the process demonstrates ways in which law teaching can, and does, draw on general theories of higher education pedagogy and practice as well as its own distinctive discourse. Above all else it has sought to show that greater creativity in teaching and learning can serve to (re)generate that sense of exploration and excitement which attracted many of us to learning law in the first place.

REFERENCES

Anderson, L W and Krathwohl, D R (eds) (2001) *A Taxonomy for Learning, Teaching and Assessing: A Revision of Bloom's Taxonomy of Educational Objectives*, New York: Longman.

Bone, A (1999) *Ensuring Successful Assessment*, Coventry: National Centre for Legal Education. Available online at <http://www.ukcle.ac.uk/resources/assessment/bone.html> (accessed 10 September 2007).

Boud, D and Feletti, G (1997) *The Challenge of Problem Based Learning* (2nd edn), London: Kogan Page.

Clegg, K (2004) *Playing Safe: Learning and Teaching in Undergraduate Law*, Coventry: UK Centre for Legal Education. Available online at <http://www.ukcle.ac.uk/research/ukcle/ncle.html> (accessed 3 September 2007).

Cowan, J (1999) *On Becoming an Innovative University Teacher*, Buckingham: Open University Press.

Directions in Legal Education (2004) 'Counting the Cost of the Law Degree'. Available online at www.ukcle.ac.uk/directions/previous/issue8/leader.html

Jenkins, A, Healey, M and Zetter, R (2007) *Linking Teaching and Research in Disciplines and Departments*, York: Higher Education Academy. Available online at <http://www. heacademy.ac.uk/resources/publications> (accessed 10 September 2007).

Kift, S, Shirley, M, Thomas, M, Cuffe, N and Field, R (2006) 'An Innovative Assessment Framework for Enhancing Learning in the Faculty of Law at QUT'. Submission for the Carrick Awards for Australian University Teaching 2006. Available online at <http://law. gsu.edu/ccunningham/LegalEd/Aus-QUT-Kift1.pdf> (accessed 10 September 2007).

Law Society/Bar Council (2004) Joint Statement on Qualifying Law Degrees. Available online at <http://www.lawsociety.org.uk/documents/downloads/becomingacademicjoint state.pdf> (accessed 9 September 2007).

Maharg, P (2007) 'The Scottish Teaching, Learning and Assessment Survey'. Available online at <http://www.ukcle.ac.uk/directions/previous/issue2/survey.html> (accessed 10 September 2007).

Maughan, C and Webb, J (1996) 'Taking Reflection Seriously: How Was it for US?', in J Webb and C Maughan (eds), *Teaching Lawyers' Skills*, London: Butterworth.

Pontin, B with Bowen, S, Hickman, J, Lloyd, I, Lopes, C and Wilkes, J (2007) 'Environmental Law History (No 1) – Tipping v St Helens Smelting Company (1865): "Antidevelopment" or "Sustainable Development"?', *Environmental Law and Management*, 19, 7–18.

Quality Assurance Agency (QAA) (2000) *Academic Standards – Law*, Gloucester: QAA.

Ramsden, P. (2003) *Learning to Teach in Higher Education*, London: Routledge.

Scott, A, 'An Introduction to Judicial Review: The Estate Agent's Problem'. Available online at <http://www.ukcle.ac.uk/resources/pbl/index.html/uea.html> (accessed 9 September 2007).

Twining, W (1994) *Blackstone's Tower*, London: Sweet & Maxwell.

FURTHER READING

Burridge, R *et al.* (2002) *Effective Learning and Teaching in Law*, London: Kogan Page. A useful collection of essays covering topics at both undergraduate and postgraduate level including: experiential learning; e-learning; teaching ethics; human rights; and teaching law to non-lawyers.

Le Brun, M and Johnston, R (1994) *The Quiet Revolution: Improving Student Learning in Law*, Sydney: Law Book Co. This is an excellent book for those interested in bridging the gap between educational theory and practice and offers a range of ideas on how to enliven undergraduate teaching.

Maharg, P (2007) *Transforming Legal Education: Learning and Teaching the Law in the Early Twenty-First Century*, Aldershot: Ashgate. A sophisticated blend of interdisciplinary theories and cutting-edge research and development work on the use of simulation and gaming in legal education. A glimpse of the direction in which legal education is going, or needs to go – perhaps?

Webb, J, and Maughan, C (eds) (1996) (See above under Maughan and Webb.) A series of essays which seek to develop both the theory and practice of teaching and assessing skills in undergraduate and vocational legal education. Some of the examples are now somewhat dated, but most of the underlying thinking and experience remains highly relevant.

24

Key aspects of teaching and learning in accounting, business and management

Ursula Lucas and Peter Milford

INTRODUCTION

This chapter aims to identify the distinctive features of education in accounting, business and management and the way in which they may impact upon teaching, learning and assessment strategies. Business education forms a significant sector within higher education. In 2005/2006 200,000 undergraduate students (some 11 per cent of the total student population) were enrolled on business, management and accounting degree programmes (HESA, 2006). To this total should be added those students who study business subjects as part of their own specialist degree studies. The diversity of students, disciplines and stakeholders within business education produces tensions that are not easily resolved and creates a complex and challenging environment for lecturers. This chapter will explore the implications of this environment for the development of learning, teaching and assessment strategies within business education. The emphasis of the chapter will be on undergraduate education in the UK, although much of the discussion may also be relevant more widely, including to postgraduate education.

DISTINCTIVE ASPECTS OF BUSINESS EDUCATION

In the United Kingdom, the **Quality Assurance Agency** Subject Benchmark Statements (QAA, 2007a) identify the purpose of general and business management programmes as threefold:

1   the study of organisations, their management and the changing external environment in which they operate;
2   preparation for and development of a career in business and management;
3   enhancement of lifelong learning skills and personal development to contribute to society at large.

The accounting **subject benchmark statements** are similar. They do not assume that all accounting students wish to qualify as accountants and an accounting degree programme is seen to provide a useful introduction to the worlds of business and finance (QAA, 2007b).

These objectives may appear straightforward but, in fact, a closer review reveals distinctive features and tensions which should be taken into account when designing teaching, learning and assessment strategies. Perhaps the most notable feature (and tension) within business education lies within the first two objectives. In 1983, Tolley (in a much-quoted statement) reflected:

> It is not clear whether the underlying concern of staff and students in these courses (i.e. Business Studies degrees) is a study of business or a study for business.
>
> (Tolley, 1983: 5)

It is apparent from the benchmark statements that business education is seen by the QAA to incorporate both of these aspects. A study *for* business recognises that there is a vocational aspect to education. Students should be adequately prepared for employment. In recent years **employability** has become a central issue within higher education (see Chapter 8). A study *about* business recognises that education can fulfil a wider role, that of allowing students to study the role of business in society, incorporating sociological, legal, economic or ethical aspects. This dichotomy in educational objectives is not new and reflects the contrasting values of a vocational versus a liberal education (for an overview and discussion of these contrasting perspectives, see Grey and French, 1996).

The business lecturer thus works within a complex and dynamic environment. Despite the view taken by the benchmark statements, business educators have to acknowledge and respond to competing demands: from government, employers, professional bodies and students. Moreover, the tradition and culture of higher education institutions and the lecturers who work within them also affect the way in which business education is provided. While there are strong influences that support a more vocational approach to business education there are also influences that support a shift towards a more liberal approach. This environment, which is illustrated in Figure 24.1, will be discussed in more detail below.

Lecturers bring with them a particular orientation to the teaching of their subject. The study of business and management does not constitute a single discipline. Rather, it comprises some traditional disciplines such as economics, mathematics, law and sociology, and newer subjects such as marketing, accounting and strategy which derive their knowledge base from a variety of traditional disciplines. Some lecturers will have

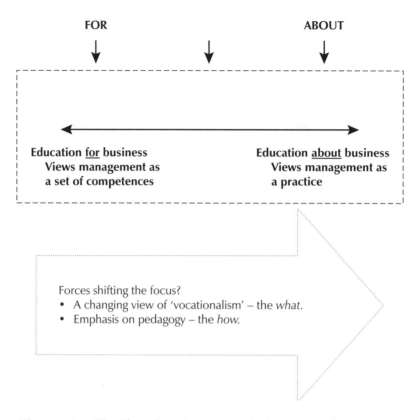

Figure 24.1 The 'for–about' spectrum in business education

come through a traditional higher educational route of doctoral specialism, tending possibly to a view of business education as being *about* business, whereas other lecturers will have entered higher education after substantial professional and business experience, tending possibly to a view of business education as being *for* business (Macfarlane, 1997). Thus even within one institution there are likely to be differing perspectives about the role of business education.

Students, too, will bring with them a particular orientation to learning. There is great diversity within the business student population. In 2005/2006 some 24 per cent of the population was represented by students studying part-time (HESA, 2006). Many of these combine employment with their studies. In addition, a substantial proportion of business students undertake some form of placement. These two categories of students will bring a quite different contextual perspective to their studies. Students will also vary according to the extent of their vocational interest: from a broad specialism to a professional qualification within a specialist area such as accounting. All of these factors have implications for curriculum design, teaching methods, approaches to teaching and assessment.

The institutional framework within which courses are designed can exacerbate the tensions between an education *about*, as opposed to an education *for*, business. The use of modular courses is widespread within the United Kingdom. The tendency within a modular structure can be towards a multidisciplinary approach within which subjects may become insular and specialist. Thus students may experience difficulty in seeing or making connections between the subjects. This problem can be mitigated but it is dependent on the willingness and ability of lecturers (with diverse views) to work in a more integrated way.

Funding agencies, government and employers emphasise the need for business graduates to be *employable* by the end of their studies, requiring business-related knowledge and skills. Skills development is emphasised in the relevant subject benchmarks. These capabilities include both attributes, such as self-reliance, and skills. The latter include skills directly related to business and accounting practice, such as business problem-solving and use of financial language, and more **transferable skills**, such as numeracy, communication and teamworking (see Chapter 8). A review of the educational literature reveals the findings of a multitude of projects which have enquired into the nature of skills, their transferability and the means of assessing them (Atkins (1999) provides a concise review of these). A key tension arises from the competition for 'space' in the curriculum: will an emphasis on skills development compromise the development of subject knowledge and conceptual understanding? Should skills be 'taught' or developed separately, or should they be embedded within subject modules?

Interrogating practice

1 Consider the balance between the development of subject knowledge and 'skills' development in a business or accounting award that you have knowledge of. Is the balance appropriate?
2 To what extent do the skills developed enhance employability?
3 To what extent do the skills developed support learning and hence the development of subject knowledge and understanding?

The changing nature of knowledge in business is an important influence on business education. Relevant knowledge includes technical expertise as well as critiques of management and accounting practices in their organisational and social context. A growing body of research on the market for ideas in business (e.g. Huszinski, 1993) reveals the contested nature of knowledge in business and management, the elements of 'fashion' both in management practices and academic approaches and the insatiable thirst of managers for new ideas to help them to deal with a complex and turbulent environment. Business curricula must therefore take account of the diversity and dynamism of subject knowledge; approaches that emphasise technique over context will develop only partial

386 Teaching in the disciplines

knowledge and understanding. Yet business educators are also under pressure to include 'useful' knowledge within the curriculum.

The trend in recent years has been a shift in focus towards an education that is *for* business. However, despite the strength of demands from government, employers, professional bodies and students, there are other forces that support a shift in focus towards an education *about* business. The first of these is a changing view of what 'vocationalism' means. The current emphasis on lifelong learning acknowledges a perception by employers that business graduates require the ability to act autonomously and to think critically. For example, during the 1990s the US-based Accounting Education Change Commission worked to incorporate principles of a liberal education into the accounting undergraduate curriculum for these reasons. This shifting view of vocationalism not only focuses on what is studied but *how* it is studied. Thus learning and teaching strategies are expected to support the development of independent learners.

A second force which shifts the focus towards an education *about* business comprises two elements: a more formal approach to programme design and an emphasis on pedagogy. The QAA requires **programme specifications** to be produced for each degree course. Programme designers have to demonstrate how the aims and the learning outcomes of the degree programme are achieved across the spectrum of modules or courses studied. This requires a clear statement of **learning outcomes** for each course and a description of how knowledge and skills are developed and assessed. In particular, the classification of skills includes cognitive skills of critical thinking, analysis and synthesis. This includes the capability 'to identify assumptions, evaluate statements in terms of evidence' (QAA, 2007a: 3) and so on. There is a growing emphasis on **pedagogy** as evidenced by the creation of a standards framework for teaching in higher education (HEA, 2006) and the growing expectation that lecturers will have engaged in some form of professional pedagogic development. Consequently there is much more support available than previously for business educators who wish to change the *how* of business education as well as the *what*.

Interrogating practice

Consider your own institution in the light of the factors discussed above.

1   Where does it lie in terms of an orientation towards an eduction *about* or *for* business?
2   How does the programme *structure* influence the orientation adopted by the programme?
3   What do *you* think the aims of a business education should be? What orientation do you adopt and why?

TWO MAJOR STARTING POINTS

Listening to students

> Insights into students' conceptions are one of the foundations of successful curriculum development, class teaching and valid assessment methods.
>
> (Ramsden *et al.*, 1993: 304)

One of the features of business education noted above is the diversity in the student population. Students will bring with them different motivations for, and different orientations to, the study of business. Some will wish for an all-round business course, some will already have a particular interest in certain subjects such as accounting, marketing or human resource management. Thus a lecturer may find that a class is composed of a variety of students who are predisposed to view their study of a particular subject in quite distinctive ways. Moreover, while the lecturer may have taken a view about where a course lies on the for–about spectrum this may differ significantly from the view taken by some (or all) of the students. Case study 1 addresses this issue. It looks at how lecturers have ascertained students' perceptions of the development of skills. In this case study the unexpected findings provided lecturers with a challenge.

Case study 1: Ascertaining students' perceptions of skills development

---

Skills development

There has been much discussion about the nature of **key skills** and the ways in which they may be developed within the curriculum. A key decision is whether skills development should be addressed separately within the curriculum or incorporated into modules. However, even if key skills are developed separately, it is important that students recognise when these skills may be relevant within individual modules. This case study describes an approach that placed a central focus on student perceptions of skills development within individual modules.

At the University of the West of England, a working group was established to design a programme specification describing the skills currently developed within the accounting and finance degree programme. Having done this, students were provided with an opportunity to discuss these skills in some depth. They were asked 'To what extent has your course helped you in developing these skills?'

The findings of the study were unexpected. Students experienced skill development as a tacit developmental process, and in some cases it was so tacit that students did not perceive it as a process of development at all. For example, having a skill was associated with being the 'kind of person you are'. Either you have a skill or you don't. Or a skill is something that 'you pick up over time', as part of the maturing process – or is developed unconsciously in higher education 'just by being here'. And whether a skill is developed within higher education 'depends on how good you are at doing that anyway'. Students varied enormously in the extent to which they arrived at university with some skills already developed. Finally, students found the language of the skills descriptors rather alien. Consequently one exclamation was 'who writes this stuff?' (for further information about this project, see Lucas *et al.*, 2004).

How students' perceptions can be taken into account in course design

How can a lecturer, even in dealing with large groups of students, take account of diverse student perceptions? First, the most positive finding of this case study was that students found the opportunity to discuss perceptions of immense value. It forced them to reflect and they started to see the course in a new light. 'It wouldn't have occurred to me that I even had those skills' was a typical response.

Finding that other students saw skills in a different way was, in itself, an eye-opener for students. Even in large groups, it is not difficult to give time for students to identify, discuss and compare their perceptions of learning or the subject. Second, the lecturer can then design learning and teaching approaches with a broader awareness of the different ways in which students approach their learning of the subject. Workshop or lecture activities may be used to address perceptions that may adversely affect learning. Third, knowledge learnt from this exercise can be referred back to later in the course. Students can then review how their perceptions have (or have not) changed during the course. An interesting account of such an approach is available in Mladenovic (2000). Although it describes an approach taken in an accounting course, it could be adopted within any other subject.

(Ursula Lucas, Bristol Business School, University of the West of England)

Asking students to reflect on their learning

While it is important that lecturers listen to students and take account of different student perceptions, it is equally important that students listen to themselves. Students need to develop self-awareness and the ability to reflect on their experience (this issue will be discussed more fully later in the chapter). **Reflection** is regarded as a central skill to be developed within under- and postgraduate education. Case study 2 discusses issues that arose when Masters students were asked to engage in reflective writing. The case highlights the issues that can arise when students are asked to undertake a novel learning activity.

Case study 2: The student experience of reflective writing at Napier University, Edinburgh

Background

Research carried out in 2004 into the student experience of reflective writing in Masters Business Management programmes at Napier University, Edinburgh undertook to explore the students' perceptions of the experience of reflective writing and to evaluate the appropriateness of reflective writing as a mechanism for encouraging critical reflection.

Data were gathered from students undertaking three different programmes of study, each of which had a required element of some form of reflective log or journal with a requirement for personal reflection. The objectives of including the reflective writing in the programmes were:

- to deepen the quality of learning, in the forms of critical thinking or developing a questioning attitude;
- to enable learners to understand their own learning process;
- to increase active involvement in learning and personal ownership of learning;
- to enhance professional practice or the professional self in practice.

Findings

The picture that emerged from the data regarding the characteristics of the students was of a group of learners who were unlikely to have had previous experience of reflective writing in their earlier studies, and while confident in their writing skills, had not often engaged in writing for pleasure.

Students were asked to rate their experience of reflective writing under three separate headings: 'Personal insight', 'Enjoyment' and 'Practical value'. Then they were asked to describe their initial view on the requirement to undertake reflective writing. It was found that students were, as a group, emphatically sceptical about the value of the reflective writing requirement at the outset. Given the high level of initial scepticism, there were a surprising number of conversions to a positive value rating on completion of the exercise. However, the overall evaluation given by the students was, at best, mildly positive.

With a few exceptions, even those who saw some benefits arising from the experience did not enjoy the process. It could therefore be concluded that they were unlikely voluntarily to use reflective writing as a mechanism for reflection in the future, although it is possible that their increased understanding of the concepts and awareness of the learning process might contribute to a reflective approach becoming a lifelong learning skill.

There were a number of key influencing factors which impacted on the student experience:

- Antipathy to the writing process, which was not the preferred medium for reflection when compared to group discussion and class activities.
- Difficulties with imposed structure, seen as overly formal or restrictive.
- Impact of assessment/submission of what was seen as a personal activity. This was the case even where considerable effort had been made to clarify the different nature of the criteria being used, and where the process had been structured to allow students to exercise their own control over personal exposure.
- Expectations of the process, which included lack of clarity and lack of common understanding.

Issues and questions

Students' willingness to engage in reflective writing will be affected by the institutional context. They may receive mixed messages about the value of reflective writing. This may occur in the following ways:

- Lack of centrality to the programme. Where the reflective writing requirement is presented as an additional feature of the programme and there is minimal integration with academic work it may be perceived as an activity that does not impinge on the 'real content' of their studies.
- Resources: quantity and quality. This relates to both staff and students. Has the time required to engage in the activity been accurately estimated and included in the student workload? If it has not then we encourage a minimalist approach by our actions, if not in our rhetoric. The necessary academic support requires both the staff time invested to develop a mentoring relationship, and the allocation of more class time for activities centred on personal reflection.
- Acceptance of the approach among teaching staff. Providing the required support also means addressing the varying commitment among staff to the principles of the process. Even where staff do appreciate the potential value of such activities, how many staff members are modelling the process that we expect students to engage in, by actually using reflective writing as part of their own personal and professional development? How many staff would be prepared to share their own reflective writing as participants within a learning community that includes the students, as suggested in the literature?
- Finally, do the compromises that we make due to institutional context fundamentally undermine our objectives in this area, and, if we are not

sufficiently convinced of the value of the practice to invest in making it more successful for our students, would we better serve their needs by recognising this?

(Fiona Oldham and Iain Henderson, Napier University Business School)

THE DESIGN OF LEARNING, TEACHING AND ASSESSMENT STRATEGIES

This section will consider ways in which learning, teaching and assessment strategies can be used to shift the focus along the for–about spectrum at both the level of the programme and the level of the individual module. Any attempt to counter the multidisciplinary tendencies of business education with a holistic approach requires integration strategies at the programme design level. However, individual lecturers can also shift the focus of teaching along the for–about spectrum in a variety of ways. Suggestions as to how the focus might be shifted are outlined in Figure 24.2. and will be discussed below.

Devices for shifting the focus?

- Curriculum and syllabus design (learning outcomes).
- Change the emphasis: increase the focus on transferable and technical subject-specific skills.
- Use professional practice to inform teaching.
- Assessment (problem-based, case studies to develop technical skills).

FOR   ABOUT

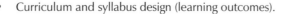

Education for business
Views management as
a set of competences

Education about business
Views management as
a practice

Devices for shifting the focus?

- Curriculum and syllabus design (learning outcomes).
- Change the emphasis: increase the focus on critical thinking and reflective skills.
- Use research to inform teaching.
- Assessment (dissertations, learning logs, case studies to question assumptions, self- and peer assessment).

Figure 24.2 Shifting the focus along the 'for–about' spectrum

Learning outcomes

The starting point for the design of learning, teaching and assessment strategies is the identification of learning outcomes. The Subject Benchmark Statements referred to above will inform these. Generic educational advice on learning outcomes often refers lecturers to Bloom's taxonomy (see Chapter 4). However, alternative taxonomies may be more relevant to vocational and professional education. For example, Carter's (1985) taxonomy of objectives for professional education and Eraut's (1994) analysis of **competence**s analyse the different types of knowledge and skills that are found within professional practice. In particular, they distinguish, as Bloom does not, between knowing how to do something and being able to do it. Thus experiential knowledge (see Chapter 2) is addressed as well as the importance of attitudes and values.

More recently it has been proposed that learning outcomes should focus on those areas of learning that are most central to a transformation of understanding within a particular subject area (i.e. on **threshold concepts)** (see Chapter 2). Initial work on threshold concepts indicates that there may be thresholds that cross subject areas and may support students in making connections between subjects. For example, one threshold identified within introductory accounting is the realisation that accounting techniques are not an objective end in themselves but represent an attempt to put a particular subjective conceptual framework into practice (Lucas and Mladenovic, 2006).

Decisions about learning outcomes have to be taken in conjunction with a decision about where the programme might lie on the for–about spectrum. Individual courses may vary in their orientation but there will be an overall approach adopted by the programme specification.

Integration

Regardless of where a programme lies on the for–about spectrum, the issue of integration must be addressed. There are several ways in which integration may be achieved. Cross-curricular themes may be identified: for example, the environment, ethics, the knowledge economy. Team-teaching might involve different subject lecturers on topics such as the business environment. Students may be asked to draw on work experience to link theory with practice and to identify the relevance of different subjects to their experience. Finally, the role of the individual lecturer in achieving integration should not be neglected. Students need constant help in locating where in the broad picture a particular subject 'fits'.

Shifts along the for–about spectrum may also be made by changing the skills emphasis of individual modules. A decision must be made as to how far learning outcomes can embrace both development of practical skills and critical review of management as a practice. It is rarely a question of 'all or nothing'. An emphasis on practical skills may be tempered by some element of critical review or vice versa. Counterbalances can be designed into the course. For example, assessments might be designed which expect students to be able to question the assumptions and theoretical frameworks underlying technical approaches. Or students may be expected to question the means by which 'professional' techniques and practice come to be accepted as the norm.

The placement period can be a valuable opportunity for students to place their academic learning in context and to experiment with the development of skills (Little and Harvey, 2006). This chapter will not consider the role of work experience further. However, Foreman and Johnston (1999), in the first edition of this handbook, discuss the use of university learning in the workplace and it is the subject of their third case study.

Synergy between research, teaching and professional practice

Lecturers can also use their professional or research practice to inform the context within which their students study. The orientation of a lecturer can be an important influence on the student's perception of the subject. Thus a lecturer might design a course that is essentially *about* business, addressing the theoretical frameworks underpinning a subject. However, even in this context, it is possible for a lecturer's professional or business experience to provide practical contexts in which that theoretical knowledge becomes relevant and thus might be effectively challenged. Similarly, a course may be essentially *for* business, and involved with the development of technical skills. However, it is again possible for a lecturer to apply a knowledge of research in the area to question the relevance and efficacy of techniques.

Once learning outcomes have been specified, assessment becomes central to the development of teaching and learning strategies. Not only should it relate directly to the learning outcomes already identified but modes of assessment should be valid, reliable and fair (see Chapter 10). Since assessment is a prime determinant of student motivation, it provides an opportunity for lecturers to channel the energies of students into what are deemed to be appropriate activities.

Assessment strategies

A good generic introduction to assessment is provided in Chapter 10, and in Macfarlane and Ottewill (2001: 53). This section will discuss aspects of assessment that are most pertinent to business education. The tensions created by diversity within business education have already been identified. A key question that might be posed is 'Can assessment assist in resolving some of these tensions?' There are various ways in which assessment may shift the focus along the for–about spectrum. Six of these will be briefly discussed below.

Where a course emphasises an education about business, assessment may focus on problems within a particular context, encouraging students to place knowledge and theories in a practical scenario, using case studies or business games. Similarly, where a course emphasises an education for business, then assessment may encourage students to place their practical studies in a conceptual framework. Dissertations provide students with opportunities to identify and critique the theory and knowledge underlying their practical studies.

Assessment may encourage students to make links between subjects. Again, case studies are an obvious choice, expecting students to take a more holistic approach to problem-solving. However, collaboration between modules to develop a joint assessment strategy is another valuable way forward.

Assessment can support the development of employment-related skills such as communication, group work or planning and organisation. However, it is critical that the marking criteria fully assess the levels of those skills. If the outcome of skills development is not easily observable, the student may be asked to reflect on its development through the writing of a reflective piece or a learning log (as in Case study 2). If there is already an emphasis on employment-related skills then assessment can also shift the focus to critical thinking and reflection. Students may be required to critically review the relevance or adequacy of those skills in a work context.

Assessment can support the development of students as critically reflective individuals. **Feedback** on assessments is central to the development of a student understanding of how they have performed. A part of the assessment might involve a reflective student piece of writing on what they have learnt from the assessment.

An important outcome of business education is often stated to be the development of students who will become autonomous individuals with a capacity to engage in **lifelong learning**. An assessment strategy may expect students to engage more independently within the assessment process throughout the three or four years of the degree course. Students can be involved in the design of assessment exercises and their marking (through self- and peer review) such that it becomes a collaborative exercise.

Case studies may be used in varying ways and may achieve quite different learning and assessment outcomes. For example, a case may be used solely for illustrative purposes, thus giving life to a highly theoretical approach. It may also be used as a problem, providing a context within which a particular problem is to be 'solved'. Alternatively, the case may be used to provide a complex context where problems are not 'bounded' and may not necessarily be 'soluble'. This chapter does not address case studies further. Foreman and Johnston (1999) consider them in some detail. Another helpful overview of the use and relevance of the case method in business education is available in Booth *et al.* (2000).

DEVELOPING CRITICAL THINKING

An essential goal of education is to support students in developing their ability to think critically. This is particularly important for business educators when faced with the diversity and tensions inherent within business education. However, students need an opportunity not just to link theory with practice, but to link an *ever-expanding* theory

Interrogating practice

- Review a course that you currently teach. To what extent do the written learning outcomes for your course reflect what you are actually trying to achieve?
- How might you change your assessment strategy in order to better align it with outcomes, or change the focus of your course or the motivation of students?

with *their* practice. As discussed above, the business environment has seen a huge expansion in the knowledge base. Moreover, we have become much more aware of the importance of students being able to identify their own personal knowledge and experiences. In this way students can identify their own personal relevances as well as those for business more generally.

The following two case studies address these issues in different contexts. Case study 3 addresses the issue of how best to support students in becoming critical readers. Case study 4 uses the notion of 'leadership' to provide a lively and meaningful context for students to reflect on their own skills and to link this with a study of the theory of leadership.

Case study 3: Supporting students in becoming critical readers

What is meant by critical reading?

Critical academic equiry can be a rather abstract concept for a student to understand. So we start with this issue and emphasise to students that being critical entails not only asking 'why' of the external world and of what one reads but also examining oneself and one's own underpinning research philosophy. We emphasise that challenging the ideas and the research conducted by others is accepted practice. However, this involves scepticism or reasoned doubt rather than destructive criticism. The aim is to achieve a constructive overview.

Barriers to critical reading

Students do not find critical reading easy. First, research (Case and Gunstone, 2003) shows that time is a dominant issue for students. Those students who take a **surface approach to learning** avoid tasks involving understanding on the grounds that they take up too much time. Those using a conceptual, or **deep, approach to learning** are willing to invest time in making sure they understand key concepts because this gains them long-term reward. Second, modular courses tend to encourage 'thinking within a course box'. The atomisation of knowledge and learning that often occurs can also create a barrier to critical reading. Third, there can be barriers to critical reading created by the cultural problems faced by students who have been educated under different educational philosophies. In cultures where knowledge is demonstrated by reiteration of published authors' work and where questioning an author's ideas is not encouraged, a more critical approach can be stressful for the student.

The development of critical reading frameworks to support students

The development of critical reading frameworks can help overcome these barriers. The frameworks discussed here were developed from the literature (Cormack, 2002; November, 2000) and augmented during years of teaching undergraduate and postgraduate business students. They provide an opportunity for the student to enter into a focused dialogue. The pro-forma structure supports the student in breaking down a seemingly intimidating body of work and in identifying the key elements of a number of different papers to form a logical review of a body of literature. Two frameworks have been developed: one for academic papers using empirical data and one for purely conceptual papers. Table 24.1 shows the critical reading framework for the former. We suggest that the frameworks should be used both formally and informally within teaching.

Formal approach

Critical reading can be embedded within the assessment of a module. At the simplest level, it can form a part of the assessment criteria of the module and this can be made explicit, with grades allocated against the criteria (Quinton and Smallbone, 2006: 87f.). This ensures that students take the requirement for critical reading seriously. Another way of encouraging critical reading is to make a critically reflective piece of writing part of the assessment. For example, students may be required, as part of an assignment (500 words out of a 2,500-word essay), to reflect on the significance, validity, reliability and extent to which they could generalise from the findings of their sources.

Informal approach

The Journals Club, a voluntary, informal lunch-time critical reading club, was set up to help students grapple with academic journal articles which they might find intimidating if attempting to read them independently. It was widely publicised to undergraduates, postgraduate students and staff. Students were given access

Table 24.1 A critical reading framework for empirical academic papers

What to look at	Student response
Date – when was the research reported on actually done?	
How current are the results?	
Where and in what context was the research carried out?	
What are the author's credentials?	
Data-collection methods – what did they actually do?	
Style	
Is it constructed clearly?	
Can you follow the argument through a logical development?	
Does the use of tables, charts and diagrams add value to the conclusions or the explanations?	
Analysis	
What is the central issue dealt with in the paper?	
What assumptions have been made (e.g. about the generalisability of the results)?	
What is the evidence supporting these assumptions?	
In what ways is this article similar or different from others you might have read?	
Reflection	
How do you respond to what the author is saying?	
How do you rate this article?	
How does it relate to other concepts you have come across?	
Does it point to further research in a particular direction?	
Is it relevant to your current work?	

to an article at least two weeks in advance on a fairly broad topic that they were likely to be studying, for example marketing strategy. Students were free to complete the frameworks and no other material was provided.

Over the course of the hour, the students and staff unpicked the article using one of the critical reading frameworks provided, and discussed the paper's merits and weaknesses. The Club has enjoyed a qualified success. Generally only the more motivated students attend. However, these students then have the chance to discuss papers with academics and with each other, increasingly rare occurrences in a fragmented modular programme.

Questions to consider

1 In what contexts might you find the use of critical reading frameworks useful?
2 What barriers to critical reading have you identified?
3 How else might you encourage deep, rather than surface, learning?

(Sarah Quinton and Teresa Smallbone, Oxford Brookes University)

Case study 4: Linking theory and practice: The leadership module at Bristol Business School (BBS)

Background

'Leadership' is seen as central to successful business practice and of interest to both academics and managers. The Leadership module therefore sits at the boundary between theory and practice. The module is designed to enable students to explore this boundary and develop both relevant subject knowledge and skills. The module is a Level 3 option offered to general business and accounting students, and has grown in popularity since it was originally designed in 1997. The module is both innovative and integrative through its design, delivery and assessment.

Objectives and approaches of module

The design of the module is informed by Kolb's (1984) experiential learning cycle (see Chapter 2) and requires students both to reflect and experiment actively. The module contains four integrated types of activity:

1 *Concrete experience*, exposing students to outdoor management and teamworking exercises focusing on leadership issues. Visiting business leaders talk to students about their leadership practice, with students being required to consider how theory informs and explains practice.
2 *Reflective observation*, requiring students to keep learning diaries that reflect on each contact session. Students perform a leadership skills audit at the end of each exercise, reflecting on their beliefs and those of the leader using an action-centred leadership framework.
3 *Abstract conceptualisation*, using traditional lectures covering concepts and theories with a textbook and guided reading.
4 *Active experimentation*, through an assessment that requires students to interview a leader and analyse the data using current leadership theory.

Evaluation of the module has demonstrated positive student feedback and evidence of deep approaches to learning in a mutually supportive learning environment owned and controlled by the learners. The experiential nature of the module has helped students to develop a strong sense of self-awareness, creativity in learning and their own leadership skills. For further information about this case, see Grisoni and Beeby (2001).

Issues/questions

- To what extent can experiential learning be used throughout the business and accounting curriculum?
- How can students be exposed to practice and theory in ways that facilitate development of theoretical knowledge, application of knowledge and self-awareness?
- How central is the notion of 'experimentation' to learning?

(Louise Grisoni and Mick Beeby, Bristol Business School, University of the West of England)

THE USE OF TECHNOLOGY IN BUSINESS EDUCATION

There is such a wide application of ICT within education that it is easy for the business educator to feel overwhelmed. Chapter 7 provides a useful overview. A valuable resource is available to the business educator in the shape of the Business, Management, Accounting and Finance Subject Centre (BMAF) – part of the Higher Education Academy. BMAF not only provides guidance for lecturers on how to approach the use of ICT within education, but it also makes a wide variety of teaching resources available online.

Case study 5: How BMAF supports lecturers

New lecturers can easily find themselves deluged with information and communications technology (ICT) acronyms, such as **VLEs (Virtual Learning Environments)** and **RLOs (Reuseable Learning Objects).** The BMAF provides a range of workshops (at no cost to the participant) on a UK-wide basis to support lecturers by giving practical advice on the range of ICT facilities in higher education and on how to use ICT in their teaching, in both distance and traditional modes. BMAF is also involved in a number of projects aimed at gaining a better understanding about how the potential of ICT can be used to improve business education in the future.

Lecturers are often concerned that today's students may have a greater grasp of web technologies such as social software than they do themselves. Moreover, students may expect the lecturer to be as familiar with these – often termed **'Web 2.0'** – technologies as they are themselves. These technologies may lead to a revolution in the design of the learning spaces themselves – which are increasingly becoming simultaneously highly social environments and highly technical environments. Students using social learning spaces may be better prepared for the socio-technical environment of the modern business workplace.

The now widespread use of ICT – particularly the internet – in business education has created a number of problems, the foremost of which is **plagiarism.** There is little to prevent a student from cutting-and-pasting from relevant text material available from all over the internet. To support the lecturer, BMAF offers workshops on such plagiarism. These workshops explore the availability and appropriate use of the detection software available (e.g. **TurnItIn**), and give practical advice on plagiarism avoidance strategies that lecturers can deploy. A second problem is that of the quality of resources available from the internet. Students often seem unaware of the varying quality of the resources available, and the lecturer will need to point them in the right direction early on in their studies. While Wikipedia is probably one of the 'safer' resources available from the internet, other less reliable and far more dubious resources exist. Here, BMAF – in collaboration with the **JISC** Intute service – provides practical guidance for lecturers on the advice they might give to students.

In late 2005, BMAF carried out a survey to establish the main concerns of lecturers, especially in teaching. Assessment, feedback, plagiarism and teaching large groups were the main concerns (also teaching international students). BMAF provides resources to assist in all these areas. The TRIBE database (Teaching Resources in Business Education) of resources is available and searchable from the BMAF website. It is currently quite small but there are plans to extend it. As well as TRIBE, lecturers may access a variety of other resources. Worthy of mention here is Google Scholar. Google Scholar is a (free) commercial offering and lecturers find it a useful resource for items such as case studies and journal papers.

(Steve Probert, Business, Management,
Accounting and Finance Subject Centre)

As discussed earlier, many business students have jobs and therefore have difficulty attending all formal sessions. The use of VLEs or intranets provides a valuable means of supporting these students, including the many MBA students who may have work commitments that prevent them from attending all scheduled classes.

In the past ten years there have been major changes in the ICT resources available for higher education. While the formats have changed from disk-based computer-based learning (CBL) through multimedia, the web and VLEs, the basic principles of implementation remain the same. Pedagogy must take precedence over the technology. Technology simply provides a new set of tools to support learning and teaching. It is important that educators do not lose sight of this.

Interrogating practice

- Access and browse the BMAF website (http://www.business.heacademy. ac.uk).
- Explore the links provided on the Resources and Publications pages.
- Explore the 'First steps in tutoring' guidance, available on the Resources page.
- How might BMAF's workshops, publications and resources support your own teaching?

WHERE DO I START? SOME GUIDANCE FOR NEW LECTURERS

For lecturers who are new to lecturing (but not necessarily new to business, management and accounting) the challenge of teaching is exciting. Yet the complexity of factors to be taken into account when preparing for teaching may be rather daunting. However, there is no need for any individual lecturer to go it alone when deciding on content and approaches to teaching. For example:

- Draw on the experience of colleagues and ask for advice. It takes some time to build up a personal portfolio of teaching materials and experience. All lecturers have benefited at some time from helpful mentors and most are willing to assist new colleagues. It is important to adopt teaching approaches that are personally meaningful but there is no need to fully 'reinvent the wheel'.
- A significant amount of teaching within business education takes place in teams. Ascertain the various skills and expertise which are available in your particular team and identify just a few aspects of teaching (or of the subject) where you would like to take responsibility for further development.
- The business syllabus is ever-expanding. Do not feel that you have to 'cover' everything (thus taking the responsibility on yourself, rather than giving it to the student). Be realistic when identifying topics for inclusion in the syllabus. More experienced lecturers often find that they reduce the number of topics as time goes on, realising that subject-specific skills are more important than comprehensive content coverage.
- Bear in mind that you do not have to be the 'expert'. Teaching is often more about facilitation than providing subject expertise. When faced with a diverse student

group, draw explicitly on their experiences (and expertise). Let the students tell their own stories or identify their own perspectives. Equally, share your own enthusiasm but also your difficulties concerning the subject. This sharing can support the mutual identification of areas for further study.

OVERVIEW

Business education is a complex, but potentially very rewarding, area in which to teach. This chapter has identified distinctive aspects of business education which must be taken into account by business educators, both at the level of the programme and at the level of the individual module. The tensions produced by the different demands of students and stakeholders and by the changing nature of the business disciplines are not, by their nature, ever likely to disappear. It is not expected that degree programmes can, or should, be created at identical points along the for–about spectrum. The Benchmark Statements do not have to be viewed as a form of national curriculum. Indeed, the diversity of students, stakeholders and educators ensures that each institution can make its own unique contribution somewhere along the spectrum. The challenge for business educators lies not in resolving such tensions but in acknowledging their nature in their own particular institutional context and in responding to them creatively as they decide on their own particular approach.

REFERENCES

Atkins, M J (1999) 'Oven-ready and self-basting: taking stock of employability skills', *Teaching in Higher Education*, 4(2): 267–280.

Booth, C, Bowie, S, Jordan, J and Rippin, A (2000) 'The use of the case method in large and diverse undergraduate business programmes: problems and issues', *International Journal of Management Education*, 1(1): 62–75.

Carter, C (1985) 'A taxonomy of objectives for professional education', *Studies in Higher Education*, 10(2): 135–149.

Case, J and Gunstone, R (2003) 'Going deeper than deep and surface approaches: a study of students' perceptions of time', *Teaching in Higher Education*, 8(1): 55–69.

Cormack, D F S (2000) *The Research Process in Nursing* (4th edn), London: Blackwell Science.

Eraut, M (1994) *Developing Professional Knowledge and Competence*, London: Falmer Press.

Foreman, J and Johnston, T (1999) 'Key aspects of teaching and learning in business and management studies', in H Fry, S Ketteridge and S Marshall (eds) *A Handbook of Teaching and Learning in Higher Education* (pp. 372–390) (1st edn), London: Kogan Page.

Grey, C and French, R (1996) 'Rethinking management education', in R French and C Grey (eds) *Rethinking Management Education* (pp. 1–16), London: Sage.

Grisoni, L and Beeby, M (2001) 'Experiential leadership development at undergraduate level', in C Hockings and I Moore (eds) *Innovations in Teaching Business and Management* (pp. 39–50) Birmingham: SEDA.

HESA (2006) Table 2e – all HE students by level of study, mode of study, subject of study. Available online at <http://www.hesa.ac.uk/holisdocs/pubinfo/student/subject0506.htm> (accessed 15 June 2007).

Higher Education Academy (HEA) (2006) *The UK Professional Standards Framework for Teaching and Supporting Learning in Higher Education*, York: Higher Education Academy. Available online at <http://www.heacademy.ac.uk/regandaccr/StandardsFramework(1).pdf > (accessed 18 May 2007).

Huszinski, AA (1993) *Management Gurus*, London: Routledge.

Kolb, D A (1984) *Experiential Learning*, Englewood Cliffs, NJ: Prentice Hall.

Little, B and Harvey, L (2006) *Learning Through Work Placements and Beyond. Sheffield: Centre for Research and Evaluation*, Sheffield: Sheffield Hallam University and Centre for Higher Education Research and Information, Open University.

Lucas, U and Mladenovic, R (2006) 'Developing new world views: threshold concepts in introductory accounting', in R Land and J H F Meyer (eds) *Overcoming Barriers to Student Understanding: Threshold Concepts and Troublesome Knowledge* (pp. 148–159), London: RoutledgeFalmer.

Lucas, U, Cox, P, Croudace, C and Milford, P (2004) ' "Who writes this stuff?": students' perceptions of their skills development', *Teaching in Higher Education*, 9(1): 55–68.

Macfarlane, B (1997) 'In search of an identity: lecturer perceptions of the Business Studies first degree', *Journal of Vocational Education and Training*, 49(1): 5–20.

Macfarlane, B and Ottewill, R (eds) (2001) *Effective Learning and Teaching in Business and Management*, London: Kogan Page.

Mladenovic, R (2000) 'An investigation into ways of challenging introductory accounting students' negative perceptions of accounting', *Accounting Education*, 9(2): 135–154.

November, P (2002) 'Teaching marketing theory: a hermeneutic approach', *Marketing Theory*, 2(1): 114–132.

Quality Assurance Agency (QAA) (2007a) *Benchmark Statement for General Business and Management*. Available online at <http://www.qaa.ac.uk/academicinfrastructure/benchmark/statements/GeneralBusinessManagement.pdf > (accessed 14 May 2007).

Quality Assurance Agency (QAA) (2007b) *Benchmark Statement for Accounting*. Available online at <http://www.qaa.ac.uk/academicinfrastructure/benchmark/statements/accounting.pdf> (accessed 14 May 2007).

Quinton, S and Smallbone, T (2006) *Postgraduate Research in Business: A Critical Guide*, London: Sage.

Ramsden, P, Masters, G, Stephanou, A, Walsh, E, Martin, E, Laurillard, D and Marton, F (1993) 'Phenomenographic research and the measurement of understanding: an investigation of students' conceptions of speed, distance and time', *International Journal of Educational Research*, 19: 301–324.

Säljö, R (1984) 'Learning from reading', in F Marton, D Hounsell and N Entwhistle (eds) *The Experience of Learning* (pp. 71–89), Edinburgh: Scottish Academic Press.

Tolley, G (1983) 'Foreword', in D Graves (ed.) *The Hidden Curriculum in Business Studies: Proceedings of a Conference on Values in Business Education*, 5, Chichester: Higher Education Foundation.

FURTHER READING

Albrecht, W S and Sack, R J (2000) *Accounting Education: Charting the Course Through a Perilous Future*, Sarasota, FL: American Accounting Association. This booklet addresses the challenges faced by accounting education, particularly the requirement for graduates who possess a broader range of skills than just the technical. While it specifically considers the US context, most of its discussion is pertinent to accounting education internationally.

Grey, C and French, R (1996) See above. This text offers alternative ways of viewing the business and management curricula; in particular, management is viewed as a complex social, political and moral practice rather than simply as a collection of competencies.

Hockings, C and Moore, I (eds) (2001) *Innovations in Teaching Business and Management*, Birmingham: SEDA. An interesting collection of innovations in business education, presented in a way that makes them easily accessible. Some of these can be adapted to a lecturer's individual needs quite quickly. Others may need more extensive adaptation, such as a change of course documentation or departmental policy.

Kaye, R and Hawkridge, D (2003) *Learning and Teaching in Business: Case Studies of Successful Innovation*, London: Kogan Page. Individual case studies range from action learning, resource-based learning, peer assessment and computer-based teaching of accounting to international consultancy assignments, developing an intranet for staff and students, and creating distributed communities of practice.

Macfarlane, B and Ottewill, R (eds) (2001) See above. This provides an excellent overview of issues affecting teaching in business and management and contains individual chapters on the teaching of particular functional areas.

25

Key aspects of teaching and learning in economics

Liz Barnett

INTRODUCTION AND AIMS

Economics in the UK is taught both in the context of single Honours degree programmes and within a wide range of joint degrees. In both cases, programmes are modular in nature, often with limited integration or cross-reference either between the main strands of economics (i.e. micro- and macro-economics) or between economics and other subjects in joint degrees. Single Honours programmes focus heavily on the development of students' theoretical and technical abilities. Joint programmes do not have the space or time to enable students to achieve such a sophisticated understanding of the discipline, and will tend to place more emphasis on applied and vocationally directed aspects, often with a bias towards the application of economics to business, accounting and finance. This chapter focuses on the single Honours context, as the business context has already been addressed in Chapter 24.

As a social science, economics will often be studied alongside disciplines such as sociology, anthropology, politics and psychology, as well as the business, accounting and finance subjects already mentioned. Readers may wish to refer to Chapter 20 in order to gain a broader understanding of the different approaches to learning and distinctive disciplinary styles to which their students may be being introduced alongside economics.

Increasingly, the teaching of economics is based on the use of analytical models that require a high level of understanding of mathematics, where in the past the subject was more discursive and text-based. Not all students are aware of this feature of economics programmes, which in recent years has led to student movement out of the discipline during the first year. Like other disciplines that require good mathematical ability (see e.g. Chapter 16), economics departments have noted declining mathematical abilities in their incoming students – an issue that is picked up later in this chapter.

The chapter will build on the basic aspects of teaching and learning in Part 1. In particular it will:

- expand on approaches to teaching and learning support which are most commonly associated with economics teaching: lecturing, the use of technologies in support of learning and small group teaching;
- summarise common approaches to assessment in economics, and explore the introduction of transferable skills into assessment;
- explore some emerging issues for teachers in economics, including addressing concerns about the mathematical ability of economics students;
- overview support for graduate teaching assistants by course tutors.

CONTEXT

Economics is an attractive degree to students, as alongside mathematics and law it offers students the prospect of high-earning graduate employment. This may give lecturers some interesting challenges in their teaching – as they face a body of learners who may be focused on what their discipline can offer them in the future rather than having an intrinsic interest in it as an area of study. On the other hand, this strong extrinsic motivation can be an effective motivator as students are aware of the need for good grades to secure the most lucrative jobs. This motivation can be harnessed particularly effectively where students take on internships or work placements during their studies, and where lecturers are able to highlight how models and techniques are applied in the 'industry'. Finally, lecturers need to keep in mind that many economics graduates, as in other disciplines, will end up working in entirely unrelated walks of life. It is consequently important to draw out more general skills and capacities the degree can foster. The recent update to the Economics Subject Benchmark Statement (QAA, 2007) highlights a number of these skills which include such concepts as opportunity cost, incentives, equilibrium, strategic thinking and numeracy skills.

Over the past ten years, the annual intake into single Honours degrees in economics from UK/EU students has remained relatively stable. However, there has been a significant increase in non-EU overseas students. This raises new challenges for lecturers in terms of ensuring that students who are working in English as a second language are effectively supported, implying the need to use examples that work effectively in an international context when working with students who may have very different prior learning experiences and expectations.

Across the UK, economics programmes have a relatively similar design, starting out with core courses that address fundamental economic principles and that enable students to develop the basic tools of economics analysis. There is a well-established theoretical core that is common to most undergraduate textbooks and fairly universal across the range of economics degrees offered in the UK. This allows for considerable sharing of teaching materials – indeed, many textbooks provide a range of teaching resources for lecturers as well as online learning support for students. Departments tend to offer a much broader and more varied range of optional courses, which build on this core by probing deeper into particular subfields (e.g. labour economics or international economics), as well as applied courses making the link to policy development and economic behaviour. As both the literature and the nature of the world economy evolve, new fields are developed (e.g. information economics) and others are de-emphasised (e.g. agricultural economics).

TEACHING ECONOMICS

A quick look at the *Guardian* league-table data based on the National Student Survey (2005) on the teaching of economics suggests that in terms of teaching methods, it is one of the lower-rated disciplines by students, alongside a number of other disciplines which are heavy on mathematics. This picture is similar in other countries. For example, research in the USA reported in Becker and Watts (1998) indicated economics among the least popular disciplines in terms of student feedback on teaching, and noted that by the 1990s, while many other disciplines had introduced much more variety and interactivity into teaching, economics remained wedded to lectures, supported by limited audiovisual input, with textbooks and possibly workbooks as the staple. However, there are promising signs of development, and recent surveys of lecturers and students run by the Economics Network (2003) have shown dramatic increases, particularly in the use of learning technologies.

Lecturing and working with large groups

Lecturing is used extensively in most economics programmes. In the survey of undergraduate economics students conducted by the Economics Network (2006), over 75 per cent indicated that they found lectures useful/very useful – the top-scoring teaching method in the discipline. The study found lectures to be most popular with older students, female students and final years rather than first years.

A number of aspects of the lecturing process have already been addressed (Chapter 5). As the core of many economics programmes is fairly stable, this is a fruitful area for sharing of resources. There is a wide range of sources for those looking for inspiration for lectures at all levels. Two particularly useful sources are the Economics Network and the Massachusetts Institute of Technology Open Courseware Project, details of which are in the references.

The Economics Network (2005) survey indicated three main areas where students felt lecturers need to improve their practice: structuring, reducing the complexity of visual materials, and making lectures more interesting.

Structuring

Introductory economics is often based on a 'building block' approach, taking students through a logical sequence of steps, building up their theoretical understanding. The sequential nature of the subject can lead to an approach to lecturing which pays so much attention to each step that the 'big picture' can be missed. The lecturer knows very clearly where he or she is heading, but may not always explain this to students. A simple guiding principle here is to ensure that each lecture starts with that 'big picture', sets the particular steps to be achieved in a broader context, and then links back to the step already covered, and forward to the next. To the experienced economist, this may often seem blindingly obvious. However, what is obvious to the lecturer may not be obvious to the student.

Reducing the complexity of visuals

PowerPoint or similar presentation software is in frequent use by economics lecturers. Many will include a range of different slide styles – text, graphical, algebraic and mathematical explanation. An article by Turner (2006) summarises the key features of effective visuals in economics as simplicity, accuracy and flexibility.

On simplicity, lecturers should pay attention particularly to graphical presentations. There may be temptation in taking a ready-made, completed graph and then trying to explain how it has been derived. A much more helpful approach is to take a complex graph and take it back to basics, starting, for example, with (labelled) axes and curve, and then building this up gradually (e.g. through using a series of slides, rather than a single slide). It can also be useful to show, for example, how the equation of the curve is turned into the actual plot, making the connection between the curve and the associated algebra. When demonstrating how changing the parameters can change the curve, again showing this in sequence, or showing the same basic graph augmented in different ways, can be helpful.

Once you have a store of basic graphical presentations, it is possible to demonstrate their flexibility to students, and also reduce your own production work – using your basic slide as a starter for a variety of explanations.

In practical terms, there are different ways in which this flexibility can be achieved. Lecture theatres may now be equipped with double projection facilities, which allow the lecturer to simultaneously use PowerPoint and a visualiser (or chalk/white board). This enables the lecturer to combine prepared outlines/notes with the practice of working through examples and ideas with students at 'writing' speed. An alternative option would be to use and annotate an interactive whiteboard. Appropriate use of technology can be a useful tool that allows, for example, gradual exposition of an idea or the development of a basic graphical form in an assortment of iterations.

On accuracy, with graphical presentations, remembering to label axes is important. If you model this good practice in your teaching, and also stress its importance to students, they should pick this up and implement it more systematically in their own work. Building accuracy of labelling and notation into assessment criteria can further reinforce this.

The other area where accuracy is important is with regard to mathematical notation. Here, economics students face many challenges, and plenty of room for confusion. Each textbook tends to adopt its own systems of notation. Each theoretical model, developed by a particular economist, will have its own notation. While experienced practitioners can understand, for example, that output is output, whether denoted by Y or Q, and that in consumer theory allocation across different goods could be denoted by g_1, g_2 or c_1, c_2 or x_1, x_2, students can become very confused. It is therefore worth paying attention to this element of detail, and ensuring that any visual materials in a lecture series have consistent notation ideally matched to the core textbook, if one is used.

Increasing interest

Clarity of structure and simplicity can enhance interest by themselves, simply by enabling students to continue following the logic of an explanation. Where structure and simplicity are absent, students may get lost at an early stage, and never have the opportunity to get back into the explanation. While it is possible to see this happening in small lecture theatres, it is much harder in large ones, and different strategies are needed for the lecturer to ensure that students are keeping up, and to know when they need to reinforce a point. In economics, as in other disciplines, a vital way of maintaining student interest is to illustrate lecture content with examples relevant to the day-to-day lives of students or to current affairs and issues of national and international interest.

Strategies for maintaining interest to keep students active through the lecture are reviewed elsewhere (Chapter 5). Technological solutions are becoming more common. A growing phenomenon in lectures is student use of laptops, enabling them to annotate lecture materials electronically. This is fuelled by increased availability of wireless technology. In the USA there are vociferous debates over the pros and cons of allowing student laptop use in lectures, and some lecturers have attempted to ban the practice. Others see it as a growing trend that can be useful for students who use it well. Some lecturers provide students with materials that are easy to annotate electronically. This may include 'incomplete' lecture notes or PowerPoint slides, which students can work on and develop as part of the session, thus keeping them alert and focused. Obviously, the same effect is possible using hard copy teaching handouts.

Interrogating practice

Think about your subject area. What examples can you draw on from current affairs, recent scandals, or day-to-day student life that could illustrate topics and grab student attention?

A more recent addition to economics lectures has been the introduction in some institutions of **Personal Response Systems** (PRS) to lecture theatres. These may be used to check student understanding and views (e.g. using **MCQs**), to encourage active participation and response to the lecture material, and to introduce alternative stimuli to keep student attention. PRS allows for rapid interaction with large numbers of students in what can at times be a passive learning situation. Case study 1 gives an example of PRS use.

Case study 1: Uses of a Personal Response System (PRS) in economics teaching

A PRS allows a lecturer or tutor the opportunity to ask questions to which the students respond by selecting an answer on a small handset. The answers are picked up by a receiver connected to a computer, with software collating the responses, and a summary of the responses given being presented as a bar chart on the computer screen (which of course can be projected on to a larger screen for the students to see).

Early versions of the PRS have been likened to the *Who Wants to Be a Millionaire* 'Ask the Audience' technology because multiple choice questions are asked. I have been using such a PRS successfully for a number of years in lectures for a second-year undergraduate Microeconomic Principles module. During the course of a 50-minute lecture, I might ask five questions at appropriate points. Questions can be asked to check student understanding of material just presented or to review material taught previously, and questions with a number of alternative correct answers can be posed to stimulate discussion. Hence, for example, in an introductory lecture on non-cooperative game theory, I may pose a question on the correct definition of a Nash equilibrium to check student understanding of the concept. Later I may show students a strategic form game, asking them to identify the number of Nash equilibria and/or the particular equilibria in the game.

The technology gives the lecturer an immediate indication of the level of under-standing of students, but can also ensure that students remain focused as they receive a variety of stimuli during a class. The PRS can be set up on an 'anony-mous mode' so that individual students' answers cannot be identified, or in a 'named mode' such that students' answers can be checked at the end of a session.

Recent updates to PRS include the opportunity to ask students questions requiring numerical or short text answers and to identify students by encouraging them to type in their name or library card number when they switch on so that their individual answers can then be recorded. This offers the prospect that the PRS may be used by students to load answers to homework exercises or tests, the software then marking the answers submitted. The software for the system may now be used in conjunction with PowerPoint, allowing users the opportunity to ask a PRS question as part of a PowerPoint presentation, the summary of responses then also appearing within the presentation.

(Dr Caroline Elliott, Department of Economics,
Lancaster University Management School)

SMALL GROUP TEACHING

Small group teaching forms an essential component in all economics programmes. The most commonly used forms are:

- classes to review pre-set problems;
- classes during which students work on problems, often in subgroups, with plenary presentation of their collective work;
- student presentations (group and individual) on both theoretical issues and their applications.

Some lecturers have started to experiment with a wider array of approaches, including the use of problem and case-based teaching (see below), games and simulations. The main purpose behind employing these different strategies is to increase active student involvement in the learning process. Since it is quite common in economics teaching for such classes to be facilitated by graduate teaching assistants, this means that module leaders need to ensure that all members of the course team subscribe to this approach.

A particular challenge for lecturers who use pre-set problems is motivating students to do the work in advance. A regular complaint from lecturers is that students come to classes unprepared, or take short cuts such as copying the answers from others, relying on answer sets from previous years, or quickly turning to answer sets provided by lecturers online. There are many reasons behind students failing to do preparatory work and it is important to distinguish between them and be prepared to address them in different ways.

Interrogating practice

Consider the group of students you are currently teaching. List the different reasons why they may not always come to class fully prepared.

A variety of approaches may be used to increase student motivation to prepare them effectively for class and reduce the opportunity for them to take short cuts with homework. For example:

- using introductory classes to establish expectations by developing a shared 'contract' between students and lecturers;
- encouraging collaboration and clarifying when and under what circumstances collaborative learning is acceptable – for example, in assessed coursework will they be penalised for working together and handing in very similar workings?
- clarifying when and how problem set answers will be released (e.g. via the **VLE**) and advising students on how best to make use of them;
- accessing the vast array of problem banks available electronically, to ensure that each year group is faced with different problems;
- designing problem sets in ways that challenge different students with different levels of ability (e.g. consider including problems which are straightforward variations on already worked examples, through to more complex and new problems, which may include past examination questions);
- rather than using classes simply to present answers to problems, actively involving students in the process, e.g. through questioning, asking them to explain the intuition behind an approach, or having students compare their work and then present their work to the class;
- giving students the challenge of designing and then solving their own problems, possibly based on worked examples.

Interrogating practice

In classes where students are expected to prepare work in advance, it is important to reward those students who come well prepared. What tactics will you use to reward those students who have undertaken the required work?

A common complaint from economics students is that their classes are not related sufficiently to real life and the application of theory to the day-to-day workings of economists in business. The increasing integration of economics into business and management programmes has led to some growth in case-based teaching and **problem-based learning**. An example of the application of problem-based learning to economics is given in Case study 2.

Problem-based learning in economics

Problem-based learning (PBL) is a teaching approach that puts students at the centre of the learning process. Working in groups, students take ownership and control of learning tasks set by the tutor of which they have no previous knowledge. The solution to the tasks involves a process of discovery and learning-by-doing through which deeper levels of knowledge and understanding are acquired. PBL has been well developed in medical education and is fully discussed in Chapter 26. Students present their findings that have developed through group activity as an interdependent process, co-coordinated by the tutor. Research (reported by Forsyth, 2002) shows that students who experience PBL retain their knowledge over a longer period of time, learn at a deeper level and develop a range of transferable skills such as presentation, communication and teamwork skills.

Case study 2: Introduction of problem-based learning into modules at London Metropolitan University

In 2005 we introduced PBL into our final-year modules. This decision was motivated by desire to experiment with alternative teaching methods, by the belief that students engage more with their learning when given greater responsibility and by the view that students should become independent learners by the end of their studies. Given this was a new initiative we decided to adopt a 'partial' approach to PBL: a mixture of directed and independent learning. In the first half semester learning is structured around a traditional lecture/seminar approach. In week 6, students are divided into small groups and are given a task designed to engage them with topics that would otherwise be covered in the rest of the semester. The task is assessed and accounts for 50 per cent of the course marks while a final examination accounts for the remaining 50 per cent. In the second half of the module lectures are replaced by presentations that report the groups' progress and form a base for class discussion that allows the tutor to direct students' attention to key issues and concepts. The tutor plays an important role in coordinating and supporting the learning process.

Economic growth module task

You have been hired as an economic consultant and policy adviser by the government of a small developing country. The country is ruled by a non-democratically elected government and open to trade with the rest of the world. The following statistics provide a snapshot of the economic situation in the country:

Statistics	Value
GDP per capita	$1.444
National saving rate	0.035%
Average investment rate	10.05%
Average years of education	4.01
% of college educated	2.12

Average years of education for females	2.97
Income share of top 20%	0.44
Income share of bottom 20%	0.07
Openness	23%
Gini coefficient	0.34
Computers for 1,000 people	2.10
FDI/GDP	2.12

The government is concerned about the state of the economy and, in particular, the standard of living, and is interested in introducing policies aimed at fostering long-run economic growth. You have been asked to produce a report that, on the basis of the country's current economic situation, suggests growth-enhancing policies. Your analysis and recommendations should be supported by references to economic theory, the use of available international evidence through descriptive statistics and graphs, and the insights provided by regression analysis. Statistical information should be used to provide indications of the likely impact of a policy change on the economy's future growth.

(Dr Guglielmo Volpe, London Metropolitan Business School)

Educational games and simulations

Some economics teachers have introduced educational games and simulations to drive student learning and to engage students in real-life economic issues. The *International Review of Economics Education* is a useful source of examples. Articles include a simulation used in an introductory monetary theory course, on the 'search-theoretic' model of money (Hazlett, 2003) and a role play/classroom experiment to demonstrate price controls and equilibration processes (Kruse *et al.*, 2005). The use of games and simulations can be highly effective in teaching complex ideas. However, they need effective integration into the curriculum, as well as a good reality check – unconvincing and trivial games can undermine the learning process. Time can be a challenge to the use of games and simulations, as many do not sit well in a standard one-hour teaching slot. Careful preparation and familiarity on how to use a game/simulation effectively is essential. For those new to using this approach, it is advisable to seek out others who are users, and observe the process before trying it. The process of debriefing is vital to ensure that students draw out lessons from the process, and see how it can apply more generally.

Using IT in economics teaching

Increasingly, Virtual Learning Environments (VLEs) and websites are used to support lectures, classes and independent study. Academic usage is growing apace: in the 2003 National Survey of Economics Lecturers, 58 per cent of respondents indicated that they were providing such online support. By the 2005 Survey on Teaching Research and

Technology, this figure had grown to 87 per cent and only 4 per cent were opposed to its use as a means of delivering learning resources. The 2005 Survey found that 90 per cent of economics lecturers already posted lecture materials online. Use is greatest in the first two years of degree programmes, where students will frequently be in large groups. Online resources will often include a range of different types of course materials (e.g. coursebooks, slides, handouts, problem sets, solutions to problems, simulations, worked examples, videos and podcasts of lectures).

ASSESSMENT

Chapter 10 outlines the fundamental principles of assessment. A National Student Survey (Surridge, 2006) suggests that students perceive this aspect of the learning experience as most problematic. Interestingly, students on the whole are confident that the assessment regimes they are faced with are fair, and that the criteria are clear, but approaching 50 per cent of them express concern about promptness (or lack of it) of feedback, similar numbers indicate that feedback has failed to help them clarify their understanding and over 40 per cent feel feedback is lacking in detail. Students studying economics are among those most critical of their assessment experience (along with engineering, medical and veterinary students). Together with later student surveys a powerful message emerges from across the sector on the need for more effective **formative assessment** of economics students.

Economics departments use a variety of assessment approaches, including examinations (which may incorporate essays, short-answer questions, case and problem-based questions, multiple choice questions), group and individual projects and online testing. The internet (e.g. the MIT Open Courseware Project) provides a wide array of examples of economics assessment tasks, which lecturers may find particularly helpful in identifying useful formative assessments – though clearly the key issue to ensure here is that any assessment tasks identified are well matched to the learning outcomes of the particular course. Volume of students on undergraduate programmes is also encouraging departments to explore the benefits and pitfalls of computer-assisted assessment (e.g. Chalmers and McCausland, 2002).

One area where there have been a number of recent developments is in the assessment of **transferable skills**. Chapter 8 has already introduced ideas on the integration of skills into curricula. An interview study of employers and alumni carried out by the Economics Network (2004) gives some insight into employer requirements. Many employers are keen to take on graduates with the appropriate technical skills, and expect them to be able to use these skills and to be able to make the results of the work intelligible to others. As one employer quoted notes: 'We are looking for economics graduates' ability to apply economic theory to policy in practical situations. They have to know enough of the theory to be able to extract it.' The 2007 Economics Subject Benchmark Statement (QAA, 2007) puts clear emphasis on the importance of skills development, noting that this should include both the broad skills such as literacy, communication and IT skills and a range of more specific transferable skills which directly build on economics, such as the ability to take account of opportunity costs, understand how incentives operate, and take strategic decisions. Case study 3 outlines one such development, focused on improving formative feedback on student writing skills, built into a core second-year microeconomics course.

Case study 3: Introducing writing skills development into a microeconomics course at the LSE

Following feedback from employers concerning the poor writing skills of some economics graduates, lecturers at the LSE decided to develop a strong written component into the formative assessment of a compulsory undergraduate micro-principles course. Five assignments were designed focusing on different styles of writing. Some of these were aimed at improving skills students need during their studies – such as essay writing and exam writing. Others involved writing short pieces that students might be expected to produce in their future employment, essentially explaining economics ideas to lay readers in an intelligible form. The development of understanding of academic integrity was also built into the exercises, and student work was submitted to the **JISC plagiarism** detection service. Any problematic work identified through the service was then discussed with students.

Some examples of writing tasks

Inferior goods: If an economist says that a good is inferior, does this mean that the good is of low quality? In 100 words, answer the question, explain your answer and support your answer with one example.

In the year 2000 there were auctions of spectrum for third-generation mobile telephones in several European countries. These auctions generated different amounts of revenue in different countries. How can this be explained? (1,000 word piece)

The course on which the development was tested was a large one (500+ students), which employed 20+ graduate teaching assistants. An important element of the implementation was to train these new teachers in how to introduce writing in economics to students, and how to give effective feedback on written work. The teaching assistants were taught to use a standard pro forma for feedback, which aided consistency of both volume and style of feedback.

(Dr Margaret Bray, Dr Jonathan Leape and Neil McLean
Department of Economics and Teaching and Learning Centre,
London School of Economics and Political Science)

Interrogating practice

Consider a formative assessment task already included in a course you teach. How could this be adapted to encourage and enable students to both practise and demonstrate their ability to communicate economics ideas to non-economists?

EMERGING ISSUES

Mathematical abilities of economics students

As noted earlier, the mathematical and statistical requirements of economics programmes have increased with the development of the discipline. Curriculum reforms in the UK have meant that students embarking on degree programmes with significant mathematical demands are hampered by a lack of technical facility, limited technical powers and an inadequate understanding of the mathematical precision needed (LMS, IMA and RSS, 1995). Curriculum reforms in 2000 appear to have made things worse rather than better, as evidenced in the report *Making Mathematics Count* (Smith, 2004) which concluded that the current curriculum and qualifications framework is failing to meet the requirements of learners, higher education and employers.

UK economics programmes have had to respond to current concerns, and have done so in an assortment of ways. Some have taken the route of keeping mathematical requirements to a minimum. This is particularly true of the more vocationally oriented business programmes, which do not expect or require high levels of mathematical ability. On the other hand, single Honours programmes have addressed this concern through a number of means:

- Making A Level mathematics a compulsory entry requirement, and increasing the incoming student awareness of the mathematical nature of the subject.
- Increasing the range and approach to the teaching of mathematics for economists, making this a larger component of the core programme, particularly in the first year.
- Introducing early diagnostic testing. Here, there is a wide variety of electronic tests that lecturers may find helpful – see, for example, Mathcentre in the references on p. 422, an initiative involving a number of UK universities, which includes some diagnostic tests appropriate to mathematics for economists.
- Establishing formal systems of support for students who are struggling. Examples here include provision of pre-sessional programmes to help incoming students get up to speed, as well as ongoing support, often through online learning. Again, there are many examples of self-learning electronic resources on the web that can be helpful in this context.
- Encouraging greater use of informal and **peer support** systems.

There is an obvious tension here between developing curricula that appeal to students and that they can succeed at (which may infer some 'dumbing down' of advanced economic analysis), and investing time and effort in ensuring that students have the necessary mathematical and statistical ability to cope. One practical consideration that economics lecturers should be aware of is that for the most part, first-year economics courses will run parallel to the accompanying mathematics and statistics courses. Consequently, lecturers need to ensure that the course structure is closely aligned with these other courses, and that they do not make inappropriate assumptions about students' numerical capabilities.

Managing diversity – dyslexia and dyscalculia

As noted earlier, the student population is increasing in diversity. New lecturers need to be well versed in both student and institutional expectations as to how they should respond to this diversity. One important area of diversity that has come to the fore in recent years is disability. The **Disability Discrimination Act** requires that students with disabilities are not treated less favourably than others; that institutions make reasonable adjustments where disabled students may otherwise be placed at a substantial disadvantage; and that institutions promote disability equality through a systematic whole organisational approach. Numerical data suggest that within the higher education system, the most commonly registered disability is **dyslexia.** Trott (2003) outlines three types of students with dyslexia/dyscalculia who may be attracted to studying economics:

1   Students who have strong mathematical capabilities, but face difficulties with language-based work, reading and short-term memory. These students may be attracted to the more mathematical elements of economics, but struggle with the more discursive and business-related elements.
2   Students who do not have problems with basic mathematics, but do find concrete to abstract generalisation problematic and face difficulties with 'remembering and retrieving symbolic material'.
3   Students who are dyscalculic, having problems with understanding numerical concepts. These students may have high levels of anxiety related to mathematics, and possibly be unaware, prior to starting a programme of study, of the level of mathematics/statistics that is required.

Given the array of economics courses and the association between economics and business on the one hand, and mathematics on the other, lecturers may well work with all three types. Universities will have specialist provision in place to support students with disabilities, and lecturers should be knowledgeable about where to direct students for additional support, and encourage openness and disclosure. In addition, the positive duty to promote equality makes it incumbent on lecturers to think and plan in advance ways of making their teaching inclusive – such that if a student chooses not to disclose a disability, he or she is still not disadvantaged. Lecturers should be aware of the importance of making any web-based materials accessible to students with disabilities. There is substantial advice on accessibility available on the web (e.g. the JISC TechDis site) and university website services should be able to advise colleagues.

Managing and supporting graduate teaching assistants

One effect of increasing pressure on resources in universities is greater use of graduate teaching assistants (GTAs) – often Ph.D. students or junior researchers starting out on their academic careers and keen to gain experience in teaching. To be effective, GTAs need an induction and support in their role and, to ensure quality of the student learning experience, careful management of them is vital. For lecturers involved in the organisation of courses that employ considerable numbers of GTAs, there is an array of tasks and responsibilities they may need to be aware of. Lecturers may need to ensure that:

- careful consideration is given to the appointment of GTAs with the necessary subject expertise and the ability to communicate effectively with students in the learning setting;
- GTAs are given appropriate initial training;
- GTAs are briefed on the objectives and expected learning outcomes of the module and its content;
- GTAs can recognise and address the likely problems students face in topics;
- GTAs know how to grade and provide feedback on student work;
- they can monitor and give feedback to GTAs on progress – which may involve observing them in class, seeking out or reviewing student feedback, and monitoring student academic progress.

Interrogating practice

Think about the course on which you are teaching. Which topics do students find particularly challenging? What aspects of those topics cause the greatest difficulties? What strategies have you found that help students to understand and overcome these difficulties?

How would you advise a co-teacher or GTA implementing these strategies?

The LSE has a successful and established programme for the induction and development of its GTAs and this is described in Case study 4.

Case study 4: Training for graduate teaching assistants at the LSE

The Department of Economics at the LSE employs around 80 GTAs each year. They provide much of the class teaching, supporting groups of up to 15 students. They grade and give feedback on coursework (which does not count towards the final degree). They also have weekly 'office hours' in which students can come to them with individual queries on their academic work.

Training and support for GTAs is a joint responsibility between the lecturer responsible for the course on which they are teaching, the department as a whole, and the Teaching and Learning Centre (TLC). Initial selection takes into account subject knowledge and communication skills. Many of the LSE's GTAs speak English as a second language. As part of initial selection and training, English language proficiency is carefully reviewed. Where additional language support is seen as necessary, this is funded by the department and required of the GTA. All GTAs must undertake some initial training, run jointly by staff from the department and TLC. GTAs are paid to attend this training, which includes a videoed teaching practice session, as well as a marking exercise using past student work.

At the course level there is some variation in approach, but the majority of course lecturers will hold briefing meetings with their GTAs, and some will hold regular meetings with their GTA teams throughout the year. Use of web-based learning resources and the institutional VLE means that most courses have comprehensive learning resources available to teachers and students. One course has a particularly sophisticated approach to monitoring student progress across its substantial numbers of classes and GTAs, using weekly online quizzes to maintain a view on variations in performance, which enable follow-up both on particular topics of concern, and where necessary with GTAs whose students appear to be having more difficulties than most.

In the first term of teaching, a lecturer from the department will observe new GTAs in class. Also in the first term, there is an online survey of student views on the quality of class teaching. Data on individual teachers are considered, and any GTAs seen to be facing difficulties with their students are contacted and provided with additional training and direct feedback on their teaching. The online survey is an annual process – hence enabling follow-up of any GTAs who face difficulties in subsequent years. Survey results are also used to identify particularly capable GTAs who may be offered additional office hours in the run-up to examinations. The best teachers may be nominated for teaching prizes, and may also be invited to contribute to the training of new class teachers in subsequent years. Some may subsequently apply for teaching fellowships of one or two years' duration. These enable GTAs to extend the range of teaching responsibilities they have, and may be seen as an important part of their career development as academics. In addition, GTAs have the option of enrolling in a Postgraduate Certificate in Higher Education, and can complete modules leading to HEA Associate and Fellow status.

(Dr Liz Barnett, Teaching and Learning Centre,
London School of Economics and Political Science)

OVERVIEW

This chapter has tried to draw attention to distinctive issues in the teaching, learning and assessment of economics. It has drawn attention to recent developments in the use of technology in teaching, approaches to handling the challenge of students' mathematical abilities, some issues relating to students with dyslexia and finally ways of effectively supporting course teams which include graduate teaching assistants. The chapter links to recent research into aspects of the student and lecturer experience in economics in the UK, conducted by the Economics Network.

REFERENCES

Becker, W E and Watts, M (1998) *Teaching Economics to Undergraduates: Alternatives to Talk and Chalk'*. Aldershot: Edward Elgar.

Chalmers, D and McCausland, W D (2002) 'Computed-assisted assessment', in *The Handbook for Economics Lecturers*, under Economics Network (2002).

Economics Network (2002) *The Handbook for Economics Lecturers*. Available online at <http://www.economicsnetwork.ac.uk/handbook/ > (accessed 14 January 2008).

Economics Network (2003) 'Is it still "chalk and talk" for economics lecturers in the UK? National survey of economics lecturers'. Available online at <http://www.economics network.ac.uk/projects/lec_survey2003_full.htm > (accessed 14 January 2008).

Economics Network (2004) 'What you need and what you got in economics higher education: results from employers' interviews and an alumni survey'. Available online at <http://www.economicsnetwork.ac.uk/projects/alumni_survey2004.pdf> (accessed 14 January 2008).

Economics Network (2005) 'Relations between teaching, research and technology in economics HE: results of the 2005 Economics Network Survey of Lecturers'. Available online at <http://www.economicsnetwork.ac.uk/projects/lec_survey2005.pdf> (accessed 14 January 2008).

Economics Network (2006) 'National Economics Students Survey (2006) Report'. Available online at <http://www.economicsnetwork.ac.uk/projects/stud_survey2006.pdf> (accessed 14 January 2008).

Forsyth, F (2002) 'Problem-based learning', in *The Handbook for Economics Lecturers*, under Economics Network (2002).

Guardian Unlimited (2007) 'Results by subject'. Available online at <http://education.guardian.co.uk/students/table/0,,1856372,00.html> (accessed 14 January 2008).

Hazlett, D (2003) 'A search-theoretic classroom experiment with money', *International Review of Economics Education* 2 (1): 80–90. Available online at <http://www.economics network.ac.uk/iree/i2/hazlett.htm > (accessed 14 January 2008).

JISC (Joint Information Systems Committee) 'TechDis'. Available online at <http://www.techdis.ac.uk/index.php?p=1_2> (accessed 14 January 2008).

Kruse, J B, Ozdemir, O and Thompson, M A (2005) 'Market forces and price ceilings: a classroom experiment', *International Review of Economics Education* 4 (2). Available online at http://www.economicsnetwork.ac.uk/iree/v4n2/kruse.pdf.

LMS (London Mathematical Society), IMA (Institute of Mathematics and its Applications), and RSS (Royal Statistical Society) (1995) 'Tackling the mathematics problem'. Available online at <http://www.lms.ac.uk/policy/tackling/report.html> (accessed 14 January 2008).

Mathcentre <http://www.mathcentre.ac.uk/search_results.php> (accessed 14 January 2008).

MIT (Massachusetts Institute of Technology) Open Courseware Project. Available online at <http://ocw.mit.edu/OcwWeb/Economics/index.htm.> (accessed 14 January 2008).

National Student Survey (2005) Reported in the *Guardian*. Available online at <http://education.guardian.co.uk/students/table/0,,1856372,00.html>.

Quality Assurance Agency for Higher Education (2007) 'Subject Benchmark Statements, Economics'. Available online at <http://www.qaa.ac.uk/academicinfrastructure/benchmark/statements/Economics.asp#p7> (accessed 5 January 2008).

Smith, A (2004) *Making Mathematics Count*. The report of Professor Adrian Smith's Inquiry into Post-14 Mathematics Education, DfES. Available online at <http://www.dfes.gov.uk/mathsinquiry/Maths_Final.pdf> (accessed 14 January 2008).

Surridge, P (2006) *The National Student Survey 2005: Findings, Higher Education Funding Council for England*, November. Available online at <http://195.194.167.100/pubs/rdreports/2006/rd22_06/NSSFindings.doc> (accessed 14 January 2008).

Trott, C (2003) 'Mathematics support for dyslexic students', *MSOR Connections* 3 (4): 17–20. Available online at <http://www.mathstore.ac.uk/newsletter/nov2003/pdf/dyslexia.pdf > (accessed 21 January 2008).

Turner, P (2006) 'Teaching undergraduate macroeconomics with the Taylor-Romer Model', *International Review of Economics Education* 5 (1): 73–82. Available online at < http://www.economicsnetwork.ac.uk/iree/v5n1/turner.pdf > (accessed 14 January 2008).

FURTHER READING

The Economics Network has two excellent resources:

Handbook for Economics Lecturers, <http://www.economicsnetwork.ac.uk/handbook/> (accessed 14 January 2008). A resource covering teaching methods, assessment, course design, etc. and useful to lecturers and teaching assistants.

International Review of Economics Education, <http://www.economicsnetwork.ac.uk/iree/> (accessed 14 January 2008). A peer-reviewed journal focused on research and practice in economics education.

Becker, W E and Watts, M (1998) See above. Based on economics teaching in the USA and written by economists for economists, with an array of practical ideas.

26 Key aspects of teaching and learning in medicine and dentistry

Adam Feather and Heather Fry

AIMS, SCOPE AND INTRODUCTION

The intention of this chapter is to elucidate some distinctive aspects of teaching and learning in medicine and dentistry for the relatively inexperienced teacher, in the context of first qualification education in British-style university medical/dental systems. There is also mention of teaching and learning in post-registration training. This chapter builds on matters considered in earlier generic chapters. Readers are especially invited to refer to the chapters on student learning, assessment, lecturing, small group teaching, e-learning and nursing.

Our general orientation is that teaching is carried out primarily to help bring about learning. **Feedback** is vital to learning, be it oral or written and from teachers, peers or patients. Self-evaluation and recognition of the need, and acquisition of the skills, to be a lifelong learner are also essential. Teaching and curriculum organisation should each create fruitful learning and assessment opportunities directed towards the production of a competent healthcare professional. These themes underpin much discussion in this chapter. We describe and comment on current practice as well as pointing to likely teaching, learning and assessment changes of the near future. This chapter focuses on:

- the curriculum and policy context in which undergraduate education takes place in the UK;
- **problem-based learning** (PBL);
- patient-centred teaching and learning;
- skills and simulation;

- using technology;
- assessment.

Despite sharing many overlapping concerns, medical and dental education also have areas of variation. Among the key differences are that at undergraduate level, dental students are more involved in invasive work with patients than their medical counterparts and that at graduation the dentist has to be capable of unsupervised, independent practice.

It is worth remembering the truism that educating doctors and dentists is a complex business. Medical and dental education involves:

- remembering a large amount of factual material;
- understanding complex mechanisms;
- competence in a range of technical skills;
- understanding and use of the scientific method;
- developing professionalism, socially responsible attitudes and ethical practice;
- deploying interpersonal skills for working with colleagues and patients;
- developing sophisticated problem-solving and diagnostic reasoning skills;
- personal skills, including self-evaluation and reflective practice.

Few educators teach all of these aspects but all need to be aware of the spectrum, and discriminating in their choice of appropriate methods for 'their' part of the curriculum, while bearing in mind that practice requires a 'holistic' rather than compartmentalised approach.

Interrogating practice

- What aims underpin an undergraduate curriculum with which you are familiar?
- Do you agree with the emphases of the aims?
- Do you think the curriculum is organised in such a way that the aims are fulfilled/attainable by most students?

THE CONTEXT OF FIRST QUALIFICATION TEACHING

The education of dentists and doctors is embedded in the practices and mores of two large service activities, namely education and the care of patients. These dual strands are present at all levels of training and are not always compatible; they are also subject to rapid policy change that impacts on how medical and dental educators can teach; we are not free agents. Other impinging matters include the unit of resource for clinical teaching and the difficulty of attracting doctors and dentists into clinical academic posts.

The General Dental Council (GDC) and the General Medical Council (GMC) have statutory responsibility for approving undergraduate/graduate entry courses and publish curriculum guidelines and recommendations. For dentistry the Quality Assurance Agency (**QAA, 2002a**) **Subject Benchmark Statement** is expected to be updated in 2007/2008, while the statement for medicine (2002b) will be subsumed into a new version of the GMC's curriculum recommendations over a similar time-scale.

In 1993 the GMC set out radical and extensive requirements for undergraduate curricula. The updated GMC document, *Tomorrow's Doctors* (2003), the outcomes of further consultation (GMC, 2006a), *The New Doctor* (GMC, 2005) and *Good Medical Practice* (GMC, 2006b), set the context and requirements for university medical curricula. Among newer expectations and recommendations are the encouragement of innovation around a core curriculum of skills, knowledge and attitudes taught in an integrated manner, interprofessional training and greater emphasis on reflective and ethical practice. Greater emphasis is also placed on learning and study skills, being curious and critical in approaching knowledge and acquiring understanding of underlying principles, concepts and mechanisms rather than the teaching and regurgitation of enormous amounts of material. This is compatible with contemporary understanding of how students and professionals learn (see Chapter 2), but also needs to be aligned with provision of high-quality and safe patient care. Today most UK schools have a 'core plus options' approach to curricula, and use case or problem-based methods of delivery (see section on PBL, p. 427). Some core skills and knowledge are now often taught with other healthcare undergraduates, including nurses, therapists and radiographers. Preparation for professional practice is emphasised. Assessment has generally lagged a little behind other curricular reforms.

Early this century the desire to change the demographics of medical student entry led to the creation of new medical schools and graduate entry programmes. These, pioneered in the UK by St George's Medical School, University of London, attract graduates from higher education. With more mature learning skills these students pass through an accelerated programme. This, the merger of several London medical schools creating year cohorts of over 350 students, and the changing knowledge of undergraduates entering higher education, have challenged curriculum leaders to devise bespoke and effective solutions, including means of accessing patients or exploring effective alternatives (see sections on simulation and technology, pp. 436, 437).

The GDC radically revised undergraduate curriculum recommendations in the late 1990s, and further updated them in 2002; these recommendations brought an evolutionary shift. The GDC emphasised its desire to see educationally progressive ideas and improved methods of study incorporated into curricula that were also to exhibit reduced congestion and earlier patient contact. The GDC recommendations are more prescriptive of 'essential elements' than the medical equivalent. The composite recommendations of the GDC visits to dental schools provide a good summary of recent practices and indicate areas in which the GDC would like to see further movement, including working in a dental team and the further development of outreach teaching that makes use of learning technology (GDC, 2006).

Postgraduate training in the UK has been the subject of much recent change and scrutiny and has increasing impact on undergraduate education. There is growing concern for a more holistic view of undergraduate and postgraduate training and for a continuum of learning and updating extending until retirement. The vocational year for newly qualified dentists is a requirement prior to independent National Health Service (NHS) practice and specialty registers were established some years ago. In postgraduate medicine several far-reaching and hugely challenging changes have occurred in political control and the structure of training. In 2005 the government set up the Postgraduate Medical Education and Training Board responsible for post-graduate training. In 2006, as a by-product of Sir Liam Donaldson's 'Unfinished business' (DoH, 2002), Modernising Medical Careers (MMC) was born. MMC saw the creation of the 'Foundation Programme', encompassing the first two postgraduate training years and the specialist 'run-through' training programmes. These were competency based, educationally supervised and structured with defined outcomes. They promised to 'improve patient care by delivering a modernised and focussed career structure for doctors' (MMC, 2007a). The Tooke Report (MMC, 2007b) is likely to result in further change.

In coming years with increasing clinical responsibilities being given to allied healthcare professionals, the further development of interprofessional practice, the shift to primary care, the growing use of evidence-based practice, enhanced use of technology, and more specialities entering the postgraduate preserve, the role of dentists and doctors will continue to evolve. All these developments have implications for undergraduate curriculum design, teaching, workplace learning and assessment. Among possibilities on the horizon are national undergraduate exit assessment and a national core curriculum.

Interrogating practice

Are you familiar with national recommendations for undergraduate and postgraduate training operating in your country and speciality?

PROBLEM-BASED LEARNING

Problem-based learning is an idea that has had currency since the 1960s (Neufeld and Barrows, 1974), but was not widely used in medical and dental education in the UK until the mid-1990s. It is now an element in many UK medical and dental undergraduate curricula, in some cases being the main organising principle and pedagogical method.

Case study 1: Problem-based learning – progressive release version

Problem-based learning (PBL) takes many forms, but there are really only two types of pure PBL – the short case version and the progressive release version. The short case format is generally used in courses designed for school leavers; the progressive release version for graduates or more mature students. Both versions use the same underlying principles (see below).

In the short case format, students are given a short trigger (e.g. a clinical case, a photograph, a newspaper or journal article), usually no more than a page long. In the progressive release version, the facilitator gives the students a much longer scenario in stages (see Figure 26.1). Students discuss each stage fully, before moving on to the next part of the scenario. Key to the process is the 'inquiry strategy' where students have to decide what history, examination, investigations and treatment would be appropriate, *prior* to receiving the results of their inquiries (i.e. students are required to think like doctors).

An example (each paragraph is a separate trigger and the whole PBL is much condensed):

Michael Hennessy, a 55-year-old architect, presented to his GP with stomach pain. He said he had been violently sick the night before after attending a celebration dinner with some friends at a local curry house.

Students hypothesise possible causes and suggest questions to ask Mr Hennessy which would help them distinguish between their hypotheses.

Mr Hennessy explained that the severe pain lasted for about five hours and then slowly subsided. He felt perfectly healthy again after a good night's sleep. He put it down to 'something he ate'. He admitted that the same thing had happened a few days before, but the pain had not lasted for quite so long. When asked where the pain was, he pointed to the epigastric region and right hypochondrium. He described the pain as colicky and griping and it seemed to move around to his back. He had taken paracetamol and that had helped the pain somewhat.

Students debate how this information has helped them and suggest what examination the doctor might carry out.

Mr Hennessy's height was 178cm and his weight was 105kg. His oral temperature was 36.6°C. Dr Oshima, the GP, noted that his sclerae were yellow, though there was no pallor of the conjunctivae. There were no signs of chronic liver disease. His mouth was dry. He had tenderness in the right upper quadrant of his abdomen and Dr Oshima could not press too deeply here. There was no demonstrable rebound tenderness. There was no organomegaly or ascites. Bowel sounds were present. Mr Hennessy's blood pressure was 130/90mmHg, and his pulse rate was 80 beats/minute. Dr Oshima asked Mr Hennessy to provide a fresh urine sample. The sample was dark brown in colour. Asked about his stools, he admitted that he had noticed they had been a bit paler than usual.

Students discuss the implications of the new information and suggest investigations which might be carried out. They discuss the relevant anatomy of the hepatobiliary tree, jaundice and the significance of the results.

The students are then supplied with the results of relevant investigations including blood tests and an ultrasound scan; they discuss the significance of these findings and suggest what further action should be taken.

An ERCP was arranged which confirmed the presence of several small stones in the common bile-duct.

The students compare and contrast the techniques for detecting stones. They discuss informed consent for ERCP and suggest treatments.

A sphincterotomy was performed to remove the stones.

The students discuss what they know about the procedure, alternatives and prognosis.

The case would then develop further with such complications as a post-operative infection, recurrence of the gallstones or perhaps a subsequent infection with hepatitis. At each stage, the students draw up a list of topics to research and feedback on. A single case usually spans three tutorials, and may be up to 20 pages long, depending on its complexity.

Students enjoy this way of learning. They are in control and decide what to research, and because they all research every learning issue, the debate during feedback is often at a very high level and enormously stimulating for the staff to listen to. The different members of the group bring different experiences to the tutorial, depending on their background knowledge. They feed off each other's skills and knowledge. This form of PBL mirrors real life, albeit in slow motion, and helps the students to think clinically, learn medical terminology and interpret clinical data (especially since they are supplied with real lab reports, radiological tests, photomicrographs and patient discharge summaries). At the same time, the students learn their basic science through these 'real' cases. Although their learning is less detailed, it is much more relevant, deeper and more lasting. Students have a problem knowing whether or not they have learnt enough in PBL. They only really find this out when they are assessed. But it is the cases, not the assessment, that drives the learning. The assessment defines the *depth* of their learning. By asking searching questions where students have to reason and apply their knowledge, they learn to reach beneath the trivial detail and get at the underlying concepts. That is what PBL is all about. And it's great fun.

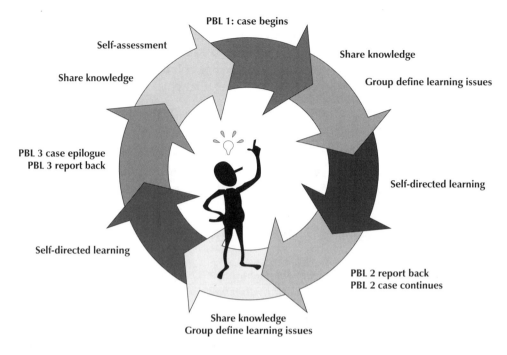

Figure 26.1 PBL at St George's

(Professor Peter McCrorie, St George's Medical School, University of London)

Boud and Feletti (1997) provide an excellent review of the range and variations of the different models of PBL. Among the most distinctive aspects are:

- learning and teaching stems from, and comes after, exposure to a scenario or trigger (the 'problem') which is presented without prior detailed teaching of all the material involved;
- students, not the teacher, make the immediate decisions about what they will research/learn in relation to a scenario;
- a non-didactic tutor/facilitator;
- interrogation of clinical and non-clinical subject matter;
- students report back and discuss their findings.

Teachers starting to use PBL often find they need to develop new skills. The following guidelines are useful pointers. The facilitator:

- is not there to lecture. The facilitator keeps the process true, guides but never leads the students (avoiding misinformation), and (in many versions) assesses performance;

- establishes or reiterates group ground rules when taking a new group;
- assists students to fulfil their roles, but does not usurp their positions;
- assists in creating an exploratory and non-threatening *learning* environment;
- ensures that students feel able to question and query each other, using an appropriate manner;
- encourages students to use and formally evaluate a wide variety of information sources, including the internet;
- assists students to present cogently;
- asks students periodically to summarise a case or aspects of it;
- at the end of each problem asks students to evaluate how they tackled the problem and suggests how the process could have been more effective;
- gives feedback to the students about their performance in a specific, constructive manner (generally within the group setting).

No matter what version of PBL is used, it is important to train staff and students in its usage, provide adequate tutorial and study rooms and ensure that learning resources are available. Like other teaching modes, PBL requires assessment methods appropriate to the expected learning outcomes and suitable evaluation (see Chapter 14). Time is needed for curriculum planning, writing, updating, and rewriting problems and assessments, and developing supporting tutorial material.

In Case study 1 the author refers to the perceived benefits of PBL. Much research into its impact has been conducted. Early classics still worth consulting include: Schmidt *et al.*, 1987; Norman and Schmidt, 1992; Vernon and Blake, 1993; Albanese and Mitchell, 1993. Challenge and counter-challenge are still occurring and more recent pieces worthy of consideration include: Dolmans (2003); Dolmans and Schmidt (2006); and Neville and Norman (2007).

There is some evidence that:

- PBL students take more of a **deep approach to learning** (see Chapter 2);
- students on traditional curricula tend to score slightly higher on conventional tests of knowledge, but PBL students retain their knowledge longer;
- students perceive PBL as more clinically relevant and rate their programmes more positively.

Interrogating practice

- Make a list of pros and cons about PBL that you think are important.
- If you use PBL now, what do you think of the way your school uses it: does it maximise its potential benefits? Why/how might that be different?
- If you do not use PBL, could you introduce it into any teaching you are connected with? Is the effort likely to be worth the rewards?

PATIENT-CENTRED TEACHING AND LEARNING

Clinical teaching is a three-way dynamic between teacher, patient and student. It occurs in the workplace environment. As the controlling factor, the teacher is obliged to maximise the situation from all perspectives. With earlier clinical exposure, students may be forced to develop a more balanced approach to the acquisition of knowledge, technical skills and professional attitudes and behaviours; it is important in initiating students into a **community of practice**.

The patient

Whenever and wherever clinical teaching occurs the patient is the most vulnerable of the three parties. Most medical patients find clinical teaching extremely rewarding, often commenting that they feel students 'have to learn'. In dentistry there is a slightly different relationship. Patients receive treatment from a novice under instruction. Their vulnerability is magnified and the teacher has added (statutory) responsibilities. The patient must be reassured that a watchful eye is being cast. In both cases, patients' attitude towards being used in teaching should always be respected and it should be reinforced that, whatever their decision, it will not affect their treatment and care. Within any teaching centre, patients should be made aware that the facility is a teaching environment and that students may be present, or, in the case of dental students, carrying out the required treatment. This allows patients to prepare for the initial encounter and to raise any anxieties they may have. At all times one needs to keep the patient informed, reach mutual agreement about the session, and most importantly, ensure that patient privacy and dignity are maintained. One should explain to the medical patient the number and level of the students who will be in attendance and the patient's proposed role. Verbal agreement should be obtained and documented. Dental sessions differ in that the patient is being treated and followed up by the student under the supervision of the teacher. The dental supervisor must approve the proposed treatment, ensure that it has been explained correctly to the patient and review its course and outcomes.

The student

With new curricula in the UK, students from a very early stage of their training will meet the challenges of the clinical environment. As with the patient, good preparation reduces anxieties, and sets out a clear level of professional conduct.

Before students are ready to interact with patients they need to practise basic clinical and communication skills. This should occur in a safe, supportive environment such as that of a clinical skills centre (see next section). For dental students, competence in core skills will have to be demonstrated prior to their introduction to the clinical arena.

The dental student is immediately faced with professional obligations, and the teacher must stress their responsibility to their patients. Punctuality, appearance, including cleanliness, background reading and practice of skills need to be emphasised. Students should be encouraged to attend clinical sessions in the right frame of mind.

Experiential learning is key in clinical learning (see Chapter 2). The teacher should make provision for teaching and learning when patients are unable to attend; **self-directed learning (SDL)** and **computer-aided learning (CAL)** will allow students to test knowledge and skills at their own pace.

For medical students, their clinical experience is all too often a rather less demanding time. However, they too should demonstrate similar professional obligation and be in possession of basic equipment such as a stethoscope. Before they go on the ward or into the clinic, students should be well briefed.

Students should not be placed in an unsupported environment or pressured into performing tasks that are beyond their level of training or conflict with cultural beliefs. Students may encounter ethical dilemmas, but they should not be asked to face them without guidance.

The teacher

For the clinician, the clinical environment will be one in which they feel comfortable. They will be familiar with the setting and staff, and hopefully aware of the potential problems that may be encountered while teaching.

Interrogating practice

Drawing on your experiences, how could you improve your own and other clinical environments to facilitate the needs of learners?

Full-time members of university staff undertake much dental undergraduate clinical teaching. Traditionally this has removed many hazards familiar to the 'part-time' medical teacher, but as dental students participate more in community settings the issues experienced by medicine are increasingly being felt. Bedside teaching often involves the teacher, patient and several students. In contrast, teaching in the dental clinic involves several students, each with their own patient, being overseen by one teacher. A teacher–student ratio of about 1:8 is common. Dental and, increasingly, medical students work closely with other healthcare professionals from an early stage of their training and the supervisor should be aware of this relationship and its development. The teacher's role is one of supervision, guidance and ensuring the safety of all participants.

On the wards it may be necessary to check that the patient(s) you wish to use in teaching are not going to be 'employed' in procedures or investigations. Check that your session does not encroach into ward routines. Locations and times may suddenly need to be changed, but the onus is firmly on the teacher to try to be punctual and prepared, or at least to inform students and patients of unavoidable changes. (Medical students often quote lack of information and disregard by the clinical staff as reasons for recurrent non-attendance.)

Whatever the setting, the teacher should not use the patient session to lecture, or use the patient as a 'chalkboard' or living text. The guiding principle in medicine should be one of demonstration and observation, with opportunities for practice as far as it is safe and ethical. Feedback on practice (from tutor, peers, self and patient where appropriate) is key but often neglected. In dentistry the chairside role is primarily that of advice and supervision. For the teacher, student–patient interactions may appear routine but for the other parties they are often complex and require a great deal of guidance, particularly in the early stages of training. Opportunistic teaching may present itself in both contexts and should never be overlooked; indeed in medicine detailed and advanced planning of much patient-based teaching is often impossible. In the medical setting clinicians need to be aware of the overall goals (**learning outcomes**) of the rotation of the student and have thought about how patient encounters may contribute to their being achieved. Questioning, from teacher to students and students to teacher, is an important skill in clinical teaching (see the section 'Questioning', pp. 81–82 in Chapter 6), but again respect for the patient needs to be considered. Good preparation and time for student **reflection** and feedback should be built into sessions.

Clinical teaching and learning is exciting and rewarding, but in the NHS of the twenty-first century it has become increasingly challenging. Points to consider when teaching in a patient-centred environment include:

- patient, student and teacher safety and anxieties;
- introduction of students to the clinical environment;
- skills acquisition, practice, feedback and assessment;
- observation, modelling and practice of professional behaviours;
- teaching versus treatment.

Clinical settings are having ever-increasing teaching demands placed upon them. This is one reason why simulation is growing as a context for learning. While it has many advantages and benefits, simulation should be used to augment and not replace the real clinical experience.

SKILLS AND SIMULATION IN TEACHING AND LEARNING

For many years clinical medicine and dentistry were taught by the principle of 'See one, do one, teach one'. The inception and use of simulation within clinical teaching and learning has allowed students to confront their anxieties within a safe environment, while

Interrogating practice

- How does the NHS of today influence the way students observe and learn clinical skills?
- How does the learning environment of the clinical skills centre differ from that of the clinical arena?

providing the teacher with a regulated, reproducible teaching arena. The simulated element will most commonly refer to materials, actors and role play.

A clinical skills centre or laboratory is incorporated into the infrastructure of most medical and dental schools in the Western world. Most now incorporate high-fidelity and virtual reality simulators, as well as SDL and CAL facilities. We found (at a medical school at which we both worked) that the employment of a dedicated skills teacher revolutionised the use and potential of the centre, as have others (e.g. at the University of Leeds Medical School (Stark *et al.*, 1998)).

Peyton, a general surgeon, describes an excellent, and widely advocated, model for teaching skills, in simulated settings and otherwise, known as the 'four-stage approach'.

Stage 1

Demonstration of the skill at normal speed, with little or no explanation.

Stage 2

Repetition of the skill with full explanation, encouraging the learner to ask questions.

Stage 3

The demonstrator performs the skill for a third time, with the learner providing the cue and explanation of each step and being questioned on key issues. The demonstrator provides necessary corrections. This step may need to be repeated several times until the demonstrator is satisfied that the learner fully understands the skill.

Interrogating practice

If you are not already using it, how could you adapt Peyton's four-stage approach to your own (simulated or non-simulated) clinical teaching?

Stage 4

The learner now carries out the skill under close supervision, describing each step before it is taken (adapted from Peyton, 1998: 174–177).

This model may be expanded or reduced depending on the background skills of the learner. Digital/video recording may be used in stages 1 and 2. As in all teaching, the learner should be given constructive feedback and allowed time for self-appraisal, reflection and practice of the skills. Within the medical clinical skills centre, particularly in SDL, we have found the use of itemised checklists useful adjuncts to learning, particularly for the novice.

Simulation

Role play is an extremely useful teaching and learning tool. Students are able to investigate, practise and explore all sides of a clinical interaction through their adopted roles; these advantages may need to be pointed out to the student. Criticisms of this technique are usually a product of poorly prepared sessions. Clear roles, with demonstration by teachers, or using preprepared videos/DVDs, are useful ways of directing student learning. Providing a supportive but quite formal environment during the sessions also encourages students to maintain their role. Prewarned, with adequate debriefing and reflection, the students usually find this a useful technique.

Simulated patients (SPs) were first used in the 1960s; their use in dental and medical undergraduate and postgraduate education has expanded rapidly since the 1980s (Barrows, 1993). They may be used instead of real patients in difficult clinical scenarios (e.g. breaking bad news and in the reproduction of acute problems that would not be assessable in traditional clinical examinations). In North America, and more recently in the UK, trained real patients (patient as educator programmes) are increasingly used (e.g. in the UK at the Sheffield University and King's College London – see references), including in training and assessing intimate clinical procedures such as vaginal speculum or breast examination. In dentistry, SPs are principally used for communication skills training and in assessment (Davenport *et al.*, 1998).

Simulation of clinical scenarios has become increasingly sophisticated. Within the safety of this setting, students can express themselves more freely while investigating the patient perspective through the eyes of the actors. The teacher must provide a clear brief for both actor and student, including detailed background scripts for the actors (see Case study 2 in Chapter 2). It is important that students feel reasonably comfortable in their given role and that the scenario is within their expected capabilities. Clear student learning objectives/outcomes are required at all stages, but excessive demands and expectations are often counterproductive. The simulation of clinical procedures and communications skills at the same time, in settings as near to the real as possible, is of increasing interest; this type of simulation also adds to realism/complexity in assessment

(Kneebone *et al.*, 2006a, 2006b). Even at undergraduate level, assessing simple clinical skills in isolation in simulated manners is unlikely to adequately prepare students for practice in the real world.

Interrogating practice

- What are the positive and negative attributes of simulation?
- How far can and should patients be used in training?
- What should be the role of simulation in assessment?

USING TECHNOLOGY IN LEARNING IN MEDICINE AND DENTISTRY

Chapter 7 considers the use of e-learning and should be read in conjunction with this section. In medicine and dentistry we are concerned with the use of computers, but also many other forms of technology, including that involved in much simulation. Most medical and dental schools in the Western world have been using various types of technology in teaching for some time, including the ubiquitous **Virtual Learning Environment**. Some schools use proprietary brands, others tailor-made products. These may be used only for information dissemination and as repositories of information, but in most instances will be used more imaginatively to include student-to-student and student-to-teacher interaction, online quizzes with feedback, use of videoed material and so on. Video material involving patients requires close attention to be paid to consent and confidentiality issues. A fairly standard approach to creating SDL e-packages is to integrate a lecture, clinical demonstration, case-based learning using anonymised patient notes, short answers, pathways through diagnosis or care, and a quiz. Such packages are costly and usually require the teacher to work with a learning technologist.

Computer-based learning opportunities exploit self-study at convenient times in a self-paced manner, may make better use of scarce resources, and solve difficulty with venues of insufficient size for a full cohort of students. But they need to be planned, designed and coordinated if they are to integrate successfully with everything else going on in a curriculum. The 'information dump' end of the spectrum has its uses (e.g. it is easy for students to look up missed lectures), but it falls into the trap of transmission rather than transformation in relation to learning (Mezirow, 1991). Another potential danger is of a depersonalised or artificial experience. Some schools are starting to experiment with second-generation technology using **wikis** and **blogs**, and other less static and teacher-controlled environments, including websites designed originally for social interaction rather than learning. Other technologies, including the use of handheld computers, mobile phones, **podcasts**, **Personal Response Systems** ('clickers'), interactive whiteboards and virtual reality, are also becoming increasingly utilised. An important issue for medicine and dentistry is to consider what any form of technology offers that particularly relates to the nature of the discipline and how students learn it. One feature of technology in teaching is that some types can be very time-consuming to set up; also an un-coordinated, non-cross curriculum approach may sometimes lead to student confusion and a lack of institutional learning about how to best use technology.

Interrogating practice

- How do any of these technologies fit into your current educational practice?
- Could you further enhance their effective use?
- What access do you have to training, a learning technologist and an e-learning strategy for your school?

Among the areas of learning in medical and dental education that are/might be enhanced by the use of technology are:

- streaming demonstrations or interviews (e.g. of clinical and communication skills, including taking a history). Filming these, provided it is done professionally, can be advantageous in many ways (e.g. making full use of scarce resources); opportunities for student activity and thought need to be added;
- the opportunity for simulated practice to precede or enhance practice in the real world, including the use of virtual reality;
- a means of maintaining a community of practice and commonality of approach when students are distributed to different clinical sites;
- handheld devices for learning logs, and computers for electronic portfolios (see Case study 3);
- capacity to represent three-dimensionally and offer manipulation (e.g. of molecules or anatomy);
- access to web information or loading reference texts on to handheld computers can aid learning, including in 'down' moments in the clinical setting, and may enhance an evidence-based approach to practice;
- many medical techniques and investigations rely on technology (e.g. imaging) and this may also be used for teaching and learning – having the additional benefit of familiarising students with how to 'read' the output.

Technology is also increasingly relevant to assessment. This ranges from the online **MCQ** that can give feedback to learners about their answers or ask learners to think about their confidence in their answer (Gardner-Medwin, 2006), to opportunities for examiners to assess at a distance.

We have not generally provided references to materials in this chapter, as they rapidly go out of date. In the UK the 01 (Medical, Dental and Veterinary) Subject Centre has much up-to-date information on its website covering new developments, open access repositories and so on (see HEA Subject Centre under Further reading). It has also been among the funders of small-scale research to investigate the efficacy and drawback of various technology-based approaches. (It is also useful for many other aspects of medical and dental education.)

Some caveats about the use of technology are appropriate. Using technology:

- can involve a high up-front cost, but can yield a good pay-off if used selectively and appropriately;
- does not (necessarily) remove the desirability/need for real-life practice;
- is expensive;
- should include promotion of thinking, learning and giving feedback, rather than just providing information.

Few university teachers are highly adept in using technology effectively; specialised training may help. Evidence for the impact and efficacy of technology is still in the early days. Technology often needs to be blended with other methods and appropriate use sought according to the topic under study. All of that said, our own experience is that students expect to use technology, take to it readily and urge on imaginative developments.

Case study 2 demonstrates how a variety of methods can be brought together to present a complete learning environment, including the incorporation of technology. This example is about anatomy teaching, but there are many other curriculum areas where technology can be used effectively and imaginatively as part of the diet of teaching and learning.

Case study 2: Anatomy teaching and learning at Peninsula Medical School

What do we do?

The Peninsula Medical School is pioneering an integrated, comprehensive and 'humanistic' approach to the teaching and learning of anatomy across all five years of our course. There is no dissection or prosection of cadavers within the programme.

Learning is triggered through exposure to common or important clinical scenarios, which may be paper-based, using simulated patients, or through real encounters in the clinical environment. Learning is intensively supported through Life Science Resource Centres in each locality. In the first two years, this student-led approach to anatomy learning is supplemented with expert-led tutorials that are clinically relevant and involve tasks to promote active learning. They incorporate living models, radiological imaging and virtual teaching tools. This approach develops an appreciation of gross anatomy from the outside (surface anatomy) inwards, aided by visual observation, body projection, palpation and auscultation. The innovative use of body projections (anatomical images projected on to the surface of a human body that may be taken sequentially, as in dissection, through the underlying layers of the body), body painting and digital surface anatomy atlases helps the students construct a 3D picture from the surface inwards.

Why do we do it?

Our approach was motivated by three main factors: (1) a desire to place the learning in a patient-centred context; (2) a concern that distinct pre-clinical/clinical phases to the programme could make it difficult to ensure that anatomy is learnt in a way that is clinically relevant and could be applied directly in medical practice; (3) the recent technological developments enable the learning of anatomy to be more authentic to modern clinical practice.

The feedback so far

Students appear to enjoy the expert-led tutorials and learning anatomy in a clinical context. Some express anxiety about their anatomy knowledge but the evidence from assessment confirms that anatomy learning increases steadily across the five-year programme. Our evaluation of the approach is ongoing but the early signs are encouraging.

(Dr Karen Mattick, Mr James Oldham, Dr Tudor Chinnah, Dr Russell Davies, Dr David Bristow, Peninsula Medical School)

ASSESSMENT

The assessment challenge is to use appropriate methods, following the basic guidelines of assessment (see Chapter 10, and Crosby, 2002). Assessment should be **valid**, **reliable**, **fair**, feasible, defendable and well conceived from the perspective of impact on learning.

Interrogating practice

List the types of assessment with which you are familiar. For each type consider if it assesses knowing, thinking, technical skills, attitudes and/or behaviour.

In the 1960s and 1970s, the assessment of medical undergraduates was similar worldwide and had remained largely unchanged since Sir George Paget introduced clinical graduating examinations in the 1840s. Written assessments consisted of free response essay questions, and clinical assessments were traditional 'long' and 'short' cases, with most schools using **viva voce**. The principal problems with these forms of assessments were that the written assessments had both weak validity and reliability and the short and long cases, despite their relatively strong validity, had poor reliability. In addition, students were able to compensate for poor performance in one domain or assessment with better performance in another. Methods for combining marks were often inadequate. The viva voce, perhaps the least reliable of all these assessments, was often used to make critical decisions around the pass/fail borderline, and for the awarding of 'excellence'.

Cynics may point to the emergence of examination litigation, notably within the USA, as a reason for change in assessment methods, but there are other, more cogent reasons, especially needing surety that we assess the main things we want students to know, do and understand and that qualifying doctors and dentists have all attained certain minimum standards. Maastricht psychometricians (notably Van der Vleuten and Schuwirth) have been prominent, along with the American National Board of Medical Education (Case, Swanson and Norcini) and the Medical Council of Canada, in introducing greater reliability into assessment in medicine, and by osmosis into dentistry.

From the early 1990s there was greater 'objectification' of medical assessment (Van der Vleuten *et al.*, 1991) and with it, an increase in reliability. Since about 2004 the pendulum has swung to put more emphasis on validity and on more difficult to assess qualities such as **reflective practice**, ethical behaviour and decision-making. Van der Vleuten and Schuwirth (2004, 2005) and Schuwirth and Van der Vleuten (2006) now counsel assessors that over-reliance on any one property pushes others out of the picture, which is also detrimental. These changes are reflected in new forms of postgraduate assessment, such as the work-based assessments (see later), all of which are having an influence at undergraduate level. In undergraduate curricula there has been a major shift away from a 'big bang' graduating examination towards continuous assessment, led by Liverpool and Dundee medical schools. This has shifted the emphasis of final examinations to 'fitness to practise'. Keys to good assessment include making it compatible with what is expected from learners (i.e. with learning outcomes) and realising that few types of test are perfect; a range is often needed both to adequately sample and to assess the different domains of knowledge, behaviours and attitudes and also to allow for variability in candidates' performance in any single assessment format.

The future of written assessment

The next ten years may signal the death of 'written'/paper-based examinations. Computer-assisted assessment can and is being used for multiple choice questions (MCQ) and **extended matching questions (EMQs),** and lends itself more easily to the testing of complex data, radiology, histology and anatomy. Virtual reality will also add to this potential. With the development of software to recognise 'handwriting', typed prose **short answer questions (SAQs)** and indeed essays/projects may be computer marked. An excellent guide to writing test questions is available online from the National Board of Medical Examiners (2007).

With MCQs, single best answer (SBA) questions have become the gold standard. At Barts and the London, UK, we have trialled the use of 'contextualised SBAs' which incorporate several positive characteristics of SAQs and MCQs. These retain a high reliability but allow greater flexibility than do conventional MCQs. MCQs and SAQs are common to many disciplines, but EMQs have been developed in medicine to assess higher levels of cognition, including diagnostic reasoning (Case and Swanson, 1996).

Updating clinical assessment: (1) the short case

The description of the **objective structured clinical examination** (OSCE) (Harden and Gleeson, 1979) heralded the demise of the long and short case. Since the early 1990s the OSCE has become widely used in both undergraduate and postgraduate assessment.

Interrogating practice

Thinking about the characteristics of a 'good' assessment, what do you believe are the advantages and disadvantages of using an OSCE?

Without doubt OSCEs potentially fulfil many of the criteria that form a 'good' assessment. However, their positive attributes must be weighed against their expense (we have calculated that they are 50 per cent more expensive than the older-style examinations), the resources required to run a single examination (venues, patients, actors, examiners and support staff) and the time. Our experience is that people can 'abuse' the OSCE format; commonly, pass/fail decisions are made using too few stations, the areas tested are sometimes unsuitable for OSCEs (and could often be more rigorously tested using other formats) and stations may lack context and complexity due to poor question setting or failure to increase the time needed.

Updating clinical assessment: (2) the long case

A more objective format of the traditional long case is the observed long case (Newble, 1991) and the **objective structured long examination record** (OSLER) (Gleeson, 1992). All the candidates are observed by examiners, see similar patients, and identical aspects of the case are assessed using an OSCE style checklist. Wass and Jolly (2001) argue that the observed long case can produce an equally reliable and valid assessment as the OSCE, while testing a more holistic approach to the patient.

Medical students commonly cite that they are rarely, if ever, observed by their tutors clerking and performing procedures on patients. As the assessments adopted in UK postgraduate training (see below) filter into undergraduate education this shortfall may be reduced.

Updating clinical assessment: (3) the viva voce

The viva voce is still used as a summative assessment tool but is regarded by many as educationally defective and indefensible. It is the least reliable of any form of clinical assessment because it uses only two examiners and its unstructured format can result in a very variable interaction. The issue of content specificity has a major effect on its reliability. It too has undergone 'objectification' and, where it is still employed, is much more structured. While it is still too unreliable to employ as stand-alone summative assessment, our view is that with station-based interviewing now becoming common-place at all stages of medical training, the viva may once again become a popular formative assessment tool.

Updating clinical assessment: (4) log-books and reflective writing

Log-books have long been used to record clinical exposure and practice. However, in their traditional form they were often subject to abuse, even in the more supervised dental environment. This abuse was often a result of short cuts, poor objectives and unrealistic targets. In response to this criticism, the use of the log-book has changed. Students should now be encouraged to use them to record and reflect upon clinical events in which they have taken part, including reflecting on and evaluating their own performance. Entries in the log-book should be monitored and commented upon, so directing the student's learning. Thus they may (also) be used as a formative assessment tool to promote learning, reflection and personal development, as described in Case study 3.

Case study 3: Reflective log-books and portfolios for dentistry

Reflective practice has been prominent in undergraduate dental studies and immediately post-qualification during the vocational training period for many years. The Dearing Report (**NCIHE**, 1997) expected that all higher education bodies would embed a Progress File by 2007 as a means to record achievement, monitor, and build and reflect upon personal development to be used throughout an individual's working life.

Dentistry developed reflective log-books, initially in paper format, and primarily as a tool to promote learning, planning and recording achievement for dental therapists in training and professional practice (Fry *et al.*, 2002). The success of this system was dependent on integration into dental programmes and cultural change within institutions and practices. The logging of daily clinical practice was supplemented by activities to encourage reflection on that practice. Characteristics such as openness of discourse, networking and a dialogue between teacher and student, including feedback, became everyday practice. There are barriers to implementing such systems and it was important for schools and deaneries to work as a team and generate a 'fit-for-purpose' approach.

Undergraduates found many benefits to using the Progress File when the scheme was extended to them (Davenport, 2005). Encouraged by this, the system has been embedded in several schools, recently in electronic form. Anecdotal evidence from graduates moving into vocational training has also been encouraging; they are keen to continue to use such tools as it enables them to map their learning needs.

The e-Progress File (ePF) has been adapted by schools to suit their needs. It is clear that time should be set aside within the curriculum to receive and give feedback about work carried out, to record clinical experience accurately and grade each session. In addition to reflective practice the e-PF encourages the student to become self-critical and develop other key skills such as communication. Such an educational tool is not static and adjustments are constantly made, if only to make it more user-friendly for student and tutor and useful into vocational training and beyond. These reflective log-books have been commended and recognised as an important learning tool by the General Dental Council and QAA visitors.

(Professor Elizabeth Davenport, Barts and the London School of Medicine and Dentistry, Queen Mary, University of London)

Updating clinical assessment: (5) work-based assessment

Interrogating practice

What are the advantages and disadvantages of work-based assessments with which you are familiar?

The rapidly changing UK postgraduate training environment has brought with it increasing direct assessment of trainees in the workplace. The assessments being used include the mini-CEX (clinical evaluation exercise), direct observation of procedures (DoPs), case-based discussion (CbD) and multisource feedback (MSF), as well as reflective logs. For a full description see MMC (2007a). While still in an evolutionary phase, these assessments give a measure of validity to an individual's training, and allow competence, excellence and perhaps most importantly underperformance to be documented, discussed and used for progression and competitive interview; they have both alternative and summative character. Recording will become increasingly electronic. The introduction of these assessment formats has not been trouble-free. Work-based assessment is becoming increasingly used at undergraduate level.

OVERVIEW

Medical and dental teaching and learning have recently undergone 'major surgery' with the aim of 'anastamozing' sound educational theory with traditional teaching and learning methods. New curricula, with student-driven learning, 'objectification' and innovation within assessment, and the changing postgraduate structure have left much for the 'jobbing' clinician and new teacher to keep up with.

Many in the older undergraduate schools question whether the revolution in medical and dental education is worthwhile. Evidence, although measured on older criteria, suggests that these major changes are not producing a 'better' graduate but are producing a different, perhaps more rounded, individual, one in whom the public can place confidence. As professionals, we are coming under increasing public scrutiny and this is never truer than in education. We must apply the same evidence-based approach to our teaching practice as we do to scientific research or clinical practice. Traditional methods do not necessarily need to be thrown away, but can be improved and brought into line with modern educational theory and practice and the requirement for a 'safe' doctor or dentist in the twenty-first century.

REFERENCES

Albanese, M and Mitchell, S (1993) 'Problem-based learning: a review of literature on its outcomes and implementation issues', *Academic Medicine*, 68 (1): 52–81.

Barrows, H (1993) 'An overview of the uses of standardized patients for teaching and evaluating clinical skills', *Academic Medicine*, 68: 443–453.

Boud, D and Feletti, G (eds) (1997) *The Challenge of Problem-based Learning*, London: Kogan Page.

Case, S and Swanson, D (eds) (1996) *Constructing Written Test Questions for the Basic and Clinical Sciences*, Philadelpia, PA: National Board of Medical Designs.

Crosby, J (2002) 'Assessment', in S Huttly, J Sweet and I Taylor (eds), *Effective Learning and Teaching in Medical, Dental and Veterinary Education*, London: Kogan Page.

Davenport, E (2005) 'Project focus: a progress file learning system', *Subject Centre Medicine, Dentistry and Veterinary Medicine, 01.8*18–19.

Davenport, E, Davis, J, Cushing, A and Holsgrove, G (1998) 'An innovation in the assessment of future dentists', *British Dental Journal*, 184 (4): 192–195.

Department of Health (DoH) (2002) *Unfinished Business: Proposals for Reform of the Senior House Officer Grade – A Paper for Consultation*, London: DoH.

Dolmans, D (2003) 'The effectiveness of PBL: the debate continues. Some concerns about the BEME movement', *Medical Education*, 37(12): 1129–1130.

Dolmans, D H and Schmidt, H G (2006) 'What do we know about cognitive and motivational effects of small group tutorials in problem-based learning?', *Advances in Health Sciences Education*, 11(4): 321–336.

Fry, H, Davenport, E S, Woodman, T and Pee, B. (2002) 'Developing Progress Files: a case report', *Teaching in Higher Education*, 7: 97–111.

Gardner-Medwin, A (2006) 'Confidence-based marking: towards deeper learning and better exams', in C. Bryan and K. Clegg, K (eds), *Innovative Assessment in Higher Education*, Abingdon: Routledge.

General Dental Council (GDC) (2002) *The First Five Years*, London: GDC.

General Dental Council (GDC) (2006) *General Visitation 2003–2005*, London: GDC.

GMC (2002 and 2003) *Tomorrow's Doctors. Recommendations on undergraduate medical education*, London: GMC.

GMC (2005) *The New Doctor*, London: GMC.

GMC Education Committee (2006a) *Strategic Options for Undergraduate Medical Education*, Final Report, London: GMC.

GMC (2006b) *Good Medical Practice*, London: GMC.

Gleeson, F (1992) 'Defects in postgraduate clinical skills as revealed by the objective structured long examination record (OSLER)', *Irish Medical Journal*, 85: 11–14.

Harden, R and Gleeson, F A (1979) 'Assessment of clinical competence using an objective structured clinical examination (OSCE)', *Medical Education*, 13: 41–54.

King's College London (2007) Patients as educators. Available online at <http://www.kcl.ac.uk/schools/medicine/learning/clinicalskills/patienteducator.html> (last accessed 22 October 2007).

Kneebone, R, Nestel, D, Wetzel, C Black, S, Jacklin, R, Aggarwal, R, Yadollahi, F, Wolfe, J, Vincent C and Darzi, A (2006a) 'The human face of simulation', *Academic Medicine*, 81(10): 919–924.

Kneebone, R, Nestel, D, Yadollahi, F, Brown, R, Nolan, C, Durack, D, Brenton, H, Moulton, C, Archer, J and Darzi, A (2006b) 'Assessing procedural skills in context: an Integrated Procedural Performance Instrument (IPPI)', *Medical Education*, 40 (11): 1105–1114.

Mezirow, J (1991) *Transformative Dimensions of Adult Learning*, San Francisco, CA: Jossey-Bass.

MMC (Modernising Medical Careers) (2007a) <http://www.mmc.nhs.uk/pages/assessment> (last accessed 10 September 2007).

MMC (Modernising Medical Careers) (2007b) *Aspiring to Excellence (the Tooke Report)*, London: MMC.

National Board of Medical Examiners (2007) <http://www.nbme.org/publications/item-writing-manual.html> (last accessed 21 October 2007).

National Committee of Inquiry into Higher Education (NCIHE) (1997) *Higher Education in the Learning Society* (The Dearing Report), London: NCIHE.

Neufeld, V and Barrows, H (1974) '"The McMaster Philosophy": an approach to medical education', *Journal of Medical Education*, 49: 1040–1050.

Neville, A J and Norman, G R (2007) 'PBL in the undergraduate MD program at McMaster University: three iterations in three decades', *Academic Medicine*, 82(4): 370–374.

Newble, D (1991) 'The observed long case in clinical assessment', *Medical Education*, 25(5): 369–373.

Norman, G and Schmidt, H (1992) 'The psychological basis of problem-based learning: a review of the evidence', *Academic Medicine*, 67(9): 557–565.

Peyton, J W R (1998) *Teaching and Learning in Medical Practice*, Rickmansworth, Herts: Manticore Europe.

Quality Assurance Agency for Higher Education (QAA) (2002a) *Subject Benchmark Statement for Dentistry*, Gloucester: QAA.

Quality Assurance Agency for Higher Education (QAA) (2002b) *Subject Benchmark Statement for Medicine*, Gloucester: QAA.

Schmidt, H, Dauphinee, W and Patel, V (1987) 'Comparing the effects of problem-based and conventional curricula in an international sample', *Journal of Medical Education*, 62: 305–315.

Schuwirth, L and Van der Vleuten, C (2006) 'A plea for new psychometric models in educational assessment', *Medical Education*, 40(4): 296–300.

Sheffield University (2007) Patients as educators. Available online at <http://www.shef.ac.uk/aume/pae_dept> (last accessed 22 October 2007).

Stark, P, Delmotte, A and Howdle, P (1998) 'Teaching clinical skills using a ward-based teacher', presentation at the ASME Conference, Southampton, September.

Van der Vleuten, C and Schuwirth, L (2004) 'Changing education, changing assessment, changing research?', *Medical Education*, 38(8): 805–812.

Van der Vleuten, C and Schuwirth, L (2005) 'Assessing professional competence: from methods to programmes', *Medical Education*, 39(3): 309–317.

Van der Vleuten, C, Norman, G and De Graaff, E (1991) 'Pitfalls in the pursuit of objectivity: issues of reliability', *Medical Education*, 25: 110–118.

Vernon, D and Blake, R (1993) 'Does problem-based learning work? A meta-analysis of evaluative research', *Academic Medicine*, 68(7): 551–563.

Wass, V and Jolly, B (2001) 'Does observation add to the validity of the long case?', *Medical Education*, 35(8):729–734.

FURTHER READING

Useful websites

General Dental Council <http://www.gdc-uk.org/ > (last accessed 21 October 2007).
General Medical Council <http://www.gmc-uk.org/ > (last accessed 21 October 2007).
Higher Education Academy Subject Centre for Medicine, Dentistry and Veterinary Medicine: <http://www.medev.ac.uk/ > (last accessed 21 October 2007). Very useful site for up-to-date news, the newsletter *01* and many other resources and reports.
Modernising Medical Careers <http://www.mmc.nhs.uk/> (last accessed 12 January 2008).
National Board of Medical Examiners <http://www.nbme.org/> (last accessed 21 October 2007).

Postgraduate Medical Education and Training Board <http://www.pmetb.org.uk/ > (last accessed 21 October 2007).

Useful journals

A list of journals follows. Each journal is international and has its own character, with *Clinical Teacher* being the most approachable and with more of a focus on the UK than the others. *Academic Medicine; Advances in Health Sciences Education; Clinical Teacher; European Dental Journal; Medical Education; Medical Teacher.*

Useful booklet series

Understanding Medical Education, a series of booklets published by the Association for the Study of Medical Education. These provide authoritative and accessible overviews of a range of key topics. May be ordered through the ASME website:<http://www. asme.org.uk/> (last accessed 6 September 2007).

Useful books

Dent, J and Harden, R (2005) *A Practical Guide for Medical Teachers*, London: Churchill Livingstone. Is comprehensive and exactly what it 'says on the tin'.

Jolly, B and Rees, L (eds) (1998) *Medical Education in the Millennium*, Oxford: Oxford University Press. Many useful chapters, especially on student learning.

Newble, D and Cannon, R (2001) *A Handbook for Medical Teachers*, London: Kluwer Publishers. A 'how to do medical education'; also useful for dentistry.

Norman, G, Van der Vleuten, C and Newble, D (eds) (2002) *International Handbook of Research in Medical Education*, London: Kluwer. Authoritative chapters by international experts.

Sweet, J, Huttly, S and Taylor, I (eds) (2002) *Effective Learning and Teaching in Medical, Dental and Veterinary Education*, London: Kogan Page. An overview compendium of basic approaches.

Key aspects of teaching and learning in nursing and midwifery

Pam Parker and Della Freeth

INTRODUCTION

This chapter aims to assist relatively inexperienced educators by exploring key issues for teaching and learning in nursing and midwifery. Educators from other disciplines may also find some aspects of the chapter helpful. It begins by discussing the ever-changing context of healthcare and implications for health professionals' education. We highlight the continual evolution of curricula before turning to teaching, learning and assessment in nine key areas: practical skills and professional judgement, developing clinical reasoning, theory and underpinning knowledge, simulation, communication skills, interprofessional collaboration, user and carer involvement, flexible approaches to learning, and large and heterogeneous student cohorts. A variety of roles that have evolved to support student learning will be described; but first we should acknowledge our own context.

The authors work in a large, inner-city school of nursing and midwifery in England. The local population is extremely diverse: ethnically, linguistically, economically and socially. Levels of international migration and national mobility are high. These factors apply just as much to the healthcare workforce as to health services' users. Naturally, this influences our perceptions.

CONTEXT

In many countries the agenda for healthcare changes rapidly due to changing political priorities and population-based changes. In much of the developed world drivers for changing services include: ageing populations, smaller households and dispersed families, increased migration, changed patterns of disease, new technologies, political intervention, changed expectations of patients/clients and their families, increased engagement with complementary therapies, increased participation in higher education, changed patterns of employment and the need to contain spiralling healthcare costs. In the UK, government and professional bodies have responded in landmark documents such as *A Health Service of All the Talents* (DoH, 2000), *Working Together, Learning Together* (DoH, 2001), *Choosing Health: Making Healthy Choices Easier* (DoH, 2004) and *Our Health, Our Care, Our Say: Making it Happen* (DoH, 2006). Nurses and midwives have developed expanded and new roles, increasingly often acting as the lead professional for particular groups of patients/clients. The consequent need for higher-level technical, professional and managerial skills increases demand for continuing professional development (CPD). However, the demand is not focused primarily upon university-based courses demanding regular attendance over several months: short courses, **work-based learning (WBL), action learning** sets (groups) and **self-directed learning (SDL)** supported by electronic resources are increasingly popular. Essential though it is to respond to changes in context as curricula are reviewed, this is not sufficient. There is a need to be proactive and anticipate the future.

Interrogating practice

For the courses to which you contribute, do you know when and how they are reviewed to ensure they remain appropriate for current and predicted service needs? How might you make effective contributions to this process?

Schools of nursing and midwifery migrated into universities about 20 years ago but continue to work in partnership with the NHS. Programmes combine practice experience or work-based learning with components addressing underpinning theory and knowledge for evidence-based practice. They are designed around national standards of proficiency but with some adaptation and flexibility to meet local needs. The nationally agreed pre-registration proficiencies arose from the *Fitness for Practice* report (UKCC, 1999) and have been revised in the light of experiences of running the programmes and the Nursing and Midwifery Council's continued focus on fitness to practice (NMC, 2004a, 2004b).

At present, pre-registration nursing programmes have a shared foundation component followed by a 'branch programme', permitting greater focus on a speciality (adult, children's, learning disability or mental health nursing). Pre-registration midwifery programmes provide two options: a three-year programme or a shortened programme for those who have first-level registration with the NMC as an adult nurse. All programmes include placements in a range of practice settings, forming 50 per cent of the curriculum, where professional skills, knowledge and attitudes are developed and assessed. Students experience patient care, from problem identification to problem-solving or alleviation; and variations in demands over the 24-hour and seven-day cycles. There is an emphasis upon strengthening the partnership between universities, students and local placement providers by linking students to 'Home Trusts' or '**Communities of Practice**' for the majority of their experience. This aims to encourage a sense of belonging and to increase local recruitment when students complete their programmes. Additional emphases include interprofessional collaboration, and user and carer involvement.

Nursing and midwifery programmes lead to academic qualifications and registration with the professional body: that is, they offer a licence to practise. Therefore, it is particularly important that the assessment of students is reliable and valid (see Chapter 10) and safeguards the public. Widened access to nursing and midwifery education and the diversity of the student population have increased the need for student support in relation to personal and academic matters. Much of this support is directed at developing or reawakening effective approaches to learning and meeting the demands of academic assessment (see Chapter 9).

Developing technology has affected all aspects of our lives, particularly health. Effective interventions can now be made where previously none were possible. Interventions can be quicker, at or near home, and are often less invasive. Expectations are higher and professionals must learn new skills to exploit new technologies competently and humanely. In addition, service users and professionals can now access (and need to evaluate) a wide range of information from the internet (e.g. the National Library for Health, 2007) or a plethora of telephone and e-mail advice services, including the nurse-led service NHS Direct. Better-informed patients/clients expect to be more involved in the planning of their care, and students must be prepared for the possibilities and tensions of this process.

In common with other disciplines, as the knowledge and skills demanded of nurses and midwives increased, curricula became overcrowded and there is concern about over-teaching students. To address this, some programmes have turned to **problem-based learning (PBL)**; sometimes termed **enquiry-based learning** (EBL) (see Chapter 26).

The falling price of technology has helped tutors and students to make greater use of blended-, mobile- and e-learning (see Chapter 7). These approaches increase flexibility for learners and can alleviate over-teaching. Flexibility is particularly important within post-registration provision since healthcare workplaces find it increasingly difficult to release staff for CPD, raising demand for work-based learning.

KNOWLEDGE, SKILLS AND ATTITUDES

The climate of continual change in healthcare requires an adaptable practitioner, committed to lifelong learning. Necessary skills include: recognising learning needs and being able to plan means of addressing these; information seeking, information management, critique and synthesis. These must be combined with experience in applying knowledge to professional practice in locally adapted ways. In addition to engagement with lifelong learning for themselves, students will need to facilitate the learning of others (peers, junior colleagues, service users): they must prepare to become educators.

Across the wide range of healthcare settings, nurses and midwives assess individual clients' needs in order to identify appropriate and effective care. They engage in clinical reasoning founded on theoretical knowledge and experience of clinical practice. Within resource constraints, they plan, coordinate, deliver and evaluate care that should be informed by the best available evidence. These core professional activities dictate most of the content of nursing and midwifery curricula, although there is scope for a variety of learning, teaching and assessment strategies to achieve these outcomes.

Healthcare professionals need to spend much of their time listening, informing and negotiating, all of which must be conducted sensitively and respectfully. Good communication skills are essential, along with attention to diversity and ethics. The complex needs of clients are best met through effective interprofessional collaboration, which requires knowledge of professional roles and responsibilities in addition to good communication. Students should learn to practise in a range of settings, learn to be effective members of multidisciplinary teams and learn to educate and support relatives or volunteers.

Interrogating practice

- In light of the knowledge, skills and attitudes desired in the healthcare professions, which approaches to learning, teaching and assessment are likely to be most effective?
- How does your programme seek to help students achieve the required knowledge, skills and attitudes?

LEARNING, TEACHING AND ASSESSMENT

Nursing and midwifery, in common with medicine, dentistry and the allied health professions, are practice-based disciplines. 'Hands-on' practical skills combined with clinical judgement based on professional experience, underpinning theory and the best available evidence are key to professional competence. This shapes learning, teaching and assessment, and a number of key issues are examined below.

Developing practical skills and professional judgement

In a spiral curriculum (Bruner, 1966), higher-level skills and more complex professional judgements are gradually mastered through repeated experiences of a variety of episodes of care. **Experiential learning** in clinical or simulated environments should be designed and supported so that the full learning cycle is completed: concrete experience, observations and reflections, formation of abstract concepts and generalisations, then testing implications of concepts in new situations (Kolb, 1984).

Supervised experience in healthcare placements typically lasts from four weeks to just over three months. The focus of learning is different for each placement and should relate to the student's level and identified learning needs. Each student is allocated a mentor from within the practice team to provide support and facilitate learning. Students should both observe care and participate in giving care. Their placements should be in a range of settings, including hospital wards, health centres and patients' homes, thus providing opportunities for developing a broad spectrum of skills and giving exposure to a variety of professional specialisations (ENB and DoH, 2001).

Providing sufficient suitable clinical placements is difficult. In many areas nursing and midwifery students compete with students from other disciplines for practice experience. Continual effort is required to identify new placements; to prepare these for students; to support the clinical staff in their roles of supervising, mentoring, educating and assessing students; and to regularly audit all practice learning environments. The large numbers of students now in placements, the pressures upon clinical staff and the fast pace of health practice make it desirable that students acquire some basic skills before entering practice areas. This protects both students and patients. Teaching these skills is best conducted in the simulated ward settings of traditional practical rooms or more sophisticated clinical skills centres.

The assessment of practical skills, clinical reasoning and professional judgement in the practice area are usually conducted by the mentor who identifies the student's level of achievement by reference to a framework. There are three common formats: practice-based assessments, skills schedules and **portfolios**. Practice-based assessments focus on specific outcomes for different stages of programmes and mentors identify if the student has achieved these at the required level. Similarly for skills schedules, the curriculum lays down threshold requirements for the number, range and level of skills acquired at milestones within the programme. Finally, portfolio formats vary but usually include **learning outcomes** and required skills with some element of **reflection**. They are a vehicle for identifying future learning needs (Gannon *et al.*, 2001).

Practice-based assessments are widely used by the health professions, practitioners generally taking a positive view of their face **validity**, authenticity and practicality. However, there is some disquiet in relation to **reliability**, objectivity and the equality of opportunity. The concerns arise due to the large number of students and the consequent number and range of placements (usually several hundred), offering variable learning opportunities. Involving several hundred mentors in assessing students presents challenges for education and updating to promote consistency and accuracy. In addition, there is often no overview for a mentor of a student's previous placement performance nor a real sense of development for students from one placement to another. Schools strive to overcome some of these concerns by moderating at least a sample of mentors' assessments; by using a single portfolio over an extended period (see Case study 1); or by augmenting mentors' assessments with more easily standardised tutor-led assessments in simulated practice settings. In addition, reflective writing, while difficult at first, provides a means through which students may develop critical analytical skills for their practice (Jasper, 1999).

Case study 1: Portfolio of practice

Portfolios of practice were developed for assessing students' practice. These replaced practice-based assessment documents with learning outcomes and a separate skills schedule. Thus all practice assessment requirements are incorporated into one document and mentors document all feedback on a student's performance in a single place. Furthermore, students have only one document to remember to take to their placements. However, it was not felt to be practical to have one portfolio for the entire programme and so portfolios were developed for each year. For nursing the first-year portfolio is common to all branches but for years two and three they are branch-specific.

The portfolios were designed with practitioners and included all the activities students needed to undertake to demonstrate achievement of the appropriate proficiencies. Some action planning and reflection were included to enable the portfolio to be graded. Using the portfolio over a period of a year has enabled mentors to review a student's performance elsewhere. Students can see their progress more clearly.

(Pam Parker and Val Dimmock, St Bartholomew School of Nursing and Midwifery, City University London)

Developing clinical reasoning

Theoretical perspectives, empirical knowledge and reflection all underpin the clinical reasoning that leads to clinical decision-making. It is good practice to begin with a client encounter (a real encounter, PBL trigger, case study or patient management scenario). This capitalises on the intrinsic motivation to provide appropriate care to be found among healthcare students. The learning trigger should be suited to students' prior knowledge and experience in order that an appropriate level of disjuncture is created. Disjuncture is the gap between what you know and understand (consciously or unconsciously) and what you feel you need to know and understand (see Jarvis (1987) for an elaborated discussion). Moderate disjuncture creates a readiness to learn and thereby closes the gap; excessive disjuncture leads to learners giving up – a 'miseducative experience' (Dewey, 1938).

Providing appropriate learning triggers is made more difficult by heterogeneous groups, or poor knowledge about the learners for whom the trigger is intended. It therefore follows that writing or selecting good triggers for interprofessional groups presents special challenges. Experience in writing triggers is often key: it may be possible to work with a more experienced colleague, or colleagues whose knowledge of the student group or field of practice exceeds yours.

The assessment of clinical reasoning also presents challenges. The dilemma is that this skill is practice-orientated but based upon theoretical or empirical knowledge. The usual assessment division of the theoretical and the practical is not helpful. Assessment approaches that can probe the various facets of clinical reasoning are required. Practice-based assessments conducted by mentoring clinical staff can be effective, as can the simulated version of this, an **objective structured clinical examination** (**OSCE**) (see Chapter 26).

Theory and underpinning knowledge

The theoretical perspectives and empirical knowledge underpinning practice for nursing and midwifery are drawn from many disciplines, including the biological sciences, psychology, sociology, ethics and philosophy, management, education and informatics. These are synthesised or complemented by research and theoretical perspectives originating directly from nursing and midwifery. To suit the wide-ranging subject matter and learning outcomes, varied approaches to learning and teaching are necessary. There is a place for the traditional lecture, for seminars, tutorials or supervision; for laboratory work, practical skills classes, experiential learning, individual and group projects; for simulation, **self-directed learning**, web-based learning, **podcasts** and portfolios; for problem-solving and PBL/EBL. A range of approaches to facilitating learning should strengthen the learning experience by capitalising on the strengths and minimising the weaknesses of each approach (see Further reading).

Assessing students' grasp of theory, recall of knowledge, and the synthesis and application of these, is best achieved through a range of approaches. Recall can be tested through unseen, written examinations or online tests via, for example, multiple choice questions, annotation of diagrams, or short structured answers. Longer written responses are required to demonstrate reflection, synthesis, application and creativity. Examinations should be augmented with assignments completed over a period of weeks, for example: essays, portfolios, learning journals, project reports and presentations. Assessment should encourage students to apply theories and empirical knowledge to client care scenarios.

With each mode of assessment it is important to ensure that the process is, so far as is possible, transparent, fair, ethical, valid, reliable and aligned with curricular intentions (see Chapter 10). The face validity of an assessment is important for maintaining student motivation.

Interrogating practice

What are the strengths and weaknesses of the approaches to learning, teaching and assessment employed in your courses? Is each approach used to best effect?

Simulation

Learning through simulation has been an established part of nursing and midwifery education for decades. Role play is discussed in the next section. Simulated environments such as traditional practical rooms or more modern clinical skills centres (Nicol and Glen, 1999) create some of the conditions of a practice environment (e.g. ward, outpatient clinic or client's home) and permit the practice of psychomotor skills, experiential learning, discussion and reflection. Advances in technology have brought increasingly sophisticated mannequins and other simulators, permitting practice of psychomotor skills such as venepuncture and suturing. Computer-based simulation enables students to, for example, listen to heart sounds and arrhythmias, or to respond to emergency situations via an interactive CD ROM. Nelson and Blenkin (2007) describe a sophisticated online role-play simulation which allows students to experience the outcomes of their decisions.

Simulation has many advantages. Learning can occur without risk to patients. Students can be allowed to make mistakes and learn from these. Practical skills can be developed in a systematic, supported manner, which can be difficult to achieve in busy practice environments (for a description of one approach to doing this, see the case study by Nicol, 2002: 186–188). Group sizes of 16 to 20 are common and manageable in a skills centre, but could not be accommodated in practice. Discussion of theoretical and ethical matters can occur in parallel with developing practical skills in a simulated setting. This would normally be inappropriate in the presence of a patient and may be forgotten later in a busy clinical environment.

The development of a key set of basic skills is possible in the early weeks of the pre-registration programme, prior to experiences in practice settings. The most important skills are those that make placement experiences safer, not only for patients but also for students and their colleagues: moving and handling, prevention of cross-infection, checking and recording patient information and so on. Other important skills are those that will allow students to feel and be viewed by qualified staff as useful members of the team, for example taking essential observations. This will improve the subsequent practice-based learning experience of students.

Later in programmes, simulated practice environments are useful for reflection upon experience in practice areas and drawing out further learning needs, many of which can be addressed through simulated practice. Thus simulation contributes to the development of clinical reasoning and to the integration of theory and practice.

Assessment of practical skills in this environment is usually undertaken using an OSCE (see Chapter 26).

Communication skills

It is almost impossible to name an aspect of practice that does not have communication as a key element; so it seems somewhat artificial to separate communication skills from the activities in which they are embedded. However, good communication is essential to promoting the well-being of patients/clients and for effective service delivery. Thus healthcare curricula contain learning outcomes related to communication to highlight this professional skill.

There may be teaching sessions labelled as 'communication skills', addressing such topics as: the psychology of communication, verbal and non-verbal communication; cultural diversity, language barriers and working through interpreters or advocates; communication with relatives, and breaking bad news. Ideally, most sessions are conducted with small groups in an undisturbed environment, with a supportive facilitator, and opportunities to experiment and practise this core skill. Discussion and role play are the dominant teaching strategies, each requiring participants to be active learners. Such 'props' as telephones or one-way mirrors may support role play; or where resources permit, input from specially trained professional actors. The actors simulate patients and then come out of role to provide feedback to the students. A communications suite permits video-recording for later self-analysis or tutor feedback. Cooke *et al.* (2003) described an interprofessional learning experience for senior students, using simulated patients and extending existing curricula in relation to breaking bad news (see also Case study 2 in Chapter 2).

Timetabled slots for the development of communication skills do not obviate the need for attention to communication issues to be integral to other teaching and learning activities. For example, it is essential to discuss and practise appropriate communication while teaching junior nursing students the practical skills of washing and feeding patients. Some teaching sessions concern psychomotor skills that are inevitably uncomfortable or embarrassing procedures. Supportive verbal and non-verbal communication is an important part of nursing and midwifery practice in these circumstances and should be considered alongside the development of the psychomotor skill. Furthermore, tutors who support students in their placements are well placed to discuss communication challenges, to observe student performance and provide formative feedback.

Communication skills are rarely the sole focus of an assessment. Since communication is integral to other activities it is entirely appropriate to assess communication skills in parallel with knowledge or psychomotor skills. The main assessment vehicles are essays, reports, practice-based assessments, OSCEs, presentations and posters. Whatever the assessment mode it is important to develop clear assessment criteria; otherwise communication assessment may be cursory and unreliable. The complex and nuanced nature of communication makes it challenging to assess.

Interprofessional collaboration

Students need to appreciate that multidisciplinary teams deliver care, possibly spanning the NHS, social services, the private sector and the voluntary sector. Effective, efficient, client-centred care requires interprofessional and inter-agency collaboration. Each team member must understand their own role and its boundaries, and seek to understand the contribution of other team members. Appropriate skills and attitudes could be developed within learning experiences confined to one profession, but multidisciplinary and interprofessional learning are often seen as key to enhancing collaborative practice (DoH, 2001; GMC, 2003; NMC, 2004a).

Implementing interprofessional learning within pre-registration education is challenging: coping with large numbers of students, differing programme lengths and academic levels, timetable and other resource constraints, meeting the requirements of professional bodies, overcoming geographical dispersion of related disciplines across universities. Nevertheless, enthusiasts regularly pioneer shared learning initiatives. Many examples may be found in Barr *et al.* (2000, 2005), Freeth *et al.* (2005) and Glen and Leiba (2002).

While many interprofessional education initiatives have been classroom or skills centre based, others seize opportunities for shared learning within practice placements. After all, this is where interprofessional collaboration matters most. The task is to coordinate the activities of students from various professions that are placed within the same environment. Facilitation for learning with and from each other should be provided. Case study 2 outlines a 'total immersion' approach to this in which supervised interprofessional student teams are given responsibility for a small caseload. This is a powerful learning experience but requires high levels of commitment, enthusiasm and supervision from the selected clinical area. Not all areas can offer this, so less intensive models are needed too. For example, student teams may be asked to 'shadow' real teams and plan care based on information drawn from talking to the patient/client and perhaps relatives, also drawing information from observing the multidisciplinary team at work in the relevant clinical area(s). The students' joint care plan can be evaluated by the university or clinical staff and it may be possible for service users to add to the evaluative discussion. In due course the students' plan can be compared with the actual course of events as recorded in notes or summarised at multidisciplinary team meetings. Barber *et al.* (1997) describe an approach like this in a 'teaching nursing home' in the USA.

Case study 2: Training wards and similar environments

Clinical training wards have been developed in Sweden and Britain (Wahlström and Sandén, 1998; Freeth *et al.*, 2001; Ponzer *et al.*, 2004). Orthopaedic wards tend to be chosen since these patients predictably require regular input from nursing, medicine, physiotherapy and occupational therapy, with opportunities for contact with other professions too. For much of their stay patients will not be acutely unwell, offering scope for student teams to learn how to manage and progress care. Normally student teams work shifts under the watchful eye of a senior nurse who works alongside them. Facilitators from each profession visit regularly to support the student team. Every two or three days the student team will have a facilitated reflection session to help them examine how well they are planning and delivering care, and to discuss emergent issues relating to team-work. Feedback from patients and students is usually very positive, although students sometimes report conflicting feelings with respect to developing their own profession-specific competence and developing interprofessional teamwork competences. Facilitators report their role as quite draining, so most initiatives rotate facilitators to prevent burnout. Universities may find that learning experiences such as these are vulnerable to difficult-to-predict changes in the clinical area; for example, reconfiguration of services may leave the area without appropriate staff to provide supervision or the caseload may change such that it becomes too complex for student teams. Constant communication between staff and managers in the clinical area and programme leaders within the university is the only way to ensure that everyone has as much notice as possible about impending changes and their likely consequences.

Similar interprofessional student placements have been described elsewhere, such as interprofessional student teams assessing and providing care for outpatients in ambulatory care clinics in the USA (Dienst and Byl, 1981). Again in the USA, Hayward (2005) describes students, supported by university tutors, using a mobile clinic to provide care and advice for older people who otherwise have limited access to services of this type.

(Della Freeth, St Bartholomew School of Nursing and Midwifery,
City University London)

User and carer involvement

It is essential that insights from service users and carers are integrated into programmes (DoH, 2001; NMC, 2004a, 2004b). This should commence when programmes are being designed by including a range of users and carers in the development groups. Where possible they should also be included in programme management teams. Users and carers can contribute to teaching in a variety of ways: this may include joining classes and discussing their experiences. This offers the advantages of interactivity and a discussion that unfolds as participants learn more about each other but it can be a demanding commitment for service users and the university staff who support them; it may also be intimidating for very junior students. Written or recorded testimonies can be excellent resources for individual study or group work; and perhaps assessment too. Sometimes you will want to create your own recordings to suit your programmes' needs, but many user and carer experiences are freely available in databases of **reusable learning objects** (RLOs). For example, the charity DIPEx (2007) has created an extensive repository of personal experiences of health and illness.

One currently underdeveloped area is the inclusion of service users and carers in assessment. It is relatively common for students to be asked to discuss users' and carers' experiences of health journeys but less common to include users and carers in practice-based assessments and assessments involving simulation. Some interprofessional placements (see section above) ask service users to contribute to the formative assessment of student teams. Whenever service users and carers are asked to contribute to educational programmes, significant personal contributions should be scrutinised within an ethical framework that prioritises the well-being of users and carers above the needs of an assessment system.

> ## Case study 3: An online discussion forum for mental health nursing students and service users

This project aimed to develop understanding and positive appreciation of mental health service users and their experiences and perspectives through mental health nursing students' participation in an online discussion forum. A secure project site was designed and piloted within CitySpace (a **Virtual Learning Environment (VLE)**). It featured folders containing welcome messages and advice on posting messages sensitively ('netiquette'); practice discussion threads ('getting to know you', 'anxiety on an acute ward' and 'respect'); pre- and post-project questionnaires; and the enquiry-based learning 'trigger'. Students and users receiving VLE training were given ongoing support by the project team, who also moderated the online discussions.

Evaluation data included pre- and post-project online questionnaires, VLE activity data, structured interviews with participants, student EBL presentations and project team reflections. Thirty-five second-year mental health nursing students and 12 mental health service users participated in the study. Overall, the project was a great success with students and service users engaging in online discussions on a range of issues, and two-thirds of EBL presentations demonstrated new-found understanding of the service user experience and perspective with implications for clinical practice identified. All interviewees stated that they would happily take part again and recommend the online forum to others. Analysis of activity data revealed that while all 35 students had taken part in practice sessions, just 15 (44 per cent) had contributed e-mails to the discussions during the 'live' debates with service users. Limitations in communication skills, sensitivity towards service users and lack of confidence in using IT appeared to limit some students' participation. Increased facilitator contact and encouragement may ease this. The service users praised the training and support provided, eagerly utilised the forum and were keen advocates of the project.

There is enormous potential to develop similar forums to promote workplace and interprofessional learning as well as wider application throughout the nursing and midwifery curriculum. Service users could take a greater lead in the design and direction of future online discussions. In addition, the anonymity and distance afforded by the online nature of interactions revealed a therapeutic potential for service users that could be further explored.

(Alan Simpson, Lisa Reynolds, Ian Light and Julie Attenborough,
St Bartholomew School of Nursing and Midwifery, City University London)

Flexible approaches to learning

As noted earlier, flexible approaches to learning such as e-learning and work-based learning are increasingly sought by students across a range of programmes so that they may more often study when and wherever they find convenient. This does not obviate the need for traditional face-to-face encounters during which contact with new people can forge new links and new ways of seeing things. Instead it means that programme developers need to think more critically about making the best possible use of more limited face-to-face course elements and what will work equally well (or even better) via online or downloaded workbooks, web links to additional materials, discussion boards and individual support via e-mail or telephone. Some tutors will need to learn new skills and it will be necessary to provide guidelines for reasonable expectations – when students can access learning materials and assessment tasks or guidelines at any time on any day, they sometimes forget that tutors cannot reasonably be expected to answer queries immediately at any time on any day! Nevertheless flexible learning will only work well if technical and academic support is available without undue delay and not always confined to traditional office hours.

Pre-registration students can find e-learning resources particularly helpful when they are on placement and cannot visit the university campus so easily. Web-based discussion boards help them to maintain contact with their peers and the learning of the group may be enhanced if tutors encourage students to share experiences of their varied practice placements. Web resources also help students to follow up learning needs that arise in the course of their placements. They will also want a means of contacting tutors to ask questions or seek advice in relation to issues that arise during placements.

Flexible work-based learning has increased in popularity with students undertaking continuing professional development. Learners and their managers value the opportunity for study and assessment that focuses on a project to enhance practice within their workplace with timing that suits individuals and practice.

Large and heterogeneous student cohorts

In addition to providing a wide ranger of smaller CPD programmes, some schools of nursing and midwifery have very large student cohorts on their main programmes, perhaps admitting over 200 pre-registration students per year, each requiring large and small group teaching, support services and an appropriately tailored range of practice placements. It is essential to subdivide cohorts, provide good academic and pastoral tutorial systems, provide learning support where needed, make good use of technology, and resist the temptation to over-lecture and over-assess.

The student population contains great diversity: age, culture, the languages spoken at home, prior educational preparation and prior work and life experience. For example, a class may contain mature students with family care responsibilities and significant work experience, often as care assistants; alongside school leavers with more up-to-date study skills but limited life and work experience; alongside graduates from other disciplines who bring a wide range of insights from their earlier studies to nursing and midwifery programmes. This vibrant diversity is likely to increase as the number of foundation degree graduates rises (both in subjects that are intended to lead people into health and social care careers and unrelated subjects). Although stimulating for learners and education providers, the extent of diversity provides some challenges for curriculum developers and tutors; and increases demand for education that can be delivered more flexibly and throughout working lives (DoH, 2001; NMC, 2006). Interprofessional education (see above) is an example of deliberately increasing the diversity of a learning group.

ROLES AND ORGANISATIONS THAT SUPPORT LEARNING

A wide range of roles support student learning and there are prescribed professional and educational requirements for some of these (Glen and Parker, 2003; NMC, 2006). This ensures that professionals who guide students' learning and assess students' performance have appropriate experience as nurses or midwives; and have studied the relevant educational principles.

Mentors

Within practice areas each student must be allocated a mentor (NMC, 2006). Mentors facilitate students' learning by providing or highlighting appropriate learning opportunities and assess the students' practice, taking responsibility for identifying whether prescribed or negotiated outcomes have been achieved. The mentor must indicate whether he or she considers the student fit to practise. The NMC requires particularly experienced 'sign-off mentors' to be allocated to students for their final practice experience.

Practice teachers

Practice teachers have been introduced for programmes that enable students to register as a specialist community public health nurse from September 2008 (NMC, 2006). This role encompasses that of mentor and sign-off mentor and, additionally, coordinating a group of mentors and student experiences.

Practice facilitators/educators

Practice educators are practitioners employed by NHS trusts and/or universities. The intention is that the practice educator is both clinically competent and familiar with students' educational programmes. The role is focused upon the theory–practice link and learning from practice experiences. Practice educators support both students and mentors and maintain close contact with the university staff responsible for managing and developing practice placements.

Lecturer practitioner

Lecturer practitioner roles are a combination of the practice educator and traditional lecturer role. They were developed as a link between trusts and universities and were seen as a useful 'stepping stone' for those who wished to move from practice into education. Many found the breadth and conflicting demands of the lecturer practitioner role difficult to manage and these positions are less popular than they once were.

Lecturers/tutors

University lecturers have multifaceted roles. For example, they deliver the theory-based teaching and assessment in students' programmes and relate this to practice. They link with service delivery settings, supporting students, mentors and their line managers, and supporting practice development. Lecturers act as personal tutors to students. They also engage in curriculum development, scholarship and research. Most lecturers in schools of nursing and midwifery are nurses or midwives, but lecturers from other disciplines are also employed to provide complementary expertise and alternative perspectives.

University-based specialist learning services

An increasing range of specialist posts that support student learning are emerging (see Chapter 9). These include library staff with expertise to support PBL/EBL, technology (IT) and media resources staff who help students harness the power of newer technologies, and tutors offering language and learning skills support. Actors, artists, poets or writers in residence are increasingly employed to improve the quality of student learning.

Interrogating practice

- Which roles support student learning in your educational programmes?
- How are people prepared for their roles?
- How does your role complement the role of others?

Organisations that support learning

The Higher Education Academy (2007) exists to help institutions, discipline groups and higher education staff in the UK to provide the best possible learning experience for their students. It has a particularly relevant subject centre for nursing and midwifery educators: the Centre for Health Sciences and Practice (2007). It also links together the work of 74 Centres for Excellence in Teaching and Learning (CETLs, 2007). There are several health-related CETLs, including some that focus on interprofessional learning, e-learning or professionalism. For those interested in researching their educational practice, useful information and contacts may be obtained from the British Educational Research Association (BERA, 2007). BERA contains a number of special interest groups (SIGs), including one for learning in the professions. Interprofessional learning has a particular champion in CAIPE (UK Centre for the Advancement of Interprofessional Education, 2007).

OVERVIEW

This chapter has discussed key aspects of teaching, learning and assessment in nursing and midwifery. It considered the context of education, the required knowledge, skills and attitudes, strategies used to develop professional expertise and the range of roles that support learning. In a single chapter it is not possible to provide more than a glimpse of these issues; those who are interested are invited to follow up some of the references and suggestions for further reading.

REFERENCES

Barber, G, Borders, K, Holland, B and Roberts, K (1997) 'Life span forum: an interdisciplinary training experience', *Gerontology and Geriatrics Education*, 18(1): 47–59.
Barr, H, Hammick, M, Freeth, D, Koppel, I and Reeves, S (2000) *Evaluations of Interprofessional Education: A United Kingdom Review for Health and Social Care*, London: CAIPE/BERA.
Barr, H, Koppel, I, Reeves, S, Hammick, M and Freeth, D (2005) *Effective Interprofessional Education: Argument, Assumption and Evidence*, Oxford: Blackwell.

British Educational Research Association (BERA) (2007) <www.bera.ac.uk> (accessed 31 July 2007).

Bruner, J (1966) *Towards a Theory of Instruction*, Oxford: Oxford University Press.

CAIPE (UK Centre for the Advancement of Interprofessional Education) (2007) <www.caipe.org.uk > (accessed 31 July 2007).

Centres for Excellence in Teaching and Learning (CETLs) (2007) <www.hefce.ac.uk/learning/tinits/cetl> (accessed 31 July 2007).

Centre for Health Sciences and Practice (2007) <www.health.heacademy.ac.uk> (accessed 31 July 2007).

Cooke, S, Chew-Graham, C, Boggis, C and Wakefield, A (2003) 'I never realised that doctors were into feelings too: changing students' perceptions through interprofessional education', *Learning in Health and Social Care*, 2(3): 137–146.

Dienst, E and Byl, N (1981) 'Evaluation of an educational program in health care teams', *Journal of Community Health*, 6(4): 282–298.

DoH (2000) *A Health Service of All the Talents*, London: Department of Health.

DoH (2001) *Working Together, Learning Together: A Framework for Lifelong Learning for the NHS*, London: Department of Health.

DoH (2004) *Choosing Health: Making Healthy Choices Easier*, London: Department of Health.

DoH (2006) *Our Health, Our Care, Our Say: Making it Happen*, London: Department of Health.

Dewey, J (1938) *Experience and Education*, New York: Macmillan.

DIPEx (2007) <www.dipex.org> (accessed 31 July 2007).

ENB and DoH (2001) *Placements in Focus: Guidance for Education in Practice for Healthcare Professions*, London: English National Board for Nursing and Midwifery/Department of Health.

Freeth, D, Hammick, M, Reeves, S, Koppel, I and Barr, H (2005) *Effective Interprofessional Education: Development, Delivery and Evaluation*, Oxford: Blackwell.

Freeth, D, Reeves, S, Goreham, C, Parker, P Haynes, S and Pearson, S (2001) 'Real life clinical learning on an interprofessional training ward', *Nurse Education Today*, 21: 366–372.

Gannon, F, Draper, P, Watson, R, Proctor, S and Norman, I (2001) 'Putting portfolios in their place', *Nurse Education Today*, 21: 534–540.

General Medical Council (GMC) (2003) *Tomorrow's Doctors*, London: GMC.

Glen, S and Leiba, T (eds) (2002) *Multi-professional Learning for Nurses: Breaking the Boundaries*, Basingstoke: Palgrave.

Glen, S and Parker, P (eds) (2003) *Supporting Learning in Nursing Practice: A Guide for Practitioners*, Basingstoke: Palgrave.

Hayward, K (2005) 'Facilitating interdisciplinary practice through mobile service provision to the rural adult', *Geriatric Nursing*, 26(1): 29–33.

Higher Education Academy (2007) <www.heacademy.ac.uk> (accessed 31 July 2007).

Hodgson, P (2000) *Clinical Placements in Primary and Community Care Project*, Leeds: National Health Service Executive.

Jarvis, P (1987) *Adult Learning in the Social Context*, London: Croom Helm.

Jasper, M (1999) 'Nurses' perceptions of the value of written reflection', *Nurse Education Today*, 19: 452–463.

Kolb, D (1984) *Experiential Learning*, Englewood Cliffs, NJ: Prentice-Hall.

National Library for Health (2007) <www.library.nhs.uk> (accessed 31 July 2007).

Nelson, D and Blenkin, C (2007) 'The power of online role-play simulations: technology in nursing education', *International Journal of Nursing Education Scholarship*, 4: Article 1 Epub.

Nicol, M (2002) 'Taking account of the starting point of students in a large group of learners with varied backgrounds and experience', in S Ketteridge, S Marshall and H Fry (eds), *The Effective Academic* (pp. 186–188), London: Kogan Page.

Nicol, M and Freeth, D (1998) 'Assessment of clinical skills: a new approach to an old problem', *Nurse Education Today*, 18: 601–609.

Nicol, M and Glen, S (eds) (1999) *Clinical Skills in Nursing: The Return of the Practical Room?*, Basingstoke: Macmillan.

NMC (2004a) *Standards of Proficiency for Pre-registration Nursing Education*, London: Nursing and Midwifery Council.

NMC (2004b) *Standards of Proficiency for Pre-registration Midwifery Education*, London: Nursing and Midwifery Council.

NMC (2006) *Standards to Support Learning and Assessment in Practice – NMC Standards for Mentors, Practice Teachers and Teachers*, London: Nursing and Midwifery Council.

Ponzer, S, Hylin, U, Kusoffsky, A and Lauffs, M (2004) 'Interprofessional training in the context of clinical practice: goals and students' perceptions on clinical education wards', *Medical Education*, 38: 727–736.

Reeves, S and Freeth, D (2002) 'The London training ward: an innovative interprofessional initiative', *Journal of Interprofessional Care*, 16: 41–52.

UKCC (1999) *Fitness for Practice: The UKCC Commission for Nursing and Midwifery Education*, London: UKCC.

Wahlström, O and Sandén, I (1998) 'Multiprofessional training at Linköping University: early experience', *Education for Health*, 11: 225–231.

FURTHER READING

Cheetham, G and Chivers, G (2005) *Professions, Competence and Informal Learning*, Cheltenham: Edward Elgar. Shows the development and application of a multifaceted model of professional competence which may help you to think about the different types of competences your curricula will aim to develop.

Freeth, D *et al.* (2005) See above. Looks in detail at the development, delivery and evaluation of interprofessional education.

Higgs, J and Jones, M (eds) (2000) *Clinical Reasoning in the Health Professions* (2nd edn), Oxford: Butterworth-Heinemann. An edited collection exploring the nature of clinical reasoning in the health professions and strategies for assisting learners.

Jacques, D and Salmon, G (2007) *Learning in Groups: A Handbook for Face-to-face and Online Environments* (4th edn), Abingdon: Routledge. An authoritative and practical guide for those wishing to develop their skills for supporting learning in groups (face-to-face or online).

Light, G and Cox, R (2001) *Learning and Teaching in Higher Education: The Reflective Professional*, London: Paul Chapman. Provides insightful scholarly analysis and practical advice.

Part 3
Enhancing personal practice

28 Enhancing personal practice

Establishing teaching and learning credentials

Heather Fry and Steve Ketteridge

SCOPE OF CHAPTER AND BACKGROUND

The focus of this chapter is on early career academics. In the UK, in most disciplines and universities, this means those who have a doctorate and hope to have a career in higher education. They may be working as (postdoctoral) researchers or as lecturers; the latter will be known in some institutions as 'probationary lecturers'. However, there are many variants of employment, with a multiplicity of patterns, so there will be others to whom this chapter is also applicable, including some more senior academics who want to have formal recognition of their teaching expertise, and in some disciplines others still taking a Ph.D.

In the UK and in several other countries early career academics are usually asked to build their research, publication, management, teaching and supervision expertise while also undertaking a formal programme of professional development. The latter usually relates largely to the teaching and supervision role, as generally a research degree will not have prepared staff for teaching, assessing and supervising different types of students. Typically in the UK at the moment, such a programme will be accredited by the **Higher Education Academy (HEA)** at the level of 'fellow', in which case it will also be at Master's level, or 'associate fellow'. In this chapter we focus on the UK experience, but much that is mentioned has wider applicability.

The early career academic is concerned not only with building a reputation for sound and well-informed teaching, but for all parts of their role. Some staff have a much heavier teaching load than others, perhaps with an expectation of scholarship in their discipline rather than research; for others, the primary emphasis is on building a reputation as an independent researcher. Whatever the emphasis, the taking of a formal programme emphasising learning and teaching is still likely to be the institutional expectation, although the timing, speed, nature, extent and level of this may vary. Both ends of the teaching/research spectrum gradually accrue a service or administrative element to their working profile and may undertake consultancy. The use of the term 'administration' under-represents the type of responsibilities many academics take on; 'academic management' may be a better term. Teaching or **academic practice** qualifications provide a foundation that can inform practice which is enhanced through **reflection** and discussion with peers, more senior staff and mentors. Larger classes, a more diverse intake, the rise of the student 'as consumer' and more pressure on staff time mean that there is less time to gradually 'learn on the job'. In the UK many doctoral students take formal courses about teaching, building on these as their career progresses.

THE UK PROFESSIONAL STANDARDS FRAMEWORK

The UK Professional Standards (UKPS) Framework for teaching and supporting learning in higher education is a national framework developed for the sector by the HEA (2006). These were developed following extensive consultation and at the request of the various funding councils and **Universities UK (UUK)**. They have been written in a form that attempts to render them relevant to all disciplines and to recognise the diversity of institutions across the higher education sector. For early career academics, the UKPS are of importance because they underpin the professional development programmes offered in teaching and learning or academic practice. The Standards (Table 28.1A) take the form of generic descriptors at three different levels of expertise. To demonstrate the Standards, individuals need to show achievement in designated areas of professional activity, core knowledge, and how they meet a set of professional values. Institutional HEA-accredited programmes have assessment requirements which relate to demonstrating the Standards.

Table 28.1A The UK Professional Standards Framework

Standard descriptor
1 Demonstrates an understanding of the student learning experience through engagement with at least two of the six areas of activity, appropriate core knowledge and professional values; the ability to engage in practices related to those areas of activity; the ability to incorporate research, scholarship and/or professional practice into those activities.
This leads to Associate of HEA status
2 Demonstrates an understanding of the student learning experience through engagement with all areas of activity, core knowledge and professional values; the ability to engage in practices related to all areas of activity; the ability to incorporate research, scholarship and/or professional practice into those activities.
This leads to Fellow of HEA status
3 Supports and promotes student learning in all areas of activity, core knowledge and professional values through mentoring and leading individuals and/or teams; incorporates research, scholarship and/or professional practice into those activities.
This leads to Senior Fellow of HEA status

Source: Adapted from http://www.heacademy.ac.uk/assets/York/documents/ourwork/professional/ ProfessionalStandardsFramework.pdf

Table 28.1B Areas of activity, knowledge and values within the Framework

Areas of activity

1 Design and planning of learning activities and/or programmes of study

2 Teaching and/or supporting student learning

3 Assessment and giving feedback to learners

4 Developing effective environments and student support and guidance

5 Integration of scholarship, research and professional activities with teaching and supporting learning

6 Evaluation of practice and continuing professional development

Core knowledge

Knowledge and understanding of:

1 The subject material

2 Appropriate methods for teaching and learning in the subject area and at the level of the academic programme

3 How students learn, both generally and in the subject

4 The use of appropriate learning technologies

5 Methods of evaluating the effectiveness of teaching

6 The implications of quality assurance and enhancement for professional practice

Professional values

1 Respect for individual learners

2 Commitment to incorporating the process and outcomes of relevant research, scholarship and/or professional practice

3 Commitment to the development of learning communities

4 Commitment to encouraging participation in higher education, acknowledging diversity and promoting equality of opportunity

5 Commitment to continuing professional development and evaluation of practice

Accredited programmes differ from institution to institution. Most commonly probationary staff are required to enroll for a postgraduate certificate or diploma that leads to national recognition at the level of 'Fellow' of the HEA. In some institutions there is a formal requirement or strong encouragement for probationary staff to complete a full Master's programme.

Accredited programmes generally 'translate' the three areas of activity in Table 28.1B into programme learning outcomes, and create a pattern of assessment suited to these and institutional circumstances. Assessment requirements therefore vary widely, but all include the demonstration of practice and reflection on it.

WAYS OF DEMONSTRATING TEACHING AND EDUCATIONAL ACHIEVEMENT

As already indicated, the teaching and learning credentials of early career academics are often demonstrated through growing practice and completion of a programme of assessed study and practice. In such programmes the distinction between **formative** and **summative** work is often blurred. Work completed for, or as part of, or able to count towards certification often contributes to the development of practice through reflection and feedback (formative) as well as demonstrating that the standard required for the qualification has been reached (summative). We comment below on a range of types of assessment commonly in use; most programmes use more than one method.

Interrogating practice

If you had to devise the formative and summative assessment requirements to demonstrate achievement of the intermediate level of the UK Professional Standards, what methods would you use? Why?

How similar are the requirements you have devised to those that your institution actually uses?

Techniques commonly used for assessment and the enhancement of practice

Observation of teaching

In its simplest form, observation of teaching is the process by which an individual's teaching is observed by another with the intention of providing feedback or eliciting a discussion that can enable the person observed to enhance the quality of their teaching and their students' learning. In higher education it is often interpreted to mean observation of lectures, but any type of teaching activity can be observed, although sometimes the logistics of this may be difficult. The observer may be a peer, colleague in the same discipline, or a specialist educationalist.

Observation of teaching is one of the most common ways by which academics are asked to demonstrate their skills as teachers and in supporting student learning. It is commonly used in a developmental way and may also be used summatively. Evidence from observation of teaching may be used to inform decisions about confirmation in post at the end of the probationary period and as part of an accredited programme.

Commonly observation of teaching follows a three-stage process (Gosling, 2005):

- *Stage 1*: Pre-observation meeting/discussion. This should be a face-to-face meeting between the observer and the observed teacher to agree the ground rules and what is to be observed. Many issues can be considered in this discussion, including intentions, teacher preferences, any special needs of the class, and teaching philosophy.

- *Stage 2*: Observing the teaching. Most universities have criteria that are used for observation, ideally based on research evidence about good teaching. There are also protocols on good practice that need to be followed (Gosling, 2005) and include informing the students about the presence of an observer and ensuring that the observer is discreet, does not participate and causes minimal disturbance to the teaching session. Fullerton (2003) provides a good general purpose form from the University of Plymouth for developmental observation of teaching.

- *Stage 3*: Post-observation meeting. The observer and the observed should meet as soon as possible after the observation (usually within a week). At this meeting the observed lecturer is prompted to reflect on the session and receives feedback on what was seen and experienced in the class. What went well and aspects that may need strengthening are both considered. The real point of this discussion is to prompt the observed lecturer to reflect on the experience so as to develop their own practice.

Teaching portfolios

A teaching **portfolio** (subsequently referred to in this chapter as a 'portfolio') is a personal record of achievement and professional development that demonstrates level of attainment, scope of experience, range of skills and activity, and/or progression as a university teacher (Fry and Ketteridge, 2003). They are commonly used at the end of the probationary period or as part of an application for promotion (see also Chapter 29). A more specific type of structured portfolio may also form part of the assessment for a professional development programme.

Portfolios need to have a clear structure and, depending on the purpose, this will usually be determined by institutional, assessment or other requirements. A portfolio should have an index or map to aid the reader or assessor in navigation and to help them find specific items of information or evidence. There will be a collection of selected illustrative materials relating to practice and providing evidence of it. It will normally include information from observation of teaching and student feedback. Most portfolios require personal reflective commentary linking evidence to specific themes, referring to the literature and showing how practice has been critically reviewed and developed. This is certainly the case for those used summatively in programmes. In portfolios it is the quality rather than the quantity of information that is always crucial.

Interrogating practice

- Does your institution use a teaching portfolio as part of a programme or for any other purpose?
- If so, do you know the required format/s of the portfolio?
- What materials have you collected for your own teaching portfolio?

Action research

Case study 1 from the University of Plymouth describes action research as part of a programme.

Essays and case studies

Essays are used in a few programmes. Here the requirement is usually for an essay in the arts or humanities style that demonstrates good powers of reasoning, knowledge of theory and/or policy, good and critical use of literature and perhaps reflection on practice. It could be argued that this method is good for demonstrating formal knowledge, but not necessarily strongly linked to developing practice. Variations on essays, such as position papers, mock grant applications and so on are also used. Case studies and reports may be used to link reflection, use of research evidence and literature with the developing teaching practice of the author.

Critical appraisal/review of journal paper

An educational journal paper(s) is set or chosen and then critiqued. This helps engagement with the concepts of learning and teaching in higher education and the research and literature, but unless linked to personal practice (e.g. through choice of paper) can also be a rather formal 'scholastic' exercise.

Reflection, reflective practice, reflective writing

Reflection involves consideration of an experience, or of learning, so as to enhance understanding or inform action. Reflective practice is the idea that 'practitioners' engage in reflection as part of their normal approach to their job. It is thus part of what drives successful professional activity, enabling it to progress, grow, respond to new ideas and introduce innovation. Not everyone 'automatically' uses reflection to enhance their performance in all areas; thus programmes for early career academics place considerable stress on using reflection to enhance teaching practice. Boud *et al.* (1985) describe reflection as 'turning experience into learning'. Reflection as it relates to **experiential learning** is discussed more fully in Chapter 2. Some programmes ask participants to reflect on their practice in writing, by keeping a diary, journal or log-book, or by writing a reflective commentary on their teaching. Reflective writing requires writing in the first person and analysis of one's own actions in the light of responses to them (including one's own) and their effectiveness. Evidence demonstrating the impact of reflective practice is hard to come by. Biggs suggests that reflection, through interpretation and integration, translates lower-order inputs to higher-order knowledge (Biggs, 1988: 190). Chapter 15 makes the pertinent point that consideration of generic knowledge about learning and teaching, personal style preferences and discipline-specific knowledge need to be brought together by reflection to develop a personal and discipline-based pedagogy. Case study 2 describes how one educational developer introduces the idea of reflection to early career academics and how he seeks to help them use reflection to enhance practice.

Case study 1: Using action research to enhance practice

The Postgraduate Certificate for Learning and Teaching in Higher Education at the University of Plymouth includes a module focused on developing professional practice specific to individual disciplines. This module is assessed by a small research/development project in which participants demonstrate some aspect of their own practice in the context of their discipline with a view to enhancing their students' learning experiences. An underlying principle is to encourage practitioners to be aware of their own practice and, by using self-critical reflection, facilitate a process of change and improvement of practice. In our experience, this was best achieved through **action research.**

There are many definitions of action research to be found in the literature. McKernan (1991: 5) suggests: 'Action research is systematic, self-reflective scientific enquiry by practitioners to improve practice.' Action research is often described as strategic, sequential and cumulative, each step informing the next. Kemmis and McTaggart (1988) see it as a spiral activity where the researcher plans, acts, observes and reflects, whereas Stringer (1996) refers to action research as a model of 'look, think, act', an iterative process carrying the researcher forward. Whichever model is chosen it is complex, and therefore the teacher-researcher needs to be flexible in approach.

At Plymouth over the years, a wide range of action research projects have been undertaken across different disciplines, focusing on various aspects of teaching practice. The titles below provide a flavour of this:

- Using video teaching to prepare students for the objective structural clinical examination in extended nurse prescribing
- Improving the learning experience of biosciences students on a first-year field course
- Improving provision of postgraduate generic research skills training
- A study of health visitor student community practice placements that critically analyses and evaluates their effectiveness in promoting student learning

While many of the participants felt overwhelmed by an approach that was, for them, very different to anything they had done before, once they embarked on the project they found it rewarding and insightful. They felt the participative nature of the action research project had led to more informative and applicable outcomes because stakeholders were involved in the data-gathering exercises. The action research made a difference to them and was rewarding and of benefit to their teaching practice.

(Dr Rachael Carkett, now at University of Teesside)

Case study 2: Reflecting – why and how

Reflection, that is conscious and purposeful pondering about our own thoughts and behaviours, is a fundamental part of life. Without reflection, we cannot make sense of what happens to us and engender actions aimed at solving the problems life throws at us. Reflecting becomes particularly important when our views and expectations are challenged.

In university life, academics are being pressurised to embrace more roles (research, teaching and management), in relation to more varied student populations and demands for a higher level of accountability. Academics are now being called upon to reflect actively on who they are and what they do, on a more conscious level, than ever before.

As a tutor and assessment adviser to academics taking an HEA accredited qualification, one area I spend a lot of time discussing with my tutees is the concept and practise of reflection. This is because some lecturers find it difficult (if not alien, at times, because of their own disciplinary domain and practices) to 'discuss' themselves. Putting such reflections in writing can be challenging, as it requires the 'I' to become central to the act of writing, when it is customary, in many disciplines, to reach for 'objectivity' by using the passive or impersonal voice. Putting oneself under the microscope, so to speak, in order to question and refine the thinking and behavioural patterns that guide one's work can be a tall order.

However, there are things that lecturers can do to reflect effectively. Here is some advice I give my tutees:

- Start getting used to describing your work environment in some detail – this will help you see things you normally do not see, as you take them for granted.
- In your interaction with your work environment, record how much this changes *you*, both as a person and as a lecturer, and how much you manage to change it.
- However, *do not stop at the descriptive level*; learn how to routinely problematise your work environment, asking yourself 'how' and 'why' things work in a certain way in your classroom, department, institution and in the higher education system. For example, if you record a problem in your teaching (say a lack of student discipline), is this due (solely) to your being unable to control a class or are there wider factors that create this problem (e.g. time of your lectures, preferred departmental mode of delivery, the way the curriculum is organised, overcrowding)?
- Remember that reflection is helped by comparisons, and these can be made at different levels. First of all, look for similarities and attrition points between

your own beliefs and views about teaching and learning (and education, in general) and those that are promoted within your own work environment; try to explain the reasons behind similarities and differences. Is the cultural (national and international) and political background something that impacts directly on the way education is perceived and practised by you and in your work environment? In what ways? In writing down your reflections, do not be afraid to use phrases such as 'I think', 'I believe', 'in my opinion'.

- Share your ideas on education and educational practices with colleagues and try to find out their views on the issues that concern you; record similarities and discrepancies between their thinking and yours, and attempt to explain the reasons behind these.
- Similarly, ask your students if teaching practices you adopt with them are useful for their learning and are well received. Students can act as a powerful mirror for your work and, ultimately, they are the ones for whom the improvement should be made – they can give you important insights that may help you to reflect about your work in an important way.
- In addition, it is helpful to compare your thinking with that canonised in educational literature; this will assist you in seeing the bigger picture and frame your thinking within wider contexts. This is a particularly valid exercise when it comes to writing about your teaching. It also has the benefit of making you see that what you may perceive as 'your own' problem is something that is part of a bigger picture.
- Finally, link your reflection to actions: once you have identified issues, think carefully about ways to resolve them, and put these into practice. Record issues that arise from the revision and try to find further solutions.

I suggest that reflection is an ongoing process which links together thinking and action; it is a never-ending cycle that helps in becoming an actor of innovation, rather than a passive recipient of change. Similarly, it helps you to see how you progress in your career and what paths may be taken to improve things for you and your working environment.

(Dr Roberto Di Napoli,
Centre for Educational Development,
Imperial College London)

Critical incidents

Some programmes ask staff to collect and reflect on key moments in their teaching. These may be moments of success, failure or puzzlement, but are instances the practitioner finds worthy of comment – they are critical in this sense. The incidents are generally reported in writing by means of description, analysis of what was happening and of the writer's reaction to it, reflection, and speculation about how to avoid or re-create similar incidents in the future. They are primarily a vehicle to encourage university teachers to think deeply about their practice.

Engaging with and using the literature

Most programmes require participants to demonstrate an introductory knowledge of appropriate literature. By displaying such knowledge, participants can demonstrate understanding and critique of key concepts (such as approaches to learning, outcomes-based curricula). A further aim is that participants read for themselves the research of some of the key figures working in higher education research and practice. The aim is not uncritical acceptance, but to promote understanding of ideas, correct use of appropriate terminology, critique of research, and critical consideration of applicability to one's own context – or any other.

Vivas

Viva voce examinations occasionally form part of the assessment of accredited programmes. In a few institutions a viva is a routine part of the final summative assessment process and is used to test breadth of knowledge and how well educational theory informs professional practice. In other cases the viva may simply be used to confirm a pass where there is uncertainty over other evidence presented by a candidate.

Commentary on programmes and demonstrating teaching credentials

Making public one's teaching and supervisory processes, demonstrating an ability to describe them in appropriate terms and analysing and reflecting upon their impact is a comparatively new concept in higher education. Long-term evidence of its efficacy as a method for personal and institutional development and student benefit is still thin. Research by Gibbs and Coffey (2004) indicates that training in teaching can be effective, showing from data collected in 22 universities in eight countries that teachers, and as a consequence their students, undergo positive changes, whereas a control group who did not receive training did not enhance their practice or in some cases made negative changes.

Another point worth considering is how effective are the assessment and 'demonstration' methods that are in use. Do they assess worthwhile things? Is the judgement that is made as a consequence of assessment **reliable**? Do they assess the areas set out in the learning outcomes and the UKPS – or any other schema? Do they also have a formative impact – or is it just assessment for the sake of assessment? It is noticeable that few assessment methods, for good or ill, can really attempt to assess 'values'. Another key area concerns how far teachers are really able to integrate theory and their own practice, as well as which assessment methods can attempt to investigate this (i.e. **validity**). Should we put so much emphasis on assessment? Aren't enhancement and engagement with practice more effective and appropriate aims which assessment can get in the way of? How far do institutional and departmental norms and hierarchies prevent the inexperienced academic from exploring and developing their teaching in innovative ways? Stephen Rowland (2000) raises a number of such critical questions about teaching and its development.

Case studies 3 and 4 consist largely of self-report by early career academics on their responses to programmes and assessments in teaching and learning. The academics come from two UK universities with profiles that are very different from each other in terms of student bodies, research ratings and staff time spent on teaching. The two accredited programmes use some common but also some differing assessment formats.

> **Case study 3: Perceptions of assessment and the Postgraduate Certificate in Learning and Teaching in Higher Education (PGCLTHE) at the University of Leeds**

This short case study has two strands. First, there is a description of the course and the assessment process. Second, there are quotes (*in italics*) from recent completers in response to the question 'What did the assessment for the PGCLTHE do for, and to, you?'

The PGCLTHE, a 60-credit, M-level qualification for staff at Leeds, may be gained by two different routes. The learning outcomes are the same for both routes but the assessment method varies: four case studies of teaching practice plus a professional development plan for one route, and a portfolio for the other. Both routes address the requirements of the UK Professional Standards Framework at standard descriptor 2 (Table 28.1A).

What participants say about the outcomes

There are five core attributes that the PGCLTHE programme aims to ingrain in those who successfully complete it. They should:

1 Develop the habit of continually reviewing their teaching practice in a critical way (reflection).

   On completion of each assignment, I became more and more aware of the need to take time out of my busy teaching schedule and reflect upon what it is that I am trying to achieve in each module, and whether I am doing that in the best possible way.

   Far from a hoop-jumping exercise, I believe it [the assessment process] has made me think more carefully about why I am doing what I am doing at every stage of the teaching process.

Carrying out and writing up the assignments, however, was hugely important in fixing critical lessons about best practice, developing practical skills and, above all, in rendering my practice reflexive.

2   Use information, as appropriate, from students, peers, colleagues, the literature and other sources of good practice to inform the review (evidence-based).

The process of writing the case studies has enabled me to discover a world of theory and scholarship in the field of applied adult learning that I was formerly unaware of.

Discussions with my mentor about each assignment became as valuable as the summative feedback.

I found carrying out both the further reading and the assignments a vital part of the learning experience. The further reading particularly served to reinforce and provide a larger evaluative context for what was learned in class.

3   Use their self-reviews to develop their practice to benefit students (enhancing student-centred learning).

The process of reflecting upon my current practice enabled me to sharpen my awareness, not only of my students' needs, but of my own needs as a practitioner.

It [the assessment process] has given me the confidence to introduce novel teaching approaches which I might have avoided previously.

4   Stay current both in what they teach and the methods they use to provide learning opportunities for students (current and relevant).

In this sense, the PGCLTHE assignments, though demanding at times, enabled me to see how important it is that I continue to read the current literature about assessment, course design, e-learning, and related subjects, in order to continue to provide an appropriate teaching and learning experience for my students.

5   Behave professionally as teachers and managers of learning, in terms of the values, norms and expectations of their discipline, institution and wider society (values-based).

The requirements of PGCLTHE assignments were such that I had to engage more fully with the language of higher education, and with the relevant quality assurance documents that pertained to my own subject area.

Participants have also made some more general comments about time commitment and value added:

Doing the assessment gave me space, and a reason, for developing my practice when I would not, otherwise, have been able to carve out time to do so.

It was a great relief to realise that my PGCLTHE assignments reflected my teaching role and therefore enhanced my practice as opposed to increasing my workload.

With so many commitments in my job, it was only the assessments that made me get into the material. If I had just attended the taught component, this would not have been enough.

The time commitment required is significant. In the time I could have written two or three research papers or four research grant applications . . . However, the list of things I have gained from the course is too long to write down here, but I feel that I am a more innovative teacher, and better aware of problems, issues and possible solutions in teaching and learning. I am a more professional assessor and module designer.

And finally, it might be a qualification in learning and teaching, but participants gain in more ways than enhancing their teaching practice:

They [colleagues in department] became more confident that I knew what I was doing. I became credible as an academic.

The reflective approach which the assessment requires has come in useful in other areas, such as staff review and setting teaching and research goals.

I now have a more critical and curious outlook, and the process of assessment has engendered more of a sense of pride in my work. . . . I now not only care 'how' and 'what', but more so, care 'why'.

(Christopher Butcher, University of Leeds)

Case study 4: Engaging with assessment in a professional development programme-appraisal and advice from practitioners at London Metropolitan University

Context

Seeking to provide course participants with experience of different forms and functions of assessment, the Postgraduate Certificate programme discussed in this case study employs a variety of methods. The assessment process is designed to promote accomplishment of the core objectives of enhancing awareness of pedagogical issues, critical reflection on academic practice and scholarly engagement with educational theory, research and policy. Three main types of assessment are reviewed, drawing primarily from a survey of the current participants, with comments from recent course evaluations.

Reflective portfolio

The portfolio encompasses four interconnected components: a critical review of an article on learning and teaching, a position paper on a theme in higher education policy, an analysis of an observed teaching session, and a reflective commentary on the entire portfolio.

The various tasks presented opportunities to engage with *'relevant literature and current debates'* and *'look at best practice'* in different subject fields. Participants appreciated the *'space and incentive'* offered to *'connect theory with practice'* and *'think more broadly'* about HE policy. This contributed to a *'better understanding'* of real issues facing teachers (such as retention or plagiarism) and how policies can *'impact in the classroom'*.

Participants reported finding the teaching observations *'very useful and formative'*, despite noting the time expenditure on setting up meetings and filling in forms, and prior trepidation. Receiving *'constructive feedback'* was *'confidence-building'* and *'a good basis for discussion and reflection'* on practice.

The advice regarding observation of teaching is that: *'it affords you the opportunity to improve your teaching practice in a secure environment'*. In order to gain full benefit, do peer observation with someone *'in a completely different discipline'* and explore the transferability of approaches; *'ensure time is allocated for feedback'* and *'do not be afraid to criticise or self-criticise'* – in an appropriately sensitive way – as *'this is a very good method of learning and becoming better teachers'*.

The global commentary on the portfolio helped to pull the learning experience together, as it meant participants had to *'reflect on* [their] *reflections'* and the essentials of *'what good teaching and learning is all about'*. Although for some people *'it may seem like a drag'*, the exercise ultimately proved *'very useful'* for most participants. It was a *'good method to audit one's teaching practice'* and plan better teaching strategies for the future.

Group presentation

Participants work in small groups to research a topic on assessment, culminating in a group presentation that is peer-, tutor- and self-assessed, using criteria devised by the presenting group.

'I hate the thought of group work but enjoy the reality' was a commonly expressed sentiment. Participants identified the benefits as gaining *'real insights'* into *'how groups can (or can't) work'* [sic] and into *'the student experience of group work'*. Overall, participants consistently acknowledged the enhanced understanding of

assessment, design and criteria they gain, and their increased interest *'to know more about ways to help students learn through the use of assessment'*.

Practice-focused project

Working on projects directly related to academic practice was for most participants a productive process. It offered the opportunity to *'research the literature'*, and *'develop knowledge and skills'*. Participants were able to apply *'theoretical work'* and *'principles of effective learning and teaching'* to practical ends such as (re)designing an assessment or a module. Some started to think *'more holistically'* about educational issues and the purpose of study in one's subject area. And advice to others is to *'use the projects to inform your actual teaching programme'*.

In doing peer reviews of draft projects, many participants found it *'valuable to look at what peers had done in different settings'* and to receive *'constructive criticism'* which could inform *'the development of* [their] *own project'*. It also enhanced awareness of the *'educative factor of feedback'*. Reviewing work for *'peers outside the subject area'* was useful as it focused attention on pedagogical elements and not just syllabus matters.

Conclusion

On a final, encouraging note: genuine engagement with the assessment process in a professional development programme can produce cumulative, enriching outcomes that become clearer with hindsight. Participants described these gains in terms of becoming *'a better reflective practitioner'*. The course assessments enabled participants *'to develop professionally in terms of the scholarly work'* undertaken and acquire *'more confidence in my own practice'*. As one participant wrote: *'It was only at the end of the whole process that it became obvious how effective the assessments were in imparting new perspectives, experience and skills. These provided a very good model for teaching and learning in one's own subject area.'*

(Digby Warren, London Metropolitan University)

OVERVIEW

This chapter has described commonly used means of enhancing, assessing and demonstrating teaching and learning expertise, especially in the context of accredited programmes aligned to the UK Professional Standards Framework. It has sounded a note of caution about the evidence base for the efficacy and psychometric properties of some assessment modes, but has also drawn on personal reports to indicate the nature of the impact they have on the practice of those who have experienced them, as participants and course tutors.

REFERENCES

Biggs, J (1988) 'Approaches to learning and to essay writing', in R Schmeck (ed.), *Learning Strategies and Learning Styles* (pp. 185–228), London: Plenum Press.

Boud, D, Keogh, R and Walker, D (eds) (1985) *Reflection: Turning Experience into Learning*, London: Kogan Page.

Fry, H and Ketteridge, S W (2003) 'Teaching portfolios', in H Fry, S W Ketteridge, and S Marshall (eds), *A Handbook for Teaching and Learning in Higher Education: Enhancing Academic Practice* (pp. 242–252), London: Routledge.

Fullerton, H (2003) 'Observation of teaching', in H Fry, S W Ketteridge and S Marshall (eds), *A Handbook for Teaching and Learning in Higher Education: Enhancing Academic Practice* (pp. 226–241), London: Routledge.

Gibbs, G and Coffey, M (2004) 'The impact of training of university teachers on their teaching skills, their approach to teaching and the approach to learning of their students', *Active Learning in Higher Education*, 5(1), 73–86.

Gosling, D (2005) *Peer Observation of Teaching*, SEDA Paper 118, Staff and Educational Development Association, London.

Higher Education Academy (HEA) (2006) The UK Professional Standards Framework. Available online at <http://www.heacademy.ac.uk/ourwork/policy/framework> (accessed 5 November 2007).

Kemmis, S and McTaggart, R (eds) (1988) *The Action Research Planner* (3rd edn), Geelong, Victoria: Deakin University Press.

McKernan, J (1991) *Curriculum Action Research: A Handbook of Methods and Resources for the Reflective Practitioner* (2nd edn), London: Kogan Page.

Rowland, S (2000) *The Enquiring University Teacher*, Buckingham: SRHE and the Open University Press.

Stringer, E T (1996) *Action Research: A Handbook for Practitioners*, Thousand Oaks, CA: Sage.

FURTHER READING

Brookfield, S (1995) *Becoming a Critically Reflective Teacher*, San Francisco, CA: Jossey-Bass. Written specially for teachers in higher education. Guides readers through many processes for becoming critically reflective about teaching.

Eraut, M (1994) *Developing Professional Knowledge and Competence,* London: Falmer. Still the single best place to read Michael Eraut's influential ideas about the nature of professional knowledge and professional expertise, but it is also worth following up his more recent work.

Schon, D (1987) *Educating the Reflective Practitioner*, San Francisco, CA: Jossey-Bass. The key text on reflection.

The Higher Education Academy website (<http://www.heacademy.ac.uk>) and its subject centres provide many useful resources for staff following accredited programmes. Some centres, such as maths, stats and OR network, offer dedicated induction courses for lecturers new to teaching in these disciplines.

29 Teaching excellence as a vehicle for career progression

Stephanie Marshall and Gus Pennington

SCOPE AND RATIONALE OF CHAPTER

Accomplished university teachers have always been well regarded by their former students and are frequently remembered with gratitude and affection in later life (Glasser, 1988; Steiner, 1997). Equally, recognition of an individual's teaching prowess by their peers and institutions has been somewhat muted and, until relatively recently, has been given little or no formal attention in the determination of professional advancement and reward. This situation is changing significantly in some countries, including the UK which is the focus of this chapter. Here national policies, funding incentives, market forces, institutional missions and the rapid growth of teaching-only posts (Court, 2007) place a new emphasis and enhanced value on competent teaching in all its forms. In virtually all UK universities and institutes, even top-flight researchers with some formal responsibilities for students are expected to possess and demonstrate continuing expertise in teaching, including the supervision of research students.

Where once the nature, volume and scope of individual professional development for teaching was a private matter it is now clearly in the public domain and subject to various forms of review and regulation. Appraisal of performance, quality assurance procedures, institutional and subject-level audits and requirements for professional body membership have exposed a once 'secret garden'. Changes in the post-Dearing (**NCIHE**, 1997) higher education landscape, such as confirmation of the role of the Quality Assurance Agency (**QAA**), the establishment of the Higher Education Academy (**HEA**) and Learning and Teaching Committees within Higher Education Funding Councils have kept learning and teaching matters to the fore and high on the national agenda. More recently, the advent, enhanced public profile and external leverage of the **National Student Survey (NSS)** has provided a fresh impetus for institutions to ensure they have structures and policies in place to assure and enhance all forms of effective academic practice. The intrinsic value of securing quality in this core element of every university's mission has been bolstered by a more demanding, fee-paying student population and the pragmatics of increased competition for students both indigenous and from overseas. Establishment of means by which they can bring about a positive student experience has led many HEIs *inter alia* to introduce a range of career paths to ensure that their most competent teachers are identified, formally acknowledged and rewarded.

A PLATFORM FOR CAREER PROGRESSION

It is against the above background that career progression needs to be considered; thus this chapter seeks to explore approaches that a number of higher education institutions (HEIs) have adopted to acknowledge these trends and to better integrate learning and teaching into career advancement once initial competence has been established. Its other concern is to provide suggestions as to how individuals might extend their experiential profile and develop a documentary evidence base to satisfy teaching-related promotion criteria. Use of paper-based or e-portfolios (Brenton, 2003; Kimball, 2005) which strike a balance between flexibility and structure, and institutional and individual needs, are ideal for this purpose (Seldin, 1997; Baume and Yorke, 2002).

What follows might usefully be augmented with ideas found in the preceding chapter as the two are complementary. In terms of its distinctive contribution, however, this chapter is based on four key propositions:

1 That continuing professional development (CPD) for learning and teaching (including supervision) can no longer be conceived as a voluntary, private activity for academics; this function of their role is underpinned increasingly by contractual requirements and the need for quality enhancement based in a nationally recognised code of practice. In essence, the management of career-long teaching competence is no longer an aspirational ideal but part of the organisational fabric of contemporary university life (QAA, 2003, 2006).

2 That whatever the specifics of CPD (and irrespective of age, career status, subject specialism or particular pedagogic expertise) it is increasingly necessary for individuals to engage with activities which ensure they are competent to perform *both* their current role (maintenance learning) *and* foreseeable future demands (anticipatory learning) (Pennington and Smith, 2002: 254).

3 That while career routes which make it worthwhile for academics to pay particular attention to learning and teaching have tended, hitherto, to be the preserve of post-1992 HEIs (see Case study 1), this trend is spreading to all parts of the UK higher education sector. Initiatives across all types of institution are accelerating the establishment of well-defined career routes based on 'teaching excellence' comparable to those for research excellence. A normative process is taking place that will be hard to resist in the long term.

4 That individuals, if they are so minded, can prepare to meet the above challenges by systematic engagement with a range of developmental activities which, when aggregated, leave them better placed to seek career advancement on the basis of their learning and teaching expertise. It is clear that if this process is started early and is

given career-long attention it has the potential to open up an attractive, alternative career route to that which has conventionally existed.

Differing requirements in different contexts

Traditionally, it has been suggested that the majority of pre-1992 universities paid lip-service only to promoting a culture where learning and teaching are formally integrated into career pathways. Indeed, a general lack of any means to demonstrate and be rewarded for excellence in teaching has been a common complaint from staff in these institutions for at least a decade. Examination of a range of promotion criteria from this group of 'research-intensive' institutions suggests, however, that a potentially far-reaching shift in policy has begun and that where career progression on the basis of teaching is now actively encouraged, detailed work has been undertaken to codify requirements, to determine appropriate indicators and to identify elements to be addressed and evidenced (see Case study 2).

Academics who work in contexts in which there is a pressure 'to publish or perish' and who are required to respond to the increased use of metrics as a major determinant of research performance may question, understandably, the wisdom of paying too much attention to teaching. Fortunately, there is growing awareness not only of the validity of promoting the teaching–research nexus as a means of 'growing' institutions' own cadres of potential research students (see Chapter 12) but also as a means of enriching a distinctive form of teaching (Elton, 2005; Jenkins *et al.*, 2007). In short, the argument has moved on and is now centred on the balance to be struck between differing permutations of individual teaching–research profiles in particular contexts.

What are the key elements?

As the first two case studies illustrate, in seeking promotion through a teaching 'route', UK HEIs aspire to an extensive profile of significant activities at a level considerably higher than the Associate and Fellow categories of the **UK professional standards** (see Chapter 28). Institutional requirements for the award of Chairs line up better with criteria established in 2007 for award of a Senior Fellowship of the HEA (see Further reading). Common components focus on personal excellence in teaching and learning, leadership, a national and/or international reputation, successful securing of competitive external funding and contributions to scholarship in the field. For many universities an established record in supervising research students through to completion in an appropriate time-scale is also essential. Despite the potentially contested nature of such concepts (Skelton, 2007), weight is given to criteria by the use of 'qualifiers' such as 'excellence', 'outstanding', 'distinguished' and 'respected'. Curriculum innovation or a distinctive approach to pedagogy are additionally identified as defining features of superior performance.

Case study 1: Northumbria University: criteria for promotion to Chair in Teaching and Learning

Production of a portfolio which includes evidence of distinctive, innovative and influential examples of programme development, pedagogy and/or learning enhancement both within the university and at national level. The Appointments Board will take into account all forms of evidence including published works and other examples of dissemination. Evidence should demonstrate some of the following:

- The delivery of nationally recognised teaching-related professional service to other universities and organisations.
- Active involvement and/or leadership of national committees relating to learning and teaching.
- Recognition of significant adoption at national level of learning and teaching innovations originally developed by the individual.
- Keynote addresses at teaching-related conferences.
- Learning and teaching leadership across the university.
- The development of appealing and innovative programmes that have attracted significant numbers of students.
- The development of successful corporate programmes.
- The development of successful short courses.
- Leading teaching collaborations with other institutions.
- Publications on teaching and learning in refereed journals, textbooks and conference papers.
- A substantial number of significant learning and teaching-related grants secured on behalf of the university.

Case study 2: University of Manchester: criteria for promotion to Chair in Teaching and Learning

Outstanding ability ... will be demonstrated by academic leadership and distinction in Teaching and Learning, including contributions to the advancement of knowledge and understanding or its creative or professional application in the field of learning at the highest level, and the ability to influence, stimulate and inspire others; and outstanding achievement in contribution to student learning as evidenced in either peer-reviewed or peer-reviewable outputs including excellence in practice in the field.

The award is designated to recognise distinguished teachers and scholars regardless of subject or pedagogic approach, and to recognise in a more formal and distinctive way the centrality of teaching and the management of learning and assessment as core activities within the university. The aim in part is to encourage teaching excellence by the creation of role models, and to aid the dissemination of good practice. But it is also to recognise outstanding performance and professional reputation in the field at an international level.

Applicants must be able to provide evidence of:

- an established reputation as an excellent teacher and scholar, in addition to showing that they are reflective practitioners, respected by peers and students for their contribution to the learning and assessment process;
- experience of leading curriculum development teams, introducing changes and innovations in teaching and learning and experienced in the evaluation of teaching, learning and assessment;
- ability to demonstrate a powerful commitment to the future development of teaching and learning within their field and a capacity to contribute to the leadership of learning development within their area of subject expertise and more broadly within the university;
- recognition in terms of a reputation that is recognised at an international level, and also scholarly outputs, which may include publications that are either peer reviewed or peer reviewable.

Applicants should include details of achievements and accountabilities which indicate that their work is of international standing, including, for example, details of successful teaching approaches, including, as appropriate, student, peer and external assessments and evaluations, and original materials used in teaching; innovations made in support of student learning; curriculum development; publications centred on teaching of the subject; participation in international conferences and so on, concerned with the development of the teaching of their subject in higher education; membership of international committees and so on, concerned with the teaching of their subject in higher education; collaboration with external bodies; evidence of their external reputation as a teacher and scholar of note.

There is no single, prescribed or guaranteed way in which individuals can satisfy the emerging criteria for appointment to a 'teaching excellence' Chair or similar type of post. The criteria for such promotion may differ widely not only among HEIs, but also among disciplines. Each case, necessarily, is judged on its merits and to a large extent is context dependent (see Case study 3). Even so, it is possible to identify a broad trend of experience from 'novice' to 'expert' which leads towards this goal (see below). A starting point is the formation of a strong personal base of effective practice, possibly initiated through successful completion of an institutional postgraduate HE teaching qualification. It is perfectly possible, of course, to build a strong subject-based competence as a teacher without recourse to a formal programme, but well-delivered, 'fit-for-purpose' programmes present opportunities for structured engagement with key issues and processes in relation to learning, teaching and assessment, skilled support, mentoring and feedback, and an initial exposure to the scholarship of the field.

MOVING ON: BUILDING A BASE OF EXPERIENCE

After achieving and demonstrating initial competence in teaching there are a number of proven ways to secure continuing career development. In broad terms these might include some or all of the following:

- Gaining experience, confidence and competence across a wider repertoire of teaching, learning and assessment methods at both undergraduate and postgraduate levels.
- Leading the design and integration of larger 'units' of learning, for example, clusters or sequences of modules across semesters; taking responsibility for the overall quality of a substantial part or the whole of a course programme.
- Leading or managing curriculum innovation, both to enhance the student experience and to provide a 'market advantage' to the institution, faculty or department.
- Securing small institutional grants and competitive national funding for developmental projects or trialling of leading-edge practice. Success of this kind develops project management and leadership capabilities as well as generating academic outputs for dissemination.
- Gaining internal teaching awards or similar external recognition such as a National Teaching Fellowship or HEA Senior Fellow status.
- Providing support, coaching and mentoring to colleagues and external, teaching-related consultancy or training to other institutions nationally and internationally. Helping to deliver a formal postgraduate teaching programme for new staff is an excellent way of sharing expertise and contributing to the next generation of teachers.
- Building a base of expertise as an external examiner, including chairing examination boards. Undertaking this kind of role exposes individuals to the fine-grained workings of a range of other institutions and helps develop more rounded judgement about teaching quality and standards.
- Significant responsibility within a graduate school.
- Contributing to the activities of, or taking a formal role in, appropriate national committees, learned societies and HEA **Subject Centres**.
- Contributing to the accreditation and CPD activities of professional, regulatory and statutory bodies. Engagement of this kind provides extensive opportunities for subject/professionally specific CPD and may be particularly relevant to career

progression in areas such as law, medicine, dentistry and social work which are regulated through a 'licence to practise'.

- Participating in internal subject reviews and QAA academic reviews and institutional audit activities.
- Undertaking further formal and accredited study to update, extend or replace initial qualifications. This may be particularly relevant where individuals feel they have 'hit a ceiling', choose to change roles or are required by their institution to add new skills to existing expertise (see Case study 3).
- Engaging in teaching-related scholarship, research and editorial activity of a generic and/or disciplinary nature.

Individuals who can demonstrate a convincing profile across most of the above categories and who additionally evidence commitment to reflection and continuous professional improvement should be well placed to respond to promotion criteria for senior 'teaching-focused' posts irrespective of institutional mission or their own teaching specialism.

Case study 3: A Master's award at Coventry University

A strategic decision at Coventry to make 'third-stream' activities the second major activity in the university led to the revision of academic contracts to include significant amounts of such activity. The opportunity was taken to review and revise an existing Master's programme that had previously focused solely on teaching and learning. New modules were introduced. Developing an Applied Research Profile offered an opportunity for participants to take stock of their expertise, to learn new skills and to plan their future applied research. The Centre for the Study of HE (CSHE) worked closely with the university's applied research support staff in order to offer the programme. A module in Academic Leadership was designed to complement existing non-certificated provision offered by human resources. The module focused on issues that were specific to leadership in an academic setting, including distributed leadership, collegiality and interdisciplinarity. An existing module, Perspectives on Professional Practice, was revised to provide a core experience for participants. Each module was made available on both a stand-alone basis and as part of a full Master's award. These changes, which brought provision into alignment with the institution's strategic plan, together with more focused and energetic marketing, have meant that Coventry staff participation in the Master's provision has increased considerably.

(Prof Paul Blackmore, now King's College London, and
Dr Andrew Rothwell, Coventry University)

What is it to be scholarly, what is it to be competent?

Demonstrable personal competence in teaching and the production of a range of appropriate scholarly outputs are interrelated and indispensable elements of appointment to a senior 'teaching excellence' post. Indeed, understanding the myriad connections and syntheses between 'doing' teaching and concepts derived from theoretical frameworks for learning and other professional literature lies at the heart of what it is 'to profess' and to earn the title 'professor' or 'professorial fellow'. It is this kind of **praxis** which promotion procedures attempt to interrogate.

It might be argued further that scholarship is the vehicle which draws the tacit knowledge (Polanyi, 1958) of excellent teachers into the public domain and, hence, makes it available to other practitioners. Moreover, scholarship is the means whereby 'reputation' is built and 'esteem' validated. It is not surprising therefore that promotion boards give it close attention, nor that valid forms of scholarship are now more frequently interpreted as 'action-' or 'policy-based' as opposed to discovery-led 'blue sky' research. It would seem that Boyer's (1990) plea for a reconsidered view of scholarship and new respect for a 'scholarship of applications and teaching' has been not only heard but enshrined in the promotion criteria of the most forward-looking HEIs.

Activities associated with reflection, action learning and action research are now well documented (see Chapter 28) and widely accepted as precursors of praxis, leading to continuing professional development.

Numerous studies of 'professionals' trace the development of practitioners from novice to expert, and Case study 4 provides an interesting account of one such journey and gives insight into the kind of profile presented for promotion to a 'pedagogic' Chair. Progression in a practice-based activity such as university-level teaching has been described as passing through a number of stages (Dreyfus and Dreyfus, 1986). Level 1, the novice stage, is characterised by adherence to taught rules and little discretionary judgement; level 2, the advanced beginner, takes more account of the global characteristics of situations but tends to treat all aspects and attributes as having equal importance. At level 3 the practitioner is considered competent, is beginning to see actions as part of longer-term goals, and is able to undertake conscious and deliberate planning and perform standardised or routine procedures. At level 4, that of proficiency, situations are seen more holistically, important aspects are more readily recognised, decision-making is less laboured and guiding axioms can be interpreted differently according to situation. The expert, the level 5 practitioner, no longer relies on rules and guidelines and has an intuitive grasp of situations based on deep understanding, knows what is possible, and only uses analytic approaches in novel situations or when new problems occur. Thus the expert stage is characterised by implicit and unconscious practice. For the experienced mid-career teacher in higher education, and particularly for those applying for promotion via the learning and teaching route, much practice will be at levels four and five. This type and level of accomplishment need to be evidenced in the documentation presented for progression to a promoted post and triangulated with data derived from students, direct peer observation and other metrics.

Case study 4: Extending experience and building expertise: a personal account

Professor Mick Healey holds a Chair in Geographical Education at the University of Gloucestershire. His main interests include links between research and teaching, learning styles, active and enquiry-based learning, and promoting the scholarship of teaching and learning.

Mick sees his career since 1980, as falling into two overlapping stages, each about 15 or so years long. The first phase was dedicated to working as an economic geographer. During this period he developed a reasonable publication record, including about 50 articles and chapters, four edited books, a textbook and a number of consultancy reports. Despite this profile he felt he was never going to develop more than a modest reputation as an economic geographer. 'I owe in large part, my chair, my National Teaching Fellowship, and my opportunity to visit universities around the world, to my involvement with the scholarship of teaching and learning', says Professor Healey. However, it was not until his mid-career that he engaged seriously with this particular aspect of academic activity. In the early 1990s, 'My interest in teaching geography led me to start investigating aspects of my practice, I gave a few conference presentations and wrote a few articles and within a few years I became a joint editor of the *Journal of Geography in Higher Education*.' But perhaps the key event was winning one of the first Fund for Development in Teaching and Learning projects in 1996, which led to directing the Geography Discipline Network and ultimately laid the foundation for the University of Gloucestershire's successful bid for a **Centre for Excellence in Teaching and Learning (CETL)** in 2005.

The other key milestone in Mick's career came in 2000 when he was awarded a National Teaching Fellowship. His project was concerned with embedding the scholarship of teaching and learning in disciplines and institutions, a 'hugely overambitious project,' he now admits, 'but it did allow me to go and discuss this kind of scholarship with people in many different parts of the world.' Mick has subsequently exploited his international network to collect examples of interesting teaching and learning practices, which he uses to inform the many workshops, keynotes and consultancies he presents and undertakes. Since 1995 he has delivered over 250 educational workshops, seminars and conference presentations in Australasia, mainland Europe and North America, as well as the UK. He has also written and edited over 100 papers, chapters, books and guides on various aspects of teaching and learning in higher education.

He talks enthusiastically about the scholarship of teaching and learning and says that 'one of the most enjoyable things is working with like-minded colleagues on a project'. He particularly values discipline-based approaches, but notes that though he started work as a geographer, nowadays he is more frequently involved with research and development projects spanning all disciplines. He gives much credit in this aspect of the development of his career to working collaboratively with a mentor, who is also a colleague and co-author, and says, 'I wouldn't be where I am now without his help and support.'

(Professor Mick Healey, in conversation with Stephanie Marshall)

For many institutions, the evidence of teaching expertise is required in the form of a teaching **portfolio**. Teaching portfolios have been written about extensively over the years (Fry and Ketteridge, 2003) and Case study 5 provides an example of the long-established use of teaching portfolios for tenure and promotion purposes from McGill University.

Case study 5: Use of teaching portfolios for tenure and promotion at McGill University, Montreal

Interest in teaching portfolios first emerged in Canada in the 1970s, with the idea developed and promoted by the Canadian Association of University Teachers. Since then, portfolio use has become relatively commonplace throughout North America. McGill University, a research-intensive university in Montreal, has had a portfolio-related policy in place since 1994 when its Senate approved the requirement of a teaching portfolio for all promotion and tenure decisions. Initially, basic requirements were outlined by the university, but by 1997, Faculties had begun developing specific protocols for portfolios that best represented the particular teaching demands of their own disciplines. Although university policy has subsequently been reviewed and refined, the basic conception remains largely the same, namely a teaching portfolio is required for any tenure and promotion decision, including (1) promotion to the rank of full professor, and (2) hiring with tenure from outside McGill.

The portfolio includes a teaching statement (five to ten pages) plus appendices of no more than 30 pages. The statement addresses: (1) an individual's teaching approach or philosophy, (2) their teaching responsibilities, (3) evidence of teaching effectiveness, and (4) teaching development activities. A full description of the relevant policies and portfolio may be found in the references (under McGill University). Policy implementation was secured with developmental support from the teaching development unit which worked with heads of departments to help define criteria for interpreting and assessing teaching portfolios. All orientations for new academics include information about the requirement. The development unit regularly offers workshops on creating and maintaining teaching portfolios; these workshops include a panel of individuals who review dossiers for tenure and promotion. The unit also works with individuals who request help in constructing such portfolios. At this point, the policy has become embedded in university practices.

(Professor Lynne MacAlpine, McGill University, Montreal)

TOWARDS THE FUTURE

In thinking about their future institutional needs, the demands of an internationalised student market and the evolving nature of academic roles, some universities have recently undertaken fundamental reviews of their selection and promotion procedures to ensure continuing fitness for purpose. Progressive human resource policies have seen the widespread adoption of job evaluation schemes aimed at parity of esteem and reward between different career routes and greater transparency in grading decisions. As HR policies and procedures have become more codified, HEIs have also recognised the imperative of retaining flexibility and responsiveness to both individual cases and their own circumstances. This is particularly true for senior appointments.

In furtherance of its strategic aim to attract and retain high-quality staff, the University of Bath (2007) recently instituted a major review of its academic career development and promotions procedures. *Inter alia,* the university has created posts with the titles of Professorial Research Fellow and Professorial Teaching Fellow; it regards each as broadly equivalent in status and contribution to the institution. Criteria have been identified in three areas: management and leadership, research and scholarship, and teaching. To facilitate promotion to Professorial Fellow, applicants need to demonstrate how they meet the criteria in different combinations for different career routes. Thus, for a Professorial Teaching Fellow applicants provide evidence of teaching as a major strength with supplementary evidence of effective performance in one of the supporting areas of 'Management and Leadership' and 'Research and Scholarship'. Appointment to a full Professorship is possible on the basis of excellent teaching and an effective contribution to both of the other elements. It is interesting to note that while an 'excellent' or 'major' teaching contribution can be evidenced in a variety of ways, considerable weight is attached to data generated from the university's own online student evaluation system.

Monash University in Melbourne, a member of Australia's Group of Eight research-intensive universities, has well-developed career routes for academic staff including promotion between Senior Lecturer, Reader, Associate Professor and Professor. Teaching portfolios are not used for promotion purposes, although the university produces clear guidelines in terms of its requirements. To make a case for promotion, staff have to identify their academic achievements under the headings 'Research', 'Education' and 'Service'. The distinctive feature of the Monash system is that candidates are able to allocate a relative weighting to each of the three areas of performance. The total weighting must add up to 100 per cent, the minimum weighting allowed for each of 'Research' and 'Education' is 30 per cent and the minimum for 'Service' 10 per cent. Candidates are advised that the relative quality and depth of supporting evidence they provide should reflect the balance of weightings declared in their application. This approach requires candidates to think carefully about the basis of their application and to analyse their individual strengths while providing the university with a flexible, consistent and transparent mechanism (for promotion guidelines, see Monash University in References).

POSTSCRIPT

Contrary to some negative (and frequently uninformed) external opinions about the capability of the UK higher education sector to manage change, many institutions have demonstrated a willingness to overhaul traditional practices. A new emphasis on teaching quality, the student experience and responsiveness to student opinion, coupled with policy-led initiatives in the area of HR management and workforce restructuring, have created a culture more inclined to innovate. Shifts in attitude and behaviour abound in relation to the valuing of human capital, the motivational dimension of performance management and the appropriateness of reward systems. The move towards the establishment of the 'Teaching Chair' or 'Professorial Teaching Fellow' is part of a dynamic which is opening up new promotional pathways for individuals at, or approaching, mid-career. It also acknowledges the almost imperceptible growth of 'teaching-only posts' in the past decade, now amounting to a quarter of all academic positions (Court, 2007).

The means deployed to test the quality of individuals seeking advancement via such routes is becoming clearer and the criteria more refined. Providing criteria are applied with rigour and integrity, and the flow of candidates is of a high calibre, there is no reason why these initiatives should not succeed and become permanent features of the HE environment. As Félix Fénéon reminds us, 'there is no such thing as the *avant-garde*; only people lagging behind'.

REFERENCES

Baume, D and Yorke, M (2002) 'The reliability of assessment by portfolio on a course to develop and accredit teachers in higher education', *Studies in Higher Education*, 27 (1): 7–25.

Boyer, E L (1990) *Scholarship Reconsidered: Priorities for the Professoriate*, Princeton, NJ: Carnegie Foundation.

Brenton, S (2003) 'Online portfolios at Queen Mary University of London' (pp. 249–250), in H Fry and S Ketteridge, 'Teaching portfolios' (pp. 242–252), in H Fry *et al.* (2nd edn), *A Handbook for Teaching and Learning in Higher Education*, London: Kogan Page.

Court, S (2007) 'Reshaping academic work and the academic workforce in the UK', paper presented at SRHE Conference, 11–13 December, Brighton.

Dreyfus, H L and Dreyfus, S E (1986) *Mind over Machine*, New York: Free Press .

Elton, L (2005) 'Scholarship and the research and teaching nexus', in R Barnett (ed.), *Reshaping the University: New Relationships Between Research, Scholarship and Teaching* (pp. 108–118), London: McGraw Hill/Open University Press.

Fry, H and Ketteridge, S (2003) 'Teaching portfolios' (pp. 242–52), in H Fry *et al.* (2nd edn), *A Handbook for Teaching and Learning in Higher Education*, London: Kogan Page.

Glasser, R (1988) *Gorbals Boy at Oxford*, London: Chatto and Windus.

Jenkins, A, Healey, M and Zetter, R (2007) *Linking Teaching and Research in Disciplines and Departments*, York: HEA.

Kimball, M (2005) 'Database e-portfolios : a critical appraisal', *Computers and Composition*, 22 (4): 434–458.

McGill University, Teaching Portfolios. Available online at <http://www.mcgill.ca/tls/policy/teachingportfolio> (accessed 18 June 2008).

Monash University, Promotion Guidelines. Available online at <http://www.adm.ed.au/sss/academic-promotion/> (accessed 18 June 2008).

NCIHE (1997) *The National Committee of Inquiry into Higher Education, Higher Education in the Learning Society*, London: HMSO.

Polanyi, M (1958) *Personal Knowledge: Towards a Post-critical Philosophy*, Chicago, IL: University of Chicago Press.

Pennington, G and Smith, B (2002) 'Career long competence: unattainable ideal or professional requirement?', in S Ketteridge *et al., The Effective Academic*, London: Kogan Page.

Quality Assurance Agency (QAA) (2003) *Handbook for Enhancement-led Institutional Review: Scotland*, Gloucester: QAA.

Quality Assurance Agency (QAA) (2006) *Handbook for Institutional Audit: England and Northern Ireland*, Gloucester: QAA.

Seldin, P (1997) *The Teaching Portfolio* (2nd edn), Bolton, MA: Anker.

Skelton, A (ed.) (2007) *International Perspectives on Teaching Excellence in Higher Education*, London: Routledge.

Steiner, G (1997) *Errata: An Examined Life*, London: Weidenfeld & Nicolson.

University of Bath (2007) 'Academic career progression: principles and framework' (May).

FURTHER READING

Barnett, R (ed.) (2005) *Reshaping the University: New Relationships between Research, Scholarship and Teaching*, Maidenhead: SRHE/Open University Press. A useful set of contributions from a range of distinguished scholars and practitioners examining such areas as 'the mythology of research and teaching relationships in universities' (Mark Hughes), and the changes taking place as a result of this convergence in global universities.

Higher Education Academy www.heacademy.ac.uk/ourwork/professional/recognition (last accessed 1 January 2008). For further reading on individual routes to further recognition.

Ketteridge, S *et al.* (2002) *The Effective Academic*, London: Kogan Page. Another set of useful contributions from a range of distinguished scholars and practitioners, exploring selected aspects of academic life that early to mid-career academics should consider when looking to career progression.

Shiach, M, Ketteridge, S *et al.* (2008) *Managing Teaching Performance*, Report of a Leadership Foundation Fellowship Project conducted at Queen Mary, University of London. The project investigates approaches to encouraging, assessing and rewarding excellent teaching in a range of research-intensive universities. Available online at www.esd.qmul.ac.uk/LFReport.pdf.

Glossary

This glossary provides two types of information. First, it provides the reader with simple explanations and definitions of technical and educational terms used in this book. Second, it provides a dictionary of many commonly used abbreviations and acronyms. The glossary has been carefully assembled by the editors. In the text, the first mention in each chapter of a glossary item appears in **bold**. The entries reflect current usage in higher education in the UK.

3D virtual world An online 3D environment in which users control a character or avatar to interact with each other and with the surrounding environment.

Academic practice A term used to describe the collective responsibilities of academic staff in higher education, namely those for teaching, learning and communicating the subject, discipline-specific research/scholarship, academic management activities and, for some, service requirements.

Access course A qualification for non-traditional, usually mature, students, as a route into higher education.

Accreditation Certified as meeting required standards (e.g. an accredited programme is one that has been approved by an external body as meeting certain standards or criteria).

Achievement motivation A desire to succeed at a task (e.g. obtaining high grades, even when the task does not inspire interest) (*see also* extrinsic motivation, intrinsic motivation).

Achieving approach to learning *See* strategic approach.

Action learning An approach to learning involving individuals working on real projects with the support of a group (set) which meets regularly to help members reflect on their experience and to plan next actions.

Action research Researching one's own practice in a cyclical manner. *See* Chapter 28, Case study 1.

Active learning A process of engaging with the learning task at both the cognitive and affective level.

Activity theory Analysing activity (especially in the workplace) as a complex phenomenon which is socially situated. May be used in relation to learning and teaching (*see also* situated learning).

Adult learning theory A range of theories and constructs claimed to relate specifically to how adults learn. Includes self-directed learning. Much of the work on reflection and experiential learning is also part of this area. Concerns over validity of some of the theories and that some aspects are not distinctively adult.

Affective domain One of the major areas of learning, the learning of values.

AIM (Alice Interactive Mathematics) ALICE stands for Active Learning In a Computer Environment.

Aims (learning aims) At the top of the hierarchy of description commonly used to define a learning experience. They are intended to provide the student, teacher and other interested parties with an understanding of the most overarching general statements regarding the intended consequences of a learning experience (*see also* objectives, learning outcomes).

Amotivation Absence of tangible motivation.

Andragogy The theory of adult learning, associated with the work of Malcolm Knowles.

API Age Participation Index.

APL/AP(E) Accreditation of prior learning. Taking into account previous 'certificated' learning gained either as whole or part of a programme, towards all or part of a new qualification. Also the counting of experience (experiential) towards obtaining a qualification.

Appraisal (as used in higher education) A formal, regular, developmental process in which the one being appraised is encouraged to review and reflect upon performance in the workplace. Usually based on a focused interview with a peer, head of department or line manager. At the interview, objectives (linked to strategic aims of the department) are set and development needs identified. Performance against these objectives is reviewed at the next appraisal interview.

Approaches to learning *See* deep, surface *and* strategic approaches to learning.

Approaches to studying inventory A device used to identify students approach to study.

Asperger's Syndrome Severe and sustained impairment in social interaction, and the development of restrictive repetitive patterns of behaviour.

Assessment Measurement of the achievement and progress of the learner (NB wider definition in North America).

Assessment centre In relation to recruitment. After first-round interviews, in which individuals are observed undertaking job-related exercises for the purpose of assessing skills, competencies and personal attributes.

Audio-visual/audio-lingual methodology Structural methodologies in language teaching developed in the 1950s and 1960s based on drilling, the formation of habit and avoidance of error.

Audit A systematic review of provision. Institutional audit is conducted by the Quality Assurance Agency on a cyclical basis.

Autonomy (of student learning) Commonly refers to students taking more responsibility for and control of themselves and their learning, including being less spoon-fed. May also include elements of students taking more responsibility for determining and directing the content of their learning.

Blended learning   A mix of face-to-face and online learning.

Blogs   Websites which allow people to set up and maintain an electronic journal without specialist knowledge of web design. Users can typically subscribe to them so that they are alerted to new entries.

Blueprinting (of assessment)   Ensures that assessment tasks adequately sample what the student is expected to have learnt.

Bologna Process   A movement to bring compatibility to degree structures that will promote recognition of qualifications outside their country of origin.

Broadband   Highspeed internet connection and transmission.

Bulletin board   An electronic version of the notice-board. Messages are left and questions asked or answered by contributing to themed or 'threaded' discussions – also called 'asynchronous communication'.

Buzz group   A small group activity, typically within a large group, in which students work together on a short problem, task or discussion. So called because of the noise the activity generates.

CAL   (computer-aided learning) Use of computers for education and training, sometimes referred to as computer-assisted instruction (CAI) or computer-based learning (CBL). In this context the computer is usually used as a discrete item of teaching.

CALL   Computer-assisted language learning.

CAS   Computer algebra system.

Centre for Excellence in Teaching and Learning (CETL)   HEFCE-funded centres bid for by universities to promote student learning.

Code of Practice   A 'series of system-wide expectations' for a range of areas (e.g. assessment) set out by the QAA.

Cognitive domain   The major area of learning in most disciplines, to do with knowledge, understanding and thinking.

Communicative approach   An approach to the teaching and learning of languages which emphasises the primacy of meaning and communication needs.

Community of practice   The community is made up of those who share common understandings and practices (e.g. in a discipline) and who may extend or create knowledge by virtue of shared practices and discussion (e.g. in the case of those working in the profession).

Competence   Most contemporary use in education relates to performing a task or series of tasks, with debate over how far such activities also require underpinning knowledge and understanding. (1) May be used generically to mean demonstrated achievement with respect to any clearly defined set of outcomes. (2) Is used to indicate both a high level of achievement and a just acceptable level of activity. (3) Something which a person in a given occupational area should be able to do.

Computer-based learning   *See* CAL.

Constructive alignment   Ensuring, at least, learning outcomes, teaching methods, learning activities, and assessment are compatible with each other.

Constructivist   A number of theories attempting to explain how human beings learn. Characterised by the idea of addition to, and amendment of, previous understanding or knowledge. Without such change, learning is not thought to occur.

Core skills   *See* transferable skills.

Course   This term is used to refer to both smaller-sized units of study (modules) and, confusingly, to larger units encompassing a set of modules that comprise a programme of study (*see also* module *and* programme).

Courseware   Software designed to be used in an educational programme. Refers to programmes and data used in CAL (computer-based learning).

Creative Commons Licence   A licence one can use to retain copyright over (digital) content but which gives users levels of flexibility in how they can reproduce one's work.

Credit accumulation and transfer (CATS)   Assigning a numerical value to a portion of learning, based on a number of notional learning hours earning one credit point. Thus modules may be said to be worth 30 credits and rated at level M (Masters). Used as a currency for purposes of transfer and equivalence (*see also* ECTS).

Crit (critique)   A form of formative and/or summative assessment widely used in art and design. Usually conducted orally and led by the learner's input.

Criterion-referenced assessment   Judges how well a learner has performed by comparison with predetermined criteria.

Critical incident (analysis)   An event which, when reflected on, yields information resulting in learning from experience.

Dearing Report   *See* National Committee of Inquiry into Higher Education (NCIHE).

Deductive teaching/learning   Working from general premises. (In language teaching, presenting grammar rules in isolation and encouraging learners to generate specific examples based on the rules.)

Deep approach to learning   Learning which attempts to relate ideas together to understand underpinning theory and concepts, and to make meaning out of material under consideration (*see also* surface approach, strategic approach).

DIUS   Department for Innovation, Universities and Skills.

Diagnostic test   A test used (possibly at the start of an undergraduate module) to identify weaknesses (e.g. in grammatical knowledge or numeracy), with a view to addressing these in a more focused manner.

Didactic teaching   A style that is teacher centred – often prescriptive, formulaic, and based on transmission.

Disability Discrimination Act   Legislation that applies to higher education to ensure non-discriminatory and equitable practices, for example in relation to access, admissions and assessment of students.

Disciplinary specificity   Characteristics of a discipline that affect what one can do when teaching it; comprising socio-cultural and epistemological characteristics of the discipline.

Distance learning   Learning away from the institution, as exemplified by the Open University. Most often students work with learning resource materials that can be paper-based, available on broadcast TV or accessed through the World Wide Web.

Domain A particular area (type) of learning. Much associated with categorising learning outcomes and the use of hierarchical taxonomies within each domain. Considerable dispute on the number and range of domains and the hierarchies of learning within them. The three domains most commonly identified are the cognitive, affective and psychomotor.

Dyslexia A specific learning disability that manifests primarily as a difficulty with written language, particularly reading and spelling. The most common disability in higher education.

ECTS European Credit Transfer System. The pan-European scheme for awarding credit to units of study (*see also* credit accumulation and transfer).

Employability A set of achievements, skills, understandings and personal attributes that make graduates more likely to gain employment and be successful in their chosen occupations.

EMQ/I (extended matching question/item) A written assessment. Each question has a theme from which lists of possible answers are placed in alphabetical order. The candidate is instructed to choose the best matching answer(s) to each of a series of scenarios, results and so on.

Enquiry-based learning Activities for students which promote enquiry rather than absorption of teacher-provided knowledge.

Evaluation Quantitative and qualitative judgement of the curriculum and its delivery, to include teaching (NB different usage in North America).

Exemplification lecture A lecture designed around a series of analytical examples.

Expansive learning Learning which transforms understanding and practice and which may occur in contexts outside formal teaching as a by-product (e.g. in the workplace, in the course of research) (*see also* activity theory).

Experiential learning Learning from doing. Often represented by the Kolb Learning Cycle.

External examiner/examining External examiners are part of UK universities' self-regulatory procedures and play a key role in maintaining standards between institutions in a particular discipline. Usually distinguished members of the profession who have the respect of colleagues and students alike. For taught programmes they serve for a fixed term. They play a similar role in examination of postgraduate dissertations and theses, leading discussion in viva voce examinations. Their function and report are part of quality assurance processes.

Extrinsic motivation Typifies students who are concerned with the grades they achieve, external rewards, and whether they will gain approval from others (*see also* achievement motivation, intrinsic motivation).

Facilitator As opposed to teacher, tutor or mentor, a role to encourage individuals to take responsibility for their own learning, through the facilitation of this process.

Fair (of assessment) Fair with respect to: (1) consistency between different markers;

(2) transparency and openness of criteria and procedures; (3) procedures that do not disadvantage any group of learners in the cohort.

FAQ   Frequently asked question.

Feedback   Oral or written developmental advice on 'performance' so that the recipient has a better understanding of expected values, standards or criteria, and can improve their performance (*see also* formative assessment).

Field trip/coursework   Practical or experimental work away from the university designed to develop practical skills (e.g. observation of natural environments), which may be for a single session or coherent period of study lasting several days. Most common in life and environmental sciences, geography, civil engineering, construction.

FL(A)   Foreign language (assistant).

Flexible learning   Often used interchangeably with the term 'open learning', but may be distinguished from it by the inclusion of more traditional modes of delivery (such as the lecture). Designed to ease student access and choice.

Focus group   A technique for pooling thoughts, ideas and perceptions to ensure equal participation by all members of a group. Requires a facilitator. Some versions of the method aim to obtain a consensus view, others the weight and thrust of opinion. More accurately called nominal group technique.

Formative assessment   Assessment that is used to help teachers and learners gauge the strengths and weaknesses of the learners' performance while there is still time to take action for improvement. Typically it is expressed in words rather than marks or grades. Information about learners may be used diagnostically (*see* summative assessment).

Foundation degrees   Two-year vocational degrees.

Framework for Higher Education Qualifications   *See* level.

Graduate attributes   The qualities, skills and understandings each university considers its students will have on exit.

Graduate demonstrators/Teaching assistants (GTAs)   Typically doctoral students who assist with teaching (e.g. as laboratory demonstrators).

Grammar-translation   A structural teaching approach whereby a grammatical point is explained and learners are drilled in its use by means of translation of numerous examples into and out of the target language.

Grounded theory   A term used originally by B. Glaser and A. Straus (*The Discovery of Grounded Theory: Strategies for Qualitative Research*, Chicago: Aldine, 1967) to describe a research method in which theory or models are developed systematically from data rather than the opposite way around.

HEA   Higher Education Academy. Supports British higher education in its endeavour to create a good 'student experience'. See web for more information (*see also* UK Professional Standards, National Teaching Fellow *and* Subject Centres).

HEFCE   Higher Education Funding Council for England.

HEFW   Higher Education Funding Council for Wales.

HESA   Higher Education Statistical Agency.

iGoogle   A personalised version of the Google homepage, which allows users to add tools and subscribe to RSS feeds within the homepage environment.

Immersion learning   Student interaction with authentic language through long periods of exposure to the second language.

Independent learning (study)   Often used interchangeably with the terms 'open learning', 'self-directed learning' and 'autonomous learning'. Has a flavour of all these terms. Perhaps most strongly associated with programmes of study created individually for each learner.

Induction   Opening period of work or study during which basic information is provided through short courses, small group activities or one-to-one meetings. The purpose is to equip participants with background information so that they may become effective in their role or in their study as soon as possible.

Inductive teaching/learning   Working from particular cases to general conclusions. (In languages learners identify recurrent use and pattern in context and work towards the formulation of rules.)

Industrial placements   A learning experience offered to students to assist them to gain applied knowledge, understanding and skills through an extended period of time based in industry.

Institutional audit   *See* Audit.

Internationalisation   Curriculum materials which include those with an international flavour. Also used to refer to the diversity of staff and students.

Internet   A decentralised global system of computer networks, in which, providing they have permission, any computer on the network can connect with any other.

Interpersonal domain   One of the major areas of learning, the learning of behaviour involved in interacting with others.

Intranet   The commonest example is the use for teaching of one of more WWW server on an *internal* network not open to the public.

Intrinsic motivation   Typifies students who enjoy a challenge, want to master a subject, are curious and want to learn (*see also* achievement motivation, extrinsic motivation).

iTunes   Popular music and video playback software made by Apple. Also allows users to subscribe to podcasts.

IWB   Interactive whiteboard.

IWLP/UWLP   Institution/University-Wide Learning Programme.

JISC   Joint Information Systems Committee, manages and develops, at a national level, ICT for teaching and learning purposes in higher education.

JORUM   A free online repository service for teaching and support staff in UK further and higher education institutions.

Key/core/common/transferable skills   *See* transferable skills.

Knowledge base for teaching   Part of what teachers draw upon when teaching; comprising the teacher's knowledge about teaching, his or her beliefs related to teaching, and his or her goals related to teaching.

L1   (of language teaching) Learner's mother tongue.

L2 (of language teaching) A second or foreign language, learnt either in the classroom or naturalistically in the country concerned.

Laboratory/practical class A type of teaching session, usually included in curricula in experimental sciences, biomedical sciences and engineering disciplines, which is broadly intended to offer training in techniques and learning how to carry out experimental investigations.

Learning and Teaching Strategy What an institution, or parts of it, wishes to achieve with regard to learning and teaching; how it will achieve it and how it will know when it has succeeded.

Learning centre A centre to which students may go to gain support for their learning (e.g. via computer-aided applications).

Learning agreement/contract A contract drawn up between teacher and learner, whereby each agrees to take on certain roles and responsibilities (e.g. the learner to hand in work on time and the teacher to return corrected work within a specified period of time). May specifically concern setting out the learning outcomes the learner undertakes to achieve.

Learning cycle Theory describing the stages of learning from concrete experience through reflection and generalisation to experiment towards new experience, often attributed to David Kolb.

Learning objectives *See* objectives.

Learning outcomes (Intended learning outcomes (ILOs)) Statements which define the learning students are expected to have acquired on completion of a session, course, programme, module or unit of study.

Learning style Used to describe how learners differ in their tendencies or preferences to learn. Recognises learning differences; a mix of personality and cognitive processes.

Level (of award)/level descriptor Used to describe a hierarchy of learning outcomes across all domains, usually L1, 2, 3, M and D. Most commonly follows classification from QAA (Framework of Higher Education Qualifications – see web).

Licensing A term often used synonymously with accreditation, especially in Europe. May also relate to a 'licence to practise'.

Lifelong learning Learning from the cradle to the grave. The modern world requires continuing professional development, constant updating and so on, irrespective of age. Universities need to consider implications for credit, flexible programmes and so on.

Mathematica A computer algebra system.

MCQ Multiple choice question.

Mentor A peer who supports and advises a new student or member of staff, helping him or her adapt to institutional culture, acting as a sounding-board for ideas and encouraging reflection on practice.

Mixed skills teaching/testing The integration of the four language skills (listening, speaking, reading and writing) in tasks which replicate real-life language use (e.g. relaying written stimuli orally, making a written note of a spoken message).

Module A discrete unit of study, credit-rated, assessed, and part of a larger award-bearing programme of study.

MSN Messenger   A tool integrated with Windows that allows users to communicate via text, audio and video, and to share content.

National Committee of Inquiry into Higher Education (NCIHE)   The Dearing Committee, set up under Sir Ron (Lord) Dearing by the Conservative government in February 1996 to make recommendations for the next 20 years about the purposes, shape, structure, size and funding of higher education. Reported in July 1997. The report commented on aspects such as organisation of programmes, quality matters, staff development and funding.

National Student Survey (NSS)   An exit survey of undergraduate student opinion on their total student experience. Intended to inform student choice.

National Teaching Fellow (NTF)   National recognition for teaching excellence (*see also* HEA).

Norm-referenced assessment   Judges how well the learner has done in comparison with the norm established by their peers.

Objectives   Originally developed by educational psychologists and known as behavioural objectives. Definition and use have become less precise in recent years. Their meaning has ranged from exact, measurable outcomes of specific learning experiences to more generalised statements of learning outcomes. The term may be distinguished from or used interchangeably (but loosely) with the term 'learning outcomes'.

OMR (optical mark reader)   A special scanning device that can read carefully placed pencil marks on specially designed documents. OMR is frequently used to score forms, questionnaires and answer sheets.

Open learning   Learning flexibly with regard to pace and location. Usually associated with delivery without a tutor being present. Will often allow learning in order of own choice, in a variety of media and may also imply no entry barriers (e.g. no prior qualifications).

Open source   Describes software available for free distribution and whose source code is available for free modification by users.

Oral examination   *See* viva voce examination.

OSCE (objective structured clinical examination)   Clinical assessment made up of a circuit of short tasks, known as stations. Several variations on the basic theme. Typically, candidates pass through a station where an examiner grades them according to an itemised checklist or global rating scale.

OSLER (objective structured long examination record)   Clinical assessment with some similarity to an OSCE, but involving one or more long case.

Passive learning/approach   As opposed to active. Learning or an approach to learning that is superficial and does not involve full engagement with the material.

Pedagogy   The practice and method of teaching and study, and research of it.

Peer assessment   Assessment by fellow (peer) students, as in peer assessment of team activities.

Peer support   A system whereby students support one another in the learning process. Students may be in informal groups or formal, designated groups.

Peer tutor/tutorial Tutorial facilitated by fellow students (peer tutors).

Performance Indicator (PI) Measures of achievement of individuals or organisations, often expressed in terms of outputs.

Personal Development Plan (PDP) A range of formal and/or informal mechanisms that promote reflection by an individual of their learning, performance and/or achievement and that encourages planned personal, educational and career development (*see also* progress files).

Personal epistemology A person's beliefs about knowledge and its development; comprising beliefs about: knowledge and knowing; knowledge construction; and the evaluation of knowledge.

Personal Response System (PRS) Individualised electronic means of 'voting' (e.g. indicating preferred answer), often used in large classes.

Placement/placement learning Placing students outside their home institution for part of their period of study, often work placement in which the student 'learns on the job'.

Plagiarism Presenting others' work as one's own.

PLE Loosely used to describe a system which allows learners to manage their own learning in a more student-centred manner than is typically encountered within VLEs. A PLE may not be a single platform or application, but may make use of various integrated tools.

Podcast A digital media file (containing sound and/or video) which is distributed over the internet and to which users can subscribe for download and playback on computers or portable playback devices such as MP 3 players.

Portfolio (teaching portfolio) A personal collection of material representing an individual's work (e.g. to demonstrate achievement and professional development as a university teacher).

Praxis Synthesis of theory and practice in which each informs the other.

Probation The initial phase in employment with a new organisation in which a member of staff 'learns the job'. In higher education, this usually involves periods of formal training and development; often the probationer is supported by a mentor. Many institutions set formal requirements that staff are expected to meet for satisfactory completion of probation.

Problem class Typically a session in the teaching of mathematics, engineering and physical science in which students work through problems and derive solutions with the support of a teacher and/or tutor/demonstrator. Not to be confused with PBL sessions.

Problem-based learning (PBL) A pedagogical method introduced in the 1960s; much used in medicine. Curriculum design involves a large amount of small group teaching and claims greater alignment with sound educational principles. Learning and teaching come after learners identify their learning needs from a trigger in the form of a scenario ('the problem').

Professional doctorates A field of studies that is a professional discipline. It is a research degree with a significant taught element plus research project published as the thesis.

Programme specification   A succinct way of describing the attributes and outcomes of a named programme of study, written to follow QAA guidelines.

Programme of study   An award-bearing collection of modules or other teaching and learning, typically running over a defined period of time (e.g. BA, M.Eng.).

Progress file   A term given prominence by the NCIHE. Comprises a transcript, or formal record of academic achievement and a developmental aspect enabling students to monitor, plan and reflect on their personal development (*see also* PDP).

Psychomotor domain   One of the major areas of learning, the learning of certain types of skill.

QAA   Quality Assurance Agency for Higher Education.

Quality   Refers to acceptable standards of teaching, student learning experience and so on in higher education.

Quality assurance   An ongoing process by which an institution (programme, department, school or faculty) monitors and confirms policies, processes and activities, and by which quality is maintained (and developed).

Quality control   Refers to the detailed checks on procedures and activities necessary for the attainment of high quality and standards.

Quality enhancement   Refers to all the activities and processes adopted to improve and develop quality, including formative activity and dissemination of good practice.

Rationalist   The belief that reason is the basis of knowledge.

Reflection   Consideration, from description to analysis, of an experience, or of learning; to enhance and improve understanding and practice.

Reflective practitioner   Someone who is continually involved in the process of reflecting on experience and is capable of continually learning from experience to the benefit of future actions.

Reliable/Reliability (of assessment)   A test which is consistent and precise in terms of factors, such as marking, quality of test and test items. The assessment process would generate the same result if repeated on another occasion with the same group, or if repeated with another group of similar students.

Reusable learning objects (RLOs)   Items of content (often web based) which may aid student learning and may be reused in a variety of contexts.

Role play   A planned learning activity where participants take on the role of individuals representing different perspectives (e.g. a mock interview) to meet learning outcomes related to empathy or to expose participants to a scenario in which they will have to take part 'for real' in the near future.

RSS   Really simple syndication. A technology used to enable people to syndicate their web content (e.g. podcasts or blogs) so that other users can subscribe to updates.

SAQ (structured/short answer question)   Also known as modified essay questions or short answers. SAQs test knowledge recall in a directed but non-cueing manner.

Scaffolding   Help and support of various types provided for students when they learn new things or are struggling.

Screen recording software   Software that records the users' computer screen. Useful for capturing and quickly making recordings of presentations.

SEDA   Staff and Educational Development Association.

Self-directed learning (SDL)   The learner has control over educational decisions, including goals, resources, methods and criteria for judging success. Often used just to mean any learning situation in which the learner has some influence on some of these aspects.

Semester   A period of study in a modular programme of study over which a set of modules are taught. Typically the academic year is divided into two semesters of equal length.

Seminar   Used with different meanings according to discipline and type of institution. May be used to describe many forms of small group teaching. Traditionally one or more students present formal academic work (a paper) to peers and a tutor, followed by discussion.

SHEFC   Scottish Higher Education Funding Council.

SI (supplemental instruction)   Originates in the USA. A means of supporting learners through the use of trained SI instructors who are also students. SI instructors take the role of facilitator and operate within a framework determined initially by the course leader. Usually SI instructors are more senior students selected for the role.

Signpost   Statements in teaching sessions that help students to see the structure and direction of the teaching, and the links. Typically in a lecture, signposts will be used to give the big picture and then to signal the end of one section, the start of the next and where it is going.

Simulated patient (SP)   An actor or other third party who plays the role of the patient in a clinical encounter with dental, medical or similar students.

Simulation   Often associated with role play, but increasingly used in the context of ICT, a learning activity that simulates a real-life scenario requiring participants to make choices which demonstrate cause and effect.

Situated learning/Situated cognition   Learning and understanding often relates to and arises from (social) contexts. Those working in similar contexts (e.g. a discipline or profession) develop understanding about that context (*see also* community of practice). In the case of language learning, assistance with vocabulary would be offered in the context of the environment rather than the other way around (*see also* activity theory).

SLA   Second language acquisition.

Small group teaching   A term used to encompass the various forms of teaching involving 'small' groups of students, ranging from one-to-one sessions to groups of up to 25 (or even more) students. Includes tutorials, seminars, problem classes.

Social software   Web-based software which allows users to communicate, collaborate, create and share content. Associated with Web 2.0 applications and messaging/conferencing tools.

Standards   The term used to refer, typically, to levels of student attainment compared to comparators (or criteria).

Strategic approach to learning   Typifies students who adapt their learning style to meet the needs of the set task. Intention is external to the real purpose of the task, as it focuses on achieving high marks for their own sake, not because they indicate high levels of learning. Also known as the achieving approach.

Student-focused approach   Teaching in which the teacher not only considers the learners and their perspectives, but which students *perceive* as being well designed to help and support them in achieving the aims the teacher indicates.

Subject benchmarking   A collection of discipline-specific statements relating to undergraduate programmes as published by the QAA.

Subject Centres   A network of 24 centres supporting the student experience in their discipline, part of the HEA.

Summative assessment   The type of assessment that typically comes at the end of a module or section of learning and awards the learner with a final mark or grade for that section. The information about the learner is often used by third parties to inform decisions about the learner's abilities.

Supervision   The relationship between a student and supervisor (member of staff) to facilitate learning and discovery.

Supervisor   Person responsible for facilitating the work of students, usually projects and research.

Surface approach to learning   Learning by students which focuses on the details of the learning experience and which is based on memorising the details without any attempt to give them meaning beyond the factual level of understanding (*see also* deep approach, strategic approach).

Target language   The particular foreign language being taught/learnt.

Team teaching   A system whereby learning is designed, delivered and supported by two or more teachers who may share the same session.

Thesis lecture   A lecture which builds up a case through argumentation.

Threshold concepts   Critical concepts in each discipline, the misunderstanding of which may impede student learning.

Transferable skills   Skills associated with employability. Variously include communication, numeracy, IT, learning to learn, values and integrity, use of technology, interpersonal skills, problem-solving, positive attitudes to change and teamworking.

TurnItIn   Online plagiarism software.

Tutorial   Used with different meanings according to discipline, type of institution, level, and teaching and learning method. Involves a tutor and one or more students. May focus on academic and/or pastoral matters.

UK Professional Standards Framework   UK descriptors of levels of teaching expertise. HEA accredited programmes map onto those descriptors (*see also* HEA).

UUK   Universities UK (formerly CVCP).

Valid/validity (of assessment)   Adequacy and appropriateness of the task/test in relation to the outcomes/objectives being assessed (i.e. it measures what it is supposed to measure).

Video-conference   A synchronous discussion between two individuals or groups of people who are in different places but can see and hear each other using electronic communications.

Virtual Learning Environment (VLE)   Web-based software which allows teachers to construct and run online courses or course areas, and students to participate in them.

Virtual seminar   A seminar which takes place over the web.

Viva voce examination   An oral examination, typically at the end of a programme of study. One part of assessment strategy if used in undergraduate programmes, principal means of assessment of postgraduate degrees. May be used to test communication, understanding, capacity to think quickly under pressure and knowledge of procedures.

Volunteering   Unpaid activities undertaken by an individual, without monetary reward, that aims to deliver measurable social and community benefit and enhance the skills base of the volunteer.

Web 2.0   No definitive definition exists, but Web 2.0 loosely describes websites and web applications which allow users to create and share content, subscribe to and aggregate content across platforms, and personalise the way they access that content.

Webcast   A live or delayed video, audio or screen capture broadcast delivered through the internet.

Wiki   Wesbite software which allows readers to edit, link and add pages.

Work-based learning (WBL)   A type of curriculum design allowing content and learning to arise from within real working contexts. Students, usually employees, study part-time and may use their workplace to generate projects. Unlike PBL, work-based learners are working on real problems in real time.

World Wide Web   A means of sharing information across the internet.

Index

Locators in **bold** refer to figures, locators in *italic* refer to tables